MARKETING DECISION MAKING

HOLT, RINEHART AND WINSTON MARKETING SERIES

Paul E. Green, Adviser
Wharton School, University of Pennsylvania

Philip Kotler, Adviser
Northwestern University

James F. Engel, David T. Kollat, Roger D. Blackwell
All of the Ohio State University
CONSUMER BEHAVIOR
CASES IN CONSUMER BEHAVIOR
RESEARCH IN CONSUMER BEHAVIOR

Ronald R. Gist
University of Denver
MARKETING AND SOCIETY: A CONCEPTUAL INTRODUCTION
READINGS: MARKETING AND SOCIETY

Charles S. Goodman
University of Pennsylvania
MANAGEMENT OF THE PERSONAL SELLING FUNCTION

Philip Kotler
Northwestern University
MARKETING DECISION MAKING: A MODEL-BUILDING APPROACH

John C. Narver, *University of Washington*
Ronald Savitt, *Boston University*
THE MARKETING ECONOMY: AN ANALYTICAL APPROACH
CONCEPTUAL READINGS IN THE MARKETING ECONOMY

Thomas R. Wotruba
San Diego College
SALES MANAGEMENT: PLANNING, ACCOMPLISHMENT, AND EVALUATION

Thomas R. Wotruba, *San Diego State College*
Robert M. Olsen, *California State College, Fullerton*
SALES MANAGEMENT: CONCEPTS AND VIEWPOINTS

MARKETING DECISION MAKING: A Model Building Approach

PHILIP KOTLER
Northwestern University

HOLT, RINEHART AND WINSTON
New York Chicago San Francisco
Atlanta Dallas Montreal
Toronto London Sydney

The author wishes to acknowledge the following:

Figure 4-2, p. 97, copyright © 1968 by The Regents of the University of California. Reprinted from *California Management Review*, vol. X, no. 4, p. 8, by permission of The Regents. *Figure 6-1*, p. 144, copyright © 1967 by The University of Chicago Press, July 1967, issue of *Journal of Business*, p. 293. *Table 11-5*, p. 315, and *Figure 17-14*, p. 557, reprinted from the *Journal of Marketing Research*, published by the American Marketing Association. *Figure 12-3*, p. 355, copyright © 1968 by the President and Fellows of Harvard College. *Table 13-8*, p. 418, reprinted by permission of the Markham Publishing Co., Chicago, Illinois, 1967. *Figure 14-3*, p. 436, copyright © Advertising Research Foundation, 1967. *Figures 14-7*, p. 457, *17-4*, p. 525, and *18-4*, p. 583, reprinted from the *Journal of Marketing*, published by the American Marketing Association. *Figure 15-3*, p. 481, from Charles C. Holt, Franco Modigliani, John F. Muth, and Herbert A. Simon, *Planning Production, Inventories, and Work Force*, © 1960; by permission of Prentice-Hall, Inc., Englewood Cliffs, N.J.

Library of Congress Catalog Card Number: 70-135637
SBN: 03-078165-5
Printed in the United States of America

1 2 3 4   22   9 8 7 6 5 4 3 2 1

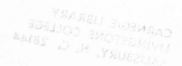

To my girls—Amy, Melissa, and Jessica—with love

Preface

A well-known marketing writer recently described his impression of the temperament of marketing men in the following words:

> A good many marketing executives, in the deepest recesses of their psyches, are artists, not analysts. For them, marketing is an art form, and, in my opinion, they really do not want it to be any other way. Their temperament is antipathetic to system, order, knowledge. They enjoy flying by the seats of their pants—though you will never get them to admit it. They revel in chaos, abhor facts, and fear research. They hate to be trammeled by written plans. And they love to spend, but are loath to assess the results of their spending.[1]

While this description has a certain amount of face validity, it overlooks the emergence of a new breed of marketing men who are turning to more analytical approaches in response to the increasing pressures on management to tie sales to profits. Marketing expenditures account for a growing part of the company's total expenses, and management increasingly wants solid analysis to back up the otherwise good intentions of marketing executives.

While the conventional wisdom of marketing still provides useful guidelines

---

[1]Lee Adler, "Systems Approach to Marketing," *Harvard Business Review* (May–June, 1967) 166.

to action, marketing executives are discovering in the quantitative sciences (and the behavioral sciences as well) valuable concepts and tools for heightening the effectiveness of marketing planning. The case for quantitative analysis in marketing rests on three expected contributions. First, the effort to formulate marketing problems in mathematical terms considerably clarifies the variables and relationships that should be researched. Someone once quipped about mathematical economics that "it doesn't say much but at least you know what is said." We shall try to make a stronger case for quantitative marketing analyses, that it "says more and says it more clearly."

Second, quantitative analysis provides a valuable collection of solution techniques. The choice of a marketing strategy out of a set of strategies becomes a matter of using an evaluation technique such as calculus, mathematical programming, or simulation. These techniques have considerable power to draw out the not-always obvious implications of complex sets of assumptions and data in which management professes to believe.

Third, quantitative analysis stimulates the development of marketing theory by distinguishing between what is assumed, what is known, and what can be inferred. The similarities and differences between competing points of view become more apparent. As theory develops, marketing management has a surer guide to action. "If you want literal realism, look at the world around you; if you want understanding, look at theories."[2]

Those who recognize these values of quantitative analysis in marketing face a rapidly growing, highly complex, and widely scattered literature that lacks systematization. The present book seeks to construct a systematic and self-contained theory of marketing analysis and decision making. As such, the book is divided into four parts. Part I is on *macromarketing decision theory*, so called because it deals with the system-level marketing decision problems facing a firm that is trying optimally to program market resources in the face of insufficient information about processes that are dynamic, nonlinear, lagged, stochastic, and interactive. The theory is constructed using the method of successive approximation. The normative analysis begins with a monopoly firm with one marketing decision variable, one sales territory, one product, one time period, one goal, and complete certainty. From this starting point, each assumption is relaxed in successive chapters to permit the study of the effect of different real world complications.

Part II is on *micromarketing decison models* and examines the separate instruments of marketing policy. Instead of viewing each instrument as a gross input of marketing effort that directly affects sales, attention is paid to the various complex links between that marketing instrument and sales. Successive chapters are devoted to distribution, pricing, sales force, and advertising; each marketing instrument is explored as a complex set of variables whose characterization and optimization become a matter of considerable challenge.

[2]Robert Dorfman, *The Price System* (Englewood Cliffs, N.J.: Prentice-Hall, Inc., 1964), p. 11.

Part III deals with *models of market behavior*, that is, with mathematical representations of buyer behavioral processes. Instead of treating sales as a gross output of the marketing process, sales are analyzed according to their components and dynamics for clues to improved marketing strategy. Sales models are built to explain total sales and brand sales for both established and new products.

Part IV is on *theory and practice* and seeks to bridge the gap between quantitative analyses of marketing problems and their actual incorporation into management decision processes. Particular attention is paid to the actual processes of information gathering, marketing planning and marketing control, management science implementation, and constructing a corporate marketing model. This writer shares the view of the relation between analysis and judgment so well articulated by Enthoven:

> Ultimately all policies are made . . . on the basis of judgments. There is no other way, and there never will be. The question is whether those judgments have to be made in the fog of inadequate and inaccurate data, unclear and undefined issues, and a welter of conflicting personal opinions, or whether they can be made on the basis of adequate, reliable information, relevant experience, and clearly drawn issues. In the end, analysis is but an aid to judgment . . . Judgment is supreme.[3]

This book is written for marketing executives, marketing researchers, operations researchers, economists, and various students of marketing who share the desire for a meaningful frame of reference for the analysis of marketing processes and problems. The emphasis on mathematical analysis is not intended to suggest that everything of importance in marketing problems can be quantified, but rather in the belief that quantification lends clarity, visibility, flexibility, and generality to assumptions and relationships deemed to be important in the phenomena. The book assumes that the reader has an elementary acquaintance with the basic ideas in calculus, linear programming, and probability theory—all of which are increasingly the subject of one or more courses taken by business school students early in their programs. This book uses these tools in the process of developing and solving mathematical statements of marketing problems and processes. Some of the more detailed mathematical arguments are developed in a separate mathematical appendix. Questions and exercises are provided at the end of each chapter to give the reader practice with the concepts developed in the book.

Many persons contributed to this book and this author feels a considerable debt to them. My past students, whose lot it was to learn their marketing analysis from my manuscript, have my gratitude for their excellent suggestions and criticisms. My particular appreciation goes to Ronald Turner, Louis Dominquez, and Gary Armstrong, who in the role of research assistants

---

[3]Alain C. Enthoven, as quoted in *Business Week* (Nov. 13, 1965) 189.

contributed their special skills to analyzing and reviewing working drafts. My colleagues at Northwestern University and elsewhere were helpful in various specific areas where "shop talk" led to a clarification of issues. Paul E. Green and Leonard M. Lodish of the University of Pennsylvania were especially helpful and insightful in their overall reviews of the manuscript. The production burden was admirably handled at different times by Edith Bass, Catherine Bullock, Marion Davis, Madeline Kluss, and Gretel Murphy. My wife, no stranger to the throes of authorship, helped provide the peaceful atmosphere so necessary to my writing.

Evanston, Illinois
January 1971

P.K.

Contents

CHAPTER 1
Marketing Analysis and Decision Making

Marketing operations are one of the last phases of business management to come under scientific scrutiny. The variables found in marketing processes do not generally exhibit the neat quantitative properties found in production and financial processes. Human factors play a larger role, marketing expenditures affect demand and costs simultaneously, and information is poor. In general, marketing effects tend to be nonlinear, lagged, stochastic, interactive, and downright difficult.

At the same time, company marketing budgets are growing at a rapid rate. Each year, American companies spend hundreds of billions of dollars to market the goods they produce and many more billions to create new goods.[1] The money is spent in promoting and distributing these goods, as well as in gathering information to help make better marketing decisions. The large expenditures for information do not change the fact that most of the marketing decisions are made in the face of substantial uncertainty. The marketing environment of most firms is characterized by keen competition, an oversupply of goods, rapidly

---

[1]Marketing expenditures account for between 40 and 50 percent of every retail dollar and support 30 percent of all the gainfully employed. Furthermore, the number of persons engaged in marketing is increasing and the number engaged in production is decreasing as a percentage of the total work force. See Reavis Cox, *Distribution in a High Level Economy* (Englewood Cliffs, N.J.: Prentice-Hall, Inc., 1965), pp. 149, 155.

shifting tastes, and a high rate of product innovation and obsolescence. Yet the science of managing marketing resources has not been advanced over the time, several decades ago, when John Wanamaker complained that he knew that half the money he spent on advertising was wasted but he didn't know which half. More than ever the firm is under pressure to improve its marketing effectiveness, and this requires substantially better concepts and tools for marketing analysis.

This chapter is divided into five sections to clarify the critical aspects of what shall here be called the problem of marketing programming. The first section isolates the major factors that contribute to the complexity of marketing phenomena, thereby laying the groundwork for further study of these factors in the first major part of this book. The second section describes various ways in which present company marketing management copes with the complexity of marketing and how each of these ways falls short of providing the needed confidence that optimal marketing programming is taking place. The third section establishes the need for theory—descriptive, prescriptive, and normative—to guide management's marketing actions. Just as the practical side of being an engineer is enhanced by knowledge of theoretical physics, the practical side of being a marketing executive is enhanced by knowledge of normative marketing theory. Section four identifies economics and operations research as to the two main sources of normative marketing theory and describes and illustrates the steps in the operations research process. Finally, section five ventures to conceptualize the marketing programming problem in an analytical statement involving notions of goal variables, a utility function, marketing decision variables, and environmental variables and constraints.

COMPLEX FACTORS IN THE MARKETING PROCESS

Merely to state that marketing decisions are made in the face of great uncertainty does not throw any light on the problém. It is necessary to go further and isolate the major complexities of the marketing process in the hope of eventually coping with them, singly or in combination.

The complexities are defined differently by different observers of the marketing scene. Businessmen see the complexity in terms of the basic variability of human nature and the insufficiency of information in any specific situation requiring action. A mathematician defines the complexity of marketing as stemming from relationships that are nonlinear, lagged, interactive, and stochastic.[2] A general systems theorist assigns the complexity of marketing to the fact that marketing is an *open system*, and therefore naturally unstable and changeable.[3]

[2]If a physicist were asked to develop optimal solutions for a system with these properties, he would put up his hands in defeat. When one of Enrico Fermi's students told the eminent physicist that he was changing his major to economics, Fermi complimented the man for his courage to venture into the harder of the two subjects.

[3]Boulding in his celebrated article distinguished among nine levels of systems analysis. [Kenneth Boulding, "General Systems Theory—the Skeleton of Science," *Management Science*, (Apr. 1956) 197–208.] The first level views a system as tantamount to its static structure. A

Our own perspective on the complexity of marketing is to isolate several problematic aspects of the marketing system that make it difficult for the decision maker to predict the market's response to variations of marketing effort. Nine perplexing problems can be distinguished; they are the subject of the following nine chapters in Part I of this book.

Shape of Aggregate Sales Response to a Single Marketing Instrument

The first problem is that the shape of the functional relationship between the market's response and the level of marketing input is typically unknown. The market is made up of buyers at various stages of awareness, interest, preference, and intention. Consequently, there is much variation in their propensity to respond to marketing offerings and efforts. Summarizing their individual behaviors into a total sales response function and specifying the ranges of increasing, constant, and diminishing returns to marketing effort is a challenging task.

Marketing Mix Interaction

The second problem is that marketing effort, far from being a homogeneous input, is a composite of many different types of activities undertaken by the firm to improve its sales. Marketing effort includes (1) pricing, (2) promotional activities such as advertising, personal selling, sales promotion, and public relations, (3) distribution activities related to the availability of goods and servicing of orders, and (4) product development and improvement activities. The firm's marketing problem is to develop a sound mix of these activities in the face of great uncertainty as to the separate and joint effects of different activities. The market's response to variations in the level of any one marketing input is conditional on the level of the other activities. Furthermore, the variation of two or more marketing activities at the same time can have synergistic effects that are greater or less than the sum of the separate effects. How to model these joint effects on a conceptual level and measure them on an empirical level is a difficult problem.

Competitive Effects

The third problem is that the market's response is a function of the competitors' efforts, as well as the firm's efforts, and the firm has imperfect to little or no

---

company's formal organizational chart would be a system at this level. The second level views a system as a simple dynamic mechanism, such as a clock or the solar system. A firm would resemble such a system if it planned its activity for an indefinite period of time and did not stray from the plan, despite variations and surprises in the environment. The third level deals with systems that have cybernetic capabilities. A firm that monitors and compares its performance to its plan and takes steps to reduce deviations is an example of such a system. Higher levels of systems analysis move into the area of open systems that have the capacity to grow and learn, and be self-conscious. Perceptual and affective elements enter the picture, as well as a larger variety of means and ends. So many variables are introduced that conceptual elegance is considerably compromised. Some analysts are not willing to work outside of mechanistic analogies and invent quasi-mechanistic models of these essentially open processes.

control over competitors' moves. The firm imperfectly forecasts the behavior and reactions of competitors and then makes the best decision possible in the light of its forecast.

Delayed Response

The fourth problem is that the market's response to current marketing outlays is not immediate but in many instances stretches out over several time periods beyond the occurrence of the outlays. A large firm such as Coca Cola can stop all of its advertising and yet continue to enjoy current and even increasing sales for a while, living off its advertising capital. The carryover effects of many marketing expenditures create a problem in the optimal timing and distribution of marketing expenditures over a planning horizon, rather than in the current year alone.

Multiple Territories

The fifth problem is that the firm typically sells in a set of territories with dissimilar rates of response to additional marketing expenditures. Should company marketing funds be concentrated in the areas where the firm is doing well or in the areas where it is doing poorly? In one form or another the question of spatial allocation of marketing funds plagues most firms, and their present methods of resolving it leave much to be desired.

Multiple Products

The sixth problem is the presence in most companies of more than one product and the consequent need to allocate limited marketing funds among them. Marketing strategies cannot be evolved for each product separately because of the strong demand and cost interactions that generally prevail among different products in the company's line. The price on a particular company product cannot be raised without considering its effect on the sale of the other products. A new product cannot be added to the product line on its own merits if it might severely reduce the revenues of existing company products. Many organizations never grapple with these critical issues and, as a consequence, achieve substantially suboptimal results.

Marketing–Corporate Interactions

The seventh problem is that marketing decisions cannot be optimized without simultaneous decision making in the production and financial areas. Whether a new advertising campaign will be profitable depends not only on the sales it produces, but also on its effect on company employment, inventories, and cash flows. Marketing, production, and financial decisions must be coordinated to achieve the corporate goals. Unfortunately, many departments are guided by considerations of departmental well-being, instead of corporate optimization, when they plan their programs.

Multiple Goals

The eighth problem is that a company tends to pursue multiple and often contradictory goals. Company presidents are often heard to say that they seek maximum sales at minimum cost. While this may be attractive rhetoric, it is fallacious logic because there is no marketing plan that simultaneously maximizes sales and minimizes costs. The firm must somehow state its objectives in such a way that a clear objective function emerges to guide the choice of a marketing strategy from a potentially large number of strategies. There is a need to consider alternative ways of resolving the multiple goal problem.

Environmental Uncertainty Effects

The ninth problem is that the marketing process is full of uncertainties beyond those just isolated. Such factors as legislation, weather, technological change, and economic fluctuation cause systematic and random disturbances in the sales response function that must be taken into account in the marketing planning process. Marketing executives have to pay attention to the variances, as well as the expected values of various forecasts and estimates of response. Several ways of handling risk and uncertainty have to be distinguished so that the executive can make an informed choice.

HOW COMPANIES COPE WITH MARKETING COMPLEXITY

Given the several complexities associated with marketing, how do marketing managers reach decisions in which they can place any confidence? Production managers in their decision making can turn to a body of engineering theory and financial managers can turn to a body of financial theory. Can the marketing manager turn to a body of marketing theory?

The general answer to this question is "no." A systematic body of normative marketing theory is still to be developed for marketing managers. It is easier to estimate responses in production and finance because the variables are subject to clearer relationships and better data. The production manager is in a fairly good position to estimate the units of output per period that would result from different combinations of men, materials, and machines. The financial manager is in a fairly good position to estimate the cash flow implications of different plans for raising, disbursing, and collecting money. But the marketing manager is *not* in a very good position to estimate the sales per period resulting from different combinations of prices, advertising message and media, sales call strategies, and product styling and packaging investments. His mean forecast error is likely to be higher, and this not only throws off his results but also the results of production and financial people.

The problem is that marketing effort works through a maze of highly unpredictable behavioral relationships, rather than through a fairly stable set of technological relationships. Market response is also subject to the vicissitudes of general economic movements and competitive forays.

What does the marketing man turn to in the face of the response uncertainties facing him as a decision maker? Four different sources of support are available.

Experience

Most marketing men say that marketing experience is the best teacher, that planning and performing a diversity of marketing activities—selling, pricing, advertising, servicing—create an ultimately sound judgment as to what will work and what will backfire. Through experience the marketing practitioner learns that inspired marketing ideas are not enough, that sales people are unevenly endowed and motivated, that customers vary immensely in their perceptions of product and company attributes, that production and financial managers greatly influence marketing outcomes, and other important lessons.

Yet experience is not enough, and herein lies the difference between the old marketing philosophy and the new. The great fault of experience is that it is unique in every man. Each man distills a message biased by his own experience and personality. It is not a random coincidence that sales managers attribute more power to personal selling and advertising managers attribute more power to advertising. When two men's experience lead to contrary conclusions, whose experience is to count? Experience cannot be the final argument for a course of action. The final argument must take the form of a stronger logic than experience.

Standard Operating Procedures

With the passage of time, companies tend to evolve standard policies and procedures to guide their decision makers. Instead of allowing individual experience to govern each decision, companies develop guidelines that codify the best management judgment and experience. Product managers are given advertising budgets that reflect safe historical ratios of advertising budgets to sales; salesmen are advised on how many calls to make to different-size customers; pricing executives abide by certain traditional markups on cost; and many other marketing activities become rule-bound over time. The unfortunate and disturbing characteristic of rules is that they typically start off as sound but almost always continue past their relevance to the situation. In any one year, a large increase or decrease in advertising expenditures may be desirable from the point of view of profit maximization. It is easier and safer, however, to follow policy and historical models than to create a compelling logic for a new policy.

Facts

Many executives act as if the answers to most marketing problems lie in the collection of facts. They will say to marketing research: "Go and find out how people like this flavor or how people view our company or how they view our competitors." It is not that these requests are wrong, but rather the implication that the facts talk for themselves and will resolve the issue. At best, they may resolve some uncertainty. Facts take on meaning only in the context of a framework of assumptions and theory. The fact that more people report a preference for one flavor over another does not mean that the first flavor is the one to produce.

It is also important to understand the strength and stability of preference, the relation of reported preference to actual behavior, the array of competitive flavors, and other factors before a decision can be made. Solutions to problems are often as sensitive to the models for analysis as the bare facts themselves. Facts are important, but like experience, they are not enough.

Assorted Theories of Market Response

Companies occasionally make a special effort to build an explicit theory of market behavior. Outside experts are called in, marketing experiments may be designed, and mathematical models may be formulated. It is at this point that it is realized that there is no shortage of company theories about market behavior. One executive believes that small amounts of advertising do not do any good, another that higher prices improve confidence in the product, and another that buyers mainly want quality. All of these have mathematical translations and could, if systematized in larger models, have important implications for the company's marketing programming. Yet one rarely sees a company in which the executives venture to integrate their theories of marketing response into an explicit system for analysis and marketing decision making.

THE NEED FOR THEORY IN MARKETING MANAGEMENT

Experience, standard operating procedures, facts, and assorted theories all make their contributions in day-to-day effective marketing management. But marketing management can also benefit from a body of explicit theory on the connection between marketing efforts of various kinds and marketing responses. Various fragments of theory are found in the published literature and in executive suites, but there has been little attempt to date to systematize and develop a coherent theory of marketing action.

By theory is meant an *explicit and coherent system of variables and relationships with potential or actual empirical foundations, addressed to gaining understanding, prediction, or control of an area of phenomena.* Considering the purposes of theory, we can distinguish between three types of theory: descriptive, predictive, and normative theory.

Descriptive Theory

Descriptive theory is the body of knowledge about the structure and functioning of an entity, process, or system. There is descriptive theory for understanding the atom, electricity, mobs, attitude formation, and a countless number of other phenomena. The marketing manager is interested in descriptive theory pertaining to the operation of a marketing system. The most elementary marketing system is made up of a company and a market. The company is related to the market through a set of four basic flows, those shown in Figure 1-1. The company dispatches (1) goods and services and (2) communications to the market; in return it receives (3) dollars and (4) information. The inner loop is an exchange of money for goods; the larger outer loop is an exchange of meanings.

A modern marketing system includes additional institutions that play a

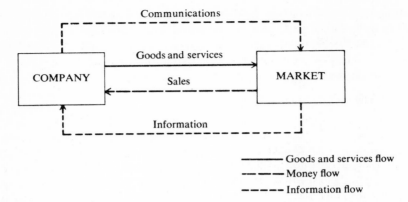

Figure 1-1 An Elementary Marketing System

crucial role in the operation of the system. (See Figure 1-2.) The behavior of suppliers has many direct and indirect effects on the company's marketing program. Furthermore, the company typically faces competitors who are seeking

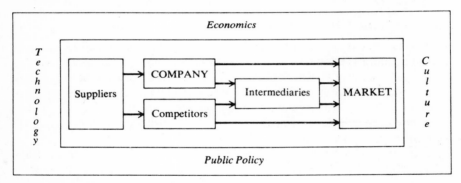

Figure 1-2 A Modern Marketing System

to satisfy the same market needs. Between the company and its market stands a host of selling, facilitating, and consulting intermediaries who add time, place, form, and possession utility to the marketplace. Finally, all of these institutions operate and respond to the larger social forces of public policy, economics, technology, and culture.

Marketing scholars, drawing on behavioral theory and organizational theory, are directing a great deal of effort toward developing models that describe the behavior of these various institutions and forces. Models have been developed of consumer[4] and industrial buyer behavior,[5] distributor be-

---

[4]See Arnold E. Amstutz, *Computer Simulation of Competitive Market Response* (Cambridge, Mass.: M.I.T. Press, 1967); John A. Howard, *Marketing Management: Analysis and Planning*, rev. ed. (Homewood, Ill.: Richard D. Irwin, Inc., 1963), Chaps. 3–4; and Francesco Nicosia, *Consumer Decision Processes* (Englewood Cliffs, N.J.: Prentice-Hall, Inc., 1966), Chap. 4.

[5]See Frederick Webster, "Modeling the Industrial Buying Process," *Journal of Marketing*

havior,[6] and competitor behavior.[7] Some companies are beginning to build computer models of their markets.[8] These models are refined over time and become a valuable tool in the development and testing of company marketing programs.

Predictive Theory

The practical value of descriptive theory is that it provides the platform for forecasting important types of behavior of interest to marketing management. Knowing how things work solves half the problem of predicting future behavior. The other half is to get good data on the independent variables that influence the course of the system. Unfortunately, data are not always available on every variable of interest, and there is the further question of cost. Some companies will settle for a highly aggregate forecasting equation that may yield an average forecasting error of x percent because a better forecasting system involving many simultaneous equations and highly disaggregative variables might cost too much in relation to the promised forecasting improvement. Predictive theory is concerned with the task of developing a practical and accurate forecasting methodology out of the materials provided by descriptive theory.

Normative Theory

While a descriptive theory provides a knowledge of the relationships between marketing system variables, and predictive theory provides a means of forecasting the outcomes of specific plans and events, the task of normative theory is to ascertain the best specific plans for realizing company objectives. Marketing management is in great need of normative theory to guide decision making in such areas as:

The best assortment of products
The best level of total marketing effort
The best allocation of marketing effort over products, territories, and customers
The best mix of different types of marketing effort
The best timing of marketing effort

The word "best" is interpreted to mean decisions that maximize the firm's objectives, subject to the constraints under which it operates. The firm must seek a simultaneous solution to the best product assortment and level, allocation,

---

Research (Nov. 1965) 370–377; and P. J. Robinson, C. W. Faris, and Y. Wind, *Industrial Buying and Creative Marketing* (Boston: Allyn and Bacon, Inc., 1967).

[6]See F. E. Balderston and A. C. Hoggatt, *Simulation of Market Processes* (Berkeley, Calif.: Institute of Business and Economic Research, University of California, 1962); and Kalman J. Cohen, *Computer Models of the Shoe, Leather, Hide Sequence* (Englewood Cliffs, N.J.: Prentice-Hall, Inc., 1960).

[7]See R. M. Cyert, E. A. Feigenbaum, and J. G. March, "Models in a Behavioral Theory of the Firm," *Behavioral Science* (Apr. 1959) 81–95.

[8]See Chap. 21.

mix, and timing of marketing effort in the light of its objectives and constraints.

SOURCES OF NORMATIVE THEORY: ECONOMICS AND OPERATIONS RESEARCH

The two disciplines that provide the fundamental concepts and tools needed in marketing programming are *economics* and *operations research*. The economic theory of the firm provides the starting point for theory construction in the area of marketing programming. The theory shows how a firm oriented toward profit maximization and characterized by efficient cost management and full information would set its *prices* (or output) under different conditions of demand and market structure. Unfortunately, the theory is considerably underdeveloped from the point of view of handling marketing complexities. It is still mainly addressed to the problem of the firm's selling a single product in a single territory, with only one or two marketing instruments, complete certainty, immediate sales response, and seeking short run profit maximization.[9] More recent developments are scattered through the literature and still have to be incorporated into the main body of theory. In 1933 Chamberlin pointed out that selling effort and product quality had to be included along with price as variables affecting the firm's demand.[10] The marginal conditions for simultaneously setting these three marketing mix variables were not elegantly worked out until 1954 by Dorfman and Steiner.[11] Work elsewhere by Koyck[12] and Nerlove[13] dealt with the issue of lagged sales response functions, but their suggested treatment still has not been joined with other marketing complexities. The theoretical interdependencies between marketing and production still have to be carefully worked out, although a useful starting point can be found in the work of Holt, Modigliani, Muth, and Simon.[14] Nordin has shown the theory of allocating the marketing budget over sales territories, but his treatment confuses the sales response function with a marketing decision rule and is also limited to simple unlagged sales response functions.[15] Theoretical development has also been deficient in modeling competitive response where more than one instrument of marketing competition exists. Also overdue is the introduction of multiple goal satisfying or constrained

[9]For an advanced example of the economic theory of the firm, see James M. Henderson and Richard E. Quandt, *Microeconomic Theory: A Mathematical Approach* (New York: McGraw-Hill, Inc., 1958).

[10]Edward H. Chamberlin, *The Theory of Monopolistic Competition* (Cambridge, Mass.: Harvard University Press, 1933).

[11]Robert Dorfman and Peter O. Steiner, "Optimal Advertising and Optimal Quality," *American Economic Review* (Dec. 1954) 826–836.

[12]L. M. Koyck, *Distributed Lags and Investment Analysis* (Amsterdam: North-Holland Publishing Co., 1954).

[13]Marc Nerlove, *Distributed Lags and Demand Analysis for Agricultural and Other Commodities*, U.S. Dept. of Agriculture Handbook 141 (Washington, D.C.: Government Printing Office, June 1958).

[14]Charles C. Holt, Franco Modigliani, John F. Muth, and Herbert A. Simon, *Planning Production, Inventories, and Work Force* (Englewood Cliffs, N.J.: Prentice-Hall, Inc., 1960).

[15]J. A. Nordin, "Spatial Allocation of Selling Expense," *Journal of Marketing* (Jan. 1943) 210–219.

profit maximization, instead of a single goal maximization. Tinbergen,[16] Theil,[17] Charnes and Stedry,[18] and others have shown how the theory of the firm could be extended to accommodate more complex formulations of the objective function, although the scattered marketing programming literature has not yet incorporated these ideas.

In short, many separate and interesting developments have been taking place in economic theory, but their integration into a unified mathematical treatment of the theory of marketing programming has still to be realized. Part I of this book is an attempt in the direction of a systematic statement. Such a statement would constitute an important contribution, both as a stimulus to further theory construction in marketing and as a guide to specific model construction in empirical marketing contexts.

The other major source of concepts and tools for examining complex marketing issues is operations research:

> Operations Research. The application of mathematical and scientific methods to problems of military, business, and man–machine systems with a view toward improving the over-all performance of such systems by analyzing the interaction of the various parts.[19]

Most experts date the beginning of operations research during World War II with the formation of British and American teams of mathematicians and scientists to study problems of supply, bombing, submarine warfare, and military strategy. When the war ended, many of the "operations researchers" left the military to join large business organizations and apply their skills to classic problems in business. The first business problems they examined were in the fields of production scheduling, inventory control, and physical distribution.[20] After scoring a number of successes in these areas, operations researchers began to apply their tools in the late 1950s to marketing problems such as advertising budgeting, sales force assignment, pricing strategy, and new product development. Early model building efforts in marketing were an attempt to fit the problem to the existing models and tools—calculus, linear programming, queuing theory, Markov processes—rather than to develop fresh models for the unique problems. For example, consumer brand selection was modeled as a simple first order Markov process, even though this left out competitive marketing strategy, in-store purchase factors, mass communications, and word of mouth

16J. Tinbergen, *On the Theory of Economic Policy* (Amsterdam: North Holland Publishing Co., 1952).

17Henri Theil, *Studies in Mathematical and Managerial Economics* (Chicago: Rand McNally & Company, 1964).

18Abraham Charnes and Andrew C. Stedry, "The Attainment of Organization Goals through Appropriate Selection of Sub-Unit Goals," in J. R. Mitchell, ed., *Operations Research in Social Science* (London: Tavistock, 1967).

19William Karush, *The Crescent Dictionary of Mathematics* (New York: The Macmillan Company 1962) p. 184.

20See Alexander Henderson and Robert Schlaifer, "Mathematical Programming: Better Information for Better Decision Making," *Harvard Business Review* (May–June 1954) 73–100.

influence in the buying process. The problem of optimal advertising media was modeled in straightforward linear programming terms, although this meant overlooking media duplication and replication of advertisements and the prevalence of nonlinear discounts. In time it was recognized that the simplified problems bore insufficient resemblance to the real problems facing marketing management. The very naïvete of these early models inspired criticism and revision and led inevitably to more complex models embodying a higher degree of realism. By the early 1960s some highly original marketing decision models had been developed. The published literature grew to include a bibliography listing over 500 marketing articles of a mathematical nature[21] and several collections of readings.[22] A number of journals such as *Management Science*, *Journal of Marketing Research* and the *Journal of Advertising Research* increasingly featured sophisticated mathematical marketing articles.

One of the first companies to finance extensive research into improved marketing decision models was DuPont. The company placed over $1 million in the hands of a specific group of company operations researchers to discover and quantify how advertising works.[23] Other DuPont operations researchers made some early applications of modern decision theory to problems in product pricing and new product introduction.

Among other early adopters of management science in marketing are such companies as Scott Paper, which conducts sophisticated field advertising experiments; Monsanto, which developed a large number of computer programs to help its executives analyze a variety of marketing problems;[24] General Electric, which has constructed a number of computer simulators of specific markets; and Ford, which carries out extensive decision analyses of major marketing policy questions. The roster also includes such companies as Pillsbury, Union Carbide, Lever Brothers, Anheuser-Busch, and Westinghouse Electric. Management science work in marketing has taken root in a number of companies in the chemical, pharmaceutical, petroleum, detergent, brewery, and consumer durable industries and is rapidly becoming attractive to companies in the airline, banking, and paper industries. Advertising agencies such as Batten, Barton, Durstine & Osborn, and Young and Rubicam, have reported the development of sophisticated models in the areas of media selection and new product development.

[21]Zenon B. Sheparovych, Marcus Alexis, and Leonard S. Simon, eds., *A Selected Annotated Bibliography on Quantitative Methods in Marketing* (Chicago: American Marketing Association, 1968).

[22]Frank M. Bass, et al, eds., *Mathematical Models and Methods in Marketing* (Homewood, Ill.: Richard D. Irwin, Inc., 1961); and Ronald E. Frank, Alfred A. Kuehn, and William F. Massy, eds., *Quantitative Techniques in Marketing Analysis* (Homewood, Ill.: Richard D. Irwin, Inc., 1962).

[23]"A Profit Yardstick for Advertising," *Business Week* (Nov. 22, 1958); see also "E. I. DuPont de Nemours & Co. (Inc.): Measurement of Effects of Advertising," in Robert D. Buzzell, *Mathematical Models and Marketing Management* (Boston: Division of Research, Graduate School of Business Administration, Harvard University, 1964).

[24]William A. Clark, "Monsanto Chemical Company: A Total Systems Approach to Marketing." in *Total Systems*, Alan D. Meacham and Van B. Thompson, eds., Detroit, Mich.: American Data Processing, Inc., 1962) 130–142.

In still another development, the Diebold Group (a firm of management consultants) in 1966 sent out an elaborate questionnaire to companies and schools doing marketing operations research in order to find out what was being done. Their summary report indicates, among other things, that the marketing areas of greatest application (in descending order) seem to be internal profit analysis, market analysis, competitive strategy, sales effort effectiveness, and pricing. Similarly, the most promising techniques (also in descending order) appear to be simulation, linear programming, and critical path analysis.

The nature of operations research is suggested by the steps through which the operations researchers go in analyzing a problem. These steps are:[25]

1. Defining the real problem
2. Collecting data on the factors affecting results
3. Analyzing the data
4. Establishing a realistic criterion for measuring results
5. Developing a model (usually but not always a mathematical one)
6. Testing the model on sample problems to make sure that it represents the system correctly
7. Developing working tools, based on the model, to achieve the desired results
8. Integrating the new methods into company operations
9. Reevaluating and revising the model as it is used

Example   The top management of a large brewery was concerned about its procedures for developing marketing budgets for the company's sales territories. Territory budgets were largely determined by recent sales and the degree of pressure and influence of the territory sales managers. Management recognized that territory sales did not necessarily indicate where additional marketing funds would do the most good. It wanted to find a better system for setting the marketing budget for each sales territory.

Defining the Problem

Management's doubts began when it discovered that a leading competitor was spending fewer promotional dollars relative to sales and achieving better sales growth and profits. Management discussions led to a feeling that the problem lay not in the level of expenditures but in its allocation to the various company sales territories.

Collecting and Analyzing Data

The problem was turned over to the company's operations research department, which decided as a first step to determine the actual procedures being used by marketing management to set up territory budgets, including the information that management had collected, the formal criteria it used, and the role it assigned

[25]"The ABC's of Operations Research," *Dun's Review and Modern Industry* (Sept. 1963) Part 2, 105ff.

to personal influence. After many interviews the operations research team was able to develop an elaborate logical flow diagram of the budgeting process. In addition the team investigated the company's historical data on company sales and market share, competitors' advertising, and sales promotion expenditures by territory, consumer brand preferences, and company and competitors' distribution coverage by territory.

Establishing a Realistic Criterion for Measuring Results

The operations research team needed a criterion for comparing various alternative ways of allocating the marketing budget. They decided to use a five-year planning horizon and estimate the impact of different allocation procedures on total discounted profit over the period.

Developing a Model

The operatons research team developed a computer model that imitated the present procedures used by management to develop budgets for the various sales territories. This model predicted actual management allocations with a fair degree of accuracy. The operations research team also developed an alternative model that based allocations to sales territories on a mathematical decision rule. The decision rule came about as a solution to a set of demand and cost equations for each territory. A territory demand equation provided a prediction of the territory's sales as a function of the amounts spent on advertising, sales promotion, and the sales force. Having equations for predicting sales and also territory cost equations, the researchers were able to develop territory profit equations and then find a decision rule for allocating the marketing budget optimally over the territories.

Testing the Model on Sample Problems

The mathematical model was tested against the company's present model on actual and hypothetical data and appeared to produce superior sales and profit results. The mathematical model helped to reduce the mean sales forecasting error by a substantial amount.

Developing Working Tools

The mathematical model required periodic data on company and competitive expenditures and sales, as well as intervening measures of consumer brand preferences. Among other things the company had to subscribe to certain standard marketing research services. In addition the model called for varying allocations away from their normal levels in a small sample of matched territories in order to get a reading on the sensitivity of sales to alternative levels of marketing expenditures.

Integrating the New Methods into Company Operations

The mathematical model now had to be converted into a system for planning and controlling territorial marketing expenditures. The final system is shown in abbreviated form in Figure 1-3. Time t signified the time when marketing management had to determine the marketing budget for each territory. They first considered territory i and its last period's sales, market share, and the marketing expenditures of the company and its competitors. Marketing management compared these results to previous predictions and adjusted the mathematical model where required. Marketing management then forecasted the future environment and competitors' strategies. These became inputs into a mathematical decision rule that produced a recommended budget and strategy for the territory, along with predicted levels of sales and profits. The same procedure was repeated for each territory. After all territory budgets and strategies were determined, they were implemented. The whole process was repeated in each period.

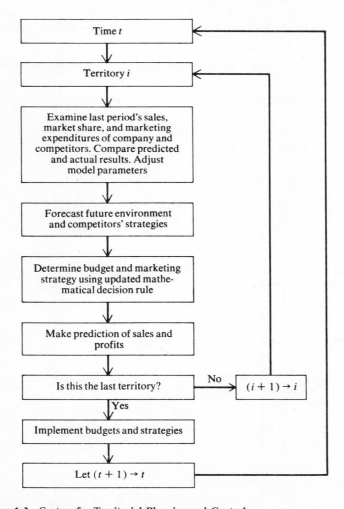

Figure 1-3 System for Territorial Planning and Control

Revaluation and Revision

A system such as this is not static; provision must be made for its continuous revision in the light of new data and insights.

ANALYTIC STATEMENT OF THE MARKETING PROGRAMMING PROBLEM

We are now ready to formulate a concise statement of the problem of marketing programming: Marketing management seeks to determine the best simultaneous settings of various *marketing decision variables* $\{X\}$ under their control (price, promotion, distribution, and product quality) over time, space, and product lines, in the face of *environmental variables* $\{Y\}$ not under their control (the economy, competitive activity, technology, and so on) and various *constraints* $\{K\}$, that will maximize the firm's long run *utility function U* as defined over a set of *goal variables* $\{Z\}$.

The following major elements stand out in this definition of the problem of marketing programming:

1. A set of goal variables $\{Z\}$
2. A utility function U
3. A set of marketing decision variables $\{X\}$
4. A set of environmental variables $\{Y\}$
5. A set of constraints $\{K\}$

These concepts are illustrated in Figure 1-4 and discussed below.

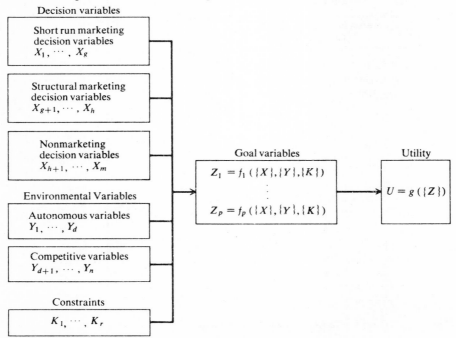

Figure 1-4   Symbolic Statement of the Marketing Programming Problem

Goal Variables

The firm is conceived to be a complex goal seeking entity that continually adjusts variables under its control in the interest of maximal achievement of its objectives. In the classic economic theory of the firm, the firm is considered to have a simple goal structure consisting of the attainment of maximum profits. The postulation of profit maximization as the firm's goal considerably simplifies the evaluation of alternative strategies. It means that the analysis can be conducted by finding an expression for profits as a function of the controllable variables and using calculus or mathematical programming to determine the optimal strategy. Profit maximization, however, has come under heavy attack as an adequate description of the firm's goal structure.[26] In more recent theories the firm is seen as seeking to satisfy multiple and changing objectives.[27] These objectives can be called the firm's goal variables and include such things as profit, sales, market share, and employee and community welfare.

A Utility Function

Typically, the firm cannot simultaneously maximize all of its objectives. Some of its objectives inevitably conflict with each other, such as is the case in trying to maximize both sales and profits, or service and profits. To handle the problem of conflicting objectives, the firm has to place a utility function over its objectives and seek to maximize this function. It could, for example, associate a weight with each objective and seek the policy $\{X\}$ that would maximize the weighted combination of its objectives.[28] Alternatively, it could set target levels for its various objectives and then seek a policy $\{X\}$ that minimizes the weighted sum of the squared deviations from these target levels.[29] As another possibility, it could select one of the objectives Z_i and seek a policy $\{X\}$ that maximizes this objective, subject to minimal achievement levels of the other variables.[30] In general the firm must find a way to convert its multiple objectives into a utility formulation that allows the decision maker to evaluate the total effect of alternative policies on its long run interest.

A Set of Marketing Decision Variables

If we consider the firm as a whole, its decision variables or policy instruments cover a broad spectrum of activities in the areas of marketing, finance, production, and administration. Management must set mutually compatible and optimizing levels for price, marketing expenditures, work force size, production rate,

---

[26]Herbert A. Simon, "Theories of Decision-Making in Economics and Behavioral Science," *American Economic Review* (June 1959) 253–283.

[27]Richard M. Cyert and James G. March, *A Behavioral Theory of the Firm* (Englewood Cliffs, N.J.: Prentice-Hall, Inc. 1963).

[28]See David W. Miller and Martin K. Starr, *Executive Decisions and Operations Research* (Englewood Cliffs, N.J.: Prentice-Hall, Inc., 1960) 161–165.

[29]Henri Theil, "Linear Decision Rules for Macrodynamic Policy Problems," in Bert G. Hickman, ed., *Quantitative Planning of Economic Policy* (Washington, D.C.: Brookings Institution, 1965), 18–42.

[30]Herbert A. Simon, "On the Concept of Organizational Goals," *Administrative Science Quarterly* (June 1964) 1–22.

capital expenditures, cash borrowing, and so forth. The theory of marketing programming concentrates on the setting of marketing decision variables but cannot neglect their interaction with nonmarketing variables.

Marketing decision variables are not all adjustable in the short run. Some subset $\{X_s\}$ are adjustable in each time period. For example, the firm can typically change its price, the number of salesmen, or advertising expenditures, within limits, in the short run. It may not be able to develop a new product, modify an old product, or alter its marketing channels, except in the long run. The fixity of some marketing variables can be traced to (1) long term commitments to keep them at certain levels, and (2) inherent difficulties in varying them continuously. Those marketing decision variables that cannot be changed in the short run will be called structural marketing decision variables $\{X_1\}$. The short run marketing decision variables must be set in the light of the structural marketing decision variables. The optimizing level and mix of marketing decision variables will be called $\{X^*\}$.

A Set of Environmental Variables

The results achieved by the firm not only depend upon its own policy settings, but also upon factors in the market that are beyond its control. Chief among these factors are the level of economic activity, competitive activity, and autonomous changes in culture, law, and technology. The firm must make two analyses of these environmental variables, one involving how these variables structurally affect the level of demand and cost, and the other involving the probable level of these variables during the planning period. The firm must then decide on the best levels of its own decision variables in the light of expected levels and effects of the environmental variable.

The problem is more complicated, in that some of the environmental variables attain levels independent of the firm's action (autonomous variables) and others are influenced by its action (competitive variables). Average temperature or gross national product are examples of the former; competitive prices and advertising are examples of the latter. The problem of short run marketing programming is then reformulated as the task of setting short run marketing decision variables that maximize the firm's utility function in the light of the structural marketing decision variables, the probable reactions of competitors, and the probable levels of the autonomous variables. The problem of long run marketing programming is the task of finding the optimal settings over time of all the marketing decision variables in the light of trends and expected levels of the environmental variables.

A Set of Constraints

Finally, this programming must be done in the context of a set of two broad types of constraints faced or self-imposed by management. First, there are constraints that delimit the range of possible settings of *decision variables*. For example, the firm may not be free to select a price outside of certain limits imposed by market forces or legal regulation. Secondly, there are constraints that delimit the range of tolerable outcomes for *goal variables*. For example, management may not accept any plan that will lead to lower sales even if it promises higher total profits.

To summarize, the firm wishing to find an optimum marketing program must go through the following steps:

1. Clarify its goal variables.
2. Formulate utility as a function of the goal variables.
3. Clarify the marketing decision variables under its control in the short run and long run and their effect on the goal variables.
4. Project the likely levels and effects of the environmental variables on the goal variables.
5. Clarify the constraints that must be observed with respect to the decision variables and goal variables.
6. Derive the decision rules or levels themselves of the marketing and other decision variables that will maximize the firm's utility function.

Questions and Problems

1. Does there appear to be any ordering by importance the of ten complexities of the marketing process listed? Are these complexities independent of each other, or are they interrelated?
2. While standard operating procedures have decided disadvantages in some instances, they do have a definite value in others. As stated in the chapter, many of these procedures are sound at the time of their inception, but become obsolete as time passes. In what types of situations are standard operating procedures most useful and feasible?
3. Give examples of descriptive, predictive, and normative theories which are applicable to marketing, providing a brief statement of their content and purpose.
4. The Tempus Company is a small producer of a laundry bleach, which has successfully competed against its larger competitors selling laundry detergents that claim to have bleaching power. Tempus management has just learned that its competitors are considering the introduction in the near future of a detergent with soaking characteristics. Management at Tempus must decide whether or not they should also develop and market such a soak product.

   Carry out a brief analysis of the problem faced by the Tempus management in the above situation, following the list of steps through which the operations researcher should go in analyzing a problem.
5. Classify the following elements in terms of the marketing programming classification in Figure 1–4: (1) profits, (2) sales volume, (3) disposable personal income (4) advertising $\leq$ \$15,000 per year, (5) competitors' advertising, (6) company price, (7) industry price level, (8) company product quality, (9) production level, and (10) company distribution channels.
6. A firm is introducing a new product. It can choose any one of each of 3 prices, 2 packages, 3 advertising campaigns, 4 distribution channels, and 2 service policies. It must contend with 5 possible strategies by competitors. How many different possible decision situations does the firm face?
7. What is the value of theory in marketing?

PART I
Macromarketing
Decision Theory

CHAPTER 2
Aggregate Sales Response to a Single Marketing Instrument

We shall start our analysis of marketing programming with the simplest possible case, so that the major concepts can be developed in a logical fashion. Each succeeding chapter in Part I will replace a previous assumption with a new real world complexity and require a more refined mathematical analysis. When this method is most fruitful, each chapter solves the new complexity along with all the old ones, with the final chapter representing a rich and complex statement and solution to the total problem. Unfortunately, the various marketing complexities are each so formidable and are subject to alternative models of expression and solution, so that a total model is in fact not achievable. Yet the reader does gain experience in handling the major analytical problems in marketing and can construct a specific model for any practical situation by synthesizing the appropriate methods described in the various chapters.

At the outset we shall assume a firm that enjoys a complete monopoly in its market. It produces one product in a fixed-size plant and sells the product in a single territory. Its physical sales volume (Q) each period is strictly determined by the level at which it sets its total marketing effort (X) in that period. In setting its marketing effort each period, the firm is guided solely by the objective of short run profit maximization. Thus the major assumptions are:

1. One marketing decision variable

2. One product
3. One territory
4. No competition
5. No carryover effect
6. Short run profit maximization

We shall proceed to consider how such a firm can determine the setting of its marketing effort so as to maximize short run profits. The analysis will consist of determining the firm's demand function, cost function, and profit function. It will be shown that the problem is one of stating profits as a function of the marketing decision variable and finding the level that will maximize profits. First, however, we have to consider alternative ways to formulate the critical demand and cost functions facing the firm.

DEMAND FUNCTION

Demand is one of the two major factors—the other is cost—that the firm considers in developing its marketing and other plans. *Demand denotes the number of units on a product or service that the market will desire to purchase per time period under varying marketing conditions.* Demand is affected by a host of variables: some under the control of the firm—the marketing decision variables; others outside of the control of the firm—the environmental variables. One of the important tasks of the marketing analyst is to isolate the major demand variables, determine the form of their relation to demand (the demand function, also called the sales response function), and estimate the actual coefficients of the demand function (the demand equation). The competent analyst recognizes that the demand equation is a highly aggregative expression for a considerably complex behavioral space and considers it to be one of several alternative levels of analysis in which order can be imposed on this complex behavioral space. In many situations the demand equation gives a good fit to available data and offers a useful way to express and manipulate one's theory of the behavior of a particular market.

For the simple economic world outlined in this chapter, demand is conceived to be affected by only one variable X within the control of the firm, that is,

$$Q = f(X) \tag{2-1}$$

where Q = demand per period in physical units
X = a marketing decision variable

Now we take up separately the case in which the marketing decision variable is negatively related to demand, as is the case with price, and where the marketing decision variable is positively related to demand, as is the case with advertising, selling effort, and product quality.

Demand as a Function of Price

One of the most basic relations in economic theory is known as the Law of

Demand, which states that the quantity demanded per period (also known as the time rate of demand) is negatively related to price. The basis for this law is the postulation of a rational consumer who has full knowledge of the goods and substitutes, a limited budget, and a singular drive to maximize his utility. For a given structure of relative prices he will allocate his income over goods (including savings) so as to maximize his utility. If the price relations change, he will normally substitute less expensive goods for the more expensive goods; this will increase his utility. For example, since a price decline will normally increase the attractiveness of that particular good in relation to other goods, he will increase his consumption of that good.[1]

The Law of Demand does not go on to state the appropriate shape of the negative relationship, implying that this varies with the particular product or product class. Yet some equation forms have become particularly popular for representing the quantity-price relationship and they are described below.

Linear demand-price function. Figure 2-1(a) shows the linear concept of the demand-price relationship whose general equation is of the form:[2]

$$Q = a - bP \qquad\qquad (2-2)$$

where Q = quantity demanded per time period
 $\quad\ a$ = positive intercept, that is, $a > 0$
 $\quad\ b$ = slope of relationship or the rate at which the quantity demanded per time period changes with respect to a unit change in price
 $\quad\ P$ = price per unit

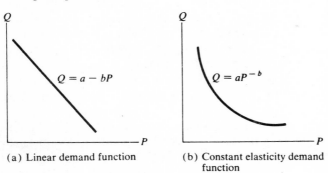

(a) Linear demand function
(b) Constant elasticity demand function

Figure 2-1   Two Alternative Demand Equation Forms

[1]However, see discussion of exceptions on pp. 29–31. For a careful statement and discussion of the Law of Demand, see James M. Henderson and Richard E. Quandt, *Microeconomic Theory: A Mathematical Approach* (New York: McGraw-Hill, Inc., 1958), Chap. 2.

[2]Most economics textbooks show P on the vertical axis and Q on the horizontal axis, as a result of a long-standing tradition in which the firm (under pure competition) sets the quantity that it will produce in the face of a going market price. Since most of the situations discussed in this book involve imperfect competition, the firm is seen as setting the price, rather than the output, as its marketing decision. Following mathematical convention, the independent variable price is shown in this book on the horizontal axis; the dependent variable, quantity, is shown on the vertical axis.

The linear relationship is not to be taken as literally applying throughout the domain of possible prices but rather as being approximately true in the neighborhood of the prevailing price. Equations in all branches of science are assumed to be valid representations of response only over the range of observed values.

Because the concept of *price elasticity* plays an important role in the analysis of marketing programming, we shall introduce its definition here and then comment on the elasticity characteristics of the linear demand function. It turns out that price elasticity varies over the linear demand function, and in fact is always higher at higher price levels.

Price elasticity is defined as the ratio of the percentage change in demand associated with a percentage change in price. In symbols:

$$e_{qp} = \frac{\text{percentage change in demand}}{\text{percentage change in price}} = \frac{(Q_1 - Q_0)/Q_0}{(P_1 - P_0)/P_0} \times 100$$

$$= \frac{\Delta Q/Q}{\Delta P/P} = \frac{\Delta Q}{\Delta P} \cdot \frac{P}{Q} \qquad (2\text{-}3)$$

where e_{qp} = elasticity of quantity demanded with respect to a change in price
$\quad\quad Q_1$ = quantity demanded per period after price change
$\quad\quad Q_0$ = quantity demanded per period before price change
$\quad\quad P_1$ = new price
$\quad\quad P_0$ = old price
$\quad\quad \Delta Q = Q_1 - Q_0$
$\quad\quad \Delta P = P_1 - P_0$

Price elasticity is understood to be negative in the normal case, although we shall drop the sign in further discussion. A price elasticity of one means that demand rises (falls) by the same percentage that price falls (rises). In this case, total revenue is left unaffected. A price elasticity greater than one means that demand rises (falls) by more than price falls (rises) in percentage terms; in this case, total revenue rises (falls). A price elasticity less than one means that demand rises (falls) by less than price falls (rises) in percentage terms; in this case, total revenue falls (rises).

The price elasticity of demand gives more precision to the question of whether the firm's price is too high or too low. From the point of view of maximizing revenue, the price is too high if demand elasticity at that price is greater than 1 and too low if demand elasticity at that price is less than 1. Whether this is also true for maximizing profits depends on the behavior of costs. If unit costs are constant over a wide range of possible outputs, it is true; but if unit costs rise with the scale of production, it may not be true.

How can the price elasticity be determined in the neighborhood of a particular price, say P_1, on a linear demand curve? Since

$$e_{qp} = \frac{\Delta Q}{\Delta P} \cdot \frac{P}{Q} \qquad (2\text{-}4)$$

is the definition of elasticity, we must proceed to make the appropriate substitutions for the terms on the right. The term, $\Delta Q/\Delta P$, when P is very small, is approximated by the first derivative of quantity with respect to price, that is, dQ/dP. For the linear demand function $Q = a - bP$,

$$\frac{dQ}{dP} = -b \tag{2-5}$$

Then

$$e_{qp} = \frac{\Delta Q}{\Delta P} \frac{P}{Q} = -b \frac{P}{a - bP} = \frac{-bP}{a - bP} \tag{2-6}$$

At "high" prices, is elasticity high or low for a linear demand function? The reader should prove that, for this elasticity function:

1. Price elasticity will be 1 when $P = a/2b$.
2. Price elasticity is high at "high" prices, making it desirable to lower price.
3. Price elasticity is low at low prices, making it desirable to raise price.

All of this pertains to a linear demand function and is subject to the usual qualifications about the use of the elasticity concept in practice. It must be recognized, in the first place, that a price will be changed in practice not by an infinitesimal amount but by a finite amount, and the magnitude of this change would make a difference in the level of response. Secondly, the effect of the price change will depend on the level of the present price, that is, whether it is "high" or "low." Thirdly, it must be recognized that short run and long run elasticity may be quite different. Buyers may have to continue with the present supplier immediately after his price increase because choosing a new supplier takes time, but they may eventually stop purchasing from him. In this case, demand is more elastic in the long run than in the short run. Stigler suggests that demand is generally more elastic in the long run because the short run is marked by the difficulty of rapid adjustment, the existence of market imperfections, and the presence of habit.[3] Or the reverse may happen in some situations; buyers may drop a supplier in anger after he increases prices but return to him later. This significance of this distinction between short run and long run elasticity is that the seller may not learn the wisdom of his price revision until some time after the change.

Constant elasticity demand-price function. There is another popular conception of the shape of this demand function, this one based on the notion of constant elasticity. This function is shown in Figure 2-1(b) and is the equation for a general hyperbolic function:

$$Q = aP^{-b} \tag{2-7}$$

It will turn out that the exponent b is the constant price elasticity and holds for every possible price.

[3]George Stigler, *The Theory of Price*, rev. ed. (New York: The Macmillan Company, 1952) 45–47.

Take the case where $b = 1$. The equation becomes

$$Q = aP^{-1} = \frac{a}{P} \tag{2-8}$$

$$PQ = a \tag{2-9}$$

But price times quantity is the definition of total revenue, R, that is,

$$PQ = R \tag{2-10}$$

For this special case, R will always equal the constant a. Thus every price change will be accompanied by an equal and opposite demand change (in percentage terms), leaving total revenue unchanged. This means that elasticity must be 1 everywhere on the curve, and it is no coincidence that $b = 1$.

We now proceed to the proof that b is the elasticity for the general hyperbolic function. We use the definition of elasticity:

$$e_{qp} = \frac{dQ}{dP} \cdot \frac{P}{Q} = (-baP^{-b-1}) \frac{P}{aP^{-b}}$$

$$e_{qp} = \frac{-baP^{-b}}{aP^{-b}} = -b \tag{2-11}$$

Thus the exponent b of price in a hyperbolic function is the price elasticity. In general the hyperbolic function form of demand has been popular among analysts because it includes an explicit term for elasticity, produces curvilinearity, and is easy to manipulate mathematically.

Other negative demand-price functions. The constant elasticity of the hyperbolic demand function, although an advantage in many ways, is thought by some to be too restrictive. There is no particular reason why the percentage change in demand is likely to be constant for a unit percentage change in price throughout the domain of possible price changes. The linear demand function shows varying price elasticity. Various nonlinear demand functions, with the exception of the hyperbolic function, would show varying price elasticity, such as the second degree polynomial,

$$Q = a - bP - cP^2 \tag{2-12}$$

the third degree polynomial,

$$Q = a - bP + cP^2 - dP^3 \tag{2-13}$$

the exponential function, where $e = 2.71 \cdots$ [4]

$$Q = \bar{Q}e^{-bP} \tag{2-14}$$

and the step function[5]

---

[4]For an explanation of the mathematical constant e, see note 16. This exponential function has two nice properties: (1) as $P \to 0$, $Q \to \bar{Q}$; $\bar{Q}$ can be called the market potential and represents the volume the market would absorb if the goods were free; (2) as $P \to \infty$, $Q \to 0$. That is, demand goes toward 0 as the price rises toward infinity.

[5]Actually, elasticity is 0 everywhere on a step demand function, except at the price breaks, where it is not defined at all. A step demand function would be used to describe situations in which buyers are indifferent to price variations within established price ranges. For example, the demand for men's suits may be Q_1 for any price within \$60–\$80, Q_2 for any price within \$80–\$100, etc.

$$Q = \begin{cases} Q_1 \text{ for } P_0 \leqslant P < P_1 \\ Q_2 \text{ for } P_1 \leqslant P < P_2 \\ Q_3 \text{ for } P_2 \leqslant P < P_3 \end{cases} \tag{2-15}$$

The analyst should be aware of these and other possible forms for the demand function because the equation he will obtain is a matter of his choice of a form fitted against the actual data—time series or cross-sectional—of prices and quantity. The scatter of the data as well as theory will suggest an equation form; then he fits it to the data.

Positively sloping demand-price functions. Even the conventional negative relation between price and quantity that is stated in the Law of Demand seems to admit of exceptions. Many situations have been observed in which the time rate of demand appears to be positively associated with price. There are four possible reasons for this paradoxical relation, each turning out to involve a third factor that is not controlled.

1. The Income Effect. If a substantial price reduction occurs on a item that particular households consume in substantial quantities, it amounts to an increase in real income for those households. With the greater purchasing power they may decide to switch altogether to more expensive products, instead of consuming more of the former product. The income effect outweighs the substitution effect. The product they abandon can be called an inferior good. Thus, if poor families consume a lot of potatoes in their diet, and the price of potatoes falls, these families might· use the savings to buy more meat and cut down on their potato consumption. A more desired good, meat now replaces potatoes because of the income effect of the price cut. All of this applies to the opposite case, in which potatoes rise in price. This cuts down family real income, so that they may have to drop meat and buy more potatoes.

2. The Veblen Effect. In the case of certain goods a higher price is likely to increase demand because of the phenomenon of "conspicuous consumption." The enjoyment felt by many buyers of higher priced furs, jewelry, cars, and so forth, partly derives from the expense of the item: its expense serves as a status symbol for the owner.[6]

3. The Expectation Effect. When a price reduction is seen as the beginning of

---

[6]In addition to the Veblen effect, there are two other related but distinguishable effects, dubbed by Leibenstein the bandwagon effect and the snob effect. "By the bandwagon effect, we refer to the extent to which the demand for a commodity is *increased* due to the fact that others are also consuming the same commodity. It represents the desire of people to purchase a commodity in order to get into 'the swim of things'; in order to conform with the people they wish to be associated with; in order to be fashionable or stylish; or, in order to appear to be 'one of the boys.' By the snob effect we refer to the extent to which the demand for a consumers' good is *decreased* owing to the fact that others are also consuming the same commodity (or that others are increasing their consumption of that commodity). This represents the desire of people to be exclusive; to be different; to dissociate themselves from the 'common herd.' " Whereas the Veblen effect describes "the extent to which the demand for a consumers' good is increased because it bears a higher rather than a lower price." For an economic analysis of these different effects, see Harvey Leibenstein," "Bandwagon, Snob, and Veblen Effects in the Theory of Consumers' Demand," *Quarterly Journal of Economics* (May 1950) 183–207.

a possible wave of further price reductions, many buyers will withold their purchases in the present, hoping to take advantage of lower prices in the future. Thus, in times of general price deflation, purchases might fall in anticipation of better values in the future. The same applies when a company known to be in trouble cuts its price; buyers might see this as the beginning of a sequence of further price cuts and hold back their purchases. By the same token the opposite situation of rising prices can cause purchases to increase on the part of buyers who expect further price increases.[7]

4.   *The Quality Effect.* In situations in which buyers are not well informed about the respective merits of competing products, and some risk is involved, buyers may take the price as an indication of quality. Thus higher priced television sets and higher priced aspirins are considered to have more quality than their lower priced counterparts. In one experiment buyers who examined several raincoats with different price tags reported quality differences even though none existed. These kinds of observations can lead an executive to recommend raising a price in the interest of selling more. But what is really lurking behind the positive sloped demand curve is this third variable, the consumer's perception of quality. The role of quality perception is shown in the four-quadrant diagram in Figure 2-2. Quadrant 1 shows the psychological relationship that might exist in the

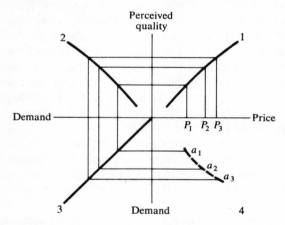

Figure 2-2   Relationship between Price, Perceived Quality and Demand

minds of buyers between product quality and price. Quadrant 2 shows the hypothetical effect of the quality factor on demand. Quadrant 3 is a redundant relation between demand and itself (a 45° line) to allow projecting the result of different prices and demand on quadrant 4. Now suppose the price was P_1.

[7]Economists use the term *elasticity of expectations* in this connection. The elasticity of expectations is the ratio of the future expected percentage change in price to the recent percentage change in price. A positive elasticity means that buyers expect a price reduction (increase) to be followed by another reduction (increase). A positive elasticity of expectation is therefore a factor in causing an apparent positively sloped demand curve.

We can trace the effect of this price through quality and quantity and project it as the point a_1. Repeat this for P_2 and P_3. These changing prices trace out a demand-price relationship in quadrant 4 that is positive.

Demand as a Function of Marketing Effort

Price is an unusual marketing decision variable, in that it is normally inversely related to demand;[8] most of the other variables such as advertising, selling effort, and product quality are positively related or positively affect the level of demand.[9] The general name we shall give to all these positive marketing decision variables is *marketing effort*. Our purpose here is to discuss how the level of demand Q varies with the level of total marketing effort (X), all other things being equal.[10]

In considering the functional relationship between total marketing effort and total market response, analysts generally dismiss the possibility that market response could be increasing exponentially or even linearly throughout the range of possible marketing efforts.[11] Most analysts assume that, after some point, additional marketing effort is associated with sales increases at a diminishing rate. Otherwise there would be a natural tendency toward monopoly in every industry. The issue is essentially one of whether diminishing marginal returns characterize market response through the whole range of marketing effort (the

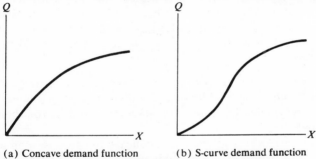

(a) Concave demand function   (b) S-curve demand function

Figure 2-3   Two Alternative Conceptions of the Positive Demand Function

[8]Economists use the term demand curve or demand function to mean the relationship between the quantity demanded and the price, i.e., $Q = f(P)$. The effect of other variables on demand is handled through shifting the demand curve. This approach, which has advantages in showing how a pure price system works, is less satisfactory for clarifying the role of nonprice factors in a modern economy. For the latter purpose, it is better to use the term *demand function* (or sales response function) to describe a multivariate relationship, that is, $Q = f(X_1, X_2, \ldots, X_n)$.

[9]It is possible to develop a positive relation between price as a marketing variable and demand by using the reciprocal of price. The reciprocal of price, $1/p$, represents the amount of product per dollar. Thd higher the reciprocal of price the higher the value received by the customer. We can call $1/p$ the *value variable* and restate the Law of Demand to read: the higher the value, the higher the demand.

[10] In Chap. 4, we shall disaggregate the marketing effort term in the demand function into particular marketing decision variables. In Part II, we shall examine the microlinkages between each marketing decision variable and sales.

[11]A possible exception is found in statements by Leonard Lavin, president of Alberto-Culver, who maintained in the past that sales could be increased at an increasing rate with advertising expenditure almost indefinitely.

concave case) or whether increasing marginal returns might be present at the beginning and later give way to diminishing marginal returns (the *S* curve case). These two competing concepts of the demand function are illustrated in Figure 2-3.

Concave demand function.   The demand function in Figure 2-3(a) shows demand starting at the origin and always increasing with marketing effort at a continuously diminishing rate.[12] This function implies that the first marketing dollar is spent in the absolutely best possible way; the second marketing dollar is spent in the next best way; and successive marketing dollars are applied in successively less productive ways—this accounts for the continuously diminishing rate of sales increase. Also implied is the idea that there are no indivisibilities in response, that there is no requirement of discrete expenditures before further investments become productive. The very first dollar of marketing expenditure is applied against the best use and is sufficient to tap it. Joel Dean has expressed the argument for this position in the following words:

> Presumably the most susceptible prospects are picked off first, and pro-gressively stiffer resistance is encountered from layers of prospects who are more skeptical, more stodgy about their present spending pattern, or more attached to rival sellers. The rise may also be caused by progressive exhaustion of the most vulnerable geographical areas or the most efficient advertising media. Promotional channels that are ideally adapted to the scale and market of firms are used first.[13]

In general this function would seem to apply to such situations as direct mail order (the best mailing lists are used first), sales calls to prospects (the best prospects are called on first), and geographical market development (the best territories are developed first).

Given the various arguments in favor of a concave function to represent the relationship between demand and marketing effort, the analyst who wishes to use this function in fitting his data has a choice among a number of functional forms all satisfying the property of concavity.[14] Three of the major, possible

---

[12]Starting the demand curve at 0 implies that company sales are 0 if marketing effort is 0. If marketing effort is defined broadly enough, to include putting in favorable product qualities, developing channels of distribution, etc., it follows that, if these things are not done, there would be no sales. If, on the other hand, marketing effort is conceived as expenses of advertising and personal selling, it is conceivable that, if these expenses were temporarily suspended, sales might remain at a positive level for a while because of a carryover effect due to past marketing expenditures. The analyst has either option and can easily modify any standard equation to produce a curve that starts at the origin or above the origin. In practical problems, the value of the curve at the origin is of little interest compared to its behavior within the range of reasonable expenditures on marketing.

[13]Joel Dean, *Managerial Economics* (Englewood Cliffs, N.J.: Prentice-Hall, Inc., 1951), p. 358.

[14]A function is strictly concave throughout if a straight line joining any two points on the graph of the function always lies below the function between the two points. A rigorous algebraic statement is that a function f is concave if for any number λ such that $0 \leq \lambda \leq 1$, and for every pair of numbers X_1 and X_2, we have $f[\lambda X_1 + (1 - \lambda)X_2] \leq \lambda f(X_1) + (1 - \lambda) f(X_2)$.

functional forms are illustrated in Figure 2-4 and discussed below.

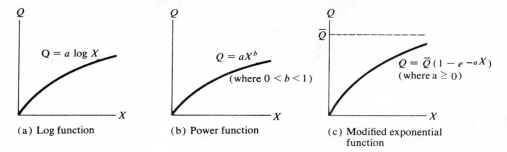

(a) Log function   (b) Power function   (c) Modified exponential function

Figure 2-4   Concave Demand Functions

1. Log Function. The first functional form is the log function $Q = a \log X$, which holds that demand varies with the log of marketing effort. Since the log of X grows slower than X itself, demand increases less rapidly than marketing effort. Specifically, to increase Q by k percent, we must increase the log X by k percent. Thus, if sales double between an expenditure of \$1 and \$2, then to double it again, \$4 must be spent; to double it again, \$8 must be spent; and so on. Constant percent increases in marketing effort are necessary to produce constant amounts of increase in sales. If Figure 2-4(a) is redrawn with the X axis in log form, then the relationship would appear as a straight line.

2. Power function. The second functional form is the power function $Q = aX^b$. A familiar example is where $b = \frac{1}{2}$, that is, $Q = a\sqrt{X}$. Here the level of demand increases with the square root of the level of marketing effort.

The function $Y = aX^b$ is one of the most versatile functions available when b is allowed to take on different values. The repertoires of possible shapes for this function is shown in Figure 2-5. If b is equal to 0, then the power function becomes

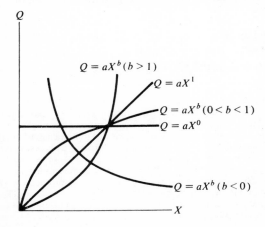

Figure 2-5   The Power Function

a horizontal line at the level a and says that marketing effort does not influence the level of demand. If $b < 0$, then demand and marketing effort are inversely related, as is the case when marketing effort takes the form of price. If $0 < b < 1$, this function produces the concave relationship mentioned above. If $b = 1$, then this function produces a straight line with the origin at 0 and the slope of a. Finally, if $b > 1$, this function produces a relationship that is increasing at an increasing rate.

One of the nice properties of this functional form is that it spells out a linear relationship on double log paper, that is, $Q = aX^b$ is the same as log Q = log $a + b$ log X.

3. *Modified Exponential Function.* The third function in Figure 2-4 can be described as exponential and asymptotic and is useful where it is believed that demand would approach a finite upper limit (Q) were marketing effort in that period to approach infinity. This finite limit is commonly called the *market potential* or the *saturation level* of demand, that is, market potential can be defined as $\bar{Q} = \lim_{X \to \infty} Q(X)$. This finite limit will be approached quite rapidly or quite slowly, depending on the product. The company's task is to estimate both the market potential ($\bar{Q}$) and the rate of approach (a) to it. Often different factors enter into each. For example, market potential may be estimated on the basis of population, national income, and other factors showing the capacity of the market to absorb the particular product. The rate of approach to this potential, on the other hand, depends on the effectiveness and amount of marketing effort expended in influencing the population to feel a desire for the product and in making it available. A useful functional form that combines these ideas is the modified exponential:[15]

$$Q = \bar{Q}(1 - e^{-aX}) \tag{2-16}$$

$\bar{Q}$ = amount demanded per period if total potential is realized

e = a mathematical constant, equal to 2.71 · · ·[16]

a = the rate at which demand approaches potential in response to marketing effort

Two things to note are that, when $X = 0$, $Q = 0$; as $X \to \infty$, $Q \to \bar{Q}$. One of the nice features of the modified exponential is that it implies that the marginal sales response will be proportional to the level of untapped potential.[17]

---

[15]An almost equivalent form without the mathematical constant e is $Q = \bar{Q} - ab^X$ where b is less than one. See Frederick E. Croxton and Dudley J. Cowden, *Applied General Statistics* (Engelwood Cliffs, N.J.: Prentice-Hall, Inc., 1955), p.298.

[16]The constant e is the base of the natural log system and very useful in higher mathematical analysis. Its value, $e = 2.71 \cdots$, is derived as the limit of a process. Suppose \$1 is invested for a year at 100 percent; at the end of a year it is worth \$2. In symbols, $Y = 1(1 + r)^1 = 1(1 + 1)^1 = \$2$. Suppose instead that it earns 100/2 per each half-year and is compounded twice. In symbols, $Y = 1(1 + 1/2)^2 = 2.25$. Or suppose it earns 100/n and is compounded n times during the period; i.e., $Y = 1[1 + (1/n)]^n$. It can be shown that as $n \to \infty$, $Y \to e$. That is, $e = \lim_{n \to \infty} 1[1 + (1/n)]^n$. Mathematically it can be shown that the initial \$1 would be worth \$2.71 · · · · through this continuous compounding process at an interest rate of 100/n when $n \to \infty$.

[17]See Appendix Mathematical Note 2-1.

It should be noted that fitting this function to company data requires an estimate of $\bar{Q}$ and a separate estimate of a. Once $\bar{Q}$ is estimated, then a can be estimated by a single observation in principle.

Many firms tend to use their estimates of market potential ($\bar{Q}$) as the basis for allocating the marketing budget to territories and products. This is a fallacious standard in itself, in that it ignores the rate of approach parameter.

S curve demand function. There is another school of thought arguing that demand may first show increasing marginal returns and then diminishing returns with respect to various alternative levels of marketing effort. This general type of function, known as an *S* curve demand function, is illustrated in Figure 2-3(b). The purpose of this type of function is to indicate why the increasing returns range exists, that is, why there may be a range of promotional economies of scale. According to Joel Dean,

> Larger appropriations may make feasible the use of expert services and more economical media. More important than specialization usually are economies of repetition. Each advertising attack starts from ground that was taken in previous forays, and where no single onslaught can overcome the inertia of existing spending patterns, the hammering of repetition often overcomes skepticism by attrition.[18]

It should be noted that the presence of promotional economies of scale is most often argued for mass advertising, rather than personal selling or direct mail. Even in the case of mass advertising, however, the threshold effect (the tendency of small doses of marketing effort not to count for much) is not without its critics. One of the most careful reviews of existing studies of advertising effectiveness concluded that there was little evidence of advertising economies of scale.[19]

The analyst who wants to fit an *S* curve demand function to his data has a choice of at least two standard equation forms that will produce this shape. Known as the Gompertz equation and the logistics equation, they are illustrated in Figure 2-6.

1. Gompertz Function. The Gompertz equation,

$$Q = \bar{Q}a^{b^X} \qquad \text{where } \log a < 0 \text{ and } b < 1 \tag{2-17}$$

will produce an *S* curve starting from a lower asymptote of $Q = a$ and rising to a higher asymptote of $Q = \bar{Q}$. If we take the logarithmic form of this curve, we get

$$\log Q = \log \bar{Q} + (\log a) b^X \tag{2-18}$$

which describes a situation in which the growth increments of the logarithms

[18]Dean, *Managerial Economics*, p. 357.

[19]See Julian L. Simon, "Are There Economies of Scale in Advertising?" *Journal of Advertising Research* (June 1965) 15–20.

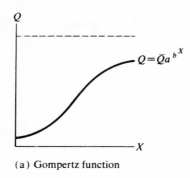

(a) Gompertz function

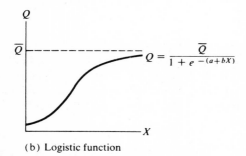

(b) Logistic function

Figure 2-6   S-Curve Demand Functions

are declining by a constant percentage b.[20] The curve can be fitted to the relationship between demand and the level of marketing effort, although its more usual application is to show a law of growth over time of populations or product demand. The reader should be careful to distinguish the difference between a demand function and a product life cycle curve, the former showing a relationship that is estimated to exist at a point in time between demand and alternative levels of marketing effort, and the latter showing the behavior of demand over time.[21]

[20]See Croxton and Cowden, *Applied General Statistics*, pp. 302–310.

[21]This distinction has often been confused. For example, Zentler and Ryde describe their *S* curve demand function in the following words: "Such a curve embodies the following ideas; when promotion is first started, the response is very small, but, once the required 'softening up' process has been performed there is a range in which response rises rapidly as promotional activity is increased. Ultimately, as promotion is increased to much higher levels, the rate of increase in response tails off again and a point is reached at which further promotion produces very little additional effect." [See A. P. Zentler and Dorothy Ryde, "An Optimum Geographical Distribution of Publicity Expenditure in a Private Organization," *Management Science* (July 1956) 337–352]. This suggests very much a process over time, rather than its proper interpretation as a set of possible alternative levels of marketing efforts and associated demands per time period. Implicit in the correct interpretation is that a particular level of marketing effort leads to a constant equilibrium rate of demand per period. A change to another level of marketing effort will lead to a different constant demand level. The demand function shows alternative equilibrium levels of demand and ignores transient dynamic effects when the firm goes from one level of marketing effort to another.

The parameters in the Gompertz equation can be made clearer by a simple example:

$$Q = 4000 \, (.2)^{.9^X} \qquad (2\text{-}19)$$

Now we can answer a few questions. What would demand be if the firm does not invest in marketing effort? If $X = 0$, then demand will be 4000 (.2), or 800 units per period. In other words, the lower asymptote of the Gompertz curve is given by $\bar{Q} = \bar{Q}a$. What would demand be if the firm invests an infinite amount of marketing effort? As $X \to \infty$, demand goes to 4000 or $\bar{Q}$. Thus demand per period for this firm will be between 800 and 4000 units per period, depending on the level of marketing effort per period.

   2.   *Logistic Function.* The logistic equation has the form

$$Q = \frac{\bar{Q}}{1 + e^{-(a+bX)}} \qquad (2\text{-}20)$$

and will produce an S curve starting from a lower asymptote of $\bar{Q}/(1+e^{-a})$ and rising to a higher asymptote of $\bar{Q}$. (Check this by substituting 0 and ∞, respectively, for X). Notice that, if $e^{-a} = 1$, then demand in the absence of marketing effort will be equal to $\frac{1}{2}$ of the potential demand. To get demand in the absence of marketing effort to be at some other ratio to potential demand, one must simply solve for the proper a exponent in the equation.

   This curve was popularized by Raymond Pearl and Lowell J. Reed in the early 1920s and is often called the Pearl-Reed curve.[22] Like the Gompertz curve, it was originally developed to describe population growth over time and it describes well many biological phenomena.[23] Yet we can use it to describe the response of demand to marketing effort. The reader may wonder when the Pearl-Reed curve is to be used instead of the Gompertz function. Technically, both functions operate between two asymptotes and describe a curve that increases at a decreasing rate of growth. The Gompertz curve involves a constant ratio of successive first differences of the log Q values, while the logistic curve involves a constant ratio of successive first differences of the $1/Q$ values. In practice, one uses the curve that gives the better fit to actual data or subjective estimates of response.

COST FUNCTION

The previous section considered a variety of functions that could relate demand per period to levels of marketing effort per period. The marketing decision maker should be interested in more than demand, however. He should be interested in

[22]See Croxton and Cowden, *Applied General Statistics*, pp. 310–316.

[23]Pearl described the curve's law of growth as appropriate for the following situation: "In a spatially limited universe the amount of increase which occurs in any particular unit of time, at any point of the single cycle of growth, is proportional to two things, viz.: (a) the absolute size already attained at the beginning of the unit interval under consideration, and (b) the amount still unused or unexpended in the given universe (or area) of actual and potential resources for the support of growth." (See Croxton and Cowden, *Applied General Statistics*, p. 315.)

maximizing the profits of the company, not its sales. Therefore he also needs the concept of cost for the analysis of marketing strategy.

Cost can be defined as the dollar value of the resources consumed in the production, promotion, and sale of the output per period. We shall introduce the simplification that the firm produces an output each period exactly equal to the demand that period, that is,

$$Q_S = Q_D \qquad (2\text{-}21)$$

where Q_S = quantity supplied

Q_D = quantity demanded

This will allow us to avoid at this early stage the complex problems of production and employment scheduling and inventory buildup that arise because of variable demand over time and imperfect forecasting. These issues will be examined in Chapter 8 in the context of the question of the joint optimization of marketing and production.

Our approach is to define an aggregate cost function that depends on the quantity of goods produced per period:

$$C = f(Q) \qquad (2\text{-}22)$$

The analysis begins with the assumption that the firm has a fixed plant size and can vary output in the short run only within the limits of zero at the low end (no output) and maximum plant capacity at the high end. The variation is possible because certain factors of production are available in variable quantities, even in the short run. Examples of variable resources, within limits, are labor and materials. Two key concepts that help to define the cost function are the production function and the factor price schedule.

The Production Function

The production function is a statement of the relationship between different levels and combinations of productive inputs (also called resources, factors of production) and the corresponding outputs per time period. Using $I_1, I_2, \cdots, I_n$ for quantities that might be used of productive inputs $1, 2, \cdots, n$ per period and Q for the quantity of output per period, the production function in its most general form is:

$$Q = f(I_1, I_2, \cdots, I_n) \qquad (2\text{-}23)$$

There are a large variety of functional forms that can serve the purpose of describing a production function, all of them satisfying the minimum condition that increases in the input of any productive factor or combination of productive factors will increase, or at least not decrease, the level of output. That is, the production function is generally represented by a class of functions that are monotonically nondecreasing.[24]

[24]It is conceivable that, if too much of any one input is added, total output might be reduced. Thus if four drivers are added to the cab of a truck, they may make it so crowded as to interfere with efficient driving.

The simplest production function would be one in which the output depended strictly on one input, call it I, that is,

$$Q = f(I) \quad \text{and} \quad \frac{dQ}{dI} \geq 0 \tag{2-24}$$

This might describe a service, such as barbering, in which the output (number of haircuts per day per shop) depends on the number of barber-hours per day. The production function for this simple case is illustrated in Figure 2-7(a). The input factor is shown on the horizontal axis and the quantity of output is shown on the vertical axis. If the curve relating input to output is a straight line with a positive slope, this would indicate a fixed relation between the number of haircuts and barber-hours per day. The curve in the illustration is not straight, implying increasing and then decreasing efficiency of output. This may be because the input factor either loses some efficiency (barbers growing tired in the latter half of the day) or the ratio between the variable input factor in relation to the fixed factors (the number of barbers in relation to the space or equipment in the shop) becomes less favorable to the variable factor.

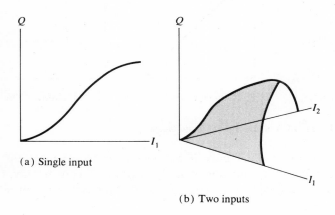

(a) Single input

(b) Two inputs

Figure 2-7 Illustrations of Production Functions

The next simplest case occurs when there are two variable inputs into the production process. The production function for this case is illustrated in Figure 2-7(b). Corresponding to every possible input combination in the $I_1 I_2$ plane is a corresponding point Q above it, representing the implied output. The points Q trace a three-dimensional output surface. To find all the input combinations that would produce a given output, say Q_0, a plane fixed at Q_0 and parallel to the $I_1 I_2$ plane can be introduced. This plane will intersect the output surface; the intersection points form a curve that can be projected down on the $I_1 I_2$ plane. The curve is known as an *isoquant* curve and shows all the input combinations that can produce the given output.

Figure 2-8 shows three isoquant curves exhibiting different degrees of input substitutability. Figure 2-8(a) shows the case where the two inputs are partially and continuously substitutable for each other. It might characterize a barber who has a variable amount of equipment he can work with (different-size scissors, different-speed electric razors, etc.). The more capital he works with, the less time he requires to produce a given number of haircuts. However, the degree of substitutability diminishes as he goes to either extreme of using all equipment or no equipment. Figure 2-8(b) shows the case in which the two inputs are completely substitutable; there are no diminishing returns in substituting one input for another. Figure 2-8(c) shows the case in which the two inputs are completely nonsubstitutable. The production function is fixed, as would be the case if one haircut always required one barber and one size of scissors. The fixed ratio of inputs case tends to characterize short run situations and is a basic supposition in the mathematical solution technique known as linear programming.

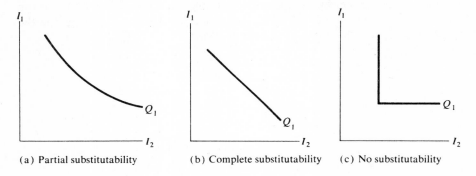

(a) Partial substitutability   (b) Complete substitutability   (c) No substitutability

Figure 2-8   Illustration of Different Degrees of Input Substitution

In the case of three or more inputs, it becomes desirable to represent the problem of the production function algebraically, instead of geometrically. One of the most popular functional forms used in this connection is the multiplicative form:

$$Q = KI_1^{i_1}I_2^{i_2}\cdots I_n^{i_n} \tag{2-25}$$

where the exponents are the elasticities of output associated with each input.[25] This functional form was popularized by Cobb and Douglas in the 1920s.[26] The Cobb-Douglas production function was originally fitted to the output of the economy as a whole (instead of a company) with the input factors being labor (L) and capital (K). One of the fittings gave:

$$Q = 1.01\, L^{.75}K^{.25} \tag{2-26}$$

[25]The argument that the exponents are elasticities can be developed in the same manner as shown earlier in this chapter on page 28.

[26]C. W. Cobb and P. H. Douglas, "A Theory of Production," *American Economic Review* (Supplement 1928) 139–165.

This equation has the following interesting properties:

1. The exponents indicate that a 1.0 percent increase in labor will yield a .75 percent increase in output, and a 1 percent increase in capital will yield only a .25 percent increase in output.

2. If labor and capital inputs are both increased by t percent, output will rise by t percent. This property is called constant returns to scale and is true only when the two exponents add to one.[27] In industries characterized by constant returns to scale, firms do not gain any unit cost advantage as they expand their plant. When firms do manage to cut unit costs through larger size plants, then increasing returns to scale are said to characterize the industry and the elasticities in the Cobb-Douglas function will sum to more than 1.

The Cobb-Douglas production function is useful here in explaining the cost function and will also be used in Chapter 3 as a model for the marketing production function. There are other functional forms that can be used to represent a variable production function, but they will not be considered here.[28]

The Factor Price Schedule

The production function shows the various ways open to the firm to produce any given level of output per period. The particular input combination chosen by the firm depends primarily on the relative prices of the different factors. Assume that each factor is purchasable in any quantity in a competitive market at a going price, that is, the firm's scale of buying does not influence the factor price. Then any two factors that the firm might buy will have a constant relative price with respect to each other. This fact can be portrayed by a straight line factor price curve drawn in the same space as the isoquants, as in Figure 2-9. The slope of the factor price curve reflects the relative market prices of the two inputs. Where this curve is tangent to the Q_1 isoquant indicates the least expensive factor combination (I_1^*, I_2^*) for producing Q_1.[29] Suppose the first input costs c_1 per unit and the second input costs c_2 per unit. Then the least cost (C) of producing Q_1 is

$$C = c_1 I_1^* + c_2 I_2^* \tag{2-27}$$

The Total Cost Function

Thus, for any given level of output, it is possible to determine the best combination of inputs in the light of relative factor prices, and the cost will be the cost of these inputs. If the firm produced this same level of output every period, the production problem would be relatively simple as long as the production function and factor prices remain stable. In practice, firms are called upon to produce different levels

[27]Given $Q = f(K, L)$, increase both K and L by a factor t. If $f(tK, tL) = t^r Q$, the function is said to be homogeneous of degree t. If $r = 1$, the function is linear and homogeneous and has the property of constant returns to scale.

[28]An advanced form is the *constant elasticity of substitution* function $Q = (aI_1^{-d} + bI_2^{-d})^{-1/d}$ developed in K. J. Arrow, H. B. Chenery, B. S. Minhas, and R. M. Solow, "Capital Labour Substitution and Economic Efficiency," *Review of Economics and Statistics* (Aug. 1961) 225–250. It is extended to cover the nonconstant elasticity of substitution case in Yehuda Kotowitz, "On the Estimation of a Non-Neutral CES Production Function," *Canadian Journal of Economics* (May 1968) 429–439.

[29]Asterisks will be used to represent optimal values of the variables.

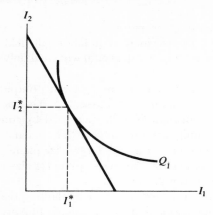

Figure 2-9   Determination of Optimum Input Combination

of output in different periods to meet variable demand. They generally work with a level of fixed resources supplemented by the amount of variable resources needed each period to keep costs as low as possible while meeting the variance of demand. However, to the extent that we can assume a stable production function and factor prices, we can express total costs directly as a function of the period's output,

$$C = f(Q) \tag{2-28}$$

The costs involved in producing any given level of output can be conveniently classified into fixed F, variable V, and discretionary X. Fixed costs are those borne regardless of the short run output level. Included in fixed costs are depreciation, management salaries, rentals, fixed interest charges, and the like. Variable costs are those whose total varies with the level of output. Variable costs include raw material, labor, fuel, packaging, delivery, and so forth. Discretionary costs are those that management freely elects to budget at the beginning of a period because they are expected to do some good. Discretionary costs include much of the outlays for advertising, personal selling, dealer promotions, and the like. Combining these costs, the total cost function is

$$C = F + V + X \tag{2-29}$$

There is no intent to suggest that all marketing costs fall in the discretionary category. Some marketing costs are in the fixed category along with other fixed costs because they are not a matter of short run decision making. Examples of fixed marketing costs are those associated with operating a branch sales office, keeping a particular product in the line, and meeting long term commitments to advertising media. Only when the marketing decision problem is one of changing the level of these costs, for example, dropping a sales branch or a product from the line, do these fixed marketing costs get reclassified into the discretionary cost category. Other marketing costs are in the variable category, that is, they vary with the level of output or sales. Necessary sales and service calls, sales commissions, delivery costs, and so on, are marketing costs that tend to vary with the level of sales. These variable marketing costs will be lumped with other variable costs because they are not a matter of short run marketing decision making. Finally, many marketing costs are discretionary such as hiring more salesmen, buying more media, and sponsoring special promotions. Our interest will focus on these discretionary marketing costs with the purpose of finding the level of these costs that are likely to maximize short run profits.

In the simplest case in which the production function and factor prices are fixed and stable, the variable cost per unit is also stable. We can talk about total variable cost being the product of *unit variable cost* c, and *total units sold* Q, that is, $V = cQ$. Then the total cost function is

$$C = F + cQ + X \tag{2-30}$$

Figure 2.10(a) illustrates the case of a linear total cost function. The corresponding average cost curve, however, is not linear. To find the average cost curve, divide the total cost by Q:

$$\frac{C}{Q} = \frac{F}{Q} + c + \frac{X}{Q} \tag{2-31}$$

This indicates that the average cost will fall at a decreasing rate toward the asymptote of the unit variable cost, as shown in Figure 2-10(b). At high levels of production, average cost will approach unit variable cost, although the two should be distinguished.

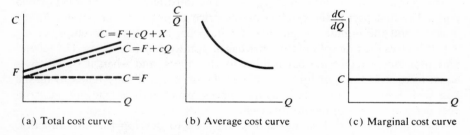

(a) Total cost curve   (b) Average cost curve   (c) Marginal cost curve

Figure 2-10   Total, Average, and Marginal Cost Curves

The marginal cost curve is a horizontal line at the level c, as shown in Figure 2-10(c). This is because the marginal cost is the cost of producing another unit, which is precisely the unit variable cost.

In more complicated cases the variable cost will not stay constant per unit of output. If factor prices vary with the scale at which the firm purchases the factors and/or if the production function changes, unit variable costs would vary with output. Then it would be necessary to use a more general functional notation for variable cost, that is, $c(Q)$. For example, suppose variable cost per unit at first falls and then rises with output. Suppose it falls at first because the firm is able to take advantage of more automated equipment and it rises later because output begins to press against capacity. This might be represented by

$$C(Q) = c_1 Q - c_2 Q^2 + c_3 Q^3 \tag{2-32}$$

with the c_1, c_2, c_3 appropriately chosen. Then the total cost function would be

$$C = F + c_1 Q - c_2 Q^2 + c_3 Q^3 + X \tag{2-33}$$

and the average and marginal cost functions would be U-shaped in appearance.

There are other ways to express cost functions, depending upon the product market being examined. Sometimes the cost function includes not only the output level, but also factor levels and prices because the latter vary. The following function was developed to describe the unit cost (per bag) of producing potato chips:

$$c(Q) = c_1 + c_2 \left(\frac{Q}{Qm} - 1 \right)^4 + (Pk) \left(\frac{W}{16} \right) \tag{2-34}$$

where c_1 = unit fixed cost
   c_2 = variable cost per unit when output deviates from capacity output
   P = price per pound of potatoes
   k = pounds of potatoes per bag of potato chips
   W = weight in ounces per potato chip bag
   Q_m = capacity output

The first term, c_1, establishes a basic unit cost per bag of potato chips to cover the cost of the bag and average labor and capital to seal it. The second term adds a small cost when the firm is not producing at capacity. When the firm is producing below or above capacity, there is an additional unit cost equal to c_2 times the fourth power of the number $[(Q/Q_m) - 1]$. The third term is the product of two parts. The first part is the product of the price of potatoes per pound, P, say 3 cents, and the number of pounds of potato per bag of potato chips, k, say 2.5; this gives the price of potatoes per bag of potato chips, 7.5 cents. The second part indicates whether the bag is filled to 16 ounces, and when it is, $W/16$ is equal to one. In times of high raw material cost, the company tends to fill the bag with less than 16 ounces, say 15 ounces, which reduces the raw material cost per bag to $^{15}\!/_{16}$ of the normal cost.

This particular cost function shows the need to develop the cost function creatively in terms of factor levels and prices, as well as the level of output, where these all vary. Normally, however, we shall treat the cost function in its simple form $C = f(Q)$.

PROFIT FUNCTION

The problem of marketing programming facing the individual firm can now be stated. It is to determine the level of marketing effort (X) that will maximize the goal attainment of the firm. The firm can have many goals, but in this chapter it will be assumed that the goal is that of short run profit maximization.

Profit maximization requires defining a profit function. Profit (Z) can be defined as the dollar difference between dollar revenue (R) and cost (C),

$$Z = R - C \tag{2-35}$$

which is the profit equation.

It is possible to refine this equation further. Sales revenue (R) can be defined as the product of price (P) and quantity sold (Q), that is,

$$R = PQ \tag{2-36}$$

which is the sales revenue equation. Substituting the sales revenue equation in the profit equation, the latter becomes

$$Z = PQ - C \tag{2-37}$$

This equation has to be developed further if we are to use it to find the impact of marketing effort (X) on the firm's profit (Z). First note that the general cost function is $C = F + c(Q) + X$. Substituting this in Equation 2-37 we get

$$Z = PQ - F - c(Q) - X \tag{2-38}$$

If we assume a constant price P and fixed cost (F), profit (Z) is a function of the quantity sold (Q) and marketing effort (X). But the quantity sold is a function of the level of marketing effort, that is, $Q = f(X)$. The substitution of this in Equation 2-38 yields

$$Z = Pf(X) - F - c[f(X)] - X \tag{2-39}$$

This equation says that profits are completely a function of marketing effort, for a given price level, cost function, and stable environment.

One more simplification is possible for the case in which the unit variable cost is a constant, that is, $c(Q) = c$. Then Equation 2-39 becomes

$$Z = Pf(X) - F - cf(X) - X \quad \text{or} \quad Z = (P - c)f(X) - F - X \tag{2-40}$$

The term ($P - c$) is called the *unit contribution to profit, overhead, and marketing*. The unit contribution multiplied by sales yields the gross margin. If the gross margin is greater than the sum of overhead and marketing expense, there is profit.

PROFIT MAXIMIZATION: SOME EXAMPLES

Once the goal variable to be maximized, in this case profits, is expressed as a function of marketing effort, the analyst can seek the profit maximizing level of marketing effort. The task of finding this level is one of applying calculus to the profit function. Two examples are developed in this section.

Finding the Best Price

A manufacturer of quality tape recorders is preparing to set a price on a new model that will be introduced into the mass home market. Marketing executives are asked to estimate probable weekly sales at different price levels and the following equation, called the demand equation, is found to give a satisfactory fit to their estimates:

$$Q = 1000 - 4P \tag{2-41}$$

The cost accountants estimate that probable total costs will be expressed, for any given sales level, by the cost equation:

$$C = 6000 + 50Q \tag{2-42}$$

These two equations provide all the information needed for finding the price that will maximize current profits. The profit equation is

$$Z = PQ - C \tag{2-43}$$

and through substitution becomes

$$Z = PQ - (6000 + 50Q)$$
$$Z = P(1000 - 4P) - 6000 - 50(1000 - 4P)$$
$$Z = 1000P - 4P^2 - 6000 - 50,000 + 200P$$

Therefore the profit equation is

$$Z = -56,000 + 1200P - 4P^2 \tag{2-44}$$

Total profits turn out to be a quadratic (i.e., second degree) function of price. In graphical terms, this function traces out the parabola shown in Figure 2-11. The point at which the curve peaks is the profit maximizing price, in this case $150.

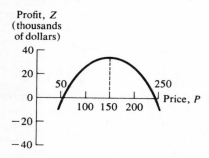

Figure 2-11   Relationship between Profits (Z) and Price (P)

The same solution is obtainable through calculus and indeed will be easier and quicker to obtain by this means.[30] It should be recognized that, at the best price, the profit function will be at a maximum and the slope of the function at this point will be 0. The slope of a function at any point is given mathematically by the first derivative, assuming that the function is differentiable and continuous. The

[30]The reader is assumed to have an acquaintance with the basic calculus notions of differentiation and integration. He should be able to find derivatives of simple functions and solve for optimum values. Most of the recent mathematics for management books contain one or two good chapters covering the essentials of calculus. See, for example, Robert C. Meier and Stephen H. Archer, *An Introduction to Mathematics for Business Analysis* (New York: McGraw-Hill, Inc., 1960), Chaps. 7–9; a more rigorous treatment is found in Burton V. Dean, Maurice W Sasieni, and Shiv K. Gupta, *Mathematics for Modern Management* (New York: John Wiley & Sons, Inc., 1963), Chaps. 6–8.

first derivative of the profit function, that is, the rate at which profit changes with respect to a very small change in price, is, for the case above:

$$\frac{dZ}{dP} = 1200 - 8P \tag{2-45}$$

The first derivative is now set equal to 0, for this will define any prices that produce a maximum, minimum, or stationary level of profits:

$$\frac{dZ}{dP} = 1200 - 8P = 0$$
$$8P = 1200 \tag{2-46}$$
$$P = \$150$$

The solution turns out to be a price of \$150. To make sure that this price defines a maximum level of profits and not a minimum or stationary level, it is necessary to test that the second derivative of the profit function is negative:

$$\frac{d^2Z}{dP^2} = -8 \quad \text{and} \quad \text{therefore} \quad \frac{d^2Z}{dP^2} < 0 \tag{2-47}$$

It is clear that this condition is satisfied and the price of \$150 will yield a higher level of profits than any other price. Specifically the profits will be

$$Z = -56{,}000 + 1200(150) - 4(150)^2 = \$34{,}000 \tag{2-48}$$

and weekly sales at this price are estimated at

$$Q = 1000 - 4(150) = 400 \text{ units per week} \tag{2-49}$$

Finding the Best Promotional Level

Suppose the same manufacturer is concerned with establishing an optimal weekly promotional budget X and assumes that there is no interaction effect between his price and his promotion. (This assumption is relaxed in Chapter 3.) On the basis of some early test market results, the sales response to promotion is estimated as

$$Q = .8\sqrt{X} \tag{2-50}$$

The same total cost function in Equation 2-42 applies again and the company plans to charge \$150. To solve for the best weekly promotional budget, the analyst forms the profit function and substitutes Equations 2-42, 2-46, and 2-50 into it:

$$Z = PQ - C - X$$
$$Z = 150Q - 6000 - 50Q - X \tag{2-51}$$
$$Z = 100\,(.8\sqrt{X}) - 6000 - X$$

$$Z = 80\sqrt{X} - X - 6000 \tag{2-52}$$

The next step is to take this profit function and set the first derivative equal to 0:

$$\frac{dZ}{dX} = 40X^{-1/2} - 1 = 0 \tag{2-53}$$

$$\frac{40}{\sqrt{X}} = 1$$

$$\sqrt{X} = 40$$

and therefore

$$X = 1600 \tag{2-54}$$

This solution says that the company should spend \$1600 a week for promotion; this will produce extra sales (compared to the case of no promotion) equal to

$$Q = .8\sqrt{1600} = .8\,(40) = 32 \text{ units per week} \tag{2-55}$$

and extra profits of

$$Z = 80\sqrt{1600} - 1600 = \$1600 \text{ per week} \tag{2-56}$$

and an average promotional cost per sales dollar of

$$\frac{X}{PQ} = \frac{1600}{(150)\,(32)} = 33\tfrac{1}{3} \text{ percent} \tag{2-57}$$

The principle of finding the best promotional outlay is illustrated graphically in Figure 2-12. The top curve describes sales revenue as growing with promotion at a diminishing rate. From this sales revenue curve is subtracted the cost of production of $50Q$; this yields the curve called gross profit before promotional cost. To find net profit after promotion, the gross profit curve is read in relation to the 45° line that represents a projection of promotion dollars on the vertical scale. The task is to find the promotional budget X, where the vertical distance is greatest between the gross profit curve and the 45° line. This is at X^*, and one of its features is that the slope of the tangent to the gross profit curve at this point will be parallel to the 45° line, which is the geometric equivalent of the fact that marginal promotional cost and marginal gross profit are equal where net profit is a maximum.

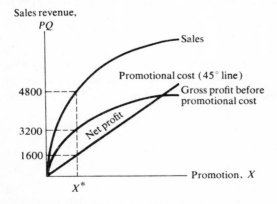

Figure 2-12   Finding the Best Promotional Outlay

SUMMARY

The problem of developing an optimal marketing program can best be seen in the simple situation consisting of (1) a monopoly firm selling (2) one product in (3) one territory, where it has available only (4) one marketing instrument that has (5) no carryover effect and where the objective is (6) short run profit maximization. This situation is analyzed by seeking an expression for the demand and cost functions, combining the two in a profit function, and applying calculus to find the value of the marketing instrument that maximizes profits.

The demand function can be illustrated in terms of price or marketing effort. Popular formulations of the inverse demand-price relationship include the linear function and the constant elasticity function. Occasionally, positive demand-price relationships are observed and they can be explained in terms of either the income effect, the Veblen effect, the expectation effect, or the quality effect. Popular formulations of the demand-marketing effort relationship are the concave function (log, power, or modified exponential) and the S curve function (Gompertz or logistic).

Cost functions are determined by first identifying the production function of the firm and then bringing in the factor price schedules to determine costs as a function of the quantity produced or sold. The total cost function can easily be manipulated to obtain the average cost and marginal cost function for further analysis.

Profits are expressed as the difference between revenues and costs as an ultimate function of the marketing decision variable. Some examples were presented, showing how to derive the best marketing decision given the demand and cost functions.

Questions and Problems

1. In 1967 Booth Appliances, Inc., sold the following numbers of units in relation to its marketing effort:

Month	Jan.	Feb.	Mar.	Apr.	May	Jun.	Jul.	Aug.	Sept.	Oct.	Nov.	Dec.
Sales (000's)	105	100	145	117	155	138	177	136	157	167	168	123
Marketing Effort (000's)	30	20	60	35	70	57	100	50	80	85	95	40

(a) Suggest some forms of demand functions which could be used to represent the data.
(b) Effort in November was $10,000 more than in October, yet sales were almost the same. To what can this be attributed?
(c) Suppose the demand function $Q = \bar{Q}(1 - e^{-ax})$ gives a good fit to the data. Assume the company has a linear cost function, $C = a + bQ$. Derive a rule for determining the optimal level of marketing effort.
(d) What would be the effect on demand of an increase in the *quality* of marketing effort per dollar?
2. Determine the shape of each of the following functions, and indicate whether it would constitute a plausible representation of the relationship between marketing effort and demand.

(a) $Q = \bar{Q}X/(a+X)$ (where $\bar{Q}$ is demand potential and X is marketing effort)

(b) $Q = \bar{Q}-a/X^b$; $X > 1$, $a/X^b < \bar{Q}$

(c) $Q = \bar{Q}e^{-x}$

(d) $Q = \bar{Q}X^2/1+X+X^2$

3. A tool manufacturer finds that the demand schedule for one of its products has the form $Q = a-bP$. Demonstrate that:

(a) Price elasticity will be unity when $P = a/2b$.

(b) Price elasticity tends to infinity at very high prices, making it desirable to lower price.

(c) Price elasticity tends to zero at very low prices, making it desirable to raise price.

4. (a) Show that the price elasticity of demand,

$$e_{qp} = \frac{dQ}{dP} \cdot \frac{P}{Q} \text{ can also be written as: } e_{qp} = \frac{d \log Q}{d \log P},$$

That is, that price elasticity is simply the derivative of the log of Q with respect to the log of P.

(b) Use this result to show that $-b$ in the exponential demand function $Q = aP^{-b}$ is the price elasticity.

5. A television manufacturer wishes to determine the price for a new portable model which will maximize the company's current profits on the model. The marketing research department's estimate of demand for the new product is represented by the function, $Q = 15,000-80P$, where Q is the quantity demanded and P is the price. In manufacturing the product the company will incur fixed costs of $300,000 and variable costs of $20 per unit.

(a) Find the optimum price and determine the level of demand, costs, and profit at this price.

(b) The demand equation shown above is a familiar one. What assumptions are implicit in such a demand equation which may greatly limit its usefulness?

6. (a) Given the following demand and cost functions for a company:

$$Q = 1000-4P+.8\sqrt{X}$$
$$C = 6000+50Q+X$$

Determine the best price (P) and promotional outlay (X).

(b) Why are these levels of P and X different from those determined in the two examples at the end of Chapter 2 ($P^* = 150$, $X^* = 1600$)?

7. The XYZ Company sets its advertising budget (A) at 10 percent of last year's sales (S). Unknown to the company, its advertising has the following impact on sales:

$$S_t = 130\sqrt{A_t}$$

The company's total cost (C) of doing business is given by the following cost equation:

$$C_t = 100+.7S_t+A_t$$

Suppose last year's sales were $1,440. What will the company's sales, cost, and profit be this period?

CHAPTER 3
Multiple Marketing Instruments

The analysis in the previous chapter assumed that the firm had available only one marketing policy instrument and its problem was to set the level of this instrument in such a way as to maximize the firm's profits. The assumption of one marketing instrument, price, is found in classical economic analysis but is quite out of line with economic reality. The modern firm must develop settings for a variety of marketing instruments; these settings constitute its "marketing mix." In this chapter we shall study the theory of determining the joint settings of various marketing factors that will maximize the firm's profits.

An Historical Note

Before 1933 economists who analyzed the problem of demand largely confined their attention to the price instrument. They maintained that under conditions of constant tastes, incomes, and technology, full information, and utility maximization, the quantity of demand per unit time would tend to vary inversely with the price, that is, $Q = f(P)$, where $dQ/dP < 0$. The concentration of economists on the price instrument is due to a number of factors, including (1) their interest in investigating and demonstrating the advantages of a free enterprise system based on the free movement of price to adjust differences in demand and supply levels; (2) the fact that price at one time had been the major marketing factor, before branding, advertising, product differentiation and other modern marketing practices came into being; and (3) the fact that price is so much more measurable, and consequently tractable, relative to other marketing variables in a formal analysis. Much of the concentration on price represents a cultural lag, because advertising, branding, product differentiation, and personal selling have been significant demand stimulants for several decades.

It was in 1933 that two, now-classic treatises were written that increased the scope and relevance of formal economic analysis for marketing problems. The first book was written by Professor Edward H. Chamberlin of Harvard University and called *The Theory of Monopolistic Competition*;[1] the second book was written by Joan Robinson of Cambridge University and called *The Economics of Imperfect Competition*.[2] Both economists pointed out that there were forms of competition taking place in the modern world that were intermediate between the two prevalent economic models of pure competition and pure monopoly. Joan Robinson was primarily concerned with variations of the monopoly model. Using geometric analysis, she refined the theory of price discrimination, showed the influence of monopsony (buyer monopolies), and so forth.

Chamberlin postulated an intermediate market structure called *monopolistic competition* in which there were many firms and each had some control over its demand because of product differentiation, either real or imagined. In the case of pure competition, on the other hand, it is assumed that all buyers see the product as identical (as a commodity) and therefore buy only on the basis of price. This means that some market price will develop that will "clear the market." No firm could charge more than this price and sell anything, nor would any firm care to sell at less than this price, since it could sell all it had at the going price. But if a firm is able to create quality, style, or feature differences in its product or use advertising or personal selling to establish a psychological preference for its brand over other brands, the firm gains some control over the price it can charge.

Having introduced the model of monopolistic competition, Chamberlin also had to analyze how the firm would handle the two new marketing instruments that he postulated, in addition to price. The first, combining all aspects of the product offering, including quality, packaging, and service, Chamberlin called "product." The second instrument he called "selling cost," which included advertising, salesmen's salaries, and promotional allowances. Chamberlin made use of graphical analysis to show how two or three of the marketing instruments could be mutually and optimally set.

Although many economists ignored or disputed this theoretical development because it introduced an element of indeterminancy into the otherwise elegant structure of price theory, some of them showed a willingness to consider the implications of nonprice instruments for economic theory. Boulding[3] in 1941

[1]Edward H. Chamberlin, *The Theory of Monopolistic Competition* (Cambridge, Mass.: Harvard University Press, 1933).

[2]Joan Robinson, *The Economics of Imperfect Competition* (London: Macmillan & Co., Ltd., 1933).

[3]Kenneth E. Boulding, *Economic Analysis* (New York: The Macmillan Company, 1941), p. 776.

and Stigler[4] in 1946 developed complex graphical solutions to the marketing mix problem. In 1951 Brems[5] extended this work, and in 1954 Dorfman and Steiner[6] showed algebraically the marginal conditions for setting price, advertising, and product quality. The theory as it stands today is primarily in the form in which it was stated by Dorfman and Steiner in 1954.[7] The theory will be reviewed later in the chapter, along with an attempt to extend it to take into account otherwise neglected interdependencies and discontinuities.

Marketing Decision Variables

Marketing decision variables (also called "marketing policy instruments," "parameters of marketing action," "sales tools," "factors of marketing") refer to all variables under the firm's control that can affect the level of demand. They are distinguished from *environmental variables*, the latter also affecting demand but not being under the control of the firm.

Ever since economists acknowledged the existence of marketing decision variables other than price, the list of variables has grown enormously in length and complexity. One of the most extensive lists is the one proposed by Borden, shown in Table 3-1.[8]

It is clear that marketing decision variables differ from each other in several ways. They differ in their degree of *divisibility*, that is, the extent to which the marketing resource is available in a continuously varying amount. Advertising, for example, can be purchased in various amounts, but a vice-president of marketing is either hired or not by the company.[9] Marketing decision variables differ in their degree of *modifiability*. Trade allowances are highly modifiable in the short run; sales force size is less modifiable; and the number of products in the line is even less modifiable. Marketing decision variables differ in their degree of *dimensionality*. A price change is closer to a unidimensional concept, whereas a change in advertising effort can refer to a change in the frequency or size of ads, the media used, or the copy. Finally, marketing decision variables differ in their *immediacy* of effect. Sales promotions tend to have their effect immediately, while corporate advertising has effects in the more distant future.

[4]George J. Stigler, *The Theory of Price* (New York: The Macmillan Company, 1946), pp. 262–263.

[5]Hans Brems, *Product Equilibrium under Monopolistic Competition* (Cambridge, Mass.: Harvard University Press, 1951).

[6]Robert Dorfman and Peter O. Steiner, "Optimal Advertising and Optimal Quality," *American Economic Review* (Dec. 1954) 826–836.

[7]Also see P. J. Verdoorn, "Marketing from the Producer's Point of View," *Journal of Marketing* (Jan. 1956) 221–235; and Gosta Mickwitz, *Marketing and Competition* (Helsingfors, Finland: Centraltrycheriet, 1959).

[8]Neil H. Borden, "The Concept of the Marketing Mix," in George Schwartz, ed., *Science in Marketing* (New York: John Wiley & Sons, Inc., 1965), pp. 386–397.

[9]It would be a mistake, however, to exaggerate the amount of indivisibility in marketing resources. There are many ways to "buy" fractional amounts of a marketing resource. For example, instead of hiring a salesman full time, the company could hire a fractional part of a salesman's time, as happens with nonexclusive sales agents or part-time salesmen.

Table 3-1.   Elements of the Marketing Mix of Manufacturers.

Product planning. Policies and procedures relating to:

Product lines to be offered—qualities, design, etc.
The markets to sell—whom, where, when and in what quantity
New product policy—research and development program

Pricing. Policies and procedures relating to:

The level of prices to adopt
The specific prices to adopt (odd-even, etc.)
Price policy—one price or varying price, price maintenance, use of list prices, etc.
The margins to adopt—for company; for the trade

Branding. Policies and procedures relating to:

Selection of trade marks
Brand policy—individualized or family brand
Sale under private brand or unbranded

Channels of Distribution. Policies and procedures relating to:

The channels to use between plant and consumer
The degree of selectivity among wholesalers and retailers
Efforts to gain cooperation of the trade

Personal Selling. Policies and procedures relating to:

The burden to be placed on personal selling and the methods to be employed in (1) the manufacturer's organization, (2) the wholesale segment of the trade, (3) the retail segment of the trade

Advertising. Policies and procedures relating to:

The amount to spend—i.e., the burden to be placed on advertising
The copy platform to adopt, (1) product image desired, (2) corporate image desired
The mix of advertising—to the trade; through the trade—to consumers

Promotions. Policies and procedures relating to:

The burden to place on special selling plans or devices directed at or through the trade
The form of these devices for consumer promotions, for trade promotions

Packaging. Policies and procedures relating to:

Formulation of package and label

Display. Policies and procedures relating to:

The burden to be put on display to help effect sales
The methods to adopt to secure display

Servicing. Policies and procedures relating to:

Providing service needed

Physical Handling. Policies and procedures relating to:

Warehousing
Transportation
Inventories

Fact Finding and Analysis. Policies and procedures relating to:

The securing, analysis, and use of facts in marketing operations

---

Source: Neil H. Borden, "The Concept of the Marketing Mix," in George Schwartz, ed., *Science in Marketing* (New York: John Wiley & Sons, Inc., 1965), pp. 389–390.

If we are to work with a long list of marketing decision variables, the demand function becomes.

$$Q = f(X_1, X_2, X_3, \ldots, X_n) \tag{3-1}$$

and the problem of finding the form of the equation and statistically estimating the coefficients becomes very formidable. A shorter classification of major decision variables would offer a theoretical advantage.

The shortest classification ever proposed is a two-factor one by Frey, who suggested that all marketing decision variables could be divided into:

1. The offering (product, packaging, brand, price, and service)
2. Methods and tools (distribution channels, personal selling, advertising, sales promotion, and publicity)[10]

Later Lazer and Kelley proposed the three-factor classification of all marketing decision variables into:

1. Goods and service mix
2. Distribution mix
3. Communications mix[11]

More recently, E. Jerome McCarthy popularized a four-factor classification of marketing decision variables, which he called the "four P's":[12]

1. Product
2. Place
3. Promotion
4. Price

This writer has found it analytically convenient to work with these four variables because they summarize succinctly the major ways in which the firm can influence sales. Table 3-2 shows the particular instruments summarized by each of the "four P's." Each of these variables is in reality several instruments but each shall be treated here as a single variable represented by a single magnitude, such as dollars per unit in the case of price, total dollars in the case of promotion or place, or an index of relative attractiveness in the case of product. The *marketing mix* of a company at any point in time will be defined as the kinds and amounts of marketing variables the firm is using. This marketing mix can be conveniently summarized by the vector:

$$(P, A, D, R)_t \tag{3-2}$$

where P = price
A = promotion (i.e., advertising and personal selling)
D = place (i.e., distribution)
R = product (i.e., rating or index of the product's overall quality in the market place)

[10]Albert W. Frey, *Advertising*, 3rd ed. (New York: The Ronald Press Company, 1961), p. 30.
[11]William Lazer and Eugene J. Kelley, *Managerial Marketing: Perspectives and Viewpoints*, rev. ed. (Homewood, Ill.: Richard D. Irwin, Inc., 1962), p. 413.
[12]E. Jerome McCarthy, *Basic Marketing: A Managerial Approach*, rev. ed., (Homewood, Ill.: Richard D. Irwin, Inc., 1964), pp. 38–40.

Table 3-2. Elaboration of the Four "P's."

Product variables
>   Quality
>   Models and sizes
>   Packaging
>   Brands
>   Service

Place variables
>   Channels of distribution
>   Outlet location
>   Sales territories
>   Warehousing system

Promotion variables
>   Advertising
>   Sales promotion
>   Personal selling
>   Publicity

Price variables
>   Allowances and deals
>   Distribution and retailer markups
>   Discount structure

If the firm is currently producing a product priced at $20, supporting it with advertising expenditures of $20,000 per period and distribution expenditures of $30,000 per period, and the product's quality is rated at $1.20, the company's marketing mix at time t is

($20, $20,000, $30,000, 1.20)$_t$

We shall now proceed to consider how the firm can determine the optimal marketing mix.

MARKETING MIX DETERMINATION IN THEORY

It should be readily appreciated that a company's marketing mix is selected from among a great number of possibilities. Suppose a company is trying to choose among three levels of price, six levels of advertising, four levels of distribution, and five levels of product quality: this means there are 360 ($3 \times 6 \times 4 \times 5$) possible marketing mix combinations. There would be many more if the variables had been permitted more possible values and/or if additional marketing variables were being considered. Even in the case of two marketing decision variables that can take on many values, there are a great number of possible marketing mix combinations. Figure 3-1 is a geometrical version of the marketing mix problem. Here two marketing variables, advertising (A) and distribution (D), are represented as axes that constitute the floor of the figure, and sales is the vertical axis. If there are no constraints on the levels of advertising and distribution, then every possible point in the A–D plane is a possible marketing mix. An arbitrary line drawn from the origin, here called a "constant mix line," shows the set of all marketing mixes where the two marketing factors are in a fixed ratio, but where the budget varies. Another arbitrary line, here called a "constant dollar line," shows a set of varying mixes that would be affordable with a fixed budget. Three specific marketing mixes are shown. The marketing mix (A_1, D_1) calls for a small marketing budget and a rough equality between advertising and distribution effort, with an estimated sales impact of Q_1. The marketing mix (A_2, D_2) involves the same budget but much more spent on advertising relative to distribution; this imbalance is expected to produce slightly higher sales, Q_2. The marketing mix (A_3, D_3) calls for a larger budget but a relatively equal splitting between advertising and distribution, and with a sales estimate of Q_3. Given these and the many other possible marketing mixes, the analyst's job is (1) to find a marketing mix demand function that describes all the Q's and (2) to embed this function into a profit function to find the optimal marketing mix. We shall first examine the second question, concerning the theory of marketing mix optimization for any demand function; in the following section we shall consider specific equation forms to represent the marketing mix demand function.

Dorfman-Steiner Theorem on Marketing Mix Optimization

Assume a company that faces the general marketing mix demand function[13]

$$Q = q(P, A, D, R) \tag{3-3}$$

and company cost function

$$C = c(Q, R)Q + A + D + F \tag{3-4}$$

Note that the unit cost c is a function of the quantity produced (Q) and the product quality (R). Thus the unit variable cost may vary with output and/or with the level of product quality. Advertising and distribution are treated as discretionary fixed costs, and F represents the sum of nondiscretionary fixed costs.

Now set up the short run profit function:

$$Z = PQ - C \tag{3-5}$$

---

[13]The marketing mix demand function is relatively new in the literature of demand functions. "It is a remarkable fact that sales, especially sales of a given brand, are not forecast with marketing variables as the principal explicit independent variables of these models." (Victor J. Cook and A. N. M. Azizur Rahman, *EMARK: An Analytical Demand Forecasting Model*, Working Paper P-43-9, Marketing Science Institute, Cambridge, Mass., p. 6). The economist's demand function tends to include price, national income, population, etc., leaving out most marketing demand instruments. The forecaster's time series approach treats demand as a multiplicative function of a time trend T, cyclical factor C, seasonal factor S, and a random component R, i.e., $Q_t = Q_{t-1}(TCSI)$. This time series equation of demand gives good predictions under certain circumstances but completely obscures the effect of the industry or firm's own decisions on demand. The marketing mix demand function is also one-sided in attempting to explain sales completely as a function of marketing effort factors, but we shall use it because its implications have been relatively neglected by past demand studies.

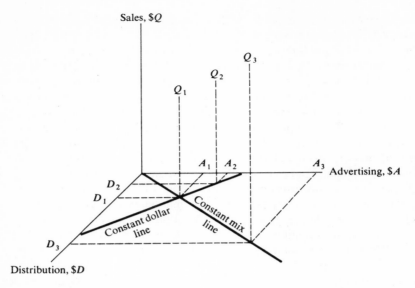

Figure 3-1   Geometric Version of the Marketing Mix Problem

$$Z = Pq(P, A, D, R) - c(Q, R)Q - A - D - F \tag{3-6}$$

$$Z = Pq(P, A, D, R) - c[q(P, A, D, R), R]q(P, A, D, R) - A - D - F \tag{3-7}$$

The profit depends in almost every way upon the levels and mix of marketing effort chosen by the firm. Both sales and costs are influenced by the marketing mix. This underscores why marketing planning must precede marketing forecasting, although some companies talk as if they first forecast sales and then develop marketing plans on the basis of their forecast.

Given the profit function (Equation 3-7) we find that it is relatively easy to determine the *necessary condition* for marketing mix optimization. Marketing mix optimization occurs when

$$\frac{\partial Z}{\partial P} = \frac{\partial Z}{\partial A} = \frac{\partial Z}{\partial D} = \frac{\partial Z}{\partial R} = 0 \tag{3-8}$$

that is, the response of profit to an infinitesimal change in any and all marketing instruments is 0. Each partial derivative of Equation 3-7 can be found and substituted into Equation 3-8, yielding after simplification[14]

$$e_P = MRP_A = MRP_D = e_R \frac{P}{c} \tag{3-9}$$

where $e_P = -\dfrac{\partial Q}{\partial P} \cdot \dfrac{P}{Q}$ = price elasticity of demand

[14]See Appendix Mathematical Note 3–1.

$$MRP_A = P\frac{\partial Q}{\partial A} = \text{marginal revenue product of advertising}$$

$$MRP_D = P\frac{\partial Q}{\partial D} = \text{marginal revenue product of distribution}$$

$$e_R = \frac{\partial Q}{\partial R}\cdot\frac{\partial R}{\partial c}\cdot\frac{c}{Q} = \text{product quality elasticity of demand}$$

In words, Equation 3-9 states that, as a necessary condition for profit maximization,[15] the values of price, advertising, distribution, and product quality must be set at such levels that price elasticity, the marginal revenue products of advertising and distribution, and the quality elasticity times price over unit costs are equal.

It must be emphasized that this theorem, known as the Dorfman-Steiner theorem,[16] does not directly give the optimal values of the marketing policy variables but rather the conditions that will be satisfied when the optimal values are found. It is too difficult to state the solutions directly for the general case, but the solutions can be found through knowledge of the first partial derivatives and working backward. Some analysts prefer to work completely with measures of elasticity, in which case it is possible to recast the Dorfman-Steiner theorem in the following form:[17]

$$e_P = \frac{PQ}{A}e_A = \frac{PQ}{D}e_D = \frac{P}{c}e_R \qquad (3\text{-}10)$$

This enables a direct comparison of the elasticities of the different policy instruments (modified by the other terms) to determine whether the marketing mix is optimum. If the equality is not satisfied at the present levels of the policy instruments, then the instruments should be adjusted in the appropriate direction. If the appropriate direction is not obvious, some trial and error may be necessary.

Advertising and Distribution: An Application of the Theory

Consider the question of whether current expenditures on advertising and distribution are in a proper balance. This type of question is almost always raised when the marketing budget is about to be divided. Advertising people ask for more money, arguing that advertising increases customer awareness, interest, and possibly preference at a low cost per customer. Distribution personnel dispute that advertising does much to create actual sales and complain that the $33,000 spent on a single, full page color ad could be better spent in increasing

---

[15]The sufficiency conditions are not stated here. For a good brief statement of sufficiency conditions, see James M. Henderson and Richard E. Quandt, *Microeconomic Theory* (New York: McGraw-Hill, Inc., 1958), pp. 271–272.

[16]Dorfman and Steiner, "Optimal Advertising and Optimal Quality," *American Economic Review* (Dec. 1954), p. 834.

[17]That is, $MRP_A = P\dfrac{\partial Q}{\partial A} = P\dfrac{\partial Q}{\partial A}\dfrac{AQ}{QA} = Pe_A\dfrac{Q}{A} = \dfrac{PQ}{A}e_A$. The same holds for MRP_D.

product availability and service. Our concern here is with the gross conditions that indicate a balance or imbalance of advertising and distribution outlays. The condition in Equation 3-10 that

$$\frac{PQ}{A} e_A = \frac{PQ}{D} e_D \qquad (3\text{-}11)$$

is the same as

$$\frac{e_A}{e_D} = \frac{A}{D} \qquad (3\text{-}12)$$

which says that, in equilibrium, the ratio of the advertising and distribution elasticities will be equal to the ratio of the respective expenditure levels.

Consider some cases. Suppose advertising and distribution have constant elasticities for all levels of expenditures and they are not necessarily the same. Assume these are the elasticities shown in Figure 3-2(a). Constant elasticities of advertising and distribution, where $0 \leqslant e_A$, $e_D \leqslant 1$, imply diminishing marginal returns to additional marketing expenditures.[18] In Figure 3-2(a), the advertising elasticity is everywhere at approximately twice the level of the distribution elasticity. According to Equation 3-12, this means that the company should be spending twice as much on advertising as on selling, that is, advertising should constitute two thirds of the marketing budget proper. The multiple exponential form of the demand function described later (see p. 68–72) is precisely one in which the elasticities are assumed to be constant; here the firm should divide the advertising and distribution funds in the same ratio as the exponents of A and D.

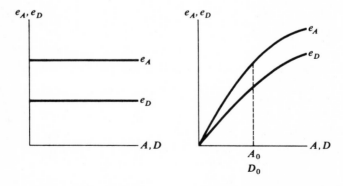

(a) Constant elasticities   (b) Increasing elasticities

Figure 3-2   Assumed Elasticities of Advertising and Distribution

[18]Since $e_A \leqslant 1$, then $dQ/dA \cdot A/Q \leqslant 1$, or $dQ/dA \leqslant Q/A$. This says that the marginal rate is everywhere less than the average rate, which implies that sales will increase at a diminishing rate. Since $e_A \geqslant 0$, then $dQ/dA \cdot A/Q \geqslant 0$, or $dQ/dA \geqslant 0$. This says that sales are an increasing function of advertising.

Now consider the case in Figure 3-2(b), where advertising elasticity is everywhere higher than distribution elasticity and both elasticities increase at a diminishing rate. Suppose the company is currently spending the same amount on advertising and distribution, that is, $A = D$. According to Equation 3-12, since $e_A > e_D$, the company should be spending more on advertising than on distribution. Given a fixed budget B, we can rework Equation 3-12 to find out the optimal fraction of the budget that should be spent on A. From Equation 3-12 we derive

$$A = \frac{e_A}{e_D}(B-A) \qquad \text{letting } D = B - A \tag{3-13}$$

$$A + A\frac{e_A}{e_D} = B\frac{e_A}{e_D} \tag{3-14}$$

$$A\left(\frac{e_D + e_A}{e_D}\right) = B\frac{e_A}{e_D} \tag{3-15}$$

$$A^* = \frac{e_A}{e_A + e_D} B \tag{3-16}$$

Thus the fraction that advertising should constitute of the total budget increases as the ratio of the advertising elasticity to the sum of the advertising and distribution elasticities.

Advertising and Product Quality: A Second Application and Some Complications

Now consider the question of developing an optimal joint level of advertising expenditures and product quality. According to Equation 3-9, optimization exists if $MRP_A = e_R(P/c)$. This condition holds true as long as we assume that advertising and product quality are independent decision variables with no influence on each other. Unfortunately, there are mutual influences between these two variables that are not taken into account in the derivation of Equation 3-9 but which affect the optimal settings. Some comments on these influences will add a sobering effect to the traditional analysis.

Take the case of a seller whose product is of average quality and whose sales are average. In an effort to improve his market share and profits, the seller is considering budgeting more for marketing effort and is trying to determine whether to spend it on improving the quality of the product or on increasing the level of advertising. If he spends the money entirely on quality improvement, he has to assume that (1) the customers want higher quality and (2) the quality improvement will be sufficiently apparent to the customers. Otherwise, he will have to appropriate some money to advertising in order to alert the market to the product's higher quality. On the other hand, if he decides to spend the money entirely on increased advertising, he has to assume that more messages about his product will improve the positive feelings of buyers toward his product. To the extent that buyers judge the quality of a brand by its relative number of advertising messages, the buildup of advertising will act to increase the appearance of more quality. Thus, to some extent, the seller can substitute expenditures on image advertising for real product quality improvement. This is a dangerous game, however, if the buyers find that the actual quality does not live up to the advertised quality. The complexity gets even worse when we realize that judgments of a product's quality are influenced not only by advertising, but also by price and distribution. If the price on a bar of soap is raised from 10 cents to $1, its packaging is revised, and it is placed in exclusive beauty salons instead of dime stores, the product has effectively been changed: it is now a beauty cream rather than a soap. All of this suggests that a form of analysis beyond that provided in the Dorfman-Steiner theorem is necessary for the joint planning of marketing effort variables.

Elasticities of Marketing Instruments at Different Stages of the Product Life Cycle

Now consider the case in which the relative elasticities of various marketing instruments change throughout the product life cycle. This would mean, according to Equation 3-10, that the relative expenditures on the different instruments should also vary through time. The only reported work on the relative elasticities of different marketing instruments at different stages of the product life cycle is that developed by the Finnish marketing economist, Gosta Mickwitz.[19] He distinguished among five competitive marketing instruments: price (P), advertising (A), service (D), product quality (R), and packaging (K). His speculations on the relative elasticities on these five instruments at different stages of the product life cycle are summarized in Figure 3-3. Each of the five panels in the figure represents the product at a different stage in its life cycle (introduction, growth, maturity, saturation, decline). The C axis represents an increase in marketing cost, and the Q axis represents the corresponding increase in sales. The slope of each line represents the responsiveness of sales (Q) to an increase in that marketing instrument's input (C) at that stage in the product life cycle. In stage 1, according to Mickwitz, product quality has the largest impact on sales. For a very small increase in the cost of more quality, sales increase substantially. The more nearly horizontal the line, the greater that instrument's impact on sales. The next most important instrument at stage 1 is advertising, followed by price. The least important instrument is service, indicating that an investment in increased service at the product introduction stage is not likely to increase sales by very much.

By stage 2 the early adopters have already purchased the product and the firm faces increasing buyer resistance. Advertising now becomes the most potent marketing instrument, while quality slips to second place. Price and service elasticity are still low.

In stage 3 most of the price-insensitive buyers have already tried the product. Furthermore, new firms have entered the market and the competition for customers is keen. The industry now makes an effort to draw in the price-sensi-

[19]Gosta Mickwitz, *Marketing and Competition* (Helsingfors, Finland: Centraltryckeriet, 1959).

tive buyers by lowering price. Price is considered the instrument with the highest elasticity at this stage, followed by advertising, quality, and service.

By stage 4 the active price competition of stage 3 has led to a low price, and there is little remaining price elasticity. Sellers try to increase the differentiation of their product. Packaging becomes important. However, the slope of even the packaging curve is high; this means that a fairly substantial investment is needed to generate more sales. Next in importance are advertising, quality, and service, which have about the same capability of increasing sales.

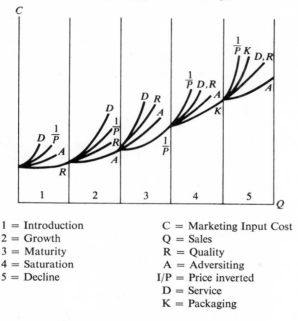

1 = Introduction	C = Marketing Input Cost
2 = Growth	Q = Sales
3 = Maturity	R = Quality
4 = Saturation	A = Adversiting
5 = Decline	I/P = Price inverted
	D = Service
	K = Packaging

Figure 3-3   Elasticity of Marketing Instruments in Different Stages of a Product's Life Cycle

Source: Mickwitz, *op. cit.*, p. 88. (Redrawn with modifications).

By stage 5 there is less to be gained through further packaging investments. The problem is one of finding new product uses and advertising them. Quality and service investments will have some impact on sales, and price cuts will have virtually no impact.

Mickwitz did not present evidence for these propositions about elasticity but relied mainly on theory and casual observation. Yet a growing number of companies are seeking to measure these elasticities. One packaged goods company has been measuring advertising elasticity for a wide range of its products at different stages of their life cycle and has found a general pattern of falling advertising elasticity as the products pass through their life cycles. These and other findings will provide the key for improving the allocations of the marketing budget to different marketing instruments at different stages of the life cycle.

SPECIFIC EQUATION FORMS FOR REPRESENTING THE EFFECTS OF THE MARKETING MIX

Having examined the necessary conditions for an optimum marketing mix for any general demand function, we shall now turn to some specific demand equation forms that convey quite different understandings of marketing mix effects. The following demand models will be examined: (1) linear marketing mix effects model, (2) the exponential marketing mix effects model, and (3) miscellaneous marketing mix effects models.

Linear Marketing Mix Effects Model

The simplest model of marketing mix effects is one that assumes that each marketing mix variable has a *constant* and *independent* effect on the level of sales. This behavior is precisely represented by the linear marketing mix equation of the following general form:

$$Q = k - pP + aA + dD + rR \tag{3-17}$$

where
$$\begin{aligned} k &= \text{a constant} \\ p, a, d, r &= \text{coefficients of sales response to different marketing decision} \\ &\qquad \text{variables} \\ P, A, D, R &= \text{marketing decision variables} \end{aligned}$$

Where sales are effected by the marketing variables in this way, it is clear that each variable has a constant and independent effect on total sales. This is shown by taking the first derivative of sales with respect to any variable, say advertising:

$$\frac{\partial Q}{\partial A} = a \tag{3-18}$$

Thus the effect of a small increase of advertising on sales is a constant a, regardless of the current level of expenditures on advertising and regardless of the levels of the other policy instruments.

A linear programming example.   If the assumptions of the linear marketing mix model are accepted, and unit costs are assumed constant regardless of the level of sales, then *linear programming* can be employed as a solution technique to finding the optimum marketing mix. We shall develop a simple example to show how linear programming may be used to find simultaneously the optimal allocation of a marketing budget between two market segments and the optimal marketing mix for each segment.

Example.   The Oxite Company produces a portable oxygen unit and sells it to two types of distributors: fire equipment distributors and surgical supply houses. Oxite's profit margin varies between the two types of distributors because of differences in selling costs, typical order sizes, and different credit policies. On the basis of a distribution cost analysis, the company estimates that the current profit margins are $15 and $10, respectively.

The company's sales are generated by a combination of personal sales force calls and selective media advertising. The company has four trained salesmen on its payroll, representing 4000 hours of available customer contact time during the next six months. Furthermore, the company has allotted $14,000 toward advertising during the next six months.

An examination of past data indicates that a unit sale to a fire equipment distributor requires about a half-hour sales call and $1 worth of advertising, while a unit sale to a surgical supply house requires a quarter-hour sales call and $2 of advertising.

The company would like to achieve sales of at least 3000 units in each customer segment. It will accept any allocation of its marketing resources, which will maximize profits, provided that these minimum sales levels are achieved.

The company's problem is to determine how much sales it should seek to develop in each customer segment to maximize its total profits. The actual amount of sales in each territory will depend upon the mix of advertising and selling resources it applies in each segment, both of which are limited. Offhand, it would seem that the company should seek more sales to fire equipment distributors because of the higher profit margin. But selling to fire equipment distributors consumes relatively more sales force time per unit sold and the limited call time may be a bottleneck.

To solve this problem, the first step is to state all the conditions in a compact mathematical form. We can distinguish between the firm's objective and the firm's operating constraints.

The objective is to maximize total profits by establishing optimal sales target volumes and marketing mixes for the two customer segments. Let Q_1 = sales target volume (in units) for fire equipment distributors, and Q_2 = sales target volume (in units) for surgical supply houses. Since every unit sold to a fire equipment distributor and a surgical supply house will yield $15 and $10 net profit, respectively, total profits will be shown by the profit function:

$$\text{profits} = 15Q_1 + 10Q_2 \tag{3-19}$$

This is called the *objective function*, which the firm wishes to maximize.

Now each possible target sales volume requires a different amount of personal selling and advertising effort. The marketing input requirements and constraints for different sales levels can be expressed mathematically. The sales force, for example, has 4000 hours of selling time available during the next six months. The estimated amount of selling time consumed will be $\frac{1}{2}$ hour (on the average) for every unit sold to fire equipment distributors and $\frac{1}{4}$ hour for every unit sold to surgical supply houses. (The numbers $\frac{1}{2}$ and $\frac{1}{4}$ are called the marketing input coefficients.) The expected amount of selling time cannot exceed the available amount, which is 4000 hours. Therefore the sales force constraint is

$$\frac{1}{2}Q_1 + \frac{1}{4}Q_2 \leqslant 4000 \tag{3-20}$$

Similarly, unit sales to fire equipment distributors and surgical supply houses require \$1 and \$2 of advertising, respectively, and cannot exceed \$14,000. Therefore the advertising budget constraint is

$$Q_1 + 2Q_2 \leqslant 14,000 \qquad\qquad (3\text{-}21)$$

In addition to these constraints, the company has decided that it must strive to sell at least 3000 units in each segment. The minimum sales quota constraints are stated as

$$\begin{aligned} Q_1 &\geqslant 3000 \\ Q_2 &\geqslant 3000 \end{aligned} \qquad\qquad (3\text{-}22)$$

At this point, the solution technique of linear programming (called the "simplex method") is used to find the values of Q_1 and Q_2 that maximize the profit function (Equation 3-19) while satisfying the constraints of Equations 3-20, 3-21, and 3-22. Because this problem involves only two unknowns, a simple graphical means of solution is available. The graphical method has the merit of offering a visualization of the problem that carries over to more complicated problems. In contrast, the standard algebraic method called the *simplex* method is used to solve larger problems, but it will not be used here.

The necessary charts are shown in Figure 3-4. First, we prepare a two-dimensional graph, where the Q_1 and Q_2 axes represent possible target sales volumes for fire equipment distributors and surgical supply houses, respectively [Figure 4(a)]. Any point in this space represents a conceivable solution before the constraints are specified. There are literally millions of such points, or solutions. In Figure 3-4(b), the constraint regarding the sales force is shown graphically. All the points in the shaded region are feasible from the point of view of the sales force constraint, that is, none will use up more than a total of 4000 call hours. (To find the shaded area corresponding to the constraint, turn the inequality $\frac{1}{2}Q_1 + \frac{1}{4}Q_2 \leqslant 4000$ into the equality $\frac{1}{2}Q_1 + \frac{1}{4}Q_2 = 4000$. The latter gives the boundary line. Algebraically:

$$\frac{1}{2}Q_1 + \frac{1}{4}Q_2 = 4000$$

$$\frac{1}{4}Q_2 = 4000 - \frac{1}{2}Q_1$$

$$Q_2 = 16,000 - 2Q_1$$

Thus the boundary line has an intercept on the Q_2 axis at 16,000 and has a negative slope of 2. This enables it to be drawn. To find which side of the boundary line represents the feasible space, place the value (0, 0), the origin, into the inequality. If it makes the inequality true—as it does in this case—then the shaded region lies on the (0, 0) side of the boundary line.

In figure 3-4(c), the advertising constraint has been added. The shaded region shows the points that satisfy both the advertising and personal selling constraints. The shaded region can be called the feasible polygon.

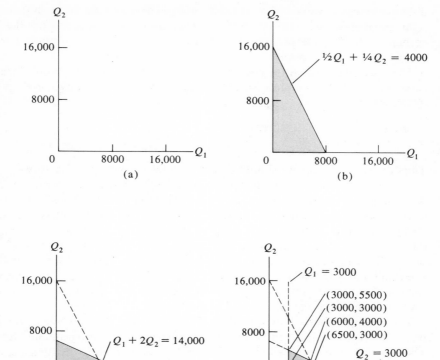

**Figure 3-4   Steps in the Graphical Solution of a Simple Linear
Programming Problem**

Figure 3-4(d) shows further modifications in the feasible polygon, resulting
from the introduction of the last two constraints regarding minimum sales
volume targets.

The problem now is to find the one best point in the feasible polygon. We
should notice that the desirability of each point in the feasible polygon can be
measured. We simply add that point to the objective function (Equation 3-19).
For example, we try the point (3000, 3000), which is at one corner of the feasible
region. Profits will be

$$\text{profit} = 15(3000) + 10(3000)$$
$$= \$75,000$$

Now, there is a helpful theorem in linear programming which says that the
optimal solution will be one (or possibly two) of the corner points of the feasible
polygon. (Graphically, the profit function $P = 15Q_1 + 10Q_2$ is drawn for

different assumed values of P. Higher values of P lead the line to shift to the right, parallel to itself. This shifting is carried on until the line touches the last corner of the feasible polygon before leaving it. This is the optimal corner point.)

The coordinates of all the corner points are shown in Figure 3-4(d). It is an easy matter in this simple case to test each. We find that the corner point (6000, 4000) gives the largest value of profits. Specifically

$$\text{profit} = 15(6000) + 10(4000)$$
$$= \$130,000$$

Thus the Oxite Company should divide its total marketing effort between the two segments so as to try to sell 6000 units to the fire equipment distributors and 4000 units to surgical supply houses. This will result in $130,000 profit. To attain sales of 6000 units to fire equipment distributors will require 3000 sales calls (because a half-hour call is required for each sale) and $6000 of advertising (because one dollar of advertising is required for each call); that is, (3000, $6000). To attain sales of 4000 units to surgical supply houses will require 1000 sales calls and $8000 of advertising; that is, (1000, $8000). These allocations just exhaust the total of the company's marketing resources. No other allocation of marketing resources can produce more profit.

This example shows how a problem in determining the best allocation and mix of marketing effort can be stated and solved in linear programming terms. The example used only two market segments, two marketing instruments, and four constraints (two of which were superfluous), but it is obvious that larger problems can be handled.

At the same time the limitations of a linear programming statement of this problem should be appreciated. The main obstacles standing in the way of more fruitful marketing applications of linear programming are nonlinearities and marketing mix interactions. A linear marketing mix function seems highly unrealistic. It is hard to believe that a marketing policy instrument will have a constant effect on sales. It seems more probable that if advertising is currently low, its doubling will have one effect; if advertising is currently high, its further doubling would have another effect. There is much evidence that, at some point, increasing the advertising outlays will increase sales at a diminishing rate. If the effect of each marketing variable were constant, management would be driven to select only one instrument, the one with the highest constant effect. Yet it is a common observation that companies diversify their marketing expenditures among different marketing instruments. This suggests that the effects of marketing decision variables are both nonlinear and interactive.

Exponential Marketing Mix Effects Model

Some of the limitations of the linear marketing mix model are overcome in the following formulation of the sales equation:

$$Q = kP^p A^a D^d R^r \tag{3-23}$$

where $\qquad$ $k =$ a scale factor

$p, a, d, r =$ constant elasticities of the respective values (price elasticity, p, is assumed negative in the usual case)

$P, A, D, R =$ marketing decision variables

The reader will note that this form is simply an adaptation of the Cobb-Douglas production function to the area of marketing.[20] Instead of stating the effects of factors of production on output, it states the effect of factors of marketing on demand. Consequently, we can prove that the exponents of marketing variables represent constant elasticities.[21] The elasticities can take on different values, leading to increasing, decreasing, or constant marginal effects.[22] The elasticities of advertising and distribution in the equation can be inserted into Equation 3-16 to determine how much should be spent on advertising out of a total budget B for advertising and distribution. Furthermore, the exponential marketing mix equation implies that the effect on demand of a change in a marketing variable will depend on the level of the other variables and the level of the variable itself. These features can be shown by taking the first derivative of sales (Q) with respect to any variable, say, advertising (A):

$$\frac{\partial Q}{\partial A} = ak P^p A^{a-1} D^d R^r = a \frac{Q}{A} \tag{3-24}$$

According to Equation 3-24, the rate at which sales will change in response to more advertising depends upon the constant elasticity of advertising (a), the current level of sales (Q), and the current level of advertising (A). The current level of sales (Q) depends on all the variables; therefore the marginal sales response is influenced by the setting of the other variables. This is called the *marketing mix interaction effect*. Furthermore, the effect of a marginal change in a variable is influenced by its present level.

An early example: Brem's equation. An early empirical example of a fitted exponential demand equation was developed by Brems in his study of Ford automobile sales.[23] Brems wished to predict the actual ratio of Ford to Chevrolet sales over the period 1932–1950 and he fitted the following equation by standard least squares regression:

---

[20]See discussion in Chap. 2, pp. 40-41.

[21]See Chap. 2. For an alternative proof, note that Equation 3–23 is written in double log form as

$$\log Q = \log k + p \log P + a \log A + d \log D + r \log R$$

Taking advertising as an example, we obtain

$$Q_A = \frac{dQ}{dA} \frac{A}{Q} = \frac{d \log Q}{d \log A} = a$$

Therefore a is the elasticity of advertising. The same proof applies to the other exponents.

[22]See Chap. 2, pp. 33-34.

[23]Hans Brems, *Product Equilibrium under Monopolistic Competition* (Cambridge, Mass.: Harvard University Press, 1951), p. 45.

$$\frac{Q_F}{Q_C} = .782 \left(\frac{R_F}{R_C}\right)^{1.51} \left(\frac{P_F}{P_C}\right)^{-1.79} \tag{3-25}$$

where Q_F = U.S. registration of new Fords
$\quad\quad Q_C$ = U.S. registration of new Chevrolets
$\quad\quad R_F$ = maximum brake horsepower of Ford
$\quad\quad R_C$ = maximum brake horsepower of Chevrolet
$\quad\quad P_F$ = price of Ford
$\quad\quad P_C$ = price of Chevrolet

This equation showed relative brake horsepower (a surrogate variable for product quality) and relative price to be the two significant predictors. According to the results, a 1 percent rise in the ratio of Ford's to Chevrolet's maximum brake horsepower would lead to a 1.51 percent rise in Ford's sales relative to Chevrolet's; a 1 percent relative rise in Ford's prices would lead to a 1.79 percent decline in Ford's relative sales. Provided that tastes have not changed, this equation, along with the relevant Ford cost data and information on Chevrolet's intentions, could help Ford determine the best price and maximum horsepower to offer the consuming public.

Deriving marketing decision rules. Under certain simplifications the exponential demand can lead to some straightforward decision rules for setting the marketing instruments. Suppose product quality is held constant and left out of the demand equation.

$$Q = kP^p A^a D^d \tag{3-26}$$

Suppose the unit cost of production is constant, so that the cost equation is

$$C = cQ + A + D + F \tag{3-27}$$

Profits (Z) will be

$$Z = (P - c)Q - A - D - F \tag{3-28}$$

Given these assumptions, the optimal settings for the marketing mix variables are given by the following decision rules.[24]

$$P^* = \frac{p}{1+p} c \tag{3-29}$$

$$A^* = a(P - c)Q \tag{3-30}$$

$$D^* = d(P - c)Q \tag{3-31}$$

The decision rules for this special case are quite interesting and worth discussing. The decision rule for price shows that the optimum price is independent of the levels of the other marketing decision variables. Price is found by simply marking up unit cost by the constant multiple $p/(p+1)$. Thus, if price elasticity

[24]See Appendix Mathematical Note 3–2.

(p) is -2, price should be marked up 100 percent of unit cost. If price elasticity is -3, price should be marked up 50 percent; if price elasticity is -4, 33 percent. In general, higher price elasticities should call for lower markups over cost.

How plausible is it that the optimal price does not depend on the level of advertising and distribution? The mathematical reason for this surprising result is that advertising and distribution expenditures are treated parametrically (as "sunk" costs) in the solution procedure for price, and hence do not affect the optimum price. A real world example will be described shortly,[25] in which price was established independently of the other variables essentially according to Equation 3-29.

It should also be noted that the optimal price does not seem to depend upon seasonal factors, competition, and other environmental variables. This is largely artificial, insofar as our model did not explicitly include environmental variables. If price elasticity (p) varies seasonally or is affected by competition, the optimal price will be affected through the variable p in Equation 3-29. We should need explicit functions for how elasticity varies seasonally or with competition.

Finally, decision rules (Equations 3-29 and 3-30) can be used to derive the optimal ratio of advertising expenditures to sales. Most sellers establish this ratio on a customary basis rather than a theoretically correct one. The theoretically correct ratio, assuming that demand response is describable by a multiple exponential function of the marketing mix variables, is given by:[26]

$$\frac{A^*}{P^*Q} = -\frac{a}{p} \tag{3-32}$$

That is, advertising and price should be set in such a way that the resulting advertising-to-sales ratio is equal to the ratio of advertising elasticity to price elasticity.

Another example. A large manufacturer of inexpensive tape recorders discovers through research that unit sales (Q) appear to be determined by the following exponential demand equation:

$$Q = 100{,}000P^{-2}A^{1/8}D^{1/4} \tag{3-33}$$

Furthermore, unit manufacturing cost (c) is estimated to be \$10 over a large range of output.[27]

Given this information, the manufacturer can proceed to determine his optimal price, advertising, and distribution. His optimal price is, according to Equation 3-25:

$$P^* = \frac{-2(10)}{-2+1} = \$20 \tag{3-34}$$

[25]See the Dial Soap example below.
[26]See Appendix Mathematical Note 3-3.
[27]For more details on this example, see Philip Kotler, "Marketing Mix Decisions for New Products," *Journal of Marketing Research* (Feb. 1964) 43–49.

His optimal advertising expenditure is, according to Equation 3-32:

$$A^* = [\tfrac{1}{8}\,{}^{(1-1/4)}(20-10)\,(100{,}000)20^{-2}(\tfrac{1}{4})^{\,1/4}]^{1/(1-1/8-1/4)} \tag{3-35}$$
$$A^* = \$12{,}947$$

His optimal distribution expenditure is, according to Equation 3-12:

$$D = \frac{e_D}{e_A}\,A = \frac{\tfrac{1}{4}}{\tfrac{1}{8}}\,12{,}947 = \$25{,}894 \tag{3-36}$$

Miscellaneous Marketing Mix Effects Models

In addition to the linear and exponential models of marketing mix effects, other models can be developed to exhibit special relationships alleged to exist between two or more marketing variables. For example, take the commonly held view that higher levels of brand advertising tend to make the demand for a brand less price-elastic. Presumably, advertising creates a psychological preference for the brand, and customers are less likely to react to small changes in price. This interaction between advertising and price can be introduced into the linear or exponential model through suitable modifications of the equations. In the linear case

$$Q = a - b_1 P + b_2 A \tag{3-37}$$

we postulate that the price-response parameter b_1, instead of being constant, depends on the level of advertising:

$$b_1 = b_1(A) \tag{3-38}$$

Assume that the exact relationship is

$$b_1 = \frac{b_1'}{A} \tag{3-39}$$

Now substitute Equation 3-39 into Equation 3-37:

$$Q = a - b_1'\frac{P}{A} + b_2 A \tag{3-40}$$

and this equation shows demand as influenced by price modified by advertising, and by advertising itself. Whether the interaction actually exists between price and advertising is something that can be tested statistically if hard data are available. A test would be conducted to see whether price alone or price interacting with advertising did a better job of fitting the data.

Now suppose that the advertising coefficient b_2 depended in turn upon the number of outlets D for the company's product:

$$b_2 = b_2(D) \tag{3-41}$$

Assume that the exact relation was one of proportionality:

$$b_2 = b_2'D \tag{3-42}$$

Now replace Equation 3-42 in Equation 3-40:

$$Q = a - b_1' \frac{P}{A} + b_2' A D \qquad (3\text{-}43)$$

and this equation shows demand as influenced by the interaction of price and advertising, and advertising and distribution.

In general, the interaction of two or more marketing variables, say X_1, X_2, and X_3, may be shown by specific interaction terms of the following form:

$$Q = a + b_1 X_1 + b_2 X_2 + b_3 X_3 + b_4(X_1 X_2) + b_5(X_1 X_3) + b_6(X_2 X_3) + b_7(X_1 X_2 X_3) \qquad (3\text{-}44)$$

Equation 3-44 shows three zero order interactions, three first order interactions and one second order interaction. Which interactions are significant can be established on theoretical and empirical grounds. Theory can lead to an appreciation of the variables that are likely to interact with each other. Statistical estimation from an adequate data base can establish those interactions that are statistically significant.

Interactions among special sets of marketing variables can also be handled by a modification of the basically exponential equation form. Starting with the exponential form,

$$Q = k P^p A^a \qquad (3\text{-}45)$$

suppose that the analyst wants to indicate that higher levels of advertising reduce the price elasticity. Assume that there is a normal level of advertising, A_n, at which the normal elasticity is p_n. Assume that the actual price elasticity, p, falls when actual advertising, A, rises above normal advertising, A_n, according to the following relationship:

$$p = p_n \frac{A_n}{A} \qquad (3\text{-}46)$$

Thus, if $p_n = -2$ and $A_n = \$100,000$, and if the company decides to double advertising to $\$200,000$, then the resulting price elasticity is reduced to -1. The substitution of Equation 3-46 in Equation 3-45 yields

$$Q = k P^{[P_n(A_n/A)]} A^a \qquad (3\text{-}47)$$

This is only the beginning of possible ways to introduce a nonconstant elasticity for one variable that depends on the level of another variable. The equation forms get harder to work with, although usually they could be fitted in logarithmic form to appropriate data by standard regression procedures. The important point is that these forms would never have been fitted in the first place nor would the appropriate data have been gathered, unless the relationships were conceived on the basis of theoretical arguments about the nature of marketing mix interactions.

Marketing Variables Considered First in Planning

At this point it is appropriate to ask whether there are patterns of logical priority among marketing decision variables in the development of the optimal marketing mix. We have been assuming up to now that any variable can be selected in any order and on any level. Thus we can conceive of a high or low price, combined with a high or low advertising program and a high or low distribution program and a high or low product quality. The equation form takes the possible decision levels and spells out the implied sales for each strategy. If certain levels of two or more variables are badly out of harmony, such as a low product quality and a high price may be, the equation type will reflect this.

Now, in many situations, management must resolve the marketing mix problem by considering the decisions in a particular order. As a case in point, consider the introduction of Dial Soap by Armour in 1948. Dial represented a new breakthrough in bathing soaps, a soap that had deodorant properties without itself being odorous; previous deodorant soaps had a slightly offensive odor. The superior quality of the product was the first fact and alone indicated a possible high price strategy. The product used the ingredient hexachlorophene, which was very expensive to manufacture. Consequently the company had no choice but to charge a high price. Management concluded that price had to be around 25c, double the price of leading soaps, to cover the higher costs of manufacture. The high price immediately stamped Dial as a specialty item and supermarkets would not give it shelf space. As a result, the product had to be distributed through drug and department stores. Once the product quality, price, and channels were established, there were clear implications for advertising. Advertising copy had to take on a prestigious tone to support the quality, price, and distribution channel policies. Advertising media had to be selected with people in mind who could afford the specialty soap and buy it in department and drug stores. In looking back at the development of the original marketing strategy for Dial, we see that the logic called for first establishing the soap's price on the basis of its quality and cost, then choosing the distribution channels, and then deciding on the advertising copy and media.

This is not the only order in which the elements in the marketing mix are decided. In some cases, certain distribution channels are initially attractive and the price and advertising are set in relation to them. In other cases, a company may come into the market to offer services that are generally not available; these services set the constraints and shape the price, quality, and advertising decisions. Some variables are decided by the market (as is price in a pure competitive market), rather than by the firm. In general, each situation may have particular patterns of priority and interaction among decision variables that call for its own unique sequence of formulating the marketing mix.

Once the basic marketing strategy is developed for a product, annual marketing planning may involve finding settings for only a few marketing variables, the rest being treated as semifixed in the short run. Consider the case of a bath oil called Tender Touch, produced by the Helene Curtis Company. When introduced in 1961, Tender Touch was endowed with certain characteristics such as moderate price and a middle-majority status quality. The company's management does not think that bath oil purchasers are responsive to price; thus, after the original price decision, subsequent price changes only reflect changes in the industry price level as the cost of living rises. Product characteristics are not tampered with to a noticeable extent, unless Helene Curtis wants to consider making a substantial change in marketing strategy. There is little Helene Curtis can do to change its distribution channels for Tender Touch, although the company might consider developing a new brand of bath oil with a marketing mix more acceptable to department store buyers and customers. Advertising is the sole marketing variable in the short run that can be freely manipulated to study its influence on sales. Helene Curtis is strongly committed to the use of network daytime television as the sole medium for its advertising. Therefore, due to the structure of the market and strategy decisions by the Helene Curtis management, the advertising expenditure level for all practical purposes is the sole variable that can be used to achieve its sales and profit targets.

ALLOWING FOR DIFFERENCES IN MARKETING EFFECTIVENESS

Mathematical marketing mix models typically express functional relationships between dollar sales and dollar amounts of advertising, distribution, and other forms of marketing effort. The use of dollar amounts is appropriate if it can be assumed that a firm is maximally and consistently efficient in its application of these expenditures and that all firms have the same efficiency per dollar spent. The assumption of perfect efficiency comes from the heritage of economic theory, in which management is assumed to operate always on the lowest, most efficient cost curve. In marketing, there is hardly anything approaching perfect efficiency, and we can safely assume that firms vary in their efficiency in spending marketing dollars.

Consider some examples. A company can reshuffle its salesmen among territories and sales may substantially increase (or decrease), although there is no change in the number of men or field sales expenditures. A company can change the graphic and structural design of its package and sales can suddenly increase (or decrease). A company can change its advertising message and sales may change drastically. In the last case, one only has to think of the Avis or Volkswagen campaigns to recognize the difference made by the sheer creative power of the advertising independent of the dollar level of expenditure. Buzzell made this observation a few years ago:

> "If we assume for a moment that the sales effects of advertising *do* depend on message content and presentation, then it is clear that mathematical models based on dollar expenditure alone leave much to be desired. Suppose, for example, that we examine historical time series data for sales and dollar expenditures, and try to ascertain some general relationship between the two. Even if we are successful in adjusting for the influence of non-advertising variables such as prices, the relationship may be seriously distorted if the creative quality of advertising in different time periods has changed."[28]

[28]Robert D. Buzzell, "Predicting Short-Term Changes in Market Share as a Function of Advertising Strategy," *Journal of Marketing Research* (Aug. 1964) 28.

Once the impact of effectiveness, as well as the level of marketing expenditures on sales is recognized, then it is clear that a firm can seek to improve its sales position in two ways. The first question the firm should ask is whether it is spending its present marketing dollars in the best possible way. Is it getting the best advertising campaign, using the best distribution channels, making the best number of sales calls, and using the best timing on sales promotions? Only after the firm is satisfied that there is no possible improvement in the content of its marketing program is it ready to consider whether it is spending the best amount of dollars. If it is presently operating at peak marketing efficiency, the only route to improved sales (and possibly profits) is through increasing marketing expenditures.

Changing the response parameters. There are two ways to introduce marketing effectiveness differences into the equations. The first approach calls for directly modifying the response parameters to reflect changes in marketing effectiveness. Suppose a firm's sales equation is

$$Q = 100,000P^{-2}A^{1/8} \tag{3-48}$$

The firm tries out a new advertising message in test markets and finds a great response. Management adopts the new message and its best estimate of the new elasticity of advertising is $\frac{1}{4}$. Consequently, management revises Equation 3-48:

$$Q = 100,000P^{-2}A^{1/4} \tag{3-49}$$

Now Equation 3-49 is used in the profit function to find the optimum price and advertising level. Thus an estimated change in marketing effectiveness is introduced by directly changing the response parameters in the demand equation before entering it in the profit function.

Using an explicit index of marketing effectiveness. The major limitation of the preceding method is that no effort is made to state *how effective* the firm is in handling each of the marketing instruments. Yet marketing practitioners will be heard to say that a particular competitor is doing the best job, another is doing a poor job, and another is doing a mediocre job. Consider the relative marketing effectiveness of Procter and Gamble, Lever Brothers, and Colgate-Palmolive. There is a commonly held belief that P. & G. gets more for its marketing dollar than the other two companies. Assume this for the sake of argument. Letting 1.00 stand for average effectiveness in this industry, we might take the next step and estimate that P. & G.'s overall marketing effectiveness is 1.10. (This may be a weighted average of P. & G.'s effectiveness with different marketing instruments.) We now postulate that a company's sales are a function of its *marketing effort* and its marketing effort is the product of its marketing effectiveness times the dollars spent. Taking advertising as an example, we have

$$A = \alpha A_D \tag{3-50}$$

where A = advertising effort
$\quad\quad\alpha$ = index of company's advertising effectiveness (1.00 = average)
$\quad\quad A_D$ = advertising budget in dollars
Substituting Equation 3-50 into Equation 3-48, we obtain

$$Q = 100,000P^{-2}(\alpha A_D)^{1/8} \tag{3-51}$$

This equation says that the elasticity of *advertising effort* is $\frac{1}{8}$, and advertising effort is the product of the quality of the effort, α, and the amount spent, A_D. For P. & G. the equation would read:

$$Q = 100,000P^{-2}(1.10A_D)^{1/8} \tag{3-52}$$

indicating that P. & G.'s dollars go 10 percent further than those of an average competitor.

Measurement of Effectiveness Differences

This still leaves the question of how to measure effectiveness differences in numerical terms. How do we know that a new advertising campaign might increase advertising elasticity from $\frac{1}{8}$ to $\frac{1}{4}$ or that P. & G. gets 10 percent more marketing impact from its marketing dollars than the average firm in the same industry.

The problem is far from solved and considerable research remains to be done. Consider advertising effectiveness as a case in point. In spite of all the research on advertising effectiveness measurement, the methods are far from satisfactory. The effectiveness of one advertising message or campaign over another is judged by opinions of experts or audience, by recall or recognition measures, or by simulated sales tests. (See Chapter 14.) Most of the proposed measures are only proxies for the ultimate item of interest, sales. Efforts are sporadically made to demonstrate a high correlation between a proxy measure of advertising effectiveness and sales. For example, Starch has offered evidence of a relationship between the level of magazine advertising recall and the brand's sales in the week following release of the ad.[29]

One recent suggestion of a measure of advertising copy quality is the *idea of relative competitive preference*.[30] This measure was developed at the Schwerin Research Corporation for evaluating TV commercials. Suppose that 15 percent of an audience prefer brand B before seeing the commercial, and 25 percent after seeing the commercial. This gain of +10 between the *prechoice percentage* and *postchoice percentage* is called the *competitive preference factor*. Now suppose that the same test for other brands in the product class yields an average competitive preference factor of +8. The conclusion is that Brand B's campaign is superior to the other brands' campaigns, and its *relative competitive preference* can be computed as $\frac{10}{8}$ = 1.25. Thus 1.25 is a proposed measure of the relative

---

[29]Daniel Starch, "Do Ad Readers Buy the Products?" *Harvard Business Review* (May–June 1958) 49–58.

[30]Buzzell, "Predicting Short-Term Changes in Market Share as a Function of Advertising Strategy," 27–31.

quality of Brand B's advertising copy to its competitor's advertising copy and may be used explicitly in the mathematical analysis of its optimum strategy.[31]

Should Increased Marketing Effectiveness Be Matched by Higher or Lower Expenditures?

When a company discovers a more effective way of using its marketing dollars, should it continue at the same expenditure level? After Avis discovered that it had a really superior advertising campaign, should it have increased or decreased its advertising budget? It may be argued that Avis can now reduce its advertising budget without hurting sales and still enjoy higher profits. Or it can be argued that Avis should increase advertising expenditures to take advantage of its increased advertising power to pass its competition.

Similarly, consider a company with a mediocre or poor advertising platform. Should it spend more to make up through repetition for what is lacking in the campaign? Or should the company spend less, since it cannot get much for its advertising dollar in relation to its other marketing activities?

One company's answer to this question was given by Thomas B. McCabe, Jr., of Scott Paper:[32]

"We set up advertising budgets on the basis of a two-year-period. But if one of our agencies comes up with a campaign that we feel has unusual merit and potential, we will increase the product budget and, frequently, the sales and profit objectives as well, if our experience and research indicate that the enlarged expenditure will produce more profit than the increase in budget."

A different answer was implied by Malcolm McNiven:[33]

"If an advertiser establishes a near-optimum expenditure level for his current advertising program, he can further improve the productivity of his advertising by better media allocation and better copy development. This should then allow him to further reduce his expenditure level since it will in a sense produce the same advertising push for him at less dollar expenditure."

A marketing consultant told the author that he would never advise cutting the advertising budget because then competitors would be able to afford the lower budget and neutralize somewhat the company's advantage.

We can go part of the way in answering the question by mathematical analysis. Much depends upon our model of the sales determination process. Suppose we assume that the model discussed in Equation 3-26 represents our understanding of this process. Suppose that the company's advertising agency develops a new

---

[31]See ibid., for the explanatory power found for this qualitative variable.

[32]Thomas B. McCabe, Jr., "How Much to Spend for Advertising," in Richard J. Kelly, *The Advertising Budget—Preparation, Administration and Control* (New York: Association of National Advertisers, Inc., 1967).

[33]Malcolm M. McNiven, "Introduction," in McNiven, ed., *How Much to Spend for Advertising* (New York: Association of National Advertisers, Inc., 1969), p. 9.

and superb advertising campaign that raises the advertising elasticity a. According to Equation 3-30, the optimal advertising level A^* depends, among other things, on the level of a. Since a has been increased, the optimal level of advertising is higher. With this model of the demand equation, a new and improved advertising campaign should be backed by *more* advertising dollars.

One can now pose an additional important question. Should the company increase its distribution expenditures as well, or leave them alone, or decrease them? We note that the optimal distribution D^* is given by Equation 3-12:

$$D^* = \frac{d}{a} A^* \tag{3-53}$$

where a, d = elasticities of advertising and distribution, respectively (also written as e_A and e_D). Accordingly, it may be desirable to increase, decrease, or leave distribution constant, depending on relative changes on the right-hand side. Although A^* has gone up, so has a, thus offsetting each other but not necessarily canceling each other. An additional facet is that the elasticity of distribution, d, is not likely to remain constant. If anything, the elasticity of distribution is likely to increase because the sales force will be enthusiastic about the new campaign and work harder, and the dealers will be more receptive. In this case, it is likely that D^* might increase on net. Therefore, the effect of finding a better advertising campaign calls for more advertising and probably more distribution, although not to the same extent.

All of these conclusions are derived from a particular model of the sales-advertising process; it is conceivable that another model will lead to other conclusions. This is why it is so important to make one's model of the sales process explicit. Only in this way can it be tested against data over time and eventually serve the company in the solution of complex marketing problems.

SUMMARY

The interrelationship among marketing mix variables is one of the most challenging questions facing marketing analysts and planners. It is a question that lies at the heart of marketing strategy and underlies the debates between advertising men, field sales managers, pricing specialists, and brand managers as to the relative emphasis that should be put on the different elements of the marketing mix.

Although the number of actual marketing decision variables runs into the dozens, we have combined them into four basic categories for analytical purposes: price, promotion, distribution, and product quality. On the basis of a general model of demand and cost, it is possible to derive the equilibrium conditions that the optimal settings of these values should satisfy. The equilibrium conditions can be expressed as a relationship among the elasticities of the various marketing instruments. To solve directly for the optimal settings, a simplified model was set up and the explicit decision rules were derived for price, advertising, and distribution.

The next task was to show alternative approaches to expressing marketing mix effects in equation form. The linear equation is simple to use but implies constant and noninteractive effects of marketing variables. The exponential equation overcomes these difficulties, although at the expense of constant elasticities of the different marketing instruments. Some additional equation types were shown that introduced special interaction effects.

The final section discussed the problem of explicitly representing differences in the effectiveness of marketing effort. The effectiveness of marketing effort can be taken into account by directly modifying the response parameters or by introducing an explicit index of effectiveness. Differences in effectiveness pose the issue of what a company should do with its dollar level of expenditures after it discovers an improved marketing approach. According to one simple model, the company should follow up the improved quality of effort by additional dollars of expenditure on both advertising and distribution.

Questions and Problems

1. The Elkton Company designs, manufactures, installs, and services pneumatic, electric, and hydraulic environmental control systems for large buildings. The Elkton Company currently has 50 percent of the large building environment control system market. Its four competitors have 30, 10, 6, and 4 percent respectively. Contracts are obtained on a bid basis. Each salesman bids as high a price as he thinks he can get, and is rated on the average markup he is able to attain.

(a) List as many company marketing decision variables as you can for the above company.

(b) Conjecture the relative importance of each of the "four P's" to the Elkton Company.

2. Given the following sales response and profit functions, determine the rules for selecting price and advertising levels, and show that the Dorfman-Steiner conditions hold at these levels:

$$Q = K - pP + aA$$
$$Z = (P - c)Q - A - F$$

3. The manufacturer of a line of inexpensive watches determines that the demand for one of his products is represented by the following equation:

$$Q = 30,000\, P^{-2} A^{1/6} D^{1/3}$$

If unit cost for the product is estimated at $8, what are the firm's optimal price, distribution, and advertising levels for this product?

4. A seller of inexpensive men's suits is currently selling one of the products in his line for $70, while spending $10,000 in advertising for this particular product. The sales and cost functions for this product can be expressed as:

$$Q = 10,000 - 100P + 5A^{.5}$$
$$C = 180,000 + 10Q + A$$

(a) What are the seller's current sales and profits?

(b) Are the current price and advertising expenditure levels optimal? If not, what are the optimal levels?

5. An industrial equipment manufacturer is trying to decide between making additional investments in advertising for his product or using this investment to improve product quality. At present he is spending about $4 (in units of $10,000) on advertising and nothing on the improvement of product quality. The relationship between profits and advertising has been determined as:

$$Z(A) = .3 + .4A - .06A^2$$

where $Z(A)$ = profits in units of $10,000 per period
  A = advertising expenditures in units of $10,000 per period
Similarly, the effect of improvements in product quality is expressed as:

$$Z(R) = .3R - .1R^2$$

where R = expenditures on improvements in quality expressed in units of $10,000 per period
The joint effect of these two variables is estimated as:

$$Z(AR) = .06AR$$

Given the above relationships:
(a) Determine the amount he should be spending on advertising and product quality improvement, respectively, to obtain maximum profits.
(b) If the manufacturer can increase his total marketing budget to $7 (in units of $10,000), how should it be split between advertising and quality improvement.
(c) Determine the marginal profit on increasing the budget of $7 (in units of $10,000) by $1.
6. Is it reasonable to expect that there is a relationship between the level of a company's advertising and the effectiveness of its salesmen? Can you illustrate this effect in a demand equation?

CHAPTER 4
Competitive Strategy

Thus far the analysis has dealt with a single firm offering a differentiated product, able to influence its sales by the quantity and effectiveness of its marketing effort. Nothing has been said about other firms that may be in the same market and their relation to this firm. Yet other firms will exercise a decisive influence on the firm's marketing policies and sales results.

Even if there were no actual competitors, a firm would face potential constraints on its marketing policies from three sources. A firm that is the only seller of a particular product or service (monopoly) (1) may be placed under legal regulation (regulated monopolies); (2) it may face the threat of antitrust action; or (3) it may face the prospect of emergent competitors if profits are too high. Thus even a monopolist must pay careful attention to an outside force in formulating its marketing strategy.

When there are many competitors present, as in *pure competition* or *monopolistic competition*, there is less need, paradoxically, to take them into account. In a purely competitive market the firm has no problem of marketing strategy, only a problem of finding the best production level. All the firms produce the same product; all the buyers have perfect information about prices and buy strictly according to price. Under these conditions no firm can charge more for its product than the market price nor would it gain anything by charging less, since it can sell its entire output at the going price. Advertising does not do any good because buyers buy strictly according to price.

Few real markets are described by pure competition and the economist's model of monopolistic competition may be more realistic.[1] Each of many producers produces a somewhat differentiated offering, at least as seen by the buyers. The offerings may differ in quality, reliability, features, or service. As a result, customers perceive different values—this gives the seller some pricing latitude and a basis for promotional investments. Because there are many firms, each firm feels more competitive independence than if there were few firms. If a firm reduces its price or increases its marketing effort, sales will probably increase without necessarily provoking competitive retaliation. If the firm increases its sales by $X, each of its n competitors has lost $X/n (if they are equally affected) and this may be too small to cause a reaction.

If this analysis is correct, the firm in a monopolistically competitive industry does not have to make explicit assumptions about competitors' reactions in its evaluation of optimal marketing strategies. It can consider largely its own demand curve and methods of increasing sales and their relative costs. The analysis in the preceding chapters can be used without much modification for the monopolistically competitive case.

The major occasion calling for explicit consideration of competitive behavior occurs when one firm's marketing actions can adversely affect the profits of another firm, that is,

$$\frac{dZ_j}{dX_i} < 0 \qquad\qquad (4\text{-}1)$$

where Z_j = profits of firm j
$\quad\quad\ X_i$ = positive marketing action of firm i

In this case, firm j is likely to retaliate by adjusting its own marketing strategy. Consequently, firm i will not consider the original move without first estimating firm j's probable reaction. The condition under which (4-1) is likely to hold is when there are few firms, for then each would be sensitive to the other's actions. The name given to such an industry is *oligopoly*, with *duopoly* reserved for the special case of only two competitors.

Not only must the oligopolistic firm worry about how competitors would react to its moves, but also about surprise moves that the competitors might initiate. Thus management must forecast environmental variables such as national income and population, as well as the active and reactive environmental variable known as competition. The firm must gather substantial and continuous intelligence about its competitors.

This chapter will examine how a firm can determine its optimal marketing

[1]For a contrary view, "We thus cannot find any examples of markets in the real world for which the model of monopolistic competition is relevant," see Kalman J. Cohen and Richard M. Cyert, *Theory of the Firm: Resource Allocation in a Market Economy* (Englewood Cliffs, N.J.: Prentice-Hall, Inc., 1965), p. 226.

program in the face of active competitors. The first step that the firm must undertake is to estimate the size of the total market, especially the influence of the number of competitors on total market size. The second step is to estimate the likely share it will capture and maintain of this total market on the basis of a given company strategy and anticipated competitors' strategies. The third step is to find the "best" marketing strategy in the light of its objectives and the forecasted countermoves of competitors. These three steps constitute the three sections of this chapter.

DETERMINATION OF TOTAL MARKET DEMAND

The individual firm facing competition must first estimate the total size of the market in which it will be selling. Total market demand turns out to be a complicated concept with eight elements, as the following definition reveals: market demand describes the *total volume* that would be *bought* of a defined *product class* by a defined *customer group* in a defined *geographical area* in a defined *time period* under defined *environmental conditions* and a defined *marketing program.*

Product class. Market demand measurement requires a careful definition of the product or product class. The seller of tin cans has to define whether the relevant market is the metal can market or the larger metal-glass container market. The seller of liquid detergents has to decide whether the relevant market is the low-sudsing household liquid detergent market or the household liquid detergent market or the household liquid and powdered detergent market. These decisions depend on how the seller views the opportunities for penetrating adjacent markets.[2]

Total volume. Market demand can be measured either in physical volume terms, dollar volume terms, or both. The market demand for automobiles may be described as 9 million cars or $27 billion. The physical volume measure is useful when the product is relatively homogeneous. Its advantage is that historical sales are not distorted by changes in the value of the dollar. But if product homogeneity is lacking or shifting, the physical volume measure can be misleading. For example, 9 million cars can have vastly varying profit implications, depending upon the mix of high priced and low priced cars.

Market demand can also be expressed in relative rather than absolute volume terms. Thus the market demand for automobiles in Greater Chicago can be expressed as 270,000 cars or as 3 percent of the nation's total demand.

Bought. In measuring market demand, it is important to define whether "bought" means the volume ordered, the volume shipped, the volume paid for, the volume received, or the volume consumed. For example, a forecast of new

---

[2]Economists use the concept of "cross elasticity" to measure the relatedness of two markets. See Chap. 7, pp. 163–164.

housing for next year usually means the number of units that will be ordered, not completed (called housing starts). A forecast of passenger automobile sales can vary, depending upon whether the measure is the number of cars delivered to dealers or the number purchased by householders.

Customer group.   Market demand may be measured for the whole market or for any segment(s) of the market. Examples of the latter are a steel producer who estimates the volume to be bought separately by the construction industry and the transportation industry, or an airline that estimates the seat-miles to be bought by business travelers and vacation travelers.

Geographical area.   Market demand should be measured with reference to well-defined geographical boundaries. A forecast of next year's passenger automobile sales will vary, depending upon whether the boundaries are limited to the United States or include Canada and/or Mexico. Market demand may be measured for cities, standard metropolitan areas, counties, states, regions, or countries.

Time period.   Market demand should be measured with reference to a defined time period. Thus one can talk about the market demand for the next calendar year, or for the coming five years, or for 1975 and so forth. Generally speaking, the longer the forecasting interval, the more tenuous the forecast. Every forecast is based on a set of assumptions about environmental and marketing conditions; the chance that some of these assumptions will not be fulfilled increases with the distance of the period forecast.

Environmental conditions.   Market demand is affected by a host of uncontrollable factors, such as technological breakthroughs, economic reversals, new legislation, and changes in taste. Different assumptions concerning the environmental conditions which are expected to prevail will lead to different estimates of market demand. Therefore it is important to list the set of environmental assumptions underlying any estimate of market demand and their assumed relative impact on demand.

Marketing program.   Market demand is also affected by controllable factors, particularly the marketing programs developed in the past and currently by the sellers. Demand in most markets will show some elasticity with respect to industry price, promotion, product improvements, and distribution effort. Thus a market demand forecast also requires assumptions about future industry prices and industry marketing outlays.

The most important thing to realize about market demand is that it is not a single number but a function. The level of total market demand, Q, at any point in time depends on two major factors: (1) the size and income of the market, and (2) the current level of total industry marketing effort. The size and income of the market sets an upper limit to what the market will consume under the most intense level of industry marketing effort. This upper limit can be called the *market potential* or *market saturation* level. The percent of the market potential that is actually realized will be determined by the current level of marketing effort.

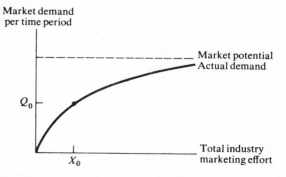

A. Static Market Demand Function

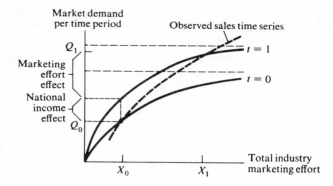

B. Dynamic Market Demand Path

Figure 4-1   Market Demand Functions

These concepts are illustrated in Figure 4-1. Market potential is represented as a constant whose level depends upon the size and income of the market at the point of time being considered. The market demand is represented as a concave function that is asymptotic to market potential and depends on the level of industry marketing effort. The actual demand in the current period will depend upon the current industry marketing effort. Thus, if the industry puts out X_0 of marketing effort, actual industry demand will be Q_0.

Stating this in functional notation will be helpful in the subsequent analysis. The basic proposition is

$$Q_t = k_t \bar{Q}_t \tag{4-2}$$

where Q_t = actual market demand at time t

k_t = fraction of realized potential at time t, where $0 \leqslant k < 1$

$\bar{Q}_t$ = market potential at time t

Both k_t and $\bar{Q}_t$ can in turn be expressed functionally. The fraction of realized potential, k_t, depends upon the current level of industry marketing effort, X_t:

$$k_t = f(X_t) \tag{4-3}$$

The market potential at time t depends upon such environmental variables as the number of customers, their interest in this product, and their purchasing power. For simplicity we shall use Y_t to represent any basic environmental determinant of market potential:

$$\bar{Q}_t = g(Y_t) \tag{4-4}$$

Then the basic proposition in Equation 4-2 can be restated, using Equations 4-3 and 4-4,

$$Q_t = f(X_t)g(Y_t) \tag{4-5}$$

Equation 4-5 says that current market demand will be the product of a marketing effort function and an environmental function.

As an example, assume that the marketing effort function and the environmental function are, respectively,

$$k_t = f(X_t) = (1 - e^{-aX_t}) \tag{4-6}$$

a concave function of marketing effort, and

$$\bar{Q}_t = g(Y_t) = bY_t \tag{4-7}$$

a linear function of national income. Then Equation 4-5 becomes

$$Q_t = (1 - e^{-aX_t})bY_t \tag{4-8}$$

According to Equation 4-8, current market demand depends upon the current levels of industry marketing effort and national income, and the parameters a and b.

The main use of this analysis is not to explain current demand so much as to forecast future demand. Therefore Equation 4-5 or Equation 4-8 must be made dynamic. Working with the general functions in Equation 4-5, suppose that a statistical analysis of past data showed the following:

$$X_t = cX_{t-1} \tag{4-9}$$

$$Y_t = dY_{t-1} \tag{4-10}$$

that is, industry marketing effort and national income grow (or decline) at the respective average rates c and d each period. If these rates hold constant, then industry marketing effort and national income t periods from the base period are given by

$$X_t = c^t X_0 \tag{4-11}$$

$$Y_t = d^t Y_0 \tag{4-12}$$

Substituting Equations 4-11 and 4-12 in Equation 4-5 we obtain

$$Q_t = f(c^t X_0) g(d^t Y_0) \tag{4-13}$$

Making this same substitution in the example of Equation 4-8, we find, after simplification:

$$Q_t = (1 - e^{-c^t a X_0}) d^t b Y_0 \tag{4-14}$$

According to Equation 4-14, market demand t periods from now depends upon projections of current marketing effort and national income according to known relationships. Presumably, all the parameters in Equation 4-14 are known and Q_t is strictly a function of t.

The dynamic analysis of market demand is shown graphically in Figure 4-1(b) for two periods. Assume that national income rises each period and is one factor causing market potential to rise. This also causes the concave curve to shift upward each period. In other words the firms would realize more sales because of the higher potential even if they did not increase industry marketing effort. This is called the income effect. Also assume that industry marketing effort increased from X_0 to X_1. This is called the marketing effort effect. As a result of the two effects, total industry sales would be observed historically to rise according to the dashed line, which is at a steeper rate than suggested by the static market demand function. This is an extremely important point because many marketing analysts and decision makers erroneously take the observed sales time series to indicate the responsiveness of sales to marketing effort (the static curve), whereas it also reflects the responsiveness of sales to environmental factors as well. In econometric work, this is called the identification problem, that is, the underlying structure is not revealed through a simple regression of observed sales on marketing effort alone.

Examples of Total Market Demand Functions

The preceding logic for expressing total market demand functions can now be illustrated with some concrete examples. The first example is taken from the Carnegie Tech Marketing Game modeled around the market for household detergents. The following total market demand function is used to generate case sales each month:[3]

$$Q_t = v_t Q_0 (1+g)^t \left(\frac{P_0}{P_t} \right)^{e_P} \left(\frac{A_t}{v_t A_0 (1+g)^t} \right)^{e_A} \cdot \left(\frac{Y_t}{Y_0} \right)^{e_Y} \tag{4-15}$$

where Q = total quantity demanded for month expressed in cases

   v = seasonal monthly index where $\sum_{t=1}^{12} v_t = 12.0$

   g = growth rate (monthly)

   P = average industry price (each brand's price being weighted by its market share)

---

[3]See Alfred A. Kuehn and Doyle L. Weiss, "Marketing Analysis Training Exercise," *Behavioral Science* (Jan. 1965) 51–67, especially p. 55.

A = total promotional expenditure for industry
Y = average income per capita
e = elasticity parameter
t = time subscript for month
0 = subscript for the values of the variables at time 0

According to Equation 4-15 the total market demand for detergents is responsive to both environmental and marketing factors. Starting with a specific demand level in the base year, Q_0, demand grows through time at the constant monthly rate, g, modified by the seasonal index, v_t. The constant growth rate term, g, implicitly represents the effect of population growth and a growing usage rate of detergents, although the model builders are not explicit on this point. A separate environmental influence on demand is wielded by the current level of national income in relation to the base level of national income, its magnitude of response being given by e_Y, the income elasticity. In passing, it should be noted that the reason for the inclusion of national income in the demand function for detergents is not obvious, since one would have expected a negligible income elasticity for this type of product.

Detergent demand is also influenced according to Equation 4-15 by two marketing variables, price and promotion. As current price rises above the base price, demand is depressed to an extent governed by the price elasticity of demand. As current promotion rises above the base promotion modified by normal growth and seasonal levels, demand is stimulated to an extent governed by the promotional elasticity of demand. It might be added that promotion in the Carnegie Tech model covers several variables such as advertising, sales force, and trade allowance activity. At the same time the total demand function omits any influence of the average quality of detergents on total demand.

The second model was developed by this author and it also is a multiplicative marketing mix demand model, with certain important modifications.[4] The market demand equation is illustrated with hypothetical parameters.

$$Q_t = G_t \cdot V_t \cdot M_t \tag{4-16}$$

$$Q_t = [4000(.2)^{.9^t}] [1 + .1 \sin (30t + 180)] \left[\sum_{i=1}^{n} \frac{P_{i,t}^{-2} A_{i,t}^{1/8} D_{i,t}^{1/4}}{n(20^{-2} \, 2500^{1/8} \, 2500^{1/4})} \right]^{2(1.05)^{-t}}$$

where

G = growth term (in number of units)
V = seasonal term (scale index)
M = marketing effort term (scale index)

Equation 4-16 says that total market demand can be found by projecting growth from an initial level of demand and modifying it each period by the seasonal

[4]Philip Kotler, "Competitive Strategies for New Product Marketing over the Life Cycle," *Management Science* (Dec. 1965) 104–119.

index and index of the effect of total industry marketing effort. The growth factor is represented by the Gompertz equation,

$$G_t = 4000(.2)^{.9^t} \tag{4-17}$$

which calls for industry sales starting at 800 units a month at $t = 0$ and growing asymptotically in S curve fashion toward 4000 units a month as $t \to \infty$. The seasonal factor is represented by the following equation:

$$V_t = 1 + .1 \sin (30t + 180) \tag{4-18}$$

which calls for the seasonal index to vary sinusoidally between .90 and 1.10. The industry marketing effort factor is represented by the following expression:

$$M_t = \left[\sum_{i=1}^{n} \frac{P_{i,t}^{-2} A_{i,t}^{1/8} D_{i,t}^{1/4}}{n(20^{-2} \, 2500^{1/8} \, 2500^{1/4})} \right]^{2(1.05)^{-t}} \tag{4-19}$$

Equation 4-19 consists of a variable numerator and a fixed denominator (since n, the number of competitors, will be fixed). The denominator is a normalizing factor, representing initial conditions. Subsequent changes in the marketing mixes are reflected in the numerator. The exponents within the brackets represent the respective marketing factor elasticities. The price has an elasticity of -2. Advertising and distribution have elasticities of $1/8$ and $1/4$, respectively, indicating that increased marketing expenditures produce increased sales at a diminishing rate.

The exponent $2(1.05)^{-t}$ [call it $f(t)$], to which the ratio in brackets is raised, produces two desirable effects. *The first effect is that, as the new market matures, total industry marketing expenditures have a diminishing influence on total product demand.* As $t \to \infty$, $f(t) \to 0$ and $M_t \to 1$. When $t = 60$, for example, M_t is very close to 1, and the total marketing expenditure level no longer influences total demand. *The second effect is that $f(t)$ reduces the cross elasticity of brand promotion from positive to negative as the market matures.* In a new market, increases in one company's promotional expenditures tend to increase the sales of other firms as well, although not proportionately. Eventually, further increases in company promotion begin to affect other companies' sales negatively. This transformation of cross elasticity from positive to negative as the market matures is accomplished by $f(t)$; in this model, it occurs at approximately $t = 14$.

Effect of the Number of Competitors upon Total Demand

The previous demand equations did not indicate any explicit effect that the number of competitors, n, had on the level of total demand. Yet there is reason to believe that total demand is stimulated in most industries by the entry of more firms. The effect of the number of competitors comes through the equation not directly in an n term, but indirectly through the effect of the number of competitors on the levels of price and promotion. Specifically, the entrance of new firms is expected to depress the price and augment total promotional expenditures, both having the effect of stimulating the level of total demand.

To appreciate this, imagine an industry that is served by one firm. The monopolist sets his price and output according to standard marginalist reasoning; this leads to higher prices and lower output than found in a comparable competitive industry. His profits are typically high. Suppose a second firm is attracted by the profit level. The second firm can enter the market, using one of several strategies.

1. *Charge the same price.* If there is no customer loyalty or other differentiating factors, then consumers will move in a random fashion between the two brands and eventually the brands will share the market equally. If unit costs are higher at lower outputs, then each firm will make less than half the profits the first firm made before the second firm appeared.

2. *Charge a lower price.* If the market is price-sensitive and well informed, then customers will switch to the new firm because of its lower price and the exmonopolist will have to lower his price in self-defense. The lower prices will expand total demand if total demand is price-elastic.

3. *Resort to heavy promotion.* The new competitor may decide to spend a substantial sum of money to call attention to its brand. This can increase total industry sales in three ways. It may increase the number of persons who are aware of the product. It may persuade some of the persons who buy substitute products to buy this product. And it may lead present buyers to increase their rate of consumption.

If additional firms enter the industry, there is further reason to expect prices to fall and total promotional expenditures to rise. However, the rate of expansion in demand is likely to slow down with each new competitor because:

1. The price is not likely to be forced down as dramatically with each new entrant.
2. The additional advertising is not likely to be so noticeable after most of the product awareness has been created and most types of messages have been used.
3. The most recent brand is likely to exhibit fewer product differences after major potential product differences have already been exploited.

Thus the effect of the number of firms on total demand works principally through the effect of the number of firms on prices and promotional effort. Equations such as 4-15 and 4-16 can be used indirectly to project these effects. A more direct way to express the effect of the number of competitors is through an expression involving n such as:

$$Q_t = \bar{Q}(1 - e^{-an}) \tag{4-20}$$

where $\bar{Q}$ = the saturation level of total demand
n = the number of competitors

The modified exponential form is used because of the previous arguments for believing that the rate of increase in total demand is likely to slow down as new competitors enter the industry.

MARKET SHARE DETERMINATION

Now that we have examined the functional representation of total demand, we turn to the problem of representing company sales. Firm i's sales, Q_i, will be some *share*, s_i, of total demand, Q; that is,

$$Q_i = s_i Q \qquad (4\text{-}21)$$

The problem now is to explain how firm i's market share is determined.

The most popular theory is that the *market shares* of various competitors will be proportional to their *effort shares*, that is, their shares of total marketing effort. The Fundamental Theorem of Market Share Determination is expressed symbolically as

$$s_i = m_i = \frac{M_i}{M} \qquad (4\text{-}22)$$

where $s_i = $ firm i's market share
   $m_i = $ firm i's effort share, that is, the share of total marketing effort
   $M_i = $ firm i's marketing effort in dollars
   $M = $ total industry marketing effort in dollars

The fundamental theorem of market share determination is illustrated for a hypothetical three-competitor situation in Table 4-1.

Table 4-1

Company i	M_i	Q_i	m_i	s_i
1	$50	$500	.50	.50
2	$30	$300	.30	.30
3	$20	$200	.20	.20

Each firm's share of market, s_i, is proportional to its share of marketing, M_i.

The idea that company market shares approximate company marketing shares is frequently expressed by businessmen. "To *get* a 10 percent share of the market, you have to spend roughly 10 percent of all marketing funds." In many industries the correlation is, in fact, high. However, this may be due to the tendency of companies to set their marketing budgets as a ratio to sales. Translated, this says: "To *maintain* a 10 percent share of the market, you have to spend 10 percent of all marketing funds." Thus high correlations where found are not necessarily of the type of causation we are trying to establish.

Now suppose that the expected correlation is not found. Consider the hypothetical data in Table 4-2.

Table 4-2

Company	m_i	s_i
1	.30	.50
2	.50	.30
3	.20	.20

In this case, company 1 spends 30 percent of total marketing expenditures and has achieved a 50 percent share of market; company 2 is in the reverse situation, spending 50 percent of the marketing funds and enjoying only 30 percent of the market; and company 3 enjoys a share of market equal to its effort share.

How can the divergence in the case of the first two firms be explained? At least four different hypotheses can be advanced.

Qualitative Effect Hypothesis

Here M_i represents the *dollars* spent by company i in marketing, and we are trying to explain the divergence between the relative dollars spent and the relative number of units sold. It may well be that the firms differ in the effectiveness with which they spend marketing dollars. Using α_i to represent the marketing effectiveness of a dollar spent by firm i (with $\alpha = 1.00$ for average effectiveness), the *effective* marketing dollars, $\bar{M}_i$, spent by firm i are

$$\bar{M}_i = \alpha_i M_i$$

Then the fundamental theorem of market share determination Equation 4-22 must be revised to read:

$$s_i = \bar{m}_i = \frac{\alpha_i M_i}{\sum \alpha_i M_i} \tag{4-23}$$

where $\bar{m}_i$ = effective effort share.

As an example, Krishnan and Gupta[5] used the following equation in their model of market share determination for a duopoly:

$$s_1 = \frac{\alpha_1 M_1}{\alpha_1 M_1 + \alpha_2 M_2} + k(P_2 - P_1) \tag{4-24}$$

The market share of firm i, s_1, is a function of its *effective* effort share relative to firm 2 and its price relative to firm 2. If prices are equal, the price term drops out. (We have been assuming this.) If firm 1's price is lower than firm 2's price, then firm 1's market share is higher by k percent of the difference $(P_2 - P_1)$.

If we assume equal prices, the hypothesis about qualitative differences in Equation 4-23 suggests the following interpretation of the data in Table 4-2:

---

[5]K. S. Krishnan and Shiv K. Gupta, "Mathematical Model for a Duopolistic Market," *Management Science* (Mar. 1967) 568–583. The symbols in their article were altered to match the notation in this book.

Table 4-3

Company	M_i	α_i	$\alpha_i M_i$	s_i
1	$30	1.67	$50	.50
2	$50	.60	$30	.30
3	$20	1.00	$20	.20

According to Table 4-3, company 1 is more than two times as efficient as company 2 in spending marketing dollars; this accounts for its disproportionately high market share. This explanation is particularly plausible when these differences persist for a long time. This formulation also permits us to work backward from effort shares and market shares to derive the relative indices of marketing effectiveness.

The existence of qualitative differences in marketing effort also helps to explain why market shares may suddenly rise for particular companies when no changes have occurred in their relative marketing expenditures. This can happen when a firm develops a better advertising platform or finds more effective advertising media, for example. Usually, the same firm will raise its advertising expenditures as well. This confounds the qualitative and quantitative effects of marketing effort; the matter is further complicated by the probable increase in advertising by competitors. Nevertheless, when market shares finally stabilize, it will be clear whether the firm performs at average or greater than average effectiveness in spending marketing funds.

Marketing effectiveness should be generalized to include qualitative advantages enjoyed by the firm that are not directly related to the quantity or quality of the firm's current marketing expenditures. For example, the firm may be located on a superior site, which can give it a long term advantage over competition. Or the firm may enjoy an unusual amount of goodwill stemming from the personality of the founder that causes better sales than could be expected simply on the basis of share of marketing expenditures. In general, where market shares and effort shares diverge for a substantial period of time, the analyst might search for the cause in qualitative advantages of the firm over competition.

Random Factors Hypothesis

If a discrepancy between current market shares and marketing shares is not explained by differences in marketing effectiveness, two other explanations may apply, both short run in nature. The *random factors hypothesis* holds that, in any particular period, the respective shares may diverge from the effort shares because of random factors. This model is a modification of Equation 4-23:

$$s_{i,t} = \bar{m}_i + u_t \tag{4-25}$$

where u_t is a random error term (expressed as a fraction) that is distributed according to a given density function, mean, and variance. Equation 4-25 says that the market share can fluctuate around its normal value for all kinds of random factors: weather, loss or gain of a few important customers, inventory stockouts, and so forth. Therefore management must be careful in interpreting and responding to current market share changes. A 2 percent decline in market share may reflect normal variation in brand loyalty or point to a real decline in the company's marketing effectiveness. If there is no evidence of the latter, management might wait to see what happens to the market share in the next period. The market share may rise again, indicating normal fluctuation, or it may fall again, indicating that some systematic factor may be at work. Any change in the market share should be judged against the known variance of market share changes; if the change appears to be a rare event in probability terms, immediate action may be necessary.[6]

Lagged Adjustment Hypothesis

A third interpretation of a discrepancy between current market shares and marketing shares is that the difference is temporary and will get smaller and disappear after a sufficient number of periods elapse. For example, a Nielsen study on new product marketing concludes that a company wishing to gain a 10 percent market share for a new product must initially spend approximately 20 percent of total industry marketing expenditures.[7] Obviously, this excessive level of marketing expenditure is only temporary in order to enable the firm to break into the market. After getting its 10 percent share of market, the firm can slowly bring down its percent of total marketing expenditures without losing its 10 percent market share. Or if it continues to spend 20 percent of total marketing expenditures, it should achieve 20 percent of the market or something is wrong with its product or marketing effectiveness.

The lagged adjustment hypothesis is described by the following equation:

$$s_{i,t} = s_{i,t-1} + k(\bar{m}_i - s_{i,t-1}) \tag{4-26}$$

where $0 < k \leqslant 1$. In words, firm i's market share at time t tends to be equal to its market share in the previous period adjusted by k times the difference between its effective effort share and last period's actual market share.

Returning to the example of divergent shares in Table 4-2, we assume under the hypothesis that for firm 2: $\bar{m}_2 = .50$ and $s_{2,t-1} = .30$. We assume a k of .4, that is, 40 percent of the discrepancy is reduced each period. This produces the following series:

$$s_{2,t} = .30 + .40(.50 - .30) = .38$$
$$s_{2,t+1} = .38 + .40(.50 - .38) = .428$$
$$s_{2,t+2} = .428 + .40(.50 - .428) = .4568$$
$$\vdots \qquad\qquad\qquad\qquad \vdots$$
$$s_{2,t+\infty} = \qquad\qquad\qquad .5000$$

[6]The theory of statistical quality control provides a useful model for the interpretation of market share change. See Edward H. Bowman and Robert B. Fetter, *Analysis for Production Management* (Homewood, Ill.: Richard D. Irwin, Inc., 1957), Chap. 6, 147–179.

[7]James O. Peckham, "Can We Relate Advertising Dollars to Market Share Objectives," in Malcolm M. McNiven, ed., *How Much to Spend for Advertising* (New York: Association of National Advertisers, Inc., 1969), pp. 23–30.

Under the lagged adjustment hypothesis, most of the discrepancy in the data of Table 4-2 will disappear in a few periods.

It is interesting to note that Equation 4-26 can be rewritten, with a little algebra, as:

$$s_{i,t} = (1-k)s_{i,t-1} + k\bar{m}_i \qquad (4\text{-}27)$$

In this formulation, company i's market share at time t is the fraction $(1-k)$ of its market share last period plus the fraction k of its equilibrium effective effort share. If k is high, say $k = 1$, then the market share will immediately adjust to effective effort share. On the other hand, if k is near 0, then the market share will adjust extremely slowly to the equilibrium effective effort share. Thus k acts as the speed of adjustment factor.

Nonlinear Market Share Hypothesis

The three preceding hypotheses all accept the fundamental theorem of market share determination in Equation 4-22 and provide reasons for observed divergences. It is conceivable that the theorem does not hold and that increased marketing effort first produces increasing, and then decreasing, returns in the way of market share. This was the conclusion drawn by a major oil company regarding the effect of its share of retail outlets on its market share.[8] Instead of finding that, as the company's share of outlets increased, its share of market increased proportionately, the company found the relationship shown in Figure 4-2. The curve was fitted through observations of the share of outlets and shares of market in different cities in its system. The practical implication of the curve is: below a certain share of outlets, the company receives a disproportionately low market share; above a certain share of outlets, it is experiencing diminishing returns. The company should place its new outlets in those cities in which they would enjoy the greatest rate of increase in market share. Instead of a distribution strategy of locating a few outlets in each of many cities, the oil company should set up a greater number of outlets in a more limited number of cities.

There are a number of factors in this industry that make the S shaped curve plausible. If the oil company has too few stations, it will find promotion and advertising a somewhat wasteful medium and may use it proportionately less than competitors. Consumers will notice the stations only infrequently and will tend to forget them, so that the company's share of mind would tend to be less than even its share of market. Consumers will have little interest in the company's credit cards because of the limited number of stations. For these reasons, it appears there would be a threshold share of stations necessary for exploitation of marketing factors. At the other extreme, when a company has a large number of stations, additional stations would tend to be located near enough to other stations of the company, so that their growth would be partially at the expense of the company's other stations; this will pull down the average volume of sales

[8]The case is reported by John J. Cardwell, "Marketing and Management Science—A Marriage on the Rocks?" *California Management Review* (Summer 1968) 3–12. For a mathematical model that rationalizes this finding, see the discussion in Chap. 11, pp. 307–312.

per company station. Furthermore, each new station will have to attract the remaining hard core customers of competitors who patronize their present stations because of locational convenience, credit cards, and so forth. For all these reasons, then, the S curve relationship between the market share and company share of outlets is a highly plausible one.

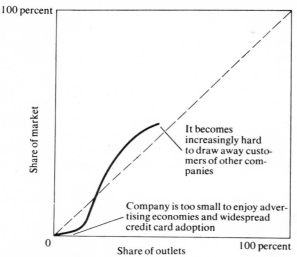

Figure 4-2   The Nonlinear Market Share Hypothesis

Source: Adopted from Cardwell, *op. cit.*, with modifications.

Market Share Determination—the Full Expression

With the exception of the expression in Equation 4-24, we have lumped all marketing effort by the company into the term M_i. If we wish to recognize the differences among marketing activities, then the fundamental theorem of market share determination in Equation 4-22 has to be amplified. If the marketing mix elements are thought to relate in a *linear* fashion, then Equation 4-22 becomes

$$s_i = m_i = \frac{k_i - pP_i + aA_i + dD_i + rR_i}{\sum_i (k_i - pP_i + aA_i + dD_i + rR_i)} \tag{4-28}$$

On the other hand, if the marketing mix elements are thought to interact in an exponential fashion, then Equation 4-22 becomes

$$s_i = m_i = \frac{k_i P_i^{-p} A_i^{a} D_i^{d} R_i^{r}}{\sum_i (k_i P_i^{-p} A_i^{a} D_i^{d} R_i^{r})} \tag{4-29}$$

Note that the denominator in both cases is a summation of the marketing effort levels of the various firms; thus Equations 4-28 and 4-29 show firm i's marketing effort as a share of the total. Although the effectiveness of the different company efforts is not shown, it can easily be included by modifying the variables in a manner similar to Equation 4-24.

As an empirical example of Equation 4-29, Glen Urban estimated the following market share function for a grocery product as a function of price and distribution (specifically the number of shelf facings):[9]

$$s_i = \frac{P_1^{-0.855} D_1^{1.13}}{P_1^{-0.855} D_1^{1.13} + P_2^{-1.245} D_2^{1.20}}$$

These elasticities, estimated by an on-line trial and error search routine, applied to a data base of 100 store audits, show the market as responding differently to each firm's price and shelf facings. These results accounted for 54 percent of the variance in the data.

Some analysts prefer to express competitive effects in a more direct fashion. Whereas Equations 4-28 and 4-29 represent the ratio of company i's whole marketing effort to the sum of competitors' efforts, it is possible to treat each decision variable separately. For example, Weiss examined market share, price, and advertising data for the brands of a low cost, frequently purchased grocery product and fitted the following four alternative formulations to the data:[10]

basic model,

$$s_i = k - pP_i + aA_i \tag{4-30}$$

differences from mean,

$$s_i = k - p(P_i - \bar{P}) + a(A_i - \bar{A}) \tag{4-31}$$

ratio to mean

$$s_i = k - p\left(\frac{P_i}{\bar{P}}\right) + a\left(\frac{A_i}{\bar{A}}\right) \tag{4-32}$$

and *log of ratio to mean,*

$$s_i = k - p \log (P_i/\bar{P}) + a \log (A_i/\bar{A}) \tag{4-33}$$

In Equations 4-30, 4-31, and 4-32, company i's market share is viewed as a linear function of the separate company decision variables. Equations 4-31, 4-32, and 4-33 express the company's settings in relation to the average of the competitors' settings of price $\bar{P}$ and advertising $\bar{A}$, each average being weighted by the relative sales volume of the companies. Equation 4-33 is as easy to work with as the other expressions because it is linear in the logs. Weiss found that Equations 4-31, 4-32, and 4-33 all improved the R^2 relative to Equation 4-30 in roughly the same amount, from approximately $R^2 = .66$ to $R^2 = .74$. There was no statistical basis to prefer any one of Equations 4-31, 4-32, and 4-33. He found that further improvement in the R^2 required introducing additional

[9]Glen L. Urban, "An On-line Technique for Estimating and Analyzing Complex Models," in Reed Moyer, ed., *Changing Marketing Systems* (Chicago, Ill.: American Marketing Association, 1967), pp. 322–327.

[10]Doyle L. Weiss, "The Determinants of Market Share," *Journal of Marketing Research* (Aug. 1968) 290–295.

variables, such as product quality, for which he employed a dummy variable proxy.

In another study, Lambin fitted a market share function similar to Equation 4-33 to the sales of a mature consumer durable good sold in three geographical markets dominated by three brands.[11] His fitted equation for market area 3 is

$$S_i = 0 \cdot 886 \tilde{P}_i^{-.255} \tilde{A}_i^{.371} \tilde{D}_i^{.322} \tilde{R}_i^{.661}$$

where each of the "tilde" variables refers to the relative ratio of firm i's marketing decision variable to the average value of its competitors' corresponding marketing decision variable. Price elasticity turns out to be low and product quality shows a higher elasticity than either advertising or distribution. The fitted values had a high $R^2 = .93$.

PROFIT MAXIMIZATION UNDER COMPETITIVE CONDITIONS

Given the functional expressions for industry demand and the company's share of total demand, the company's task is to find the marketing program that promises to maximize its profits. In order to formulate a program, the company must estimate its competitors' plans and possible reactions to the company's plan. At one extreme we can assume that the competitors prepare their plans independent of the company's plans and do not react to the company's plans. This means that there is no competitive interdependence and the company has to discover the independent criteria used by the competitors to set their marketing plans. At the other extreme the competitors can be assumed to be very sensitive to the company's marketing plan, particularly its price and somewhat less its advertising expenditures.[12] In this case the company must consider for any contemplated plan i, the competitors' most probable response, the company's reaction, the competitors' next move, the company's move, ad infinitum. The situation resembles that of a chess game and each player at some point must stop the estimation of the likely sequence of moves and countermoves. Short of using the power of a computer to enumerate and evaluate the many possible maneuvers, there is no satisfactory analytical method unless we make some specific simplifying assumptions about competitive behavior. One simplifying assumption is that the competitors are rational and also seek profit maximization. This leads to an analytical solution based on the concept of *competitive equilibrium*. An alternative simplifying assumption is that the competitors use

[11]Jean-Jacques Lambin, *Optimal Allocation of Competitive Marketing Efforts: An Empirical Study*, private draft, 1968. An abbreviated version of the paper is reported in J. J. Lambin and K. S. Palda, "Parameter Estimates for Optimal Marketing Decisions," in Robert L. King, ed., *Marketing and New Science of Planning* (Chicago, Ill.: American Marketing Association, 1969), pp. 69–74.

[12]Whereas company prices are very visible, company advertising expenditures are more difficult to estimate. Furthermore, many companies maintain their advertising expenditures at a certain percentage of sales, regardless of competitors' expenditures, and may prefer to meet high competitors' advertising expenditures with other types of marketing effort. In general, advertising interdependency is probably less pronounced than price interdependency.

explicit decision rules to set their marketing plans that are known to the company. This leads to a solution through the medium of simulation. Both approaches are described and illustrated in the following sections. For simplicity the other firms are treated as one competitor and the analysis is carried out in terms of competition between duopolists.

The Competitive Equilibrium Approach

Assume a situation consisting of two competitors who independently set three policy instruments, P, A, D, in such a way as to maximize their own profits. Each competitor is aware of the other firm's profit function at any time and hopes to use this knowledge to improve its profits. Assume that, after a series of moves and countermoves, neither duopolist makes any further adjustment in its marketing mix. This means that neither duopolist sees a gain coming from a further adjustment of its own marketing mix, that is,

$$\frac{\partial Z_i}{\partial X_{ik}} = 0 \qquad \text{for all } i \text{ and } k \tag{4-34}$$

where Z_i is the profits of the ith firm ($i = 1, 2$) and X_{ik} is the kth instrument used by the ith firm ($k = 1, 2, 3$). When Equation 4-34 is satisfied, a competitive equilibrium is said to exist.

The competitive equilibrium solution can be found in principle through calculus.[13] The steps are as follows:

1. Formulate the profit function faced by each firm.
2. Differentiate the profit function for each firm with respect to each marketing instrument. Given two firms and three instruments each, we find that this leads to six first derivatives.
3. Set the six first derivatives equal to 0 and solve the resulting six equations for the optimal marketing values for each firm.
4. Check the second derivative conditions to make sure that profits are at a maximum.

Once these marketing mix values are found, neither firm could improve its profits by departing from these values. Hence these values define a competitive equilibrium.

Illustration of competitive equilibrium. As an example of competitive equilibrium reasoning, assume two firms facing somewhat different demand situations and each influenced by the other's marketing mix settings. Assume that the first firm's sales show decreasing returns to scale with respect to advertising, negative returns with respect to its own price, and constant returns with respect to its competitor's price; that is:

$$Q_1 = 3A_1 - A_1{}^2 - 2P_1 + 3P_2 \tag{4-35}$$

[13]For complicated profit functions, the solution may be difficult to find in practice. Optimal search techniques may have to be used.

The second firm estimates that it gets constant returns to scale with respect to its own advertising, negative returns with respect to its competitor's advertising, negative returns with respect to its own price, and constant returns with respect to its competitor's price; that is:

$$Q_2 = 3A_2 - 3A_1 - 3P_2 + P_1 \tag{4-36}$$

Each firm will set its own marketing mix variables to maximize its profit function. Assume that each firm has a unit variable cost of \$1 and that fixed cost can be ignored. The profit functions of the two firms are, respectively:

$$Z_1 = (P_1 - c_1)Q_1 - A_1 = (P_1 - 1)(3A_1 - A_1{}^2 - 2P_1 + 3P_2) - A_1 \tag{4-37}$$

$$Z_2 = (P_2 - c_2)Q_2 - A_2 = (P_2 - 1)(3A_2 - 3A_1 - 3P_2 + P_1) - A_2 \tag{4-38}$$

Thus each firm's profits will depend upon its own marketing decisions and those of its competitor. Each firm will attempt to maximize its own profit function by taking the first derivatives of its own profit function with respect to each of its controllable marketing decisions variables and setting these first derivatives equal to zero. This results in four equations:

$$\frac{\partial Z_1}{\partial P_1} = 3A_1 - A_1{}^2 - 4P_1 + 3P_2 + 2 = 0 \tag{4-39}$$

$$\frac{\partial Z_1}{\partial A_1} = 2A_1 - 2P_1 A_1 + 3P_1 - 4 = 0 \tag{4-40}$$

$$\frac{\partial Z_2}{\partial P_2} = 3A_2 - 3A_1 + P_1 - 6P_2 + 3 = 0 \tag{4-41}$$

$$\frac{\partial Z_2}{\partial A_2} = 3P_2 - 4 = 0 \tag{4-42}$$

By solving Equations 4-39 to 4-42 simultaneously, the following competitive equilibrium marketing decisions and profits emerge:[14]

	Firm 1	Firm 2
	$A_1 = \$1$	$A_2 = \$2$
	$P_1 = \$2$	$P_2 = \$1.33$
	$Z_1 = \$2$	$Z_2 = -\$1.67$

Thus at competitive equilibrium, firm 1 spends less on advertising than firm 2 and charges a higher price. It ends up with positive profits while firm 2 ends up with a loss. Nevertheless neither firm 1 or 2 can improve its situation by unilaterally changing to another marketing mix. As long as either competitor sets his marketing variables at the indicated solution, the other competitor would be best off by setting his variables at the indicated solution for him.

[14]See Appendix Mathematical Note 4-1.

The Competitive Simulation Approach

The preceding analytical solution to the competitive marketing strategy problem works well as long as the relevant demand and cost functions of the competitors can be stated simply. Very often however, competitive response patterns are quite complex and require complex modeling that is not amenable to an analytical solution technique. In these cases, the analyst seeks to understand the competitive relationships by running his complex model through time and noting the pattern of consequences resulting from different pairings of competitive marketing strategies. Although simulation represents a promising approach to understanding competitive marketing dynamics, only a few models have been reported in the literature. Three models will be described here which exhibit quite different approaches to modeling competitive marketing strategies. These models have been developed by the author, Roman Tuason, and Cyert, Feigenbaum, and March, respectively.

Kotler simulation.[15] Not all firms seek short run profit maximization or are able to obtain all the information they need for finding the profit maximizing mix. Instead they may follow specific rules for setting marketing mix levels that lead on the average to satisfactory results. A *competitive marketing strategy* will be defined as *a set of decision rules* or program that adjusts $(P, A, D)_t$ from period t to period $t+1$, for all t.

Competitive marketing strategies differ according to which elements of the environment they emphasize, the nature and complexity of the response, and the objectives they embody. At least nine classes of marketing strategy can be distinguished.

Nonadaptive strategy. This defines a strategy in which the initial marketing mix is held constant throughout the product's life cycle. The completely non-adaptive strategy has the form:

$$P_{i,t} = P_{i,t-1}$$
$$A_{i,t} = A_{i,t-1} \tag{4-43}$$
$$D_{i,t} = D_{i,t-1}$$

The three following nonadaptive equations are examples:

$$P_{i,t} = \$20$$
$$A_{i,t} = \$2500 \tag{4-43a}$$
$$D_{i,t} = \$2500$$

$$P_{i,t} = \$25$$
$$A_{i,t} = \$3500 \tag{4-43b}$$
$$D_{i,t} = \$3500$$

$$P_{i,t} = \$15$$
$$A_{i,t} = \$3500 \tag{4-43c}$$
$$D_{i,t} = \$3500$$

[15]This section is adapted with modifications from Philip Kotler, "Competitive Strategies for New Product Marketing over the Life Cycle," *Management Science* (Dec. 1965) 104–119.

Strategy 4-43a represents a perpetuation of an introductory marketing mix used by both firms at $t = 0$. Strategy 4-43b represents a "market skimming" strategy, in relation to Strategy 4-43a, whereby the firm hopes to capture the quality-conscious segment of the market by a high price and high promotion. Strategy 4-43c represents a "market penetration" strategy, in relation to Strategy 4-43a, whereby the firm hopes to gain a large market share through a low price backed by high promotion.

Time-dependent strategy.   This defines any strategy that provides for automatic marketing mix adjustments to take place through time. Its general form is

$$P_{i,t} = f(t)$$
$$A_{i,t} = f(t) \qquad\qquad (4\text{-}44)$$
$$D_{i,t} = f(t)$$

The basic condition for using this type of strategy is that management has some prior knowledge of the likely course of market growth and of the pattern of seasonal variation. Decision rules are provided that change the elements in the marketing mix from month to month to meet anticipated time-dependent changes in total sales.

The first example of a time-dependent strategy is

$$P_{i,t} = 5(.95)^t + 15$$
$$A_{i,t} = 1.01 A_{i,t-1} \qquad\qquad (4\text{-}44a)$$
$$D_{i,t} = 1.01 D_{i,t-1}$$

The first equation causes price, which initially stands at $20, to fall exponentially and asymptotically to $15 as $t \to \infty$. By $t = 60$, P_i will be quite close to $15. The objective of this pricing decision rule is to earn a premium initially by selling the product to the less price-conscious, more affluent consumers. Further sales gains are made by gradually reducing the price to stimulate sales among more price-conscious segments of the market. The price is never permitted to be reduced below some lower limit (here $15), which represents unit variable production costs (here $10) plus some margin (here $5) which, at planned sales levels, would cover overhead and yield some profit. Strategy 4-44a also provides that advertising and distribution expenditures be increased by 1 percent each month to take advantage of the expected growth in the market.

A second example of a time-dependent strategy is

$$P_{i,t} = 5(.95)^t + 15$$
$$A_{i,t} = 12,500(.2)^{.9^t}\{1 + .1[\sin 30(t + 180)]\} \qquad\qquad (4\text{-}44b)$$
$$D_{i,t} = 12,500(.2)^{.9^t}\{1 + .1[\sin 30(t + 180)]\}$$

Equation 4-44b differs from Equation 4-44a in providing for marketing expenditures to match the expected movements in industry sales due to growth (G) *and* seasonal (V) variation. This strategy is based on two assumptions: (1) that the company's marketing research department is able to estimate accurately the course of industry sales and the likely pattern of seasonal variation; and (2) management believes that marketing expenditure changes should *coincide* with, rather than lead or lag, changes on account of G and V.

The last assumption is modified in still a third time-dependent strategy:

$$P_{i,t} = 5(.95)^t + 15$$
$$A_{i,t} = 12{,}500(.2)^{.9t}\{1 + .1[\sin 30(t + 270)]\}$$
$$D_{i,t} = 12{,}500(.2)^{.9t}\{1 + .1[\sin 30(t + 270)]\}$$

(4-44c)

The only change from Equation 4-44b is that marketing expenditures are phased to reach their peak and trough before sales reaches its peak and trough, respectively.

Competitive adaptive strategy.   This defines any strategy in which firm i adjusts its marketing mix *because* of marketing mix changes made by firm j in previous periods. It has the general form:

$$P_{i,t} = f(P_{j,t-1}, P_{j,t-2}, \ldots, P_{j,t-k})$$
$$A_{i,t} = f(A_{j,t-1}, A_{j,t-2}, \ldots, A_{j,t-k})$$
$$D_{i,t} = f(D_{j,t-1}, D_{j,t-2}, \ldots, D_{j,t-k})$$

(4-45)

The first example of this strategy is

$$P_{i,t} = P_{j,t-1}$$
$$A_{i,t} = A_{j,t-1}$$
$$D_{i,t} = D_{j,t-1}$$

(4-45a)

Equation 4-45a provides for a *one-period lagged imitation* of a competitor's strategy. The firm using it wishes to maintain a competitive parity with the other firm, so that prospective customers can hardly distinguish between the two product offerings. This is a "safe" strategy, in that if it is successful, it should lead to almost equal division of the market.

Another example of a competitively adaptive strategy is

$$P_{i,t} = .6P_{j,t-1} + .3P_{j,t-2} + .1P_{j,t-3}$$
$$A_{i,t} = .6A_{j,t-1} + .3A_{j,t-2} + .1A_{j,t-3}$$
$$D_{i,t} = .6D_{j,t-1} + .3D_{j,t-2} + .1D_{j,t-3}$$

(4-45b)

In this case the firm sets its marketing mix variables for the current period as a weighted average of its rival's last three period marketing mix levels, with greater weight being given to the rival's more current levels.

Still a third example of a competitively adaptive strategy is given below:

$$P_{i,t} = .95P_{j,t-1}$$
$$A_{i,t} = 1.02A_{j,t-1}$$
$$D_{i,t} = 1.02D_{j,t-1}$$

(4-45c)

Here the firm seeks to "out-appeal" its rival in every possible way, in the interest of achieving the larger market share. It sets its price 5 percent below its rival's price, and sets its advertising and distribution expenditures 2 percent above those of its rival. Because of the one period lag, however, the firm's price and expenditures may not actually bear the intended relationships to the rival's current price and promotion.

Sales-responsive strategy. This defines any strategy that leads a company to adjust its marketing mix on the basis of its past sales results. Its general form is

$$P_{i,t} = f(Q_{i,t-1}, Q_{i,t-2}, ..., Q_{i,t-k})$$
$$A_{i,t} = f(Q_{i,t-1}, Q_{i,t-2}, ..., Q_{i,t-k}) \qquad (4\text{-}46)$$
$$D_{i,t} = f(Q_{i,t-1}, Q_{i,t-2}, ..., Q_{i,t-k})$$

Although this shows the marketing mix being adjusted as a function of the last k periods of unit sales, a past series of company dollar sales or market shares may be substituted for unit sales.

The first example of a sales-responsive strategy is

$$P_{i,t} = P_{i,t-1} \frac{Q_{i,t-1}}{Q_{i,t-2}}$$

$$A_{i,t} = A_{i,t-1} \frac{Q_{i,t-2}}{Q_{i,t-1}} \qquad (4\text{-}46a)$$

$$D_{i,t} = D_{i,t-1} \frac{Q_{i,t-2}}{Q_{i,t-1}}$$

This strategy calls for adjusting marketing mix variables according to whether sales rose or fell in the latest period. If sales rose by X percent, then the last price is raised by the same percent to take profit advantage of the favorable shift in sales, while advertising and distribution costs are reduced. These decision rules tend to stabilize a company's market share in the interest of enlarging current profits.

A second sales-responsive strategy is given by the following decision rules:

$$P_{i,t} = 20$$
$$A_{i,t} = .0625 P_{i,t-1} Q_{i,t-1} + .25(.95)^t P_{i,t-1} Q_{i,t-1} \qquad (4\text{-}46b)$$
$$D_{i,t} = .0625 P_{i,t-1} Q_{i,t-1} + .25(.95)^t P_{i,t-1} Q_{i,t-1}$$

In this case, the firm refuses to compete along price lines and relies completely on adjustments in marketing expenditures to achieve its objectives. Marketing expenditures are adjusted in each period so as to maintain some desired ratio to current sales revenue. The practice of setting marketing expenditures as some percentage of sales (either past, current, or expected) is quite common in business, although the rule has little logical defense. As in Strategy 4-46b, *the desired ratio* between total marketing expenditures and sales revenue is programmed to decline asymptotically over time from an initial value of .6250 to .1250. The initial value seems inordinately high unless one realizes that new product marketing costs necessarily loom large in the total cost picture until sales can be stimulated to greatly increased levels, at which point marketing costs bear a more normal ratio to total costs.

A final sales-responsive strategy, this time geared to market share changes, is shown in the following logical flow diagram form:

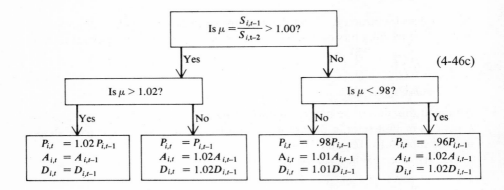

(4-46c)

This strategy calls for marketing mix adjustments to current market share changes that attempt to stabilize or expand the company's market share, s_i. Sales management often plays the "market share" game. Strategy 4-46c calls for examining whether the company's share of the market rose or fell in the latest period. For example, if its market share increased by more than 2 percent, then price is raised by 2 percent to take profit advantage of this development, while marketing expenditures are maintained at their previous levels. The other boxes are similarly interpreted.

Profit-responsive strategy. This defines a strategy in which the marketing mix is adjusted in response to "significant" interperiod changes in company profits, Z. The adjustments are made without distinguishing the causes of any recent changes in profits. An example of a profit-responsive strategy is shown below:

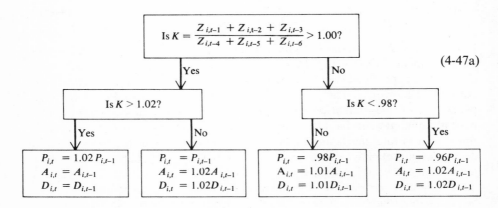

(4-47a)

This strategy is very similar to Strategy 4-46c, except that (1) it is responsive to profit changes rather than market changes, and (2) it responds to quarterly profit changes rather than monthly profit changes.

Completely adaptive strategy. A completely adaptive strategy is one that produces monthly changes in the marketing mix by responding to all current developments, including the passage of time, changes in one's own and one's competitor's sales and profits, and changes in the competitor's marketing mix. The completely adaptive strategy would amount to a complicated information processing and decision-making system.

Diagnostic strategy. A diagnostic strategy is one that produces changes in the marketing mix only after distinguishing among possible causes of current developments. All the previous strategies were nondiagnostic. Strategy 4-46c, for example, did not distinguish between a decline in market share due to a normal seasonal contraction and a decline due to a competitor's price cut. Strategy 4-46c could be made diagnostic by introducing diagnostic questions and branching operations into the flow diagramming.

Adaptive profit maximizing strategy. An adaptive profit maximizing strategy is one that would lead to optimal marketing mix responses to the marketing mix moves of the competitor. If the rival's next P, A, D were known each time, there is a setting for the adapting firm's P, A, D that would maximize its profits. The profit maximizing strategy for the adapting firm can be found by taking its profit function, finding the first partial derivatives with respect to its own P, A, D, setting these derivatives equal to 0, and solving the three equations simultaneously. By inserting the rival's expected P, A, D into the solution, the firm can determine its best P, A, D each time.

If the rival's next move is not known with certainty, there are two alternatives. One is to assume that the rival's mix adjustments from one period to the next tend to be small. On this assumption, his last mix, rather than his next (but unknown) mix, would be used to formulate the adapting firm's optimal response. The other alternative is to guess what the rival will do next. This expectation would be used to compute the optimizing P, A, D.

Joint profit maximizing strategy. Although an adaptive profit maximizing strategy is the best offensive against a rival's moves, it will not necessarily lead to maximum profits. Ethical questions aside, unfortunately the firm may do better by convincing its rival to collude. Then both duopolists could choose in each period the *pair of mixes* that maximized the *sum* of their profits over the next sixty months. This may involve dissimilar mixes each period, in which case the two firms would have to agree in advance on how they would divide the total profits.

Illustration. The first five classes of competitive strategy and their thirteen variants (Strategies 4-43a, b, c; 4-44a, b, c; 4-45a, b, c; 4-46a, b, c; and 4-47a) were simulated in pairs for a hypothetical market over a sixty-month period for the purpose of exploring their properties. Sixty months represented the investment horizon—when the plant and equipment would be fully depreciated—and also a point in time when the product was expected to be well into the maturity stage of its life cycle. Since there were thirteen specific strategies, seventy-eight unique pairs could be tested in all, according to the combinatorial formula $_{13}C_2 = 13!/(2! \ 11!)$. The printout for each of the seventy-eight pairs provided a month by month description of the marketing mix of each duopolist, the level of total industry sales, each firm's sales and market share, and each firm's profits. In addition, the monthly profits of each duopolist were cumulated with compound interest (at 6 percent) and the total was posted at the end of the play. Thus the cumulative, compounded net profits of firm i using strategy m for sixty months was given by:[16]

$$Z_{i,m} = \sum_{t=1}^{60} Z_{i,t}(1.06)^{60-t}$$

$Z_{i,m}$ served as the index of the strategy's success. Since earlier profits weighed more heavily in this index—the result of interest compounding—this index favored those strategies that led to the realization of earlier profits. This is realistic, since two streams of money are not equally desirable simply because they might sum to the same total at the end of the game.

The results of the seventy-eight strategy confrontations are summarized in Table 4-4. Each cell represents a unique strategy pair and gives total net profits and terminal market shares for the two duopolists at $t = 60$. For example, when duopolist X used the nonadaptive strategy 4-43a and duopolist Y used the time-dependent strategy 4-44a, duopolist X accumulated compounded net profits of $331,000 and duopolist Y accumulated compounded net profits of $269,000. Thus strategy 4-43a is superior in a confrontation with strategy 4-44a if *profits* serve as the criterion. On the other hand, it should be noted that duopolist Y held 68 percent of the market at $t = 60$. This is not surprising, because while duopolist X held his price and promotion expenditures constant, duopolist Y kept reducing his price and increasing his promotional expenditures. Thus strategy 4-44a makes good sense for the firm seeking the larger market share, but this same firm must be prepared to accept a lower percent of total profits if its competitor uses the nonadaptive strategy 4-43a.

Other generalizations can be drawn from Table 4-4 about the consequences of different strategies. A few points, however, should be kept in mind. Each inference is conditional upon the particular parameters employed in the strategy descriptions, as well as the operational characteristics and parameters of the market and cost models.[17] No sensitivity testing of the same strategies with

[16]Inadvertently, the writer used a 6 percent rate per month instead of per annum as intended. The rate should have read (1.005). This exaggerated the levels of the final compounded profits but not their relative ranks. Therefore all the conclusions drawn in the text hold.

[17]For market and cost models, see Kotler, "Competitive Strategies for New Product Marketing over the Life Cycle," 104–119.

Table 4-44. Cumulative, Compounded Net Profits (in Thousands) and Terminal Market Shares at $t = 60$. From Kotler, "Competitive Strategies for New Product Marketing over the Life Cycle," *Management Science* (Dec. 1965) 115.

Duopolist X	Duopolist Y												
	4-43a	4-43b	4-43c	4-44a	4-44b	4-44c	4-45a	4-45b	4-45c	4-46a	4-46b	4-46c	4-47a
4-43a→	505(.50) 505(.50)	559(.42) 583(.58)	219(.67) 332(.33)	269(.68) 331(.32)	−286(.76) 224(.24)	−282(.75) 225(.25)	503(.50) 505(.50)	505(.50) 505(.50)	476(.53) 478(.47)	* *	425(.53) 459(.47)	505(.50) 505(.50)	530(.55) 552(.45)
4-43b→		673(.50) 673(.50)	254(.74) 323(.26)	309(.75) 323(.25)	−251(.81) 189(.19)	−248(.81) 190(.19)	645(.50) 673(.50)	676(.50) 674(.50)	657(.53) 635(.47)	* *	493(.62) 477(.38)	491(.68) 445(.32)	632(.63) 624(.37)
4-43c→			128(.50) 128(.50)	168(.52) 124(.48)	−382(.61) 56(.39)	−378(.60) 57(.40)	128(.50) 127(.50)	129(.50) 125(.50)	68(.53) 111(.47)	* *	261(.32) 217(.68)	151(.52) 117(.48)	14(.82) 88(.18)
4-44a→				164(.50) 164(.50)	−387(.50) 88(.41)	−381(.58) 89(.42)	167(.50) 165(.50)	169(.50) 165(.50)	121(.53) 147(.47)	* *	270(.30) 262(.70)	−12(.62) 99(.38)	229(.64) 223(.36)
4-44b					−467(.50) −467(.50)	−464(.49) −466(.51)	−455(.50) −468(.50)	−448(.50) −468(.50)	−524(.53) −487(.47)	* *	173(.20) −277(.80)	−86(.55) −469(.45)	−109(.78) −455(.22)
4-44c→						−463(.50) −463(.50)	−452(.50) −464(.50)	−446(.50) −464(.50)	−521(.53) −484(.47)	* *	174(.21) −274(.79)	−89(.56) −468(.44)	−75(.77) −437(.23)
4-45a→							505(.50) 505(.50)	505(.50) 505(.50)	−774(.50) −719(.50)	* *	391(.50) 389(.50)	505(.50) 505(.50)	835(.51) 833(.49)
4-45b→								505(.50) 505(.50)	−504(.52) −452(.48)	* *	389(.49) 392(.51)	505(.50) 505(.50)	917(.51) 916(.49)
4-45c→									−2551(.50) −2550(.50)	* *	368(.47) 364(.53)	−59(.49) −95(.51)	628(.49) 647(.51)
4-46a→										* *	* *	* *	* *
4-46b→											391(.50) 391(.50)	249(.72) 269(.28)	373(.80) 373(.20)
4-46c→												505(.50) 505(.50)	318(.46) 324(.51)
4-47a→													724(.50) 724(.50)

* Equation 4-46a produced such wild fluctuations in P, A, D that the results were not included.

alternative parameters has been conducted. Secondly, *only two characteristics* are being analyzed for each strategy playoff: cumulative profits and terminal market shares. Some other characteristics of a playoff that may be of interest, but which are not analyzed here, are (1) cumulative industry sales for the sixty months, (2) the mean level and variance of each firm's market share for the sixty months (in some cases, the terminal market share represents a late reversal of the duopolist average share during most of the game), and (3) the variance of each firm's sales and profits for the sixty months (high variance may be regarded as an undesirable characteristic of an otherwise good strategy).

The implications of Table 4-4 will be presented in the form of answers to a series of questions.

1. *Which long run strategy is the best to adopt if the firm wanted to guarantee a minimum return regardless of what its competitor did?* On the assumption that duopolist X has no knowledge of duopolist Y's strategy, it may choose a strategy that guarantees some profit even under the worst eventuality (maximum criterion). According to Table 4-4, strategy 4-43a fulfills this criterion best. The least duopolist X might make is $224,000, and this would happen only if duopolist Y were to adopt strategy 4-44b. It might be added that duopolist Y would not knowingly adopt strategy 4-44b because it would then put itself in the red to the amount of $286,000. In fact, if duopolist Y knew that duopolist X planned to adopt strategy 4-43a, it would be in Y's interest to adopt strategy 4-43b, thus making cumulative profits of $559,000. This would be fine for X, too, who would make $583,000.

Inspection of the three nonadaptive strategies 4-43a, 4-43b, and 4-43c shows them all to be relatively safe courses of action. This seems to contradict the idea that the initial marketing mix will require dynamic adjustment over the life cycle of the new product. It shows that if a nonadaptive mix with good parameters is chosen at $t = 0$, it may constitute a safe and fairly profitable strategy for several years.

2. *Which long run strategy subjects the firm to the greatest amount of risk?* The worst recorded losses occurred when both firms independently chose to use strategy 4-45c, that is, to always charge less and spend more than its competitor. The result is endless price cutting and endless expansion of promotion. The strategy of outdoing the rival (strategy 4-45c) is also ruinous if the competitor chooses strategies 4-44b, 4-44c, 4-45a, 4-45b, or 4-46c. Even where it functions well, strategy 4-45c is almost always dominated by strategy 4-43a or strategy 4-47a and therefore should not be considered further.

Strategies 4-44b and 4-44c should also be avoided because they almost guarantee ruin. They both require the firm to budget too much for promotion in relation to sales for too long a time. The firm's sales in month 1 were $9717; it spent $5579, or 57 percent, for advertising and distribution. This high promotion/sales budget is understandable at the launching of the new product, but it should be brought down to a more reasonable percentage over time. Strategies 4-44b and 4-44c prolong the exaggerated percentage through time by providing that the starting budget must grow at the same rate as the industry growth rate. In addition, the firm using strategy 4-44b or strategy 4-44c brings down its price too quickly and thus does not capitalize enough on the rapidly growing sales. True, it managed to end at month 60 with 76 percent of the market, but this was no compensation for the $286,000 in cumulative losses.

3. *Which strategy offers the chance of greatest profit?* Under the right circumstances, the profit-responsive strategy 4-47a would produce more cumulative profits than any other strategy. Cumulative profits would be as high as $917,000, $835,000, or $628,000 if the rival used the imitative strategies 4-45a, 4-45b, or 4-45c, respectively. Or if the rival used the same profit-responsive strategy, each firm would enjoy profits of $724,000. Thus there are four chances out of thirteen (if the rival chose his strategies with equal probabilities) that strategy 4-47a would lead to an exceptionally high return.

The strategy would be used, however, at the risk that a loss as high as $109,000 might be incurred if the rival used strategy 4-44b. But as we saw earlier, strategies 4-44b and 4-44c are likely to be removed from the strategy set because both are inferior strategies. Practically speaking, the least profitable consequence of using strategy 4-47a might be $14,000, which would result if the rival used the nonadaptive strategy 4-43c.

Since the large potential gains from this strategy seem to be more than worth the small risks, both duopolists may be tempted into choosing it, at a handsome profit of $724,000 to each. Yet even more would be gained ($917,000) through collusion if one of the duopolists used strategy 4-47a and the other used the weighted lagged imitative strategy 4-45b.

How does the profit-responsive strategy 4-47a compare to the similar market-share-responsive strategy 4-46c? *It seems better to let the specified adjustments be made in response to profit changes rather than in response to market share changes.* This has to be qualified, however, because strategy 4-47a involved a response to six past profit levels, while strategy 4-46c involved only two past market share levels. Thus strategy 4-47a led to slower and smaller adjustments than strategy 4-46c, and this may be a factor in the superior results using strategy 4-47a.

4. *If the rival's strategy is known in advance with certainty, what is the best adaptive strategy?* The best adaptive strategy will not only vary with the rival's strategy, but also with the *objectives* of the adapting firm. Suppose it is known that the rival will adopt strategy 4-44a. If the objective is to *maximize profits*, then strategy 4-43a should be adopted; this will yield $331,000 (and yield the rival $269,000). No other strategy could produce more profits. If the objective is to adopt the *course of action that would minimize the rival's profits*, strategy 4-44b would keep down the rival's cumulative profits to $88,000; unfortunately this would be accomplished at the price of a loss to one's own firm of $387,000. If the objective is to *maximize market share*, the terminal market share could be maximized by adopting strategy 4-47a. Profits would be $229,000 (in contrast to $331,000 if the objective had been profit maximization). If the objective is to maximize *the ratio of the firm's profits to the rival's profits*, strategy 4-43a satisfies this and yields 1.24 times the cumulative profits ($331,000/$269,000) of the

rival. The motive for this decision rule is to maximize the difference between the terminal positions. A variant would be to *choose the strategy that maximizes the dollar difference between cumulative profits*, which also happens to be satisfied by strategy 4-43a in this case. The converse strategy would be to *minimize the difference between the outcomes*, and here an imitative strategy would be effective.

This illustration shows how simulation can be used to evaluate competitive strategies. Further modifications can be introduced to add realism:

1.   The model can be revised to include carryover effects of promotion.
2.   Instead of a homogeneous market, the model can be refined to exhibit distinct market segments, thus posing an additional challenge to strategy.
3.   Instead of two equally endowed firms, both entering the market at $t = 0$, an examination can be made of what a late comer can do to secure a reasonable share of market and what the earlier firm can do to maintain its own profits.
4.   Instead of using the same elasticities for the two firms, one firm can be assigned higher promotional elasticities to represent greater product appeal.
5.   Instead of constant costs throughout the sixty months, a declining cost function can be introduced to explore the implications for marketing strategy.
6.   Instead of using the same decision rule for advertising and distribution expenditures, they will be treated differently.
7.   Instead of only two firms, the same model will be used to explore oligopoly behavior.

Tuason simulation.[18]   Tuason carried out a simulation of the household coffee market in which he tested the competitive efficacy of a particular adaptive, diagnostic strategy. His model described a large coffee company which made decisions on price, deals, and product blend each week. The decisions are made according to the strategy shown in Figure 4-3. Essentially the coffee company considers whether the last period results satisfy its market share and profit goals. If not, the firm considers appropriate changes in its marketing program or product. These changes are guided by a diagnosis of any changes in the marketing program of competitors. The company evaluates the expected costs, sales, and profits from the contemplated marketing plan, and, if these meet its goals, the plan is adopted.

Other programs (not shown) generate the actions of competitors, retailers, and customers. For example, competitors are combined and represented as a single competitor whose marketing program is generated stochastically each period. Retailers react to the marketing programs of the company and its competition by making adjustments in retail price and shelf space. Finally, different segments of the market respond differently to the competitive and

[18]Roman V. Tuason, *Experimental Simulation on a Pre-determined Marketing Mix Strategy*, Ph.D. dissertation, Northwestern University (1965).

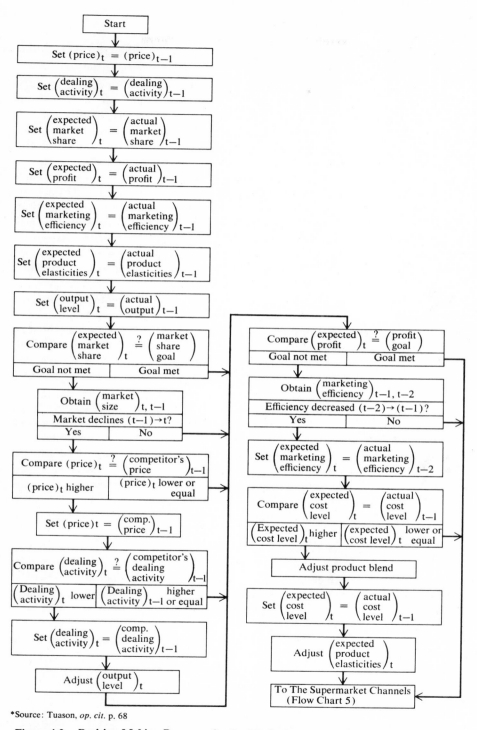

Start

Set $(\text{price})_t = (\text{price})_{t-1}$

Set $\left(\dfrac{\text{dealing}}{\text{activity}}\right)_t = \left(\dfrac{\text{dealing}}{\text{activity}}\right)_{t-1}$

Set $\left(\begin{array}{c}\text{expected}\\\text{market}\\\text{share}\end{array}\right)_t = \left(\begin{array}{c}\text{actual}\\\text{market}\\\text{share}\end{array}\right)_{t-1}$

Set $\left(\begin{array}{c}\text{expected}\\\text{profit}\end{array}\right)_t = \left(\begin{array}{c}\text{actual}\\\text{profit}\end{array}\right)_{t-1}$

Set $\left(\begin{array}{c}\text{expected}\\\text{marketing}\\\text{efficiency}\end{array}\right)_t = \left(\begin{array}{c}\text{actual}\\\text{marketing}\\\text{efficiency}\end{array}\right)_{t-1}$

Set $\left(\begin{array}{c}\text{expected}\\\text{product}\\\text{elasticities}\end{array}\right)_t = \left(\begin{array}{c}\text{actual}\\\text{product}\\\text{elasticities}\end{array}\right)_{t-1}$

Set $\left(\begin{array}{c}\text{output}\\\text{level}\end{array}\right)_t = \left(\begin{array}{c}\text{actual}\\\text{output}\end{array}\right)_{t-1}$

Compare $\left(\begin{array}{c}\text{expected}\\\text{market}\\\text{share}\end{array}\right)_t \overset{?}{=} \left(\begin{array}{c}\text{market}\\\text{share}\\\text{goal}\end{array}\right)$

Goal not met | Goal met

Obtain $\left(\dfrac{\text{market}}{\text{size}}\right)_{t,\,t-1}$

Market declines $(t-1) \rightarrow t$?

Yes | No

Compare $(\text{price})_t \overset{?}{=} \left(\begin{array}{c}\text{competitor's}\\\text{price}\end{array}\right)_{t-1}$

$(\text{price})_t$ higher | $(\text{price})_t$ lower or equal

Set $(\text{price})_t = \left(\begin{array}{c}\text{comp.}\\\text{price}\end{array}\right)_{t-1}$

Compare $\left(\dfrac{\text{dealing}}{\text{activity}}\right)_t \overset{?}{=} \left(\begin{array}{c}\text{competitor's}\\\text{dealing}\\\text{activity}\end{array}\right)_{t-1}$

$\left(\dfrac{\text{Dealing}}{\text{activity}}\right)_t$ lower | $\left(\dfrac{\text{Dealing}}{\text{activity}}\right)_{t-1}$ higher or equal

Set $\left(\dfrac{\text{dealing}}{\text{activity}}\right)_t = \left(\begin{array}{c}\text{comp.}\\\text{dealing}\\\text{activity}\end{array}\right)_{t-1}$

Adjust $\left(\begin{array}{c}\text{output}\\\text{level}\end{array}\right)_t$

Compare $\left(\begin{array}{c}\text{expected}\\\text{profit}\end{array}\right)_t \overset{?}{=} \left(\begin{array}{c}\text{profit}\\\text{goal}\end{array}\right)$

Goal not met | Goal met

Obtain $\left(\dfrac{\text{marketing}}{\text{efficiency}}\right)_{t-1,\,t-2}$

Efficiency decreased $(t-2) \rightarrow (t-1)$?

Yes | No

Set $\left(\begin{array}{c}\text{expected}\\\text{marketing}\\\text{efficiency}\end{array}\right)_t = \left(\begin{array}{c}\text{actual}\\\text{marketing}\\\text{efficiency}\end{array}\right)_{t-2}$

Compare $\left(\begin{array}{c}\text{expected}\\\text{cost}\\\text{level}\end{array}\right)_t = \left(\begin{array}{c}\text{actual}\\\text{cost}\\\text{level}\end{array}\right)_{t-1}$

$\left(\begin{array}{c}\text{Expected}\\\text{cost level}\end{array}\right)_t$ higher | $\left(\begin{array}{c}\text{expected}\\\text{cost level}\end{array}\right)_t$ lower or equal

Adjust product blend

Set $\left(\begin{array}{c}\text{expected}\\\text{cost}\\\text{level}\end{array}\right)_t = \left(\begin{array}{c}\text{actual}\\\text{cost}\\\text{level}\end{array}\right)_{t-1}$

Adjust $\left(\begin{array}{c}\text{expected}\\\text{product}\\\text{elasticities}\end{array}\right)_t$

To The Supermarket Channels
(Flow Chart 5)

*Source: Tuason, *op. cit.* p. 68

Figure 4-3. Decision Making Processes for the Marketing Firm of Brand M

retail developments in a manner specified by empirically derived equations from a study by Massy and Frank.[19]

Tuason's main purpose was to see how well the particular marketing strategy shown in Figure 4-3 would perform under different conditions, such as rapid versus slow market growth, high versus low market variability, high versus low marketing costs, high versus low weight given to the market share objective, and so forth. This meant designing a set of experiments involving rerunning the model under many different combinations of conditions. To make the matter more complicated, the model would have to be rerun many times within each experimental setting in order to measure the average effectiveness of the decision program in that circumstance. To keep down the computer cost and time involved in exploring every possible experimental setting, Tuason used a fractional factorial experimental design similar to that used by Bonini.[20] It permitted the testing of a more limited number of experimental settings while providing sufficient information for estimating the effect of different parametric settings on the outcome. Through this procedure, he was able to draw various conclusions about the effectiveness of this marketing strategy under different conditions. He found, for example, that this strategy performed more effectively in an environment of high sales variability than low sales variability. Thus Tuason demonstrated that a computer program could be designed that would develop weekly decisions on pricing, dealing, and product blend that produced satisfactory profits and market share in the face of unpredictable changes in competitive and environmental conditions.

This work can be extended in several ways. Tuason generated competition's strategy stochastically, although in reality it is developed in much the same way as the company's strategy. This suggests the possibility of including two elaborate strategy decision programs and simulating the results. Furthermore, the study was based on artificially generated data, and a logical next step would be to try to develop an explanation of an actual set of data describing competitive marketing activity in the coffee industry. Executives could be interviewed about their actual decision processes as a way of refining the computer program.

The Cyert, Feigenbaum, March Simulation.[21]   In 1959, Cyert, Feigenbaum, and March published a complex model simulating the competition between the American and Continental Can companies during the period 1913–1956. American Can, the original firm in the industry, had enjoyed a monopoly status. Then Continental Can was formed. From the beginning the two competitors operated somewhat differently. The splinter firm, Continental Can, faced lower costs because of newer and more efficient equipment; furthermore it assumed

---

[19]William F. Massy and Ronald E. Frank, "Short Term Price and Dealing Effects in Selected Market Segments," *Journal of Marketing Research* (May 1965), 171–185.

[20]Charles P. Bonini, *Simulation of Information and Decision Systems in the Firm* (Englewood Cliffs, New Jersey: Prentice Hall, 1963), especially Chapter 7.

[21]Richard M. Cyert, Edward A. Feigenbaum, and James G. March, "Models in a Behavioral Theory of the Firm," *Behavioral Science* (Apr. 1959), 81–95.

that demand was more price-elastic. These differences in behavior were built into the model and marked a departure from analytic models, which usually impute the same behavior to all competitors.

The major decision made by each duopolist in the model is his level of output. In making this decision the market price must be estimated for various output levels. Since the product is homogeneous, only one price will prevail at any time. The model assumes that the market absorbs all of the output at an appropriate price, so that no inventory problem is recognized.

Although the elements of the marketing mix are not manipulated in this model, the set of decision rules does recognize market processes; in this sense the model may be considered to illustrate competitive marketing strategy. Thus each duopolist estimates the amount that his competitor can sell. Further, each duopolist forecasts a demand curve that is a linear function of total output and which depends on his own estimate of the slope.

Specifically, the forecasting phase involves generating estimates of the competitor's behavior and demand. To forecast the splinter firm's output, the exmonopolist first estimates

$$V_{m,t} = \frac{Q_{s,t} - Q_{s,t-1}}{Q_{m,t} - Q_{m,t-1}} \tag{4-48}$$

where
$\quad V_{m,t} =$ conjectural variation term describing ratio of change in splinter firm's output to exmonopolist's output

$Q_{s,t} - Q_{s,t-1} =$ the actual change in the splinter firm's output during period t

$Q_{m,t} - Q_{m,t-1} =$ the actual change in the exmonopolist's output during period t

Similarly, the splinter firm estimates

$$V_{s,t} = \frac{Q_{m,t} - Q_{m,t-1}}{Q_{s,t} - Q_{s,t-1}} = \frac{1}{V_{m,t}} \tag{4-49}$$

Now, for the exmonopolist, he estimates $V_{m,t}$ as a weighted average of the splinter firm's behavior over the last four time periods. The equation used is

$$V'_{m,t} = V_{m,t-1} + \frac{1}{7}\left[4(V_{m,t-1} - V_{m,t-2}) + 2(V_{m,t-2} - V_{m,t-3}) + (V_{m,t-3} - V_{m,t-4})\right] \tag{4-50}$$

The splinter firm is expected to be more responsive to recent shifts in its rival's behavior; thus the splinter firm is assumed to use simply the information from the last two periods. The equation used is

$$V'_{s,t} = V_{s,t-1} + (V_{s,t-1} - V_{s,t-2}) \tag{4-51}$$

In forecasting demand, both firms assume that demand is a falling linear function of the total industry output. The exmonopolist imagines the demand curve to be less elastic than the splinter firm because of its past history of dominating the industry. The actual market demand curve is linear but its slope is somewhere between both imagined demand curves. The competitors reposition their estimate of the intercept of the demand curve after each period but do not change their ideas on its slope.

The firms are not assumed always to operate at their lowest costs. When achieved profits have exceeded profit goals for two periods, the company is assumed to face 5 percent higher average costs due to looser control over costs. The authors call this "organizational slack" and define it as a "situation within an organization in which individual energies potentially utilizable for the achievement of organizational goals are permitted to be diverted."

Each competitor has established a particular profit goal. The exmonopolist, because of its size, substantial computational ability, and established procedures for dealing with a stable, rather than a highly unstable, environment will tend to maintain a relatively stable profit objective; specifically, the objective is considered to be the moving average of the realized profit over the last ten time periods. The splinter firm's profit objective, on the other hand, is a moving average of the realized profit over only the last five time periods because it has not reached a state of relative stability.

If the firms forecast that their plans will satisfy their profit goals, the plans are implemented. Otherwise the firms reexamine, in order, their costs, demand projections, and objectives to see if a feasible plan can be found.

Using these decision procedures and a set of initial conditions and parameters, the model was simulated for the period 1913–1956. The results of the duopoly model in terms of comparisons of market shares and profit ratios for American and Continental Can are shown in Figure 4-4. Cyert, Feigenbaum, and March comment on these results that "the fit of the behavioral model to the data is rather surprisingly good, although we do not regard this fit as validating the approach."[22]

On an absolute basis, the theory as shown in Figure 4-4 surpassed what might have been expected by chance, although this conclusion is not based on rigorous statistical evidence. The authors did not use, or at least report, any standard measure such as chi-square. Figure 4-4 shows similar trend movement between the actual and predicted series but substantially less period to period change. Success in reproducing trends, of course, is much easier than success in reproducing fluctuations. The computer-generated series in both Fig. 4-4(a) and 4-4(b) show some false leads not found in the real data, making it all the more important to include the results of appropriate statistical tests.

Even if the authors had secured a better fit, this would fall far short of providing the type of validation needed to establish the theory, for the model and parameters were entirely constructed from the very data that were used later. Admittedly, it is no mean task to find the right parameters to recreate the time series as well as they did. But strictly speaking, a better test would have been to measure parameters from the first half of the data and test the model against the second half of the data. This would have constituted a predictive test.

[22]Ibid., p. 90.

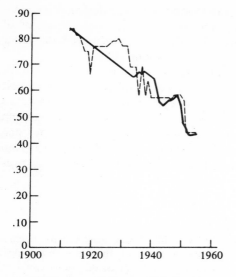

(a) **Comparison of Share of Market Data.**

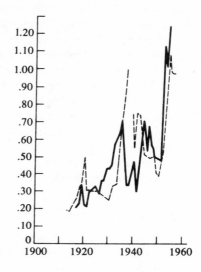

(b) **Comparison of Profit-Ratio Data.**

Figure 4-4

None of this is meant to detract from the pioneering quality of the Cyert, Feigenbaum, and March simulation. It opened a whole new style of inquiry in the study of business competition.

SUMMARY

This chapter considered the problem of competitive strategy as it appears in those markets in which each firm must consider the reactions of its competitors when preparing to choose a marketing strategy. The first step in evaluating a marketing strategy is the determination of total market demand. This is conceptualized as a concave function that is asymptotic to a limiting industry potential and depends on the level of industry marketing effort. More specifically, actual market demand at a particular time is seen to be the product of a marketing effort function and an environmental function. The dynamic nature of industry demand is demonstrated by expressing the demand relationship as a function of the time period. Examples of more sophisticated demand functions were examined in which environmental factors such as national income, seasonal and growth factors, and marketing variables played an important part. The effect of the *number* of competitors works principally through the marketing variables.

The next step is the estimation of an individual firm's market share. The fundamental theorem of market share determination holds that market share is proportional to effort share, that is the share of total marketing effort. Apparent deviations from proportionality are explainable by the following hypotheses:

qualitative differences in effectiveness, random fluctuations, lagged adjustment effects, and nonlinear or "threshold" response of market share. An extension of the relationship between market share and effort share expressed the latter variable in terms of the elements of the firm's marketing mix.

The last step is to determine the marketing program that maximizes the firm's profits. The competitive equilibrium approach is one of two solution approaches; it calls for taking partial derivatives of each firm's profit function with respect to each marketing variable, setting the derivatives equal to zero, and solving them simultaneously for the optimal marketing mix for each firm. The other approach calls for simulating the marketing strategies of the competing firms over a given time period and examining the results in the light of the firm's objectives regarding return and risk.

Questions and Problems

1. A large appliance manufacturer, dissatisfied with its current market share, decides to increase its marketing effort substantially. As a result, the marketing budget is increased by 20 percent over a two-year period. What assumptions could be drawn if, after a sufficient length of time:
(a) The company had increased its sales volume, but not its market share.
(b) The company's market share had increased, but its sales volume was unchanged?
   In which of these cases does the increase in marketing effort appear to have had the greatest effect?
2. Current market demand for an industry is given by $Q_t = k_t \bar{Q}_t$, where $\bar{Q}_t$ is market potential at time t. Total market potential for the industry is a linear function of per capita income Y_t, specifically, $\bar{Q}_t = 1,000 Y_t$. The percentage of total potential realized, k_t, is given by $k_t = 5 \times 10^{-7} X_t$, where X_t is total industry marketing effort in time t and where $0 \leqslant X_t < 2 \times 10^6$.
(a) If $Y_t = \$8,000$ and $X_t = \$500,000$, what is the market demand for the industry at time t?
(b) The marketing expenditures of each firm and the index of effectiveness of these expenditures are provided below. Determine each firm's market share.

Firm	M_i = marketing expenditure (in thousands)	α_i = effectiveness of marketing expenditure ($\alpha = 1.00$ = average)
1	100	1.00
2	100	.90
3	150	1.05
4	150	1.00

3. Assael and Day reported a study in which they had some success explaining the level of market share of different brands in terms of the following equation:

$$s_{i,t} = a + bV_{i,t} + cs_{i,t-1}$$

where $V_{i,t}$ = relative attitude index toward brand i at t. (See Henry Assael and George A. Day, "Attitudes and Awareness as Predictors of Market Share,"

Journal of Advertising Research, Dec. 1968, 3–10). Their market share equation does not explicitly show any marketing decision variables. Does this mean that no such variables are operating?

4. There are only two firms in a particular industry. The sales response function and profit function for firm 1 are given by:

$$Q_1 = 500 + (1/6)A_1 - 460P_1$$

and

$$Z_1 = P_1Q_1 - F_1 - A_1$$

For firm 2, these functions are:

$$Q_2 = 300 + (1/7)A_2 - 275P_2$$

and

$$Z_2 = P_2Q_2 - F_2 - A_2$$

Determine the values of P_1, P_2, A_1, and A_2 at competitive equilibrium.

5. Two competitors face each other with the following demand functions:

(a) $$Q_1 = 15A_1^{.6} - 15P_1^{-.2}$$

(b) $$Q_2 = 20A_2^{.4} - 10P_2^{-.1}$$

The profit function for each competitor is:

$$Z_i = P_iQ_i - A_i - F_i \qquad i = 1, 2$$

(For convenience, unit variable cost has been left out: Assume the industry sells services and F represents the total fixed cost of the source of the services.) Determine the prices and advertising levels that each competitor will establish under competitive equilibrium.

CHAPTER 5
Carryover Effects

Up to now, we have been describing functional relationships between sales and various marketing instruments on the assumption that the effects of marketing expenditures are immediately and fully realized in the period that the marketing expenditures take place. The marketing decision maker is seen as choosing among alternative levels of marketing expenditure, and the chosen level is seen as having its entire impact in that period. But a deeper look at the question of cause and effect in marketing makes it clear that current sales relate only loosely to current marketing effort.

Consider a situation in which management makes a decision to spend $50,000 this month on sales promotion. The effect of this expenditure on sales will depend on levels of company sales promotion expenditure in previous months. If the company has been spending $50,000 on sales promotion every month, the $50,000 can be thought of primarily as an expense of maintaining sales at the present level, rather than as a stimulus of additional sales. If, on the other hand, the company spends $50,000 on sales promotion for the first time, and if sales rise above their previous level, it is easier to talk about the $50,000 as "causing" a certain increase in sales. The effect of the current $50,000 sales promotion expenditure on current sales cannot be considered in isolation from the previous pattern of expenditures on sales promotion. This leads to the concept of the *carryover effects* of marketing expenditures, that marketing expenditures have effects on sales that carry over into future periods.

This concept has been alluded to in the literature as "the sales decay effect,"[1] "the holdover effect,"[2] "the distributed lagged effect,"[3] and "the carryover effect."[4] These terms are used in different ways by different writers who often fail to distinguish between quite different marketing processes giving rise to carryover effects.

Carryover effects will be used as the general term to describe the influence of a current marketing expenditure on the sales in future periods. Two types of carryover effects can be distinguished. One type of carryover effect arises from the fact that delays occur between the time marketing dollars are spent and the time induced purchases occur. This can be called the *delayed response effect*. The other effect arises from the fact that new customers that have been created by the marketing expenditures remain customers for many subsequent periods. Their later purchases should be credited to some extent to the earlier expenditures. This can be called the *customer holdover effect*.[5] Some percentage of the new customers will be retained each period and this gives rise to the notion of the *customer retention rate* and its converse, the *customer decay rate* (also called attrition or erosion rate).

To begin to make sense of carryover effects in marketing, we shall first examine the delayed response effect and then the customer holdover effect. Following this, an attempt will be made to represent carryover effects, regardless of their source, in single equation form. Finally, a particular aggregate model of carryover effects will be examined in detail and solved for measures of the short run and long run profitability of alternative marketing expenditure levels.

DELAYED RESPONSE MODEL OF CARRYOVER EFFECTS

A major reason for needing to relate marketing expenditure in one period to sales in subsequent periods is the presence of several types of time delays or lags between the occurrence of a marketing expenditure and its ultimate realization in the form of company sales.

The first time delay occurs between the period when the marketing expenditure is made and the marketing stimulus appears: this is called the *execution*

---

[1]M. L. Vidale and H. C. Wolfe, "An Operations-Research Study of Sales Response to Advertising," *Operations Research* (June 1957) 370–381, especially pp. 371–372.

[2]Alfred A. Kuehn, "How Advertising Performance Depends on Other Marketing Factors," *Journal of Advertising Research* (Mar. 1962) 2–10, especially p. 4.

[3]Roy N. Jastram, "A Treatment of Distributed Lags in the Theory of Advertising Expenditure," *Journal of Marketing* (July 1955) 36–46.

[4]Donald S. Tull, "The Carry-over Effect of Advertising," *Journal of Marketing* (April 1965), 46–53.

[5]Most authors fail to make this distinction. Tull, "The Carry-over Effect of Advertising" talks about . . . "a *carry-over (lagged) effect* of advertising" and Kuehn, "How Advertising Performance Depends on Other Marketing Factors," talks about "the budgeting implications of *lagged (carry-over) effects* of advertising and habitual brand choice behavior by consumers . . ." (Italics mine). Kuehn hints at the distinction if one considers his lagged (carryover) effects to be the delayed response effect and his habitual brand choice behavior to be the holdover effect.

delay.[6] For example, a company may spend $50,000 to prepare an ad that does not appear until the following month. This alone would mean that it is illogical to try to relate this month's marketing expenditures and this month's sales.

The second time delay may take place between the appearance of the marketing stimulus and the time of its noting by potential buyers. This can be called the *noting delay.* Thus a full page magazine ad may appear in this month's edition of a magazine, but some readers will see and read the ad for the first time only in succeeding months. This is another reason why it may be illogical to relate this month's marketing expenditures and sales. Because people read their magazines at different times, any ad may be expected to have effects distributed over a number of future periods. (Not all marketing stimuli are subject to a noting delay. A television commercial or a salesman's call involve no noting delay: these stimuli are noted when they occur or not at all.)

A third time delay may take place between the time of perception and the time of purchase: this is called the *purchase delay.* The motivating effect of a marketing stimuli will lead to a time varying placement of orders or purchases. One person might make a purchase as soon as he is exposed to the stimuli; another person might not act for days or weeks. Salesmen often hear from prospects weeks or months after they make their initial call. The purchase delay is still another reason why current marketing expenditures can be expected to have a distributed lagged impact on future sales.

Finally, a fourth delay occurs between the time an order is placed or a purchase is made somewhere in the distribution system and the time the sales are recorded in the company: this is called the *recording delay.* It actually can work in two opposite ways, depending on the situation. The recording delay is positive if an order is received by a company but is not recorded as a sale until the merchandise is shipped. For companies with backlogged orders, the sales recording delay may be quite substantial. On the other hand, many companies fill the distribution pipelines with their goods in advance of orders and count them as sales. Here sales occurred in advance of orders and the recording delay is negative. In principle, a company should date sales as of the time orders are placed if it wants to relate accurately its marketing expenditures to their effects on customers. The difficulty of doing this is another complication in ascertaining marketing instrument effectiveness.

When all of these lags are combined, the sales impact of current marketing expenditures may extend far into the future. The problem is one of determining the percentage of total induced sales that take place in the current period and each of the succeeding periods. Graphically, the problem can be considered in the following way. Figure 5-1(a) shows a hypothetical sequence of marketing events over three time periods. The first period begins with a marketing expenditure, followed by the marketing stimulus occurring a little later but still in the same period. A particular buyer perceives the marketing stimuli for the first time in period 2. The impression settles in his memory and he finally places an order in period 3. The order will be interpreted as the sale if we ignore the reporting lag.

[6]This may also be a *lead* if the marketing stimuli occurs before it is paid for.

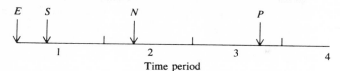

(a) An example of different delays involving one marketing stimulus and one buyer, where E = marketing expenditure, S = marketing stimulus, N = noting, and P = purchase.

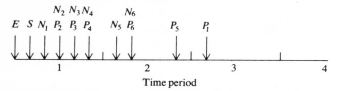

(b) An example of different delays involving one marketing stimulus and six buyers with different noting and purchase times.

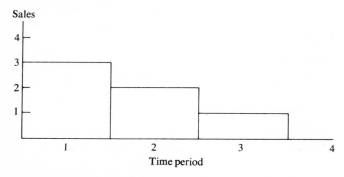

(c) Sales in succeeding periods due to a marketing stimulus in period O.

Figure 5-1   The Delayed Response Model of Carryover Effects

Figure 5-1(b) shows a similar picture this time involving six buyers instead of one. As before, the marketing expenditure and the marketing stimuli both occur in the first period. Four buyers note the stimulus in this period (N_1, N_2, N_3, N_4) and three of them place orders immediately (P_2, P_3, P_4). The other buyer makes his decision to buy in the third period. Meanwhile, two new buyers are exposed in the second period, one buying immediately and the other buying a little later but still in the second period.

Figure 5-1(c) summarizes the sales occurring in Figure 5-1(b) in the form of a histogram. The histogram shows that three sales occurred in period 1, two sales in period 2 and one sale in period 3. The sales in period 1 are said to represent the current effect of the marketing expenditure and the sales in periods 2 and 3 represent a one- and two-period lagged effect of the marketing expenditure.

The hypothetical example showed the current effect as being largest, with the succeeding lagged effects growing progressively smaller. Marketing analysts commonly make this assumption and try to fit an exponential decay function to the observed pattern.[7] This is analytically convenient because a single parameter can be used to describe the diminishing pattern of lagged effects, as will be shown later.[8] But it should be stated that there is no intrinsic reason why the current effect should be the largest followed by successively smaller effects. It depends on the length of the execution, noting, and purchase delays and their clustering pattern. When the stimulus and noting occur simultaneously and orders are placed shortly after noting, the common pattern of diminishing sales effects is defensible. When noting occurs at quite different times after the stimulus, and orders come at quite different times after the noting, then other lagged sales patterns are possible. The pattern of lagged sales effects could very conceivably follow a bell-shaped course, first rising and then falling.

CUSTOMER HOLDOVER MODEL OF CARRYOVER EFFECTS

Beside lags, there is another factor that leads to attributing a carryover effect to current marketing expenditures. Suppose that a marketing stimulus is paid for today, appears today, is noted today, and leads to purchase today. No delayed response is involved. The buyer finds the product agreeable and decides to remain with this brand. On this basis it can be said that the marketing stimulus this period affected sales this period *and* for many future periods. This customer holdover effect is the second sense in which we talk about the carryover effect of a marketing expenditure today. It is an effect that can take two different, pure forms.

New Buyer Holdover Effect

To analyze the holdover effect, we shall assume a market consisting of a fixed number of buyers buying at a constant average purchase rate per week.

Suppose that a particular seller has just sold to N customers this week, each customer having bought one unit of the product. The seller loses a constant percentage of his customers per week in the absence of any new stimulus (called the sales decay effect or competitive erosion effect). Assume that the percentage of customers he holds over from week to week is c, and as long as they continue as customers, they buy one unit a week.

In the absence of any new marketing stimuli, the seller's number of customers in any future time period can be predicted from:

$$N_t = c^t N_0 \tag{5-1}$$

where N_t = number of customers in period t

c = customer holdover rate $0 \leqslant c \leqslant 1$

t = number designating for the time period ($t = 0$ is period before the stimulus occurs)

N_0 = number of customers in period 0.

---

[7] See Vidale and Wolfe, "An Operations-Research Study of Sales Response to Advertising," or Kuehn, "How Advertising Performance Depends on Other Marketing Factors,"
[8] See the Koyck model later in this chapter.

For example, if the customer holdover rate is $c = .8$, and there are at present 100 customers, there would be eighty customers left at $t = 1$, 64 customers left at $t = 2$, and so on.

Suppose a one-shot marketing expenditure is made at the beginning of period $t = 1$ and its entire effect takes place in the same period (no delayed response effect and no word-of-mouth follow-up). The expenditure increases the number of new customers by ΔN. In period 2, the stimulus has been withdrawn but the remaining number of new buyers who first bought in period 1 would be $c\Delta N$. By period m, the remaining number of new buyers would be $c^{m-1}\Delta N$.

If all the purchases through time induced by the transient marketing stimulus in period $t = 1$ are accumulated, we have

$$
\begin{aligned}
\sum \Delta N &= \Delta N + c\Delta N + c^2\Delta N + \ldots + c^{m-1}\Delta N + \ldots \\
\sum \Delta N &= \Delta N(1 + c + c^2 + \ldots + c^{m-1} + \ldots) \\
\sum \Delta N &= \Delta N\left(\frac{1}{1-c}\right)
\end{aligned}
\tag{5-2}
$$

by the rule for the limit of the sum of an infinite power series when $0 \leqslant c < 1$.

Thus, if a marketing stimulus is introduced in some past period and increases the number of customers, its effect on sales lingers on through infinity. Even though no additional marketing expenditure may be made, the number of customers is higher today than it would have been if no marketing expenditure had taken place in $t = 1$. We call this type of holdover effect the *new-buyer holdover effect*.

Increased Purchases Holdover Effect

A holdover effect can occur even if the number of customers does not increase as a result of the marketing expenditure. This can happen if the marketing stimulus increases the average quantity purchased per period by a customer. Suppose the average quantity purchased is a function of the average level of brand awareness. If R represents the average purchase rate, and A the average level of customer brand awareness, then:

$$R_t = f(A_t)$$

For simplicity assume a proportional relationship between R and A,

$$R_t = bA_t \tag{5-3}$$

The total quantity sold by this company in time period t will be

$$Q_t = R_t N \tag{5-4}$$

where N is the fixed number of customers.

Now assume that the average customer awareness erodes in the absence of new marketing stimuli, specifically, only c percent of awareness carries over each period. At the same time a fresh marketing stimulus during a period will increase the level of customer awareness. The combination of erosion and regular new stimuli produces the pattern of average customer awareness shown in Figure 5-2(a). Here the erosion is represented as linear, the stimuli as occurring at regular intervals, and their effect on awareness as constant. By way of contrast, Figure 5-2(b) shows a pattern of exponential erosion punctuated by irregularly occurring stimuli of varying impact on awareness.

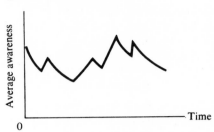

(a) Linear erosion, regularly spaced stimuli, and constant and immediate effect.

(b) Exponential erosion, irregularly spaced stimuli, and varying and distributed effect.

Figure 5-2   Pattern of Average Customer Awareness in Market

A change in market awareness, ΔA, will lead to a change in the average quantity purchased, ΔR, according to Equation 5-3:

$$\Delta R = b\Delta A$$

The full effect on the average quantity purchased over time of this one-shot marketing stimulus will be

$$\sum \Delta R = \Delta R + c\Delta R + c^2\Delta R + \ldots + c^{m-1}\Delta R + \ldots$$
$$\sum \Delta R = \Delta R(1 + c + c^2 + \ldots + c^{m-1} + \ldots)$$
$$\sum \Delta R = \Delta R\left(\frac{1}{1-c}\right)$$

by the rule for the limit of the sum of an infinite power series when $0 \leqslant c < 1$. This increment in the purchase rate can be translated into the corresponding sales increase by using Equation 5-4:

$$Q = \left(\frac{\Delta R}{1-c}\right) N \tag{5-5}$$

The reader will see that this result is comparable to the case in which the marketing stimuli at $t = 1$ created new buyers instead of greater awareness.

In general, a marketing stimulus introduced during a certain period as a pulse will have an effect not only on sales that period, but also on sales in all subsequent periods. This effect takes place either because new customers are created in that period, many of whom linger on as customers in subsequent periods, or because a new awareness is created in that period, leading to a higher average purchase rate, part of which continues through all subsequent periods. The total effect of the stimulus may also take the form of a combination of new buyers and a higher purchase rate. Whichever the rationale, the result is the same in suggesting that the quantity bought today is a function not only of today's marketing effort, but also of past levels of marketing effort.

REPRESENTING THE CARRYOVER EFFECT IN EQUATION FORM

Having explored the theoretical sources of the carryover effect, we next consider its measurement from empirical data. The empirical task is one of taking data on sales (Q) and marketing expenditures (X) and using least squares regression to determine the coefficients of the following equation:

$$Q_t = a + b_t X_t + b_{t-1} X_{t-1} + b_{t-2} X_{t-2} + \ldots \qquad (5\text{-}6)$$

The carrying out of the statistical estimation is expected to yield two interesting pieces of information. The first is how far back in the past does a marketing expenditure still have an influence on current sales. By testing the regression coefficients for their statistical significance, it is usually found that most of the influence on current sales is accounted for by the most recent terms. For example, Massy and Frank found, in their statistical estimation of the effect of previous price deals on current sales, that only the price deals in the two immediately preceding periods had an effect on current sales.[9] The other piece of information concerns the pattern of weights. As stated earlier, most analysts expect to find the b regression terms getting progressively smaller, indicating that the current marketing expenditure has the greatest effect, followed by successively smaller effects from previous expenditures. This has exceptions, however, and the weights may also appear to increase first and then decrease.

Estimating the coefficients for this equation is handicapped by the problem of multicollinearity. Multicollinearity is said to exist when some or all of the explanatory variables are so highly correlated among themselves that it is statistically difficult, if not impossible to disentangle their separate influences and obtain a reasonably precise estimate of their relative effects.[10] In the case of fitting a time series of sales to a time series of marketing expenditures, lagged several times, there will generally exist high multicollinearity among the lagged series of marketing expenditures. This is because the marketing expenditure time series is not likely to be a random time series but one characterized by serial correlation because of trend and seasonal factors. Therefore the correlation between a time series of marketing expenditures and itself lagged 1, 2, ... n periods is likely to be high. The consequence of multicollinearity is that the standard errors of estimate are very large and the estimated effects of different lagged levels of marketing expenditures are very imprecise.

Because of this problem, analysts have searched for alternative ways to

---

[9]William F. Massy and Ronald E. Frank, "Short Term Price and Dealing Effects in Selected Markets," *Journal of Marketing Research* (May 1965) p. 178.

[10]For a full discussion, see J. Johnston, *Econometric Methods* (New York: McGraw-Hill, Inc., 1963) pp. 201–207. Also see William F. Massy and Ronald E. Frank, "*Estimation Methods for Distributed Lag Models*," Research Report No. 7, Graduate School of Business, Stanford University, Stanford, Calif., Dec. 1963.

summarize the pattern of distributed lagged effects of one variable upon another. At least four different conceptual models are available: (1) Koyck's model, (2) marketing investment model, (3) exponential smoothing model, and (4) Vidale-Wolfe model.

Koyck's Model

In 1954 Koyck proposed a weighting pattern for the coefficients of previous marketing expenditures that could be described with two parameters.[11] He proposed that the initial sales effect of a previous expenditure is b and that this effect declined each period by a constant percentage, c, that is:[12]

$$b_{t-1} = cb_t \tag{5-7}$$

where c is the carryover effect and $0 \leqslant c < 1$. Substituting Equation 5-7 in Equation 5-6 we get

$$Q_t = a + bX_t + cbX_{t-1} + c^2bX_{t-2} + \ldots + c^nbX_{t-n} + \ldots \tag{5-8}$$

where b = current effect of today's marketing expenditure
c = carryover effect, $0 \leqslant c < 1$
c^nb = current effect of a marketing expenditure made n periods ago (assumes that every marketing expenditure has a constant effect b)

Now, with a little algebra, this expression can be simplified. The objective is to express Q_t as a function of only one X term, X_t, and one other term that is lagged to express the carryover effect. Take Equation 5-8 and lag it one period:

$$Q_{t-1} = a + bX_{t-1} + cbX_{t-2} + c^2bX_{t-3} + \ldots \tag{5-9}$$

Multiply Equation 5-9 by c:

$$cQ_{t-1} = ca + cbX_{t-1} + c^2bX_{t-2} + c^3bX_{t-3} + \ldots \tag{5-10}$$

Subtract Equation 5-10 from Equation 5-8:

$$Q_t = cQ_{t-1} + a + bX_t - ca \tag{5-11}$$

Rearrange Equation 5-11:

$$Q_t = (1-c)a + bX_t + cQ_{t-1} \tag{5-12}$$

This yields the important result that if the current influence of past marketing expenditures decreases at a constant rate, the current sales level (Q_t) is related to a constant $(1-c)a$, the current marketing expenditure level (X_t), and a

---

[11]L. M. Koyck, *Distributed Lags and Investment Analysis* (Amsterdam: North-Holland Publishing Co., 1954).

[12]He also showed how the case could be handled in which the weights first increased and then decreased, in the latter case according to a convergent geometric series. Irving Fisher, who first introduced the concept of distributed lags, recommended a weighting pattern based on the log normal distribution involving weights that increased rapidly at first and then diminished slowly. See Irving Fisher "Note on a Short-Cut Method for Calculating Distributed Lags," *Bulletin de l'Institut International de la Statistique*, 39 (1937) 323–327.

fraction c of last period's sales level, where c represents the carryover effect. To discover the sizes of the current and carryover effects, current sales are fitted to current marketing expenditures plus last period's sales. Last period's sales, Q_{t-1}, acts in the equation as a weighted moving average of all past marketing expenditures.

Even though Equation 5-12 obviates the need to lag marketing expenditures several periods, it too is subject to some serious statistical estimation problems. If sales are highly autocorrelated, this equation will yield a spuriously good fit with the c coefficient of Q_{t-1} representing the autocorrelation factor as much as the carryover effect.[13] Furthermore, c may measure the carryover effect only if we assume that executives decide on the level of marketing expenditure without reference to current sales. If they set marketing expenditures as a strict function of current sales, then the equation may be reflecting the dependence of expenditure levels on sales levels as much as the reverse effect. When mutual influence between Q and X exist, at least two structural equations should be fitted to separate the two effects.[14]

Marketing Investment Model

Some analysts find it useful to think of marketing expenditures as building up a capital asset called marketing goodwill, and it is the current value of this asset that directly influences the current level of sales.[15] It can be shown that this is equivalent to the Koyck model under certain assumptions and provides additional insights about the carryover effect.

Assume that current sales, Q_t, are a linear function of the current values of marketing goodwill, $\overline{X}_t$:

$$Q_t = a + b\overline{X}_t \tag{5-13}$$

The task is to define a functional relationship between the current value of marketing goodwill and current and past marketing expenditures:

$$\overline{X}_t = f(X_t, X_{t-1}, X_{t-2}, \ldots, X_{t-n}, \ldots) \tag{5-14}$$

Since $\overline{X}_t$ represents a capital asset, it is reasonable to assume that it depreciates each year at some rate d. The percentage of value carried into the next year is $c = 1 - d$. The relationship between the value of this asset this year and the preceding year, in the absence of any new marketing expenditure, is

$$\overline{X}_t = c\overline{X}_{t-1} \tag{5-15}$$

If, however, there is a new marketing expenditure of $\overline{X}_t$ dollars, the value of

[13]See Appendix Mathematical Note 5-1.

[14]See Frank M. Bass, "A Simultaneous Equation Regression Study of Advertising and Sales of Cigarettes," *Journal of Marketing Research* (Aug. 1969) 291–300.

[15]This investment approach to marketing expenditures is found in Marc Nerlove and Kenneth J. Arrow, "Optimal Advertising Policy under Dynamic Conditions," *Economica* (May 1962) 129–142; Lester G. Telser, "Advertising and Cigarettes," *Journal of Political Economy* (Oct. 1962) 471–499; and Joel Dean, "Measuring the Productivity of Investment in Persuasion," *Journal of Industrial Economics* (Apr. 1967). Their conceptual models, however, exhibit some differences.

marketing goodwill is assumed to increase by this amount and Equation 5-15 is modified to

$$\overline{X}_t = X_t + c\overline{X}_{t-1} \tag{5-16}$$

Returning to the linear relationship between this period's sales and the value of this period's marketing goodwill, Equation 5-13 becomes

$$Q_t = a + bX_t + bc\overline{X}_{t-1} \tag{5-17}$$

$$Q_t = a + bX_t + bcX_{t-1} + bc^2X_{t-2} + \ldots + bc^nX_{t-n} + \ldots \tag{5-18}$$

And Equation 5-18 is nothing other than the Koyck model shown in Equation 5-8. Thus the marketing investment model provides an independent justification for regressing current sales on current marketing expenditures and last period's sales as derived in Equation 5-12.

Exponential Smoothing Model

Neither of the previous models provides an explicit indication of the *relative* influence of the current expenditure versus the sum of all past marketing expenditures on current sales. Note that the b coefficient of current marketing expenditures in Equation 5-18 is not a fraction showing the relative influence of current expenditures but a number showing the sales effect (in dollars or units) of a current marketing dollar. This number is not necessarily between 0 and 1. To develop a model showing relative influence, we shall again use the concept of the current value of marketing goodwill but this time define it not as in Equation 5-16 but as:[16]

$$\overline{X}_t = (1-c)X_t + c\overline{X}_{t-1} \tag{5-19}$$

where $0 \leqslant c \leqslant 1$. That is, the current value of marketing goodwill is a weighted average of the current marketing expenditure and last period's marketing goodwill. If the carryover effect, c, is .8, then the current value of marketing goodwill equals 20 percent of the period's marketing expenditure plus 80 percent of last period's goodwill. In the extreme case when $c = 1$, the current value of goodwill depends entirely on past expenditures. At the other extreme, if $c = 0$, the current value of goodwill depends entirely on this period's marketing expenditure. In fact, $c = 0$ implies that no goodwill is built up over time.

What general weighting pattern does Equation 5-19 imply? Extending the terms in Equation 5-19, we have

$$\overline{X}_t = (1-c)X_t + c(1-c)X_{t-1} + c^2(1-c)X_{t-2} + \ldots + c^n(1-c)X_{t-n} + \ldots \tag{5-20}$$

If $c = .8$, the weights become

$$\overline{X} = .2000X_t + .1600X_{t-1} + .1280X_{t-2} + \ldots + .8^n(.2)X_{t-n} + \ldots \tag{5-21}$$

This general way of weighting past marketing expenditures has two useful characteristics:

[16]As an alternative to the concept of marketing goodwill, Equation 5–19 can be interpreted as defining the *effective current level of marketing expenditures*.

1. The weights continuously diminish, with the most current marketing expenditure receiving the most weight.
2. The sum of the weights approaches 1 as $t \to \infty$.[17]

The current value of goodwill comes from smoothing the past time series of marketing expenditures through the use of exponential weights, hence the term exponential smoothing model.

This exponentially smoothed measure of marketing goodwill, $\overline{X}_t$, may be assumed to have a linear relationship to current sales, although other relations are also possible. Combining the assumptions of Equations 5-13 and 5-20, we have

$$Q_t = a + b(1-c)X_t + bc(1-c)X_{t-1} + bc^2(1-c)X_{t-2} + \ldots + bc^n(1-c)X_{t-n} + \ldots$$
$$(5\text{-}22)$$

Note that this is a somewhat different weighting pattern from Equation 5-18. This model indicates that the marginal sales effect of current marketing expenditures is $b(1-c)$, instead of simply b, where $(1-c)$ is the percentage influence of current marketing expenditures on current sales.

Vidale-Wolfe Model

Each of the previous models represented the effect of lagged marketing expenditures on current sales in a linear fashion (see Equations 5-8, 5-18, and 5-22). Vidale and Wolfe proposed an interesting model in which they sought to explain not the level of sales directly but the rate of change in sales.[18] Lagged effects were handled through a single sales decay term. Their studies of the sales-advertising relationship in several major companies led them to formulate the following differential equation:

$$\frac{dS}{dt} = \left[\frac{rA(M-S)}{M} \right] - \lambda S \qquad (5\text{-}23)$$

where
$\quad S$ = rate of sales at time t
$\quad dS/dt$ = change in the rate of sales at time t $\Big\}$ variables
$\quad A$ = rate of advertising expenditure at time t

$\quad r$ = sales response constant (sales generated per advertising dollar when $S = 0$)
$\quad M$ = saturation level of sales (the maximum sales that can be profitably achieved via a given campaign) $\Big\}$ parameters
$\quad \lambda$ = sales decay constant (proportion of sales lost per time interval when $A = 0$)

The right-hand side of the equation shows that the increase in the rate of sales depends on several factors: it will be greater for higher levels of r, A, and $(M-S)/M$, and it will be smaller for higher levels of λ and S. In words, the

[17]See Appendix Mathematical Note 5–2.
[18]Vidale and Wolfe, "An Operations-Research Study of Sales Response to Advertising."

equation says that the increase in the rate of sales, dS/dt, is equal to the response of sales per dollar of advertising, r, times the number of advertising dollars being spent, A, reduced by the percentage of unsaturated sales, $(M-S)/M$, less the sales being lost through decay, λS.

The parameters r, M, and λ, are taken as constant for a given product and campaign. The response coefficient, r, can be measured by observing the rate of change in sales that takes place under controlled conditions with a given campaign. The saturation level M is estimated from data on the absolute size of the market. The sales decay constant, λ, is measured by observing sales declines in areas where A has been set at 0 for measurement purposes.

If the three parameters have been measured, Equation 5-23 may be solved for the rate of advertising necessary to maintain sales at any specified growth rate. A rate of sales growth of k units per period could be achieved by substituting k for dS/dt in Equation 5-23 and solving for A:

$$A = \frac{k+\lambda S}{rm} \tag{5-24}$$

where $k = dS/dt$, the change in sales per time period
 $m = (M-S)/M$, the remaining sales potential

Thus more advertising expenditure would be necessary the higher the desired sales growth rate, the higher the sales decay constant, the higher the present sales level, the lower the sales response constant, or the lower the remaining sales potential. All of these relations accord with intuition. By setting $k = 0$ in Equation 5-24, this equation also indicates the rate of advertising expenditure necessary to maintain constant sales.

Equation 5-23 can also be used to forecast future sales for any rate of advertising expenditure maintained for duration T. The rate of sales is obtained by integration of Equation 5-23 and the solution is as follows:

$$S(t) = \left[\frac{M}{(1+\lambda M/rA)}\right][1-e^{-(rA/M+\lambda)t}]+S_0e^{-(rA/M+\lambda)t} \qquad t \leqslant T \tag{5-25}$$

where S_0 is the rate of sales at $t = 0$, the start of the advertising campaign.[19]

After advertising has stopped, sales decrease exponentially:

$$S(t) = S(T)e^{-\lambda(t-T)} \qquad t > T \tag{5-26}$$

The forecast of future sales is shown in Figure 5-3. Sales increase most rapidly at $t = 0$ and taper off as saturation is approached; after T, sales decline exponentially. Total additional sales generated by the campaign can be found by integrating the area under the curve from $t = 0$ to $t = \infty$, less the area under the curve representing sales that would have taken place at an alternative planned rate of advertising expenditure.

[19]For the mathematical derivation, see Frank M. Bass, et al., eds., *Mathematical Models and Methods in Marketing* (Homewood, Ill.: Richard D. Irwin, Inc., 1961), pp. 375–377.

The model can also be analyzed to show the total additional sales generated by an advertising pulse of negligible duration, representing the short, intense campaign. Vidale and Wolfe show that the total additional sales would be approximately $(ra/\lambda)\,(M - S_0)/M$ for sales initially well below saturation.[20] The authors also use investment theory to determine the optimal advertising outlay for a short, intense campaign.

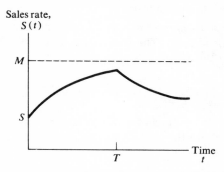

Figure 5-3   Sales Response to an Advertising Campaign of Duration T:
Vidale-Wolfe Model

Our main interest here is in their representation of the carryover effect in terms of a sales decay constant. Their sales decay constant, λ, can be shown to be related to the carryover rate c in Equation 5-1:

$$N_t = c^t N_0 \qquad\qquad\qquad (5\text{-}27)$$

Let $c = e^{-\lambda}$ where $e = 2.71 \ldots$ the base of the natural logarithms. Then Equation 5-27 becomes

$$N_t = e^{-\lambda t} N_0 \qquad\qquad\qquad (5\text{-}28)$$

and instead of talking about the carryover rate c, we can talk about the sales decay constant λ. The sales decay constant is presumably low for well-established brands, and these brands need not spend as much to maintain their sales level. Brands with a high sales decay constant must be continuously supported by advertising money to offset competitive inroads. Furthermore, the sales decay constant is likely to vary over the product's life cycle, probably decreasing as the product passes from the introductory stage to the maturity stage, and then increasing as the product passes to the saturation and decline stages.

DERIVING MEASURES OF RESPONSE FROM CARRYOVER MODELS

Once a particular carryover model is specified and statistically fitted, it is possible to derive several measures of short run and long run response to marketing expenditures. Using the Koyck model Equation 5-12 as an example,

[20]See ibid. for mathematical derivation.

we shall show how to derive the marginal effect of marketing expenditures on sales, the marketing expenditure elasticity, and the marginal rate of return to marketing effort. These measures will be derived for both the short and the long run, the distinction being based on the current effect and the full term effects of a marketing expenditure.[21]

Marginal Effect of Marketing Expenditures on Sales

The *marginal effect of marketing expenditures on sales* is the sales increase caused by a $1 increase in marketing expenditures. The short term marginal effect is directly given by b in Equation 5-12 because:

$$\frac{dQ}{dX} = b \tag{5-29}$$

The long run sales effect of a marketing expenditure will be larger than the short run effect because it affects sales in both the current and future periods. In fact, long run sales, Q_∞, are given by

$$Q_\infty = (b + cb + c^2b + c^3b + \ldots)\, X_t = \frac{b}{1-c}\, X_t \quad \text{where } 0 \leqslant c < 1 \tag{5-30}$$

since the sum of a converging geometric series reduces to the expression on the right.

The long run sales effect of a marketing expenditure can be derived in another way. The long run effect would be manifest when sales attain their equilibrium level (Q_∞). Using Equation 5-12, sales attain their equilibrium level when

$$Q_\infty = (1-c)a + bX_t + cQ_\infty \tag{5-31}$$

Gathering the Q_∞ terms, simplifying, and solving, we get

$$Q_\infty = a + \frac{b}{1-c}\, X_t \tag{5-32}$$

The long run marginal effect can be found by differentiating Equation 5-32:

$$\frac{dQ_\infty}{dX_t} = \frac{b}{1-c} \tag{5-33}$$

And this is the same result as derived in Equation 5-30.

The expression $1/1-c$ can be called the *long run marketing expenditure multiplier*. For example, if the carryover effect is as high as .8, the long run marketing expenditure multiplier is 5. That is, the long run sales effect is 5 times the size of the short run sales effect. On the other hand, if $c = .2$, which signifies a rapidly declining promotional effect, the long run multiplier is 1.25. In this case, the long run effect is only 25 percent higher than the short run effect.

---

[21] For a fuller discussion and application, see Kristian S. Palda, *The Management of Cumulative Advertising Effects* (Englewood Cliffs, N.J.: Prentice-Hall, Inc., 1964).

Marketing Expenditure Elasticity

It is also of interest to derive the marketing expenditure elasticity, so that the effectiveness of various marketing instruments can be compared in terms of the Dorfman-Steiner theorem. Elasticity of sales with respect to a change in marketing expenditure is defined as

$$e_{qx} = \frac{dQ}{dX}\frac{X}{Q} \tag{5-34}$$

We have already found that $dQ/dX = b$, the marginal effect of marketing expenditure on sales. For X/Q, the average ratio of marketing expenditure to sales, $\overline{X}/\overline{Q}$, will be used. Therefore the short run marketing expenditure elasticity is

$$e_{qx} = \frac{b\overline{X}}{\overline{Q}} \tag{5-35}$$

and the long run elasticity is

$$e_{qx}^{\infty} = \frac{b}{1-c}\frac{\overline{X}}{\overline{Q}} \tag{5-36}$$

Marginal Rate of Return on Invested Marketing Dollar

The final task is to measure the marginal rate of return on the investment of a dollar in marketing effort. According to Equation 5-8, a dollar invested in marketing effort today will have an impact on this period's sales and all future period's sales, with the impact decaying geometrically over time toward 0. The marginal sales effect of today's marketing dollar on current sales is b; on next period's sales, cb; on the following period's sales, c^2b, and so on; that is,

Sum of future sales
created by $1 invested $\quad = b+cb+c^2b \ldots \tag{5-37}$
in marketing this period

The marketing manager is ultimately interested in profits, not sales. Suppose that all other costs than promotion are a constant percentage, k, of sales. Then $z = 1-k$ represents the gross profit margin. The marketing manager is really interested in

Sum of future profit
created by a marketing $\quad = zb+zcb+zc^2b \ldots \tag{5-38}$
dollar invested this period

Furthermore, profit dollars have diminishing value the further into the future they are earned. Future profit dollars should be discounted, say, at rate r, where r represents the company's opportunity cost or target rate of return. The measure that results from discounting a stream of future income is called the present value (PV) of the stream.[22] The present value of the future income

[22]See Chap. 9.

stream in Equation 5-38 is given by

$$PV = \frac{zb}{(1+r)^0} + \frac{zcb}{(1+r)^1} + \frac{zc^2b}{(1+r)^2} + \ldots \tag{5-39}$$

Since it is an investment of \$1 that generates the future income stream, then $PV = 1$. The task is to solve the following equation for r:

$$\$1 = \frac{zb}{(1+r)^0} + \frac{zcb}{(1+r)^1} + \frac{zc^2b}{(1+r)^2} + \ldots \tag{5-40}$$

and the solution is:[23]

$$r = \frac{c}{1-zb} - 1 \tag{5-41}$$

According to Equation 5-41, the marginal rate of return on an invested marketing dollar will be higher, the higher the marketing dollar's carryover rate, the higher the gross profit percentage, or the higher the short run marginal sales effect on advertising. All of these conclusions are in accord with common intuition.

Duration Time of Marketing Expenditure Effect

Another question that might be examined is how much of the long run sales effect of a marketing expenditure is accomplished in the first few periods after the expenditure. Suppose that we want to learn how many periods it will take for 95 percent of the total long run effect to occur. Recall from Equation 5-30 that the total future sales produced by a marketing expenditure today is the sum of the infinite convergent geometric series:

$$Q_\infty = (b+cb+c^2b+\ldots+c^nb+\ldots)\, X_t = b\left(\frac{1}{1-c}\right) X_t \text{ where } 0 \leqslant c < 1 \tag{5-42}$$

The total sales produced by this marketing expenditure in the first n periods is:[24]

$$Q_n = (b+cb+c^2b+\ldots+c^{n-1}b)\, X_t = b\left(\frac{1-c^n}{1-c}\right) X_t \tag{5-43}$$

The problem is to find the number of periods n when

$$\frac{Q_n}{Q_\infty} \geqslant .95 \tag{5-44}$$

Then

$$\frac{Q_n}{Q_\infty} = \frac{b[(1-c)^n/(1-c)]X_t}{b[1/(1-c)]X_t} = 1-c^n \geqslant .95 \tag{5-45}$$

[23] See Appendix Mathematical Note 5-3.
[24] See Charles D. Hodgman, ed., *Standard Mathematical Tables*, 12th ed. (Cleveland: Chemical Rubber Publishing Company, 1959), p. 357.

Solving Equation 5-33 for n, we have:[25]

$$n \leqslant \frac{\log .05}{\log c} \tag{5-46}$$

Thus the number of periods that must elapse before a marketing expenditure has had .95 of its total effect is directly related to the carryover effect c. As c increases, log c also *increases*, but its absolute value *decreases* (it becomes a smaller negative number), hence n *increases*. Where marketing expenditures have a high carryover effect, most of the total effect will occur over a long time.

An Application of Koyck's Model: The Lydia Pinkham Case

One of the first and most thorough applications of Koyck's model to the lagged effects of marketing expenditure was carried out by Palda in 1964.[26] The objective of his study was to determine the effect of Lydia Pinkham's advertising on the sales of its Vegetable Compound between 1908 and 1960. Palda gave the following reasons for choosing this product.

> The firm spent a very high proportion (40–60 percent) of its sales on advertising. Furthermore it did not employ many of the customary "parameters" of marketing action: sales force, credit, discounts, frequent changes in package, point of purchase efforts, special offerings, etc. The assumption thus could safely be made that advertising had a measurable effect on Pinkham's sales. The product itself, Lydia Pinkham's Vegetable Compound, had no close substitutes. Competitors' marketing action was not, therefore, a complicating factor to be coped with. By the same token certain allied issues, such as the geographic distribution of Pinkham's marketing effort could be ignored. During the detailed examination which followed the decision to delve into the Pinkham case, further factors were discovered which added to the simplicity of the ultimate quantitative analysis. On the whole the conclusion was reached that there was remarkable stability (between 1908–60) in the universe from which the sample observations were obtained.[27]

Palda fitted several different equations and was able to demonstrate that the Koyck distributed lagged models gave a better fit to the Pinkham data and a better forecast than models that did not incorporate lagged effects.

The following demand equation, for example, gave a fairly good explanation of the variations in the sale of Lydia Pinkham's Vegetable Compound between the years 1908–1960:[28]

$$Q_t = -3649 + 1180 \log X_t + .665 Q_{t-1} + 774D + 32t - 2.83 Y_t \tag{5-47}$$

where Q_t = sales in thousands of dollars in year t

X_t = advertising expenditures in thousands of dollars in year t

[25]See Appendix Mathematical Note 5–4.
[26]Palda, *The Management of Cumulative Advertising Effects.*
[27]Ibid., p. 87.
[28]Ibid., pp. 67–68.

D = a dummy variable, taking on the value 1 between 1908–1925 and 0 from 1926 on

t = year (1908 = 0, 1909 = 1, ...)

Y_t = disposable personal income in billions of current dollars in year t

The five independent variables on the right appeared to explain 94 percent of the yearly variation in the sale of Lydia Pinkham's Vegetable Compound between 1908 and 1960. This equation is essentially the same as Equation 5-12 with three additional variables, D, t, and Y, that help explain some of the variance. Note that advertising expenditures, X_t, predicts best in log form, indicating that sales increase at a diminishing marginal rate with increased advertising. The dummy variable D shifts the sales intercept downward after 1925 to express a discontinuity in Lydia Pinkham's sales history. To find the average short run marginal sales effect of advertising, b, take the first derivative of sales in Equation 5-47 with respect to advertising expenditure:

$$b = \frac{dQ_t}{dX_t} = \frac{dQ_t}{d \log_{10} X_t} \cdot \frac{d \log_{10} X_t}{dX} = 1180 \frac{\log_{10} e}{X} = \frac{1180(.4343)}{X} = \frac{512.47}{X} \tag{5-48}$$

The following estimates are based on planned advertising expenditures in 1961 of \$695 (in thousands) and forecasted sales of \$1,257 (in thousands). The short run sales effect of 1961 advertising will be, according to Equation 5-48,

$$b = \frac{512.47}{695} = .737 \tag{5-49}$$

Equation 5-47 shows the carryover effect to be

$$c = .665 \tag{5-50}$$

Therefore the long run marginal sales effect of 1961 advertising expenditures will be

$$\frac{b}{1-c} = \frac{.737}{1-.665} = 2.20 \tag{5-51}$$

The short run advertising elasticity is given by Equation 5-35:

$$b \frac{X_{1961}}{Q_{1961}} = .737 \frac{695}{1,257} = .407 \tag{5-52}$$

The long run advertising elasticity is given by Equation 5-36:

$$\frac{b}{1-c} \frac{X_{1961}}{Q_{1961}} = \frac{.737}{1-.665} \frac{695}{1,257} = 1.216 \tag{5-53}$$

The final item of interest is the rate of return that would be yielded to the company by its marginal advertising dollar. The company's gross profit margin, z, after all expenses but before advertising and taxes, averaged a high 75 percent of sales. Therefore its long run marginal rate of return on 1961 planned advertising expenditures, according to Equation 5-41, is

$$r = \frac{c}{1-zb} - 1 = \frac{.665}{1-.75\times.737} = .487 \tag{5-54}$$

Palda carried out this computation for each year in the period 1908–1960 and found the mean long run marginal rate of return to be $r = .53$. Since corporate taxes ran about 30 percent of profits during this period, this yielded an after-tax rate of return on advertising of .37, a not implausible rate for a well-established firm in the pharmaceutical industry.

SUMMARY

Marketing analysts and practitioners recognize that current marketing expenditures are not limited in their effects to current sales but influence many periods of future sales as well. A confusing variety of terms and models have been used to describe carryover effects. Their relationship to each other and the underlying processes giving rise to carryover effects have generally not been clarified.

Carryover effects can be defined as the effects that current marketing expenditures have on sales beyond the current period. Two quite different processes underlay carryover effects. Carryover effects arise in the first place because of various types of time lags between the spending of marketing funds, the appearance of stimuli, the noting of them, and the purchase action of buyers. Carryover effects arise in the second place because new buyers or higher buying rates caused by the marketing stimuli tend to persist and affect future sales levels.

Marketing analysts usually examine the carryover effect by regressing current sales on current *and* past marketing expenditures, retaining as many past marketing expenditure terms as are statistically significant. Fitting the equation involves tough statistical issues of autocorrelation and direction of influence. As a partial solution, analysts have sought simplified schemes involving only one lagged term that carries the weight of all past expenditures. For example, the Koyck model is built on the assumption that the carryover effects diminish at a constant rate. This yields an equation in which current sales are explained by current advertising and last period's sales. The marketing investment model yields equivalent results, although here the key idea is the existence of a level of current marketing goodwill that depreciates at a constant rate but is renewed by new marketing expenditures. The exponential smoothing model also relies on a single marketing expenditure variable that in this case is a weighted average of current versus all past marketing expenditure. The Vidale-Wolfe model utilizes a sales decay constant to express a steady decay of sales in the absence of new marketing expenditures.

Once a carryover model is specified and measured, it is possible to derive measures of short and long run marginal sales effects, marketing expenditure elasticities, and the long run rate of return on marketing expenditure. These measures were derived for the Koyck model and illustrated with an actual study of the effects of advertising on the sales of Lydia Pinkham Vegetable Compound between 1908–1960.

Questions and Problems

1. Analyze your own purchase behavior in terms of the problem of delayed response effects with respect to a product you have recently purchased. Try to determine the marketing efforts which influenced your decision to buy and the immediacy of their effects.

2. The president of a large soft drink company claims that advertising money spent on the company's biggest seller is a bad investment. He maintains that the response in sales is not sufficient to justify the current high level of advertising expenditures. To prove his point he suspends all advertising for a period of six months. Sales do not drop significantly during this period, and the president feels that his claims are sustained. Are they?

3. Suppose the current expected value of "b" is produced in the following way:

$$b_{t+1} = kb_t + (1-k)\bar{b}_t$$

(a) Show how b_{t+1} depends upon b_{t-1}, b_{t-2}, and $\bar{b}_{t-2}$

(b) For $k = .7$, find the actual weight given to b_{t-1}, b_{t-2}, and b_{t-3}, in determining b_{t+1}.

4. Suppose the current effective level of a brand's advertising depends 70 percent on the current expenditures and 30 percent on past expenditures exponentially weighted. Suppose past advertising expenditures have been 6 (most recent), 4, 3, and 0. What is the current effective level of advertising?

5. A manufacturer wishes to determine the level of advertising which will maintain his current sales growth rate at 4 percent. Current sales are $50,000 and it is estimated that sales could reach a level of $150,000 at saturation. Sales response to advertising dollars is estimated at 1.1, and it has been determined that the company would lose .2 of its sales per period if no advertising expenditure were made.

(a) How much advertising is needed to maintain the desired growth rate?

(b) What rate of growth would be sustained if $20,000 was spent per period for advertising?

6. A Koyck model is fitted to company sales data using 20 periods over which marketing expenditures and sales (in thousands of dollars) summed to 45,000 and 192,000 respectively. The carryover rate is found to be .8, and the short-run marginal effect of marketing expenditures on sales is .5. Find:

(a) The long-run marginal effect

(b) The short and long run marketing expenditure elasticities

(c) The marginal rate of return on the marketing investment (assume a gross profit margin of .7)

(d) The number of periods which must elapse for 95 percent of the total effect of a marketing expenditure to be realized.

7. A seller is interested in determining the effects of marketing expenditures on sales. Through previous studies it is known that the company's carryover rate is .8 and that the short-run marginal effect of marketing expenditures on sales is .6. If the company has average sales of $2,000,000 and its marketing expenditures average $500,000, compute:

(a) The long-run marginal effect

(b) The long-run marketing expenditure elasticity

(c) The marginal rate of return on marketing effort (assume that the gross profit margin is .5).

CHAPTER 6
Multiple Territories

Up to now we have considered how a company operating in a single market area might set its marketing mix in the presence of competitors and carryover effects so as to maximize its profits. The vast majority of firms, however, do not operate in a single market area but rather sell in a multitude of areas that are organized as sales territories. A market of any size is customarily divided into geographical units called sales territories. The territories themselves may be combined into districts that in turn may be combined into regions. We shall ignore the different tiers and use the term *territory* to describe any geographical area for which the company develops separate marketing plans and budgets.[1]

The question might immediately arise as to why the existence of multiple territories calls for any new principles. It would seem that each territory's demand function and cost function provide all that is needed to determine the optimal marketing expenditure in each territory. It turns out that this is true provided that the company has enough funds to carry out the optimal expenditure in each territory. Very often, the company lacks sufficient funds to develop each territory optimally and must ration its funds among these territories. Should the company put most of its funds in its already strong territories for the

---

[1]The problem of designing optimal sales territories is examined in Chap. 13, pp. 371–378.

purpose of strengthening them still further? Or should it devote a large portion of its budget to developing its weaker territories? The territorial allocation of marketing funds is one of the key practical problems facing marketing management and one on which a lot of confusion exists.

This chapter will first describe some of the more common rules of thumb used by companies to allocate their marketing funds over territories. After describing these practices and their limitations, the chapter will describe the theory of optimal allocation of a marketing budget between two territories for which the demand and cost functions are known and the objective is current profit maximization. The two-territory solution is then generalized into the n territory solution. The chapter will conclude with two numerical examples to illustrate the theory.

COMPANY PRACTICES IN ALLOCATING THE MARKETING BUDGET TO TERRITORIES

Very few companies use the notion of territorial demand functions (sales response functions) to allocate their marketing budgets to territories. Instead they rely on a variety of other bases for allocating the money, such as estimates of sales potential, industry sales, or company sales for each territory.

A common practice of many companies is to base their allocation on territorial *sales potential* (or market potential), which is an estimate of the territory's absolute or relative capacity to buy the particular industry's product. We can conveniently think of sales potential as the upper asymptote of an industry sales response function, that is, the level toward which industry sales would move under maximal industry marketing effort. Sales potential is not the same as actual sales (except in those cases in which actual sales are maximal sales) and has to be inferred from various territorial indicators thought to be directly related to the territory's sales potential.[2] In this connection, many companies rely on the "Survey of Buying Power," which is published semiannually by *Sales Management* magazine. The survey presents estimates of the relative buying potential of different counties and cities in the United States. The relative buying potential is constructed as a weighted index in the following manner:

$$Q_i = .5Y_{1i} + .3Y_{2i} + .2Y_{3i} \qquad (6\text{-}1)$$

---

[2]Many investigators attempt to identify the appropriate indicators by performing a statistical regression of territorial sales on various territorial indices, such as income, population, etc. This procedure is conceptually faulty, in that the regression variables explain actual sales, not potential sales. Since the latter series does not exist, the results of statistical regression can only suggest the appropriate indicators. A conceptually more satisfactory approach is to estimate territory sales potentials by factor analysis, which attempts to extract the factors underlying a whole set of indices describing an entity. The first extracted factor from a set of territorial indices of income, population, etc., can be thought of as the territorial sales potential. Factor analysis as a statistical technique is described in Chap. 18, pp. 605–610. For its application to sales potential estimation, see Fritz Kafka and Benjamin Lipstein, "A New Approach to Geographic Sales Potentials," a paper presented at a meeting of the Northern New Jersey Chapter of the American Marketing Association, May 26, 1959.

where Q_i = percentage of total national buying power found in area i
Y_{1i} = percentage of national disposable personal income originating in area i
Y_{2i} = percentage of national retail sales in area i
Y_{3i} = percentage of national population located in area i

Sales Management claims that the specific weights (i.e., .5, .3, .2) yield a sales potential measure that represents the buying power of many consumer goods that fall between low priced staples and high valued luxury goods. Sellers are free to modify these weights to reflect their own conception of the relative contribution of these three variables to territorial sales potential.

Other companies base their allocations on actual industry sales by territory rather than estimated sales potential by territory. They may allocate their funds on a proportional basis to actual industry sales or on a disproportional basis. Some companies feel that territories with high industry sales levels should receive disproportionately more company funds because the gains stand to be larger; other companies feel that the weaker territories deserve disproportional support. A slightly more sophisticated approach is to examine the difference in each territory between estimated industry potential and actual industry sales level. Then the marketing budget is allocated in some relation to each territory's unrealized sales potential.

None of these allocational alternatives, however, are conceptually defensible because they all ignore the marginal response of sales to additional marketing effort. Current levels of industry sales and/or sales potential in different territories do not have any necessary connection with the probable marginal sales response of a territory to additional marketing inputs, which is only revealed in the full sales response function for the territory.

This leads some companies to prefer to base their allocations on current *company sales* by territory, rather than industry sales, on the assumption that this is a better reflection of the likely sales response of a territory to company marketing effort. Current company sales reflect the number and vigor of competitors, the availability of middlemen, the degree of buyer awareness and loyalty, and other territorial characteristics. The view is that the stronger the company's position in a territory, the more benefit it would derive from further expenditures in the territory. In this connection, Hartung and Fisher found that oil companies begin to enjoy promotional economies after opening up more than a certain threshold percentage of service stations in a given area.[3] Kuehn seems to have drawn a similar conclusion:

> Increased advertising where the brand is relatively strong generally appears to be more profitable in the short run, unless the brand is already near its maximum potential penetration of the consumer market. . . . By concentrating on a few markets, a brand frequently has a better chance of forcing distribu-

[3]See Philip H. Hartung and James L. Fisher, "Brand Switching and Mathematical Programming in Market Expansion," *Management Science* (Aug. 1965) 231–243. Their study is discussed here in Chap. 11, pp. 307–312.

tion and increasing its over-all short term profitability, thereby obtaining the means for subsequent investment expenditures in other territories. It can be expensive to hold one's own in every market simply as a matter of principle, especially if this prevents the brand becoming firmly established and profitable in any one region.[4]

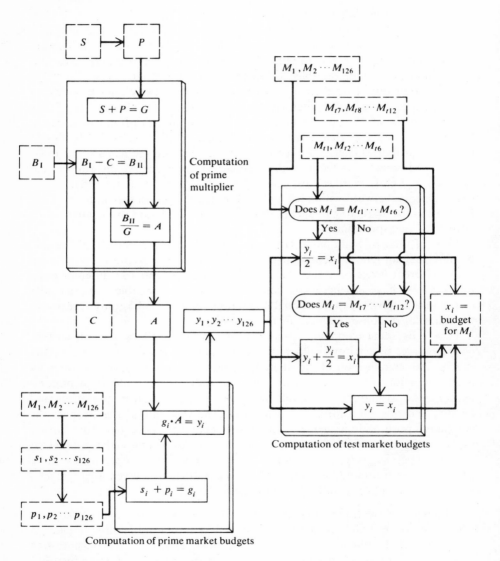

Figure 6-1 Guardian Oil: Allocating Advertising Funds to Territories

[4]See Alfred A. Kuehn, "How Advertising Performance Depends on Other Marketing Factors," *Journal of Advertising Research* (Mar. 1962) 7.

Key

$B_I =$	advertising budget, approved by management for the coming time period.
$C =$	estimated media production costs to put B_I into effect.
$B_{II} =$	space and time budget, to be apportioned.
$S =$	total sales of branded "Guardian" gasoline, including both regular and premium grades, in U.S. direct-supplied territory during the previous year.
$P =$	total sales of "Guardian Premium" gasoline, same.
$M_1, M_2 \ldots M_{126} =$	listing of markets where Guardian gasoline is sold on a direct basis
$s_1, s_2 \ldots s_{126} =$	branded "Guardian" gasoline sales, regular and premium grades, in $M_1, M_2 \ldots M_{126}$, through direct-supplied service stations, during the previous year.
$p_1, p_2 \ldots p_{126} =$	"Guardian Premium" gasoline sales, same.
$M_{t1}, M_{t2} \ldots M_{t6} =$	selected 50 percent test markets, in which advertising expenditures are to be kept at a constant level for an indefinite period in order to test the impact of advertising.
$M_{t7}, M_{t8} \ldots M_{t12} =$	selected 150 percent test markets, same.
$A =$	prime multiplier.
$G =$	total "profit" gallons, giving double weight to premium gallons.
$g_i =$	"profit" gallons sold during the previous year in M_i (any market).
$y_1, y_2 \ldots y_{126} =$	prime market budgets.
$x_i =$	budget for M_i.

From Marschner, p. 293.

However, others argue that disproportionate marketing effort should go into the company's weaker sales territories in order to build them into profitable markets. Still others argue that many factors should be considered besides company and industry sales before determining the budget allocation to territories.

Examples of Company Practice: The Marschner Study

One of the few detailed studies of how companies actually apportion their marketing budgets to sales territories was made by Don Marschner.[5] He spent several weeks interviewing the executives of an oil company and later a coffee company to determine the procedures each company used to allocate its advertising budget to its geographical markets. His initial assumption was that these large profitable companies allocated their funds on the basis of a sophisticated model that included such factors as the territory's sales response constant, saturation level, and sales decay constant as in the Vidale-Wolfe study,[6] or at least proxies for these variables. However, in carrying out his study he found that these companies used quite primitive criteria that omitted most of the theoretically correct factors in the normative model. He found that both companies treated advertising largely as a dependent variable to sales, rather than as one of the independent variables affecting sales.

[5]See Donald C. Marschner, "Theory Versus Practice in Allocating Advertising Money," *Journal of Business* (July 1967) 286–302.

[6]See M. L. Vidale and H. B. Wolfe, "An Operations Research Study of Sales Response to Advertising," *Operations Research* (June 1957) 370–381. This study was described in Chap. 5.

Marschner's flow diagram for the procedure used by the Guardian Oil Company (name is disguised) is shown in Figure 6-1. First, it should be pointed out that it took him some time to establish the procedure, since few executives at the company really understood how the allocation was being determined. In fact, it took several reconstructions of his interview notes to produce this final flow diagram. The flow diagram shows the process starting with an advertising budget B_I. Estimated media production costs C are subtracted to leave a net advertising budget B_{II}. Then the company estimates its total gasoline sales volume S (which combines regular and premium gasoline) and adds premium sales volume P back to this figure to yield $G = S + P$, so that G represents "profit" gallons (thus double weight is given to premium gasoline sales). The company then takes the ratio of the net advertising budget to the profit gallons to establish a figure for advertising dollars per profit gallon A. It calls this the prime multiplier.

Next this oil company divides its markets into 126 prime markets and 12 test markets. Each prime market receives an advertising budget equal to its previous year's profit gallons sold, multiplied by the prime multiplier. In other words, the advertising budget is allocated largely on the basis of last year's company sales in the territory, where premium gasoline sales receive twice the weight of regular gasoline sales. As for the twelve test markets, they are subdivided into two groups, the territories in the first group receiving only 50 percent of their normal advertising budget and the territories in the second group receiving 150 percent of their normal advertising budget. This allows the company presumably to determine experimentally the effect of different levels of advertising expenditure. However, there is no evidence that the resulting information is actually used to alter the future territorial allocations.[7]

When it was pointed out to the oil company executives that their procedure, in spite of its complex appearance, reduced to one of setting advertising budgets on the basis of sales, they justified it by saying that the company lost a certain percentage of its customers in each market each year and that advertising's most important job was to get new customers to replace them. But this assumes that the company loses the same percentage of customers in all of its markets. Furthermore, this implies that the company wants the same rate of sales growth in each market and that sales response to advertising is similar in all territories.

In the case of the coffee company, King's Crown (name is disguised), the advertising allocation procedure was more complicated:

> King's Crown has found that a close correlation appears to exist between the degree of brand acceptance that has already been achieved in a given market

---

[7]The setting aside of some markets to test the effect of alternative levels of marketing expenditure is a sophisticated approach to estimating the sales response function; the results can become part of an adaptive control system for determining advertising expenditure. See John D. C. Little, "A Model of Adaptive Control of Promotional Spending," *Operations Research* (Nov. 1966) 1075–1097. Little's model is discussed here in Chap. 10, 279–282.

and the responsiveness of sales volume to advertising expenditures in that market. Therefore, one of the major factors used in determining how much money is to be allocated is the market's "BD Rating" (Brand Development Rating), based upon unit sales per thousand population (or per thousand households). Empirical evidence indicates that advertising expenditures fall on most fertile ground where BD Ratings are already highest; therefore, King's Crown tries to allocate its money where brand penetration (i.e., sales *density*, rather than sales *volume*) is greatest, regardless of the size of the market. [8]

Marschner examined the procedure in detail and concluded that King's Crown actually was assigning money on the basis of sales volume already achieved, rather than sales density, because the latter was estimated from the former. The company's spending procedures also ignored the possibility that a point of diminishing marginal returns might be reached.

On the basis of this and other studies, it can be concluded that company practices in allocating marketing budgets to territories are far from ideal, even in large progressive companies. Practice is handicapped by frequent confusions between actual sales and sales potential, industry sales and company sales, and average sales and marginal sales. With this as background, we can now examine the principles of optimally allocating the marketing budget to sales territories.

THEORY OF ALLOCATING THE MARKET BUDGET TO TERRITORIES

It was stated earlier that the average level of current sales in a territory has no necessary connection with the probable marginal sales response of the territory to additional marketing inputs. In general, size rules for allocation are wrong because they confuse "average" and "marginal" sales response. Figure 6-2 shows the difference between the two and the fact that there is no reason to assume they are correlated. The two dots in the figure show present company sales and marketing expenditures in two territories. Company sales are $40,000 in territory 1 and only half, or $20,000 in territory 2; the company spends $3000 on marketing in both territories. The average sales response to a dollar of marketing effort is thus greater in territory 1 than territory 2; it is 40/3 as opposed to 20/3, respectively. It might seem desirable, therefore, to shift funds out of territory 2 into territory 1, where the average response is greater. Yet the real issue is one of the marginal response. The marginal response is represented by the *slope* of the sales function through the points. A higher slope has been drawn for territory 2 than for territory 1. The respective slopes show that another $1000 of marketing expenditure would produce a $10,000 sales increase in territory 2 and only a $2000 sales increase in territory 1. Clearly, marginal response, not average response, should guide the allocation of marketing funds.

Marginal response is indicated along the sales response function for each territory. We shall assume that a company is able to estimate territorial sales response functions by statistical regression or expert query techniques.[9] Suppose that the sales response functions for two territories are those shown in Figure 6-3. The company wishes to allocate its budget B to the two territories to maximize profits. When costs are identical for the two territories, then the allocation that will maximize profits is the one that will maximize sales. The funds are optimally allocated when (1) they exhaust the budget, and (2) the marginal sales response is the same in both territories. Geometrically, this means that the slopes of the tangents to the two sales response functions at the optimal allocations will be equal. Figure 6-3 shows that a budget of $6 million would be allocated in the amount of approximately $4.6 million to territory 1 and $1.4 million to territory 2; at this level the marginal sales response to new dollars would be the same in either territory.

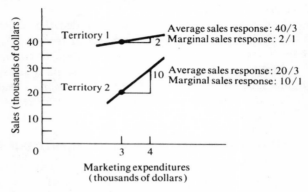

Figure 6-2 Average and Marginal Sales Response

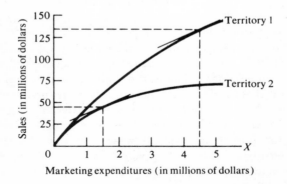

Figure 6-3 Sales Response Functions in Two Company Territories

[9]See Chap. 19 for a discussion of data gathering and estimation methods.

Having examined the principle of optimal allocation in geometric terms, we shall now develop an algebraic solution that includes territorial cost differences, as well as sales response differences in the analysis. Consider two company territories with the following sales response functions:[10]

$$Q_1 = a_1 X_1^{b_1} \tag{6-2}$$

$$Q_2 = a_2 X_2^{b_2} \tag{6-3}$$

where Q = number of units demanded
  X = marketing dollars
  a = scale coefficient, $a > 0$
  b = elasticity exponent, $0 < b < 1$

Thus sales response in the two territories may differ, both in their elasticities and in their scale. The effect of the elasticity versus the scale coefficient on the shape of the demand function is shown in Figure 6-4. The closer the elasticity approaches 1, the more linear and constant the sales response; whereas the higher the coefficient, the greater the magnitude of the sales response.

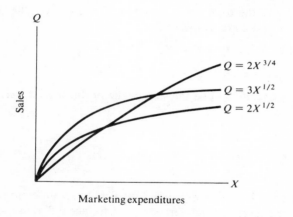

Figure 6-4 **Illustrations of the Demand Function** $Q = aX^b$ (with $0 < b < 1$)

In the case of cost, assume that total costs start at a certain positive level (F), increase at a decreasing rate at first because of economies of scale, and then increase at an increasing rate as production approaches capacity. This type of cost function is illustrated in Figure 6-5 and can be expressed by a cubic equation. The total cost functions for territories 1 and 2 are

$$C_1 = F_1 + c_1 Q_1 - d_1 Q_1^2 + e_1 Q_1^3 + X_1 \tag{6-4}$$

$$C_2 = F_2 + c_2 Q_2 - d_2 Q_2^2 + e_2 Q_2^3 + X_2 \tag{6-5}$$

---

[10]Other forms of the sales response function could have been used, leading to different specific solutions, although the general solution method is the same.

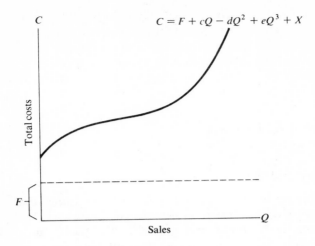

$$C = F + cQ - dQ^2 + eQ^3 + X$$

Figure 6-5   A Cubic Total Cost Function

The next step is to derive the total profit function, $Z = PQ - C$. The profit functions for territories 1 and 2 are, respectively,

$$Z_1 = (P_1 - c_1)Q_1 + d_1 Q_1^2 - e_1 Q_1^3 - F_1 - X_1 \tag{6-6}$$

$$Z_2 = (P_2 - c_2)Q_2 + d_2 Q_2^2 - e_2 Q_2^3 - F_2 - X_2 \tag{6-7}$$

The total profit for the company will be the sum of the profit in each territory, that is,

$$Z = Z_1 + Z_2 \tag{6-8}$$

$$Z = (P_1 - c_1)Q_1 + d_1 Q_1^2 - e_1 Q_1^3 - F_1 - X_1 + (P_2 - c_2)Q_2 + d_2 Q_2^2 \tag{6-9}$$
$$- e_2 Q_2^3 - F_2 - X_2$$

Note that the profit function Equation 6-9 allows the firm to set different prices and marketing expenditure levels in each territory and to face different costs.

A Digression on Constrained Maximization; the Lagrangian Multiplier Technique

At this point, the condition is introduced that the firm has a certain budget B that it wishes to allocate between the two territories in the amounts (X_1, X_2) in such a way that $X_1 + X_2 = B$ and profits Z are maximized. The general solution procedure for this type of problem in which a differentiable and continuous function is to be maximized (or minimized) subject to one or more constraints (here, a given budget level) is known as the Lagrangian technique.[11] The

---

[11]See Charles R. Carr and Charles W. Howe, *Quantitative Decision Procedures in Management and Economics: Deterministic Theory and Applications* (New York: McGraw-Hill, Inc., 1964), pp. 248–252. If the functions are not continuous and differentiable, mathematical programming is an alternative technique for finding solutions to constrained maximization problems. For an example involving products, see Chap. 7, pp. 170–173.

technique calls for forming a function called the Lagrangian expression and maximizing this expression in the ordinary way, that is, by finding the first derivatives of all the decision variables, setting each equal to 0, and solving the resulting set of equations simultaneously. The Lagrangian expression consists of the original profit function with a term added for each constraint. The added term is formed in the following way. First note that the constraint in our problem is

$$X_1 + X_2 = B \tag{6-10}$$

that is, the dollars allocated to both territories should exhaust the budget. This constraint can be restated as

$$B - X_1 - X_2 = 0 \tag{6-11}$$

This constraint is now multiplied by an unspecified parameter λ called the Lagrangian multiplier:

$$\lambda(B - X_1 - X_2) \tag{6-12}$$

This term is now added to the original profit function, and the new profit function is called the Lagrangian expression L:

$$\begin{aligned} L = {} & (P_1 - c_1)Q_1 + d_1 Q_1{}^2 - e_1 Q_1{}^3 - F_1 - X_1 \\ & + (P_2 - c_2)Q_2 + d_2 Q_2{}^2 - e_2 Q_2{}^3 - F_2 - X_2 \\ & + \lambda(B - X_1 - X_2) \end{aligned} \tag{6-13}$$

We must now describe how finding the pair (X_1, X_2) that would maximize this expression would succeed in maximizing profits subject to the budgetary constraint. The central theorem of Lagrangian multiplier theory is that any values (X_1, X_2) which maximize the value of the profit function subject to the stated constraint(s) will also maximize the Lagrangian expression, and vice versa. In the discussion it will be helpful to think of the Lagrangian multiplier as standing for the amount that would be added to profit if the marketing budget were increased by \$1. Suppose that a solution appeared in which the budget was fully allocated and yet extra budget dollars had a positive marginal profitability, that is $\lambda > 0$. Then,

$$\lambda(B - X_1 - X_2) = 0 \qquad \lambda > 0; \ (B - X_1 - X_2) = 0 \tag{6-14}$$

and this term in the Lagrangian expression has no effect on the original profit equation. Now suppose the solution called for spending less money than was available, that is,

$$B - X_1 - X_2 > 0 \tag{6-15}$$

This could only mean that the marginal profit potential of the unused budget dollars is 0 (or else they would have been used), that is, $\lambda = 0$. Then

$$\lambda(B - X_1 - X_2) = 0 \tag{6-16}$$

and this term in the Lagrangian expression has no effect on the original profit function.

Figure 6-6 Finding the Optimal Marketing Expenditure With and Without a Budget Constraint

Typically, budgets are constraining and the marginal profitability of extra budgetary resources will be positive. Figure 6-6 shows a hypothetical profit function estimated for different levels of total marketing expenditure. The global maximum profit would be attained with a budget of B_3, and this would be revealed by ordinary maximization calculus applied to the function. However, if the budget is constrained to B_2, the Lagrangian technique will locate the highest profit within the constrained range of marketing expenditure. There is one important exception: the Lagrangian technique does not evaluate the end points because they are not differentiable. Since B_0 is such an end point, it would not be evaluated, even though it turns out to be the profit maximizing marketing expenditure within the constrained range. Also, B_2 would have been yielded as the profit maximizing marketing expenditure by the Lagrangian technique. Note that the slope of a tangent to the profit function at B_2 is positive, that is, $\lambda > 0$; therefore a larger budget than B_2 would add profits. To check on the possibility that end points are sometimes the maxima/minima, they should be examined separately by inserting them in the Lagrangian expression, calculating the resulting profits Z for these values, and comparing these profit figures with those derived after the maxima/minima of the function have been determined using the Lagrangian function. In the normal case, the Lagrangian technique yields two useful results:

1. The allocation of marketing effort (X_1, X_2) that will just exhaust the budget and maximize profits under the given constraint
2. The marginal profitability of one extra dollar above the budget, that is, λ

Having examined the logic of the Lagrangian expression for problems in constrained maximization, let us return to the maximization of Equation 6-13. The task is to find the first three partial derivatives of the Lagrangian expression (Equation 6-13) with respect to X_1, X_2, and λ, and set each equal to 0:

$$\frac{\partial L}{\partial X_1} = (P_1 - c_1)a_1 b_1 X_1^{b_1-1} + 2d_1 a_1{}^2 b_1 X_1^{2b_1-1} - 3e_1 a_1{}^3 b_1 X_1^{3b_1-1} - 1 - \lambda = 0$$

$$(6\text{-}17)$$

$$\frac{\partial L}{\partial X_2} = (P_2 - c_2)a_2 b_2 X_2^{b_2-1} + 2d_2 a_2{}^2 b_2 X_2^{2b_2-1} - 3e_2 a_2{}^3 b_2 X_2^{3b_2-1} - 1 - \lambda = 0$$

$$(6\text{-}18)$$

$$\frac{\partial L}{\partial \lambda} = B - X_1 - X_2 = 0 \qquad\qquad (6\text{-}19)$$

Now rewrite Equation 6-19 with X_2 on the left-hand side, substitute this in Equation 6-18, and equate Equations 6-17 and 6-18, since both are equal to 0:

$$(P_1 - c_1)a_1 b_1 X_1^{b_1-1} + 2d_1 a_1{}^2 b_1 X_1^{2b_1-1} - 3e_1 a_1{}^3 b_1 X_1^{3b_1-1} \qquad (6\text{-}20)$$
$$= (P_2 - c_2)a_2 b_2 (B - X_1)^{b_2-1} + 2d_2 a_2{}^2 b_2 (B - X_1)^{2b_2-1} - 3e_2 a_2{}^3 b_2 (B - X_1)^{3b_2-1}$$

This whole expression is a function of X_1 and there exists one or more X_1, given a budget B, that satisfies the expression. The X_1 is (are) the root(s) of this equation, and one of these roots will yield a constrained maximum Z. Once we find X_1^*, it can be placed in Equation 6-10 to find X_2^*, and the territory allocation problem is solved.

To find the roots of Equation 6-20 is a formidable task. Assuming that all the coefficients and elasticities have been measured, the analyst might use grid search techniques, trying out successive values of X_1 to locate the value(s) that bring equality between the two sides of the equation.[12]

Solution with Linear Costs and Equal Marketing Expenditure Elasticities

Another approach is to simplify some of the assumptions underlying the equation to produce a modified equation that is solvable. For example, if we assume that (1) total costs increase linearly rather than nonlinearly with sales and (2) the marketing expenditure elasticities are the same in both territories, then Equation 6-20 reduces to the following solution:[13]

$$X_1^* = B\left[\frac{(m_1 a_1)^\alpha}{(m_1 a_1)^\alpha + (m_2 a_2)^\alpha}\right] \qquad (6\text{-}21)$$

where $\alpha = 1/1 - b$ and $m_i = P_i - c_i$, the gross margin. The bracketed term shows the fraction of the budget B that should go into territory 1. To gain some insight into this fraction, consider three cases.

Case 1. Assume that the two territories have the same scale response to marketing expenditures (i.e., $a_1 = a_2$) and yield the same gross margins (i.e., $m_1 = m_2$). Then Equation 6-21 becomes

$$X_1^* = \frac{B}{2} \qquad\qquad (6\text{-}22)$$

---

[12]For a good discussion of optimal seeking methods in the face of analytically intractable functions, see Douglass J. Wilde, *Optimum Seeking Methods* (Englewood Cliffs, N.J.: Prentice-Hall, Inc., 1964).

[13]See Appendix Mathematical Note 6–1.

Since the assumptions made the two territories identical, it is not surprising that optimal allocation consists of dividing the funds equally between the two territories.

Case 2. Assume that the two territories differ only in the scale of response to marketing expenditures (i.e., $a_1 \neq a_2$). Then Equation 6-21 becomes

$$X_1^* = B\left(\frac{a_1^{\alpha}}{a_1^{\alpha}+a_2^{\alpha}}\right) \tag{6-23}$$

The bracketed term shows the proportion of B that should be allocated to territory 1 for an optimum solution. Clearly, more than half of the budget should go to territory 1 whenever $a_1 > a_2$. Equation 6-23 shows the specific form of the fraction of the budget that should go to territory 1 and how it depends on the relative scales of response.[14]

Case 3. Assume that the two territories differ in the scale of response (i.e., $a_1 \neq a_2$) and in gross margin (i.e., $m_1 \neq m_2$). Note that if the gross margins in the two territories are equal, we have the solution in Case 2. In fact, when the gross margins are equal, the allocation that maximizes total profits is the same as the allocation that maximizes total sales. When gross margins are unequal as a result of different costs and/or prices in the two territories, this obviously affects the solution. In fact, the solution is the one shown in Equation 6-21; its only difference from Equation 6-23 is that the a_1 are weighted by their respective gross margins. If $m_1 > m_2$, that is, territory 1 yields more unit gross margin than territory 2, then territory 1's share of the budget is further increased from one half, though not proportionately. In fact, whether territory one or two gets more than one half of the budget depends strictly upon whether

$$m_1 a_1 \underset{<}{\overset{>}{\gtrless}} m_2 a_2 \tag{6-24}$$

Thus a territory that is 10 percent better than another territory in the scale of sales response but 10 percent worse in unit gross margin would receive half of the budget.

The case of n territories. The solution shown in Equation 6-21 generalizes to

---

[14]The solution in Equation 6–23 is almost identical to the one developed by J. A. Nordin in his "Spatial Allocation of Selling Expenses," *Journal of Marketing* (Jan. 1943) 210–219. The small difference is caused by the fact that Nordin defines his sales function in a reversed fashion (using our notation):

$$X = aQ^b$$

where X = marketing expenditure level, Q = quantity sold, and a, b = parameters.

Nordin states the problem as one of determining the level of marketing expenditures necessary to achieve a given level of sales, rather than as one of sales being determined by the level of marketing expenditures. His formulation can be confusing because one could interpret his equation as the company decision rule for determining how much to spend on marketing as a percentage of current sales. It is important to put the "effect" variable on the left-hand side and make it a function of the "cause" variables on the right-hand side. As a result of his using a company decision rule instead of a sales response function, his solution is slightly different from the one presented here.

n territories. Given a linear cost function and equal marketing expenditure elasticities in all territories, Equation 6-21 becomes:[15]

$$X_1^* = B\left[\frac{(m_1 a_1)^\alpha}{\sum_{i=1}^n (m_i a_i)^\alpha}\right]$$
(6-25)

Example.   Assume that a company sells in two territories and the estimated demand functions are, respectively,

$$Q_1 = 6X_1^{1/2}$$
(6-26)

$$Q_2 = 3X_2^{1/2}$$
(6-27)

Territory 1 shows twice the response to promotional marketing expenditures as territory 2, although in both cases there are diminishing marginal returns. The total costs of selling in the two territories are

$$C_1 = 60 + 4Q_1 + X_1$$
(6-28)

$$C_2 = 28 + 5Q_2 + X_2$$
(6-29)

Territory 1 can be thought of as the company's home territory and territory 2 as a distant territory. The fixed cost is substantially higher in territory 1 because of the presence of the main plant and headquarters, but the unit variable cost is lower because of lower shipment costs to customers. Now assume that average prices in the two territories are $P_1 = \$7$, $P_2 = \$9$. The average price is lower in the home territory because it is a larger market and has attracted more competition.

The company's sales in the last period were $407 (in thousands). Management typically sets the promotional marketing budget (i.e., advertising and personal selling) at 16 percent of sales. This means that the promotional budget for the coming year is $65 (in thousands). The company is seeking to divide funds optimally between the two territories. How much of the budget should be spent in the home territory, considering that it responds better to promotion and shows lower unit variable costs but, on the other hand, shows higher fixed costs and brings in a lower price per unit?

The solution will be developed using the Lagrangian approach. (We shall assume that the general solution in Equation 6-21 is not available.) First the Lagrangian profit function is formed as in Equation 6-13:

$$L = (7-4)6X_1^{1/2} - 60 - X_1 + (9-5)3X_2^{1/2} - 28 - X_2 + \lambda(65 - X_1 - X_2)$$
(6-30)

$$L = 18X_1^{1/2} - 60 - X_1 + 12X_2^{1/2} - 28 - X_2 + \lambda(65 - X_1 - X_2)$$
(6-31)

Then find the first three partial derivatives of L in Equation 6-31 with respect to X_1, X_2, and λ, and set each of them equal to 0:

$$\frac{\partial L}{\partial X_1} = 9X_1^{-1/2} - 1 - \lambda = 0$$
(6-32)

[15]See Appendix Mathematical Note 6–2.

$$\frac{\partial L}{\partial X_2} = 6X_2^{-1/2} - 1 - \lambda = 0 \qquad (6\text{-}33)$$

$$\frac{\partial L}{\partial \lambda} = 65 - X_1 - X_2 = 0 \qquad (6\text{-}34)$$

Setting Equations 6-32 and 6-33 equal to each other, we have

$$9X_1^{-1/2} = 6X_2^{-1/2} \qquad (6\text{-}35)$$

Substituting Equation 6-34 as solved for X_2 into Equation 6-35, we find that Equation 6-35 becomes

$$9X_1^{-1/2} = 6(65 - X_1)^{-1/2} \qquad (6\text{-}36)$$

Solving Equation 6-36 for X_1^*, we find $X_1^* = \$45$ (this and the following dollar figures are in thousands of dollars). Thus territory 1 receives $45 and territory 2 receives the remaining $20. This allocation of the $65 will generate total profits of $21.40, according to Equation 6-31. Total sales will be $402.50 and the company's profits to sales ratio will be 5.3 percent.

We might question whether this return on sales can be increased by changing the size of the promotional budget. For, while the company has divided the budget of $65 in the optimal way, it cannot be sure that the budget itself is at the optimal level. One way to check this is to determine the value of an extra dollar of promotional expenditure by solving the same problem again, except using a budget of $66.

Rather than carry out this lengthy calculation, a more direct method of checking is available. This consists of calculating the marginal profit. The Lagrangian multiplier λ shows the change in profit that would result from adding one more $1(000) to the budget. It can be solved using Equation 6-32:

$$\lambda = 9X_1^{-1/2} - 1 = \frac{9}{\sqrt{45}} - 1 = 1.34 - 1 = 0.34 \qquad (6\text{-}37)$$

Since the marginal profit is positive, this means that increasing the promotional budget will produce additional profit. Specifically, an increase to $66 will produce $0.34 additional profit. However, we still do not know how much the promotional budget should be increased.

To determine the optimal budget level, we make use of the fact that λ, the marginal profit on an extra $1(000), will be 0 when the budget is optimal. Substituting $\lambda = 0$ into Equations 6-32 and 6-33, we get, after rearranging terms:

$$9X_1^{-1/2} = 1 \quad \text{or} \quad X_1 = 81 \qquad (6\text{-}38)$$

$$6X_2^{-1/2} = 1 \quad \text{or} \quad X_2 = 36 \qquad (6\text{-}39)$$

Therefore the optimal budget will be $117 divided between X_1 and X_2, as shown. This will yield a profit of $29, sales of $540, and a resulting profit to sales ratio of 5.4 percent, an increase of 0.1 percent over the return on the constrained budget.

A Second Example.[16]   The XYZ Company is a medium-size hardware manufacturer employing a direct sales force of forty-two salesmen. Forty of the salesmen work in the company's Eastern territory, where its plant and facilities are located; two of the salesmen work in the Western territory, which the company opened up a few years earlier. The forty Eastern salesmen sell direct to retailers, while the two Western salesmen sell to wholesale distributors who in turn sell to retailers. Because the two Western salesmen sell through distributors, they each account for approximately five times the sales volume sold by the average Eastern salesman. Specifically, the forty Eastern salesmen in the previous year accounted for $6 million of sales ($150,000 a man), while the two Western salesmen accounted for $1.5 million of sales ($750,000 a man). The company felt that it should reconsider whether it had divided the forty-two salesmen in the best ratio between the two territories. Specifically, should more of its men be selling in the West? The company also wanted to examine whether forty-two men constituted the optimal size sales force.

The first step taken by the management was to estimate the demand function in each territory. Management strongly felt that potential company sales had an upper limit of approximately $12 million in each territory. Management also felt that, as more salesmen were assigned to either market, actual sales would approach the saturation level asymptotically and exponentially. These two assumptions meant that the demand function was taken to have the form of a modified exponential equation:[17]

$$S = \bar{S}(1 - e^{-aN}) \tag{6-40}$$

where S = estimated sales per period (in dollars)
$\bar{S}$ = saturation level of sales per period
e = the mathematical constant 2.718 ...
a = the rate at which sales approach the saturation level of sales
N = number of salesmen in the territory

To employ this equation form, management needed to estimate $\bar{S}$ and a for each of the two territories. For each territory, $\bar{S}$ had already been estimated as $12 million, the estimate presumably being based on the number of customers in the territory, their buying rate, competitive activity, and other factors entering into an estimate of sales potential. This left the task of estimating the response coefficient a for each territory. Some members of management felt that this should be estimated by forming educated guesses as to the likely level of sales with different numbers of salesmen, plotting the estimates, and fitting the appropriate modified exponential curve through the estimates. Other members of management felt that it would be more objective to use last year's sales and

---

[16]The example is patterned after a case described in Robert D. Buzzell, *Mathematical Models and Marketing Management* (Boston: Division of Research, Graduate School of Business Administration, Harvard University, 1964), pp. 136–156. The case dealt with an analysis of the optimum mix of direct and wholesale salesmen for the Engineered Products Corporation (fictional name).

[17]See Chap. 2, Figure 2–4(c).

sales force size in each territory as the key observation for finding a.[18] It takes only one historical observation to fit a curve that depends on only one parameter. This latter view prevailed and the equation for the Eastern region (E) was solved in the following way. Since the company estimated $\bar{S}$ at \$12,000 (in thousands) and forty Eastern salesmen sold \$6000 (in thousands) last year, they inserted this information in Equation 6-40:

$$6000 = 12{,}000\,(1 - e^{-a_E(40)}) \tag{6-41}$$

This leaves only a_E to be estimated. Since there is one equation and one unknown, a_E can be solved:

$$1 - e^{-40a_E} = .5 \tag{6-42}$$

$$e^{-40a_E} = .5 \tag{6-43}$$

$$e^{40a_E} = 2 \tag{6-44}$$

$$a_E = .01725 \tag{6-45}$$

Therefore the demand equation for the Eastern territory is

$$S_E = 12{,}000\,(1 - e^{-.01725N_E}) \tag{6-46}$$

A similar analysis for the Western territory (W), this time using the information that two men sold \$1500 (in thousands) last year, yields $a_W = .065$. Therefore the demand equation for the Western territory is

$$S_W = 12{,}000\,(1 - e^{-.065N_W}) \tag{6-47}$$

The next step called for estimating the cost of selling in each of the territories. The company's fixed costs were estimated at \$2000 (in thousands). The company's salesmen averaged \$12,000 in salary and commissions. The company's expenses of distribution were lower in the East than in the West, so that when these were added to the unit production costs, the company's production and distribution expense for every dollar of sales in the East was \$.623 and in the West was \$.682. The total cost equation therefore is

$$C = 2000 + 12(N_E + N_W) + .623S_E + .682S_W \tag{6-48}$$

The preceding estimates of the demand and cost functions permitted management to express the profit function:

$$Z = S_E + S_W - 2000 - 12(N_E + N_W) - .623S_E - .682S_W \tag{6-49}$$

$$Z = .377S_E + .318S_W - 2000 - 12(N_E + N_W) \tag{6-50}$$

$$Z = .377[12{,}000(1 - e^{-.01725N_E})] + .318[12{,}000(1 - e^{-.065N_W})] \\ - 2000 - 12(N_E + N_W) \tag{6-51}$$

Given the profit function, we can now estimate the optimal allocation of the

---

[18]These two contrasting philosophies of fitting a function, the subjective and the objective, are discussed in detail in Chap. 19.

forty-two salesmen between the two territories and the optimal total number of salesmen.

Optimal allocation of the salesmen. This problem calls for finding the number of salesmen in each territory (N_E, N_W) that will maximize the profit function Z subject to the constraint that $N = N_E + N_W = 42$. The solution is found by forming the Lagrangian profit function:

$$L = .377[12,000(1 - e^{-.01725N_E})] + .318[12,000(1 - e^{-.065N_W})]$$
$$- 2000 - 12(N_E + N_W) + \lambda(N - N_E - N_W) \qquad (6\text{-}52)$$

Now find the first three partial derivatives with respect to N_E, N_W, and λ and set them equal to 0:

$$\frac{\partial L}{\partial N_E} = 78.039e^{-.01725N_E} - 12 - \lambda = 0 \qquad (6\text{-}53)$$

$$\frac{\partial L}{\partial N_W} = 248.04e^{-.065N}{}_W - 12 - \lambda = 0 \qquad (6\text{-}54)$$

$$\frac{\partial L}{\partial \lambda} = N - N_E - N_W = 0 \qquad (6\text{-}55)$$

Setting Equations 6-53 and 6-54 equal to each other and rearranging Equation 6-55 to read $N_W = N - N_E$, we get

$$78.039e^{-.01725N_E} = 248.04e^{-.065(N - N_E)} \qquad (6\text{-}56)$$

Solving Equation 6-56 for N_E, we obtain

$$N_E = .79N - 14.07 \qquad (6\text{-}57)$$

Substituting $N_E = N - N_W$ into Equation 6-57, we obtain

$$N_W = .21N + 14.07 \qquad (6\text{-}58)$$

This solution is general and enables the optimal territorial allocation to be solved for any size sales force N. Since the sales force in the example is forty-two, then:

$$N_E = .79(42) - 14.07 = 19 \qquad (6\text{-}59)$$

$$N_W = .21(42) + 14.07 = 23 \qquad (6\text{-}60)$$

This suggests that the company should assign twenty-three of its forty-two men to the West, leaving nineteen in the East. The men in the West will sell to distributors and the men in the East will sell to retailers. This reallocation is estimated to increase profits from $215 (in thousands) to $1714 (in thousands), ignoring any costs of changeover. Naturally, this conclusion should be thoroughly reviewed in the light of the assumptions and data before implementing it.

The solution also permits the determination of the optimum territorial allocation for any other size salesforce. Figure 6-7 shows the optimum territorial allocation of other possible sales force sizes. Note that, with a small sales force, most of the men should be in the West; with a large sales force, most of the men should be in the East. Another way of putting this is that a small company should rely primarily on selling through distributors, while a large company should rely primarily on selling direct.

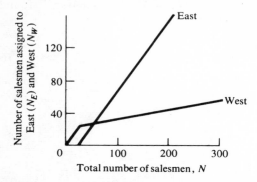

Figure 6-7   Most Profitable Allocation of Salesforce to East and West for Various Sizes of Total Sales force

Optimal number of salesmen. The other question concerns the optimal-size sales force for this company. For this solution, we differentiate the original profit function without the Lagrangian budget constraint with respect to N_E and N_W and set the derivatives equal to 0 and solve:

$$\frac{\partial Z}{\partial N_E} = 78.039e^{-.01725N_E} - 12 = 0 \tag{6-61}$$

Therefore $N_E \cong 110$.

$$\frac{\partial Z}{\partial N_W} = 248.04e^{-.065N_W} - 12 = 0 \tag{6-62}$$

Therefore $N_W \cong 46$.

This solution says that, if each territory is considered a separate profit maximizing opportunity, the company should expand its Eastern sales force to 110 men and its Western sales force to 46 men. While this conclusion should be reexamined very carefully for its sensitivity to different assumptions, it does suggest that the company has been operating far below its profit potential and should plan to expand its sales force substantially over the next several years.

SUMMARY

A great number of companies operate in several geographical areas, called territories. In principle, each territory could be analyzed separately in terms of its demand and cost characteristics and the marketing budget set, so as to optimize the company's profits from the territory. The company's total marketing budget is thus built up as the sum of the separate territorial budgets. In practice, companies tend to set up a total marketing budget first (what is affordable, traditional, etc.) and then seek to divide it among the territories. The budget is divided among the territories according to relative sales potential, relative industry sales, or relative company sales, although all of these bases are faulty in theoretical terms. Companies act as if their stronger territories (or their weaker territories) deserve proportionately more support, although there is nothing in the logic of being a strong or weak territory that indicates the proper support level.

The theory of allocating a fixed budget optimally to different territories requires the use of the territorial sales response functions and territorial cost function. A complicated solution was found for the case of two territories with different marketing expenditure elasticities and nonlinear costs. A simplified solution was then found for the case of two territories with the same marketing expenditure elasticity and linear costs. The best allocation was found to depend on the two territories' respective gross margins and scales of response. The solution was then generalized for the case of n territories. Two numerical examples were presented to illustrate the method, which largely consists of solving problems in constrained maximization through the use of the Lagrangian multiplier technique.

Questions and Problems

1. An executive recently recommended allocating advertising expenditures to various markets in proportion to sales in these markets. His reasons were as follows: In the absence of further company advertising a fixed (but unknown) percentage of sales in each market would be lost to competitors. The role of advertising is to hold present customers or to replace them. Therefore, the promotional level in each market should be proportional to the sales level. Do you agree?

2. A manufacturer estimates the relationship between sales and marketing expenditures for each of three major sales regions A, B, and C. The estimated sales volumes (in millions) for different levels of marketing expenditure are shown below:

		Regions		
		A	B	C
	1	10	2	5
Marketing	2	14	8	6
Dollars	3	16	9	10
	4	17	9	12
	5	17	9	13

The manufacturer's marketing budget for the year is $5 million. How should he allocate this budget to maximize his total sales?

3. A manufacturer of men's dress shirts has a promotional budget of $80 (in thousands) and wishes to determine which allocation of this budget between his two

territories will maximize profits. The demand functions for territories 1 and 2 are:

$$Q_1 = 10X_1^{1/2}, \quad Q_2 = 5X_2^{1/2}$$

where X_i is the amount of promotional dollars spent in territory i. The respective cost functions are:

$$C_1 = 100 + 6Q_i + X_1, \quad C_2 = 30 + 4Q_2 + X_2$$

(a) If $P_1 = \$7$ and $P_2 = \$8$, what is the optimal allocation of the budget between the two territories?

(b) Could additional profits be made by increasing the budget?

(c) What is the optimal budget?

4. A company wishes to find the optimal budget allocation rule for its two territories. These territories share a common elasticity of sales response to promotional dollars of $b_1 = b_2 = 1/2$. They differ, however, in gross margins (m) and scale response coefficients (a), that is, $m_1 = 2$, $m_2 = 3$, $a_1 = 6$, and $a_2 = 5$. What portion of the promotional budget should be allotted to each territory?

5. A manufacturer is preparing his advertising budget for next year. He has been operating at capacity and has made no plans to expand capacity because of high interest rates. He sells in two territories and wants to maintain the same sales level in each territory. The following information exists about each territory:

	Territory 1	Territory 2
Sales response coefficient	4	5
Remaining sales potential as a percentage of total potential	.2	.4
Sales decay coefficient	.1	.2
Present level of sales	100,000	200,000

How much should he spend on advertising?

6. The example on pages 157–160 suggests a reallocation of the company's 42 salesmen in its two territories. Review this recommendation in the light of the assumptions made, and indicate the considerations which are neglected in the mathematical solution.

7. Given the sales response function $S_w = \bar{S}_w(1 - e^{-a_w N_w})$, and $N = 2$, $S_w = 1500$, and $\bar{S}_w = 12,000$, prove that $a_w = .065$.

CHAPTER 7
Multiple Products

We have considered several complications in the theory of marketing programming that are all related to the case of a single product. Yet most companies produce two or more products and the problem of allocating company budgets and developing marketing strategies for the individual products occupies much of management's time. Therefore it behooves us to look at effective marketing decision making in the context of multiple products.

It might seem strange at first that the management of two or more products poses new analytical problems that cannot be handled in ways previously discussed. If the question is one of how much to spend on each product, could this not be settled separately for each product on the basis of its own demand and cost function? Or if the question is how much each product should receive of a given budget, could this not be solved in the same way as the multiple territory problem?

The new elements in this problem are the *demand and cost interdependencies* found among the products in a company's line. This is not true of multiple territories, where we can usually assume that the demand in each territory is independent of the demand in every other territory and the cost of serving each territory is independent of the cost of serving every other territory. On the other hand, two company products are likely to be interrelated in demand and/or cost. *Two company products are said to be interrelated in demand when the price or some other element of the marketing mix of one affects the demand for the other.* Economists use the concept of "cross elasticity of demand" to express and measure the interdependence.[1] A positive cross elasticity means that two products are substitutes, a negative cross elasticity means that two products are complements, and a zero (or low) cross elasticity means that two products are unrelated in demand. If a television manufacturer lowered the price of his color television sets, this would decrease the demand for his black and white sets (substitutes), increase the demand for his color TV table stands (complements), and probably would not affect the demand for his pocket radios. Before changing the price of any single item in his line, the seller must consider the various product cross elasticities to determine the likely overall impact on his total profits.[2]

Two products are said to be interrelated in cost when a change in the output of one affects the cost of the other. By-products and joint products are related in this sense. If the output of pork is cut down, so will the output of ham. As a result, the unit cost of the ham that is produced will rise because the overhead is spread over fewer units. More generally, any two products using the same production facilities are interrelated on the cost side even if they are not joint products. This is true under any cost accounting practice that requires a full allocation of costs. Thus management must examine various cost interactions among products before it considers changing the output level of any product in its line.

Management faces three basic types of problems in the management of multiple products. One can be called the *multiproduct marketing strategy problem* and deals with the issue of determining optimal budgets and marketing strategies for all the products *currently* in the product line. Some of the firm's current products are highly profitable, others are of medium profitability, and still others are of low or negative profitability. Furthermore, the company's products are likely to have interrelationships both on the demand and on the cost side. The products also tend to be managed by different product or brand managers who are very competitive in their budget requests for company funds. For all these reasons the allocation of company marketing funds to different products and the development of effective marketing strategies is a formidable task. The job, however, must be done, and we shall consider in this chapter the logic of developing marketing budgets and strategies for company products with demand and cost interrelationships.

The second basic problem is called the *production rate problem* and deals with the issue of how much the company should plan to produce and sell of each of

---

[1]Technically, the price cross elasticity of demand (e_{cp}) is the percentage change in the quantity sold of product A associated with a percentage change in the price of product B. In symbols, we have

$$e_{cp} = \frac{\Delta Q_A / Q_A}{\Delta P_B / P_B}$$

The concept of cross elasticity is equally applicable to any other element of the marketing mix.

[2]An example of the measurement and use of price cross elasticities is developed in Chap. 12, pp. 362–364.

its existing products in the coming planning period. In one sense, this problem has already been solved by the choice of budgets and marketing strategies. The budgets and marketing strategies lead to a certain expected sales level of each product that manufacturing should be prepared to supply. Yet, in practice, marketing and production people use different standards in planning the sales and output mix. Marketing managers tend to emphasize relative profit margins as a guide to setting relative outputs; production managers tend to emphasize fixed production resources as a guide to setting relative outputs. An example and analysis of this problem will be presented in the second section of this chapter.

The third basic problem, called the *product mix* problem, deals with the issue of which products to add, retain, and drop. Some of the company's products are just starting out; others are in the peak of their performance; and still others are becoming weak. The firm must consider which new products to add to its line and which old products to phase out. We shall not evaluate individual products here; instead we shall discuss the optimal portfolio of products in the third section of this chapter.[3]

Allocating Marketing Funds to Products in Practice

Before examining these three product management problems, it would be helpful to consider how companies typically divide their total marketing budget among the products in their line. We will leave out the role of purely political factors such as negotiation and persuasion that managers use to influence the size of their budget.[4] Instead we shall concentrate on the overt criteria for allocating the budget over products in the line.

One way to describe the annual budgeting of funds to products is to say that the allocations are heavily precedent-oriented. The starting point for the new budgets seems to be the previous year's allocations. If the company decides on a 10 percent overall budget increase, it may make a 10 percent increase in funds available to every product manager. An across the board increase, although completely indefensible in theory, is often resorted to because it entails the least political complication, for there can be no charge of favoritism or any implied criticism of individual managers' performance. However, it is a decision that avoids evaluation, and this is its main weakness.

More frequently, management will make some adjustments away from a strictly across the board solution. Some of the products that are doing poorly may be given proportionately less support and indeed they may be set up for phasing out altogether; products doing extremely well may get a proportionately greater increase than 10 percent; and the remaining products will get an across the board increase of 10 percent.[5] The reasoning still takes place around the use

---

[3]The evaluation of individual products to add to the line is discussed in Chap. 17; the evaluation of individual products to phase out of the line is discussed in Philip Kotler, "Phasing Out Weak Products," *Harvard Business Review* (Mar.–Apr. 1965) 107–118.

[4]However, see the discussion in Chap. 19.

[5]Sometimes there is an opposite tendency to increase the funds going to products that have sustained a drop in market share. This may be rationalized on grounds that competition must have stepped up its expenditures and must be emulated, whereas in fact it may be that the product is failing on its own "merits."

of last year's allocations as precedents instead of what each product actually deserves in the way of support, which in many cases may be quite different.

The precedent levels themselves generally originate from company rules regarding reasonable ratios of product budgets to sales. A common decision rule is to allocate the total budget proportionately to each product's recent or anticipated sales:

$$X_j = \frac{R_j}{\sum_{j=1}^{n} R_j} B \tag{7-1}$$

where X_j = amount of funds to be allocated to the jth company product
$\qquad R_j$ = sales revenue of the jth company product ($R_j = P_j Q_j$)
$\qquad B$ = budget dollars

While this rule is simple to implement, it contains a number of obvious weaknesses; there is no reason to believe that it would maximize profits, which is the real concern of the firm. For example, suppose that one of the company's products contributes 50 percent of the total revenue but only 20 percent of the total profit. This is often the case with high volume, small margin products. This type of product is also a frequent cause of bottlenecks in the production of other products. In this situation it is possible that profits might be enhanced by reducing the emphasis on this product and increasing the emphasis on other products. The simple decision rule in Equation 7-1 is not likely to result from a normative analysis of this problem.

A rule that allocates the marketing budget in proportion to the gross margins, rather than sales, of the various products would be an improvement but is still not likely to maximize profits.[6] The final marketing budgets will influence the respective product sales levels and also the respective output levels. Therefore the gross margins are only approximate and represent standard costs rather than actual costs. The solution would have to be reexamined on the basis of actual costs. A mathematical programming computation may be required in the end to develop the normative solution.

The real data needed for optimization are not the relative sales or gross profits of different products but the probable marginal responses to different levels of company marketing effort. Companies may recognize this intuitively when they adjust product budgets away from pure proportionality rules in the direction of variables that indicate differential marginal responses, such as rapidly rising sales, increased distribution penetration, and so on. We shall look at this principle more formally in the following section.

THE MULTIPRODUCT MARKETING STRATEGY PROBLEM

The general problem that will be considered here is that of finding the set of simultaneous price levels and marketing efforts for all products in the line for

---

[6]See John U. Farley, "An Optimal Plan for Salesmen's Compensation," *Journal of Marketing Research* (May 1964) 39–43.

the coming period that would maximize current period profits subject to (1) a given total marketing budget; (2) a given total production capacity; (3) given minimum levels of outputs, prices, marketing expenditures and costs; and (4) stated demand and cost interactions among products in the line. The problem is expressed in mathematical programming terms in Table 7-1.

Table 7-1. Statement of Multiple Marketing Strategy Problem.

Maximize $Z = \sum_i (P_i - c_i)Q_i - \sum_i X_i - F$
subject to:

(1) $\sum_{i=1}^{n} X_i \leqslant B$ 　 } budget constraint

(2) $\sum_{i=1}^{n} k_i Q_i \leqslant K$ 　 } production capacity constraint

(3) $\begin{cases} Q_i \geqslant 0 \text{ for all } i \\ P_i \geqslant 0 \text{ for all } i \\ X_i \geqslant 0 \text{ for all } i \\ c_i \geqslant 0 \text{ for all } i \end{cases}$ 　 } nonnegativity constraints

(4) $\begin{cases} Q_i = f(P_1, \ldots, P_n, X_1, \ldots, X_n) \text{ for all } i \\ \qquad\qquad\qquad\qquad\qquad i = i, \ldots, n \\ c_i = f(Q_1, \ldots, Q_n) \qquad\qquad \text{for all } i \\ \qquad\qquad\qquad\qquad\qquad i = 1, \ldots, n \end{cases}$ 　 } demand response and interaction conditions
　 } cost response and interaction conditions

Note

Z = total profit per period in the whole product line
Q_i = demand per period for product i
P_i = price of product i
X_i = marketing effort per period for product i
c_i = cost per unit of producing quantity Q_i
F = fixed cost
B = total budget per period for marketing effort
K = total production capacity (that is, machine hours) per period
k_i = amount of production capacity used by unit of output of product i

This is a complicated problem to express and solve analytically, especially in real product line situations.[7] Heuristic modeling and solution procedures may offer some help. We shall make the problem more manageable by examining special cases, showing the means available for solving each special case in principle. The three special cases are as follows:

1. Optimal pricing of two or more products exhibiting demand and/or cost interactions

[7]For two interesting simplifications of this problem, see Norbert Lloyd Enrick, "Sales Production Coordination through Mathematical Programming," in American Institute of Certified Public Accounts, *New Techniques for Business Planning, Systems, and Control* (New York, 1967), 29–37; and James T. Godfrey, W. Allen Spivey, and George B. Stillwagon "Production and Market Planning with Parametric Programming," *Industrial Management Review* (Fall 1968) 61–75.

2. Optimal allocation of the marketing budget among two or more products exhibiting demand and/or cost interactions

3. Optimal output levels for two or more products in the face of limited production and marketing resources

Optimal Pricing of Interacting Products

We shall first consider a simplification of the problem of multiproduct marketing strategy for the case in which there are two products and a price interaction between them. The two products are denoted by the subscripts i and j. The price interaction can be represented in several ways, two of the more common of which are: the *linear price interaction model*,

$$Q_i = k_i - a_i P_i + b_i P_j$$
$$Q_j = k_j - a_j P_j + b_j P_i \tag{7-2}$$

and the *exponential price interaction model*,

$$Q_i = k_i P_i^{-a_i} P_j^{b_i}$$
$$Q_j = k_j P_j^{-a_j} P_i^{b_j} \tag{7-3}$$

In both models, the k term represent scale effects, the a terms represent own-product price sensitivity, and the b terms represent cross product price sensitivity. In the exponential model, the a's and b's are literal elasticities instead of general sensitivities. It should also be noted that the models in their present forms deal with products that are substitutes: an increase in the price of the other product will *increase* the sales of the reference product. The case of complements can be treated with no further difficulty by simply reversing the signs of the cross product sensitivities.

If the production or marketing of the two products involves cost interactions as well as demand interactions, a useful total cost function is the following one:

$$C = F + c_i Q_i + c_j Q_j + c_{ij} (Q_i Q_j)^{-d} \tag{7-4}$$

This cost function comprises a fixed overhead charge (F), which is independent of levels of output, constant marginal costs of producing and distributing products i and j (not necessarily equal, that is, $c_i \neq c_j$), and a cost interaction factor consisting of a constant cost factor (c_{ij}) divided by the exponentiated product of the two products' production levels. This cost function is particularly useful in situations where costs rise with departures from an equal output of both products, such as might be found in casting or blending operations. Thus, if $c_{ij} = 48$ and $d = 1$, the interaction cost of producing $(4, 4)$ of the two products would be \$3 whereas the interaction cost of any other combination of 8 units, such as $(2, 6)$ would be more (here \$4).

While the use of the particular cost interaction formulation $c_{ij}(Q_i Q_j)^{-d}$ can flexibly represent a wide variety of cost interaction situations, we will drop it from the following analysis because of the mathematical complications it presents in seeking a solution to the general problem. That is, assume $c_{ij} = 0$ although in working with specific data where cost interaction is present, the cost interaction factor should be introduced and manipulated.

Example. The problem we shall now illustrate is that of finding the pair of prices (P_i, P_j) that maximizes the current profit rate in the face of price interaction but no cost interaction. The first step is to form the profit function:

$$Z = P_iQ_i+P_jQ_j-(F+c_iQ_i+c_jQ_j)$$
$$Z = (P_i-c_i)Q_i+(P_j-c_j)Q_j-F \tag{7-5}$$

Now substitute the linear price interaction model of Equation 7-2 into Equation 7-5:

$$Z = (P_i-c_i)(k_i-a_iP_i+b_iP_j)+(P_j-c_j)(k_j-a_jP_j+b_jP_i)-F \tag{7-6}$$

Differentiating this function with respect to P_i and P_j and setting the first derivatives equal to 0, we obtain the following solution for P_j:[8]

$$P_j^* = \frac{(k_i+c_ia_i-c_jb_j)(b_i+b_j)+(k_j+c_ja_j-c_ib_i)(2a_i)}{4a_ia_j-(b_i+b_j)^2} \tag{7-7}$$

(The optimal price of product i can be derived through substituting P_j^* into an earlier step in the mathematical proof.) We see that the optimal price of product j, under the assumption of linear price interaction, depends upon all the information in the two demand functions and the cost function. The result would have been even more complex if a cost interaction factor had also been included. Since Equation 7-7 is only meaningful if it yields a positive price P_j^*, the following condition must be satisfied in the normal case:

$$4a_ia_j > (b_i+b_j)^2 \tag{7-8}$$

Optimal Allocation of Marketing Effort among Interacting Products

Now assume a firm that has set prices on its products which it does not wish to alter. At the same time the firm can affect its sales by the amount of promotional funds that it devotes to each product. The firm has a promotion budget B for the period, and it will divide the budget between the two products in the amounts X_i and X_j, where

$$X_i+X_j = B \tag{7-9}$$

Furthermore, assume that the amount spent on each product will affect the sales of both products. Let this marketing expenditure interaction be represented by the following exponential demand equations:

$$Q_i = k_iX_i^{a_i}X_j^{-b_i}$$
$$Q_j = k_jX_j^{a_j}X_i^{-b_j} \tag{7-10}$$

In this case the two products compete, since the effect of increased funds on one product reduces the demand for the other product. (To handle the case of

[8]See Appendix Mathematical Note 7–1.

complementary products, omit the negative signs in front of the b's.) Form the Lagrangian expression of the profit function Equation 7-5 using Equations 7-9 and 7-10:

$$L = (P_i - c_i)(k_i X_i^{a_i} X_j^{-b_i}) + (P_j - c_j)(k_j X_j^{a_j} X_i^{-b_j}) - F + \lambda(B - X_i - X_j) \quad (7\text{-}11)$$

Differentiating this expression, we obtain the following implicit solution to the optimal level of X_j:[9]

$$\frac{a_i(B - X_j)^{a_i - 1} X_j^{-b_i} + b_i(B - X_j)^{a_i} X_j^{-b_i - 1}}{a_j(B - X_j)^{-b_j} X_j^{a_j - 1} + b_j(B - X_j)^{-b_j - 1} X_j^{a_j}} = \frac{(P_j - c_j)k_j}{(P_i - c_i)k_i} \quad (7\text{-}12)$$

Equation 7-12 is as far as we can go in simplifying the solution. Note that the right-hand side is a constant and the only variable on the left-hand side is X_j, the amount of the marketing budget going to product j. In a real problem, all the parameters would be actual numbers and the solution approach would be to try out different values of X_j to identify the form of the solution space. If the form is well-behaved, it will be fairly straightforward to locate the optimal product budget, X_j. This result can then be subtracted from the budget B to find X_i.

Optimal Allocation among Noninteracting Products Subject to Nonlinearities and Constraints

The two previous problems assume continuity and substitutability of inputs and marketing responses. Their solution glosses over the technical problems of specific resource limitations and the lack of complete substitutability and continuity. Linear programming represents an alternative approach that in some ways is more in tune with the multiproduct strategy problem. For this reason we shall develop a specific illustration of the use of linear programming as a solution technique.

Assume that the XYZ company sells two products, 1 and 2, and uses two marketing instruments to stimulate demand, advertising (A) and selling (D). In each planning period the company must decide on the amount of advertising and selling resources (A_1, A_2, D_1, D_2) to devote to the two products. The total advertising and selling resources of the company for the planning period are $A = \$22,600$ and $D = 6000$ man-hours. On the basis of historical records and experienced judgment, the management has arrived at tentative productivity coefficients for its advertising and selling efforts for each product. A dollar of advertising is estimated to yield \$6 profit when spent for product 1 and \$10 profit when spent for product 2.[10] Assume that this holds over the whole range of the advertising budget, that is, there are no increasing or diminishing returns

---

[9] See Appendix Mathematical Note 7-2.

[10] To find this, we estimate the number of units sold per dollar of advertising and multiply this by the profit margin per unit. Thus if a dollar of advertising tends to sell approximately $\frac{1}{2}$ unit of product and the profit margin per unit is \$12, the profit per unit is \$6 ($\frac{1}{2} \times 12$). The reader may wonder why the firm does not spend an infinite amount of money if each dollar of advertising yields pure profits in excess of \$1. This characterization is artificial because of the linearity assumption (actually diminishing marginal profits per dollar of advertising would be expected and the problem is avoided by postulating a finite budget).

to advertising. In the case of personal selling, assume that the effect is more complicated and characterized by diminishing returns. If the company devotes up to 2000 of the 6000 available man-hours in selling product 1, the profit margin per selling hour is $24; if the company devotes between 2000 and 6000 man-hours to selling product 1, the profit margin per selling hour is $18. The profit margin is not $18 for all hours spent in selling product 1 but just for those hours over 2000. To describe this decline in productivity, we invent the auxiliary variables D_{11} and D_{12} to represent the amounts of selling effort against product 1 at the higher and lower level of productivity, respectively. Then the range of the auxiliary variables are constrained as follows:[11]

$$0 \leqslant D_{11} \leqslant 2000$$
$$0 \leqslant D_{12} \leqslant 4000 \qquad (7\text{-}13)$$

Note that, even if all the selling time is devoted to product 1, the amount $(D_{11} + D_{12})$ will not exceed the available selling time of 6000 man-hours. The conditions in Equation 7-13 amount to defining a "piecewise linear" approximation to a concave function as shown in Figure 7-1.

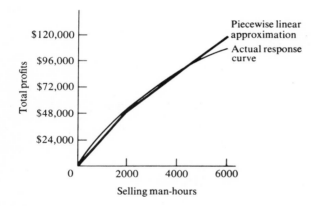

Figure 7-1   Approximating a Concave Function With Two Linear Segments

Similarly, assume that if the company devotes up to 1500 hours in selling product 2, the profit margin per selling hour is $40; if the company devotes between 1500 and 6000 hours to selling product 2, the profit margin per selling hour in this range falls to $20. In symbols, we obtain

$$0 \leqslant D_{21} \leqslant 1500$$
$$0 \leqslant D_{22} \leqslant 4500 \qquad (7\text{-}14)$$

[11]For a fuller description of the method of convex programming, which amounts to inventing auxiliary variables and approximating a non-linear function by linear segments so that the problem can be solved by the simplex method, see the description in Andrew Vazsonyi, *Scientific Programming in Business and Industry* (New York: John Wiley & Sons, Inc., 1958), Chap. 7.

Finally, assume that the management imposes some policy constraints on the minimum and maximum amounts of advertising and personal selling to be devoted to each product. These minimums and maximums are imposed to ensure the continuation of both products in the product line because in some way they support each other. Specifically, assume that management insists that at least 2200 man-hours and \$5000 advertising dollars, and no more than 4500 man-hours and \$18,000 advertising dollars, be devoted to each product. With the latter condition, the whole problem is stated in mathematical programming terms in Table 7-2.

Table 7-2 Linear Programming Statement of Marketing Resource Allocation Problem.

Find the allocation of marketing effort (A_1, A_2, D_{11}, D_{12}, D_{21}, D_{22}) that maximizes

$$Z = 6A_1 + 10A_2 + 24D_{11} + 18D_{12} + 40D_{21} + 20D_{22} \qquad \} \text{ profit function}$$

subject to the following conditions:

$$\left. \begin{aligned} A_1 + A_2 &\leq 22{,}600 \\ D_{11} + D_{12} + D_{21} + D_{22} &\leq 6{,}000 \end{aligned} \right\} \begin{aligned} &\text{marketing resource} \\ &\text{constraints} \end{aligned}$$

$$\left. \begin{aligned} D_{11} &\leq 2{,}000 \\ D_{12} &\leq 4{,}000 \\ D_{21} &\leq 1{,}500 \\ D_{22} &\leq 4{,}500 \end{aligned} \right\} \begin{aligned} &\text{auxiliary variable} \\ &\text{constraints (for} \\ &\text{productivity} \\ &\text{changeovers)} \end{aligned}$$

$$\left. \begin{aligned} D_{11} + D_{12} &\geq 2{,}200 \\ D_{21} + D_{22} &\geq 2{,}200 \\ D_{11} + D_{12} &\leq 4{,}500 \\ D_{21} + D_{22} &\leq 4{,}500 \\ A_1 &\geq 5{,}000 \\ A_2 &\geq 5{,}000 \\ A_1 &\leq 18{,}000 \\ A_2 &\leq 18{,}000 \end{aligned} \right\} \begin{aligned} &\text{policy constraints} \\ &\text{(minimum and} \\ &\text{maximum usage} \\ &\text{levels)} \end{aligned}$$

$$A_1, A_2, D_{11}, D_{12}, D_{21}, D_{22}, \text{ all} \geq 0 \qquad \left. \right\} \begin{aligned} &\text{nonnegativity} \\ &\text{constraint} \end{aligned}$$

The problem has been stated in a form appropriate for solution by the simplex method of linear programming.[12] The optimal program turns out to be:

$$A_1 = \$5{,}000$$
$$A_2 = 17{,}600$$
$$D_{11} = 2{,}000$$
$$D_{12} = 200$$
$$D_{21} = 1{,}500$$
$$D_{22} = 2{,}300$$

And this will produce total profits of \$363,600, more than any other resource allocation strategy could produce.

[12]See any standard reference text on linear programming. For example, G. Hadley, *Linear Programming* (Reading, Massachusetts: Addison-Wesley Publishing Company, Inc., 1962).

The same technique can be extended in a straightforward manner to cover any number of products and any number of marketing decision variables. As shown for the case of personal selling, it can handle nonlinear sales response functions as well. All that is required is an estimate of the shape of the sales response function and its approximation by linear segments. Any number of linear segments can be used to get as close to approximating the curve as desired, although this increases computation time and computer storage requirements.

At the same time we should be clear about what the preceding formulation does not handle. The formulation implies constant market prices, although with some difficulty it is possible to introduce the negative price demand relationship. The formulation does not readily handle product interaction on the demand or cost side and, even if the interactions were formulated, the problem could not be solved by the simplex method of linear programming. Calculus is more effective than mathematical programming for problems with few products, product interaction, few constraints, and high substitutability and continuity in the functions. Mathematical programming is more effective in handling linear and discontinuous responses, many constraints, and noninteraction among products.

When the conditions of the problem point to linear or mathematical programming, the technique yields some valuable by-products. The first is that the technique produces not only the optimum allocations (primary solution), but also information about the cost of imposing each resource and policy constraint (dual solution).[13] This information allows management to answer such questions as the following.

1. What is the relative value of adding sales call hours versus advertising dollars to the company's marketing resources? (For the problem in Table 7-2, an added sales call hour will produce $20 and an added advertising dollar will produce $10.)
2. What would the company gain by relaxing each of the minimum and maximum usage constraints? (Effective constraints appear to be the selling of products 1 and 2 at the first level, that is, D_{11} and D_{21}; also the A_1 minimum.)
3. What would the company gain by increasing its total market budget by a small amount? (The company could gain $20 net profit for the marginal cost of another sales call hour.)

The second benefit of linear programming is that this method makes it easy to test the sensitivity of the optimal solution to alternative estimates of the relative effectiveness of selling and advertising. The alternative estimates are fed in and the computer immediately produces a new optimum solution that can then be compared with the original solution. In many cases the optimal solution is relatively insensitive to minor changes in the estimated response coefficients.

---

[13]For a discussion of the dual solution, see G. Hadley, *Linear Programming* Chap. 8.

PRODUCTION RATE PROBLEM

We now turn to a different problem than that of determining the optimal marketing strategies for two or more products in the company's line. This problem concerns how much to produce of each product and will be called the Production Rate Problem. This problem can be stated as follows: Given n products that the firm produces, how much of each ($Q_1, Q_2, \ldots, Q_i, \ldots, Q_n$) should the firm plan to produce and sell to maximize current profits in the light of its resource endowments, resource consumption rates, and profit margins.

This is the problem faced by every company in each planning period when it reviews its sales, current inventory levels, and available resources and then seeks to develop a sales and production plan for the coming period. The planning is typically carried out by a committee that includes representatives from production and marketing. Very often, opinion splits between these two groups regarding desirable production and sales goals. The major issues can be illustrated with the hypothetical data in Table 7-3.

Table 7-3. Productive Inputs, Costs, Supplies, and Requirements for Two Company Products.

1	2	3	4	
			Production requirements per unit of output	
	Cost per unit of input	Available supply		
Productive inputs			Product 1	Product 2
1. Material in pounds	$3	28,000	3	1
2. Machine hours	$50	3,000	.1	.2
3. Labor hours	$6	4,000	.3	.2
4. Selling hours	$20	6,000	.5	.2
5. Advertising dollars	$1	22,000	2	1
Price per unit (P_i)			$40	$30
Cost per unit (c_i)			$27.80	$19.20
Profit margin per unit (z_i) = ($P_i - c_i$)			$12.20	$10.80

Five inputs that enter into the production and sale of two company products, 1 and 2, are listed in this table. The first three inputs are production factors and the last two are sales factors. The five inputs are stated in appropriate units; the cost per unit of each input is shown in the second column. For example, a pound of material used in this product cost the company $3, a machine hour $50, a labor hour $6, a selling hour $20, and an advertising dollar, $1. The third column lists the amount of each resource available for the planning period. Some of these resources are limited in amount because they take time to expand (such as machine hours and possibly selling hours), and others are limited by policy and the budgeting mechanism.

The last two columns in Table 7-3 show the amount of each resource required for the production and sale of one unit of output of each product. The estimates of required production inputs are based on fairly hard engineering data, while the estimates of required sales inputs (the last two items) is based on average experience in selling the product. The management estimates that it takes about a half-hour of selling time and \$2 of advertising to sell a unit of the first product and a quarter hour of selling time and \$1 of advertising to sell a unit of the second product.[14]

In comparing the production requirements for the two products, it is clear that product 1 uses more material and labor per unit of output than product 2, while product 2 uses more machine hours. In fact, the company could produce at most 9333 units of product 1 because this product uses 3 pounds of material for every unit of output and the company has available up to 28,000 units of material. The other factors are not a bottleneck to the production of product 1 at this point. Similarly, the company could produce at most 15,000 units of product 2 because this product uses $\frac{1}{5}$ of a machine hour per unit of output and only 3000 machine hours are available. Now consider these limitations in relation to the market prices of product 1 (\$40) and product 2 (\$30). If the company were to produce only one of the two products, which should it be? If the company wanted to maximize sales revenue, then it could make \$373,320 (\$40 × 9333) with product 1 or \$450,000 (\$30 × 15,000) with product 2. It would produce product 2.

Of course, a company is not interested in maximizing sales revenue but rather profits. To find profits, it must deduct the unit costs of producing and selling each of the products. The cost (c_i) per unit of output of each product is found by multiplying the cost per unit of each input by the required input level and summing these input costs. The unit cost for each product is shown below:

$$\text{Cost per unit of output, product 1}\Big\} = (\$3)(3)+(\$50)(.1)+(\$6)(.3)+(\$20)(.5)+(\$1)(2) = \$27.80$$

$$\text{Cost per unit of output, product 2}\Big\} = (\$3)(1)+(\$50)(.2)+(\$6)(.2)+(\$20)(.2)+(\$1)(1) = \$19.20$$

Having calculated unit costs, the respective profit margins can now be stated:

$$z_1 = P_1 - c_1 = \$40 - \$27.80 = \$12.20$$
$$z_2 = P_2 - c_2 = \$30 - \$19.20 = \$10.80$$

This information is summarized at the bottom of Table 7-3.

In planning production and sales, marketing management is likely to look at the profit margin per unit in recommending which products to emphasize, while production management is likely to emphasize bottleneck factors in production and call for a joint set of output levels that balance production requirements. Neither criterion is sufficient for an optimal solution. When there are many products in the line, each consuming scarce resources at different rates, the optimal solution is difficult to arrive at intuitively or through simple decision

---

[14]In principle, the marginal and not the average productivity of these inputs should be used. It is assumed here that the average productivities are constant over a wide range of inputs and therefore average productivity is a satisfactory measure of marginal productivity.

criteria. The difficulty is aggravated further if additional constraints are present. For example, suppose management insists on producing at least 3000 and 2000 units of products 1 and 2, respectively, and no more than 8000 and 12,000 units of products 1 and 2, respectively. The lower policy limits are established because the company must produce a minimum of each product to meet essential market demand and gain the advantages of a full product line. The upper policy limits are established because they represent the company's concept of the sales potential of each product. A complete mathematical programming statement of this problem is shown in Table 7-4.

Table 7-4. Linear Programming Statement of Optimal Production Levels Problem.

Find the set of outputs (Q_1, Q_2) that

$\qquad$ maximize $Z = 12.20Q_1 + 10.80Q_2$ $\qquad\big\}$ profit function

subject to
$$3Q_1 + Q_2 \leqslant 28,000$$
$$.1Q_1 + .2Q_2 \leqslant 3,000$$
$$.3Q_1 + .2Q_2 \leqslant 4,000 \qquad\bigg\}\ \text{resource constraints}$$
$$.5Q_1 + .2Q_2 \leqslant 6,000$$
$$2Q_1 + Q_2 \leqslant 22,000$$

$$Q_1 \geqslant 3,000$$
$$Q_2 \geqslant 2,000$$
$\qquad\qquad\qquad\qquad\big\}$ minimum product line constraints

$$Q_1 \leqslant 12,000$$
$$Q_2 \leqslant 9,000$$
$\qquad\qquad\qquad\qquad\big\}$ market potential constraints

The linear programming solution to the problem in Table 7-4 calls for the production of 5000 units of product 1 and 12,000 units of product 2. The profit on this output mix is 190,600 and higher than any other feasible output mix. Furthermore, most of the selling and advertising effort will go to product 1. However, neither marketing resource is fully utilized.

As noted earlier, the linear programming approach provides useful information beyond the optimal quantities that should be produced. The *dual solution* to the problem provides a means of evaluating the imputed cost of each of the constraints, and *sensitivity analysis* indicates how sensitive the optimal program is to variations in the estimates of the productivity coefficients.[15] A special benefit of using linear programming for this problem is that it provides an objective standard for resolving differences between production and sales management in the planning of sales.

At the same time the limitations of this statement of the problem should also be recognized. The model assumes that market prices are not affected by the quantity sold. It also assumes that all the inputs are available at constant costs

---

[15]Sensitivity analysis is the examination of the pattern of change in the solution of a problem as a result of systematic variation in the parameters of the problem. See Richard B. Maffei, "Mathematical Models, Values of Parameters, and the Sensitivity Analysis of Management Decision Rules," *Journal of Marketing* (Apr. 1957), pp. 419–427.

and their productivity levels are constant. The model also assumes no product interactions on the demand or cost side, a simple short run profit maximization objective, and no inventory problem. Some of these restrictions can be relaxed but at the expense of complicating the statement of the problem and perhaps making it difficult or impossible to solve for an optimum.

The statement of the production rate problem is commonly applied in solving the product blending problem. Candy manufacturers use it to determine the optimal mix of different candies to put in candy boxes each day in the face of changing ingredient prices; oil companies use it to determine the optimal blending of fuel; and feed manufacturers use it daily to determine optimal feed mixes.[16] The innovative aspect of the statement in Table 7-4 is that it includes marketing costs in the statement of the problem. That this makes a difference becomes apparent by solving the problem without the inclusion of the two sales inputs. If these are ignored, the optimal production rate vector would appear to be (5333, 12,000) and the total profits are $194,667. While higher problems are indicated, this solution is not feasible. This highlights a central point developed more fully in Chapters 8 and 9, that any model limited to only one functional decision area such as marketing is liable to yield a solution which suboptimizes from the point of view of the firm. Chapters 8 and 9 indicate how marketing decisions can be embedded in total firm models.

PRODUCT MIX PROBLEM

The previous section considered a given product line and raised the question of how much of each product the company should plan to produce and sell in the current planning period. Now we turn to a more basic type of problem, namely, which products the company should produce in the first place. The optimal product mix problem can be stated as follows: Given n possible products that a firm can produce or sell, which m of them (where $m \leqslant n$) will maximize the company's profits?[17]

Some of the situations in which this problem is faced by real firms are listed below.

1. A supermarket has to select a product subset out of all possible items because of limited shelf space.
2. A television manufacturer has to design a few basic models out of a large set of possibilities.
3. A company facing a prolonged labor shortage must decide which of its products to continue to produce and which to drop.
4. A company evaluating a large set of new product ideas must select some subset for actual development.

---

[16]Hadley, *op. cit.*, Chap. 12, especially pp. 458–463.

[17]Technically, the issue is not one of maximizing current profits but the value of the firm. Each product mix implies a unique earnings stream and risk. Here we shall use a current profit criterion and Chaps. 9 and 10 will deal with more realistic criteria.

5. A company facing the need to prune its product line because of product proliferation must decide on the best products to retain.

All of these situations involve the selection of some subset of possible products. Imagine the following set (N) of all possible products that can be produced or sold.[18]

$$N = 1, 2, \ldots, i, \ldots, n \qquad (7\text{-}15)$$

There are 2^n different subsets (i.e., product lines) that the decision maker can select. The jth subset (S_j) will be denoted by an n element vector of 1's and 0's, the ones standing for the items included in the subset. The set of all possible subsets is

$$S_1, S_2, S_3, \ldots, S_{2^n}$$

where $S_1 = (0, 0, 0, \ldots, 0)$
$S_2 = (1, 0, 0, \ldots, 0)$
$S_3 = (0, 1, 0, \ldots, 0)$
$\vdots \qquad\qquad \vdots$
$S_{2^n} = (1, 1, 1, \ldots, 1)$

The number (m) of products in the jth subset can be represented by $(S_j) = m$.

The problem is to find that subset of products which maximizes the firm's profits. One possible solution approach is to evaluate every subset but this is prohibitive if 2^n is large. In this case, some other technique is needed to simplify the combinatorial universe.[19]

Before turning to this question, we must consider the more basic question of how the profit for any particular subset is to be evaluated. If there is complete product independence, we should estimate the expected profit for every product in the line and then sum the profits for each subset. If there is product interdependence, the profits of any product depends on the other products in the subset and the problem becomes extremely complicated. For this reason, the analysis of this problem is conducted on the following pages under different sets of assumptions.

The Case of Product Independence and a Budget Constraint

Suppose the company is to choose m out of n possible products and each product involves a certain marketing mix (P, A, D) that will lead under an assumed state of the environment, Y, to a certain average level of sales, Q, a certain average total cost, C, and a certain level of initial investment, I.

---

[18]The formal statement of the problem is adapted with modification from Donald B. Rice, *Product Line Selection and Discrete Optimizing* (Herman C. Krannert Graduate School of Industrial Administration, Purdue University, Institute Paper No. 66, Jan. 1964), p. 3.

[19]Rice shows how the problem can be solved using discrete optimization, *op. cit.*

If we assume that demand and cost for each product depend only on its own decision variables and sales, the average rate of return, r, for product i will be

$$r_i = \frac{P_i Q_i - C_i}{I_i} \tag{7-17}$$

Now take the array of all possible products and prepare a new vector N' which lists the estimated r for each product, where the products have been rearranged according to their r's from highest to lowest:

$$N' = (r_{1'}, r_{2'}, r_{3'}, \ldots, r_{i'}, \ldots, r_{n'}) \tag{7-18}$$

The final step is to select the first m of these products, stopping at the point where $m + 1$ products would involve an investment that would just exceed the available budget, B.[20]

As an example, suppose that a manufacturer of electronic equipment has a new investment budget of \$1.5 million and wishes to develop a subset of products from a set of eight product proposals, including tape recorders, transistor radios, tapes, phonograph needles, and so forth. These product opportunities are shown in Table 7-5, along with each product's price (column 2),

Table 7-5. Hypothetical Characteristics of Eight Products for An Optimal Product Line Selection Problem.

1	2	3	4	5	6	7
Product	Price P	Annual sales[a] Q	Annual cost[a] C	Initial investment I	$\dfrac{PQ - C}{I}$	Rank of product according to column 6
1	\$ 10	10,000	\$ 80,800	\$160,000	.12	4
2	1	500,000	480,000	400,000	.05	7
3	1,000	200	190,000	250,000	.04	8
4	40	100,000	3,920,000	800,000	.10	5
5	3	1,000	2,500	2,000	.25	1
6	20	80,000	1,530,000	500,000	.14	3
7	500	50	20,200	30,000	.16	2
8	20	200,000	3,960,000	500,000	.08	6

[a] These figures assume implicitly that the optimal marketing mix has been decided for each product and is reflected in each product's sales and costs.

estimated sales (column 3), cost (column 4), and investment (column 5). Column 6 shows the estimated r for each product and column 7 shows its rank according to rate of return. This ranking shows that the products stand in the following order: (5, 7, 6, 1, 4, 8, 2, 3). The investment cost of each of the corresponding products is

[20]For a general discussion of this problem, see Harold Bierman, Jr. and Seymour Smidt, *The Capital Budgeting Decision* (New York: Macmillan, 1960).

$(2000; 30,000; 500,000; 160,000; 800,000; 500,000; 400,000; 250,000)$.

The cumulative investment cost is shown in the following vector:

$(2000; 32,000; 532,000; 692,000; 1,492,000; 1,992,000; 2,392,000; 2,642,000)$

Since the investment budget is $1.5 million, the optimal product line consists of the first five products and the weighted average rate of return is .117.

This solution technique is based on the following assumptions:

1. There are no product interactions on the demand or cost side.
2. All products have the same investment time spans.
3. The figures for price, quantity, and cost are stable on an annual basis.

These assumptions can be relaxed and solutions sought for more realistic cases.

The Case of Product Independence and Several Constraints

Integer programming can serve as a model for representing the problem of optimal product line selection in the face of several constraints. An example of an integer programming statement is shown in Table 7-6. This problem state-

Table 7-6. Integer Programming Statement of Optimal Product Line Selection Problem.

Find the vector $(U_1, U_2, \ldots, U_i, \ldots, U_n)$ where $U_i = 1$ or 0 for each i, that

maximizes $Z = z_1 U_1 + z_2 U_2 + \ldots + z_i U_i + \ldots + z_n U_n$ } profit function

subject to
$$a_1 U_1 + a_2 U_2 + \ldots + a_i U_i + \ldots + a_n U_n \leqslant A$$
$$b_1 U_1 + b_2 U_2 + \ldots + b_i U_i + \ldots + b_n U_n \leqslant B$$
$$\vdots$$
$$k_1 U_1 + k_2 U_2 + \ldots + k_i U_i + \ldots + k_n U_n \leqslant K$$

resource and policy constraints

ment calls for finding the n element vector of 1's and 0's that maximizes profits subject to various constraints. The constraints can be of different kinds. One constraint may represent the available amount of labor hours and the rates at which different products use up labor hours. Another constraint may involve the available amount of advertising dollars and the rates at which different products use up advertising dollars. Still another constraint may represent a maximum amount of sales instability that a company would tolerate and the rates at which different products contribute to instability.

The Case of Product Independence and Dynamic Product Selection over Time

The previous formulation is static in assuming that the company will make a one-time selection of the best subset of possible products and introduce them simultaneously into the product mix. Suppose the problem is more dynamic and calls for the company to select a certain group of new products today, another group next year, another group in the third year, and so forth, so as to maximize long run return subject to some budget and policy constraints. In other words, the company is trying to develop a dynamic program of future product investments. How can this problem be stated and solved?

For each product under consideration, the company calculates its *excess present value* today, next year, and for each year in its planning horizon.[21] Excess present value is defined as

$$E_{it} = V_{it} - I_{it} \qquad (7\text{-}19)$$

where E_{it} = excess present value of product i at time t

V_{it} = present value of product i's future profits at time t[22]

I_{it} = investment required for product i at time t

Only projects with $V_{it} > I_{it}$ are worth considering; a measure of their relative merit is given by $E_{it} = V_{it} - I_{it}$, their excess present value. Notice that for any project i in the set, the company can estimate not only the project's excess present value if adopted at time t, but also its excess present value for any future time period when it might be adopted.

$$E = E_{1t}U_{1t} + E_{2t}U_{2t} + \ldots + E_{nt}U_{nt} + E_{1,t+1}U_{1,t+1} + \ldots + E_{n,t+k}U_{n,t+k} \quad (7\text{-}20)$$

where U = a binary variable taking on the value 1 (when product i should be adopted at time t) and 0 otherwise

The objective is to find the set of $U_{it} = 1$ that will maximize Equation 7-20. It is necessary to state constraints that will prevent any project i from being adopted in both year t and $t+j$, where $j = 1, 2, \ldots, k$. The following conditions prevent this from happening:

$$
\begin{aligned}
U_{1,t} + U_{1,t+1} + U_{1,t+2} + \ldots + U_{1,t+k} &= U_1 \\
U_{2,t} + U_{2,t+1} + U_{2,t+2} + \ldots + U_{2,t+k} &= U_2 \\
\vdots \\
U_{n,t} + U_{n,t+1} + U_{n,t+2} + \ldots + U_{n,t+k} &= U_n
\end{aligned}
\qquad (7\text{-}21)
$$

where the U_i's themselves represent binary variables, taking on the value 1 if the ith project is selected in some year and the value 0 if the ith project is not selected at all. Since U_i is constrained to be 0 or 1, no project can be selected more than once.

In addition, various types of management constraints are introduced into the problem. Management generally likes to show its stockholders a steady earnings growth. Suppose management wants to choose new products over time in such a way that the earnings each year are at least 5 percent higher than the previous

[21]See Eugene M. Lerner and Alfred Rappaport, "Limit DCF in Capital Budgeting," *Harvard Business Review* (Sept.–Oct. 1968) 133–139.

[22]V_{it}, present value of product i at time t, is the estimated discounted value of the earnings stream over the product's life discounted at the company's cost of capital. See Chap. 9, pp. 233–237 for details on this concept.

year's earnings. Let Z_t represent total profits on all the products in the line at time t. Then these conditions state:[23]

$$Z_{t+1} - 1.05Z_t \geqslant 0$$
$$Z_{t+2} - 1.05Z_{t+1} \geqslant 0$$
$$\vdots$$
$$Z_{t+k} - 1.05Z_{t+k-1} \geqslant 0$$

(7-22)

Other management constraints can also be introduced. The main purpose of the discussion is to show that some progress can be made in formulating the problem of dynamic project selection over time.

The Case of Multiproduct Sales Interdependence

When the condition of product independence no longer holds, the product selection problem becomes quite formidable. Unfortunately, product interdependence is a fairly common phenomenon. Three types of product interdependence can be distinguished.

1. *Product interaction:* the case in which the marketing mix developed for each project influences the sales and/or costs of the other products
2. *Sales covariance:* the case in which major environmental forces (such as seasonal or cyclical demand) cause two or more company products to move in the same way
3. *Risk covariance:* the case in which returns on different products are subject to uncertainty and the measures of uncertainty are intercorrelated.

Situation 1 was examined earlier in the chapter; here we shall consider situations 2 and 3.

The case of sales covariance. Suppose that a firm is evaluating several product opportunities and estimates each product's future sales and cost history under the assumption of a particular marketing strategy and particular environment for each product. For simplicity, assume that the product projections are accurate and that the firm will use the specified marketing strategy for each selected product. The marketing environment assumption consists of a general forecast about the economy and specific forecasts of seasonal and cyclical demand facing each product. Some products are expected to show high growth rates and others low growth rates; some are expected to vary positively with economic cycles, others negatively, and others not at all; and some are expected to have high seasonal demands and others low or no seasonal demands.

[23]The condition that $Z_{t+1} - 1.05 \, Z_t \geqslant 0$ is actually written as

$$\sum_{i=1}^{n} (Z_{i,t+1} \, U_{i,t+1}) - 1.05 \sum_{i=1}^{n} (Z_{i,t} \, U_{i,t}) \geqslant 0$$

In selecting a subset of products, the company has to pay particular attention to positive correlations in the pattern of future sales. For example, if two products are estimated to face highly volatile and correlated demand, this would place a burden on the firm's production facilities and cash flow. The company would find itself needing many men, materials, and money at certain times of the year and few at other times. When output peaked, costs would rise more than proportionately and profits would fall more than proportionately. The company would clearly be concerned with the covariance of sales among the products in its line.

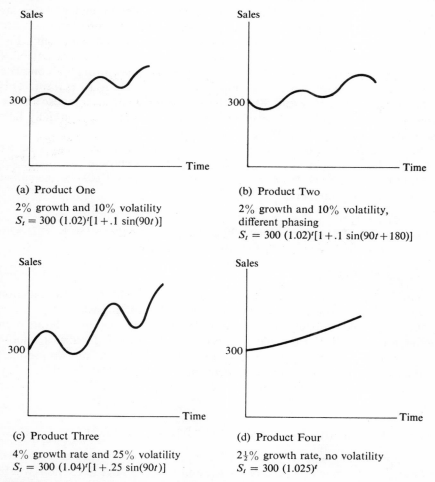

(a) Product One

2% growth and 10% volatility
$S_t = 300 \ (1.02)^t[1 + .1 \ \sin(90t)]$

(b) Product Two

2% growth and 10% volatility,
different phasing
$S_t = 300 \ (1.02)^t[1 + .1 \ \sin(90t + 180)]$

(c) Product Three

4% growth rate and 25% volatility
$S_t = 300 \ (1.04)^t[1 + .25 \ \sin(90t)]$

(d) Product Four

$2\frac{1}{2}$% growth rate, no volatility
$S_t = 300 \ (1.025)^t$

Figure 7-2 Sales Projections for Four Products

To illustrate these issues, assume that the firm wishes to add two products to its line from among four which it is evaluating. Figure 7-2 shows the projected future sales history of each of the four products. The general equation describing future sales is

$$S_t = S_0 (1+g)^t[1+v \sin (at+b)] \tag{7-23}$$

where S_0 = sales at time $t = 0$

$\quad\quad g$ = percentage annual increase in sales

$\quad\quad t$ = time variable, in years

$\quad\quad v$ = percentage volatility of sine curve

$\quad\quad a$ = sine curve angle parameter

$\quad\quad b$ = sine curve phasing parameter

The four products in Figure 7-23 all start at the same sales level of 300 (assumed for convenience). They are expected to grow at different annual rates, as represented by the different g's in the equation. The first three products are subject to cyclical fluctuation as represented by the sine curve expression. For example, the expression $[1+.1 \sin (90t)]$ in Figure 7-2(a) produces an index number centered around 1.00 that initially rises and goes through a complete cycle every four years, where the amplitude of the cycle is 10 percent. This cyclical index varies between .90 and 1.10. The foregoing is true also of the expression $[1+.1 \sin (90t+180)]$ in Figure 7-8(b), except that it initially falls and moves exactly opposite to the previous expression.

Now in selecting two of the four products, the firm faces 4!/2!2!, or six possible subsets: $S_{12}, S_{13}, S_{14}, S_{23}, S_{24}, S_{34}$. Let us consider the total sales picture that would result from selecting particular subsets. Consider the subset S_{12}. We form the summation:

$$S_{12} = S_1 + S_2$$
$$S_{12} = 300(1.02)^t[1+.1 \sin (90t)] + 300(1.02)^t[1+.1 \sin (90t+180)] \tag{7-24}$$
$$S_{12} = 600(1.02)^t + 300(1.02)^t[.1 \sin (90t) + .1 \sin (90t+180)]$$

$$S_{12} = 600(1.02)^t \tag{7-25}$$

because $[.1 \sin (90t) + .1 \sin (90t+180)] = 0$ for all t. The result in Equation 7-25 is a smooth growth in sales at the rate of 2 percent annually.

The firm would probably not be satisfied with the 2 percent growth rate even though it is smooth. For it could elect product 4 by itself and realize a smooth growth rate of 2.5 percent. At the same time, it wishes to take on two products in order to operate at capacity, which currently is above \$600. Suppose it considers the subset consisting of products 1 and 3, S_{13}:

$$S_{13} = S_1 + S_3 \tag{7-26}$$

$$S_{13} = 300(1.02)^t[1+.1 \sin (90t)] + 300(1.04)^t[1+.25 \sin (90t)] \tag{7-27}$$

It is not possible to simplify Equation 7-27 but the conclusion is clear: sales will grow at an initial rate of 3 percent but the amplitude of sales fluctuation will be greatly aggravated. The company can gain an improved growth rate in sales but at the price of larger fluctuations. Since larger fluctuations raise costs disproportionately, it is not clear that S_{13} will lead to greater profits than S_{12}.

In a similar manner, the product subset S_{34} could be evaluated. A casual examination indicates that it would offer a still higher initial growth rate (approximately 3.25 percent) and an amplitude of sales fluctuation somewhere between that found for S_{12} and S_{13}. It would be necessary to examine the remaining product subsets on an individual basis because there is no mathematical programming algorithm for selecting the best subset. In general, for subsets made up of two products of relatively equal sales size, the findings are:

1. If the two products have coincident sales fluctuations, the fluctuation of the total sales is increased.
2. If two products have equal and oppositely phased sales fluctuations, total sales will grow smoothly.
3. If one product shows sales fluctuation, and the others show none, total sales will fluctuate but with a lower percentage amplitude.

How is the firm to choose among alternative subsets that differ in their rate of sales growth and volatility? There are two approaches to the problem. The first consists of defining management's utility function for sales growth and volatility:

$$U = g - kv \tag{7-28}$$

where U = utility of a particular sales growth rate and volatility
  g = percentage annual growth rate
  k = company discount rate for volatility
  v = percentage volatility

Equation 7-28 shows management's utility as equal to the percentage annual growth rate g less some fraction k of the percentage volatility v. Suppose that the firm were to choose only one of the four products shown in Figure 7-2 and the discount rate for volatility was .05. Then the utility of the four products would be

$$U_1 = .02 - .05(.10) = .0150$$
$$U_2 = .02 - .05(.10) = .0150$$
$$U_3 = .04 - .05(.25) = .0275$$
$$U_4 = .025 - .05(.00) = .0250$$

and product 3, in spite of having the highest volatility, offers the highest utility. Naturally, the utility rankings of the four products are highly sensitive to the choice of the volatility discount rate k.

This method of evaluating product alternatives is not ultimately satisfactory because profits have not been measured. To measure profits, it would be necessary to subtract the projected cost estimates based on historical data from the sales history for each product. For product subsets, the joint costs caused by the amplitude of fluctuation in production and cash flow must be subtracted from gross profits. The resulting profit projections for each subset over the planning horizon should then be discounted by the company's cost of capital. The resulting present value of each subset should be used as the figure of merit for choosing the best subset.

In general, management must find a systematic way to project its sales and profit future with different configurations of products. Too often companies add one product at a time, largely on individual merits, and after several years find that the overall product line has too much sales volatility. Or the company may find that the products are overconcentrated in one or two stages of the product life cycle. This section has shown that it is possible to examine in advance the future overall sales and profits implied in particular policies of product selection.

The case of risk covariance. The preceding case assumed that future sales and costs for each product could be estimated with accuracy. Now let us drop the assumption of perfect certainty and assume that management can only estimate an average rate of return on each product subject to a certain amount of variance. The symbols $E(r_i)$ and $V(r_i)$ will stand for the estimated annual return and variance of return, respectively, for product i. The optimal product selection problem can now be stated:

Given n possible products, each with an estimated mean and variance[24] of annual return, and with possible covariances[25] of returns between pairs of them, choose an efficient subset that produces the highest expected return with a given variance, *or* that produces a given expected return with the lowest variance.

This is an adaptation of the "expected value—variance of return" (*E-V*) model for portfolio selection that has been applied mainly to stocks.[26] The purpose of the model is to show how investors can reduce their risk by diversifying their investments in a way that takes advantage of the covariances of returns between pairs of investments (stock or products). The fundamental theorem of this analysis is that it is always possible to select an investment subset that would yield a given return at less risk than the lowest risk of a single investment yielding that return.

[24]For a set of numbers, r, the $V(r)$, is given by

$$V(r) = E[(r-\bar{r})^2] = \frac{1}{n} \sum_{i=1}^{n} (r_i-\bar{r})^2$$

where $\bar{r}$ is the arithmetic mean of the numbers. Thus the variance is a measure of expected average squared deviation of the numbers from their mean. The square root of the variance is known as the *standard deviation* and is a frequently used measure of dispersion.

[25]The covariance is a measure of the expected degree of association between two sets of variables (X and Y) such as height and weight, income and education, and so forth. Using the symbol $V(XY)$ for the covariance between variables X and Y, the covariance is measured by

$$V(XY) = E[(X-\bar{X})(Y-\bar{Y})] = \frac{1}{n} \sum_{i=1}^{n} (X-\bar{X})(Y-\bar{Y})$$

The covariance is also defined as $E(xy)/N$ in the expression $\rho = E(xy)/N\sigma_x\sigma_y$ where ρ is the symbol for the coefficient of correlation and $x = X-\bar{X}$ and $y = Y-\bar{Y}$. Thus ρ can be considered as the covariance divided by the product of the standard deviations of the two variates, i.e., the normalized covariance.

[26]Harry Markowitz, "Portfolio Selection," *Journal of Finance* (Mar. 1952) 77–91. See also Kalman J. Cohen and Frederick S. Hammer, *Analytical Methods in Banking* (Homewood, Ill.: Richard D. Irwin, Inc., 1966), pp. 271–280, for a discussion of the Markowitz article.

To show how this is accomplished, consider a set of n potential products and a vector of their expected returns

$$(r_1, r_2, \ldots, r_i, \ldots, r_n), \tag{7-29}$$

a vector of their relative shares of the total investment

$$(a_1, a_2, \ldots, a_i, \ldots, a_n) \qquad \text{where } \sum a_i = 1, \tag{7-30}$$

a vector of their variance of returns

$$(\sigma_1{}^2, \sigma_2{}^2, \ldots, \sigma_i{}^2, \ldots, \sigma_n{}^2), \tag{7-31}$$

and a matrix of covariances between the returns on all pairs of products:

$$
\begin{array}{c}
 \\
1 \\
2 \\
\vdots \\
i \\
\vdots \\
n
\end{array}
\begin{array}{cccccc}
1 & 2 & & i & & n \\
\left[\begin{array}{cccccc}
\sigma_{11} & \sigma_{12} & \cdots & \sigma_{1i} & \cdots & \sigma_{1n} \\
\sigma_{21} & \sigma_{22} & \cdot & \cdot & \cdot & \cdot \\
\vdots & & & \vdots & & \vdots \\
\sigma_{i1} & \cdot & \cdot & \sigma_{ii} & \cdots & \sigma_{in} \\
\vdots & & & \vdots & & \vdots \\
\sigma_{n1} & \cdot & \cdot & \sigma_{ni} & \cdots & \sigma_{nn}
\end{array}\right]
\end{array}
\tag{7-32}
$$

The diagonal elements in the covariance matrix are all 1's because the covariance of any number with itself is unity. The matrix is symetrical, that is, the covariances in the lower left half are mirror images of the covariances in the upper right half because $\sigma_{ij} = \sigma_{ji}$.

With this information, it is possible to estimate the expected return and variance of any subset m of products, where $m < n$. Use is made of well-known probability theorems regarding the means and variances of sums of random variables.[27] First, the expected value of a sum of weighted random variables is equal to the sum of the weighted expected values:

$$E\left(\sum_{i=1}^{m} a_i r_i\right) = \sum_{i=1}^{m} (a_i E r_i) \tag{7-33}$$

Secondly, the variance of a sum of weighted random variables is equal to[28]

$$V\left(\sum_{i=1}^{m} a_i r_i\right) = \sum_{i=1}^{m} a_i{}^2 V(r_i) + 2 \sum_{i=1}^{m} \sum_{j=1}^{m} a_i a_j V(r_i r_j) \qquad \text{for } i \neq j \tag{7-34}$$

Equation 7-34 provides the key to the fundamental theorem stated earlier. If the portfolio of products is so selected that the covariance term in Equation 7-34 is negative, then the variance of the portfolio will be less than the variance of a single product with this return.

Assume that a firm can find the minimum risk portfolio for any specified

---

[27]William Feller, *An Introduction to Probability Theory and its Applications, Vol. I*, (New York: John Wiley & Sons, Inc.) 3rd ed., 1968, Chap. 9.
[28]See Appendix Mathematical Note 7–3.

return level;[29] then the set of all minimum risk portfolios is called the *efficient set*. The shape of the efficient set is illustrated on the return-risk chart in Figure 7-3(a). It shows that higher return portfolios are accompanied by proportionately higher risks.

The final question is which portfolio of products is the best one for the company to select. It turns out that there is no best portfolio outside of the utility of management for return and risk.[30] Suppose management is willing to express its return risk indifference curve as the one shown in Figure 7-3(b). Only now is it possible to find the *E-V* portfolio that would maximize management's utility, in this case the one indicated by the point of tangency of the efficient set and the return-risk indifference curve, $E'_m V'_m$.

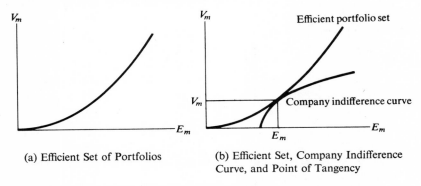

(a) Efficient Set of Portfolios

(b) Efficient Set, Company Indifference Curve, and Point of Tangency

Figure 7-3   Efficient Set of Portfolios and Company Indifference Curves

Thus we have defined the optimal product mix for situations in which the following conditions are satisfied:

1.   The mean and variance of return can be estimated for every product, as well as the covariance of return for each pair of products. (This implies that the best marketing strategies have been predetermined.)

2.   The mean and variance of return are assumed constant for the planning horizon, that is, there are no cycles or trends in the returns.

3.   The efficient set of product mixes can be found; furthermore, the company can define a return-risk indifference curve.

SUMMARY

This chapter has treated the problem of developing marketing budgets and strategies for products having demand and cost interrelationships. Management

---

[29]See Appendix Mathematical Note 7–4 on determining the least risk portfolio for a given return.

[30]See Chap. 10, pp. 264–267.

tends to use simple rules of thumb such as allocating the budget in proportion to the revenue generated by each product.

The basic problem is to find the set of simultaneous price levels and marketing efforts for all products that will maximize profits subject to budget and inter-action constraints. Three separate cases were considered. In the first case the optimal prices were determined, assuming no constraints and with the marketing effort given, by invoking the first order conditions of calculus. Second, the optim-al allocation of marketing effort was determined when the prices are given and using the Lagrangian method to accommodate the budget constraint. The third case used linear programming to compute the optimal levels of marketing instruments and product outputs among non-interacting products subject to constraints, but without assuming substitutability and continuity of the relevant functions as the first two methods did.

The next problem considered was the determination of the relative amounts of the products in the line to produce in order to maximize profits, given certain resource constraints. The linear programming format for the solution to this problem demonstrated how an objective standard can resolve differences between sales and production objectives.

A more fundamental question in the above context is which products the company should have in its product line. Three approaches to this problem were examined under the assumption of product independence. The first approach illustrated a method of selecting products according to a criterion such as profitability until a budget constraint is satisfied. The second approach used integer programming to illustrate how several constraints can be satisfied. In the third approach a technique that emphasizes the dynamic nature of the selection problem was used. For each product the excess present value of future profits over investment was computed, and an excess present value function was formulated using binary coefficients. The objective of this approach was to maximize the function subject to constraints such as the growth rate of profits over time.

The existence of product interdependencies was next considered, first in the context of sales covariance, and then of risk covariance. When environmental factors cause the sales of various products to move in the same way, manage-ment can avoid the volatility of such correlated demand by appropriate product selection. Sales functions that embody growth rate and volatility were postulated, and the need for management to project systematically the sales and profit future for different lines was underlined.

Finally it was recognized that estimates of the rate of return on products are subject to some variance. If each product has an estimated mean return, vari-ance, and possible covariance with other products, the problem was seen as choosing the product subset that maximizes the expected return for a given risk level or minimizes the expected risk for a given return. A graphical method was employed for determining the optimal product portfolio to satisfy management's criteria of utility.

Questions and Problems

1. A large West Coast air conditioning sales and service company is considering the discontinuation of its servicing operations. The company's accountants indicate that in the previous year the company made 163,822 service calls at an average cost of $9.27 per call. Because of the high level of competition in the air-conditioning service business, the company's average service charge is only $7.85.

An analysis of the company's sales records, however, indicate that on the average, about 12 percent of the service calls result in the sale of a new air-conditioning unit as a replacement for the existing unit. Such sales would almost invariably be lost to competition if the company were to discontinue service activity.

(a) If the company realizes a profit of $23.00 on each new unit sold, should the company discontinue its service operations?

(b) Analyze the above problem in terms of concepts developed in the chapter.

2. A monopolist produces two goods in quantities X_1 and X_2 in a given time period. The demand for each product is:

$$Q_1 = 20,000 - 400P_1 + 200P_2$$

$$Q_2 = 18,000 - 300P_2 + 100P_1$$

The cost of producing the two products is:

$$C = c_1Q_1 + c_2Q_2 + F = 50Q_1 + 40Q_2 + F.$$

Determine the profit maximizing prices and production quantities.

3. A manufacturer produces two products which yield profits of $3 and $2 per unit, respectively. Each product goes through three processes. Each unit of product 1 requires 8 hours in process 1, 2 hours in process 2, and 4 hours in process 3. Each unit of product 2 requires 4, 2, and 2 hours in the respective processes. The amount of time available each day in processes 1, 2, and 3 are 320 hours, 120 hours, and 160 hours. State the above as a linear programming problem and determine the solution graphically.

4. Below are the characteristics of 5 products from which management wishes to select an optimal product line.

Product	Price	Annual Sales (units)	Annual Cost	Initial Investment
A	$ 4	5,000	$ 18,000	$ 20,000
B	20	30,000	546,000	450,000
C	90	1,000	85,000	25,000
D	150	400	52,000	60,000
E	15	100,000	1,400,000	400,000

If the company's investment budget is $500,000, in which projects should it invest? (Assume no product interaction, and that the products have the same investment time spans.)

5. A manufacturer is trying to select the best subset of products for his line from a set of 10 possible products.

(a) How many subsets does he have to choose from?

(b) If he wishes to handle exactly 4 products, how many subsets are there to choose from?

(c) If he wishes to handle no more than 4 products, how many subsets are there to choose from?

6. A ski manufacturer produces a line of snow skis, but finds demand to be very seasonal, as shown below. Suggest a logical solution and evaluate your solution in terms of the concepts of sales covariance, product interaction, and risk covariance.

	Fall	*Winter*	*Spring*	*Summer*
Sales (units)	12,000	6,000	500	600
Profit (dollars)	$160,000	$10,000	− $78,000	− $50,000

7. The following are sales projections for 4 products being considered by a company for addition to its product line:

(a) $200 (1.03^t)[1 + .2 \sin (50t)]$

(b) $200 (1.04^t)[1 + .4 \sin (50t)]$

(c) $200 (1.02^t)$

(d) $200 (1.03^t)[1 + .2 \sin (50t + 180)]$

The company wishes to choose 2 of the 4 products which will yield the best results in terms of growth rate and sales stability. What combination would appear to be the best?

CHAPTER 8
Joint Marketing and Production Planning

We have examined various complexities in the marketing process, such as multiple territories, products, instruments, and carryover and competitive effects, with a view toward determining the profit maximizing marketing strategy. While considering marketing decisions and costs in some detail, we have been content to express nonmarketing activities and costs at a highly general level. For example, we have assumed that production activities could be arranged in a straightforward manner to supply the required output. We have also assumed that financial activities could be arranged in a straightforward manner to generate the required cash flow and investment. Nonmarketing costs were all lumped indistinguishably in a single equation cost expression.

When one looks more closely at production and financial activities, it becomes clear that they involve highly complicated decision issues whose resolution will make a difference to overall company marketing strategy and profits. Production involves decisions on levels of employment, inventory, capital, and output that are affected by, and affect, marketing decisions. Finance involves decisions on sources and uses of funds that are affected by, and affect, marketing decisions. Although many production and financial decisions can be made after the marketing plan has been established, many other production and financial decisions must be considered jointly with marketing decisions if overall company profits are to be maximized.[1]

In spite of the desirability of joint interdepartmental decision making for many types of company decisions, there is a strong departmental bias in practice. Each department generally has a primary objective; its personnel are rewarded on how well they achieve this objective. The marketing department takes the viewpoint of sales revenue maximization; production takes the viewpoint of keeping down unit manufacturing costs; purchasing seeks to keep down material and inventory costs; and finance tries to keep down money capital costs. As long as each department is rewarded on the basis of how well it achieves its primary objective, departments will resist incurring higher costs, even if this might save still more for another department. Examples abound of the conflict of interests between departments that often lead to a suboptimization of company profits:

1. The marketing department might want to concentrate its promotional effort during the months of peak demand, even though this tends to place strains on the manufacturing system. The manufacturing department must either vary employment and production rates to keep a constant inventory level or vary the inventory level to maintain fairly continuous employment and output. Either alternative might entail more expense than the company would bear if promotional spending were more uniform throughout the year.

2. The marketing department benefits when the company carries a high level of inventory because this means that customers can be promised early delivery. The department responsible for controlling the level of inventory has the opposite inclination of keeping inventory levels low, especially if they are not charged with the costs of stockouts. Obviously, the proper level of inventory must come out of an analysis that takes into account all departmental costs.

3. The marketing department favors high cost physical distribution methods such as a large number of warehouses and rapid modes of transportation. Others in the company such as the freight department and controller's office have a strong interest in keeping down the costs of physical distribution.

4. The marketing department favors a steadily growing budget for market development to insure continuously growing sales. On occasion the financial officer will recommend reducing market development funds in order to improve the picture of current profits in the interests of attracting additional capital.

5. The marketing department generally favors liberal credit arrangements for customers. A liberal credit policy, however, tends to increase the absolute amount of bad debts and reflects unfavorably on the credit department.

6. The marketing department sometimes favors dropping or "taxing" the lowest 20 per cent of the customers who account for only, say, 5 percent of the sales but a much greater percent of marketing expense. But the manufacturing department recommends holding on to these marginal customers because the

[1]For a pioneering effort to integrate various decisions of the firm in terms of microeconomic theory, see Douglas Vickers, *The Theory of the Firm: Production, Capital, and Finance* (New York: McGraw-Hill, Inc., 1968).

5 percent additional output may bring down unit production costs through fuller utilization of capacity.

7.   The marketing department often favors producing a product in several models or sizes to increase customer appeal. The manufacturing department may resist this because of the extra tooling and inventory costs entailed by variety.[2]

8.   The marketing department wants the manufacturing department to exercise the highest standards of quality control. But manufacturing must keep this expense within reason and is less concerned with the cost of customer dissatisfaction.

9.   The marketing department prefers to set a low price on a new product to stimulate its sales. This goes along with recommending building a large plant to prepare for a high sales volume. The controller, however, might like to proceed more cautiously by setting a high price on the product and building a small plant.

10.   The marketing department favors direct cost accounting because this results in lower estimated product costs and gives the marketing department more pricing latitude. The accounting department favors full costing to make sure that all costs are recovered through the pricing structure.

These and other interdepartmental conflicts are summarized in Table 8-1. The universality of these conflicts suggests that business decision making, when conducted entirely on a departmental basis, is likely to be highly suboptimal. While departments are an efficient means for carrying out and controlling specific types of business activities, they are less defensible as a source of policy on issues that have interdepartmental significance. Such issues require a corporate model, not a departmental model, for their resolution.

This chapter will limit itself to examining a set of company problems that are of deep common concern to the marketing and manufacturing departments. It will illustrate some models for resolving these problems in the company's interest, rather than according to the narrow interests of either the marketing or manufacturing department alone. The next chapter will take up company problems involving marketing activities in relation to a variety of financial goals that the company might have beside current profit maximization.

The five joint marketing-production problems that will be considered in this chapter are:

1.   Selecting the best inventory policy in the face of uncertain demand

2.   Developing the best production schedule in the face of a predictable pattern of seasonal demand, and attempting to influence the seasonal pattern by an off-season discount

3.   Determining which marginal customers to drop in the interest of effecting marketing and production economies

4.   Designing a system on feedback principles to smooth out production fluctuations

---

[2]See Martin K. Starr, "Product Planning from the Top: Variety and Diversity" in *Systems: Research and Applications for Marketing*, Daniel M. Slate and Robert Ferber, eds. (Urbana, Ill.: University of Illinois, Bureau of Economic and Business Research, 1968), pp. 71–77.

Table 8-1 Summary of Organizational Conflicts between other Departments and Marketing

Other departments	Their emphasis	Emphasis of marketing
Engineering	Long design lead time Functional features Few models with standard components	Short design lead time Sales features Many models with custom components
Purchasing	Standard parts Price of material Economic lot sizes Purchasing at infrequent intervals	Nonstandard parts Quality of material Large lot sizes to avoid stockouts Immediate purchasing for customer needs
Production	Long order lead times and inflexible production schedules Long runs with few models No model changes Standard orders Ease of fabrication Average quality control	Short order lead times and flexible scheduling to meet emergency orders Short runs with many models Frequent model changes Custom orders Aesthetic appearance Tight quality control
Inventory management	Fast moving items, narrow product line Economic levels of stock	Broad product line Large levels of stock
Finance	Strict rationales for spending Hard and fast budgets Pricing to cover costs	Intuitive arguments for spending Flexible budgets to meet changing needs Pricing to further market development
Accounting	Standard transactions Few reports	Special terms and discounts Many reports
Credit	Full financial disclosures by customers Low credit risks Tough credit terms Tough collection procedures	Minimum credit examination of customers Medium credit risks Easy credit terms Easy collection procedures

Source: Philip Kotler, "Diagnosing the Marketing Takeover," *Harvard Business Review* (Nov.–Dec. 1965) 70–72.

5.   Determining whether marketing-production planning is best coordinated in a centralized or decentralized way

INVENTORY PLANNING UNDER UNCERTAIN DEMAND

Our analysis of optimal marketing programming to this point has assumed that the manufacturing department would produce in each period the exact amount demanded in each period, that is,

$$Q_s = Q_d \qquad (8\text{-}1)$$

If the market purchased the company's product at a constant rate, then the company could produce at a constant rate. Each day the factory would produce exactly the daily quantity ordered or sold and this would involve the firm in a zero or low level (constant) inventory position.

Unfortunately, a constant sales rate is the exception rather than the rule. Company sales are typically subject to both *random* and *systematic* variation. In this section we shall confine our attention to the case of random sales variation and appropriate policies for dealing with it.

Nature of Random Sales Variation

Virtually every time series of sales tends to exhibit some randomness in addition to whatever systematic properties are exhibited. Orders can be affected by a great variety of factors, such as the weather, world news, competitors' actions, governmental legislation, and so forth. Each firm or person about to place an order may or may not execute it on a particular day or in a particular period, for a variety of reasons. Random variation is a fairly common property of a sales time series.

The analyst who recognizes random variation in a sales time series will try to represent it analytically as a first step to examining appropriate marketing and production policies. Three major types of random variations are illustrated in Figure 8-1. In the first case, current demand, Q_t, is equal to a constant demand level, $\bar{Q}$, plus a small current deviation, u_t. The current deviation cannot be predicted but presumably it comes from a distribution whose characteristics can be analyzed. Very commonly, the deviation is assumed to come from a normal distribution whose mean is 0 and whose standard deviation is σ, that is, u_t is distributed $P_n(0, \sigma)$. (Of course, other probability distributions can be assumed in order to generate more complicated sales time series.) If the standard deviation of u_t is small in relation to $\bar{Q}$, then this demand behavior does not pose too serious a problem for effective production planning. Employment and output could be kept fairly steady during the year with a buffer inventory stock to absorb the small fluctuations. If the standard deviation of u_t is fairly large, then the buffer inventory stock would have to be larger and might become a significant cost of doing business.

The second example of random variation shows demand growing by a constant amount, a, each period and subject to a random disturbance. It is fairly easy for the firm to adapt to this demand picture by planning a steady growth in labor, materials, and capital over the planning period. The problem is more difficult if capital is available in only discontinuous doses, in which case the firm will have to operate with insufficient or excess capacity at certain times.

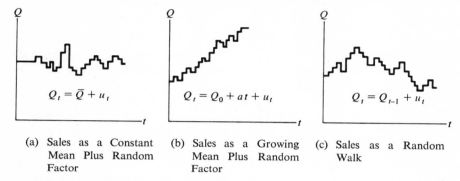

(a) Sales as a Constant Mean Plus Random Factor

$$Q_t = \bar{Q} + u_t$$

(b) Sales as a Growing Mean Plus Random Factor

$$Q_t = Q_0 + at + u_t$$

(c) Sales as a Random Walk

$$Q_t = Q_{t-1} + u_t$$

Figure 8-1   Three Types of Random Sales Series

The third example shows demand following the course of a "random walk." Sales of the last period become the base on which is added the new disturbance. This means that it is very difficult to forecast future sales. The current sales level is the best estimate of future sales, but actual future sales may be higher or lower as a result of the cumulative impact of many factors. For this situation it is possible to derive a probability distribution for the possible states of demand in any future period. The variance of this distribution is typically larger than the variance to which u_t is subject, making the random walk situation more difficult to plan for than either of the first two situations.[3]

Whenever there is significant variation in the sales rate, a company will usually find it desirable to carry a certain level of finished goods inventory. This is true whether the variation is systematic and predictable or random and unpredictable. The basic reason, from production's point of view, is that the provision of inventory enables the manufacturing department to smooth its employment and production rates. Another basic reason, from marketing's point of view, is to prevent stockouts and assume a continuous and uninterrupted supply of product to dealers and customers. It is very important for the company to determine the proper level of inventory to carry, for too little inventory can lead to stockouts and lost customers and too much inventory can lead to excessive inventory costs.

[3]See William Feller, *An Introduction to Probability Theory and Its Applications* (New York: John Wiley & Sons, Inc., 1958), vol. 1, 3rd ed., pp. 354–359. Feller develops expressions for unrestricted random walks in connection with diffusion processes. The sum of n independent random variables (i.e., the distance "walked") when each step can take the values $+1$ or -1 with probabilities p and q, respectively, is $S_n = X_1 + X_2 + \ldots + X_n$. The expectation of S_n is $E(S_n) = (p-q)n$ and the variance is $V(S_n) = 4npq$. Thus the expectation is a minimum and the variance is a maximum when $p = q = \frac{1}{2}$. The above might be compared with the variance of a simple binomial process $= npq$, i.e., it is four times as great.

The Classic Inventory Model under Certainty

To appreciate the effect of sales uncertainty on the proper inventory level, we shall first review briefly the classic inventory model under certainty. All inventory models require setting up a cost expression as a function of order quantity or order time and seeking the order quantity or time that will minimize it. We shall consider the problem from the point of view of how much to order (order quantity). The larger the quantity ordered, the less often an order has to be placed. Placing orders involves *order processing costs*; maintaining large inventories involves *carrying costs*. It is through a comparison of these opposing costs that the decision on order quantity can be made.

The costs of placing an order are somewhat different for the distributor and the manufacturer. The distributor's processing costs consist of whatever materials (stamps, order forms, envelopes, etc.), machine accounting time, and labor are used up every time an order is placed, received, and inspected. Distributors have estimated their order processing costs as low as $1 in some cases and as high as $20–$30 in others. The figure settled upon can make quite a difference in the final determination of optimal order quantity. Some of the variance in the estimates of different firms is real—based on actual operating cost differences; and some is artificial—based on different accounting methods. Generally speaking, only variable processing costs should be measured. This avoids the problem of highly arbitrary overhead charges, which is usually at the basis of estimating ordering costs to be as high as $30 an order. If any overhead is included, it should reflect the costs clearly attributable to the level of ordering activity, and not to other operations that would go on anyway.

Order processing costs for a manufacturer consist of setup costs and running costs for the item. If setup costs are very low, then the manufacturer's cost per item would be generally constant and approximately equal to the running costs. However, if setup costs are high, then the manufacturer can reduce the average cost per unit by producing a large run. In this case, the company would prefer to produce large runs infrequently.

Against the order processing costs must be placed the costs of carrying the inventory. The larger the average stock carried, the higher the inventory carrying costs. These carrying costs fall into four major categories:

Storage space charge.   Inventories are held in special facilities that require heat, light, and security. These facilities may be rented or owned. In either case, decisions to carry high levels of inventory will raise the space costs (actual or opportunity costs).

Cost of capital.   Inventories represent a form of investment of corporate funds. As a result, the company foregoes the opportunity rate it could make on its money in other uses. This is a very important cost but one over which there is much disagreement, both on concept and measurement.[4] Some companies make a very low charge, slightly above the bank interest rate of 6 percent, for their

[4]See Ezra Solomon, ed., *The Management of Corporate Capital* (New York: The Free Press, 1959).

cost of capital. Other companies consider their cost of capital to be as high as 30 percent. Decisions to carry higher inventory levels will, of course, raise the total capital costs.

Taxes and insurance.   Inventories are typically insured and also bear tax charges. The variable cost of tax and insurance should enter into the decision on order quantity.

Depreciation and obsolescence.   Goods in inventories are subject to a number of risks that can reduce their value, among which are damage, price devaluation, and obsolescence. Although these costs are difficult to measure, the larger the inventory carried, the higher the write-off may have to be.

These costs make up total inventory carrying charges. They have been estimated to be about 25 percent of the inventory value.[5] This is generally higher than the estimate used by many businessmen, but there is growing recognition that the cost is this high. It means that marketing management in particular must be more persuasive about the sales impact of carrying large inventories. A company that increased its inventory investment from $400,000 to $500,000 without a corresponding increase in sales would bear an incremental cost of $25,000 in making this move. The question is whether the resulting higher service standard would increase sales by enough so that the gross profit on these sales would exceed $25,000. This is the issue each company must face.

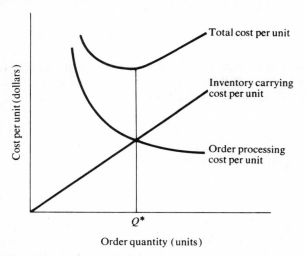

Figure 8-2   **Determining Optimal Order Quantity (Q*)**

The optimal order quantity can be derived either graphically or mathematically. Figure 8-2 shows how the two opposing costs, processing and carrying costs, behave with different order quantities. The order processing cost per unit

[5]For sources and a breakdown of this estimate, see J. L. Heskett, Robert M. Ivie, and Nicholas A. Glakowsky, Jr., *Business Logistics: Management of Physical Supply and Distribution* (New York: The Ronald Press Company, 1964), pp. 13–15.

is shown to fall with the number of units ordered because the order costs are spread over more units. Inventory carrying charges per unit are shown to rise with the number of units ordered since each unit will remain longer in inventory. The two cost curves can be summed vertically into a total cost curve. The lowest point on the total cost curve can be projected down on the horizontal axis to find the optimal order quantity Q^*.

This same order quantity can be derived mathematically. The first task is to express the components of total cost. The following five elements are involved:

Q = order quantity in units
C = price plus variable order costs per unit
I = percentage of annual carrying cost per unit to unit value
S = set up or order cost (fixed per order)
D = annual demand

From these, we derive the following three variables:

$Q/2$ = average quantity on hand
D/Q = number of orders placed per year
IC = annual carrying cost per unit

Total variable inventory costs (TC) can be defined as:

TC = annual processing costs + annual carrying costs
TC = number of orders per year x cost to place one order + average quantity carried (in units) x carrying cost per unit

$$TC = \frac{D}{Q}S + \frac{Q}{2}IC \qquad (8\text{-}2)$$

The only policy variable in Equation 8-2 that management controls is the order quantity Q. To find the Q that minimizes total annual inventory costs, proceed to differentiate Equation 8-2 and set it equal to 0:

$$\frac{dTC}{dQ} = -\frac{DS}{Q^2} + \frac{IC}{2} = 0 \qquad (8\text{-}3)$$

This yields the following optimal order Q^*:

$$Q^* = \sqrt{\frac{2DS}{IC}} \qquad (8\text{-}4)$$

This formula was developed early in the century and is called the economic lot size or economic order quantity (EOQ) formula. It is used widely in industry, often in modified form to take into account certain real world complications. For example, the formula assumes a constant ordering cost, a constant cost of carrying an additional unit in inventory, a known demand, no quantity discounts, and so forth. When these are modified, the formula is correspondingly altered.[6]

[6]For a comprehensive analysis and derivation of inventory formulas, see Martin K. Starr and David W. Miller, *Inventory Control: Theory and Practice* (Englewood Cliffs, N.J.: Prentice-Hall, Inc., 1962).

The Inventory Model Modified for Uncertainty

Here we shall specifically consider only one of the several complications that could be introduced: the effect of uncertainty. Two classes of uncertainty will be considered, that concerning the *lead time for delivery*, and that concerning the *annual demand, D*.

If the lead time for delivery is 0, then the company would never incur a stockout cost. It could replenish stock instantly. If the lead time is finite and constant, the company would simply place its order L days before the known stockout date. If the lead time is finite and uncertain, the company would face some probability of stockout if it simply ordered $\bar{L}$ days in advance (where $\bar{L}$ is average delivery delay). Whether this would involve a heavy expense depends upon the *penalty cost of stockout per unit, p*. If the penalty cost is 0, as when customers are completely willing to wait, then the seller need not order more than Q^*. If the penalty cost is high, as when customers are likely to switch to competitors, the seller must order something more than Q^*, the excess amount being called a safety stock R. The higher the penalty cost, the higher the optimum safety stock, all other things being equal. Carrying the safety stock costs money, and incurring stockouts also costs money; the two costs must be balanced.

If the annual demand is uncertain, this further complicates the problem of optimum order quantities and safety stocks. The greater the variance of demand, the higher the optimum order quantity safety stock, other things being equal. Lead time uncertainty plus annual demand uncertainty calls for modifying the total cost expression in Equation 8-2 to read

$$TC = \frac{D}{Q}\left[S+pE(u>R)\right]+IC\left[\frac{Q}{2}+(R-\bar{u})\right] \qquad (8\text{-}5)$$

where
$\quad p = $ penalty cost per unit of stockout
$\quad u = $ demand during lead time
$\quad R = $ safety stock
$E(u>R) = $ the expected number of units of stockout
$pE(u>R) = $ the expected stockout cost
$\quad u = $ mean demand during lead time

Comparing Equation 8-5 to the certainty case in Equation 8-2, we find that the annual order processing costs have been increased by the expected cost of stockouts and the annual carrying costs have been increased by the amount of safety stock carried. To find the optimal order quantity, we differentiate the total cost with respect to Q in Equation 8-5, set it equal to 0, and solve

$$\frac{dTC}{dQ} = -\frac{DS}{Q^2}-\frac{DpE(u>R)}{Q^2}+\frac{IC}{2} = 0 \qquad (8\text{-}6)$$

$$Q^* = \sqrt{\frac{2D[S+pE(u>R)]}{IC}} \qquad (8\text{-}7)$$

According to Equation 8-7, the company should increase its order quantity by a factor proportional to the square root of the expected stockout cost. That is, the optimal order quantity in the case of uncertainty does not rise as fast as the expected stockout cost. The expected stockout cost depends upon the safety stock, R, which is another decision variable of the firm. The optimal safety stock, R^*, is that stock such that the cost of carrying one or more units of safety stock exceeds the expected reduction in cost. The cost of carrying one more unit of safety stock is IC. The expected reduction in stockout cost is the penalty cost weighted by the probability that demand will exceed R times the number of lead times per year; that is, $[D/Q]pPr(u > R)$. The marginal conditions can be expressed as

$$\frac{D}{Q}pPr(u > R) \leqslant IC \tag{8-8}$$

$$Pr(u > R) \leqslant \frac{ICQ^*}{Dp} \tag{8-9}$$

To find R, first compute Q^* using Equation 8-7 on the assumption that the expected number of stockouts is 0. Then turn to an appropriate cumulative probability table and find the value of R^* that satisfies Equation 8-9. Introduce this R^* into Equation 8-7 and recompute Q^*. Continue the procedure until the Q's converge and the R's converge.

Equations 8-7 and 8-9 show how the optimal Q^* and R^* depend intimately on the penalty cost per unit of stockout, p. The higher the assumed penalty cost of stockout, the higher the company's inventory should be. Marketing men tend to exaggerate the penalty cost of stockouts, while controllers tend to understate it.[7] In general, penalty cost will be higher in industries marked by keen competition and a fairly undifferentiated product. Companies in such industries will have to carry larger inventories, adding to their out-of-pocket costs. They will more often find themselves tempted to break the price to reduce excess inventories. A still better strategy for the long run is for the individual company to seek product differentiation. To the extent that it can increase customer loyalty, it can afford more occasional stockouts without suffering as high a penalty.

PRODUCTION PLANNING FOR SEASONAL DEMAND

As mentioned earlier, companies will tend to carry inventories even where demand is perfectly predictable, provided that it shows some systematic variation. A good example of systematic variation in demand is seasonal demand.

---

[7]The cost of stockout is extremely difficult to measure, and some consider this to be a sufficient reason for ignoring it. But ignoring this cost is probably more biasing to the solution than assuming a positive cost lying somewhere between the extreme estimates of different "experts." In examining this cost, a distinction should be drawn between the immediate effect of a stockout, some *lost sales*, and the ultimate effect of frequent stockouts, the possibility of some *lost customers*. The second cost is far more serious. The company should adhere to a customer service standard at least up to the average of the industry so as not to raise the probability of lost customers.

For the sake of illustration, seasonal demand can be represented by the sine function:

$$Q_t = a \sin (kt + \theta) \tag{8-10}$$

The firm can adapt to seasonal demand in three different ways:

1. By varying the employment and output level in consonance with demand variations.
2. By varying the overtime and undertime level and output in consonance with demand variations.
3. By varying the inventory and order backlog levels, keeping employment and output constant.

It is clear that each policy emphasizes different costs and the company makes its choice on the basis of holding down the more significant costs. If inventory carrying costs are high, the company might favor policy one or two. If skilled labor is scarce or overtime rates are high, the company might favor policy three. In practice, companies may not adopt a pure strategy but rather allow two of the three variables to vary in some mix to reduce the costs of demand variations.

The Holt, Modigliani, Muth, and Simon Solution

One of the best-known solutions to the problem of optimal production policy is the one developed by Holt, Modigliani, Muth, and Simon.[8] They assume that management is interested in maximizing profits and proceed to show that the problem of determining optimal employment, output, and inventory is tantamount to a cost minimization problem. They do this by assuming that the company makes a forecast of demand for the next T periods. If there are no forecast errors, then this forecast determines at least the revenue part, PQ, of the profit equation:

$$Z = PQ - C \tag{8-11}$$

Therefore the problem of maximizing Z is translated into the problem of minimizing C.[9]

The authors go on to assume that all the costs of production can be measured and fitted approximately well by a quadratic cost function. The costs that they measure are: (1) regular payroll costs, (2) hiring and layoff costs, (3) overtime costs, and (4) inventory-connected costs. They show how these costs can be expressed as a quadratic function of output and state the problem to be: Find the W_t and $Q_{s,t}$ that will minimize the quadratic cost function $C = f(W, Q_s, I)$ subject to the constraints

$$I_{t-1} + Q_{s,t} - Q_{d,t} = I_t, \qquad t = 1, 2, \ldots, T \tag{8-12}$$

[8] See their *Planning Production, Inventories, and Work Force* (Englewood Cliffs, N.J.: Prentice-Hall, Inc., 1960).
[9] The authors, it should be noted, are implicitly assuming constant or zero level marketing activity during the period. Tuite's model, to follow, does not make this assumption.

where W_t = work force to hire this period
$Q_{s,t}$ = rate of production this period
I_t = inventory level this period
$Q_{d,t}$ = forecasted sales this period

The solution to this problem turns out to consist of two linear decision rules, one for setting $Q_{s,t}$, the production rate, and the other for setting W_t, the work force level:

$$Q_{s,t} = \left(\sum_{i=0}^{T-1} \alpha_{i+1} Q_{d,t+1} \right) + bW_{t-1} + c + dI_{t-1} \tag{8-13}$$

$$W_t = \left(\sum_{i=0}^{T-1} \beta_{i+1} Q_{d,t+1} \right) + fW_{t-1} + g + hI_{t-1} \tag{8-14}$$

where $\alpha, \beta, b, c, d, f, g, h$ = coefficients determined by the actual costs of changing production and work force levels and deviating from the optimal inventory level

Table 8-2 Illustration of Solution to Optimal Production Rate and Work Force Problem

$$Q_{s,t} = \begin{cases} +0.458 Q_{d,t} \\ +0.233 Q_{d,t+1} \\ +0.111 Q_{d,t+2} \\ +0.046 Q_{d,t+3} \\ +0.014 Q_{d,t+4} \\ -0.001 Q_{d,t+5} \\ -0.007 Q_{d,t+6} \\ -0.008 Q_{d,t+7} \\ -0.008 Q_{d,t+8} \\ -0.007 Q_{d,t+9} \\ -0.005 Q_{d,t+10} \\ -0.004 Q_{d,t+11} \end{cases} + 1.005 W_{t-1} + 153.0 - 0.464 I_{t-1}$$

$$W_t = 0.742 W_{t-1} + 2.00 - 0.010 I_{t-1} + \begin{cases} +0.0101 Q_{d,t} \\ +0.0088 Q_{d,t+1} \\ +0.0071 Q_{d,t+2} \\ +0.0055 Q_{d,t+3} \\ +0.0042 Q_{d,t+4} \\ +0.0031 Q_{d,t+5} \\ +0.0022 Q_{d,t+6} \\ +0.0016 Q_{d,t+7} \\ +0.0011 Q_{d,t+8} \\ +0.0008 Q_{d,t+9} \\ +0.0005 Q_{d,t+10} \\ +0.0004 Q_{d,t+11} \end{cases}$$

Note: $Q_{s,t}$ the number of units of product that should be produced during the forthcoming month, t

W_{t-1} the number of employees in the work force at the beginning of the month (end of the previous month)

I_{t-1} the number of units of inventory minus the number of units on back order at the beginning of the month

W_t the number of employees that will be required for the current month, t (the number of employees that should be hired is therefore $W_t - W_{t-1}$)

$Q_{d,t}$ a forecast of number of units of product that will be ordered for shipment during the current month, t

$Q_{d,t+1}$ the same for the next month, $t+1$, etc.

Source: Holt, Modigliani, Muth, and Simon, *Planning Production, Inventories, and Work Force*, p 61.

These two rules are illustrated for a particular set of costs (not shown) in Table 8-2. The optimal rate of production this month according to Equation 8-13 is positively related to a weighted (decreasing weights) forecast of future sales and last period's work force, and negatively related to last period's inventory. The desirable work force this period turns out to be positively related to the level of last period's work force and the weighted sales forecast, and negatively related to the level of last period's inventory.[10]

In general, problems in minimizing a quadratic cost function usually yield a solution in the form of linear decision rules. Of special interest to the marketing analyst is that the solution is perfectly general and can include as one of the inventory costs the cost of stockouts, which are a cost of prime importance to marketing executives.

At the same time, the solution fails to indicate the optimum joint plan for marketing and production. The Holt, Modigliani, Muth, and Simon model is a prime example of a departmental optimizing model, which assumes other departmental decisions and plans have already been determined. It shows how to find the W_t and Q_{st} that will minimize production costs for a given demand forecast based on a specific marketing plan. But a company usually can make a choice from a potentially large set of alternative marketing plans. In principle it could forecast future demand under each alternative marketing plan, find the optimal production plan via the Holt, Modigliani, Muth, and Simon model for each marketing plan, and determine the one that results in the highest profits.

Tuite's Example

The desirability of selecting a marketing strategy and production scheduling plan *simultaneously* was recently illustrated by Tuite for the case of a seasonal discount offered to customers on purchases made during the slack seasons.[11]

[10]"There is a fairly complex interaction between these two decisions rules. The production of one month affects the net inventory at the end of the month. This in turn influences the employment decision in the second month which then influences the production decision in the third month. Thus there is a continual dynamic interaction between the two decisions. The influence of net inventory on both the production and employment decisions produces a feedback or self-correcting tendency which eventually returns net inventory to its optimal level regardless of whether or not sales have been forecasted accurately.

"The weights that are applied to the sales forecasts and the feedback factors in the two decision rules determine the production and employment responses to fluctuations of orders and thereby indicate how much of these fluctuations should be absorbed by work force fluctuations, overtime fluctuations, and inventory and back order fluctuations in order to minimize costs. The work force responds only to fairly long-term fluctuations in orders, but production responds strongly to the orders in the immediate future and to the inventory position. Thus it appears that short-run fluctuations in orders and the disturbances that are caused by forecast errors are absorbed largely by overtime and undertime fluctuations. Extremely sharp fluctuations in orders are absorbed almost entirely by inventory and back order fluctuations.

"Implicit in these optimal decision rules is the answer to a question which is frequently raised: how should production be varied when orders follow a predictable seasonal fluctuation? The decision rules are designed to minimize costs despite predicted and unpredicted fluctuations of orders—predictable seasonal fluctuations are no exceptions." (Ibid., p. 62.)

[11]Matthew F. Tuite, "Merging Marketing Strategy Selection and Production Scheduling: A Higher Order Optimum," *Journal of Industrial Engineering* (Feb. 1968) 76–84.

Companies that are concerned with the amplitude of seasonal sales fluctuation often seek to smooth their sales curve by offering a discount, k, on orders placed in slack months.[12] If the customer sees where the discount would yield more than the cost of his carrying inventory for a longer period, he will take advantage of the discount. The higher the discount rate, the more the goods purchased on discount and the smoother sales will be through the year. This means that the company can reduce some of the undesirable fluctuations and costs associated with normal seasonal variation in the production rate, work force levels, and inventory carrying levels.

The company's problem is to find the optimal seasonal discount k. Suppose that the discount rate does not affect total sales during the planning period but only reshuffles the levels of monthly sales. Let $\$K_t$ represent the total discount taken by customers in month t, that is, K_t is the product of the discount rate k times the amount purchased on discount that month. Let K_T represent the total discount over the planning period T, resulting from a particular discount level k. Total revenue for the planning period is therefore

$$R = PQ_T - K_T \qquad (8\text{-}15)$$

The marketing department studies the relationship between the discount rate k and the actual opportunity cost K_T of offering the discount (see Figure 8-3(a)).

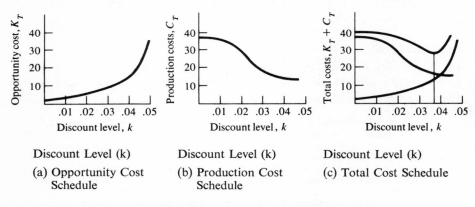

Discount Level (k)

(a) Opportunity Cost Schedule

Discount Level (k)

(b) Production Cost Schedule

Discount Level (k)

(c) Total Cost Schedule

Figure 8-3 Illustration of Joint Selection of Marketing and Production Strategy

Source: Tuite "Merging Marketing Strategy Selection and Production Scheduling: A Higher Order Optimum," *Journal of Industrial Engineering* pp. 79, 83.

The production department determines the optimal production plan for the seasonal pattern resulting from each discount level k (at discrete intervals) using the Holt, Modigliani, Muth, and Simon solution; the resulting minimum production costs (C_T) are shown in Figure 8-3(b). Revenue losses (K_T) mount,

[12]Another demand smoothing strategy is that of countercyclical promotion, which should be evaluated against other demand smoothing strategies before deciding on a policy.

of course, as the discount rate (k) is increased, while production costs (C_T) fall with higher discount rates because of demand smoothing. The best discount rate would be the one that minimizes the total cost:

$$TC = K_T + C_T \tag{8-16}$$

This discount rate can be either found graphically as in Figure 8-3(c) or by differentiating the total cost function with respect to k, setting the derivative equal to 0, and solving for k. This problem illustrates how an interdepartmental determination is required for selecting the best marketing strategy (here discount rate) and production plan.

OPTIMAL POLICY TOWARD MARGINAL CUSTOMERS

Most companies will find, in examining their distribution of sales, that a high proportion of sales is contributed by a small proportion of customers, products, territories, and so forth. An often-heard complaint is that "80 percent of our sales come from 20 percent of our customers" (not that there is any connection between the two figures). This finding leads a company to examine more closely its weak customers, products, and territories; it will seriously consider removing the weaker ones, particularly if the cost of servicing the weak sales segments exceeds their contribution to profit.

Different departments in the company exhibit varying attitudes toward the weak customer. (We shall concentrate on the weak customer problem, although the analytical approach also applies to the problem of weak orders, products, or territories.) The sales department may want to maintain the weak customer, first because the small customer eventually may become a large customer and, secondly, because the sum of small customers may add a substantial amount to total sales and thus reflect to the credit of the sales department. The production department may also want to maintain the small customers because they make possible a higher level of output, enabling fixed costs to be spread over more units and unit costs to be brought down. The financial department, on the other hand, generally prefers to drop many small customers who seem to be costing the company more than they are worth in sales and whose credit practices are often not dependable. Because of these conflicting interests, it is important that the decision to drop small customers be considered in the framework of total company's profits, long run as well as short run.

To give the problem a concrete setting, consider a truck manufacturer who sells his trucks through a national network of independent franchised dealers. Some dealers are large and sell many trucks each year; others are small and hardly sell any. The size distribution of his dealers is given by

$$n = n(x) \tag{8-17}$$

where x = number of trucks sold by a dealer each year

$n(x)$ = number of company dealers selling x trucks

Figure 8-4(a) illustrates one possible version of the distribution of dealers by size, where there are many small dealers and a declining number of large ones. Dealer size is treated as a continuous variable for analytical convenience, although in principle it is actually integer and the curve in the figure is an approximation to a discrete set of frequencies.

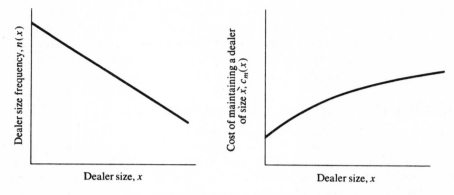

(a) Frequencies of different size dealers   (b) Cost of serving various size dealers

Figure 8-4   Illustration of Frequencies and Costs of Varying Size Dealers

Now assume that the company bears a cost of serving each dealer, consisting of sales calls, paperwork, financing, and so forth. Although this cost depends upon many factors, it will be closely related to the size of the dealer, that is,

$$c = c(x) \tag{8-18}$$

where c = cost of maintaining a dealer of size x.

Typically, this function consists of a minimum fixed cost for maintaining any dealer; beyond this the cost rises with the size of the dealer. The rate of rise typically declines, that is, unit marketing cost to a dealer falls with size of dealer. This is illustrated in Figure 8-4(b).

The two functions in Figure 8-4 allow a calculation to be made of the total selling costs. The total number of trucks sold by the company can be found by integrating the product of the number of dealers in a size class and the size class:

$$Q = \int xn(x)dx \tag{8-19}$$

where Q = total number of trucks sold.

The total selling cost can be found by integrating the product of the number of dealers in a size class and the cost of selling to that size class over all size classes:

$$C_s = \int n(x)c(x)dx \tag{8-20}$$

where C_s = total selling cost

Equation 8-20 can also be used to find the total cost of selling to fewer than all of the existing dealers. Suppose that the company drops all dealers who sell fewer than $x = k$ trucks. In addition, the largest dealers sell $x = m$ trucks. Then the total cost of selling to dealers who sell k or more trucks per year is given by the definite integral of Equation 8-20 between the limits k and m, that is,

$$C_{s(k)} = \int_{k}^{m} n(x)c(x)dx \tag{8-21}$$

In addition to the selling cost, there is the cost of producing the total number of trucks that the company will sell:

$$C_p = h(Q) = h\left(\int_{k}^{m} xn(x)dx\right) \tag{8-22}$$

where C_p = total production cost

This production cost function is illustrated in Figure 8-5, for the typical case in which there are fixed costs at zero output and additional costs rising at a varying rate for higher levels of outputs.

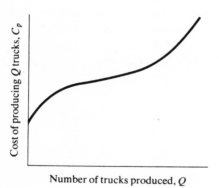

Figure 8-5   Illustration of a Production Function

We are now ready to combine these three functions into a simple model of profit as a function of the number of trucks the company decides to sell. Total profit (Z) will equal the total revenue from selling Q trucks minus the total cost of producing Q trucks (C_p) minus the total cost of serving the number of dealers required to sell Q trucks (C_s). In symbols, we have

$$Z = PQ - C_p - C_s \tag{8-23}$$

or

$$Z = P\int_{k}^{m} xn(x)\,dx - h\left(\int_{k}^{m} xn(x)\,dx\right) - \int_{k}^{m} n(x)c(x)\,dx \tag{8-24}$$

To find the optimal number of dealers to drop amounts to determining the k that maximizes profits in Equation 8-24. If the function in Equation 8-24 is well behaved, this amounts to finding the derivative of profits with respect to k, setting the derivative equal to 0, solving for k and checking the second order conditions; in other cases, sequential search procedures may have to be used. If k turns out to be greater than 0, that is, $k > 0$, then some of the marginal dealers should be dropped in the interest of increasing company profits.

A computer program called *Mardlr* (Marginal Dealer) was written to be used on a time sharing computer to make it easy for the analyst to solve the preceding kind of problem. The computer output is shown in Table 8-3. The first part shows how the computer terminal is activated. The analyst sits down at a terminal connected to the company computer and dials a special number for a line. Then the computer types a request for his user number, which he types in. (The analyst's inputs are all italicized in Table 8-3.) Then the computer asks what language system he will use and he answers *Bas* (for *Basic*, an elementary programming language). The computer asks if the analyst wants to develop a new program or call an old program from storage. He answers *Old*. The computer asks for the name of the program and he types in *Mardlr*. The computer says it is ready and the analyst types in *Run*.

At this point (Part 2) the computer types a description of what it needs to solve the problem. It tells the analyst that it needs three equations entered in a particular format and two numbers. In Part 3, the analyst types in the information according to the suggested format. The equations are: size distribution of dealers,

$$n = 10 - \frac{x}{10}$$

cost of selling to a dealer of size x,

$$C_1 = 8000 + 50x$$

and cost of producing Q units,

$$C_2 = 500{,}000 + 3000Q$$

He types in the largest number of units sold by a dealer, 100, and the price of a truck $5,000. He also types *Run*, which activates the computer to solve the problem.

In a very short time, the solution is printed out. Part 4 shows the total revenues, costs, and profits with different numbers of dealers. Profits are highest when the retained dealers sell five or more units. There are 456 such dealers and the profits are $28,159 thousands. In Part 5, the analyst types in *Bye* and this disconnects his service.

Thus Table 8-3 shows a conversational program that makes it very easy for the analyst to solve the marginal dealer problem on the computer through a computer program (not shown) that carries out the necessary calculations. At the same time the analyst should be aware of the following aspects of the problem that are not solved by the model.

Table 8-3 Use of a Time Sharing Program to Solve Marginal Customer
Problem

---

1 {
User number—U50001
Northwestern University

System—*Bas*
New or old—*Old*
Old problem name—*Mardlr*
Ready

Run
}

2 {
Mardlr   11:38   Wed.   08–20–69

Enter the equations that depict, [1] N = the frequency distribution of dealers
as a function of X, where X is the number of units sold by a dealer, [2] C_1 = the
cost of selling to a dealer as a function of X, [3] C_2 = the cost of producing Q
units; [4] X_m = the largest number of units sold by a dealer, [5] P = the price
per unit to the dealers. Enter this information in the following form . . . .

10 [Leave the remainder of the line blank]
190 Let N = [Type in the proper functional expression]
220 Let C_1 = [Type in the proper functional expression]
250 Let C_2 = [Type in the proper functional expression]
260 Let X_m = [Type in number]
290 Let P = [Type in price]
Run
Time: 3 secs.
}

3 {
10
190 Let $N = 10 - X/10$
220 Let $C_1 = 8000 + 50X$
250 Let $C_2 = 500000 + 3000Q$
260 Let $X_m = 100$
290 Let $P = 5000$
Run
}

4 {
Mardlr   11:40   Wed.   08–20–69

For Dealers selling	Total No. of Dealers evaluated	Total revenues (in thousands)	Total costs (in thousands)	Total profits (in thousands)
1 or more	495	83,325	55,288	28,036
2 or more	485	83,275	55,178	28,096
3 or more	475	83,177	55,040	28,136
4 or more	466	83,032	54,874	28,157
5 or more	456	82,840	54,680	28,159
6 or more	446	82,602	54,459	28,143

Dealers selling 5 or more units should be retained
Time: 13 secs.
}

5 {
Bye

Timesharing disconnected at 11:41   Wed.   08–20–69
}

The model assumes that all the sales of terminated dealers are lost to the company. Realistically, some proportion of these sales may be transferred to other company branches. To the extent that this takes place, the solution is not optimal and the company could afford to drop somewhat more than k dealers. This factor could be formally built into the model but is not included here.

Another assumption is that the present sales levels of the various dealers are stable through time. In fact, some of the marginal dealers are new and their volume can be expected to increase over time. The analytical model should be refined to take future sales patterns into account.

Finally, the model assumes that selling costs are a result of dealer size, rather than a partial cause of dealer size. The company can vary the level of its marketing attention to dealers between, and within, different-size classes and affect their sales to some extent. A practical option facing a company confronting a marginal dealer is to increase the dealer's sales training in the hope that it will lead to improvements in his sales; alternatively the company might consider reducing the sales calls to the particular dealer in the hope that his sales remain level but a cost saving is effected. Introducing the functional relationship between marketing effort and sales would call for modifying the preceding analysis.

These are considerations that enter into the analysis of the small dealer problem and that also bear on the weak territories and products problem as well. The analytical function is designed to bring together marketing and production costs at a company system level, so that the company could determine the rough magnitude of suboptimization caused by the presence of weak dealers; actual termination decisions require a host of additional data surrounding each case.

MARKETING-PRODUCTION PLANNING IN THE FACE OF SYSTEM DYNAMICS

Up to now, we have viewed the question of marketing-production interaction in terms of seeking joint decisions that would optimize some objective, such as total profits. The optimal decisions have been defined under largely static assumptions, with little or no attention paid to market growth, information delays and distortions, and feedbacks of various kinds. Yet these are important concerns in the actual coordination of marketing and production policy; they will be examined in this section.

Jay Forrester of the Massachusetts Institute of Technology deserves much of the credit for calling attention to industrial dynamics and presenting methods for their analysis and control.[13] His models dramatize how information delays and distortions, as well as uncoordinated decision making, can induce costly fluctuations in sales and production. His models are often too complicated to be amenable to optimization techniques but they do provide a tool for estimating the consequences of different company policies that might be used in the system.

[13]See Jay W. Forrester, *Industrial Dynamics* (Cambridge, Mass.: The M.I.T. Press, 1961).

Forrester's early models were concerned with the response of company production flows (men, material, machinery, and money) to different patterns of exogenously determined sales over time. His main interest was to find the set of company production decision rules that could satisfactorily respond to a wide variety of different sales input patterns to which the company might be exposed. In his later models, he began to emphasize the role played by company promotional policy in shaping the sales input pattern and began to include marketing decision rules along with production decision rules as jointly needing simultaneous determination in order to achieve satisfactory profits.[14] Here we shall examine first a model in which marketing policy is assumed to be set and sales patterns are generated exogenously. Later we shall introduce marketing policy as an active element.

An Example of a Simple Industrial Dynamics Model

The following miniature system explores the relationship between retailers and wholesalers, although it could easily be extended to include manufacturers and other agents in a total distribution system.[15] Assume that the retail sector constantly receives orders that arrive in some exogenously determined pattern. These orders go into an unfilled order bin and after some time lag are filled from retail inventory. The retailers in turn place stock replenishment orders with wholesalers according to the following retailer ordering rule:

$$PSR_{KL} = RRR_{JK} + \frac{1}{2}(IDR_K - IAR_K) \tag{8-25}$$

where PSR = purchase orders sent from retail
   RRR = requisitions received at retail
   IDR = inventory desired at retail
   IAR = inventory actual at retail
   J, K, L = time subscripts, where J is the moment marking the beginning of last week, K is the beginning of this week (now), and L is the beginning of next week. JK is the period of time between the beginning and end of last week and KL is the period of time between the beginning and end of this week.

This rule says that retailers will order an amount of new stock each week equal to the quantity bought by customers during the week plus one half of the difference between the desired inventory and the actual inventory at the end of the week. As noted earlier, RRR will be generated in some particular pattern determined exogenously, and the analyst is interested in the characteristics of the system's response. The inventory desired at retail, IDR is developed out of

---

[14]Ibid., Chap. 16.
[15]This specific example is adapted from the discussion of Forrester's Industrial Dynamics in Claude McMillan and Richard F. Gonzalez, *Systems Analysis: A Computer Approach to Decision Models*, 2nd ed., (Homewood, Ill.: Richard D. Irwin, Inc., 1968), Chap. 16.

experience or an economic lot size rule and represents the average retailer's policy.

Consider the following rule:

$$IDR_K = 6\frac{2}{3}\left[\frac{RRR_{JK-2}+RRR_{JK-1}+RRR_{JK}}{3}\right] \tag{8-26}$$

which says that the retailer prefers to maintain an inventory level of almost seven times the size of the average weekly order rate (average based on last three weeks).[16] As for the determinants of the actual inventory level, IAR, the following simple relationship holds:

$$IAR_K = IAR_J + SRR_{JK} - SSR_{JK} \tag{8-27}$$

where SRR = shipments received at retail
SSR = shipments sent from retail

Thus the actual level of retail inventory today is equal to the inventory last week adjusted upward by new stock arriving and downward by inventory depletion during the week. The system is still not complete because Equation 8-27 introduced two new variables, SSR and SRR; these in turn must be determined in some manner:

$$SSR_{JK} = RRR_{JK-2} \tag{8-28}$$

that is, retailers fill their customers' orders two weeks after they arrive. Then

$$SRR_{JK} = PSR_{JK-3} \tag{8-29}$$

that is, retailers receive their replenishment stock three weeks after placing their orders.

Drawing the system together, we have:

$$PSR_{KL} = RRR_{JK} + \frac{1}{2}(IDR_K - IAR_k) \qquad \text{ordering rule} \tag{8-25}$$

$$IDR_K = 6\frac{2}{3}\left(\frac{RRR_{JK-2}+RRR_{JK-1}+RRR_{JK}}{3}\right) \qquad \text{desired inventory} \tag{8-26}$$

$$IAR_K = IAR_J + SRR_{JK} - SSR_{JK} \qquad \text{actual inventory} \tag{8-27}$$

$$SSR_{JK} = RRR_{JK-2} \qquad \text{shipments sent} \tag{8-28}$$

$$SRR_{JK} = PSR_{JK-3} \qquad \text{shipments received} \tag{8-29}$$

This is a system of five equations and six distinct variables (ten variables when time is introduced). In order for the system to be closed, the number of unknowns (ten) must be reduced to the number of equations (five). There are two basic ways this can be done. One is to recognize that past time-dated variables already have their values determined (in this case, four: RRR_{JK-2}, RRR_{JK-1}, PSR_{JK-3}, and IAR_J). This reduces the number of remaining unknowns to six, one more than the number of equations. At this point we make the assumption

[16]The time subscript notation should be explained: JK-1 will represent the week just preceeding the present week, JK-2 two weeks preceding the present week, and so on.

that RRR_{JK}, the sales rate, is determined exogenously, and we proceed to study how the system responds to a variety of different sales patterns.

Of the variety of possible sales input patterns, three are particularly interesting. The first is one in which a steady level of sales suddenly rises to a permanently higher level. This is described as a step input function and is illustrated in Figure 8-6(a). The second occurs when sales increase momentarily and then settle back to the former level. This is called an impulse input function and is illustrated in Figure 8-6(b). In the third case, sales fluctuate in a cyclical way over time. This is called a sinusoidal input function and is illustrated in Figure 8-6(c).

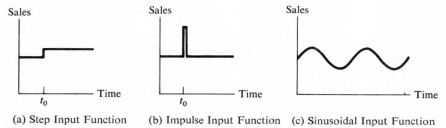

(a) Step Input Function   (b) Impulse Input Function (c) Sinusoidal Input Function

Figure 8-6 Three Major Patterns of Sales Input

Any one of these sales patterns, or other types, can be examined for their temporal impact on other variables in the retail, wholesale, and manufacturing segment of the industry by simulation. Take the case of a step function in which sales suddenly increase by 10 percent over the previous level. Before the sales increase, assume that a steady state was achieved with RRR and SRR standing at 300, UOR (unfilled orders at retail) standing at 600, and $IAR = IDR = 2000$. These conditions are shown in the first few rows of Table 8-4. Assume that the 10 percent permanent sales increase occurs in period 4. Variables such as SSR, UOR, and IDR shortly move up and achieve a new steady state. Other variables such as PSR, SSR, and IAR show oscillatory behavior with a tendency toward damping. Actual inventory at retail, for example, increases initially by a much higher percentage than the sales increase, a phenomenon that Forrester calls *amplification*. Amplification stems from the structure of delays and feedbacks in the system and can be costly to the firm.

Figure 8-7 shows a graphical summary of the system's responses to the 10 percent sales increase, this time for a larger model (not shown) that includes the factory level, as well as the retail and wholesale level. Each curve is differently defined and is to be read with respect to a particular vertical scale. The main thing to notice is how amplified several of the responses are to a simple 10 percent sales increase. For example, factory production output rose 45 percent in response to the 10 percent sales increase. Assuming that it is costly to increase factory production output by 45 percent within a five-month period (and then have to reduce output), Forrester would search for changes in the structure of company policies and feedbacks to reduce costly production fluctuations.

Table 8-4 The System's Responses to a 10 Percent Sales Increase

	Week	RRR	SSR	PSR	SRR	UOR	IAR	IDR
	—3			300				
	—2	300		300				
Time	—1	300		300				
Zero	1	300	300	300	300	600	2000	2000
	2	300	300	300	300	600	2000	2000
	3	300	300	300	300	600	2000	2000
	4	330	300	364	300	630	2000	2067
	5	330	300	397	300	660	2000	2133
	6	330	330	445	300	660	1970	2200
	7	330	330	428	364	660	2004	2200
	8	330	330	395	398	660	2071	2200
	9	330	330	337	445	660	2186	2200
	10	330	330	288	428	660	2284	2200
	11	330	330	255	395	660	2349	2200
	12	330	330	252	337	660	2356	2200
	13	330	330	273	288	660	2314	2200
	14	330	330	310	255	660	2239	2200
	15	330	330	350	252	660	2161	2200
	16	330	330	378	273	660	2104	2200
	17	330	330	388	310	660	2084	2200
	18	330	330	378	350	660	2104	2200
	19	330	330	354	378	660	2152	2200
	20	330	330	325	388	660	2210	2200
	21	330	330	301	378	660	2258	2200
	22	330	330	289	354	660	2282	2200
	23	330	330	292	325	660	2277	2200
	24	330	330	306	301	660	2248	2200

Source: McMillan and Gonzalez, *Systems Analysis,* p. 444.

How does all of this concern marketing management and the problem of developing marketing programs? The answer is that these different sales patterns are partly influenced by marketing management. For example, a firm facing a sinusoidal sales pattern could adopt demand smoothing strategies (seasonal discounts, counter cyclical promotion, etc.) to reduce costly production fluctuations. We have seen earlier how a seasonal discount policy could be evaluated analytically. When the system is too complicated to be solved analytically, because of nonquadratic cost functions, various information delays and distortions, and so forth, an Industrial Dynamics model can be built to explore the implications of the proposed policy through simulation.

A Second Example of Industrial Dynamics

In his more recent work, Forrester has treated marketing policy together with production policy as endogenous variables in the total system. Consider the case of a company that introduces a new product and backs it up with a certain

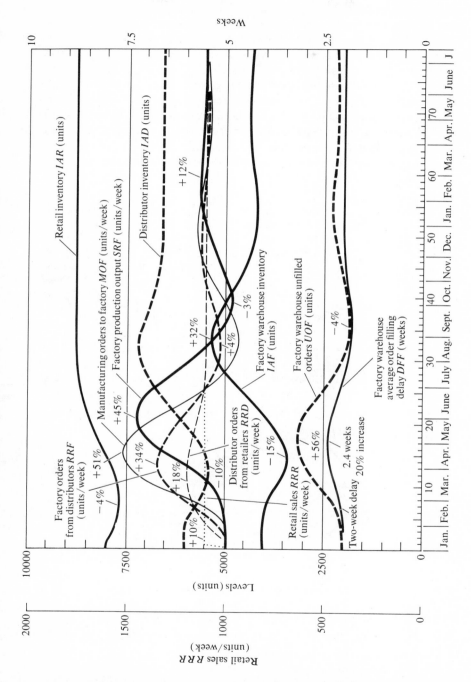

Figure 8-7 Graphical Illustration of a System's Responses to a 10 Percent Sales Increase
Source: McMillan and Gonzales, p. 441, taken from Forrester, *op. cit.*, p. 24.

amount of sales effort.[17] This amount of sales effort, taking place with a certain level of sales effectiveness, produces a certain increase in the rate of sales. See Figure 8-8(a). If this sales rate is profitable, the sales budget will be increased and this will lead to an increase in sales effort, a further increase in sales, and a further increase in the sales budget. This can go on for a long time and produce continuous sales growth. The rate of sales growth depends on the level of sales effectiveness and the fraction of the sales revenue going to the support of sales effort, among other things. If sales had been unprofitable, this could have led to a cut in the sales budget and a further reduction in sales. In either case the variables are related in a positive feedback loop, as shown in Figure 8-8(a), which can produce either continuous growth or continuous decline.

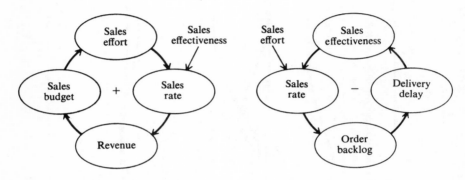

(a) Positive Feedback in Sales Growth   (b) Negative Feedback Limiting Sales

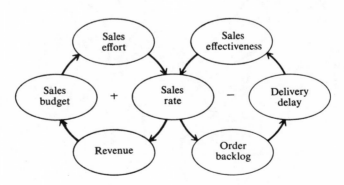

(c) Coupled Negative and Positive Feedback Loops

Figure 8-8   Positive and Negative Feedback Loops in Sales Growth

Source: Jay Forrester, "Modeling of Market and Company Interactions," *ibid*, pp. 357, 358, 361.

[17]This example is adapted from Jay W. Forrester, "Modeling of Market and Company Interactions," in Peter D. Bennett, ed., *Marketing and Economic Development*, Proceedings of the 1965 Fall Conference of the American Marketing Association (Chicago: American Marketing Association, 1965), pp. 353–364.

Now suppose that production capacity has not been expanded and that sales begin to press against capacity. This increases the order backlog and, in turn, the delivery delay. See Figure 8-8(a). Some customers are resentful about the delay and start switching some of their business to competitors. This is tantamount to a reduced level of sales effectiveness, which results in a lowering of the sales rate. Now sales fall, the order backlog is reduced, delivery is improved, and sales effectiveness rises. Sales again start to rise, but eventually and in short order sales will again reach the ceiling of production capacity and cause a reversal. This oscillation process, triggered by the barrier of a constant level of production capacity, is illustrated as a negative feedback loop in Figure 8-8(b). It is a negative feedback loop because, as sales increase, forces are brought into being that eventually work against a continued sales increase. The function of a negative feedback loop is to bring variables back to a particular level, the force for returning them often growing stronger the greater the deviation.

The complete system is described by joining both feedback loops as shown in Figure 8-8(c). The role of the positive feedback loop is to cause sales to grow as long as there is slack production capacity. Eventually, however, capacity is reached and the negative feedback loop is activated, causing sales growth to stop and sales fluctuation to take over. A time series of the key variables and their behavior as a result of this simple system is shown in Figure 8-9.

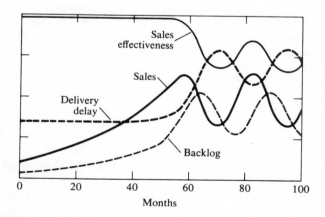

Figure 8-9 Results of the Interaction between Sales Growth and a Production Capacity Constraint
Source: Forrester, *ibid.*, p. 361.

This example underscores the need for coordinated company planning, instead of separate departmental planning. It is of no help for marketing to plan for larger and larger sales levels unless top management at the same time is planning to create the capacity to meet the sales targets. This model is particularly helpful in exploring the question of timing the introduction of the new capacity. Capacity cannot generally be acquired in infinitesimal amounts. Very often, the greatest economy is achieved when large scale revisions are made in plant and production layout. A decision made at one point in time to expand capacity will yield the new capacity some periods later. If the decision is made too early in relation to actual demand, it will lead to underutilized capacity; if the decision is made too late, it will lead to lost sales and customers. By simulating the positive feedback loop and trying different timings and amounts of new capacity, it is possible to determine jointly a satisfactory marketing and production capacity policy.

CENTRALIZED OR DECENTRALIZED MARKETING-PRODUCTION PLANNING

We have discussed several examples of marketing-production interaction without examining organizational mechanisms for interdepartmental coordination. In this last section, we want to consider three different methods of coordinating decision making between the marketing and production departments. Consider a single product firm that has a marketing department and a production department.[18] The marketing department has two decision variables, price (P) and advertising (A). The demand function for the firm is given by $Q_d = f(P, A)$. There are initially no constraints on the marketing department's policies, except that price and advertising must be nonnegative. The production department has two decision variables: standard hours employed w and overtime hours w_0. The production department faces three constraints, the first consisting of a finite number of available standard hours $\overline{W}$, the second consisting of the requirement that overtime must not exceed some fraction k of the standard hours employed, and the third consisting of the nonnegativity of w and w_0. The firm's production function is $Q_s = g(w, w_0)$. In any period, the firm is assumed not to produce more than the quantity demanded, that is,

$$f(P, A) \geqslant g(w, w_0) \tag{8-30}$$

In this situation, there are three different mechanisms that can be used to develop joint marketing-production plans, called centralization, coherent decentralization, and decentralization by guidelines. Each of these shall be examined in turn.

Centralization calls for the decisions to be made by the central authority who is aware of these interdependent departmental functions and can find the global solution. The global solution is found by forming the company profit function:

$$\max Z = Pg(w, w_0) - A - cw - c_0 w_0 \tag{8-31}$$

(where c and c_0 are the wages for standard and overtime hours, respectively), subject to the standard hour constraint,

$$\overline{W} - w \geqslant 0$$

[18]This section is largely adapted from David P. Baron, "Joint Decision Technologies in a Marketing-Production Context," an unpublished working paper, Northwestern University, Evanston, Ill., 1969.

the supply constraint,

$$f(P, A) - g(w, w_0) \geqslant 0$$

the overtime constraint,

$$kw - w_0 \geqslant 0$$

and the nonnegativity constraints,

$$P, A, w, w_0 \geqslant 0$$

Note that the production function is used in Equation 8-31, rather than the demand function because company profits will depend upon the number of units produced, not demanded, and the company may not produce to meet the full demand when output is constrained by available labor hours. The problem of the central authority is to set (P, A, w, w_0) in such a way so as to maximize profits without violating any of the constraints. This calls for forming the Lagrangian expression and maximizing it. The result will show the various conditions that are satisfied by an optimal solution and the dual values, namely, the value of relaxing each of the constraints. Because the solution involves extended algebra, it will not be shown here and the reader is referred to the original paper.[19]

For the centralized solution to be achieved, the central authority must receive from the two departments the respective functions and the wage rates. After it solves the problem, the separate departments must agree to implement the solution. Because of the chance that (1) the central authority might not receive accurate information and/or (2) the solution may not be implemented because the respective departments may not agree with it or be motivated, companies have sought alternatives to direction from the top.

This leads to *coherent decentralization* as a second possible coordinative mechanism.[20] The idea of coherent decentralization is that each department is

[19]By way of contrast, Vickers constructs a somewhat different function for the central authority to solve, this one involving financial as well as marketing and production variables. The firm is seen as having the task of setting the decision variables in such a way as to maximize the Lagrangian expression:

$$Z = Pf(X_1, X_2) - c_1 X_1 - c_2 X_2 - r(D)D + \lambda[\bar{K} + D - g(Q) - g_1 X_1 - g_2 X_2]$$

where $f(X_1, X_2)$ = the quantity produced as a function of two factors of production, 1 and 2
$\quad c_1, c_2$ = the unit cost of factors 1 and 2, respectively
$\quad r(D)$ = interest cost as a function of the amount of debt
$\quad D$ = amount of debt
$\quad \lambda$ = Lagrangian multiplier
$\quad \bar{K}$ = amount of equity capital held by firm
$\quad g(Q)$ = money required to finance output (working capital)
$\quad g_i X_i$ = money required to finance factor of production i

It can readily be seen that management faced a difficult problem in finding the optimal settings of the decision variables P, X_1, X_2, and D. See Douglas Vickers, *The Theory of the Firm: Production, Capital and Finance* (New York: McGraw-Hill, Inc., 1968), 160.

[20]A. Charnes, R. W. Clower, and K. O. Kortanek, "Effective Control through Coherent Decentralization with Preemptive Goals," *Econometrica* (Apr. 1967) 294–320.

given a separate objective function to maximize; to the extent that each succeeds in maximizing its own "profits," the company will achieve maximal profit. The problem is to find the appropriate separate objective functions. The key need is to find an appropriate internal transfer price, β. Consider the following departmental subprograms:

Marketing Department

$$\max Z_1 = (P-\beta)f - A$$

subject to

$$P, A \geqslant 0$$

(8-32)

Production Department

$$\max Z_2 = \beta g - cw - c_0 w_0$$

subject to

$$\overline{W} - w \geqslant 0$$
$$kw - w_0 \geqslant 0$$
$$w, w_0 \geqslant 0$$

(8-33)

In this formulation, the marketing department is treated as a profit center, and its job is to set price and advertising in such a way as to maximize marketing department profits. Note, however, that the marketing department pays β dollars to the production department for every unit it sells. In turn, the production department is a profit center, its profit being the difference between what it sells to the marketing department (receiving as it does β dollars per unit) and its production costs. It will be motivated to produce as much as it can, subject to the constraints and the behavior of production costs with more output. Thus, under coherent decentralization, both departments make their own decisions and are motivated to maximize their own profits—this is expected to yield to maximal company profits. The key lies in finding the right transfer price β, which requires extended mathematical analysis.

Coherent decentralization usually has two problems, one arising from the time and cost that might be involved in finding the optimal transfer price and the other arising from the possibility that the departments might "game" the system by exaggerating their costs in order to gain a better transfer price. To get around these problems, a third organizational arrangement has been proposed, called *decentralization by guidelines*. Here the central authority leaves decision making up to the two departments but imposes constraints on the range of acceptable decisions. Consider the following subprograms that might be developed for the two departments under decentralization by guidelines:

Marketing Department

$$\max Z_3 = Pf - A$$

subject to

$$0 \geqslant P_L \geqslant P \geqslant P_U$$
$$\bar{A} - A \geqslant 0, \; A \geqslant 0$$

(8-34)

Production Department

$$\min Z_4 = cw + c_0 w_0$$

subject to

$$g = \bar{f}$$
$$\overline{W} - w \geqslant 0$$
$$kw - w_0 \geqslant 0$$
$$w, w_0 \geqslant 0$$

(8-35)

In this case, the marketing department is again a profit center, this time the profits being equal to the gross revenue minus the advertising cost. The marketing department is kept from raising price too high because this would reduce demand: it is interested in maximizing the product of price times revenue. The department is kept from spending too much on advertising because advertising subtracts from its profits and should not be used beyond the point where its effect on demand is not worth the extra cost. To make sure that marketing does not set a misguided price on advertising, the central authority requires that these be set within a particular range. Price must be set somewhere between a lower price limit (P_L) and an upper price limit (P_U). Likewise, a maximum advertising budget, $\bar{A}$, is specified, so that marketing does not overspend in relation to what the central authority sees as the economic level of advertising.

As for the production department, its task is to minimize the cost of production subject to producing at least what marketing says will be the level of demand, that is, $\bar{f}$, and to meeting the other conditions on resource utilization. Each department is free to pursue its own goals, however, with constraints put on the range of decision variables for each. The advantage of decentralization by guidelines is that the individual departments can make their own decisions and they have little incentive to "game" the system, since a transfer price is not being established. On the other hand, the main problem is that the coordinator has to have some knowledge of the range of optimal values to establish the guidelines. This method produces not necessarily the best solution but one that is hopefully not too far from the optimal level.

Thus we have examined three different ways to bring about joint marketing-production planning in the interests of achieving good or optimal profits. Each arrangement has its advantages and disadvantages and in the end a judicious amount of experimentation by a company is needed to determine which coordinative mechanism works best in the long run for the company.

SUMMARY

The activities of the marketing department affect, and are intimately affected, by the activities of other company departments. Marketing production interactions are a particular source of problems for which joint planning procedures must be found. This chapter used five problems to illustrate how marketing planning is affected by production considerations.

The first problem is that production must be planned in practice not to vary with daily sales, but rather in a way that will provide adequate inventories to meet unstable patterns of demand. The discussion showed how to derive an optimal economic lot order formula that produces inventories which minimize the total cost including the stockouts.

The second problem is that of gearing production to meet a known seasonality of sales in such a way that takes into account overtime costs, layoff costs, and inventory costs. The well-known linear production decision rules of Holt, Modigliani, Muth, and Simon were examined. An extension of these rules by

Tuite that takes into account the determination of an optimal off-season discount was then reviewed.

The third problem is that of determining which customers to maintain when some of them are costing the company more than they are worth. Mathematical functions were set up showing the relation between the size of a customer and the cost of servicing him and the cost of producing a given level of output. An optimal solution was found and it was made accessible to the average executive in the form of an easy to use conversational computer program.

The fourth problem is that of determining the impact of alternative marketing-production arrangements and policies on total sales and profits. Forrester's Industrial Dynamics approach was illustrated as a tool for studying the system level effects of various alterations of a system. Industrial Dynamics produces a time profile of the reaction of the various parts of a system to a sudden increase in sales, a sudden or gradual fall in costs, or other exogenous variations.

The fifth problem is that of determining whether marketing-production decisions are best made by a central authority, or by each department separately. The trouble with a centralized solution is that the central authority may not get adequate and accurate information, and the departments may not be motivated to perform at their best levels. Alternatively, coherent decentralization leaves each department free to make its own decisions and maximize its own profit function, subject to a transfer price that links their activities. Decentralization by guidelines also leaves the decision making to the departments, this time placing constraints on the range of possible decisions that might be chosen by the departments.

Questions and Problems

1. (a) A small manufacturer is attempting to determine the optimal order quantity for one of its products. Demand for the product is known to be 5000 units, while carrying cost per unit is $5 and order cost per order is $1000. Assuming that these costs are constant, determine the optimal order quantity.

   (b) Prove that the order quantity which minimizes total variable inventory costs must occur at the point where inventory carrying cost per unit equals order processing cost per unit (as depicted in Figure 8-3).

2. The following demand equations depict two different demand situations:

$$Q_{t,1} = 20,000 + \mu_{t,1}$$
$$Q_{t,2} = 20,000 + \mu_{t,2}$$

In the above, $\mu_{t,1}$ and $\mu_{t,2}$ are normally distributed random variables representing current deviations from a constant demand level, and are specifically defined as:

$$\mu_{t,1} = f_n(0, \sigma = 4,000)$$
$$\mu_{t,2} = f_n(0, \sigma = 2,000)$$

Which situation would require a larger buffer inventory stock? Prove your answer by determining the probability that demand will be between 15,000 and 25,000 units for each situation and comparing the probabilities.

3. A manufacturer of large farm equipment estimates that sales of his product in the coming month (period t) will be 10,000 units. He expects the sales in each of the coming 12 months will grow at a rate of 2 percent over the preceding month's sales. He anticipates that at the end of the current month (period $t-1$) he will have a work force of 800 employees and an inventory of 5,000 units. Using the decision rules provided in Figure 8-4, determine the number of units of the product that should be produced in the coming period and the number of additional employees that will be required.

4. In the Tuite example, suppose that the company determines the following relationships between the total discount over the planning period (K_T), production costs (C_T), and the discount rate (k):

$$K_T = 100,000k + 1,000,000k^2$$
$$C_T = 500,000 - 170,000k$$

Determine the best discount rate.

5. The problem of coordinating marketing and other company functions such as production and finance is a formidable one. Each area has its own objectives, which often conflict to the detriment of overall company operations. Can you suggest ways in which such conflict can be reduced or resolved? How can such diverse areas be coordinated toward a common goal?

CHAPTER 9
Company Goals

Up to now, complex issues in marketing programming have been described and resolved on the basis of finding the solution that would maximize current profits. Current profits is an appealing and frequently stated goal and has the additional advantage of providing an easily quantified objective function to guide policy determination.[1] Yet the use of this criterion has come under increasing attack by businessmen, economists, and operations researchers.[2]

The attack has been of two basic kinds. There are those who prefer to impute a single overriding objective to the firm but wish to make it something other than current profit maximization. The most frequently nominated alternative is *long run profit maximization*. As a standard, long run profit maximization provides a justification for many current investments and expenses whose immediate effect is to reduce profits but whose long run effect is expected to increase profits. Included are gifts to universities, investments in research and development, investments in opening up new market territories, and so forth. By the same

[1]See the case for profit maximization in the author's *Marketing Management: Analysis, Planning and Control*, (Englewood Cliffs, N.J.: Prentice Hall, 1967) 130.

[2]Adolph A. Berle, Jr., and Gardiner C. Means, *The Modern Corporation and Private Property* (New York: The Macmillan Company, 1932); A. D. H. Kaplan, Joel B. Dirlam, and Robert F. Lanzillotti, *Pricing in Big Business* (Washington, D.C.: The Brookings Institution, 1958); and Herbert A. Simon, "A Behavioral Model of Rational Choice," *Quarterly Journal of Economics*, 89 (1952) 99–118.

token, long run profit maximization involves many difficulties in application. It requires that a multiperiod framework be substituted for a single-period framework and the use of highly uncertain estimates of future effects.

The other attack has been directed against the whole notion that the company is motivated by a single organizational goal that remains dominant through time. *Survival* might be such a goal but it is too vague to provide a guideline to the resolving of specific company problems. These critics advance the proposition that the company generally pursues several goals simultaneously. The goals are not all of equal weight and the weights do not stay constant through time. At any point in time, however, the goals may have a specific weighting that permits some formal analysis to be made of the best course of action.

Our purpose in this chapter is to explore the variety of formal ways in which the company goal or goals can be stated to provide a clear guide for policy analysis. The "best" policy turns out not unexpectedly to be sensitive in most cases to the particular statement of company goals.

SINGLE-GOAL FORMULATIONS

In this section, we take the position that the company is motivated by a single goal that it wishes to maximize. The company accepts no other goals or constraints, save the observance of legal and ethical rules as governing its conduct. The goal it seeks to maximize can be called *profits* (also earnings, cash flow, rate of return, etc.). The company is seen as applying a profit yardstick to all of its decisions. The profit yardstick enters into making a choice among mutually exclusive courses of action. It also enters into rating different opportunities or projects where a best subset of them is sought.

Even "profits" turn out to be ambiguous. A company can pursue profits in one of four forms, depending on whether absolute or relative profits are sought and on whether current or long run profits are sought. The four distinctions are illustrated in Figure 9-1 and discussed in the following paragraphs.

	Current	Long run
Absolute	Current absolute profits	Present value
Relative	Current rate of return on investment (ROI)	Internal rate of return on investment

Figure 9-1 Four Types of Profit

Current Absolute Profits

Our analysis of marketing policy in the previous chapters relied exclusively on the use of current absolute profits as the objective criterion. Current absolute profits (Z) are defined as the difference between the company's sales revenue (R) and the cost (C) of producing and selling the goods and services that constitute these sales, that is,

$$Z = R - C \tag{9-1}$$

The revenue and cost components of Equation 9-1 in turn can be further elaborated by recognizing that sales revenue is the product of price times quantity, PQ, and that costs can be classified into fixed, variable, and discretionary costs:

$$Z = PQ - F - c(Q) - X \tag{9-2}$$

This equation seems straightforward enough, but the analyst who is actually engaged in preparing a profit estimate for a proposed company marketing action must take a number of additional factors into account. He must deal with certain accounting and financial aspects of each of the components in Equation 9-2 before rendering a final profit estimate.

The first issue arises with respect to price, P. The analyst engaged in evaluating alternative company courses of action must estimate the most likely average price at which the merchandise will be sold in the market. Price must reflect any discounts applicable to the list that customers are expected to take. Many companies offer a discount to the customer for early payment such as 2/10, net 30, which means that a customer can deduct 2 percent of the bill if he pays in 10 days and otherwise must pay the whole bill by the end of a month. This is a considerable discount for the company that takes advantage of it, amounting to a saving of 36 percent if annualized. The seller receives less revenue to the extent that customers take advantage of these terms and the analyst must make some estimate of the percentage of customers that will take advantage. This is important if the company is considering alternative marketing strategies that will affect the kinds of customers it will have. This arises, for example, if a company is trying to decide whether to sell through large dealers or small dealers where they have different likelihoods of taking advantage of early payment terms.

The next issue arises in connection with estimating the quantity sold, Q. There is the question of whether sales should be said to take place at the time of order arrival or order shipment. Because shipment may lag several weeks after orders are received, especially in markets where demand is strong, this can make a difference in end of the year profit levels. If sales are recorded on the basis of orders received, then they will be overstated to the extent that some backlogged orders may be subsequently canceled by customers who decide not to wait for merchandise. Even recording sales as of the time of shipment may lead to an overstatement because some merchandise may be returned. If the company is considering marketing alternatives that are likely to be characterized by different rates of canceled or returned merchandise, this factor should be introduced into the estimation.

Fixed costs, F, raise a very important question that has been debated ever since the accounting fraternity began. Any product produced by a multiproduct firm can look good or bad depending upon the proportion of overhead that is charged to the production and sale of the product. In principle the product should be charged with its "fair" share of the overhead. The question revolves around defining its fair share. Certainly any part of the present overhead that would eventually disappear if the product was dropped from the line can be said to be a cost that is properly charged to the product. For example, if three of the company personnel spend all their time managing this product, their salaries should be charged to this product. It is less clear how much of the company president's salary should be charged to this product. If the company president devoted an average of 10 percent of his time to this product, this might be a fair basis for charging 10 percent of his salary to this product. But executive time sheets are often too hard to gather, and accountants take the easier and perhaps more reasonable course of charging each product with a percent of the non-allocable costs equal to the percentage of its sales to total sales. This is based on the assumption that costs vary largely in proportion to sales; therefore each product should bear nonallocable fixed costs in proportion to sales.

It should be noted that the estimate of fixed costs will affect the estimate of absolute profits but not necessarily matter to the determination of the profit maximizing course of action. Suppose the company is trying to decide among three different prices to charge for a new product. The price will affect the sales revenue, variable cost, and profits. But assuming that the fixed cost is not affected, the different courses of action will exhibit the same ranking according to profits. From the point of view of calculus, $dF/dP = 0$ and therefore fixed costs do not affect the determination of the profit maximizing course of action. However, it must be said that if fixed costs are high, the company may decide to drop the product.

One must be sure, though, that fixed costs will not change with different policy choices. In one published analysis of the optimal number of salesmen, the operations research department developed a profit equation that included a fixed cost of $2 million.[3] At the time the company had a sales force of 40 men. The profit equation was optimized with respect to the number of salesmen and it turned out that the optimal number of salesmen was 156. But if the company really accepted the finding and increased its sales force to 156 men, its plant investment would have to be greatly expanded and the $2 million would seriously understate the fixed cost. Here is a case where the fixed cost should be included in the equation on a semivariable basis.[4]

The next issue that arises is the estimation of variable costs, $c(Q)$. Most companies establish standard costs for different production operations and these are the costs that enter the books. This means that the measured costs may not

[3]See "Engineered Products Corporation," p. 115, in Robert D. Buzzell, *Mathematical Models and Marketing Management* (Boston: Harvard University, Division of Research, Graduate school of Business Administration, 1964).

[4]This mistake was neatly avoided by Semlow in his article on optimizing the number of salesmen. He adjusted the fixed cost for different sizes of the proposed salesforce. See Walter J. Semlow, "How Many Salesmen Do You Need?" *Harvard Business Review* (May–June 1959) 126–132.

be affected by the scale of operations although the scale can make a difference to true costs. Departments complain periodically about the level of particular standard costs and this often leads to their review and possible revision.

Unit variable costs are not only affected by the current scale of output but also by the accumulated output overtime. Management is increasingly recognizing the phenomenon of "experience curves" (also called progress curves, production learning curves, etc.) as they arise in the area of new products and new processes.[5] In the first round of production, many problems will be encountered and the workers will need time to master the processes. As they do, costs are brought down. Many of the published studies show unit variable costs (C) falling linearly with the logarithm of the cumulative amount of output, that is,

$$c = a\bar{Q}^{-b} \tag{9-3}$$

where c = unit cost
$\bar{Q}$ = log of cumulative output

There is also an experience curve for many marketing tasks, but this has not been studied or reported in the literature. The significance of experience curves is that estimates of future profits, when they extend beyond one year, should take into account the possibility of declining costs, not simply those occasioned by a higher level of production and sales, but those due to the increased proficiency resulting from accumulated experience. If the decline in costs with accumulated production is expected to be substantial, this would indicate that a company with a new product should price it low and spend a lot on promotion to gain as much market share as possible because this means bringing down its unit costs faster and hence having an edge over competition.

The final issue concerns the estimating of discretionary marketing costs, X. In principle, each alternative marketing program implies a level of marketing cost. The estimate of marketing cost is of course subject to some uncertainty. Many costs arise that are hard to anticipate, such as the need to change the packaging, meet a competitive attack, or support a weakening price structure. Total marketing costs must be estimated as accurately as possible, not only because of the effect they will have on costs but also the difference they will make to sales because $Q = f(X)$.

Use of net cash value.   Many analysts prefer to estimate the *net cash value* of each policy alternative rather than profits, Z. Net cash value, Z', is defined as profits after taxes plus accounting depreciation charges, that is,

$$Z' = Z(1-t)+d \tag{9-4}$$

where t = corporate tax rate
d = estimated depreciation

[5]Winifred B. Hirschman, "Profit from the Learning Curve," *Harvard Business Review* (Jan.–Feb. 1964) 125–139.

This gives the company an idea of the actual net cash increase (or decrease) it is likely to experience with a particular policy alternative. Although depreciation is an expense, it does not represent a cash outlay and therefore it can be added back to profits to find the cash value. Furthermore, the firm's particular depreciation policy will affect its before-tax profits, Z. If the firm decides to use a declining balance method of depreciation instead of a straight line method, this reduces the company's before-tax profits and its tax bill in the early years of the investment. Analysts will work with cash flow in order to consider the net effects of depreciation strategies on corporate taxes and cash availability. Whether the analyst will come to different rankings of alternative marketing strategies if he uses current profit or cash value measures will depend upon the circumstances of the problem. In many cases, the rank order of different policy alternatives will not be affected by which measure is used; only the absolute levels will be affected. If, however, the depreciation policy opportunities are differentially affected under alternative marketing strategies, then the selected criterion can affect the final rankings.

Cash value is the criterion chosen by Pessemier in his model for simulating the profit consequences of different strategies for introducing a new product. He used the following formulation of net cash value:[6]

$$Z' = (1-t)[(P-c)Q-i-u]+d \qquad (9-5)$$

where c = full unit cost
$\quad\quad i$ = interest cost
$\quad\quad u$ = nonrecurrent costs

Other terms are as defined previously. In this expression, unit manufacturing costs, c, are treated as constant, whereas our expression in Equation 9-3 left it more general. Interest costs, i, are singled out for two reasons. First, different marketing strategies will imply different working capital levels that imply different levels of interest cost. Secondly, interest costs are affected by the company's debt/equity strategy in financing the new product and hence will make a difference to its before-tax profits and hence total tax bill. By introducing interest as a separate cost, its effect can be explicitly considered in evaluating different strategies. Finally, it should be noted that Equation 9-5 also singles out nonrecurring start up costs for separate estimation.

Many analysts feel that net cash value as a criterion should be confined to short run analysis rather than to long run analysis. A company is usually concerned about its cash position in the short run and therefore wants to consider the cash flow consequences of different policies. But in the long run, earnings are what matter. Depreciation, although only a book estimate each year, is a *real* expense and the company's performance will ultimately be attested to by its earnings, not its cash flow.

[6]Edgar A. Pessemier, *New-Product Decisions: An Analytical Approach* (New York: McGraw-Hill, Inc., 1966), p. 155.

Current Rate of Return on Investment—ROI

Most companies recognize the importance of relating current absolute profits (or cash flow) to the relevant investment base to determine how efficiently they are investing their funds. This is important for the company as a whole, as well as for various operating divisions within the company. Obviously, top management cannot learn much from information on the absolute profit in the different divisions because each division has a different amount of resources committed by the firm to its operation. The logical basis is to consider the *return on investment* (popularly called ROI) for each division. Many companies use division ROI rates as (1) a basis for executive promotion and compensation plans and (2) a basis for appropriating investment funds among the divisions.

To estimate ROI involves using items found on both the income statement and balance sheet of a company. Figure 9-2 shows these items and how they are combined by the DuPont Company to estimate divisional ROI's. ROI is expressed definitionally as the product of two ratios, sales turnover and the profit margin. Each of these in turn are spelled out in further detail in the chart.

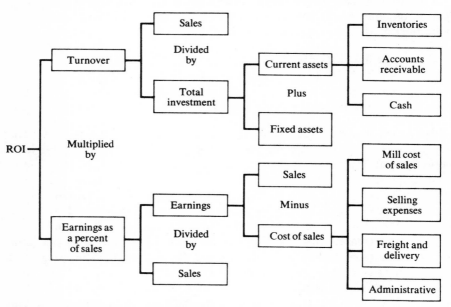

Figure 9-2 The du Pont System of Financial Control
From *Financial Executive* (July, 1965) p. 41.

Actually ROI can be looked at usefully as the product of three ratios:

$$\text{ROI} = \frac{\text{net sales}}{\text{total assets}} \times \frac{\text{net profits}}{\text{net sales}} \times \frac{\text{total assets}}{\text{net worth}} = \frac{\text{net profits}}{\text{net worth}} \qquad (9\text{-}6)$$

The three ratios suggest the three profit paths available to an enterprise.

The firm seeking to improve its return on net worth can seek to increase its rate of sales turnover (capital management), or its profit margin (margin management), or its financial leverage (financial management). The model dramatizes the need for the firm to interrelate its capital, margin, and financial plans effectively.

The ROI criterion is widely used by major companies to measure the return earned in different company divisions. Efforts have been made to extend ROI to various types of company activities, such as advertising and selling operations. For example, a sales branch represents an investment and management may be interested in the return on this investment. Or an individual salesman may be viewed as a profit center and the company may wish to relate the profit to investment. A major advertising campaign may be treated as an investment and be evaluated in a ROI way. Two major issues arise in the effective implementation of the profit center idea. First, the company must be able to identify the sales attributable to the investment activity; this is particularly hard in the case of marketing activities. Secondly, the company must be able to determine the value of the investment. Too many companies use book value figures instead of going concern values. Thus the sales branch that has depreciated more of its assets will automatically appear to have a higher ROI. Problems such as these have to be solved.

Companies that use ROI performances within the company to allocate resources and reward promotions must be careful to recognize that individual managers have some control over ROI. The marketing manager is often able to take a set of actions to produce a ROI that looks good in a particular year, perhaps by cutting down certain marketing expenditures or pushing substantial amounts of merchandise into distributor's pipelines. He may even get promoted. His successor then inherits the job and confronts a bundle of problems left by his predecessor. ROI provides no protection against the temptation of some marketing managers to sacrifice long run profits to short term gains in a particular year. For this reason, more long run criteria have been proposed.

Internal Rate of Return on Investment

In most cases in which marketing policy alternatives are being compared, their financial consequences extend beyond one year, and in fact into the indefinite future. This is certainly true for the evaluation of alternative new product strategies, channel strategies, advertising strategies, and logistics strategies. In these cases, management should estimate the earnings (or cash flows) for each year in the future to determine the best course of action. In practice, management only makes the estimate for a finite number of future years, say five or ten years, and this period is called the *planning horizon*. Management is willing to ignore the years beyond the planning horizon for at least three good reasons. First, there is the great uncertainty that surrounds estimates of events that take place far into the future, making the estimates of low value to management. Second, dollars earned in the future are worth less to management than those earned now because they cannot be put to work. Third, there are the rapid depreciation procedures that render many assets worthless in a relatively short period. For these reasons management is willing to accept the verdict of estimated earnings for the first five or ten years.

The estimated earnings streams themselves are often not sufficient to indicate the best alternative. Consider the two hypothetical earnings streams in Table 9-1.

Table 9-1

	Year				
	1	2	3	4	5
Alternative 1	$5	$7	$8	$4	$2
Alternative 2	$7	$4	$2	$8	$5

Which is the more attractive earnings stream? When more than two alternatives are involved, the difficulties of comparing projected earnings streams increase even more. The analyst is in need of some single number to represent the overall value of a given earnings stream.

The simplest measure that comes to mind is the sum of the earnings over the planning period. Unfortunately, this turns out to be the same for both alternatives shown in the table. Moreover, this measure commits two fallacies that make it a poor criterion in judging among marketing policy alternatives. In the first place it ignores the possibility, indeed probability, that each alternative involves a different level of investment: all other things being equal, the alternative is preferred that yields the greatest rate of return on investment. Second, the operation of summing the annual earnings ignores the varying value of money that is received at different points in time.

These two deficiencies are overcome in the criterion known as *the internal rate of return on investment*, r. Consider a marketing opportunity that requires an investment of I dollars today and that is expected to yield a sequence of annual earnings over the next n years of $Z_1, Z_2, \ldots, Z_n$. The internal rate of return on this investment is given by solving for r in the formula:

$$I = \frac{Z_1}{1+r} + \frac{Z_2}{(1+r)^2} + \cdots + \frac{Z_n}{(1+r)^n} \tag{9-7}$$

The logic of this formula is as follows. Z_1 earnings will be received at the *end* of the first year (this is assumed for simplicity). Since the firm will not receive this amount for a year, its *present value*, V_0, is less than its dollar value, Z_1. In fact, if the firm is able to earn r percent on its investments, then it would be indifferent between receiving a sum V_0 now and Z_1 a year from now, that is,

$$V_0(1+r) = Z_1 \tag{9-8}$$

or

$$V_0 = \frac{Z_1}{1+r} \tag{9-9}$$

Thus V_0 is the present value of Z_1 dollars that is expected to be received at the end of a year. Similarly, the firm would be indifferent between a sum V_0 which will earn r for two years and a sum Z_2 that it will receive two years from now, that is,

$$V_0(1+r)(1+r) = Z_2 \tag{9-10}$$

$$V_0 = \frac{Z_2}{(1+r)^2} \tag{9-11}$$

Continuing the same logic, we see that the rate of return formula (9-7) simply converts future sums into their present value equivalent through discounting them at the rate that the firm is able to invest its money.[7] Because the Z's in the numerators vary, there is no simple solution formula for r as a function of the Z's and I.[8] Instead the analyst tries out an arbitrary r; if as a result, the left-hand side of the equation exceeds the right, then r is too large. A smaller r is then tried, and if the right-hand side of Equation 9-7 now exceeds the left, then the new r is too small. Through iterations of this sort (now easily performed by a computer), an r can be found that just equilibrates the two sides of the equation. This r represents the internal rate of return.

By calculating r for each policy alternative, these policies can be ranked. The policy alternative ranking highest is presumably the most desirable course of action, provided that its internal rate of return exceeds the company's target rate of return. If the company's target rate of return is 20 percent, and the best policy alternative promises only a 15 percent rate of return, the company will presumably want to search for better alternatives.

The internal rate of return criterion, however, is not without some conceptual difficulties. For example, the best policy alternative might be estimated to yield 35 percent but involve only a small investment, whereas the next best policy alternative might yield 25 percent on a much larger investment. Before preferring

---

[7]Equation 9–7 has a useful continuous analogue if certain assumptions can be made. First, assume that the future earnings stream can be approximately represented as growing or declining by a constant percentage g:

$$Z_0 (1+g)^t$$

where Z_0 = profit at time 0

g = annual percent of growth ($g > 0$) or decline ($g < 0$)
t = time variable

Then Equation 9–7 can be rewritten as

$$I = \sum_{t=1}^{n} \frac{Z_0 (1+g)^t}{(1+r)^t} \tag{9-7b}$$

In continuous space, Equation 9-7b is equivalent to

$$I = \int_0^n \frac{Z_0 e^{gt}}{e^{rt}} \, dt = \int_0^n Z_0 e^{(g-r)t} \, dt \tag{9-7c}$$

where e = mathematical constant, 2.718 . . . . The internal rate of return, r, is that number which brings the integral into equality with the investment.

[8]If $Z_1 = Z_2 = \ldots = Z_n$, then Equation 9-7 becomes $I = Z\,[1/(1+r)+1/(1+r)^2+ \ldots +1/(1+r)^n]$ and a standard table can be used to solve for r.

the first alternative, management has to consider what it can earn in the next best opportunity with the remaining investment money. If it could earn very little, this takes the luster off the $r = 35$ percent policy alternative and makes the $r = 25$ percent alternative look better. Another complication arises when different policy alternatives involve earning streams of different longevities. In comparing their merits, some assumption must be made about the likely rate at which money can be reinvested at the time the shorter projects expire. It has also been shown that, in certain special cases, a proposed investment may have more than one rate of return.[9] There are still other difficulties that may or may not matter to the particular application of internal rate of return analysis that the analyst is considering.[10]

Present Value (Discounted Cash Flow)

These and other difficulties with the internal rate of return formula have led a number of analysts to prefer a *present value* measure for appraising alternative courses of action.[11] This criterion does not involve any change in the estimation of future annual earnings. The only difference is that the company assumes a discount rate d and solves for present value, PV, in the formula:

$$PV = \frac{Z_1}{1+d} + \frac{Z_2}{(1+d)^2} + \cdots + \frac{Z_n}{(1+d)^n} \tag{9-12}$$

Present value means the present worth of an annuity of n future annual payments, where future dollars are discounted at d percent.

In evaluating a particular opportunity, the company estimates its future earnings stream, discounts it at rate d, and compares the resulting present value (PV) to the present dollar investment (I) required to take advantage of the opportunity. If $PV > I$, the estimated earnings stream will more than return the rate of return assumed in d. The theory is that the firm should invest in all opportunities that have a *positive excess present value*, assuming that it can borrow all the funds it needs at a cost of no more than d percent. If the firm is not able to borrow all the funds it needs, or if the borrowing cost increases for more funds, then the firm will want to consider only a subset of opportunities. Instead of using absolute excess present value, it would be better to find the ratio of each opportunity's estimated present value to its required investment, that is, PV/I. The opportunities can be ranked according to these ratios and all the opportunities above some cutoff point can be considered.

[9]James H. Lorie and Leonard Savage, "Three Problems in Capital Rationing," *Journal of Business* (Oct. 1955) 229–239.

[10]For a good discussion, see Harold Bierman, Jr., and Seymour Smidt, *The Capital Budgeting Decision* (New York: The Macmillan Company, 1960).

[11]Terborgh has shown through four examples that present value can produce a ranking of projects opposite to that produced by a rate of return evaluation. Present value assumes that the funds from projects will be reinvested at the company's cost of capital, not at the project's rate of return and this is a more reasonable assumption. See George Terborgh, "Some Comments on the Dean-Smith Article on the MAPI Formula," *Journal of Business* (Apr. 1956) 138–140.

There are at least two different views on what the discount rate should represent. One view holds that the company should use its *cost of capital* as its discount rate. Thus if a company can borrow money from debt and/or equity sources at an average cost of d, then this figure might be used to discount the future earnings stream. A positive excess present value indicates that the project would return more than the annual cost of the borrowed funds. The use of d to represent the company's cost of capital, however, involves all the intricate conceptual problems in measuring a company's cost of capital. Others hold that the company should discount the future earnings stream at the rate of return it seeks to earn as a corporation. This will lead it only to accept projects that will maintain this rate of return, whereas using the cost of capital for the discount rate may lead the company to accept projects that might dilute the target rate of return.

In special cases the company may wish to modify the discount factor in evaluating future courses of action because of some additional objective. For example, suppose a company is planning to "go public" soon. This means that it wants its profits to look as high as possible in the immediate future. This means that the company might want to use a higher discount rate on profits that are earned further in the future on comparing the merits of different investments. Or consider an opposite case, in which a company anticipates a future tax cut. In this case, the company may place more weight on future profits than on present profits. This means that the company might want to use a higher discount rate for near-term profits than profits into the far future in comparing the merits of different projects. In principle, it need not be even assumed that every firm has a continuously decreasing time preference for future profit dollars. At any point in time, a firm might feel extreme impatience (discounting all future profits) or no time preference, treating all future returns equally.

The present value approach has its share of problems, particularly in connection with determining the appropriate discount rate, and also in considering interrelated opportunities. In the end, the analyst must understand the different approaches, their limitations, and the sensitivity of the evaluations to the different objective criteria. In many cases, the merits of alternative courses of action may not be too sensitive to the use of a rate of return approach or a present value approach.

MULTIPLE GOAL FORMULATIONS

Although profit in some form is an overriding goal of the business firm, it is not the only factor that an organization considers when trying to decide among alternative plans of action. An organization is a complex hierarchical social system pursuing a variety of organizational and personal goals. The top management of the firm must deal with, and satisfy, many interest groups, including customers, stockholders, workers, bankers, suppliers, and the community at large. All of these groups can affect the firm's survival and progress and therefore are relevant objects to be satisfied. The problem that arises is that company actions designed to increase the satisfaction of one group such as employees may diminish the satisfaction of another group such as stockholders. The company therefore typically makes its decisions within a framework of constraints and tradeoffs. Recognizing that it cannot advance every group's interest with the same decision, management focuses on satisfying different groups at different times as the circumstances vary, subject to providing basic satisfaction levels for the other groups.

Generally the announced or published objectives of the company are of little operational help in choosing among alternative plans. In an exploratory survey of stated corporate objectives, it was found that:

A number of firms cited their objectives in such broad terms that it was difficult to know what they had in mind other than to sound virtuous. Such statements as: "... our company's objective is to be the best in the industry," "... the company will strive for the most effective use of capital," and "... to serve the common good" are typical.[12]

Even if specific objectives are mentioned, often there is no indication of their relative importance. Furthermore, there is typically no recognition that the stated objectives are in competition, that one can be pursued only at the expense of another. Consider the following sample of statements that businessmen make:

"We want to maximize our sales and our profits."
"We want to achieve the greatest sales at the least cost."
"We want to keep down inventory costs and maximize sales."
"We want to design the best possible product in the shortest time."

All of these statements involve attractive rhetoric but faulty logic. Consider the first objective, joint maximization of sales and profits. To show the difficulty of finding a marketing strategy that will simultaneously maximize both objectives, we shall work with the simple problem described in Chapter 2, pp. 45 to 47. The problem involved finding the profit maximizing price, given the following information: the demand equation,

$$Q = 1000 - 4P \tag{9-13}$$

the cost equation,

$$C = 6000 + 50Q \tag{9-14}$$

and the profit equation (derived from Equations 9-13 and 9-14),

$$Z = -56,000 + 1200P - 4P^2 \tag{9-15}$$

Differentiating the profit function, the profit maximizing price is $150. Now

[12]Reported in an unpublished paper, "On the Setting of Corporate Objectives," by Harper W. Boyd, Jr., and Sidney J. Levy.

suppose that the company had wanted to maximize sales revenue, PQ. The sales revenue equation is

$$PQ = 1000P - 4P^2 \tag{9-16}$$

Differentiating the sales revenue function with respect to price, we find that the sales revenue maximizing price is \$125. Thus the same price does not simultaneously maximize profits and sales revenue.

This leads us to state formally the problem of multiple goals: If we have a set of n objectives, $Z_1, Z_2, \ldots, Z_n$, all of which cannot be simultaneously maximized by any one conceivable plan, how can the goals be operationalized in such a way as to provide an unambiguous ranking or rating of alternative plans?

Analysts who have examined the problem of multiple goals have not come up with any consensus on the solution. Instead of one major method of operationalizing multiple goals, at least three different approaches have been proposed. They are described and compared in the remainder of the chapter.

Utility Function Maximization

One approach to the problem of multiple goals is to try to combine the goals into a single expression that itself is to be maximized. We can do this by introducing the concept of utility. Suppose the company wants to achieve high profits, high sales, high market share, low production costs, and some other goals, that is, $Z_1, Z_2, \ldots, Z_n$. Each of these goals has a utility associated with it: $U(Z_1), U_2(Z_2), \ldots, U_n(Z_n)$. Furthermore, the utility increases monotonically with the amount of the goal achieved, that is, the monotonic utility assumption is

$$\frac{dU_i}{dZ_i} > 0 \quad \text{for all } i \tag{9-17}$$

Also assume that the utility derived from each goal is independent of the utility received from any other goal, that is, the independence assumption is

$$U_i(Z_i \mid Z_j) = U(Z_i) \tag{9-18}$$

Finally, assume that the utilities received from the various goals are *additive*; the additivity assumption is

$$U = U_1 + U_2 + \ldots + U_n \tag{9-19}$$

If these assumptions are accepted, we can argue that the firm seeks to maximize the utility function (Equation 9-19).

As an illustration, suppose the firm seeking the "best" price to charge decides that it gets twice the utility from the achieved profit level as the achieved sales revenue level. This firm would want to charge the price that would maximize the utility function:

$$U = 2Z + PQ \tag{9-20}$$

In terms of the example in Equations 9-13, 9-14, and 9-15, Equation 9-20 becomes

$$U = 2(-56,000 + 1200P - 4P^2) + (1000P - 4P^2) \tag{9-21}$$

$$U = -112,000 + 3400P - 12P^2 \tag{9-22}$$

Differentiating Equation 9-22 and setting it equal to 0, we have

$$\frac{dU}{dP} = 3400 - 24P = 0 \tag{9-23}$$

$$P = \$141 \frac{2}{3} \tag{9-24}$$

If we assume that management imputes twice as much utility to profits as sales, the best price to charge is $141 2/3. It should be noted that this price is exactly 2/3 of the way between the sales revenue maximizing price of $125 and the profit maximizing price of $150. This procedure of formulating an additive utility function is equivalent to finding a weighted mean between the various maximizing solutions, the weights reflecting the various utility coefficients.

The transformation of goals into an additive utility function suffices to solve the problem, although it is a highly artificial approach. The assumptions of monotonicity, independence, and additivity are difficult to accept. Businessmen find it particularly hard to attach meaning to the notion that one goal is twice as important as another. The notion of twice as important implies the existence of a *ratio scale*, which is the highest form of measurement scale, valid only for variables that have a nonarbitrary zero point, such as weight and distance.[13] Temperature, for example, is only an *interval scale* concept, since it has an artificial origin. It cannot be said that something is twice as warm as something else, since this would not be true independent of the scale (Fahrenheit or Centigrade). When we come to things like business goals, we are operating with only an *ordinal scale*; again no operational meaning can be attached to one goal's being twice as important as another. We can do this, mathematically, but must recognize its artificiality.

The problem of combining multiple goals into a single maximand function is made even more difficult when the goals are expressed in incommensurate units. In the previous example, the two goals of profits and sales revenue both had a dollar measure. Suppose instead that the firm wished to maximize the sum of profits (in dollars) and quantity sold (in units), both having equal weight, that is,

$$U = Z + Q \tag{9-25}$$

Again drawing on Equations 9-13, 9-14, and 9-15, we have

$$U = (-56,000 + 1200P - 4P^2) + (1000 - 4P) \tag{9-26}$$

[13]See S. S. Stevens, "Mathematics, Measurement and Psychophysics," in S. S. Stevens, ed., *Handbook of Experimental Psychology* (New York: John Wiley & Sons, Inc., 1951), pp. 1–41.

$$U = -55,000 + 1196P - 4P^2 \tag{9-27}$$

$$\frac{dU}{dP} = 1196 - 8P = 0 \tag{9-28}$$

$$P = \$149.50 \tag{9-29}$$

We should want this solution ($P = \$149.50$) to be insensitive to the units in which the different variables are expressed. Would it have made a difference if profit dollars had been stated in tens of dollars or quantity sold had been expressed in dozens? Let us assume that dollars were restated in terms of tens of dollars. Then,

$$U = (-5600 + 120P - .4P^2) + (1000 - 4P) \tag{9-30}$$

and the solution, using the same procedure as before, is $P = \$145$. Thus the units do make a difference and the additive utility function fails to meet the dimensionality test.

A dimensionality-free method has been proposed by Bridgeman.[14] Instead of using the additive utility function

$$U = U(Z_1) + U(Z_2) + \ldots + U(Z_n) \tag{9-31}$$

formulate the problem multiplicatively as

$$U = Z_1^{U_1} Z_2^{U_2} \ldots Z_n^{U_n} \tag{9-32}$$

To see how this works, consider the company that is trying to choose between two new products and is concerned with the profits (in dollars), Z_1, the probable growth rate of sales (in percent), Z_2, and the goodwill that the product will gain for the company (in scale points), Z_3. See Table 9-2. Management estimates the respective contributions of products 1 and 2 to each goal, and the importance of each goal. Using Equation 9-32, the utility of product 1, $U(P1)$ and two, $U(P2)$ are, respectively,

$$\begin{aligned} U(P1) &= 3,000,000^3 \cdot 3^2 \cdot 6^1 = 1458 \times 10^{18} \\ U(P2) &= 2,000,000^3 \cdot 4^2 \cdot 8^1 = 1024 \times 10^{18} \end{aligned} \tag{9-33}$$

Table 9-2

Goal	Product 1	Product 2	Importance
Profits (in dollars in first year)	3,000,000	2,000,000	3
Growth rate of sales (in annual percent)	3	4	2
Company goodwill gain (in scale points; 10 best, 1 poorest)	6	8	1

[14]P. W. Bridgeman, *Dimensional Analysis* (New Haven, Conn.: Yale University Press, 1922), pp. 21–22. See the description and example in David W. Miller and Martin K. Starr, *Executive Decisions and Operations Research* (Englewood Cliffs, N.J.: Prentice-Hall, Inc., 1960), pp. 161–164.

Product 1, in spite of a lower expected sales growth rate and contribution to company goodwill, is carried by the higher profit expectation into having the higher utility ranking. The ratio of the utility of the two outcomes is

$$\frac{U(P1)}{U(P2)} = \frac{1458 \times 10^{18}}{1024 \times 10^{18}} = 1.424 \qquad (9\text{-}34)$$

Furthermore, it can be shown that this same ratio of the two utilities would have emerged even if different units had been used in the problem. Thus Equation 9-32 provides a dimensionality-free method of comparing the utilities of two or more alternatives when two or more goals are involved.

Loss Function Minimization

The problems associated with imposing a utility function over the multiple goals have led analysts to search for other formulations. Instead of maximizing a utility function, the same problem can be handled by trying to minimize a loss function. Called *target programming or goal programming*,[15] this approach calls for management first to specify target values for each of its goals, that is, $Z_1^*, Z_2^*, ..., Z_n^*$. At the end of the planning period, each discrepancy of an actual performance from a desired performance, that is $(Z_i - Z_i^*)$, produces regret, and the regret is positively related to the size of the discrepancy. The task is to formulate a function that expresses the total loss (regret, disutility, penalty) felt by management with a plan that fails to attain all target values. For simplicity, let us assume:

1. The loss felt by management is symmetrical whether the estimated result of the plan exceeds or falls short of the target value.
2. The loss felt by management is proportional to the square of the deviation between actual and desired results.
3. The losses felt for the various goal discrepancies are additive.

The loss function that satisfies the preceding three assumptions is

$$L = (Z_1 - Z_1^*)^2 + (Z_2 - Z_2^*)^2 + \ ... \ + (Z_n - Z_n^*)^2 \qquad (9\text{-}35)$$

A geometrical interpretation of this loss function can be provided. First, take the square root of both sides and we will recognize that the right-hand side is the standard definition of distance:

$$\sqrt{L} = \sqrt{(Z_1 - Z_1^*)^2 + (Z_2 - Z_2^*)^2 + \ ... \ + (Z_n - Z_n^*)^2} \qquad (9\text{-}36)$$

This function is illustrated in Figure 9-3 for the case of two goals. The center of

[15]See J. Tinbergen, *On the Theory of Economic Policy*, 2d ed. vol. 1, Contributions to Economic Analysis (Amsterdam: North-Holland Publishing Company, 1952); H. Theil, "Linear Decision Rules for Macrodynamic Policy Problems," in B. G. Hickman, ed., *Quantitative Planning of Economic Policy* (Washington, D.C., The Brookings Institution, 1965), pp. 18–42; and A. Charnes, W. W. Cooper, and Y. Ijiri, "Breakeven Budgeting and Programming to Goals," *Journal of Accounting Research*, vol. 1, 1963, pp. 10–43.

the circle represents the target values (Z_1^*, Z_2^*), and for these values, $L = 0$, that is, there is no loss felt. For all deviations from the target value whose distance is $\sqrt{L_1}$, which gives the trace of a circle, the results are equally regrettable. The further away the estimated results of a plan are from the center of the circle, the greater the regret L, with regret growing as the square of the distance.

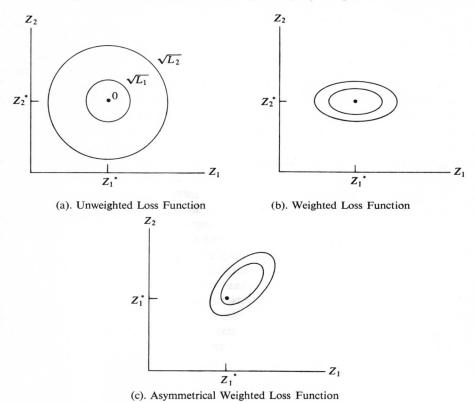

(a). Unweighted Loss Function

(b). Weighted Loss Function

(c). Asymmetrical Weighted Loss Function

Figure 9-3   Geometric Interpretation of Different Loss Functions

There are certain problems with the loss function in Equation 9-35 that can be met by relaxing some of the assumptions. For example, the loss function treats all the goal deviations as equally serious, whereas management might consider a unit deviation from target profits to be twice as serious as a unit deviation from target sales. To reflect the different weights that management may wish to attach to different goal deviations, Equation 9-35 can be modified into

$$L = W_1(Z_1 - Z_1^*)^2 + W_2(Z_2 - Z_2^*)^2 + \ldots + W_n(Z_n - Z_n^*)^2 \qquad (9\text{-}37)$$

For the two-goal case, this modification has the effect shown in Figure 9-3(b). The effect is to transform the circle into an ellipse, in this case showing that deviations from goal 2 are considered more serious than deviations from goal 1.

Another problem with the original formulation in Equation 9-35 is that over- and underachievement of goals are equally regrettable. If the goals are such things as sales and profits, certainly the management would be far less unhappy about a plan for which sales and profits were expected to exceed the target values than when they were expected to fall short. In fact, management would be delighted. But we must remember we are assuming that the company cannot find any plan that can fulfill all the targets at the same time, let alone over- achieve all of the targets. At best the company can find a plan that will under- achieve on some of the target values and overachieve on others. Clearly, the company pays a price to overachieve on some of the values (because this leads to underachievement elsewhere) and this is the reason that overachievement also involves a penalty. But the loss felt for overachievement of a goal is generally less than that felt for underachievement. Suppose that the loss function for both types of discrepancy is that illustrated in Figure 9-4. Underachievement is represented by a quadratic loss function and overachievement is represented by a linear loss function. This asymmetrical treatment leads to the following formulation:

$$\begin{aligned}
L = {} & W_1(Z_1 - Z_1^*)k_1 + W_1(Z_1^* - Z_1)^2(1 - k_1) \\
& + W_2(Z_2 - Z_2^*)k_2 + W_2(Z_2^* - Z_2)^2(1 - k_2) + \ldots \\
& + W_n(Z_n - Z_n^*)k_n + W_n(Z_n^* - Z_n)^2(1 - k_n)
\end{aligned} \tag{9-38}$$

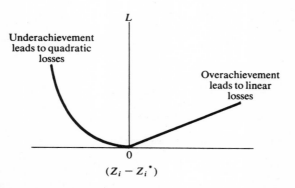

Figure 9-4 Asymmetric Loss Function

Every feasible plan will imply under- or overachievement for each goal, in which case the loss can be calculated by setting k_i to 1 for overachievement of the ith goal or to 0 for underachievement of the ith goal. In the case of over- achievement, the loss is considered equal to the absolute deviation; in the case of underachievement, the loss is considered equal to the squared deviation. Alternative asymmetric loss functions can also be formulated. The asymmetrical loss function in Equation 9-38 is illustrated in Figure 9-3(c), where it has the effect of distorting the isoloss curves away from the center. Large deviations in the direction of overachievement are of equal loss to small deviations in the direction of underachievement.

Once management has specified the target values and accepted the formulation of the loss function, the analyst can proceed to determine the plan that would minimize management's regret. For example,

$$L = 2(Z-33{,}000)^2 + (R-61{,}000)^2 \qquad (9\text{-}38)$$

would indicate that management wanted profits to be as close to \$33,000 as possible and sales revenue to be as close to \$61,000, with twice as much loss felt for profit deviation as revenue deviation. To solve this for the optimum marketing plan, it is necessary to substitute the relevant profit and revenue functions into the equation, simplify the equation, differentiate L with respect to the marketing decision variables, set each derivative equal to 0, solve the equations simultaneously, and test that the solution is a minimum. There is no difficulty in doing this in principle, although finding the solution to the system in practice may be difficult and require numerical approximation techniques.

The problem may even be more difficult if this quadratic loss function is to be minimized subject to certain constraints. The simplex technique of linear programming cannot be depended upon to find the plan that produces the globally minimum regret. This is because the minimum value is not guaranteed to lie at a corner point of the feasible space, even assuming that the feasible space is convex. Figure 9-5(a) shows a case in which the minimum loss solution in the feasible space lies on the boundary of the feasible space rather than at an extreme point. Figure 9-5(b) shows a case in which the minimum loss solution in the feasible space lies within the interior of the feasible space. To solve such problems of minimizing a quadratic function over a convex feasible space, advanced methods in quadratic programming must be used.

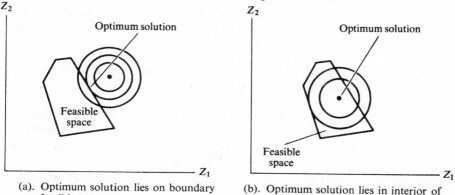

(a). Optimum solution lies on boundary feasible space.

(b). Optimum solution lies in interior of feasible space.

Figure 9-5   Constrained Loss Function Minimization

Constrained Maximization Formulation

There is still a third way to handle multiple goals, and this way is the most consistent with management's way of thinking about the problem.

The starting point is an earlier statement that management focuses on different goals at different times, subject to providing minimum satisfaction levels for the other goals.[16] If the management just turned in a poor profit showing, management will be most worried about the stockholder's attitude and probably will seek a plan that will maximize profits in the coming year, subject to achieving satisfactory levels of the other goals. If, in the next year, sales stay constant and profits grow, management may want to maximize sales growth, subject to meeting particular levels of profits and other goals. Whereas, in loss function analysis, we specified maximal aspirations (targets), in constrained maximization, we specify minimal aspirations and one goal. In this connection, Baumol has advanced the hypothesis that companies typically seek to maximize sales revenue subject to a profit constraint, rather than the reverse.[17] He bases this on a variety of observations: (1) declining sales may cause customers to think the product is declining in popularity, banks to refuse to lend money, and distributors to give less attention to the product; (2) "executive salaries . . . are far more closely correlated with the scale of operations of the firm than its profitability"; (3) executives seem to talk more and worry more about the level of sales than anything else; and (4) companies continue to keep unprofitable segments of their business, instead of performing the surgery necessary to increase profits. Baumol quickly adds that management is not unconcerned with profits but treats them as a discretionary constraint that must be met by the company's plan. "So long as profits are high enough to keep stockholders satisfied and contribute adequately to the financing of company growth, management will bend its efforts to the augmentation of sales revenues rather than to further increases in profits."

Another example of constrained maximization thinking is reported in a case study of the use of the DEMON model.[18] The case concerned the testing of a new product and the decision on whether to go national. Management was asked to state its objectives as a guide to determining the best marketing plan. Management set the following objectives:

1.   The payout period had to be no more than three and a half years.
2.   The minimum acceptable profit had to be no less than $4 million.

Beyond this, management would accept the plan that maximized its profits.

Sometimes management will discover that there is no plan that can satisfy all the constraints simultaneously, and this means that some constraints have to be relaxed. Mathematical programming will produce information on the cost of keeping each constraint where it is. For example, the "dual" solution will show

[16]See this interpretation of the multiple goal problem in Herbert A. Simon, "On the Concept of Organizational Goals," *Administrative Science Quarterly* (June 1964) 1–22.
[17]See William Baumol, *Business Behavior, Value and Growth* (New York: The Macmillan Company, 1959) Chap. 6.
[18]See David B. Learner, "DEMON New Product Planning: A Case History," Proceedings of the *48th National Conference of the American Marketing Association*, Frederick E. Webster, Jr., ed., June 1965. The model is reviewed in Chap. 17, pp. 519–563.

whether the payout period requirement of three and a half years, if relaxed to four years, might not lead to a plan with a higher profit potential.

In the case of our sample problem, suppose the multiple goals of management are stated in terms of maximizing one of the goals, say profits, subject to achieving minimal acceptable levels of other goals, say sales revenue and number of units sold; that is, in the profit equation, we maximize

$$Z = -56,000 + 1200P - 4P^2$$

subject to the revenue equation constraint

$$1000P - 4P^2 \geqslant 50,000 \tag{9-40}$$

and the quantity sold constraint,

$$1000 - 4P \geqslant 300$$

and the price nonnegativity constraint,

$$P \geqslant 0$$

This problem says that management wants to find a price such that the company is at least able to gross \$50,000 in sales revenue and sell at least 300 units. The price constraint, $P \geqslant 0$, insures that the mathematical solution technique does not permit a negative price to come into the solution. At this point the analyst is ready to solve the problem. Using calculus with Lagrangian technique, the optimum price is \$175 and the profit is \$31,500.[19]

As mentioned earlier, an advantage of expressing multiple goals in the form of a constrained maximization problem is adaptability. As the dominant interest of the firm, and the pressures and problems it faces change through time, it can redefine the goal and the constraints. The new goal and constraints can be easily expressed and lead management to the plan that is most calculated to meet its current needs.

SUMMARY

When we look closely at company goals, we see that enterprises define their objectives in a variety of ways that defy the simple formulation used in the analysis until now. The central issue is whether the analysis of optimal marketing policy should be based on maximizing a single goal or some function of several goals. If a single goal formulation is to be used, there are four choices. One is to treat current profits as the objective function, which we have been doing up to now. As a variant of this, current cash value rather than current profit might be used, the former including depreciation and excluding taxes and consequently expressing better the firm's possible interest in the cash impact of the marketing plan. A second choice is to maximize ROI, the ratio of current profit to investment or net worth. A third choice is to measure the internal rate of return of the

[19]Appendix Mathematical Note 9-1.

proposed marketing plan, where the internal rate of return is the interest rate that reconciles the anticipated earnings stream and the current required investment. This is closely related to the fourth choice, that of present value, which is found by discounting the anticipated earnings stream by either the company's cost of capital or desired rate of return. There are a few special circumstances in which the internal rate of return and present value may not produce the same rankings of projects, and hence a careful choice must be made between them.

Analysts are increasingly recognizing that the formulation of the company's objective function may require combining two or more goals. There are three different methods of building a multiple goal formulation. The first calls for developing a utility function of the separate goals, which is then maximized. The second calls for formulating a loss function that is to be minimized. Deviations of performances from targets are squared, summed, and weighted to form the loss function. The third calls for treating one of the goals as the objective function and the other goals as a set of constraints to be satisfied at specified levels. These three ways of handling multiple goals lead to different results, and this underscores the importance of giving careful thought to the problem of what the company is really trying to achieve by its plans.

Questions and Problems

1. A company is considering opening two new retail outlets, each of which will require an initial investment of $400,000. Management has calculated that these stores will produce the following earnings:

Year	1	2	3	4	5
Store 1 (000)	200	150	100	50	50
Store 2 (000)	50	100	100	150	50

   Assuming that the company can borrow all of the required funds at a rate of 5 per cent, should it proceed with the investments?

2. The XYZ Company has just gathered estimates for making a business analysis of a new product. Variable costs are constant at $5 a unit; additional plant can be obtained at a cost of $28,000 and depreciated over 4 years; the new product can be charged $14,000 a year for its share of general overhead; the marketing program calls for an annual advertising expenditure of $15,000 on advertising, $20,000 on distribution, and a price of $9. How many units per year will the firm have to sell to break even?

3. Large organizations often espouse such lofty goals as "to be the leader in the industry," or "to attain rapid growth through the implementation of dynamic management practices." Discuss the value of such goals. What are the attributes of good organizational goals and objectives?

4. Show that Bridgeman's utility functions are dimensionality-free by recasting the problem following Equation 9-32 so that:
(a) Profits are expressed in millions of dollars rather than in dollars and company image is on a scale of 1 to 20 points (that is, each value doubles).
(b) Profits are expressed in thousands of dollars and growth rates in decimal numbers

rather than percentages. Do these dimension changes change the ratio of utilities?
(c) Prove this dimensionality-free property in the general case.
5. Top executives of a camera company are trying to decide which of two possible cameras to introduce. One is a low-priced, easy-to-load camera (P_1) and the other is a medium-priced camera (P_2) whose sales will be lower but which will not invite strong competitive retaliation.

The executives have settled on the following values for company goals, rated from 0 to 1:

G_1	company survival	0.6
G_2	profits	0.3
G_3	utilization of present capacity	0.5
G_4	increased market share	0.4
G_5	quality image	0.2

They have also rated each product on its capacity to satisfy these goals:

G_j	P_{1J}	P_{2J}
survival	0.2	0.4
profits	0.8	0.5
capacity use	0.6	0.3
market share	0.4	0.2
image	0.1	0.6

(a) Show the utility function.
(b) Choose the best product.
6. The primary product of the Holden Manufacturing Company has suffered greatly from falling sales in recent years due to poor quality. Top management, realizing this, has taken action resulting in substantially improved product quality. They now feel that product exposure is critical in reestablishing a quality image. They are anxious to increase the quantity of the product sold, even at the expense of current profits, and would receive 10 times as much utility from high unit sales as they would from a high percentage increase in current profits.

Using the demand and profit equations in 9–13 to 9–15 and the multiple goal formulation in 9–19, determine the best price to charge for the product.

CHAPTER 10
Uncertainty

One of the factors that makes modern marketing so frustrating and at the same time so intriguing is the presence of uncertainty. Up to now the marketing executive was assumed to know exactly the nature of the demand and cost functions facing the firm. His problem was to find the marketing program that would maximize some utility function of the company's set of goals. Because of the presence of carryover effects, product interactions, nonlinear responses, and other complications, finding the solution was not always easy even under the assumption of certainty. Now that the additional possibility of uncertainty is introduced, finding the optimum marketing program seems even less attainable.

Uncertainty faces every business executive but few executives cope with uncertainty in any formal way. They absorb the uncertainty through a variety of organizational and individual devices ranging from committee decision making, through substantial investments in marketing research, through the use of risk reducing criteria.[1] For example, management may decide against considering any new product that would not pay back its investment in three years. Or management may refuse to consider new markets, in which they lack intimate

---

[1]For a discussion of uncertainty-absorption devices, see Richard M. Cyert and James G. March, *A Behavioral Theory of the Firm* (Englewood Cliffs, N.J.: Prentice-Hall, Inc., 1963), pp. 118–120.

experience. They tend to make various rules of thumb to screen out the high risk investments.

Some executives make their decisions under assumed certainty. They make their best single estimate of every relevant factor in the situation and compute the value of the outcome. They consider whether the outcome is attractive and, if it is, they adopt the course of action.

Conservative executives often choose to imagine the worst possible case in which demand is lower than expected and costs are higher than expected. If the investment still appears attractive, they may go ahead. Their opposite counterparts are the executives who tend to be optimistic about the future of a project and prefer to take the risk.

Many executives make three estimates of the relevant variables: an expected, an optimistic, and a pessimistic estimate. But in few cases do they proceed to process these estimates in a formal way that may be described as leading to the "best" decision by some criteria. Instead they ponder these and other possibilities and then somehow make up their minds.

Executives interested in more formal ways of decision making under uncertainty can turn to a growing body of literature known as "decision theory." Decision theory encompasses a variety of methods for coping with various levels of uncertainty. At least three levels of uncertainty should be distinguished by the decision maker. The first level is known as *risk* and describes the case in which the possible events following the decision and their respective probabilities are known to the decision maker. Dice and roulette games, as well as life and automobile insurance, are classic examples of situations of risk. The second level is known as *uncertainty* proper and describes the case in which the possible events following the decision are known to the decision maker but not their probabilities. Most marketing decisions fall into this class. For example, in raising his advertising budget or cutting his price, the decision maker knows the range of possible reactions of customers and competitors but not the respective probabilities. Because each situation is somewhat unique, the marketing executive cannot rely on a set of past frequencies of various responses as a guide to objective probabilities. He can express and use subjective probabilities but they should not be confused with the objective probabilities that are present in situations of risk. The third is known as *ignorance* and describes the extreme case in which neither the possible events following the decision nor their probabilities are known. Ignorance characterizes the decision maker's state of mind when some bold unprecedented move is about to be taken that has an uncountable number of ramifications. A management that is considering merger with another firm knows that there are going to be a great many consequences following this move, many of which cannot be anticipated. A management that is considering a new product introduction knows that many consequences are beyond its ken at the time of the decision. Situations characterized by ignorance by their very definition defy formal decision making, whereas situations characterized by risk and/or uncertainty have spawned many formal solution proposals.

This chapter will consider how the analysis used in previous chapters must be modified to handle uncertainty. The first section will carefully consider the various points in the formulations of demand and cost functions where uncertainty can arise. The second section will consider six different decision criteria that have been proposed for handling situations of risk and/or uncertainty. The third section will describe a particular philosophy, known as adaptive model building, for designing decision systems whose parameters are updated periodically in the light of experiments to measure key uncertain variables.

SOURCES OF UNCERTAINTY

Once uncertainty is admitted into the discussion of analytical demand and cost functions, it becomes clear that uncertainty can appear in several places. Consider the following simple demand function:

$$Q = 10 + 5\sqrt{X} + 3Y \tag{10-1}$$

where Q = quantity demanded per period
X = company promotional expenditure
Y = national income

If the decision maker is not completely confident that this expression would predict demand exactly, it is because he feels that uncertainty is rooted in one or more of six sources, respectively named: (1) exogenous variable uncertainty; (2) form of the variable uncertainty; (3) coefficient uncertainty; (4) structural form uncertainty; (5) omitted variable uncertainty; and (6) stability uncertainty.

Exogenous Variable Uncertainty

The demand equation in Equation 10-1 requires the decision maker to know X and Y before he can forecast Q. Promotional expenditures (X) pose no problem in this connection because promotional expenditure will presumably be set by the firm. On the other hand, the future level of national income (Y) is subject to some uncertainty. Some uncertainty as to the level of national income and other exogenous variables generally must be faced.

There are different ways to cope with exogenous variable uncertainty. The decision maker can always introduce the "most probable" estimates of the exogenous variables and carry out the analysis. Conservative decision makers may want to introduce pessimistic estimates for the levels of the exogenous variables to see whether this would change the best course of action. If the exogenous variable is treated as a random variable with a known mean ($\overline{Y}$) and variance (σ_Y^2), it is possible to derive the mean and variance of demand ($\overline{Q}$, σ_Q^2) using familiar theorems on probability.[2] For Equation 10-1 the expected value of demand would be

$$\overline{Q} = 10 + 5\sqrt{X} + 3\overline{Y} \tag{10-2}$$

and the variance of demand would be

$$\sigma_Q^2 = 9\sigma_Y^2 \tag{10-3}$$

[2] See Chap. 7, p. 187.

since var $(bY) = b^2$ var (Y), provided that b and Y are uncorrelated. Knowing the mean and variance of demand, the decision maker can proceed to compute the mean and variance of profit and then decide on the basis of these return and risk characteristics of the investment whether to go ahead. The use of return and risk criteria for decision making under uncertainty is discussed later in this chapter.

Form of the Variable Uncertainty

Equation 10-1 makes assertions about the form of each variable as it affects demand. For example, demand is shown to have a square root relation to promotion and a linear relation to national income. The square root relation suggests that demand is subject to diminishing marginal increases with increases in promotion, whereas increases in national income will lead to proportional increases in demand. These forms of the relationship are surmised on the basis of intuition and basic economic theory. If the decision maker is in the enviable position of having sufficient historical or cross-sectional data, he can try out different forms of the variables for their respective effectiveness in explaining the data. Statistical tests of significance in this case will help reduce his uncertainty concerning the proper form of the variables.

Coefficient Uncertainty

Equation 10-1 provides coefficient measures of the magnitude of response of demand to both promotional and national income. Thus every dollar increase (after taking the square root) of promotion increases demand by five units, and every dollar increase in national income increases demand by three units. These coefficients presumably come from a maximum likelihood statistical fitting of the equation to data. In any event the response coefficients are statistically estimated and therefore subject to some estimation error.

The conservative way to cope with this uncertainty is to reduce each of the response coefficients to a pessimistic level to see how much this depresses the demand estimate, and whether this is sufficient to change the best course of action. Unfortunately management generally has weak intuition regarding the appropriate size of the response coefficients and may not be able to propose reasonable pessimistic estimates for the response coefficients or evaluate the reasonableness of the statistically fitted ones.

The decision maker may wish to use the statistically measured variance of the response coefficient for promotion as a reflection of his uncertainty about the true response level. Suppose he believes that the response coefficient for promotion (call it $a = 5$) is a random variable that is positively correlated with national income. That is, he believes that promotional expenditures are more effective, the higher the level of national income. In this case, demand will also be a random variable with a variance given by

$$\sigma_Q{}^2 = X\sigma_a{}^2 + b\sigma_Y{}^2 + 2\rho X^{1/2}\sigma_a b\sigma_Y \qquad (10\text{-}4)$$

where $\sigma_Q{}^2$, $\sigma_a{}^2$, and $\sigma_Y{}^2$ are the variances of demand, the response coefficient, and national income, respectively, and ρ is the correlation coefficient between the promotional response coefficient and national income.[3] Given the variance of demand, the analyst can then find the variance of profits for any intended level of promotional expenditures and use it along with the mean of profits to arrive at his decision on promotion.

Structural Form Uncertainty

Equation 10-1 calls for summing the effects of different variables, rather than multiplying them or handling them in some other way. We saw in Chapter 2 that the demand equation can take many forms. This question of the proper structural form of the equation is therefore another source of uncertainty. Here as before, the analyst must rely on management intuition, economic theory, and statistical criteria for getting at the best equation form.

Omitted Variable Uncertainty

Equation 10-1 attempts to portray the main factors affecting demand but obviously does not include every factor. In leaving out some factors, the analyst recognizes that Equation 10-1 is not going to be a perfect predictor of demand. He hopes that the omitted factors are individually small in their influence on demand; the net effects of all of them tend to cancel out. He does not expect them exactly to cancel out and tries to estimate the average error and the distribution of error. For example, his model of demand may be

$$Q' = 10 + 5\sqrt{X} + 3Y + u \tag{10-5}$$

where u = random normal error term with mean of 0 and standard deviation of σ, that is, u is distributed $P_n(0, \sigma)$

Or the error may be postulated to be distributed according to a different probability distribution function (p.d.f.) than the normal one. In any event, the postulation of a random error term subject to a known or assumed p.d.f. allows the analyst to go from an estimate of demand uncertainty to profit uncertainty, using standard probability theory. He can advise on the best course of action on the basis of the decision maker's feelings about the return, risk, and other characteristics of the profit p.d.f., as shall be described later in the chapter.

However, omitted variables can cause a serious problem when they exert a large and systematic influence upon demand but are not accounted for in the equation. For example, suppose demand in Equation 10-1 is also influenced by the number of retail outlets carrying the firm's product. For simplicity, assume that company promotional expenditures and national income remain the same year after year. Yet demand will change from year to year, given changes in the number of retail outlets. Management can assume that its forecasting errors represent random error, that is, the effect of many small factors. It will be advisable, however, to test the time series of errors to see whether they are

[3]See Appendix Mathematical Note 10–1.

normally distributed,[4] as would be expected under the assumption of random error. In this case, the error will appear nonrandom; this provides a clue to the analyst to look for some important systematic factor that may have been omitted. If he stumbles upon the number of retail outlets as a possible omitted variable, its correlation with the error term will be large and significant enough to demonstrate that this variable should have been included.

Stability Uncertainty

For Equation 10-1 to be useful, it is necessary to assume that there is period to period stability in the functional form and in the response coefficient. Stability in turn implies that the underlying behavior of customers, competitors, and channels, as well as the characteristics of the product, are unchanging or not changing dramatically. This is a fairly safe assumption to make for established markets and products, where customer habits are strong and competitors tend to pursue constant strategies. The assumption is an unsafe one to make in new or highly competitive markets. Demand forecasting in new markets requires a more complex and microanalytic model that goes beyond the single equation and contains built-in dynamic features. Such models will be investigated in Chapter 17.

An example. The analyst who works with a single equation function to represent total demand, as in Equation 10-1, must examine the six sources of uncertainty just described to anticipate the kinds of problems that may have to be dealt with. He may have to develop new ways of expressing the particular uncertainty and formally incorporating it into the analysis. Consider the following example.

A light bulb manufacturer decided to enter into the production of bulbs for photographic darkroom use and was trying to decide how much burning life to build into the bulb. He could build in more burning life by increasing the quality of the filament but felt that burning life had a diminishing marginal impact on demand. His best estimate of the relationship between bulb burning life (X) and sales (Q) is given by

$$Q = aX^b \tag{10-6}$$

where a = scale factor, $a > 0$

b = bulb burning life elasticity, $0 < b < 1$

This relationship is illustrated in Figure 10-1.

At the same time the manufacturer feels some uncertainty about the effect of bulb burning time on demand and says he is less confident of his sales estimates for high levels of bulb burning time than for low levels of bulb burning time.

---

[4]An appropriate statistical test may be the Durbin-Watson d statistic. For a discussion of this test and estimation methods in the presence of autocorrelation, see J. Johnston, *Econometric Methods* (New York: McGraw-Hill Inc., 1963), pp. 192–200.

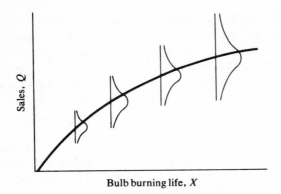

Bulb burning life, X

Figure 10-1   Hypothetical Relationship between Bulb Burning Life and Sales

This is because the competitors' bulbs were short lived and he could guess pretty well the share of market he would get with his own introduction of short-lived bulbs. It was harder to estimate his share of market with a better quality bulb because it depended upon whether customers acknowledged the difference, were willing to pay more for it, and whether competitors reacted. He felt that the standard deviation of his sales estimate (i.e., his uncertainty regarding sales) increased proportionately with the bulb burning time:

$$\sigma_Q = mX \tag{10-7}$$

where m = factor of proportionality and $m > 0$.

He decided to incorporate this relationship, along with other demand and cost information, into a complex marketing strategy simulator. The simulator required the random generation of demand estimates for different settings of bulb burning life. To achieve this, he combined Equation 10-6 and a chance-determined amount of Equation 10-7:

$$Q = aX^b + kmX \tag{10-8}$$

where k = a random normal deviate, where $P(-3 < k < +3) = .99^+$. This equation is used in the following way to generate a level of demand. The manufacturer decides to test the profit implications of setting bulb burning life at $X = X_0$. Since a and b are assumed known, the first term on the right-hand side of the equation is a known number. Then a random normal deviate k is drawn from a table of random normal numbers. If it is 0 (this is k's expected value but it has a very low probability), then the second term drops out. Otherwise k is multiplied by the known mX, and the result is added to the first term. This is a single stochastically generated demand estimate and can be converted through further steps into a profit estimate. By repeating this process many times, it will yield many estimates of demand and profit for a bulb whose burning life has been set at X_0. In this way the manufacturer can better visualize the expected result and range of results that might occur with a particular marketing policy.

DECISION CRITERIA UNDER UNCERTAINTY

When a decision maker knows with certainty all the factors entering into his problem, he can proceed to solve it using short run profit maximization or multiple goal criteria discussed in Chapter 9. Finding the best course of action may require considerable mathematical analysis, but usually the choice of the objective function is fairly limited. Decision making under uncertainty also requires the selection of an objective function, but here the range of choice is much larger. *Men do not all feel the same way about risk.* As a result, a variety of decision criteria is available for guiding the decision maker who faces uncertainty. Some decision criteria appeal largely to the conservative executive and others to the risk taking executive. They can lead to vastly different evaluations of the best course of action. No criterion is dominant and best in all circumstances, although each has its merits in certain circumstances. This section will examine and illustrate the following six decision criteria:

1. Expected monetary value criterion
2. Expected utility criterion
3. Return risk criterion
4. Probability distribution of return criterion
5. Minimax criterion
6. Minimum regret criterion

Expected Monetary Value Criterion

In situations of genuine risk, where the possible events and their objective probabilities are known, most decision makers will use the long run *expected monetary value* of the "game" as a guide to actions subject to certain qualifications described later. The expected monetary value is easy to calculate. Suppose a decision maker is offered the opportunity to spin the lottery wheel in Figure 10-2 on a repeated basis for as long as he wants. Each time one of three events will happen. There is a .30 probability that he will win $30.40, a .50 probability that he will win $14.20, and a .20 probability that he will lose $28.90. Suppose he is allowed to play the game at no cost. Will he play?

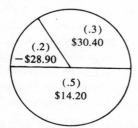

Figure 10-2   A Hypothetical Gambling Situation

If he is allowed to play the game only once, he might decline if the possible loss of $28.90 looms larger in his mind than the possible gains. This might happen if he is impoverished and cannot afford to lose $28.90. Most players would not be in this situation; furthermore they would be impressed at the .80 probability of winning something. If they could play the game continuously, they would recognize that they would inevitably come out ahead. For example, in ten plays they would expect to earn:

$$3 \times \$30.40 + 5 \times \$14.20 - 2 \times \$28.90 = \$104.40$$

This means that their average gain per game is $10.44. This is what we mean by the expected monetary value of the game. The expected monetary value (EMV) could be computed directly by multiplying the event payoffs (Z_i) by their respective probabilities (p_i) and summing:

$$EMV = p_1 Z_1 + p_2 Z_2 + \ldots + p_n Z_n \tag{10-9}$$

$$EMV = \sum_{i=1}^{n} p_i Z_i$$

In the example:

$$EMV = .3 \times 30.40 + .5 \times 14.20 - .2 \times 28.90 = 10.44$$

Since the executive expects to earn $10.44 in the average play over the long run, he will want to play, especially if there is no charge for playing. In fact he would normally be willing to play even if there is a charge per play, as long as the charge does not exceed $10.44. Expected monetary value indicates the most he would pay to play, since he is interested in net gain and this must be positive.

Suppose there is no charge to play the game and he could buy information before each play that would perfectly forecast the outcome. What is the most he should pay for this information? The information is only of value when it warns him that a loss of $28.90 is about to occur. This happens .20 of the time. Therefore the expected value of perfect information (EVPI) is $5.78, that is, .20 × 28.90; he should not pay more than this for information each time before a play if the game is otherwise free.[5]

Now let us apply these concepts to a real business situation. To the extent that a real business situation contains objectively known risks and is played repeatedly as in insurance, the sellers of insurance will set their price to cover expected long run beneficiary costs, as they can be estimated from mortality tables, plus selling costs. Expected monetary value is a reasonable decision criterion in these situations. To the extent that the business situation departs from the assumptions of (1) objective risks and (2) repeated play, expected monetary value becomes less attractive than other criteria to be discussed later.

Nevertheless, many executives have used EMV in single decision situations in which the risks were subjectively estimated. Consider the following cases.

Example.[6]   A large chemical company was pondering what to do with a new

[5]See Robert Schlaifer, *Probability and Statistics for Business Decisions* (New York: McGraw-Hill Inc., 1959).
[6]This example is a simplified version of one reported in Wroe Alderson and Paul E. Green, *Planning and Problem Solving in Marketing* (Homewood, Ill.: Richard D. Irwin, Inc., 1964), pp. 216–233.

product that had been under development for several years. The product was estimated to have approximately twenty major uses. The personnel responsible for making the commercialization decision felt great uncertainty regarding the product's potential profitability. They were uncertain about the best size plant to build if they introduced the product nationally.

To analyze this problem formally, the company's operations research director met with the product manager and marketing personnel. This committee agreed on the following ground rules:

1. The executives would consider three alternative pricing policies: a skimming pricing policy, a penetration pricing policy, and an intermediate pricing policy.
2. The executives would consider two alternative initial plant sizes, with capacities of 10 million pounds and 25 million pounds, respectively. They also agreed that if demand exceeded capacity, there could be up to three years delay before the additional capacity could be developed.
3. The analysis would be limited to a thirteen-year planning horizon.
4. The executives would judge among the alternative possible decisions on the basis of which appeared to have the highest expected present value.

Using these ground rules, the executives prepared three different forecasts of annual sales covering the thirteen years, representing, respectively, a pessimistic, optimistic, and most-likely outlook.

The next step involved computing the expected present values of seventy-two different possible developments (two initial plant sizes, three pricing policies, three sales forecasts, and four capacity addition delay levels). An illustration of eighteen of these developments is shown in Figure 10-3. The dollar figure at the end of each of the eighteen branches represents an estimate of the present value of the expected cash flow during the thirteen year period. For example, management expects a cash flow whose present value is $30.4 million if it employs a skimming pricing policy, builds a small plant of 10 million pounds annual capacity, and experiences very good sales.

The numbers in parentheses preceding the present value estimates are the probabilities assigned by management to the optimistic, most probable, and pessimistic forecasts, respectively (0.3, 0.5, 0.2). The next step calls for computing the expected present value for each alternative facing management. This is found by multiplying each of the three present values by their respective probabilities as outcomes. Thus the expected present value of the skimming price, small plant alternative is $10.44 $[= 0.3 \times \$30.4 + 0.5 \times \$14.2 + 0.2 \times (-\$28.9)]$. Note that these are the figures used in the previous lottery example, except they are now in millions of dollars. The expected monetary value of the other five strategies are also shown at the right in Figure 10-3.

Examining Figure 10-3, it turns out that the large plant size yields the highest expected present value under all pricing policies and sales forecasts; the skimming pricing policy dominates the others under all conditions. Thus, if the company decides to introduce the product commercially and wants to earn maximum expected profits based on the model, it should build a 25 million pound plant initially and use a skimming pricing policy. This move, P_1F_2, has an expected present value of $12.03 million.

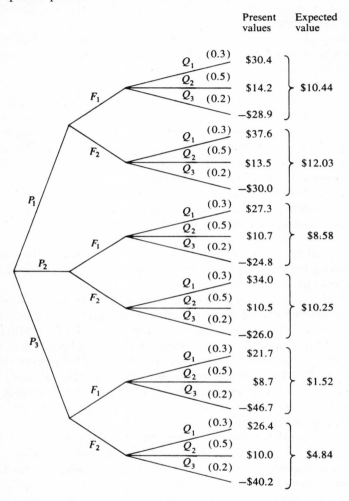

Figure 10-3 Decision Tree for New Product Decision Problem

Explanation:
P_1, skimming pricing policy; P_2, intermediate pricing policy; P_3, penetration pricing policy; F_1, small plant; F_2, large plant; Q_1, optimistic demand forecast; Q_2, most probable demand forecast; and Q_3, pessimistic demand forecast.

The use of EMV by the large chemical company to decide among alternatives is not surprising because they have the resources to withstand a major loss ($30.0 million, with a .20 probability); this decision criteria, applied consistently to all their ventures, should yield the highest EMV in the long run. Managements in other circumstances, however, may prefer other criteria.

Expected Utility Criterion

While men may tend to use EMV in decision situations where the gamble is small in relation to their assets, the criterion tends to be modified in higher risk situations. Most men will not accept a gamble, even if it has a positive EMV, if it involves investing all their capital in a venture that had a small probability of gaining an enormous amount and a high probability of losing all. Swalm[7] shows evidence that many executives would not take gambles at the mathematical expectation. One particular executive he interviewed would not accept a proposal that had a 50–50 chance of either making his company $300,000 or losing $60,000, in spite of the fact that the mathematical expectation is $120,000.

The disinclination of an executive to use EMV in high risk situations can be explained in a number of ways. If the executive is in middle management, he may want to avoid risky situations because a poor decision on his record might spoil his future in the company. His chances of promotion may be better through a series of sound decisions, even with modest results, than a series of gambles that might not pay off. In organizations that place a premium on conservative decision making, executives often do not even take normal risks.

If the executive is the top decision maker in the company, he may want to avoid risky decisions because the possible satisfaction of winning may be less than the tension and effort of living with the decision. The utility of money for him does not rise as rapidly as the amount of money itself. If diminishing marginal utility for income is fairly common among top business executives, then this fact must be incorporated in any analysis. The executive, instead of being assumed to maximize expected income, seeks to maximize expected utility.

The use of expected utility maximization as a means of explaining choice behavior under risk makes the following two assumptions:

1. It is possible to get a consistent utility curve for money for any executive through his willingness to express his preferences between situations or how much he would pay or accept for a situation.
2. The executive will decide (or should decide) between new situations on the basis of which has a higher expected utility according to his utility curve for money. In other words, the executive tries to maximize his expected utility.

Each of these assumptions will now be illustrated.

Constructing the decision maker's utility curve for money. The decision maker will be viewed as a man trying to choose between two or more alternatives involving known amounts of risk. He will be asked how he feels about gambles involving amounts of money in a dollar range that is familiar to him. A salesman may be asked to think about gambles of gaining or losing $100,000 for the company, while a company president may be asked to think about gambles of

---

[7]Ralph O. Swalm, "Utility Theory—Insights Into Risk Taking," *Harvard Business Review* (Nov.–Dec. 1966) 123–136.

gaining or losing $10 million. The decision maker's upper reference level will be Z_G (G for gain) and his lower reference level will be Z_L (L for loss). A third useful reference level will be zero gain, Z_0.

The problem is to develop corresponding utility numbers for all dollar amounts in the executive's reference range. It is convenient to think of the utility of a zero dollar gain as 0, that is,

$$U(\$0) = 0 \qquad\qquad (10\text{-}10)$$

As for the utility of the upper dollar reference amount Z_G, this is arbitrary. Let it be set at 120, that is, $U(Z_G) = 120$, because this number can be repeatedly divided in half and yield whole numbers. Now the executive is asked to react to a series of simple gambles. The first question might be:

Suppose you have a 50–50 chance of making either $400,000 (upper reference level) or nothing and somebody offers to buy this chance from you. What is the least amount of money you would want?

Suppose the decision maker says he would settle for $110,000. This figure can be called his *certainty equivalent* because he is indifferent between $110,000 and the risky opportunity. His *utility* for a gain of $110,000 can be found by solving the equation representing his indifference:

$$
\begin{aligned}
U(\$110{,}000) &= .50\ U(\$400{,}000) + .50\ U(0) \\
U(\$110{,}000) &= .50\ (120) + .50\ (0) \qquad\qquad (10\text{-}11) \\
U(\$110{,}000) &= 60
\end{aligned}
$$

Thus his utility for a gain of $110,000, in a scale from 0 to 120, is 60. As a result of this question, his utility curve is known to pass through the three points shown in Figure 10-4.

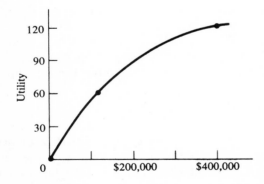

Figure 10-4   The Decision Maker's Utility Curve

It should be noted that the executive's certainty equivalent value of $110,000 differs from the mathematical expectation of $200,000. It can be said that this executive is willing to pay a premium for avoiding risk. His *risk premium* is the difference between the EMV and the certainty equivalent CE, or

$$EMV - CE = \$90,000 \tag{10-12}$$

Further points on the utility curve can be determined by asking the decision maker to respond to additional gambles. For example, he might be asked:

Suppose you have a 50–50 chance of making either $400,000 or $110,000 and somebody offers to buy this chance from you. What is the least amount of money you would want?

Suppose he gives $200,000 as his certainty equivalent. The utility of $200,000 for him can be calculated in the following way:

$$
\begin{aligned}
U(\$200,000) &= .50U(\$110,000) + .50U(\$400,000) \\
U(\$200,000) &= .50(60) + .50(120) \\
U(\$200,000) &= 90
\end{aligned}
\tag{10-13}
$$

This point can be added to Figure 10-4; hopefully, it is consistent with the approximation already established. Additional utilities can be estimated through further questions although four or five points usually suffice for curve fitting.

To arrive at the decision maker's negative portion of the utility curve, let us arbitrarily set the lower reference level, Z_L, at $-\$100,000$ and assign it a disutility of -120, that is, $U(-\$100,000) = -120$. Then the executive can be asked the following question:

Suppose you have a 50–50 chance of losing either $100,000 or nothing. What is the most you would pay to be released from this risky situation?

Suppose that the decision maker says he would pay $60,000 to avoid this situation because he cannot afford to take the chance of losing $100,000. Then the disutility of a $60,000 loss to him is

$$
\begin{aligned}
U(-\$60,000) &= .5U(-\$100,000) + .5U(-\$0) \\
U(-\$60,000) &= .5(-120) + .5(0) \\
U(-\$60,000) &= -60
\end{aligned}
\tag{10-14}
$$

This point can be used to extend the utility curve in Figure 10-4 down into the third quadrant (not shown). Further questions about gambling situations can help improve the approximation of the executive's total utility function.

If the points give a reasonably consistent curve, the next step calls for fitting an equation to the curve. Fitting a standard second-degree equation by least squares,[8] we get

$$U = -13.74 + .0008138Z - .00000000122Z^2 \tag{10-15}$$

The equation can now be used as an alternative to the graph to derive the decision maker's utility for any possible gain or loss of income.

Using the decision maker's utility curve for money. Suppose that the decision

---

[8]Other equation types could alternatively be fitted such as a root function or a logarithmic function.

maker is trying to decide between the two courses of action described below and he wants to maximize his expected utility, where his utility function is given by Equation 10-15:

A: .70 probability of a $200,000 gain and .30 probability of a $50,000 loss
B: .90 probability of $140,000 gain and .10 probability of a $40,000 loss

The executive can now proceed to find the expected utility (EU) of each alternative:

$$EU_A = .70U(\$200,000) + .30U(-\$50,000) = .70(90.4) + .30(-36.7) = 52.27$$
$$EU_B = .90U(\$140,000) + .10U(-\$40,000) = .90(76.0) + .10(-29.5) = 65.45$$

Thus *B* has a higher utility than *A* for this decision maker. This is in spite of the fact that *A* has the higher expected monetary value (EMV$_A$ = $125,000 and EMV$_B$ = $122,000). Since the executive is going to face this exact situation only once, he attaches a little more weight to the amount and probability of the possible loss than the possible gain.

Return-Risk Criterion

In both the case of expected monetary value and expected utility, the decision maker is content to use a single value for judging the merits of a proposed course of action. This single value comes out of collapsing the possible outcomes of a course of action into a single figure by using the respective probabilities as weights. Whatever risk is associated with the course of action influences the expected value but is not made an explicit parameter in itself. Yet many executives who have to evaluate courses of action with uncertain outcomes ask for information on both the expected return and expected risk. Given these two parameters (instead of only the first) about a prospective strategy, they show their first preference for strategies that promise a high return and a low risk. They shun strategies that portend a low return and high risk, and they maintain mixed attitudes toward intermediate strategies. Return and risk become a language for characterizing opportunities and strategies.

Executives will sometimes complain that their subordinates do not take enough risk, or take too much risk, in relation to the return level. Can this common business parlance about return and risk be translated into rigorous concepts for use in formal marketing decision making under uncertainty?

To think about this question concretely, suppose the analyst had to translate the strategy P_1F_1 in Figure 10-3 into return and risk terms. What two numbers might he use? For return, the expected monetary value (i.e., mathematical expectation) of $10.44 would be a natural measure to use. For risk, it would be desirable to use some measure of the dispersion among the possible outcomes. According to the reasoning, the greater the uncertainty, the greater the risk to which the firm will be exposed. Among the possible measures of dispersion are the range, the variance, or the absolute deviation. Because the variance has a number of mathematically desirable properties, it will be used in this analysis as the measure of risk.

Returning to strategy P_1F_1 in Figure 10-3, the variance (in millions) is $20.88 (calculation not shown here). The expected return and variance of return for all six strategies (in millions) are shown in Table 10-1.

Table 10-1.

	P_1F_1	P_1F_2	P_2F_1	P_2F_2	P_3F_1	P_3F_2
Return (R)	$10.44	$12.03	$8.58	$10.25	$1.52	$4.88
Variance ($\sigma_R{}^2$)	$435.97	$550.97	$330.15	$432.22	$613.08	$558.38

If we assume that the decision maker is favorably disposed toward return and averse to risk, then he would prefer the course of action that portends the highest return and the lowest variance. Since none of the six strategies has this enviable quality, the executive must redefine his criterion. He may, for example, prefer the strategy with the greatest ratio of return to risk: this is strategy P_2F_2. Or he may prefer the strategy with the highest return providing that risk (variance) does not exceed $400 million: this is strategy P_2F_1. Or he may prefer the strategy with the least risk, given that the return is at least $10.40 million: this is strategy P_1F_1.

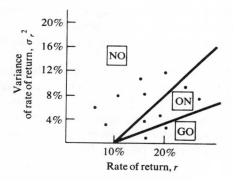

Figure 10-5   Return-Risk Grid

We have seen how return and risk could be used to choose among mutually exclusive courses of action. It probably has an even greater usefulness in the context of the problem of evaluating a whole set of marketing projects or investments in which they have to be ranked and only some subset can be adopted. Top management can use these concepts along with a simple graphical device to communicate to its general managers the average level of risk they should be assuming in marketing investments. The graphical device is shown in Figure 10-5. Instead of dollar return and dollar risk, the diagram uses estimated rate of return (shown on the horizontal axis) and estimated variance of the rate of return (shown on the vertical axis). Every investment project is rated in terms of its expected rate of return and risk, and is then characterized as a point in the space. Figure 10-5 shows the return risk characteristics of a dozen projects. The return risk space is subdivided into three linear regions. The region at the lower right is called the GO region because management looks favorably upon projects with these return and risk characteristics. Projects in this region promise a high return and a low risk. The line defining the GO region starts at an intercept of 10 percent because management does not want to consider any investments, even if riskless, that would yield less than 10 percent. It would prefer to keep the money invested in liquid or semiliquid form at this rate. The slope of the line defining the GO region rises at a rate showing management's psychological terms of trade for return and risk. For every rise in the expected return of 1 percent management is willing to accept more risk for higher expected returns but at a decreasing rate.

The second region called ON represents investment opportunities that are of dubious value to the company, while the third region called NO represents investment opportunities that are definitely unattractive to the company.[9] NO opportunities pose too much risk for the expected rate of return. As for ON opportunities, the company suspends judgment or makes an effort to gather more information about them. Marketing research studies are expected to clarify management's estimate of return and reduce its estimate of uncertainty, with the net result that projects in the ON region are expected to fall more clearly into the GO or NO region after marketing research. This form of analysis therefore not only groups projects according to relative initial attractiveness but also points out which projects would benefit the most from additional marketing research.

This still leaves open the question of how various projects within the GO region rank in terms of each other. This is particularly important if the company has less investment funds than good investment opportunities. The ranking can be accomplished by postulating a management utility index that is some function of the return and risk parameters. This function will yield a single number for each project and thus permit a ranking of all GO projects. For example, consider the following utility function:

$$U_i = r_i - .8\sigma_{r_i}^2 \tag{10-16}$$

where
U_i = utility of product i
r_i = expected rate of return on product i
.8 = company's risk aversion coefficient
$\sigma_{r_i}^2$ = variance of rate of return on product i (square of standard deviation)

Essentially the formula says that management's utility for the project is equal to the expected rate of return less an amount representing the risk. Risk is represented by the variance weighed by a risk aversion coefficient reflecting the particular company's level of risk aversion. The formula as a whole yields the certainty equivalent of a risky investment.

[9]It is assumed that all projects are mutually independent. Otherwise, some projects in the ON or NO region might have to be accepted because of their positive effect on projects in the GO region. Project interdependence would call for a modified analysis not developed here.

Now consider this function in connection with evaluating the two projects shown in the GO region of Figure 10-5, where the return risk vectors are approximately (15 percent, 1 percent) and (20 percent, 3 percent), respectively. Let us call these projects $G1$ and $G2$. The utilities of these two projects are, respectively,

$$U(G1) = 15 - .8(1)^2 = 14.2$$
$$U(G2) = 20 - .8(3)^2 = 12.8 \qquad (10\text{-}17)$$

Even though $G2$ has a higher estimated return, it has the lower utility for management because of the high discounting for risk. If the management had adopted a lower risk aversion coefficient, say .4, $G2$ would have looked better:

$$U(G1) = 15 - .4(1)^2 = 14.6$$
$$U(G2) = 20 - .4(3)^2 = 16.4 \qquad (10\text{-}18)$$

A utility function for return and risk is useful in that it can be easily communicated to various operating heads of company divisions as a guideline to rating and ranking various projects. Top management's choice of the risk aversion coefficient is its way of formally expressing to the various managers how much risk they should be taking.

At the same time, the return risk criterion raises some serious problems. The use of the variance to measure risk is not entirely satisfactory. A high variance means that the outcome may be unusually good or unusually bad in relation to the expectation. Someone has suggested that the left half of the probability distribution be labeled risk and the right half be labeled opportunity. Some executives are attracted by high variance because of the high payoff it implies if they are lucky. For this reason, a better measure of risk might be the *semivariance* that measures the downside risk. Alternatively, risk may be defined as the *expected value of the loss function* and this too will avoid including the opportunity side of variance.[10] Still another alternative is to define risk as *the probability of losing R dollars*, where R is the level of ruin for the decision maker. This last alternative allows the decision maker to set up the problem of choosing between risky investments using a chance constrained formulation, that is, one in which one of the constraints is that losing R dollars is not allowed to exceed a certain probability.

A still more basic problem with the return risk criterion is that these two characteristics of a probability distribution do not tell all about it that the decision maker might like to know. Consider Figure 10-6 showing two investment opportunities A and B, with approximately the same expected return and same variance of return. Executives should be indifferent between these two opportunities insofar as the return and variance are identical. Both opportunities yield the same utility as calculated by Equation 10-16. Yet executives who are asked to make a choice generally are not indifferent. This means that they are at least sensitive to the third moment of the distribution, if not to the whole shape.

[10]This definition of risk is illustrated in Chap. 11, p. 301.

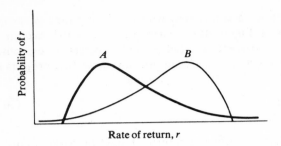

Figure 10-6 **Two Investments with Identical Means and Variances and Opposite Skewness**

Probability Distribution of Return Criterion

The preceding limitations of the return risk criterion point to the possible desirability of developing and displaying the whole probability distribution of return for any strategy or investment, rather than one or two parameters characterizing this distribution. The advantage of showing the whole distribution is that executives have different attitudes toward uncertainty, some being more interested in the grave loss it might imply and others in the excellent gain it might imply. They have different attitudes toward skewness and peakedness characteristics of the probability distribution of return; the best way to accommodate these different attitudes is for the analyst to present the full profile of uncertainty surrounding any course of action.

This leads to two questions. The first concerns the method of obtaining the probability distribution of returns for any proposed strategy. The second concerns the criterion for ranking strategies after their individual probability distributions of returns are estimated.

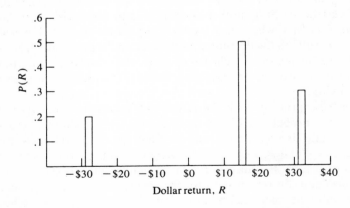

Figure 10-7 **Discrete Probability Distribution of Sales for Strategy $P_1 F_1$**
Source: See Figure 10-3.

Estimating the probability distribution of return. Let us return to strategy $P_1 F_1$ in Figure 10-3. The tree diagram presents a discrete probability distribution for the random variable sales, Q. The probability distribution is recast into a conventional probability distribution diagram in Figure 10-7. Presumably, management will be shown the probability distribution for each strategy and seek the one that best satisfies its attitudes toward return and risk.

How were the probabilities and payoffs in Figure 10-7 arrived at? Executives were asked to consider three different specific sales outcomes, Q_1, Q_2, and Q_3. (These are not shown but the implied return has been calculated for each: \$30.4, \$14.2, and $-$\$28.9, respectively.) They were also asked to distribute a total probability of one over the three possible outcomes, and these turned out to be .3, .5, and .2 for Q_1, Q_2, and Q_3, respectively. It is not made clear how the original three specific sales outcomes were chosen or how discrepant probability evaluations of different executives were resolved.

There are other, more satisfactory ways to obtain subjective probability distributions of sales; they are reviewed in detail in Chapter 18. When sales are the only variable treated as uncertain, then the analyst can immediately translate the uncertainty over sales into the implied uncertainty over final return. All that is necessary is to subtract costs (treated as known) and perform whatever other operations are necessary to bring about the desired payoff measure. In many cases, however, such as new product introductions and site selections, uncertainty characterizes a host of factors. For example, uncertain variables might include market price, unit variable cost, and total investment, in addition to quantity sold. Executives may be willing to formalize their uncertainty for each of these variables in the form of a three-point (pessimistic, most likely, optimistic) estimate. The question then becomes how to combine all of these uncertain estimates about productive inputs into a final probability distribution of return. This problem is dramatized in Figure 10-8.

Mathematical analysis would ordinarily serve the purpose of determining the probability distribution of some payoff measure from the known probability distributions of demand and cost inputs. If all the probability distributions are independent and normal, it is not too difficult to find the final probability distribution of return by using theorems on the distribution of sums and products of normal random variables. However, in most practical applications, the executives will render distributions that are not all normal. Furthermore, some random variables will be functionally related such as price and quantity sold. Consequently, it is usually too difficult or impossible to determine the probability distribution of returns from mathematically manipulating the input distributions.

The technique that analysts have resorted to in this case is Monte Carlo simulation. One variation of the application has been called Risk Analysis[11], and another Venture Analysis.[12] Pessemier has used the technique in the context of the new product decision problem, and we shall briefly describe his approach.[13]

[11]David B. Hertz, "Risk Analysis on Capital Investment," *Harvard Business Review* (Jan.–Feb. 1964) 95–106.

[12]Sigurd L. Andersen, "Venture Analysis: A Flexible Planning Tool," *Chemical Engineering Progress*, (Mar. 1961) 80–83.

[13]Edgar A. Pessemier, *New-Product Decisions: An Analytical Approach* (New York: McGraw-Hill, Inc., 1966), Chap. 4.

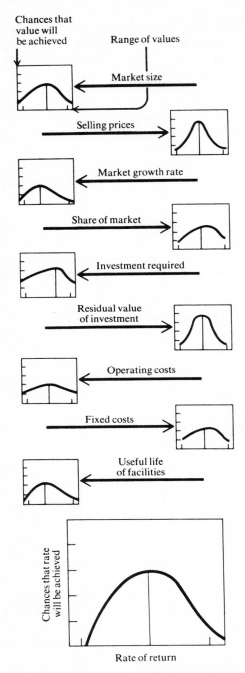

Figure 10-8   Problem of Deriving a Probability Distribution of Rate of Return from a Whole Set of Input Probability Distributions
Source: David B. Hertz, "Risk Analysis in Capital Investment," *Harvard Business Review,* January-February 1964, p. 102.

Pessemier's approach calls for the decision maker to assume some marketing environment (the state of the economy, technology, distribution channels, etc.) and some marketing strategy for each of the years in the planning horizon. The decision maker estimates expected values and the 0.1 and 0.9 decile values for unit sales, price, unit cost, and investment for each year in the planning horizon. These data permit the derivation of probability distributions for all the uncertain variables.[14] The computer now takes over and draws a sample value for each uncertain variable for the coming year. These sample values are drawn in a Monte Carlo fashion, that is, through the selection of random probability numbers that can be translated into a value for each variable.[15] The sample values for the coming year permit the determination of first year profits. Sample values are then drawn for the second, third, … n year and profit is determined for each year. The profit stream is then solved for the internal rate of return that brings it into equality with the company's investment.

The computer repeats the same process many times, producing as a result many internal rates of return for this marketing strategy and environment. These r's are summarized in a frequency distribution and this becomes the probability distribution of return expected with the particular marketing strategy in the particular environment. The same process can be repeated using a different marketing strategy and/or marketing environment. This Monte Carlo approach to estimating the probability distribution of return is summarized in flow diagram form in Table 10-2.

Table 10-2   Monte Carlo Simulation Model (Pessemier)

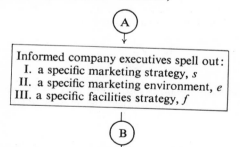

Ⓐ

Informed company executives spell out:
I. a specific marketing strategy, s
II. a specific marketing environment, e
III. a specific facilities strategy, f

Ⓑ

The executives then estimate the annual expected values of the following variables over the i years in the new product planning horizon:
1. unit sales (Q_i)
2. unit price (P_i)
3. unit cost (c_i)
4. investment (I_i)

In addition to the expected values of these variables, the executives estimate the respective 0.1 and 0.9 decile values. The decile values enable the analyst to treat each variable as subject to a lognormal probability distribution with a known mean and variance. (These will be used later.) Finally, the

[14]See Chap. 18, p. 589.
[15]See Appendix Mathematical Note 10–2.

Table 10-2—(contd.)

executives estimate annual expected values, but not quantile values, for the following three variables:
   5.   depreciation (d_i)
   6.   opportunity costs in dollars (h_i)
   7.   nonrecurring startup costs (u_i)

The analyst now generates by Monte Carlo methods a sample value for each variable (Q_i, P_i, c_i, and I_i) for each year during the product planning horizon. (A device is used to permit serial correlation of successively generated values of unit sales.)

These values enable a computation to be made of the positive cash flows (Z_i) each year. The formula is

$$Z_i = (1-t)[(P_i - c_i)Q_i - i_i - u_i] + d_i$$

where t stands for the tax rate. In other words, the profit contribution in year i is found by first taking the difference in year i between price (P_i) and full unit cost (c_i) times unit sales (Q_i). This gives the unadjusted before-tax profit. Then interest costs (i_i) and nonrecurring startup costs (u_i) are subtracted. The after-tax profit is found by applying the profit retention rate. Depreciation (d_i) is then added back to the cash flow to cancel the effect of its being subtracted implicitly as part of c_i.

The investment cash flow stream is discounted back to the present by the firm's opportunity cost of capital to yield the present value of the firm's investment flow (I)

Successive approximation is used to find the rate of return (r) that will discount the profit flow to an amount equal to the discounted investment

Have enough r's been generated yet?

 No   Yes

Table 10-2—(contd.)

Return to Step C

Order the r's in a frequency distribution and show graphically. This is the approximate probability distribution of rates of return for marketing strategy s, marketing environment e, facilities strategy f, and various expected values and quantile estimates

Are the probability distribution (return risk) characteristics satisfactory for making a GO decision?

 Yes

$\boxed{L}$ No

Launch the product

Investigate the desirability of gathering more information, Estimate the expected value of perfect information (EVPI) by weighing the conditional cost of incorrect action and sum the results. Is EVPI "high enough?"

 Yes

$\boxed{N}$ No

Estimate the expected gain from different marketing research studies designed to reduce the uncertainty surrounding Q, P, c, and I, respectively. (This is done by substituting various values of a particular random variable and repeating the Monte Carlo simulation.) Is the expected net gain from the best study greater than 0?

 Yes

$\boxed{P}$ No

Gather additional information. Then go back to B

Is there another marketing strategy or facilities strategy that should be considered?

 No

$\boxed{R}$ Yes

Drop the product

Return to A

Source: This flow diagram has been developed by the author from Pessemier's discussion, *New-Product Decisions*, Chap. 4.

One important set of limitations in the particular version of risk analysis described in Table 10-2 should be noted. In the present version, no matter what price is drawn the sales volume distribution is unaffected. It would seem more accurate to change the mean of the sales volume distribution, depending on the outcome of the price drawn. Thus, if a high price is drawn, there should be a greater chance of drawing a small sales volume. Similarly, the mean of the unit cost distribution should be made dependent on the sales volume that is drawn. In addition to linking the variables in the current year, a case could be made for linking the variables through time. Thus, if a high price is randomly drawn this year, this should affect the mean of the price distribution from which price is drawn next year. Chance is still allowed to operate, but the outcome of a drawing is used to affect the mean level of future drawings. These two types of dependencies, the cross-sectional and the longitudinal, are lacking in early versions of risk analysis but can be built in with some additional effort.

Determining the best strategy.   After the probability distribution of return is determined for each strategy, the task still remains of ranking them in terms of desirability of outcome. The problem is much harder than when the merit of each strategy was summarized by a single number (expected monetary value or expected utility) or by two numbers (expected return and risk). Consider for example the five rate of return probability distributions in Figure 10-9. They were estimated for the problem of branch bank location, using the Monte Carlo simulation method outlined above.[16] The officers of a major bank were trying to decide which of five locations would be best for locating a new branch. Estimates of the mean and standard deviation of demand, investment, and costs were made for each site for each year of the planning horizon. The corresponding probability distributions were sampled in Monte Carlo fashion on a repeated basis and these probability distributions of rates of return were built up. Which branch seems to be the most attractive?

The first thing to look for is whether any probability distribution dominates all other probability distributions. This would happen if one probability distribution is entirely to the right of all the others. That is, its lowest possible estimated rate of return is superior to the best possible rate of return with any other branch. This does not characterize any branch's probability distribution in Figure 10-9. We might next look for individual probability distributions that are strongly or weakly dominated by another and remove it from consideration. For example, most executives would feel that Branch B dominates Branch A because it has a higher expected rate of return, a higher possibility of a very high return, and a lower probability of a very poor return. Therefore Branch A can be removed from the set of alternatives. Beyond this instance of weak dominance, no others seem apparent, so that it is now necessary for the executives to compare the remaining distributions as a whole.

---

[16]See E. Eugene Carter and Kalman J. Cohen, "The Use of Simulation in Selecting Branch Banks," *Industrial Management Review* (Spring 1967) 55–70.

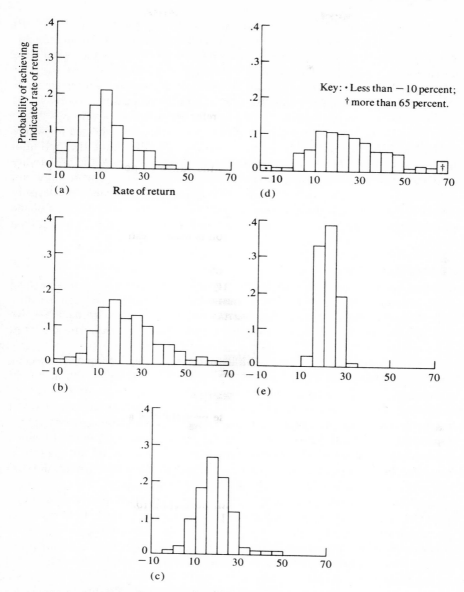

Figure 10-9 Five Probability Distributions of Rates of Return

Source: Carter and Cohen, *op. cit.*, p. 65.

The executives' taste for risk becomes the critical factor. Consider Branch D and Branch E. Some decision makers would prefer Branch E because it portends a return of about 20 percent subject to only a small amount of uncertainty. Branch D, on the other hand, involved considerable uncertainty. Its expected return is also around 20 percent, but the branch may yield as little as -10 percent return on investment or as much as a 70 percent return on investment. The conservative decision maker would prefer Branch E and the speculative decision maker would prefer Branch D. This underscores the main advantage of displaying the whole probability distribution of returns for each strategy. It allows the decision maker to realize fully the range of possible results of his action without any concealment behind one or two major parameters.

At the same time, as long as an objective function cannot be defined for whole probability distributions, it is without meaning to talk about the optimum marketing strategy. Monte Carlo simulation is used to estimate the probability distribution of return for any strategy contemplated by management but is not conceived as a tool for searching for improved strategies. Only when the decision maker can express his utility function in terms of simple characteristics of the probability distribution of returns is it possible to define and seek an optimal strategy.

Minimax Criterion

The four previous criteria all assume that the decision maker knows the statistical odds governing the contingencies surrounding his choices. They assume that, even if he does not know the objective probabilities, he has a strong subjective feeling for them and is willing to use these probabilities as an intrinsic part of the analysis.

In many cases, the decision maker will not have a strong feeling or any feeling for these probabilities. In the case of a new product that might sell at one of three levels, Q_1, Q_2, and Q_3, he may find the marketing research results very confusing: the results may leave him with no feeling for the ultimate level of market interest in the new product. In such situations executives may be tempted to assume that all three events are equally likely. The assignment of equal probabilities, known as the LaPlace criterion (or criterion of rationality), is appealing in that it would seem to be the set of probabilities that would minimize the error if all possible sets of probabilities were equally likely.[17] Many persons think that assigning equal probabilities is the least biased assumption they can make in the face of total ignorance. At the same time, they recognize that their assignment of equal probabilities is completely arbitrary.

Many decision makers would prefer to abandon altogether the use of probabilities in situations of complete uncertainty. Once probabilities are abandoned in the analysis, the decision maker no longer expects to use a single figure as a measure of the merit of a proposed course of action. Probabilities produced a single figure of merit through the operation of arithmetically weighing the various possible outcomes. Once they are abandoned, the decision maker must look at the raw outcomes themselves.

For example, conservative decision makers will tend to be very interested in

[17]For some background on this criterion, see David W. Miller and Martin K. Starr, *Executive Decisions and Operations Research* (Englewood Cliffs, N.J.: Prentice-Hall, Inc., 1960), pp. 90–94.

the worst possible outcome of every possible action they might take. This is particularly true if a bad decision could topple the whole enterprise. In the area of military planning, many generals will choose the strategy that would leave the military strength as intact as possible even if the worst outcome took place. In the area of corporate planning, many officers will want to choose the strategy that would have the least worst consequence on the future of the firm. This interest is known as the minimax decision criterion (or criterion of pessimism).[18]

As an example, let us return to the chemical company that had to decide on the "best" strategy for launching a new product. The alternative strategies and payoffs were shown in Figure 10-3. The same information, ignoring the probabilities, has been recast in matrix form in Figure 10-10. This is commonly described as a *payoff matrix* in the decision theory literature. As a matter of convention, strategy alternatives are typically listed at the left and states of nature are listed at the top. *States of nature* refer to various values that the chance variable (in this case, sales) can take on that will affect the payoff. The chance variable is beyond the control of the firm, falling under the influence of competition or "nature". The values inside the cells represent best estimates of the payoffs for various strategy state combinations. The payoffs may represent current annual profits, present values, rates of return, and so forth; hence the general name payoffs instead of profits.

States of Nature

	Q_1	Q_2	Q_3
$P_1 F_1$	\$30.4	\$14.2	\$$-$28.9
$P_1 F_2$	37.6	13.5	$-$30.0
$P_2 F_1$	27.3	10.7	$-$24.8
$P_2 F_2$	34.0	10.5	$-$26.0
$P_3 F_1$	21.7	8.7	$-$46.7
$P_3 F_2$	26.4	10.0	$-$40.2

(Strategies)

Figure 10-10   Payoff Matrix for New Product Decision Problem

As stated earlier, the decision maker who wants to insure himself of not going bankrupt will concentrate primarily on the maximum possible loss with each strategy. The minimum of these maximum possible losses, \$24.8 million, would occur with strategy $P_2 F_1$. The strategy $P_2 F_1$ is therefore the best strategy as defined by the minimax criterion.

[18]This decision criterion has also gone under the name of the *maximin* criterion in situations in which the decision maker would gain from every possible strategy and wishes to choose the strategy that will maximize the minimum possible gain. A strategy opposite to minimax (or maximin) is known as *maximax* and describes the use of only the best possible results from each strategy to maximize the decision criterion of the business executive who prefers to take risks.

Minimum Regret Criterion

There is still another way to look at the information in Figure 10-10 and cope with the uncertainty characterizing the three possible sales outcomes. The decision maker might consider the best strategy under each possible state of nature. For example, if he knew that sales would be Q_1, his best strategy would be P_1F_2. All other decisions would have produced some amount of regret. For simplicity, assume that the amount of regret he would experience for not selecting the payoff maximizing strategy given the state of nature is equal to the dollar difference between the payoff under the best strategy and the strategy he selected. Thus, if he chose P_1F_1 instead of P_1F_2 when Q_1 occurred, his regret would have been $37.6 - 30.4 = 7.2$. The regrets can be computed for all the other cells in a similar way; they have been gathered in a matrix shown in Figure 10-11. Note that the best strategy in each column is assigned a zero for zero regret and all the other strategies are assigned a dollar regret number, representing the difference between their payoff and the best payoff in the column.

	States of Nature		
	Q_1	Q_2	Q_3
P_1F_1	7.2	0	4.1
P_1F_2	0	.7	5.2
P_2F_1	10.3	3.5	0
P_2F_2	3.6	3.7	1.2
P_3F_1	15.9	5.5	21.9
P_3F_2	11.2	4.2	15.4

Strategies (label at left of table rows)

Figure 10-11   Regret Matrix for New Product Decision Problem

The next step calls for the executive to examine the most regret that he might feel with each strategy. For example, strategy P_1F_1 might lead to as much as $7.2 regret and this would happen if Q turned out to be Q_1. If we look at the worst regret for each strategy, the series is

7.2, 5.2, 10.3, 3.7, 21.9, 15.4

The minimum of these maximum regrets is 3.7, corresponding to strategy P_2F_2. We conclude that the executive who wants to minimize his maximum regret would choose strategy P_2F_2.[19]

In effect, the minimum regret criterion calls for applying the minimax criterion to the regret matrix instead of the payoff matrix. Regrets are measured by the dollar differences between the best strategy and other strategies for given

[19]The idea of minimizing the maximum regret was first proposed by Savage. See L. J. Savage, "The Theory of Statistical Decision," *Journal of the American Statistical Association* 46 (1951) 55–67.

states of nature. Since regret is directly but not necessarily linearly related to dollar opportunity costs, the criterion could be modified by introducing the decision maker's utilities for dollars.

ADAPTIVE MODELS FOR HANDLING UNCERTAINTY

Having examined different sources of uncertainty and different criteria for policy selection in the face of uncertainty, we shall now consider the possibility of designing a decision system in which the parameters are updated periodically on the basis of new information about sales response. The decision maker is conceived not only as making a decision each period, but also conducting an experiment to learn of the latest state of the system.

We shall illustrate the principles involved by describing John D. C. Little's example of an adaptive model.[20] Assume a company whose profits are described by the following model:

$$Z = mS - X - F \tag{10-19}$$

where Z = profit rate (dollars/household/year)
  S = sales rate (dollars/household/year)
  X = promotion rate (dollars/household/year)
  F = fixed cost rate (dollars/household/year)
  m = gross margin, the incremental profit as a fraction of sales (dimensionless)

To the best of the company's knowledge, its sales are determined by the promotion rate in a simple quadratic relationship:

$$S = a + bX - cX^2 \tag{10-20}$$

Given this information, it can easily be shown that the optimal promotion is given by:[21]

$$X^* = \frac{(mb - 1)}{2mc} \tag{10-21}$$

If the company spends something other than X^*, the loss rate, L, relative to maximum profit is given by:[22]

$$L(X) = mc(X - X^*)^2 \tag{10-22}$$

Now suppose the company did not have accurate information about the parameters of the sales function in Equation 10-20. There are two cases to consider. The first is where the sales response function is not known accurately

---

[20]J. D. C. Little, "A Model of Adaptive Control of Promotional Spending," *Operations Research*, (Nov. 1966) 1075–1097.
[21]See Appendix Mathematical Note 10–3.
[22]See Appendix Mathematical Note 10–4.

but is thought to be stable through time. In this case, it would pay for the company to put in a big effort to measure the function as soon as possible and as accurately as possible, because the benefits in achieving optimization of X would extend far into the future. The other case is that in which the sales response function is not known accurately and furthermore is expected to shift through time. The shifts can be caused by new developments in competitive activity, advertising copy, product changes, and economic changes. In this case, it would not pay to invest heavily in learning the exact parameters of the sales response function in the current period. Suppose, in particular, that the parameters change slowly through time. Then the best research strategy would be to collect some new information each time about the current level of the parameters of the sales response function and combine this with the old information to produce new estimated parameters for the sales response function on which the current outlay for promotion can be based.

To illustrate this approach, Little develops a simple model of how the sales response function changes each period. He assumes that, in any period t, the sales rate for the product will be given by

$$\tilde{S} = \tilde{a} + \tilde{b}X - cX^2 \tag{10-23}$$

where tilde ($\sim$) means the variable is treated as a random variable. Thus Little is assuming that a and b vary from period to period, while c is constant and known. Although c is the term that regulates the curvature to the sales response function, Little showed through sensitivity analysis that knowing c is not critical. Little assumes that $\tilde{a}$ has a high variance from period to period. However, this is not too critical because $\tilde{a}$ does not affect the optimal setting of X even if a were perfectly known. Little assumes that $\tilde{b}$ follows a random walk governed by the following process:

$$\tilde{b}(t) = kb(t-1) + (1-k)\bar{b} + \tilde{u}_b(t) \tag{10-24}$$

where k = a constant, $0 \leqslant k \leqslant 1$
            $\bar{b}$ = the long run average value of $\tilde{b}(t)$
            $\tilde{u}_b(t)$ = a random variable with mean = 0 and variance = σ_b^2

Thus the current $\tilde{b}(t)$ is a weighted average of the previous period $b(t-1)$ and the long run average $\bar{b}$, perturbed by a random disturbance term $\tilde{u}_b(t)$. If k is close to 1, then $\tilde{b}(t)$ is highly dependent on $b(t-1)$ and wanders more freely from $\bar{b}$. If k is close to 0, $\tilde{b}(t)$ stays close to $\bar{b}$ and is not very affected by last period's value.

Now the problem facing the company is to design an experiment each period to attempt to measure the current value of b. The company has picked a promotion rate X_0 for the coming period on the basis of applying profit maximization criteria to its most current information on the sales function, as in Equation 10-21. The experiment consists of using this promotion rate in all markets, except a subset of $2n$ of them randomly drawn. In n of the test markets, the company will plan to spend a deliberately low amount of dollars, X_1; in the other n test markets, the company will plan to spend a deliberately high amount of dollars, X_2, where:

$$X_1 = X_0(t) - \frac{d}{2} \tag{10-25}$$

$$X_2 = X_0(t) + \frac{d}{2} \tag{10-26}$$

and d is a design constant to be selected. This experiment is illustrated in Figure 10-12.

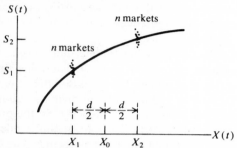

Figure 10-12   A Sales Experiment to Estimate b

The point of the experiment is that it will yield information on the average sales created by a low level of promotion and the average sales created by a high level of promotion and by averaging them in the following way, an estimate of current incremental sales response, $\hat{b}(t)$, is found:

$$\hat{b}(t) = \frac{\bar{S}_2 + cX_2{}^2 - \bar{S}_1 - cX_1{}^2}{d} \tag{10-27}$$

where $\hat{b}(t)$ = an estimate of $\tilde{b}(t)$

$\qquad \bar{S}_i$ = observed mean sales in group i

This estimate $\hat{b}(t)$, in principle, could be used for determining the optimal promotional rate in the next period; but it would lead to a smoother tracking system if the current estimate $\hat{b}(t)$ were combined in some fashion with the last estimate, $\tilde{b}(t-1)$. In other words, the last estimate, $\tilde{b}(t-1)$ will be treated as a prior estimate; the present estimate, $\hat{b}(t)$, would be treated as sample evidence; and the two would be combined to form the posterior estimate, $\tilde{b}(t)$. Little suggests the use of an exponential smoothing process for finding the posterior $\tilde{b}(t)$:

$$\tilde{b}(t) = g\hat{b}(t) + (1-g)\tilde{b}(t-1) \tag{10-28}$$

where g = the exponential smoothing constant and $0 \leqslant g \leqslant 1$

Then the optimal promotion expenditure constant in period $t+1$ is given by

$$X^*(t) = \frac{(m\tilde{b}(t) - 1)}{2mc} \tag{10-29}$$

which is an adaptation of Equation 10-21.

Thus this adaptive control model works in the following way. Each period the company decides on the optimal promotional level based on the latest estimate of the b coefficient (and the other coefficients). At the same time the company plans to spend somewhat less than this rate in one subset of markets, and somewhat more than this amount in another. This experiment gives the company a new estimate of b that might have changed for any number of reasons. The new estimate of b is combined with the last estimate of b into a new b that is then used for determining the optimal rate of expenditure in the next period. This procedure is repeated from period to period and should produce promotion level decisions that are not far from the optimal, given the shifting nature of the sales response function. Little provides a numerical example of how well this tracking system would work in a particular case.

As part of the optimal analysis, the company has to determine several things in addition to the optimal promotion rate. First, it must determine the best number of markets to set aside for the experiment. Every market that is removed from the set receiving the normal level of promotion is receiving a suboptimal level of expenditure if the normal level is the appropriate level. So the problem is to withdraw as few markets as possible from the mainstream, while withdrawing enough to get sensitive information on any basic shifts in b. The second problem is that the company must determine how much less and how much more it should spend in each of the two sets of test markets. Again, the greater the deviation of the amount spent from the normal, the more suboptimal the expenditures might be, while at the same time the more sensitive the experiment might be in catching a shift in b. A third problem is to choose the smoothing constant g carefully. The closer g is to 1, the closer promotion spending will be tied to last period's spending and therefore appear to be less responsive to real shifts in b. On the other hand, the closer g is to 0, the more responsive promotion will be to the latest experimental results (compounded with random error) and the more promotion is likely to shift around from period to period.

It should be appreciated that these results are tied to a particular model of the sales response function created by Little to illustrate the philosophy of adaptive control. The point, of course, is that the model could be changed, more marketing mix variables added, and the same principles applied to a case of greater realism. All this is possible because of the basic contribution of Little in opening up this type of adaptive model building in a marketing context.

SUMMARY

The difficulties faced in the analysis of marketing problems when facts and relationships are assumed known are compounded greatly when the real fact of uncertainty is added. Taking an ordinary sales response function that hitherto has been treated as known, we have been able to identify at least six sources of possible uncertainty: (1) exogenous variable uncertainty, the uncertainty surrounding the future level of an exogenous variable; (2) form of the variable uncertainty, the difficulty of establishing whether a certain variable's effect on another is linear, squared, logged, and so forth; (3) coefficient uncertainty, the variance that surrounds any estimate of the response coefficient; (4) structural form uncertainty, the uncertainty surrounding the basic structure of the equation; (5) omitted variable uncertainty, the question of whether the model includes all the important variables; and (6) stability uncertainty, the basic issue of whether the equational relationship is stable through time.

Given these several sources of uncertainty, we next considered six different criteria that the decision maker can use to select a policy in which uncertainty is faced: (1) expected monetary value criterion, calling for the executive to estimate the expected monetary value of each alternative and to choose the one with the highest EMV; (2) expected utility criterion, calling for the executive to select the alternative with the highest expected utility; (3) return risk criterion, calling for the executive to rank all the alternatives according to their return and risk, and then to choose the most favorable return risk combination (it was shown that a certainty equivalent formula could be used to find the utility of any return risk combination); (4) probability distribution of return criterion, calling for the executive to examine the whole probability distribution of return for each strategy and to choose among them in a way that reflects his own preference for different characteristics of the distribution; (5) minimax criterion, calling for the executive to choose the alternative that would leave him least worst off if the worst happened; and finally (6) minimum regret criterion, calling for the executive to choose the alternative that would minimize his postdecision regret.

For those decisions that are made regularly, such as setting the promotion budget, it would pay to design a decision procedure that includes collecting new estimates of sales response each time, so that the parameters of the profit function might be updated. Little has shown, for a system in which the sales response function shifts in a random walk fashion from period to period, that the company would benefit from setting up some test markets, in half of which it spends less than the normal rate of promotion and in the other half more than the normal rate of promotion. The resulting estimate of sales response could be combined with the prior estimate to lead to a smoothed estimate that is used in next period's determination of optimal promotion. Adaptive control models thus offer a way to cope with a situation in which it is felt that the sales response function shifts in an uncertain way each period and current measurement is required if promotional expenditures are to be optimally adjusted.

Questions and Problems

1. An individual has an opportunity to participate in a game for which there is a $10 entry fee each time he plays. In this game he stands to win $50, $20, or $8 with the respective probabilities of .3, .1, .4, and has a probability of .2 of losing $45. If there is no limit to the number of times he can play, should he play the game?

2. A company executive is asked, "If you have a 50-50 chance of making either $400,000 or nothing, what is the least amount of money for which you would sell this chance?" The executive's answer is $200,000. He is then asked, "If you have

a 50-50 chance of making \$200,000 or nothing, how much money would you accept for this chance?" He answers \$100,000. Finally, he is asked, "If you have a 50-50 chance of losing \$100,000 or nothing, how much would you pay to be rid of the gamble?" His answer is \$50,000.

If the utility of the upper dollar reference amount, $U(Z_G)$, is set at 160, and the utility of the lower dollar reference amount, $U(Z_L)$, is set at -40, and it is assumed that $U(0) = 0$:

(a) Determine the executive's utility for \$200,000, \$100,000, and $-$\$50,000, respectively.

(b) Determine the equation which represents the executive's utility curve for money.

(c) Using this equation, determine the executive's utility for (1) \$150,000, (2) $-$\$75,000, (3) \$50,000.

(d) How reliable do you think this interviewing method is in obtaining an accurate utility curve?

3. A company faces two possible investment projects, I_1 and I_2. The returns on these projects are expected to be $r_1 = 15$ percent, $r_2 = 10$ percent. The standard deviations of these rates of return are $\sigma_{r_1} = 4$, $\sigma_{r_2} = 2$. Using the return-risk criterion outlined in the chapter, calculate management's utility for each project for three different risk aversion coefficients (.2, .5, .8) and analyze the results.

4. You are the chairman of a new product committee facing a decision with respect to a new product which has just been test marketed by your company. Each of the 10 company executives who has been closely involved in the product's development is asked to make an independent forecast of the product's most likely rate of return. The results, in percents, are: 10, 12, 12, 12, 15, 15, 15, 15, 18, 18, 20.

The company generally invests in products where the estimated rate of return exceeds 14 percent. Considering the estimates above, determine the character of the distribution of the estimates and indicate whether you would invest in the product.

5. Suppose the top manager of a firm is asked to give an "educated guess" about the most probable level of sales (Q_e) for a given period (assuming a specific state of marketing environment and a specific marketing strategy). Suppose that he indicated that his average expectation (Q_e) is \$500. Further, assume that his pessimistic estimate is $Q_p = $ \$450 such that the probability of a sales level lower than Q_p would be .20; and that his optimistic estimate is $Q_o = $ \$550 such that the probability of a sales level higher than Q_o is .20. Suppose further that the probability distribution of demand is normally distributed. Determine the mean and the standard deviation of the distribution.

6. A company must choose from three investment strategies I_1, I_2, and I_3. Management knows that the return realized on its investment choice will depend upon which of the three corresponding strategies B_1, B_2, or B_3 is chosen by its competitor. The company's payoff matrix is shown below (figures in percent ROI).

	B_1	B_2	B_3
I_1	12	8	5
I_2	10	20	-5
I_3	-10	10	15

Determine the company's best investment strategy:

(a) Using the minimax criterion

(b) Using the minimum regret criterion.

PART II
Micromarketing Decision Models

CHAPTER 11
Distribution Decision Models

The previous chapters developed tools and models for analyzing various types of complexities found in the marketing system. Each successive chapter added another problem facing the marketing model builder and showed the means for handling it. The marketing decision maker's sights were kept at the macrolevel, where he sought to determine the optimal marketing expenditures for maximizing his objectives. Very little was said about the rich content within each marketing decision variable and the clues they afford to setting optimal marketing plans.

In this second major part of the book, we shall take up four of the major marketing decision areas—distribution, pricing, sales force, and advertising—and explore a series of models involved in effective decision making in each. These marketing decision areas are by no means exhaustive, although they are probably the most important categories dealt with by marketing management. Some of the other marketing decision areas, such as sales promotion, product assortment, and so forth, have either been described in other sections of this book or share sufficiently similar logic to the major decision areas, so that they do not warrant separate discussion.

Of the four marketing decision areas, distribution is a logical place to start. The distribution decision involves the seller in determining the most profitable ways to reach the markets he wants to serve. If he decides to sell direct, this has implications for the size and type of sales force, the size of his advertising budget, and his prices, among other things. If he decides to sell through middlemen, this decision will call for a different plan of sales force activity, advertising, and pricing. The distribution decision is basic to the planning of the other marketing efforts. At the same time, we shall not want to lose sight of the *interrelatedness* of all marketing decisions.

We shall divide the distribution decision into four major components. The first is called *distribution strategy*, which is the problem of determining the basic way in which the company will try to *sell* its products to designated end markets. The company has options ranging from direct selling, through bulk supply, to using a variety of intermediaries (manufacturers' agents, brokers, jobbers, wholesalers, retailers, etc.). The second is called *distribution location*, which concerns the determination of the number and location of outlets that the seller wants to work through. Here the company considers how many outlets will maximize its return, and their best locations. The third is called *distribution logistics*; this is the problem of determining the best way to *supply* products to the intermediary sellers or final buyers. Here the company seeks to balance considerations of high service to customers with considerations of holding down inventory, warehousing and transit costs. The fourth is called *distribution management* and this is the problem of developing, managing, and controlling a trade mix (mix of gross margins, allowances, and services) that will motivate the distribution system to perform at peak level. Given the fact that many resellers are independent profit maximizers themselves, the company must choose trade terms calculated to win preferential treatment from middlemen and customers.

Before examining models useful in analyzing these specific and interrelated decisions, the reader should note the following general points about distribution channels. First, there is nothing sacrosanct or necessarily permanent about the particular institutions that constitute the company's distribution system at a point in time. The important thing about a distribution channel is not the institutions that make it up so much as the functions they perform. To get goods to actual or potential customers involves work. There is work involved in making the goods physically available in different locations (sorting, assorting, storage, and transportation); in searching for buyers and communicating information about product features and availability (sales force and advertising); and in closing sales and delivering goods (negotiation, order handling). These functions can be performed in different ways and any distribution channel is a particular configuration for performing these functions, operating at a certain level of costs and with a certain generation of sales.[1] The major reason for channel change is timely discoveries by entrepreneurs of more effective or efficient ways to accomplish the same work. For example, the early success of the self-service supermarket is explained by the fact that it is able to perform more work than the corner grocery and enable prices to be brought down.

---

[1]This point of view on channels has led to a mathematical analysis of the equilibrium number of middlemen that will appear in a channel. This analysis is presented in Appendix Mathematical Note 11–1.

In the second place, channels of distribution are not always "captained" by manufacturers. At one time, wholesalers were dominant in many distribution channels. Today we find examples of channels managed by every conceivable type of agent. The old individualistic marketing channel—consisting of independent manufacturers, wholesalers, and retailers—is finding increasing competition from corporate, administrative, and contractual channels (or vertical marketing structures). A *corporate channel* is a centrally owned and operated vertical marketing system that is programmed for concerted action and the achievement of certain economies. An example is Hart, Schaffner, and Marx, the clothier, which owns some basic raw material sources, factories, and a chain of over 200 retail stores. An *administered channel* is one in which an agent is able to exercise administrative control over a vertical network by dint of its economic power. For example, Kraftco and Campbell Soup are two examples of companies that have carved a pipeline from raw materials to finished products and enjoy space management privileges in supermarkets to administer their end point marketing mix. A *contractual channel* is one in which independent firms have joined together on a contractual basis to achieve buying and selling power through combination. Examples of contractual channels include voluntary retail associations led by a wholesaler, farm cooperatives, and franchise organizations. The most important point to note is that channel competition increasingly means the competition of alternative vertical marketing structures, rather than the competition between individualistic firms such as wholesalers or retailers.[2]

A third important point about channels is that a firm cannot always put together the channel it wishes. For example, a firm producing a new food product will find it extremely difficult to obtain shelf space, unless it has considerable economic power or the new product appears to be a sure winner. A machine manufacturer may try to hire outstanding sales agencies to handle its products, only to be turned down. A furniture manufacturer may have to offer exclusive distribution in order to get certain retailers to carry its goods. The main point is that a seller may finally arrive at a sound distribution strategy, only to learn that the particular middlemen are not available at all or on the terms contemplated.

In the fourth place, middlemen do not always perform in the expected way, even after they have agreed to work with the seller. The seller has to recognize, especially in individualistic marketing channels, that the middlemen are independent profit seeking firms that will behave first in their own self-interest. If middlemen do not think highly enough of the seller, they may fail to set up displays, follow the seller's price policies, or supply adequate records. There is good evidence that many middlemen are more oriented toward the satisfaction of their customers than the satisfaction of their suppliers, especially when the various suppliers each account for small shares of the middleman's business.

---

[2]For further discussion of these channel types, see Bert C. McCammon, Jr. and Albert D. Bates, "The Emergence and Growth of Contractually Integrated Channels in the American Economy," in P. D. Bennett, ed., *Economic Growth, Competition and World Markets* (Chicago: American Marketing Association, 1965), 496-515.

The suppliers in this case must be skillful in finding ways to motivate the middlemen.

Fifth, the seller must select the channels of distribution with an eye not only on the economics, but also the control aspects of channels and their adaptability. A channel decision is a long term commitment to a way of doing business and it influences product development, marketing communication strategy, sales force territories and plans, pricing, and so forth. It is important that the company consider how much control it is likely to achieve through the desired channels. It is also important that the company show some preference for channels that are easier to disengage from, in the event that more viable channels appear.

DISTRIBUTION STRATEGY

Distribution strategy is the problem of determining the basic way in which the company will try to sell its products to designated end markets. It is not simply a matter of whether to sell through one type of retailer versus another (say department vs. discount stores) but whether the firm should use retailers at all in relation to other possible systems of distribution. The management must try to distinguish all of its major channel alternatives and use some method of analysis to evaluate the worth of each alternative. An excellent way to appreciate the issues involved and a methodology for their solution is to consider the following case.

Choosing a Distribution Strategy for a New Product

The Commodity Chemical Company is an old-line manufacturer of chemicals that had enjoyed a period of high profits but more recently has experienced a profit slump.[3] A growing number of stockholders has become critical of the company's management for an allegedly too narrow product line. The management has consequently sought new products and in this connection has expanded its research and development program. The first fruits of its new research program are perchlorotrombones (name fictitious), a new class of chlorinated organic chemicals that function as bleaches, germicides, and oxidants. The diversification committee of the Commodity Chemical Company is considering marketing a product based on this chemical for the swimming pool germicide market. It believes that its product has superior qualities to existing pool germicidal chemicals. At the same time, the company has never done any previous consumer marketing and its present channels of distribution are far from ideal for tapping the swimming pool market. During the committee's discussion, the research director, sales manager, commercial development manager, advertising agency representative, and company consultant came up with quite different proposals for the marketing of this product. Here the reader should try to list some major alternative distribution strategies before reading on.

---

[3]Edward C. Bursk and Stephen A. Greyser, *Advanced Cases in Marketing Management* (Englewood Cliffs, N.J.: Prentice-Hall, 1968), 156–165.

One way to think about this question is to visualize alternative ways in which swimming pool owners could purchase this product. The swimming pool owner may buy this product in at least the five ways shown in Figure 11-1. The seller will want to study these five alternative retailing channels, especially the relative volumes of swimming pool germicidal that move through each, their relative rates of growth, and their relative profitability as channels. Management will want to interview swimming pool owners about the value they place on price, convenience, packaging, germicidal effectiveness, and so forth, to determine which retailing channel or channels are the most promising. Management has the option of concentrating on one of these channels, perhaps one that is relatively underutilized in relation to its future potential, or marketing through several of these channels.

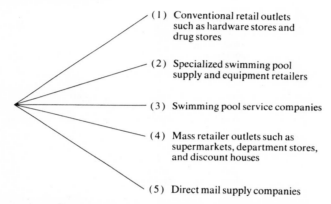

(1) Conventional retail outlets such as hardware stores and drug stores

(2) Specialized swimming pool supply and equipment retailers

(3) Swimming pool service companies

(4) Mass retailer outlets such as supermarkets, department stores, and discount houses

(5) Direct mail supply companies

Figure 11-1   Commodity Chemical Company: Alternative Retailing Strategies

The analysis should be pushed back a step because there is the question of more basic relationships that the company can have to the retailing of the germicidal chemical. Figure 11-2 illustrates five radically different ways in which the company might market the new product. Distribution strategy 1 (Present Distributors Alternative) calls for the company to use its present distribution channels to market the product to retailers and service people in the swimming pool market. This approach was advocated by the sales manager who felt that the present distributors would be upset if they were by-passed by the company and not allowed to participate in the potential profits on this new product. He felt that the company had an obligation to its present dealers, that it had good control over them, and that they would be enthusiastic and competent in cultivating new retailing contacts in the swimming pool germicide market.

Distribution strategy 2 (New Distributors Alternative) calls for the company using swimming pool supply distributors to bring its new product into the various retail channels. The commercial development manager favored this alternative because he felt that the company's present chemical distributors lacked contacts and experience in dealing with the kinds of retailers who sold swimming pool germicides. He felt that swimming pool supply distributors would be more effective in getting the company's product into fast and broad distribution. Furthermore, he felt that these new distributors could be granted higher margins than the company found it desirable to give to their present distributors who might ask for higher margins on the company's other products.

Distribution strategy 3 (Acquisition Alternative) calls for acquiring a small company that is already well entrenched in the swimming pool supply market and using its established distribution system. The research director favored this method of breaking into the market.

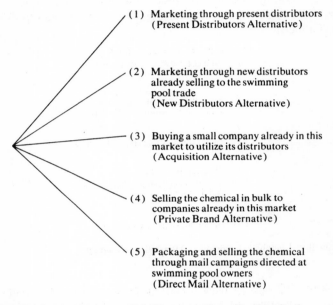

(1) Marketing through present distributors
(Present Distributors Alternative)

(2) Marketing through new distributors already selling to the swimming pool trade
(New Distributors Alternative)

(3) Buying a small company already in this market to utilize its distributors
(Acquisition Alternative)

(4) Selling the chemical in bulk to companies already in this market
(Private Brand Alternative)

(5) Packaging and selling the chemical through mail campaigns directed at swimming pool owners
(Direct Mail Alternative)

Figure 11-2   Commodity Chemical Company: Alternative Distribution Strategies

Distribution strategy 4 (Private Brand Alternative) calls for the company to sell the new chemical in bulk to companies that are already in the pool supply business. This alternative is likely to yield lower profits but at the same time reduces the company's risk. The company's consultant suggested that this alternative be given serious consideration.

Distribution strategy 5 (Direct Mail Alternative) calls for packaging the chemical under a company brand name and using a direct mail approach to selling it. This strategy would be evaluated through a preliminary test in some major cities. This strategy was advocated by the advertising agency representative as a sound way to evaluate the size and interest of the market in this new germicide.

The committee members obviously held a broad range of viewpoints, largely rooted in factors associated with their particular positions in the company.

What was particularly frustrating in their committee discussions was the lack of any analytical framework for rating the different proposals. The discussion moved back and forth over the different qualitative implications of each proposal, such as the feelings of present dealers, the problems of acquiring a sound small company, and so forth. But no common profit framework was developed for making meaningful comparisons of the different proposals.

This is unfortunate because there are at least three different techniques that could be fruitfully applied to help management think about the best strategy. They are respectively the weighted factor score method, the hierarchical preference ordering method, and the method of strategy simulation.

Table 11-1   Weighted Factor Score Method Applied to Distribution Strategy 1

Factor	(A) Factor weight	(B) Factor score .0 .1 .2 .3 .4 .5 .6 .7 .8 .9 1.0	Rating (A × B)
1. Effectiveness in reaching swimming pool owners	.15	✓ (.3)	.045
2. Amount of profit if this alternative works well	.25	✓ (.5)	.125
3. Experience company will gain in consumer marketing	.10	✓ (.2)	.020
4. Amount of investment involved (high score for low investment)	.30	✓ (.8)	.240
5. Ability of company to cut short its losses	.20	✓ (.7)	.140
		Total score	.570

Weighted factor score method.   This method calls upon management to list the major factors that the company should consider, assign weights to reflect their relative importance, rate each distribution strategy on each factor, and determine the overall weighted factor score for each distribution strategy. In this way, the five distribution strategies could at least be ranked and the lowest ranking ones could be dropped. An example of this method is shown in Table 11-1. Suppose the company's diversification committee came up with the five factors listed in the first column as the most important considerations bearing on all the alternatives. These factors concern the distribution strategy's likely effectiveness, profitability, experience value, investment level, and possible losses. Associated with each factor is a weight reflecting its subjective importance to the company. The table shows a hypothetical rating of the first distribution strategy (Present Distributors Alternative). We note that it scores modestly on the first three factors and highly on the last two factors. The factor scores are multiplied by the factor weights to arrive at an overall score of .57 for this strategy according to the following formula:

$$V_i = \sum_{j=1}^{n} W_j F_{ij} \qquad\qquad (11\text{-}1)$$

where V_i = strategy i's total score

W_j = weight associated with factor j, where $j = 1, 2, \ldots, n$,

$\quad 0 \leqslant W_j \leqslant 1$, and $\sum_{j=1}^{n} W_j = 1$

F_{ij} = strategy i's score on factor j, where $0 \leqslant F_{ij} \leqslant 1$

Each of the distribution strategies would be rated against the same criteria to find its total score; and the distribution strategies would then be ranked according to their total scores.

This method represents an improvement over simply listing the pros and cons of each alternative. It attempts to quantify the qualitative attributes of the different proposals in a common measurement framework. It is useful at an early stage of evaluation when little data are available. The method has had considerable application in the rating of new product proposals and has undergone many refinements.[4] At the same time, it is subject to several limitations, as noted by Alderson and Green:[5]

1. This method misleadingly uses an interval scale for data that are properly only ordinal.

2. The factor weights may not be independent of the factor scores.

3. The factors themselves may not be independent.

4. The procedure assumes that the rater has equal competence in rating all the factors and strategy alternatives.

Hierarchical preference ordering method. A second technique, formulated by Eduardo L. Roberto,[6] avoids the criticism of misapplying an interval scale to ordinal data. It calls for management to (1) rank, not rate, the five factors in order of importance, (2) set a minimum level from 0.00 to 1.00 for each factor which a distribution strategy must satisfy, in order to be considered, and (3) examine all the distribution strategies against the first important factor, then the second, etc., eliminating those strategies at each stage that fail to satisfy that factor. An application of this technique to our problem is shown in Table 11-2. The rows list the five factors in order of importance (see factor weights in Table 11-1). For each factor, a minimum pass level is established by management. The five distribution strategies are listed in the remaining columns.

---

[4]See Barry M. Richman, "A Rating Scale for Product Innovation," *Business Horizons* (Summer 1962) 37–44; John T. O'Meara, Jr., "Selecting Profitable Products," *Harvard Business Review* (Jan.–Feb. 1961) 83–89; and Marshall Freimer and Leonard Simon, "The Evaluation of Potential New Product Alternatives," *Management Science* (Feb. 1967) 279–292.

[5]Wroe Alderson and Paul E. Green, *Planning and Problem Solving in Marketing* (Homewood, Ill.: Richard D. Irwin, Inc., 1964), p. 206.

[6]Unpublished paper at Northwestern University.

Looking at the minimum pass level for the first factor, .3, all but strategy three pass. Therefore, strategy three is eliminated from further consideration because it requires too much investment. Looking at the second most important factor, strategy five is now eliminated because it fails to promise enough profits.

Table 11-2   Hierarchical Preference Ordering Method Applied to Five Distribution Methods

Factors in order of importance	Minimum pass level	Strategy one	Strategy two	Strategy three	Strategy four	Strategy five
1. Amount of investment involved	.3	.8 = P	.6 = P	.2 = F	.9 = P	.9 = P
2. Amount of profit if this alternative works well	.5	.5 = P	.8 = P	.6 = —	.5 = P	.4 = F
3. Ability of company to cut short its losses	.5	.7 = P	.6 = P	.1 = —	.8 = P	.8 = —
4. Effectiveness in reaching swimming pool owners	.3	.3 = P	.7 = P	.8 = —	.6 = P	.3 = —
5. Experience company will gain in consumer marketing	.4	.2 = F	.5 = P	.6 = —	.2 = F	.4 = —
Ranking		3rd	1st	5th	2nd	4th

Note: P = Pass
      F = Fail

Continuing this procedure, successively less important factors are brought in until only one strategy remains, strategy two. In essence this method proceeds on the theory that "Choice aims at satisfying the greatest number of wants starting with the most important and going down their hierarchy. Therefore, choice is determined by the least important want that could be reached."[7] The relative standings of the five strategies are shown in the bottom row.

Roberto's method has certain advantages over the weighted factor score method. It does not make the mistake of multiplying numbers which are essentially ordinal. Further, it represents a process that probably comes close to how many managers tend to think about choosing among alternatives, namely eliminating strategies as they fail to satisfy successively less important factors at minimum levels. On the other hand, hierarchical preference ordering gives no credit to how well a particular distribution strategy exceeds a minimum level required by some factor. A particular strategy may be almost perfect on the most

[7] N. Georgescu-Roegen, "Choice, Expectations, and Measurability," *Quarterly Journal of Economics*, November 1954, 518.

important criterion and slightly below the minimum level on a minor criterion and as a result be eliminated, whereas some tradeoff should actually be established.

Strategy simulation method. Both of the previous methods fail to produce an actual estimate of profit and risk for each strategy. There is no visualization of what is expected to happen under each strategy to revenues, costs, and investment over some suitable planning horizon. To accomplish this, it would be desirable to create a simulation model for examining the estimated monetary consequences of each strategy under different assumptions and sets of data.

To show the power of a computer simulation to assist in the comparison of alternative distribution strategies, plausible data were developed for this problem on the basis of the reported facts in the case. Table 11-3 shows some of the data inputs used in the marketing simulation.[8] For example, the Acquisition Alternative was considered to require the highest investment while the Private Brand Alternative required the lowest level of investment. Each distribution strategy involved a somewhat different pricing policy and contribution margin.

Table 11-3 Example of Data Input for Simulation of Alternative Distribution Strategies

| | Distribution Strategies | | | |
| | (1) | (2) | (3) | (4) |
Variables	Present distributors alternative	New distributors alternative	Acquisition alternative	Private brand alternative
Investment	$300,000	$500,000	$2,500,000	$100,000
Price per bag	$2.7	$2.5	$2.7	$2.2
Contribution margin per bag	$1.2	$1.0	$1.2	$0.7
Mean monthly advertising budget	$5,000	$50,000	$10,000	$5,000
Advertising effectiveness coefficient	1/2	1/1.8	1/1.9	1/2
Initial number of distributors	80	20	60	60
Growth rate per month in number of distributors	.02	.04	.01	.02
Maximum number of distributors permitted	150	150	150	150
Distribution effectiveness coefficient	1/2.5	1/2.0	1/2.2	1/2.2

Each distribution strategy also involved a different level of advertising expenditure and a different expected level of advertising effectiveness. Under the Present Distributors Alternative, the company would start out with the highest number

---

[8]These data and the following analysis are not part of the original case but were developed at Northwestern University by Michael Vialle to illustrate a simulation analysis of the problem.

of distributors but would acquire additional distributors slowly; whereas under the New Distributors Alternative, the initial number of distributors would be low but their growth rate would be high because it is assumed that potential distributors would react favorably to the large advertising budget and the higher margin given to them under this alternative.

Other inputs not shown deal with the rate of growth in demand expected under the different distribution strategies, a provision for substantial competitive reaction if the company's market share starts to exceed a certain figure, and a provision for the effect of test marketing before making a decision. The particular distribution strategies are simulated for a forty-eight month period and the computer program calculates three different measures of performance over this period. The results are shown in Table 11-4.

Table 11-4   Results of Simulation of Alternative Distribution Strategies

	(1) Present distributors alternative		(2) New distributors alternative		(3) Acquisition alternative		(4) Private brand alternative	
Criterion	Value	Rank	Value	Rank	Value	Rank	Value	Rank
Pay-back period (months)	14	3	8	1	25	4	9	2
Share of potential	44%	4	100%	1	62%	2	43%	3
Accumulated discounted profit (millions)	3.25	3	6.10	1	5.60	2	1.99	4

Pay-back period refers to how many months will pass before the accumulated revenue covers the accumulated cost to the company. The share of potential refers to the percent of the company's potential share of the market that is realized by the particular distribution strategy. Accumulated discounted profit refers to the present value of the forty-eight month earnings stream discounted at 10 percent. The reader should note that in this example the New Distributors Alternative ranks highest on all three criteria. It is estimated to lead to full pay-back within eight months, enable the company to realize 100 percent of its potential market share, and lead to the highest level of accumulated profits. The Present Distributors Alternative is the poorest strategy on all criteria; the Acquisition Alternative is attractive on accumulated discounted profits and the share of potential but not on pay-back period; and the Private Brand Alternative is attractive on pay-back but not on the ultimate share of potential or profits. In addition to these results, the alternative of first running a market test and then choosing a strategy was tested on the computer model and was always dominated by the strategies calling for an immediate decision. This was because management felt that a high price would be paid for delaying the introduction of the product on a national basis.

In summary, this company faced several alternative distribution strategies and the company executives held diverse and not entirely disinterested views on the appropriate strategy. No proposal was backed up by any hard-headed profit calculation nor was there an agreed-upon framework for comparing and ranking the alternative strategies. Our discussion showed that one framework is provided by the weighted factor score model and another by the hierarchical preference ordering method. These methods, while an improvement over simply listing advantages and disadvantages of each strategy, lack a profit calculation and suffer from other shortcomings. It was then proposed that computer simulation would be a better method in requiring the executives to think hard about sales, costs, marketing programs, and investment for each strategy. It would permit management to project the logical consequences of its estimates and readily test the effect of introducing new assumptions.

Changing from One Distribution Strategy to Another—The Case of Direct Selling versus Manufacturers' Representatives

Companies that have already chosen a distribution strategy and are using it must nevertheless be alert to new opportunities to alter the distribution strategy where money can be made or saved. Very often, this occurs when a seller feels he can eliminate a middleman and take over this function. The type of analysis to accompany this decision will be examined here.

Companies that wish to establish rapid distribution of their product often hire sales agents (also called manufacturers' representatives). A sales agency is a firm with one or more salesmen that will represent the lines of a number of non-competing manufacturers and be compensated on a commission basis. It often has good connections in the markets sought by the manufacturer.

As a seller grows in size, he is tempted to replace sales agents in high sale potential areas with a sales force of his own because a company sales force might produce more sales (since it concentrates on selling only the company's products), or because this may involve less cost than the compensation system, or because the seller can exercise more control over a company sales force. A case situation will be presented involving this contemplated change in distribution strategy, and use will be made of Bayesian decision theory to formulate and resolve the channel decision problem.[9]

[9]The following case is adapted with certain modifications from Alderson and Green, *Planning and Problem Solving in Marketing*, pp. 311–317.

The term Bayesian comes from Reverend Thomas Bayes, an eighteenth-century minister and mathematician who proposed the basic probability theorem for combining information on prior probabilities plus sample results into new posterior probabilities. This theorem is employed in the analysis if the decision maker actually collects further information and wishes to revise his probabilities (called *posterior analysis*); if the decision maker only engages in formulating the problem in order to decide which course of action to take, not including the possibility of collecting further information, this is called *prior analysis* and does not involve Bayes theorem. If the decision maker includes the gathering of further information as one of the alternatives, this is called *preposterior analysis* and does involve Bayes theorem. Although modern decision theory may or may not involve Bayes theorem in a particular application, the field has settled on the term Bayesian decision theory to represent the general framework that calls for distinguishing alternatives, placing probabilities on uncertainties, developing loss functions, and choosing alternatives according to expected values.

The XYZ Company is presently using a sales agent to sell its product to retailers. The sales agent is compensated at 6 percent of the sales price per case to retailers. Since the sales price is $10 per case, the sales agent receives a commission of 60¢ per case. The agent presently sells 200,000 cases per year and this is expected to continue. The company itself earns a $1 profit on each case sold.

The company is considering replacing the sales agent by a direct company sales force, which, after sufficient training, is expected to cost the company only 50¢ per case. Furthermore, the company believes that there is some chance that its own sales force would be able to sell more than 200,000 cases per year. On the other hand, the company will have to bear $35,000 in cost to train the new sales force and phase out the sales agent. The company would be willing to make this decision if it felt that it could recover the transition costs of $35,000 in one year. Should it change its distribution strategy?

The first step is to establish the number of cases that a company sales force would have to sell in the first year to break even on the transition costs. Let this figure be called S_b. Note that the company will save 10¢ on every case sold under the new system and also will make an extra dollar on every case sold under the new system in excess of 200,000 cases. The number of cases sold under the new system must be such that it yields an extra $35,000 in profit. In other words, we have

$$\$35,000 = .10S_b + 1(S_b - 200,000) \qquad (11\text{-}2)$$

Therefore $S_b = 213,634$

Thus the new sales force must manage to sell 13,634 cases more the first year than the sales agent, in order to recover the transition costs of $35,000.

The next task is for management to estimate whether they think the new sales force could sell at least 213,634 cases in the first year. If management felt certain that the new sales force could sell substantially more than this break-even number of cases, then it would not hesitate to change to a direct sales force. However, in practice, management can envision a range of possible sales results, some which would favor adopting the new system and others favor retaining the old system. Management, though, does not think all sales results are equally likely. Suppose that management is asked for an estimate of the most probable level of first year sales with a company sales force and replies 250 (in thousands of cases). Management is next asked for a sales estimate on the low side such that there is only one chance in four in their mind that sales might even be lower than this figure: management responds with the estimate 200. Finally, management is asked for a sales estimate on the high side such that there is only one chance in four in their mind that sales might even be higher than this figure: management responds with the estimate 300.

From these three sales estimates—most probable, pessimistic, and optimistic —plus the assumption that the probability of different sales levels will conform to a normal distribution, management's view of sales can be characterized by the sales probability distribution shown in Figure 11-3(a). It should be noted that 25 percent of the area in the tail of a normal distribution conforms to .67 standard deviation units from the center of the distribution (see a normal table in any basic statistics book). From this information it is possible to infer the number of cases that implicitly conform to one standard deviation in management's mind: Since

$$.67\sigma = 50,000$$

then

$$\sigma = 75,000$$

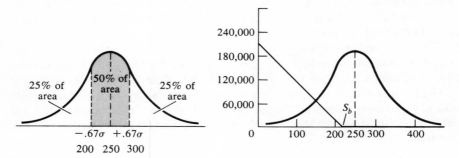

(a) Probability Distribution of Sales (b) Conditional Value of Perfect Information
    (in thousands of cases)

Figure 11-3   Probability Distribution of Sales and Conditional Loss Function for the Company Sales Force Alternative

If it is assumed that management expects sales to be drawn from a normal distribution with a mean of 250 and a standard deviation of 75, should management adopt a company sales force? A company sales force is clearly the preferred alternative if no further information is available because the expected sales level exceeds the break-even level of sales. Nevertheless, there is some chance that the company might lose money if it takes this step. The company might well ask about the size of the expected loss if it hired a company sales force. If the expected conditional loss is low, then management might proceed to hire its own salesmen. If the expected conditional loss is high, management might choose to study this alternative further before making a decision.

There will only be a loss if the company sales force sells less than 213,634 cases. The amount of the loss will depend upon how much less they sell. Each case under 213,634 means the loss of $1.10 ($1 for profit and 10¢ for difference in distribution cost). Letting S stand for the number of units sold, the loss function is

$$L = 1.10 \,(213,634 - S) \qquad \text{where } S \leqslant 213,634 \qquad (11\text{-}3)$$

This loss function is linear and is illustrated in Figure 11-3(b).

From this figure, we note two important points: (1) lower sales levels involve higher losses, and (2) lower sales levels are less probable. A good measure of risk is *expected loss*, which is equal to the sum of all the possible losses times their corresponding probabilities. Since there is a very large number of possible sales levels, it would be very tedious to carry out all of the necessary calculations. Fortunately, there is a shortcut formula for estimating the expected loss wherever there is a linear function and a normal probability distribution. (Shortcut formulas are also available for a limited number of other situations.) The expected loss, L, is given by

$$\bar{L} = C \cdot \sigma \cdot N(D) \tag{11-4}$$

where $\bar{L}$ = expected loss (in thousands of dollars)

C = absolute value of the slope of the loss function; here 1.10

σ = standard deviation of the normal distribution; here 75,000

D = absolute distance of expected sales from break-even sales, expressed in terms of standard deviations; here

$$D = |S_B - \bar{S}|/\sigma = |213,634 - 250,000|/75,000 = .48$$

$N(D)$ = a derived loss function for the standardized normal curve. This value is looked up in a unit normal loss integral table: for $D = .48$, $N(D) = .204$.[10]

This formula makes sense, in that it says that the expected loss will be greater, the greater the absolute value of the slope of the loss function, the greater the standard deviation of the normal distribution, and the closer the break-even sales level to the mean sales level. The expected loss can now be calculated using Equation 11-4:

$$\bar{L} = 1.10 \, (75,000) \, (.204)$$
$$\bar{L} = \$16,830$$

Thus if the company went ahead and hired a sales force and this sales force did not sell at the break-even level, the company would lose different amounts depending on the actual sales level; the expected value of these possible losses is $16,830. This figure is extremely useful, in that it sets an upper limit to the value of collecting additional information before making a decision. Since the company might expect to lose $16,830 if it went ahead and hired a company sales force without further research, it should not spend more than this sum on researching this alternative. It would be wiser just to hire the company sales force. If the company could purchase perfect information for less than $16,830 that would tell it exactly what a company sales force would sell, it would be worth buying this information to avoid the larger expected loss. For this reason, the expected loss has also been called the expected value of perfect information (EVPI) in the Bayesian literature. Information, of course, is less than perfect most of the time and so the company should even scale down further the amount it is willing to spend on research.

[10]See Robert Schlaifer, *Probability and Statistics for Business Decisions* (New York: McGraw-Hill, Inc., 1959), p. 706.

This example illustrates a common distribution strategy problem, switching from sales agents to a company sales force, and a useful framework for analyzing the issues of uncertainty and the value of information. The Bayesian decision framework has been developed and applied to a wide variety of marketing problems, including pricing, new product introductions, and so forth, and is coming into rapid favor and use by marketing decision makers in many companies.[11]

DISTRIBUTION LOCATION

As part of determining its distribution strategy, that is, the basic way it will sell its products to the market, a company must decide on the *degree of market exposure* desired. Specifically it must decide on the number of sales outlets to use and their locations. The company could decide on a policy of *intensive distribution* in which it will place its product in every available outlet; or *selective distribution* in which it will place its product in a more limited number of outlets; or *exclusive distribution* in which it will place its product in the hands of a few exclusive agents. Intensive distribution appears to be a rational policy for goods that people wish to purchase frequently and with minimum effort; examples are tobacco products, soap, newspapers, chewing gum, and gasoline. Selective distribution can be used for goods that buyers might seek out; the advantage to the seller is that he gains more control over distribution and does not have to spread his merchandising and servicing effort over too many outlets. Exclusive distribution is used to bring about a greater partnership between seller and reseller in the fortunes of the product and is commonly used in the distribution of new automobiles, some major appliances, and some brands of apparel.

Let us take the point of view of a national company (automobile manufacturer, gasoline retailer, food chain, national franchiser, etc.) that has adopted a particular market exposure policy and presently operates a network of sales outlets. Each year this company has to consider new investment in facilities improvement and expansion. Suppose it establishes a budget of B dollars for investment in facilities. The company will find that it can invest this money in four possible ways or any mixture:

1. The money can be spent in expanding the size of the present outlets.
2. The money can be spent in remodeling the present outlets.
3. The money can be spent in relocating some of the present outlets.
4. The money can be spent in opening up new outlets.

In principle, the company will allocate the budget over the four alternatives in such a way that the marginal dollar yields the same return in all uses. In practice, management will feel compelled to make certain specific facility investments out

---

[11]For references, see Alderson and Green, *Planning and Problem Solving in Marketing.*

of what appears to be necessity or indisputable soundness. Some stores have to be expanded, renovated, or relocated, and some new sites are too good to pass up. Various rules of thumb are used in management circles to make these decisions. Let us suppose that the first three categories of facility decisions are made first at a cost of B_1 dollars. This leaves $B - B_1$ dollars for opening up new outlets. Now suppose that the average new outlet costs the company X dollars to build. This means that the company is considering developing n new outlets in the coming year, where $n = (B - B_1)/X$. The problem facing the company is determining where to locate these new outlets and their specific sizes. Actually, the company faces a sequence of four decisions:

1. Of all the potentially promising areas in the country for locating one or more new outlets, which areas should be selected? (Market selection decision.)
2. How many new outlets should be located in each selected area? (Number of outlets decision.)
3. In which particular sites should the new outlets be located? (Site selection decision.)
4. What size and characteristics should each particular outlet have? (Store size and characteristics decision.)

The remainder of this section will take up these decisions in order.

Market Selection Decision

A company planning to develop n new outlets must determine in which market areas to place them. A market area is a city, country, state, or region in which company outlets can be opened. This can be called the macroproblem in contrast to site location, which is a microproblem. Some of the outlets may be placed in market areas in which the company is already established, where it wants to increase its market share; the others can be placed in new market areas deemed promising by the company. In both cases, the company will be guided by the same consideration, that is, the profit potential latent in each market area. The task is one of developing a good measure of market area profit potential.

Most practitioners are able to come up with a large list of indicators of market area profit potential. According to a Sears executive,

> I could easily fill a book describing the full extent of the field work, statistical analysis and projections that go into the study of a single Sears market. All important factors which bear on how customers spend their retail dollars are carefully examined and evaluated. Briefly, I can tell you that we analyze not only our existing stores in a market, but we carefully study competition, population density and growth (which includes age distribution), housing growth (past and future), the diversity and stability of the local economy, unemployment, and a long list of other factors, some major, some minor, that might influence retail business.[12]

[12]Statement by Arthur Rosenbaum, director of Sears Business Research Department, in a company news brochure.

What is rarely found is an explicit formula that combines all of the important indicators of profit potential into a specific profit measure for the area. Here we would like to propose such a measure.

The proposed measure involves the following three concepts:

S_i = company sales potential of market area i
Z_i = company profit potential of market area i
$V(Z_i)$ = present value of company profit potential in market area i

The basic approach will be to estimate the company sales potential of market area i and then subtract estimated selling costs to find the company profit potential of the area. The profit potential will be assumed to grow or decline at a certain rate over a given number of years, leading to a projected earnings stream for n years that will then be discounted at the company's target rate of return to find the present value of the company profit potential in market area i. Each of these steps will now be spelled out in greater detail.

Estimating company sales potential of market area i. The first step is to estimate the probable sales that a new or additional company store of average size and average location is likely to realize in this market area. Suppose the company examines the statistics on its other stores and calculates the average annual household expenditures spent by each income class at a typical company outlet. This provides a starting point for estimating the expected sales of a new outlet in this market area. Suppose that the market area has a known frequency distribution of households by income class. Then the company can estimate that unadjusted sales of a new company store in this market area would be S_i dollars, where:

$$S_i = \sum_{j=1}^{n} s_j p_{ij} N_i \qquad (11\text{-}5)$$

where S_i = estimated annual sales of a new company outlet in market area i (unadjusted)
  s_j = average annual household expenditures of income class j at a company outlet
  P_{ij} = percentage of total households of market area i in income class j
  N_i = number of households in market area i

At this point, the company introduces certain adjustments in the sales estimate to compensate for the oversimplifications. Since this figure was based on the spending patterns of different income classes at an average company store now existing in the system, it should be adjusted for any factors present in this market area that are likely to increase or decrease this average level of expenditure. The most important factor calling for an adjustment in this figure is the amount of competition that exists in this market area relative to that in an average market area. If the company estimates that competition will be unusually light, then it should increase estimated sales by an appropriate percentage to reflect this.

Conversely, if the company estimates that competition will be unusually heavy, then it should reduce estimated sales by an appropriate percentage. Let I_c represent an index of competitiveness that normally stands at 1.00. Then, adjusted estimated company sales potential in market area i for a new store of average size is given by

$$S_i' = I_c S_i \qquad\qquad (11\text{-}6)$$

Estimated sales should be further adjusted for any additional factors that could cause sales to be different from those in an average company store. Adjustments could be made for an atypical product assortment, store size, pricing policy, customer services, management quality, location, impact of the number of existing company outlets on sales at the new outlet, and so forth. In fact, management may wish to form its estimate directly by visualizing the kind of store that it would put into this market area, finding data for an analogous store and market area, and using these data to estimate sales for the new market area. However this is done, the company will end up with an adjusted sales potential estimate for a new store or another store in market area i.

Estimating company profit potential in market area i. The company now estimates its expenses of doing business in this market area. A good way to proceed is to express each major category of expense as a percentage of sales somewhere around the normal percentage, except for cost differences expected in the particular market area. Several expenses are likely to be in their normal relation to sales in all market areas, such as depreciation, heat, light, salaries, and so forth. These can be lumped together as a single percentage of sales. At least three other expenses may vary considerably from the normal percentage and should be stated separately. The first is the shipment cost to this market area. If the company has its major plant in market area k, then the cost of operating an outlet in market area i will be directly related to the distance between area k and i, the cost of transportation between these points, the issue of whether estimated sales will support carload shipment or less than carload shipment, and so forth. Thus shipping cost to market area i may turn out to be more or less than the average percentage of sales. A second expense deserving separate estimation is advertising and promotion. If the company is already well established in this area, the advertising cost may be relatively low as a percentage of estimated sales; if the company is new in the area, the advertising cost may be relatively high as a percentage of estimated sales. A third cost that might warrant separate treatment is real estate costs which may be unusually high or low in this market area relative to the average market area.

The profit potential of market area i can now be expressed as

$$Z_i = S_i' - (n_i + t_i + a_i + l_i)S_i' \qquad\qquad (11\text{-}7)$$

where Z_i = profit potential of market area i

S_i' = company sales potential of market area i (adjusted)

n_i = estimated normal expenses of selling in market area i as a percentage of sales (excluding transportation, advertising, and real estate)

t_i = transportation expense of selling in market area i as a percentage of sales

a_i = advertising expense of selling in market area i as a percentage of sales

l_i = real estate expense of selling in market area i as a percentage of sales

Estimating the present value of company profit potential in market area i.   The final step calls for forming an estimate of the expected trend in profit over the planning horizon in market area i. An area that is growing rapidly in population and income may mean healthy and growing profits for a number of years; a more stable area may mean profits that will continue at their first year level. The estimation of future profits could actually be made in some detail, through separate estimates of sales growth and each cost item. For our purposes, we shall proceed to make a macroassumption about the behavior of future profits by assuming they will grow or decline at the rate g for n years. Furthermore, it will be assumed that the company discounts future earnings at the rate r. Therefore, the net present value of the future earnings stream for market area i is estimated as

$$V(Z_i) = \frac{\sum_{k=1}^{n}(1+g_i)^k(Z_{ik})}{(1+r)^k} - I_i \tag{11-8}$$

where $V(Z_i)$ = net present value of the company profit potential of market area i

Z_{ik} = profit potential of market area i in year k

g_i = growth rate of profit potential in market area i

r = company discount rate

I_i = present value of outlet investment cost in market area i

Armed with these net present value estimates, the company can rank the market areas in order of attractiveness. In principle, the company should open a new or additional outlet in every market area in which the net present value is positive. If the sum of the investments exceeds the original budget B for new outlet development, the company can either borrow the additional funds needed or cut off new store openings at the point where the budget is exceeded.

The method just outlined requires one modification to accommodate an important issue that might arise. Up to now, we have assumed that the company would locate zero or one outlet in each candidate market area. This justified the use of an evaluation model based on estimating the profit value of one additional outlet per market area. Yet the company might plausibly consider opening more than one outlet in the more promising market areas. If new outlets yielded constant returns, then the company would place all the outlets it could build this year in that market area coming out first in present values. Yet constant returns are most improbable: additional outlets in the same area may bring about increasing or decreasing returns, as we shall see in the next section. The present method does not yield any information about the value of a second, third, and so forth, outlet in the same market area. Fortunately, a company rarely considers opening more than one or a few outlets in the same market area in the same year. And management can always use the preceding method to consider a second or third store in the more promising market areas. From the point of view of long range planning of outlets, the company should consider the appropriate long run number of outlets per market area. To this problem we now turn.

Number of Outlets Decision

Imagine a company that is planning to open twelve new outlets over the next several years in four new market areas. In this case, there are 455 different possible assignments of the twelve outlets to the four areas. In general, the number of ways, k, in which r outlets can be distributed to n markets is given by

$$k = \frac{(n+r-1)!}{(n-1)!r!} \tag{11-9}$$

Among the 455 alternatives are placing all the outlets in one of the cells, dividing the outlets equally between the cells, and a multitude of unequal division assignments. The question is clearly one of the behavior of sales and profits with more outlets in an area. There have been very few reported studies of this problem, but one has been published that is extremely thoughtful. This is the study by Hartung and Fisher on the optimal number of service stations that an oil company should build in any particular metropolitan area.[13] Earlier in Chapter 4, a relationship was reported between the metropolitan market shares of an oil company and its percentage of stations in the metropolitan area (see pp. 96-97). This relationship was found by fitting a curve to data on a large number of cities in which the oil company operated. The best fitting curve was found to be an S-shaped function (see Figure 4-2) and several theoretical reasons were advanced to support the empirical shape of the curve that was found. Now we shall look at a mathematical model of brand choice behavior in this industry that leads to an alternative measurable empirical relationship. On the basis of this model and an empirically fitted curve, the company would have a tool for setting the optimal number or percentage of its stations in a given metropolitan area.

Hartung and Fisher base their analysis on a Markovian model of customer brand switching behavior. Consider Company A's market share. They postulate that Company A's market share in the next period will be made up of some percentage of last period's customers who repurchase the brand and of some

[13]Philip H. Hartung and James L. Fisher, "Brand Switching and Mathematical Programming in Market Expansion," *Management Science* (Aug. 1965) 231–243.

percentage of noncustomers who switch to this brand. Specifically, their market share model says:

$$X_{t+1} = aX_t + bY_t \tag{11-10}$$

where X_t = market share of Company A in time period t

Y_t = market share of all competitors in time period t (thus $X_t + Y_t = 1$)

a = probability that a purchaser of product A in time period t will repurchase it in time period $r+1$

b = probability that a purchaser of a competitive product in time period t will purchase product A in time period $t+1$

If these probabilities remain constant through time,[14] the brand switching process will eventually lead to steady state market shares. Company A's market share will reach its steady state equilibrium when the number of customers switching from product A will exactly equal the number of customers switching to product A. When this happens, Company A's market share will remain the same in all subsequent time periods. The steady state market share can be found by letting $X_{t+1} = X_t = X$ in Equation 11-10:

$$X = aX + bY \tag{11-11}$$

and, since $X + Y = 1$ or $Y = 1 - X$, by substitution:

$$X = \frac{b}{1-a+b} \tag{11-12}$$

The next task is to explain the determinants of the two probabilities. The staying probability, a, depends on customer satisfaction with product A, maintained customer interest in product A, and other factors; the switching probability, b, may reflect customer dissatisfaction with the other brands, special promotions by brand A, and other factors. The staying probability in the normal case of a satisfying product will be several times the size of the switch-in probability. Here we are particularly interested in the relationship of these two probabilities to Company A's percentage of outlets in the area. It is reasonable to postulate that each probability will vary directly with the company's percentage of outlets, that is,

$$a = k_1\left(\frac{P}{O+P}\right) \qquad b = k_2\left(\frac{P}{O+P}\right) \tag{11-13}$$

where P = number of outlets carrying product A

O = number of outlets carrying competing brands

k_1, k_2 = constants

For example, if k_1 is greater than k_2, it would mean that the rate of staying with brand A is greater than the rate of switching to brand A.

---

[14]This is a heroic assumption, since deals, promotions, and price wars will affect these probabilities.

Equations 11-13 can now be substituted in the steady state Equation 11-12 with the following result:

$$X = \frac{k_2 P}{O + (1 + k_2 - k_1)P}$$

(11-14)

The equation can also be rewritten to show the equilibrium average sales per company A outlet for any given total market size. First note that

$$X = \frac{S}{T}$$

(11-15)

where S = sales of product A

T = total sales of all brands

Substituting Equation 11-15 in Equation 11-14 and simplifying, we get

$$\frac{S}{P} = \frac{k_2 T}{O + (1 + k_2 - k_1)P}$$

(11-16)

This equation is the key to predicting the effect of the relative number of company A's outlets on its average sales per outlet. The effect of more company A outlets will depend critically on the quantity $(1 + k_2 - k_1)$. If this quantity is negative, an increase in the number of outlets will increase the average sales per outlet. Conversely, if this quantity is positive, an increase in the number of outlets will decrease the average sales per outlet. Therefore the task becomes one of finding a way to measure k_1 and k_2.

Hartung and Fisher rearranged Equation 11-16 to read:[15]

$$\frac{\bar{S}}{\bar{O}} = k_2 + (k_1 - k_2)X$$

(11-17)

where $\bar{S} = \dfrac{S}{P}$ = average sales per company A outlet

$\bar{O} = \dfrac{T}{O + P}$ = average sales per industry outlet

This equation says that the ratio of company A's average volume to the industry's average volume is a linear function of market share. The authors went on to fit this equation statistically to a sample of observed market areas in which they had data on a company's volume per outlet, industry's volume per outlet, and the company's market shares. The linear function was borne out with a coefficient of determination $R^2 = .64$. For their data, $k_1 = 4.44$ and $k_2 = .64$, which meant that a company with 10 percent of the outlets would find that 44.4 percent of its customers stayed and that it attracted 6.4 percent of the customers of competitors. Since $(1 + k_2 - k_1) = 1 + .64 - 4.44 = -2.8$, additional outlets in this area will increase the average sales of all company outlets in this area.

[15]See Appendix Mathematical Note 11–2.

This would therefore be a good area in which to build additional outlets, in comparison to areas in which the difference between k_1 and k_2 was less. In fact, the total additional sales that company A would enjoy by building one more outlet (assuming competitors did not increase their number of outlets) can be found by taking the derivative of S with respect to P. First we rearrange Equation 11-16 to find the sales equation:

$$S = \frac{k_2 TP}{O + (1 + k_2 - k_1)P} \tag{11-18}$$

This equation is then differentiated:

$$\frac{dS}{dP} = \frac{k_2 TO}{[O + (1 + k_2 - k_1)P]^2} \tag{11-19}$$

Letting $k_1 = 4.44$ and $k_2 = .64$ as before, we suppose that a large metropolitan area is serviced by 500 stations, of which 25 (or 5 percent) belong to Company A. (i.e., $O = 475, P = 25$). Further suppose that total sales in the area are 5 million gallons per month (i.e., $T = 5$ million); each station sells an average of 10,000 gallons per month. On the basis of this information, opening up an additional station will create additional sales of 9.266 gallons per month:

$$\frac{dS}{dP} = \frac{.64(5,000,000)475}{[475 + (1 + .64 - 4.44)25]^2} = 9266 \tag{11-20}$$

Interestingly enough, if this company had been operating 15 percent of the stations instead of 5 percent, opening up an additional station will create additional sales of 29,200 gallons per month:

$$\frac{dS}{dP} = \frac{.64(5,000,000)425}{[425 + (1 + .64 - 4.44)75]^2} = 29,421 \tag{11-21}$$

Thus a new outlet is able to add substantially more sales to the company A chain when the company occupies 15 percent of the market, instead of only 5 percent. This has two important policy implications:

1. Management would be better off to place new outlets in its high market share areas than in its low market share areas. If everyone followed this practice, it would lead to strong regional marketers.
2. The company should not enter new areas just to gain some representation. It should only enter areas in which it plans to become a dominant marketer in the area.

At the same time, it should be recognized that the k_1, k_2 parameters of the equation are valid only in the range in which the market shares were observed. They should not be used to infer that average outlet sales would continue to grow if outlets are added in areas in which Company A's market share is very substantial.

Hartung and Fisher caution:

Note that we are neglecting the influence of risk and, in addition, we have neglected the influence of saturation. This neglect is probably not serious so long as market shares do not go beyond 25 to 35 percent. At that point one should consider the saturation effect and the internal competition that one station of a brand has on another station of the same brand.[16]

Hartung and Fisher also show how a company that is willing to take a long range view of its facility development decision can formulate a model for determining the optimum number of outlets and locations. Specifically the problem is to determine the number of outlets to build in each of M marketing areas in each of the next Y years, where Y is the planning horizon. Assume that the company has decided on an affordable facilities budget for each of the Y years. The number of new outlets to be built in area i in year j will be N_{ij}. The total number of company outlets in area i in year j (assuming no closed outlets) is given by

$$P_{ij} = P_{io} + \sum_{k=1}^{j} N_{ik} \tag{11-22}$$

where P_{ij} = the total number of company outlets in area i, year j
$\quad\quad P_{io}$ = the number of current outlets in area i

Let us assume that the company's objective in developing its facilities plan is to maximize its discounted income over the Y years. This can be expressed as maximize

$$Z = \sum_{i=1}^{M} \sum_{j=1}^{Y} \frac{1}{(1+r)^j} R_{ij} \bar{S}_{ij} P_{ij} \tag{11-23}$$

where Z = discounted income over the Y years
$\quad\quad r$ = the discount rate
$\quad\quad R_{ij}$ = return from the sale of one unit of the product in area i, year j
$\quad\quad \bar{S}_{ij}$ = average sales per outlet, that is, $\bar{S}_{ij} = S_{ij}/P_{ij}$

The company's problem is to choose N_{ij}'s in the objective function—the N_{ij}'s are in the equation implicitly[17]—that will maximize the company's discounted earnings. The N_{ij}'s that can be chosen are themselves subject to at least two types of constraints. The first set of constraints says that the sum of new outlets

---

[16]Loc. cit., p. 242.

[17]The substitution of Equation 11–22 into 11–23 and the rearrangment of terms yields the following objective function: maximize

$$\sum_{i=1}^{M} \left[\sum_{j=1}^{Y} \left(N_{ij} \sum_{k=j}^{Y} \frac{1}{(1+r)^k} R_{ik}\, \bar{S}_{ik} \right) + P_{io} \sum_{j=1}^{Y} \frac{1}{(1+r)^j} R_{ij}\, \bar{S}_{ij} \right]$$

each year times their construction costs cannot exceed the available budget for that year:

$$\sum_{i=1}^{M} C_{ij}N_{ij} \leqslant B_j \qquad j = 1 \ldots Y \tag{11-24}$$

where C_{ij} = construction cost of one outlet in area i, year j
B_j = total capital allocated for building outlets in year j

The second set of constraints says that there is an upper limit to the number of outlets that can be built in each area in each year because of a limited number of locations and company-imposed limitations on facilities investment:

$$N_{ij} \leqslant L_{ij} \qquad i = 1 \ldots M, j = 1 \ldots Y \tag{11-25}$$

where L_{ij} = upper limit on the number of outlets that can be built—or that the company is willing to build—in area i, year j

Finally, it should be noted that, in the objective function Equation 11-23, a functional relationship between $\bar{S}_{ij}$ and P_{ij} should be specified. According to Hartung and Fisher's findings,

$$\bar{S}_{ij} = \frac{k_2 T_{ij}}{O + (1 + k_2 - k_1)P_{ij}} \tag{11-26}$$

(See Equation 11-16.) Equation 11-26 must be estimated for each market area in each year and substituted into the objective function. Thus the problem is to find the set of N_{ij}'s that maximizes Equation 11-23, subject to Equations 11-24, 11-25, and 11-26. Hartung and Fisher discuss a number of methods for solving this nonlinear programming problem. The primal solution to this problem will represent an optimal facilities development plan. The dual solution will show the costs to the company of adhering to each of the policy constraints and will function to stimulate management to reconsider its constraint levels. Hartung and Fisher have made an excellent methodological attack on the number of outlets decision problem in their synthesis of Markov processes and nonlinear programming techniques.

Site Selection Decisions

After determining the most attractive market areas in which to place new outlets, the company faces the problem of selecting specific sites. Both sales and cost will be affected by the specific location of the outlet; in the case of service stations, even the particular corner can make a significant difference. For years, site selection by major organizations has been based on primitive criteria at best. Very often, a site would be selected because it represented an unusually good real estate buy rather than out of consideration of the demand characteristics of the site; this is a case of the tail wagging the dog. The demand characteristics themselves would be measured in a most elementary way, chiefly by considering the socioeconomic makeup of the surrounding population, traffic size and flow, parking conditions, location of competition, and a dozen other factors. The practitioners rarely turned to location theory because much of it was abstract and bent on explaining the location of economic activity[18] or the trading area boundary between two cities[19] rather than helping them estimate sales at a particular site.

The problem of site selection is actually two problems: that of site search and that of site evaluation. *Site search* describes the procedures used by the company to discover potentially good sites for its outlets. Large companies usually work through real estate agents or through a company real estate department to search out good sites. This usually produces a number of new real estate opportunities each period. Some of these sites, however, will fail immediate tests and the others have to be evaluated more thoroughly. Our discussion will center on the problem of *site evaluation*, for which it is possible to distinguish at least three different approaches. They can be called, respectively, the checklist method, the analogue method, and the gravitational method. Each of these will be examined below.

Checklist method of site selection.   The most elementary method of evaluating a potential site is to visit it, observe the various factors that are likely to affect sales and costs, and make an intuitive judgment of its potential success. It was not unusual some years ago for the successful president of a growing chain to get in his Cadillac, drive to a site that came to his attention, watch the traffic and makeup of the shoppers, peer into competitive outlets, check some of his impressions with local real estate people, and integrate this information intuitively into a decision about the site. Although this can best be described as casual

---

[18]A. Losch, *The Economics of Location* (New Haven, Conn.: Yale University Press, 1954, translation); and Walter Isard, *Location and Space Economy* (New York: John Wiley & Sons, Inc., 1956).

[19]Paul D. Converse, "New Laws of Retail Gravitation," *Journal of Marketing*, Oct. 1949. In this connection, studies were conducted, starting in 1927, by William J. Reilly and subsequently by Paul D. Converse to measure the retail trade influence of a city. The original "law" developed by Reilly reads like an adaptation of the law of planetary attraction. According to Reilly: "Two cities attract retail trade from any intermediate city or town in the vicinity of the breaking point approximately in direct proportion to the population of the two cities and in inverse proportions to the squares of the distances from these two cities to the intermediate town." Mathematically this can be expressed as

$$\frac{B_a}{B_b} = \left(\frac{P_a}{P_b}\right)\left(\frac{D_b}{D_a}\right)^2$$

where B_i = the proportion of retail trade from the intermediate town attracted by city i; P_i = the population of city i; D_i = the distance from the intermediate town to city i; and a, b = the particular cities being compared.

Subsequent empirical investigations revealed that the exponents may vary because of other variables not explicitly included in the equation. Population and distance are still considered the primary variables, but other variables may warrant different exponents. Among these second order variables are lines of transportation and communication; business, social, and amusement attractions of the two cities; psychology of distance prevailing in that part of the country; differences in promotional intensity; parking facilities, etc. For a good exposition of the various laws of retail gravitation, see George Schwartz, *Development of Marketing Theory* (Cincinnati, Ohio: South-Western Publishing Company, 1963), pp. 9–34.

research, many early company presidents had good instincts and managed well without formal research. As their companies grew larger in size, however, the site search and evaluation function had to be formalized. The company would hire a real estate consulting firm or establish a company real estate department. Now first-hand observations at the site would be augmented with formal study of census and other data on population, income and expenditure trends, local zoning practices, highway plans, and so on. More systematic observation would be made on traffic by day of week and hour of day. Shoppers would be surveyed as to their residential addresses, travel patterns, attitudes toward shopping facilities, and so on.

Because so many factors are pertinent in the evaluation of a site, real estate advisors have developed checklists to assist the firm in covering all the factors that affect the potential success of a site.[20] Nelson has published one of the most thorough checklists, which includes eight major site factors (trading area potential, accessibility, growth potential, business interception, cumulative attraction potential, compatibility, competitive hazards, and site economics), each of which is divided into several subfactors. Each listed factor is checked separately for the proposed site and given a rating of excellent, good, fair, or poor. The result of these ratings, based on as much hard data collection as possible, is a profile of the strengths and weaknesses of the proposed sites.

Nelson did not carry this farther, but there exists a significant possibility for a quantitative refinement of his procedure. A quantitative rating scale, ranging from 1 to 4, say, can replace the use of rating adjectives. Then individual weights can be assigned to the various factors based on the subjective judgments of experienced company analysts or a statistical regression analysis of the characteristics of successful existing locations. If we let F_{ij} represent the numerical rating for site i on factor j and W_j, the factor's weight or importance, then the value of the ith proposed site (V_i) would be given by

$$V_i = \sum_{j=1}^{n} W_j F_{ij} \tag{11-27}$$

(See Equation 11-1.) Some of the data for estimating V may be quite subjective; yet the relative standing of V for the ith site may be a good indicator of its relative desirability.

Analogue method of site selection. This method of site evaluation is associated with the name of William Applebaum and represents a more sophisticated research procedure than checklists for estimating the potential sales at a site.[21]

---

[20]Among the better known examples are: Richard Nelson, *The Selection of Retail Locations* (New York: F. W. Dodge Corporation, 1958); Bernard J. Kane, Jr., *A Systematic Guide to Supermarket Location Analysis* (New York: Fairchild Publications, Inc., 1966); and Victor Gruen and Larry Smith, *Shopping Towns USA: The Planning of Shopping Centers* (New York: Reinhold Publishing Corporation, 1960).

[21]See William Applebaum, "Methods for Determining Store Trade Areas, Market Penetration, and Potential Sales," *Journal of Marketing Research* (May 1966) 127–141, for the most complete description of his method. See also Saul B. Cohen and William Applebaum, "Evaluating Store Sites and Determining Store Rents," *Economic Geography* (Jan. 1960) 1–35.

The method calls for developing zones around the proposed site and estimating the sales that the proposed store is likely to attract from each zone. Estimates of sales from each zone are based on the drawing power rates of similar stores in the company's chain; hence this method is called the analogue method.

Table 11-5 presents Applebaum's illustration for a real but disguised location.

Table 11-5 Illustration of Applebaum's Site Evaluation Method Applied to Location X.

(1) Zone (miles)	(2) Population in zone	(3) Estimated per capita sales	(4) Estimated weekly sales	(5) Computed drawing power, %
.00– .25	4,700	$2.00	$9,400	28
.25– .50	12,900	.76	9,804	29
.50– .75	23,000	.22	5,060	15
.75–1.00	36,300	.12	4,356	13
Beyond	—	—	5,051	15
			$33,671	100

Source: Applebaum, "Methods for Determining Store Trade Areas, Market Penetration, and Potential Sales," *Journal of Marketing Research* (May 1966) 140.

The area surrounding the proposed site is divided into quarter-mile zones (column 1). Census tract data are used to estimate the population residing in each zone (column 2). The first use of analogues comes into play to estimate per capita sales from each zone (column 3). The store location analyst chooses a subset of other stores in the chain (not shown) that are located at sites resembling the proposed new site. Presumably, "customer spotting" techniques have been applied at the other sites and have revealed the drawing power and per capita expenditures for different zones surrounding each of these other stores. In practice, customer spotting means taking a random sample of 300–400 customers of an existing store and finding out their addresses, weekly food expenditures, and so forth. This allows building a prospectus for each store of the percentage of customers who come from each quarter-mile zone surrounding the store and their weekly expenditures. This information is averaged for the subset of analogous stores chosen by the analyst and used to develop column 3. Column 3 may be the literal average per capita sales of the analogous stores or may be slightly modified to compensate for factors not found in the other stores.

Column 4, estimated weekly sales by zone, is then found by multiplying zone population by zone per capita expenditures. Totaling these figures provides the estimated weekly sales, here $33,671, for the new outlet. As a check, column 5 is computed by recasting column 4 as percentages. Column 5 says that the new store is expected to draw 28 percent of its total sales from the nearest zone, 29 percent of its total sales from the second zone, and so forth. These drawing power percentages are compared to the average of the analogous stores (not shown); to the extent that they match, the analyst has increased confidence in the sales estimate.

The estimate of sales of $33,671 is now divided by the planned store size, say 10,000 square feet, to find the estimated sales per square foot, here $3.37. A further calculation is made of profit per square foot by subtracting all the estimated costs, including the site cost, from estimated sales, and expressing this figure on a square foot basis. If the company is satisfied that the estimated sales and profits per square foot meets its site acceptance criteria, there is one additional estimate that must be made before bidding on the site. The issue arises as to whether any of the company's present stores currently draw sales from the trading area of the new site, and if so, how much volume they might lose to the new store. If three company stores are now drawing a total of $18,000 from the trade area and are expected to draw only $8000 after the new store is developed, then the differential new store sales is only $23,671 ($33,671–$10,000), a figure that yields substantially lower estimates of sales and profit per square foot. This underscores the importance of estimating not the gross sales and profits of a new store, but the differential sales and profits added to the chain by the new store.

This method meets the complexities in the problem of site evaluation by basing estimates on the experience of analogous company outlets. The method relies heavily on the analyst's ability to make judicious selections of analogous stores and to make further modifications for unrepresentative aspects. The method, therefore, cannot readily be used when analogous stores cannot be found or the customer spotting data on the analogous stores are obsolete.

Gravitational method of site selection. This method is associated with the name of David L. Huff,[22] who, following the retail gravitation concepts of Reilly and Converse,[23] developed a series of mathematical models designed to evaluate a proposed site and to select an optimum site from a number of alternatives. He utilizes the basic gravitational notion that the attraction exercised on a consumer in area i by a retail center at location j is directly proportional to the size of the retail center and inversely proportional to the customer's distance from the center. The reasoning is as follows. Suppose stores or shopping centers[24] are pretty much alike except for size and distance. A larger center means a larger product assortment and hence a greater utility for the consumer. Distance, on the other hand, represents a cost or disutility to the consumer. On the assumption that the consumer wants to be an efficient shopper, he will be attracted to any particular center in proportion to the ratio of utility to disutility. Huff expressed the consumer's attraction in the following probability terms:

$$p_{ij} = \frac{S_j/D_{ij}^{\lambda}}{\sum_{j=1}^{n} S_j/D_{ij}^{\lambda}} \tag{11-28}$$

[22]See David L. Huff, "A Probabilistic Analysis of Consumer Spatial Behavior," in William S. Decker, ed., *Emerging Concepts in Marketing* (Chicago: American Marketing Association, 1963) 443–461; and "A Programmed Solution for Approximating an Optimum Retail Location," *Land Economics* (Aug. 1966) 293–303.

[23]See note 19 above.

[24]Huff's method is primarily adapted to estimating sales potentials for shopping centers.

where $p_{ij} =$ the probability of a consumer in area i shopping at a particular location j

$S_j =$ the size of the retail center in location j

$D_{ij} =$ the distance between i and j

$\lambda =$ an estimated sensitivity parameter relating kinds of shopping trips and distance

$n =$ the number of retail locations

As an illustration, suppose λ is 2 and the consumer is able to shop at two retail centers, the first consisting of 100,000 square feet at a distance of 1 mile from his home and the second consisting of 50,000 square feet at a distance of 2 miles. According to Huff's formula, the probabilities of the consumer's shopping at each store are .89 and .11, respectively, as shown by the following calculation:

$$p_{i1} = \frac{100,000/1^2}{100,000/1^2 + 50,000/2^2} = .89$$

$$p_{i2} = \frac{50,000/2^2}{100,000/1^2 + 50,000/2^2} = .11$$

These probabilities are subject to two different interpretations, although both lead to the same analytical results in practice:

1. Each consumer in location i will shop 89 percent of the time at center 1 and 11 percent of the time at center 2.
2. Eighty-nine percent of the consumers in location i will shop at center 1 while 11 percent will shop at center 2.

The value of λ is obviously a key factor in this model. For many years, analysts tended to use the squared distance as the negative factor, partly because this is the parameter in the planetary gravitational formula and partly because early work by Reilly and Converse supported this. Later work showed that λ varied for different types of retail centers and should be independently fitted rather than assumed. Huff suggested an iterative fitting technique for estimating λ. First, λ is set arbitrarily at some number greater than 1. Then Equation 11-28 is used to calculate the p_{ij}'s for different consumer locations. Then the actual number of consumers at each location is found from census data and used to estimate the expected number of consumers from each location who will shop at center j, that is,

$$E_{ij} = p_{ij} \cdot C_i \qquad (11\text{-}29)$$

where $E_{ij} =$ the expected number of consumers originating at i and terminating at j

$C_i =$ the total number of consumers at i

These expected values are compared with the actual relative frequencies obtained from survey data and a correlation coefficient is calculated. The object is to obtain the highest correlation coefficient possible, or to arrive at an error term between the estimate and the actual that is less than a specified amount. Successive values of λ are estimated between a lower and upper bound according to terms of the Fibonacci search.[25] This technique assumes convergence to an optimum value in a finite number of search steps. The iterative procedure is continued until a satisfactory value of λ is obtained (i.e., when the error factor reaches a minimum) for the particular situation. Using a number of samples from similar areas, an average λ value may be calculated to be used in estimating potential for new sites.

After estimating λ, Huff proceeds to expand his model to calculate the expected annual sales originating at i and terminating at location j, using information on average amounts budgeted by the consumers for a particular class of goods. A further extension allows for the determination of market area potential as follows:

$$N_j = \sum_{i=1}^{m} n_{ij} \tag{11-30}$$

$$Q_j = \sum_{i=1}^{m} q_{ij} \tag{11-31}$$

where N_j = the total number of consumers from all of the origin points shopping at j
n_{ij} = the number of consumers at location i shopping at store j
Q_j = the total expected volume of sales at j
q_{ij} = the sales expenditures of consumers from location i at store j
m = the number of statistical areas involved

The trading area for a specific center location can be represented as a series of equiprobable contour lines that diminish smoothly in intensity, although not regularly, as the distance increases from the center. This contrasts with the more traditional primary, secondary, and tertiary scheme used by Applebaum and others, which are zones arbitrarily containing varying percentages of nearest shoppers.

Huff's methodology can then be used to select an optimum location from a specified number of potential locations for a retail development. The steps involved in this analysis consist of: (1) estimating total sales volumes for different size centers in each location, (2) determining the operating profit as a percentage of sales for each center, (3) calculating the net operating profit for each size operation in each potential location, and (4) selecting the location that yields the highest net operating profit. A computer program has been devised to carry out this analysis.[26]

Huff's method, compared to that of Applebaum, has more analytical character,

[25]For a detailed discussion of the Fibonacci search technique, see Douglas J. Wilde, *Optimum Seeking Methods* (Englewood Cliffs, N.J.: Prentice-Hall, Inc., 1964), 24–30.

[26]David L. Huff and Larry Blue, *A Programmed Solution for Estimating Retail Sales Potentials* (Lawrence, Kans.: University of Kansas Center for Regional Studies, 1966).

in that it uses a few principles to derive a rich set of estimates. This is also a possible source of weakness because it omits many factors that might belong in a total evaluation of a site. For example, the probability contours usually should be modified to reflect natural barriers and distortions of the particular terrain. Furthermore, retail centers are not likely to appear the same in the consumers' minds, but rather strike them as having different images, accessibilities, and prices that create a basis for differential store preference. The empirical drawing power ratios used by Applebaum are more likely to reflect the impact of store difference variables than anything in Huff's method. At the same time, Huff's formula could be expanded to include these additional factors in the following way:

$$p_{ij} = \frac{S_j^{\lambda_1} I_{ij}^{\lambda_2} A_{ij}^{\lambda_3} / D_{ij}^{\lambda_4} P_{ij}^{\lambda_5}}{\sum_{j=1}^{n} S^{\lambda_1} I_{ij}^{\lambda_2} A_{ij}^{\lambda_3} / D_{ij}^{\lambda_4} P_{ij}^{\lambda_5}} \tag{11-32}$$

where p_{ij} = the probability of a consumer in area i shopping at a particular location j

S_j = the size of the retail center in location j

I_{ij} = the image of retail center j perceived by a consumer in area i (an index number reflecting the center's reputation, product assortment, and decor)

A_{ij} = the accessibility of center j to the consumer in area i (an index number reflecting the center's relative parking space, ease of entrance and exit, and position in relation to traffic flow)

D_{ij} = the distance or time between location j and consumer area i

P_{ij} = the perceived price level of retail center j to consumer in area i

λ = various sensitivity parameters

By restating this formula in log form and fitting it to the data on existing company outlets, it may be possible to estimate the λ's and thus derive insight into the relative influence of the different variables on store shopping probabilities. Short of including these additional variables, it is felt by many analysts that Huff's Equation 11-28 is of limited value in estimating sales potential for single stores. Individual store size per se has not been found to have the great influence claimed on drawing power.[27] Size appears to be more of a factor in explaining drawing power differences of shopping centers and here is where Huff's method may be most effective.

One notable effort to introduce other factors into a gravitational model was developed by Hlavac and Little and is concerned with estimating the sales potential of sites for automobile dealerships.[28] In their model, an auto dealer's

[27]Bernard J. LaLonde, "Differentials in Supermarket Drawing Power," Marketing and Transportation Paper 11, Bureau of Business and Economic Research, Michigan State University, East Lansing, 1962.

[28]T. E. Hlavac, Jr., and J. D. C. Little, "A Geographic Model of an Automobile Market," Working Paper 180–66, Alfred P. Sloan School of Management, Massachusetts Institute of Technology, Cambridge, 1966.

"pull" is a function of the consumer's make preference, the dealer's local image independent of make, and the consumer's distance from the dealer. Specifically, the probability that consumer i will purchase an auto from dealer j is given by

$$p_{ij} = \frac{L_{im}I_j e^{-b_j D_{ij}}}{\sum_{k=1} L_{im}I_k e^{-b_k D_{ik}}} \tag{11-33}$$

where

p_{ij} = the probability of consumer i's purchasing an auto from dealer j

L_{im} = the make preference of consumer i for auto maker m

$\quad L_{im} \geqslant 0, \; \Sigma_{m=1}^M L_{im} = 1,$ and $m = 1, 2, \ldots, M$

I_j = dealer j's local image independent of make (as affected by advertising, service, size, etc.)

$e^{-b_j D_{ij}}$ = the effect of distance on the probability, where D_{ij} is the distance between consumer i and dealer j, b_j tells how fast sales fall with distance, and e is the constant 2.71 ...

k = a subscript for the dealer, where $k = 1, \ldots, n$

This formula is similar to Huff's formula in Equation 11-28 with the nominal difference that the effect of distance on the purchase probability is expressed through an exponential decay factor rather than a λ distance term. Hlavac and Little proceed to use the p_{ij}'s to find expected sales in the same manner as Huff did in Equation 11-29. To fit the model, the authors used 1963 new car registration data for Cook County, Illinois, covering 17,670 purchases, eight major makes, and 184 dealers. Market shares in Cook County were used to represent make preferences, L_{im}. Dealer images, I_j, and the effect of distance, b_j, were estimated by maximum likelihood procedures. The resulting equation yielded sales predictions that came quite close to actual sales, showing that dealer sales are largely explained by the three postulated factors of brand preferences, dealer images, and shopping distances.

One particularly notable feature of this model is that it is available for executive use on an interactive computer basis for on-line investigation of a variety of site selection and interbrand competition questions. An executive can sit at a computer terminal, dial this program, and use it to estimate the sales and market share effect of adding, eliminating, or relocating a dealer. This kind of model even makes it possible to investigate the impact of an overall locational pattern strategy, as well as a single site selection. Too often, companies add one site at a time on ad hoc criteria, instead of developing a competitive pattern of locations that takes maximum advantage of the distribution of sales potential throughout a metropolitan area, while being optimally adapted to the locational patterns of competitors. Although this is not emphasized by Hlavac and Little, gravitational models in general are most promising for the evaluation of overall locational pattern strategies.

Store Size and Store Characteristics Decisions

The previous discussion indicated that the sales potential of a new store will be affected by a number of factors in addition to the store's location. In its detailed analysis of a location opportunity, management will be thinking not so much of the effect of an average company store in that location as of a store of a particular size, layout,[29] product assortment, decor, parking capacity, and so forth. All of these factors will be considered by management with a view toward identifying those levels of the various factors that will have a maximum impact on profits.

Of all the outlet characteristics, store size is traditionally singled out as being of prime importance. The larger the store, the greater its product assortment and neighborhood conspicuousness, and therefore the larger its trading area and sales penetration. Yet sales may not increase with store size in a proportional manner. Management needs some measure of the relationship between store size and store sales in order to build stores of the right size. If small stores yield higher returns on investment than large stores, the company may be better off building several small stores, instead of a few large ones with a given budget.

Baumol and Ide developed a model in which store size had both a positive and negative effect on store sales as size increased.[30] Instead of using store size directly, they focused on a correlated variable, the number of different items, N, that the retailer carried. They argued that the greater the number of different items, the more likely the shopper will be attracted because he would have greater confidence in finding the items he wanted. On the other hand, the greater the number of different items, the more the time required by the shopper to get to the spot in the store where the items he wants are kept. Their particular formulation of the two effects of the number of items is as follows:

$$f(N, D) = k_1 p(N) - k_2(c_d D + c_n \sqrt{N} + c_i) \tag{11-34}$$

where $f(N, D)$ = a measure of the consumer's expected net benefit from shopping at a store with N different items and a distance D

$p(N)$ = probability that consumers will find some set of items in the store that will make his trip successful

c_d, c_n, c_i = cost parameters

k_1, k_2 = respective weights for benefit and cost of shopping where $0 \leqslant k_i \leqslant 1$ and $\sum k_i = 1$

Their formulation permits a number of conclusions to be drawn. First, the expected net benefit of shopping in a store with very few items may be negative. Second, the expected net benefit of shopping in a store with a tremendous number of items may also be negative because the first term in Equation 11-34 can never exceed k_1, while $k_2 c_n \sqrt{N}$ grows indefinitely large. (This explains, for example, why a Sears store is never built so large that it carries all the items listed in its catalog.) Third, sales are likely to increase with store size at an increasing and then diminishing rate and eventually a negative rate, with the exact shape dependent on the parameters in the equation.

[29]The demand creation effects of store layout are analyzed in an original way by John U. Farley and L. Winston Ring, "A Stochastic Model of Supermarket Traffic Flow," *Operations Research* (July 1966) 555–567.

[30]William J. Baumol and Edward A. Ide, "Variety in Retailing," *Management Science* (Oct. 1956) 93–101.

In a practical context, management will build different-size stores to serve different purposes. For example, Sears will build stores ranging from a catalog sales office of approximately 5000 square feet to a hard-line store with approximately 18,000 to 20,000 square feet of selling area, a small full-line department store of approximately 36,000 square feet of selling area to a major "A" store with an approximate 150,000 square feet of selling area. The choices of store size and location are obviously interdependent decisions, and it is difficult to say which comes first. We can imagine where good sites are sought first; when found, they dictate a particular store size because of the available space and the character of the area. Conversely, we can imagine situations in which the company has decided on a desirable mix of store sizes and seeks to acquire a corresponding mix of sites.

As for store characteristics other than size, their relative impact on demand varies with the nature of the business. A company can sometimes make headway on this question by collecting data on its existing stores and fitting a regression equation to explain sales or market share variations. Such an analysis was carried out, for example, by the Rayco Manufacturing Company, a manufacturer of automobile seat covers that operated a distribution network of independently financed, franchised dealers who merchandised Rayco products exclusively.[31] In 1955, Rayco had over 150 dealers operating in sixty different cities. Data on over 300 variables that might have some logical connection with past or potential sales were assembled for each Rayco outlet. However, 300 variables could not be accommodated in the multiple regression analysis because of their high intercorrelation and the availability of only 150 observations (stores). The Research Division examined carefully the logical rationale for each variable and was able to reduce the set to 74. Included among them were such variables as "average January temperature," "percent of the dwellings that were one-unit detached structures," and an "index for the physical appearance of a store." The reduction of the number of variables to 74 permitted a meaningful fit in terms of the number of observations. An equation was fitted and yielded a coefficient of multiple determination (R^2) of .98. However, several of the variables failed to pass tests of statistical significance; in the final equation, 37 variables were retained, yielding an R^2 of .92. This equation revealed the major store characteristics that affected sales and their relative importance. Presumably, the formula would permit Rayco to introduce the specific characteristics or decisions contemplated for any new site and estimate potential sales.

This author applied a similar analysis to determine the relative importance of two dozen different store characteristics in accounting for the trade area market shares of fifty-four stores belonging to a medium-size food chain.[32] Several qualitative variables were rated in index number form, such as the caliber of the

---

[31]The discussion that follows is adapted from "Rayco Manufacturing Company, Inc.: Pinpointing Store Locations by Electronic Computer," Case 3M38, Intercollegiate Case Clearing House, Harvard Graduate School of Business Administration, Boston, by permission of the author, Charles H. Dufton, Northeastern University, Boston.

[32]Unpublished study.

store's management, the quality of its meats, store cleanliness, and so forth. Subjective ratings of the store's and competitors' standings on these variables were provided by management. The equation was fitted in logged linear form and six variables appeared to account for 74 percent of the variance in company store market shares ($R^2 = .74$). These variables are shown in the order they appeared in stepwise regression in Table 11-6. In this study, store size and store

Table 11-6 Relative Importance of Variables Influencing Area Market Shares of a Food Chain

	Cumulative R^2
1. Selling space	$R^2 = .25$
2. Convenience to shoppers in trading area	$R^2 = .57$
3. Number of competitors in trading area	$R^2 = .63$
4. Store tidiness	$R^2 = .66$
5. Store lighting	$R^2 = .71$
6. Extent of advertising	$R^2 = .74$

convenience accounted for the lion's share of market share determination, and this is consistent with the assumptions of the gravitational model. At the same time, this technique helps identify additional variables that account for some of the remaining variance and may turn out to be useful in planning and forecasting for new site locations.

This brings us to the end of the discussion of distribution location decisions, specifically those involving market area selection, number of outlets, site selection, and store and other characteristics determination. Now we turn to models for distribution logistics decision making.

DISTRIBUTION LOGISTICS

In addition to establishing locations for its outlets, a company must also design an efficient physical distribution system for getting goods to its outlets and customers. The physical distribution system is made up of decisions on *warehouse locations, inventory levels, packaging and handling procedures,* and *transportation carriers.* These decisions have both a cost and demand aspect. The cost aspect of physical distribution has received the most attention, and many successful operations research models have been developed in this area. The demand aspect has come to the foreground more recently and deserves the serious attention of designers of physical distribution systems.

Marketing executives, of course, are particularly interested in the demand aspect of physical distribution. Each component physical distribution decision can affect company sales. Warehouse locations are a promotional tool, in that they give confidence to local buyers of better availability and company service. Inventory level policies affect availability and hence sales. Packaging and handling procedures, insofar as they affect the damage goods rate, will affect the number of customers. Transportation modes, insofar as they can mean faster or slower arrival of goods, will affect buyer satisfaction and sales.

Physical Distribution System Optimization

The demand creation aspects of physical distribution can either be treated on the revenue side of the equation or as a form of costs. Many analysts find it convenient to develop a cost term to represent the lost sales associated with a particular level of physical distribution service. The problem of designing an optimal physical distribution system is then seen as one of choosing those levels of physical distribution services that minimize the total cost of physical distribution, including the cost of lost sales. The objective function might read:[33]

$$C = T + F + I + L \tag{11-35}$$

where C = total distribution cost of proposed system
T = total freight cost of proposed system
F = total fixed warehouse cost of proposed system
I = total inventory cost of proposed system
L = total cost of lost sales associated with the proposed system

If the cost of lost sales, L, were left out, then the company would tend to minimize warehousing, inventory, and carrier costs, overlooking the negative effects this would have on revenue. Admittedly, the cost of lost sales is the most difficult of the four costs to measure, yet this is no excuse for leaving it out of the equation. The way to think about it is to identify the levels of the warehousing, inventory, and transportation service at which there would be no lost sales. Then management makes an educated guess as to how much sales would be lost at lower levels of product availability and customer service. It is also useful to distinguish between lost sales and lost customers. A temporary stockout condition can result in customers' switching some of their purchases temporarily to others; a continually recurring stockout condition can lead to dissatisfied customers who undertake to do business on a permanent basis with a competitor.

Given the objective cost function in Equation 11-35, management seeks to find the number of warehouses, inventory levels, and modes of transportation that will minimize it, subject to at least three constraints: (1) customer demand must be satisfied; (2) factory capacity limits must not be exceeded; and (3) warehouse capacity cannot be exceeded. A variety of mathematical solutions to this problem has been proposed. The Baumol-Wolfe solution leaves out fixed warehouse costs and takes a several stage linear programming approach to arrive at an approximate solution to this nonlinear programming problem.[34] Balinski and Mills also use a piecewise linear programming approach and employ a different set of assumptions and solution techniques.[35] Shycon and Maffei use the technique of simulation to evaluate the cost of alternative arrangement of a physical distribution

[33]This equation is a simplification of the equation in Alfred A. Kuehn and Michael J. Hamburger, "A Heuristic Program for Locating Warehouses," *Management Science* (July 1963) 657–658. The costs in their equation are subscripted: they depend on $X_{h,i,j,k}$, i.e., the quantity of good h shipped from factory i via warehouse j to customer k.

[34]W. J. Baumol and P. Wolfe, "A Warehouse Location Problem," *Operations Research* (Mar.–Apr. 1958) 252–263.

[35]M. L. Balinski and H. Mills, *A Warehouse Problem*, prepared for Veterans Administration, Mathematica, Princeton, N.J., Apr., 1960.

system.[36] Their computer program can evaluate a system of up to 40 warehouses, 4000 customers, and 10 factories, which is an advantage over some of the more mathematical techniques. One of its novel features is the use of latitudes and longitudes of various potential locations to calculate air miles to estimate approximate shipping costs between various points. However, a major drawback of simulation is that it does not provide a systematic method of moving toward the optimal physical distribution solution. Unfortunately, most of these models failed to include the cost of lost sales in the formulation.

In contrast, the Kuehn-Hamburger solution does include the cost of lost sales in the formulation.[37] Their model is based on three heuristics that efficiently reduce the number of feasible solutions at a substantial cost saving in computer time and yet produce a good solution. The three heuristics are as follows. First, it is assumed that warehouses in the system will normally be located at major metropolitan centers, rather than between any centers. Second, it is assumed that a good solution can be obtained by adding one warehouse at a time to the system, the one that produces the greatest cost savings for the entire system. Third, it is assumed that only a small subset of all possible locations have to be evaluated in searching for the next warehouse. Figure 11-4 shows the overall computer program. The first part of the program locates warehouses one at a time, until no additions can be made to the system without increasing total distribution costs. Then the bump and shift routine examines all of the activated sites to see if any have been rendered uneconomical by the addition of subsequent warehouses. It also checks to see whether any warehouses may be profitably shifted to other sites. The Kuehn-Hamburger heuristic model for selecting warehouses was run on a certain set of data and performed as well as, or better than, other models that claimed optimization.

Waiting Line Optimization

One important marketing aspect of a physical distribution system and channels of distribution is how much time customers have to wait for service. The customer who waits in a line in a supermarket, bank, gasoline station, or airline bears a cost in terms of more desirable uses of time. If the customer regards the waiting time as excessive, he may decide to do business elsewhere, causing lost sales to the company.

While waiting time is a cost to the customer and possibly to the company, so is the effort to reduce waiting time. The supermarket could reduce waiting time by adding more counters or personnel, or both. The decision problem is one of balancing the cost of lost sales against the cost of additional facilities. In marginal terms the supermarket should increase its servicing facilities up to the point at which the cost of an additional facility would just overtake the profits lost due to customer impatience.

[36]H. N. Shycon and R. B. Maffei, "Simulation—Tool for Better Distribution," *Harvard Business Review* (Nov.–Dec. 1960) 65–75. For a more technical description, see M. L. Gerson and R. B. Maffei, "Technical Characteristics of Distribution Simulators," *Management Science* (Oct. 1963) 62–69.

[37]Kuehn and Hamburger, "A Heuristic Program for Locating Warehouses," *Management Science* (July 1963) 657–658.

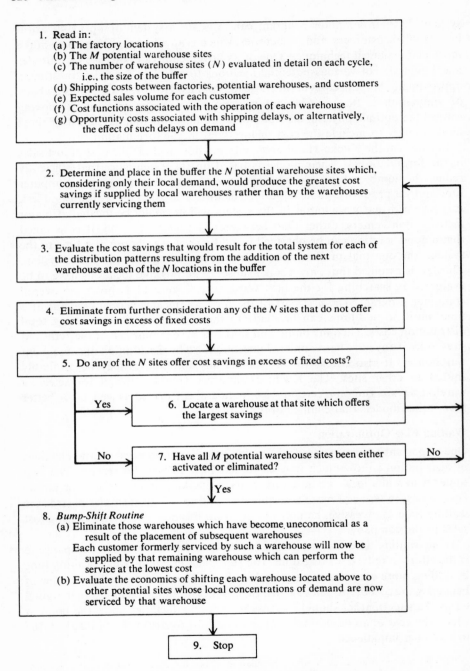

1. Read in:
   (a) The factory locations
   (b) The M potential warehouse sites
   (c) The number of warehouse sites (N) evaluated in detail on each cycle, i.e., the size of the buffer
   (d) Shipping costs between factories, potential warehouses, and customers
   (e) Expected sales volume for each customer
   (f) Cost functions associated with the operation of each warehouse
   (g) Opportunity costs associated with shipping delays, or alternatively, the effect of such delays on demand

2. Determine and place in the buffer the N potential warehouse sites which, considering only their local demand, would produce the greatest cost savings if supplied by local warehouses rather than by the warehouses currently servicing them

3. Evaluate the cost savings that would result for the total system for each of the distribution patterns resulting from the addition of the next warehouse at each of the N locations in the buffer

4. Eliminate from further consideration any of the N sites that do not offer cost savings in excess of fixed costs

5. Do any of the N sites offer cost savings in excess of fixed costs?

Yes

6. Locate a warehouse at that site which offers the largest savings

No

7. Have all M potential warehouse sites been either activated or eliminated?

No

Yes

8. *Bump-Shift Routine*
   (a) Eliminate those warehouses which have become uneconomical as a result of the placement of subsequent warehouses
      Each customer formerly serviced by such a warehouse will now be supplied by that remaining warehouse which can perform the service at the lowest cost
   (b) Evaluate the economics of shifting each warehouse located above to other potential sites whose local concentrations of demand are now serviced by that warehouse

9. Stop

Figure 11-4   Kuehn-Hamburger Heuristic Warehouse Location Program

Source: Kuehn and Hamburger, p. 647.

The decision problem is illustrated graphically in Figure 11-5. The higher the average waiting time in the system, the greater the cost of lost sales (1), but the

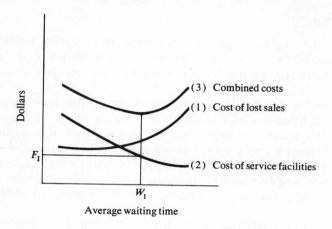

Figure 11-5 **System Costs as Related to Average Waiting Time**

lower the cost of facilities and personnel (2). The two cost curves are added vertically to derive a combined cost curve (3). The lowest point on this combined cost curve indicates the optimal waiting time to be built into the system (W_1) and the optimal investment in service facilities (F_1). The lowest point can be found graphically or through differential calculus if appropriate cost equations can be found.

The cost of additional facilities is not difficult to measure, but it is very difficult to measure the cost of lost sales that take place due to customer impatience. In the first place, people vary considerably in their attitudes toward waiting. In the second place, customer impatience is a function of the difference between anticipated and actual waiting time, and anticipated waiting varies by situations. Also, customers who feel impatient may not abandon the store if alternative stores are no better.

Waiting line theory, also called queuing theory, is not designed to answer *how much* waiting time *should* be built into a system. This is primarily an economic question as shown in Figure 11-5. The theory is designed instead to handle two preliminary questions: What amount of waiting time may be expected in a particular system? How will this waiting time change as a result of particular alterations in the facilities?

The waiting time depends on four dimensions of the system:

Interarrival time. The time between arrivals into the system has a probability distribution that can be estimated from frequency data. The mean, standard deviation, and other characteristics of interarrival time can then be derived from the probability distribution.

Service time.   The time between the initiating of a service and its completion can also be viewed as having a probability distribution.

Number of service facilities.   The greater the number of service facilities, the shorter the waiting time.

Servcie method.   Usually customers are serviced in the order in which they arrive (called first-in, first-out). But other methods are service to the most important customers first, service for the shortest orders first, and service at random.

The analyst studying a particular system must determine the empirical values and probability distributions of the components of the system. Figure 11-6 shows various alternatives that might exist or be postulated. Any particular system can be analyzed for its queuing characteristics such as expected waiting time, expected queue length, and the variability of waiting time and queue length. For certain simple queuing situations, it is possible to derive these answers mathematically; for more complicated systems, estimates can be derived by simulation.

If the existing system breeds long queues, the decision maker can simulate the effects of different proposed changes. In the case of a supermarket with a serious queuing problem on Saturdays, four possible methods are indicated: (1) the supermarket can try to influence its customers to do their shopping on other days; (2) the supermarket can decrease the service time by employing baggers to aid the cashiers; (3) more service channels can be added; and (4) some of the channels can be specialized to handle smaller orders.

Most of the literature about queuing deals with facility planning for telephone exchanges, highways and toll roads, docks, and airline terminals. Yet retailing institutions such as supermarkets, filling stations, and airline ticket offices also face critical queuing problems, so that marketing executives can be expected to show increased interest in waiting line models.

DISTRIBUTION MANAGEMENT

We have examined the successive questions of distribution strategy, location, and logistics and reviewed the analytical techniques available to aid decision making in these areas. Let us assume that the company's distribution system is now designed, implemented, and operating. The company's task is to motivate its outlets—both company-owned and independent—to operate at the highest level of performance. The company would like to see the outlets order as much as possible, give the most prominent display space to its merchandise, cooperate wholeheartedly in special promotions, boost its products over competitors' products, and provide excellent customer service. To encourage these practices, the company has available a certain number of sales tools, the more important ones of which are retail margin, special retail allowances, number of company service calls, cooperative advertising allowances, dealer training programs, dealer literature and sales aids, and so on. Each tool will have a certain incentive value that varies with its own level and the level of the other tools. The company's challenge is to find the proper mix of incentives that will optimize its profits through the dealer. Fortunately, the appropriate decision models do not differ substantially from those developed for other marketing tools. At the same time, some specific comments on model building in this area are offered to suggest the types of problems encountered.

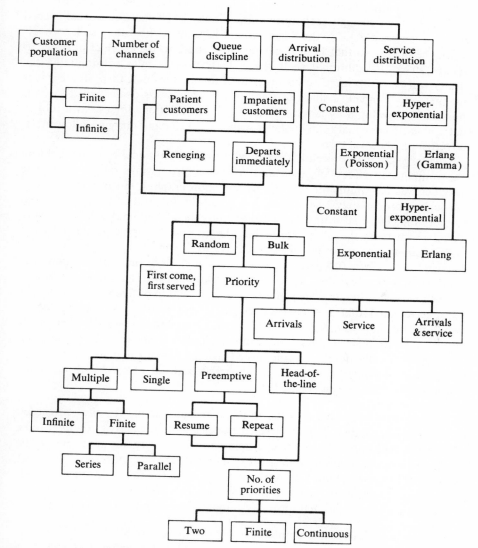

Figure 11-6   Queuing Models Available

From James M. Moore, "To Queue or Not to Queue," *Journal of Industrial Engineering,* March-April 1961, p. 118.

Companies would like to obtain as much dealer shelf space for their products as possible. Shelf space, along with the price and image of the product are major factors affecting the level of retail sales. To the extent that the dealer has latitude in setting the price, he will be influenced by the manufacturer's price and any allowances offered at the time. Allowances can lead the dealer to set a lower retail price or devote more shelf space to the product or both. Shelf space is also influenced by the amount of retail advertising, because dealers expect products with higher advertising to sell more units. Finally, shelf space is also influenced by any overstock held by the dealer. Some salesmen deliberately seek to overstock the dealer, so that he will devote more space to the product in order to reduce stock. If additional shelf space does increase sales substantially, the dealer will be led to increase his order level for the product; then, in a circular manner, the company's share of total sales through this dealer will rise. It is possible to develop a dynamic model of these interactions for use as a tool to determine effective marketing policies with respect to retail margins, allowances, advertising, and overstocking.

One large company recently developed a simulation model to throw light on the complicated effects of trade and consumer promotions on its sales. The product was flashbulbs for use in amateur photography; and distribution was through approximately 2000 wholesalers who sold the product through approximately 100,000 retail stores. The need to study its promotional policies in more detail arose from the observation that the company shipments ranged from 5–75 million units a month, while incentives to distributors, retailers, and consumers, ranged from 0–8 percent a month. An analysis of the gross data on sales and promotions revealed no consistent relationship. The same promotion seemed to have different effects at different times and in different situations. The idea germinated that a simulation model could possibly be constructed to represent this industry, particularly the response differences of various channels associated with their volume, cost of money, and min-max inventory rules. The model was finally developed and tested against historical data on company promotion; it yielded predictions that correlated at the .96 level with historical sales results. The analyst concluded:

> Some past programs now began to make sense as to why they succeeded and why they failed. In some areas the sales promotion activity thought to be effective had failed because it had points in it that were not appealing to the channels of distribution as far as carrying inventory was concerned. The price weighted by the volume was not in accordance with their needs or desires. It was also found that, in the trade, the capital structure of the channels of distribution was such that terms were more appealing than discounts.[38]

The company has used this simulator to pretest alternative sales plans consisting of allowances, terms, and discounts and is satisfied that its value as an analytical device has more than justified the cost of developing it.

[38]Quoted from a private document.

SUMMARY

A company's channels of distribution represent a foundation for its other marketing policies. For this reason, management will want to exercise great care in its basic decisions on distribution strategy, location, logistics, and management. The first of these, distribution strategy, is the task of determining the basic way in which the company will sell to buyers. Here the company should carefully distinguish all of the alternatives and evaluate them, either through the weighted factor score method, the hierarchical preference ordering method, or preferably through simulating future sales, costs, and profits under given assumptions about each alternative.

The second decision area, distribution location, is concerned with four interrelated decisions: market selection, number of outlets, site location, and store size and other characteristics. The first task is to determine the most attractive market areas in the country in which to locate new outlets. A good procedure is to estimate discounted cumulative profits on a new average size outlet that might be opened in each area. The company can then concentrate its store location research in the highest ranking areas. The company should then turn to the question of the optimal number of outlets per market area. The Hartung and Fisher study showed how Markov theory and nonlinear programming can be used to examine this question. As for site location, current techniques range from primitive checklists, through the analogue method used by Applebaum, through gravitational models originally developed by Reilly and Converse and, in more recent times, reformulated by Huff, Hlavac, and Little. Also, store size was shown to be an important factor in affecting the level of sales. Other characteristics of the outlet such as its decor, caliber of management, product assortment, and so forth, will also affect demand. One way to examine the relative influence of all these factors on demand is by a regression analysis performed on the data describing existing company stores. Two examples of store sales regression analyses are described in the chapter.

Distribution logistics, the third area of distribution decision making, is concerned with determining the best way to supply company outlets with product. Distribution logistics involves four major variables: the number of warehouses, inventory levels, packaging and handling procedures, and transportation carriers. To determine the optimal physical distribution system, it is necessary to formulate the appropriate cost function, including the cost of lost sales. Once the cost of lost sales is included along with the other physical distribution costs, the task is to minimize the distribution cost function subject to certain constraints. Among the techniques that have been used to solve this problem in an optimal, or at least satisfactory, way are heuristic programming, variants of linear programming, and simulation. Queuing theory is another technique that is useful in distribution system planning, where waiting time is a concern to the customers and threatens to get out of hand.

The fourth area, distribution management, is the problem of motivating the outlets to perform at the highest possible level. Here management can formulate a dynamic analysis of the interaction of trade allowances, advertising, and overstocking and use the power of computer simulation to pretest the effects of alternative promotional programs to the trade.

Questions and Problems

1. Use the weighted factor score method to evaluate distribution strategy III in Figure 11-2, using the factors and weights suggested in Table 11-1. Suppose distribution strategy III receives the following ratings on the five factors: .8, .6, .7, .3, and .2. What is the total score for distribution strategy III?

2. The ABC Corporation currently sells one of its products directly to retailers through its own sales force. Present sales are 100,000 units per year and the company's profit margin is $2.00 per unit. Management estimates that the cost of maintaining the sales force is $1.00 per unit.

   The company is considering the use of wholesalers, rather than selling directly to retailers. The wholesaler's commission would be 75c per unit, but sales force costs per unit sold would be cut by one half.

   (a) If the initial cost of converting to the wholesaler distribution system is $18,000, how many additional units would the company have to sell to cover its transition costs in one year?

   (b) If management's estimates of the pessimistic, most likely, and optimistic levels of sales for the coming year under the wholesaler strategy are 100,000, 110,000, and 120,000 respectively, should the company change its distribution channels?

3. A large fish and chips restaurant franchiser is considering opening a new outlet in a large metropolitan area. There are presently 200 fish and chips outlets in the area, of which 20 hold his company's franchise. Each outlet in the area has average monthly sales of $10,000.

   (a) Using the Hartung-Fisher model, determine the amount of additional sales that would be created by opening up a new outlet in this area (assume $k_1 = 4.44$ and $k_2 = .64$)

   (b) What would be the amount of additional sales if 30 of the 200 stores in the area were company franchises?

4. A men's shoe manufacturer plans to establish a new outlet in one of its two major market areas: A_1 and A_2. The company and its competitors currently sell a total of 100,000 pairs of shoes in each area. There is a total of 250 outlets in A_1 (of which 25 are company outlets) and 200 outlets in A_2 (40 of which are company outlets). In a recent study the company found that it was able to retain about 30 per cent of its customers in A_1 and about 40 per cent in A_2 from purchase to purchase. It was also found that the company was able to persuade 10 per cent of its competitor's customers in A_1 (8 percent in A_2) to switch to its own brand. Should the new outlet be established in A_1 or A_2?

5. A company is considering the development of one of two new market areas. Estimates of potential sales, expenses and growth rates for each area are presented in the following table:

	Area 1	Area 2
Adjusted annual sales potential, S_i	$500,000	$750,000
Transportation expenses (percent of sales), d_i	.20	.15
Advertising expenses (percent of sales), a_i	.25	.30
Real estate expenses (percent of sales), l_i	.10	.12
Other expenses (percent of sales), n_i	.29	.35
Expected growth rate of profit potential	.04	.06

It is estimated that it would cost the same amount to develop either area (I_i = $150,000). Suppose the company's cost of capital is 10 percent. Which area offers the more attractive rate of return over a 3 year planning horizon?

6. Huff's gravitational model assumes that the consumer's marginal utility with respect to distance varies according to the value of the exponent λ. For instance, λ = 2 indicates that the consumer experiences diminishing marginal utility with respect to increases in distance. The model, however, assumes that the consumer experiences constant marginal utility with respect to increases in store size.

Suppose that the consumer actually experiences diminishing marginal utility with respect to increases in store size. Using an exponent as the parameter which accounts for the consumer's marginal utility of store size, modify Huff's formulation to accommodate this diminishing marginal utility.

In the example used in the chapter to illustrate Huff's model (Center I = 100,000 sq. ft., 1 mile; Center 2 = 50,000 sq. ft., 2 miles) suppose that it is found that the consumer shops only 60 percent of the time at Center I. Determine the value of λ in this instance.

CHAPTER 12
Price Decision Models

Of all the marketing decision variables that influence the sales of a product, price has received the most analytical attention by professional economists with the result that theoretical formulations abound. Much of microeconomic theory consists of analyses of the price that would be set by sellers operating under different market structures, such as pure competition, monopolistic competition, oligopolistic competition, and monopoly. These formulations, although interesting in their own right, are of limited helpfulness to the seller facing a problem of setting a price for the first time, initiating or meeting a competitive price change, or developing a structure of prices on all the products in the line that maximizes total profits. To show how the seller might proceed, we have to turn to various operations research models that have been developed for specific pricing situations.

Pricing may, or may not, be an important element in the marketing mix in any particular product situation. There are situations in which the seller has little pricing latitude—in commodity markets, many food products, public utility services, and so forth; in these cases, pricing is one of the less important concerns in developing marketing plans.[1] There are other situations in which pricing is an

---

[1] See Jon G. Udell, "How Important Is Pricing in Competitive Strategy?" *Journal of Marketing* (Jan. 1964), 44–48. Udell sent questionnaires to a sample of 200 producers of industrial and consumer goods, seeking to determine the rated importance of price versus other marketing policy variables in competitive strategy. Udell concluded: "It appears that business management did not agree with the economic views of the importance of pricing— one-half of the respondents did *not* select pricing as *one of the five most important* policy areas in their firm's marketing success."

acute concern, such as those where there is production overcapacity (gasoline industry), where forms of distribution are rapidly changing (the advent of the discount house in retailing), where competition is keen (appliance industry), and where jobs must be bid for (military and private construction industry). In these and other situations, price decisions require considerable skill and experience.

At what stage in marketing planning for a new product is the price decision made? This will vary with the product and situation. Sometimes a "high" price is made necessary by the very design and quality of the product; the price is set high to cover the higher cost and to establish psychologically the product's quality in the buyers' minds. Sometimes the prior necessity or desirability of using certain distribution channels effectively dictates the price to be charged. Sometimes the seller's intentions on services to be provided with the product necessitate a certain price level.

In most cases, the determination of a price or price zone is necessary before the company can develop a communication and personal selling strategy. For the price will define the segments of the market that will be interested in the product. Only when these segments are defined is it possible to prepare the appropriate messages and media for promoting the product.

Earlier chapters of this book have described the theory of optimal pricing under circumstances in which the demand and cost functions are known with certainty by the seller.[2] While this theory calls our attention to the right factors, it omits many considerations that the marketing decision maker must deal with in practice. Therefore this chapter will begin with a discussion of important factors that must be considered in actual pricing situations but which were not explicitly considered in the theoretical model. The second section describes three different bases—cost, demand, and competition—used in practice by businessmen to set their actual prices. The third section considers one particular situation in which prices have to be set new each time, that of sealed bidding for contracts, and some of the models that have been developed to aid decision makers in this area. The fourth section probes into models and methods for deciding whether to initiate or meet price changes. The last section deals with the problem of setting individual prices in the product line in which the products exhibit demand and/or cost interactions.

LIMITATIONS OF THE THEORETICAL PRICING MODEL

The theoretical pricing model described in earlier chapters is built on at least four restrictive assumptions that severely limit the model's applicability to actual pricing problems. They are:

The firm's objective in setting a price is to maximize the short run profits on the particular product.

The only party to consider in setting the price is the firm's immediate customers.

[2]See Chap. 2 and Chap. 7.

The price can be set independent of the levels set for the other marketing variables.

The demand and cost equations can be estimated with sufficient accuracy.

These assumptions shall be examined in turn.

The Problem of Objectives

The theoretical pricing model assumes a single product for which the seller is trying to determine the price that would maximize current profits. Current profits, rather than long run profits, are at issue because of the use of stable demand and cost assumptions. In reality, demand can be expected to change over time (as a result of changes in tastes, population, and income), and cost can be expected to change over time (as a result of changes in technology and input prices). Pricing to maximize long run profits would have to utilize projections of the likely long run course of demand and cost. A more sophisticated model would be required to solve the problem of pricing optimally over the product's life cycle.

A limitation of quite another sort is that profit maximization, whether current or long run, is not always the immediate pricing objective of a firm. It may be the ultimate goal, but conceptions of the means for achieving it may differ. At least five different pricing objectives of a more concrete sort can be found in practice.[3]

Market penetration objective.   Some companies set a relatively low price in order to stimulate the growth of the market and to capture a large share of it. Any of several conditions might favor setting a low price:[4]

1.   The market appears to be highly price-sensitive; that is, many additional buyers would come into the market if the product were priced low.
2.   The unit costs of production and distribution fall with increased output. (Whenever a product is favored by scale economies, it is desirable to give serious consideration to all measures that would stimulate sales, including a low price.)
3.   A low price would discourage actual and potential competition.

Market skimming objective.   Some firms seek to take advantage of the fact that some buyers always stand ready to pay a much higher price than others because the product, for one reason or another, has high present value to them. The objective of skimming pricing is to gain a premium from these buyers and only gradually reduce the price to draw in the more price elastic segments of the

---

[3]For a documentation of pricing objectives, see the Brookings study by A. D. H. Kaplan, Joel B. Dirlam, and Robert F. Lanzilloti, *Pricing in Big Business* (Washington, D.C.: The Brookings Institution, 1958).

[4]See Joel Dean, *Managerial Economics* (Englewood Cliffs, N.J.: Prentice-Hall, Inc., 1951), pp. 420ff.

market. It is a form of price discrimination over time rather than over space. It makes good sense when any of the following conditions are present:

1. There is a sufficiently large number of buyers whose demand is relatively inelastic. (Were the company to set a low price initially, it would forego the potential premium from this segment of the market.)
2. The unit production and distribution costs of producing a smaller volume are not so much higher that they cancel the advantage of charging what some of the traffic will bear.
3. There is little danger that the high price will stimulate the emergence of rival firms. (Where barriers to entry are high, because of patents, high development costs, raw material control, or high promotion costs, the innovating firm can proceed with relative safety to pursue a market-skimming pricing policy.)[5]

Early cash recovery objective.   Some firms seek to set a price that will lead to a rapid recovery of cash. They may be either strapped for funds or regard the future as too uncertain to justify patient market cultivation.

Satisficing objective.   Some companies describe their pricing objective as the achievement of a satisfactory rate of return. The implication is that, although another price might produce an even larger return over the long run, the firm is satisfied with a return that is conventional for the given level of investment and risk. Target pricing (discussed later in this chapter) is an example of this.

Product line promotion objective.   Some firms seek to set a price that will enhance the sales of the entire line rather than yield a profit on the product by itself. This has often been called loss leader pricing, although if it succeeds in enhancing total profits by increasing sales of the entire line, it should more properly be called profit leader pricing.

The Problem of Multiple Parties

In addition to taking a narrow view of pricing objectives, the theoretical pricing model assumes that the only significant group to consider in the pricing of a product is the firm's customers. But, in reality, several parties have to be considered simultaneously in setting the price.

Intermediate customers.   The firm must think through its pricing not only for its ultimate customers, but for its intermediate customers as well. Some companies in fact set a price for distributors and allow them to set whatever final price they wish. This is done when it is thought that each distributor is in the

---

[5]A high initial price offers two other advantages. First, it leaves room for reducing the price if a mistake has been made; this is always easier than increasing a price if it had been set too low initially. Second, a high price may create an impression of a superior product. A home permanent kit, originally marketed at 39c in dime stores, did not sell, but caught on when it was repriced at $1.98 and marketed through drugstores.

best position to determine the price suited to local conditions and to set it high enough to provide sufficient selling incentive. The disadvantage is that the manufacturer relinquishes control over the final price. The other approach is for the manufacturer to determine the final price and how much of a distributor's margin is necessary to provide sufficient distributor incentive. The distributors must recognize that the important incentive variable is not the difference between the distributor's and final price (the margin), but rather the margin times the sales stimulated by the particular final price.

Rivals. The theoretical pricing model did not consider competitive reactions explicitly. It can be argued that whatever assumption is made about competitive reactions can be incorporated in the shape of the demand function, but this treatment of competitive reaction is too implicit and static. The price set by the manufacturer influences the rate of entry of new rivals and the pricing policies of existing rivals. The traditional demand curve is too summary a way to represent the dynamic reactions and counterreactions occasioned by a pricing policy.

Suppliers. The company's suppliers of materials, funds, and labor also must be considered in setting the price. Many suppliers interpret the product's price as indicating the level of the firm's revenues (and profits) from the product. Labor unions will act as if a high price, or price increase, constitutes grounds for higher wages. Farmers believe they deserve higher cattle prices if retail meat prices are high. The firm's bank often feels uneasy if the firm's price is on the low side. Thus various supplier groups may have to be considered by the firm in setting a price.

Government. Another price-interested party is the government. Under the Robinson-Patman Act, the seller cannot charge different prices to comparable customers unless the price differences are based strictly on cost differences. Under the Miller-Tydings Act, the seller may or may not be able to require retailers to sell his branded product at a uniform list price, depending upon the state laws. Public utilities must justify their rates before regulatory commissions. The steel industry must move cautiously with price increases because of the government's interest in price stability. At various times, pricing in the meat, drug, and heavy equipment industries has been subject to government pressure. The prices of agricultural goods and of imported goods are affected by agricultural and tariff legislation, respectively. And various state and local governmental units pass legislation and rulings affecting the prices that can be set by sellers.

Other company executives. Price is a concern of different parties within the company. The sales manager wants a low price, so that his salesmen can "talk price" to customers. The controller likes to see a price leading to an early payout. The price makes an important difference in copy and media tactics to the advertising manager. The production scheduling manager is interested because the price will affect the rate of sales. These and other executives in the organization can be expected to have strong views on where to set the price.

The Problem of Marketing Mix Interaction

The theoretical pricing model also assumes that other marketing variables are held at some constant level, while the effect of price on sales is being examined. This is evident in the usual treatment of the demand function as a relationship only between quantity demanded (*Q*) and price (*P*). But this begs the whole question of how optimal values can be set on advertising, personal selling, product quality, and other marketing variables before price is set. As emphasized throughout this book, the several marketing variables have to all be considered simultaneously to arrive at the optimal mix. This task is missing or assumed away in the theoretical pricing model.

The Problem of Estimating Demand and Cost Functions

Serious statistical problems handicap the determination of actual demand and cost functions. In the case of a new product, there is no experience upon which to base these estimates. Unless data are available on a similar established product, estimates are likely to take the form of guesses rather than hard facts. Data on established products are usually not much more satisfactory.

Johnston has described the major econometric techniques for estimating cost functions from existing data.[6] Demand functions are more difficult to determine because several of the variables are not quantifiable: they are typically highly intercorrelated; both demand and cost have been shifting during the period; and the random errors tend to be large. Because some of the "independent" variables are also dependent (sales depends on advertising, and advertising depends upon sales), a system of simultaneous equations, rather than a single equation estimate of demand, seems to be required.[7] Finally, even were these hurdles to be overcome, there are always lingering doubts about whether the relationships measured from historical data apply to today's situation.

Since the demand and cost equations are estimated with an unknown degree of error, the criterion of maximizing profits may have to be replaced with the criterion of maximizing *expected* profits (where probability distributions are put on the estimated functions) or the criterion of maximizing the minimum possible gain. In any situation of risk and uncertainty, the pricing executive will want to see how sensitive the theoretically calculated price is to revisions in the estimated data.

METHODS OF PRICE SETTING IN PRACTICE

The fault with the economist's pricing model is not one of illogic but of oversimplification. The pricing models used in practice also for the most part tend

[6] See Jack Johnston, *Statistical Cost Analysis* (New York: McGraw-Hill, Inc., 1960).
[7] See Richard E. Quandt, "Estimating Advertising Effectiveness: Some Pitfalls in Econometric Methods," *Journal of Marketing Research* (May 1964) 51–60.

to be based on a limited view of the pricing problem and opportunities. They tend to emphasize one of the factors, such as cost, demand, or competition, to the neglect of the other factors. Nevertheless, they meet some of the more practical requirements for price determination in the presence of imperfect information and multiple parties. We shall examine cost oriented, demand oriented, and competition oriented pricing.

Cost Oriented Pricing

A great number of firms set their prices largely or even wholly on the basis of their costs. Typically, all costs are included, including a usually arbitrary allocation of overhead made on the basis of expected operating levels.

Markup pricing. The most elementary examples of this are markup pricing and cost-plus pricing. They are similar, in that the price is determined by adding some fixed percentage to the unit cost. Markup pricing is most commonly found in the retail trades (groceries, furniture, clothing, jewelry, and so forth), where the retailer adds predetermined but different markups to various goods he carries. Cost-plus pricing is most often used to describe the pricing of jobs that are nonroutine and difficult to "cost" in advance such as construction and military weapon development.

Markups vary considerably among different goods. Some common markups in department stores are 20 percent for tobacco goods, 28 percent for cameras, 34 percent for books, 41 percent for dresses, 46 percent for costume jewelry, and 50 percent for millinery.[8] In the retail grocery industry, items like coffee, canned milk, and sugar tend to have low average markups, while items like frozen foods, jellies, and some canned products have high average markups. In addition, quite a lot of dispersion is found around the averages. Within the category of frozen foods, for example, one study showed the markups to range from a low of 15 percent to a high of 213 percent.[9]

Many hypotheses have been advanced to explain the variations in markups within selected product groups. Lee E. Preston conducted a detailed study to examine how much of the markup dispersion within common grocery product groups could be explained by three commonly used rules of thumb:

> Markups should vary inversely with unit costs.

[8] *Departmental Mechandising and Operating Results of 1962* (New York: National Retail Merchants Association, 1963), pp. 16, 20, 28. An interesting study of markup pricing practices in a department store was reported by Richard Cyert, James G. March, and Charles G. Moore. They interviewed a shirt buyer about how he set prices for standard, exclusive and import items, on a normal markup basis and in periods of regular sales and markdowns. They designed a computer program which imitated his procedures and tested it on a random sample of 197 invoices. Over 85 percent of the computer program's price predictions were correct to the penny. This demonstrated the highly routinized, rule-bound character of much price decision making in retailing. See R. M. Cyert and J. G. March, *A Behavioral Theory of the Firm* (Englewood Cliffs, N.J.: Prentice-Hall, 1963), pp. 128–148.

[9] See Lee E. Preston, *Profits, Competition, and Rules of Thumb in Retail Food Pricing* (Berkeley, Calif.: University of California Institute of Business and Economic Research, 1963), p. 31.

Markups should vary inversely with turnover.

Markups should be higher and prices lower on reseller's (private) brands than on manufacturer's brands.[10]

Using multiple regression analysis with 5 percent levels of significance, he could only conclude that "some of the . . . rules of thumb were followed to some extent in some of the product groups." In one product group a single rule helped explain 61 percent of the variance in percentage markups, and in two groups a combination of two rules helped explain over 60 percent. Evidently, store managers used at least rough rules of thumb to avoid "getting lost" in a maze of individual pricing decisions. But the principal finding was that a large amount of variation remained unexplained and was probably due to erratic decisions, random factors, and frequently better adaptations to the current market than could be provided by the rules.

Does the use of a rigid customary markup over cost make logical sense in the pricing of products? Generally, no. Any model that ignores current demand elasticity in setting prices is not likely to lead, except by chance, to the achievement of maximum profits, either in the long run or the short run. As demand elasticity changes, as it is likely to do seasonally, cyclically, or over the product life cycle, the optimum markup should also change.[11] If markup remains a rigid percentage of cost, then under ordinary conditions it would not lead to maximum profits.

Under special conditions, however, a rigid markup at the right level may lead to optimum profits. The two conditions are that average (unit) costs must be fairly constant over the range of likely outputs and price elasticity must be fairly constant for different points on the demand curve and over time.[12]

Both conditions—fairly constant costs and fairly constant elasticity—are apt to characterize many retailing situations. This may explain why fairly rigid markups are in widespread use in retailing and why this may not be inconsistent with optimal pricing requirements. In manufacturing, however, it is less likely that the two special conditions obtain; here fixed markup pricing is more difficult to justify on logical grounds. In particular, marginal costs are likely to differ from average costs because of scale economies. When manufacturers set prices on the basis of average costs, they are not likely to arrive at the profit maximizing price.

Still, markup pricing remains popular for a number of reasons. First, there is generally less uncertainty about costs than about demand. By pinning the price

---

[10]Ibid., pp. 29–40.

[11]For example, housing contractors generally price by marking up their estimated costs by some percentage, but they show a willingness to accept a lower percentage when demand falls, as in the winter. In a study of the pricing policies of a sample of eighty-eight small businesses, William Haynes found that most of the firms did not adhere strictly to rigid markups but modified them under different circumstances. See William W. Haynes, *Pricing Decisions in Small Business* (Lexington: University of Kentucky Press, 1962).

[12]See Appendix Mathematical Note 12–1.

to unit costs, the seller simplifies his own pricing task considerably; he does not have to make frequent adjustments as demand conditions change. Second, when all firms in the industry use this pricing approach, their prices are likely to be similar if their costs and markups are similar. Price competition is therefore minimized, which would not be the case if firms paid attention to demand variations when they priced. Third, there is the feeling that most markup pricing is socially fairer to both the buyer and the seller. The seller does not take advantage of the buyer when his demand becomes acute; yet the seller earns a fair return on his investment. Thus the popularity of a cost oriented approach to pricing rests on considerations of administrative simplicity, competitive harmony, and social fairness.

Target pricing. A common cost oriented approach used by manufacturers is known as *target pricing*, in which the firm tries to determine the price that would give it a specified target rate of return on its total costs at an estimated standard volume. This pricing approach has been most closely associated with General Motors, which has publicly stated that it prices its automobiles so as to achieve a long run average rate of return of 15–20 percent on its investment.[13] It is also closely associated with the pricing policies of public utilities, which have a large investment and are constrained by regulatory commissions, in view of their monopoly position to seek a fair rate of return on their costs.

The pricing procedures used in target pricing can be illustrated in terms of the break-even chart in Figure 12-1. Management's first task is to estimate its total costs at various levels of output. The total cost curve is shown rising at a constant rate until capacity is approached. Management's next task is to estimate the percentage of capacity at which it is likely to operate in the coming period.

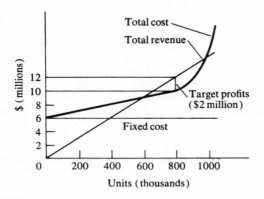

Figure 12-1 Breakeven chart for determining target price

Suppose that the company expects to operate at 80 percent of capacity. This means that it expects to sell 800,000 units if its capacity is 1 million units. The

13Kaplan, et al., *Pricing in Big Business.*, pp. 48–55; 131–135.

total cost of producing this volume, according to Figure 12-1, is $10 million. Management's third task is to specify a target rate of return. If the company aspires for a 20 percent profit over costs, then it would like absolute profits of $2 million. Therefore one point on its total revenue curve will have to be $12 million at a volume of 80 percent of capacity. Another point on the total revenue curve will be $0 at a volume of 0 percent of capacity. The rest of the total revenue curve can be drawn between these two points.

Where does price come in? The slope of the total revenue curve is price. In this example, the slope is $15 a unit. Thus, if the company charges $15 a unit and does manage to sell 800,000 units, it will attain through this price the target rate of return of 20 percent, or $2 million.

Target pricing, however, has a major conceptual flaw. The company used an estimate of sales volume to derive the price, but price is a factor that influences sales volume. A price of $15 may be too high or too low to move 800,000 units. What is missing from the analysis is a demand function, showing how many units the firm could expect to sell at different prices. With an estimate of the demand curve and with the requirement to earn 20 percent on costs, the firm could solve for those prices and volumes that would be compatible with each other. In this way, the firm would avoid setting a price that failed to generate the estimated level of output.

Demand Oriented Pricing

Cost oriented approaches rely on the idea of a standard markup over costs and/or a conventional level of profits. Demand oriented approaches look instead at the intensity of demand. A high price is charged when or where demand is intense, and a low price is charged when or where demand is weak, even though unit costs may be the same in both cases.

Price discrimination. A common form of demand oriented pricing is price discrimination, in which a particular commodity is sold at two or more prices.[14] Price discrimination takes various forms, according to whether the basis is the customer, the product version, the place, or the time.

Pricing that discriminates on a *customer basis* is illustrated in the retail selling of automobiles and major appliances. A car buyer may come into an automobile showroom and pay the list price for the automobile. Ten minutes later, another car buyer may hold out for a lower price and get it.[15] The automobile may be identical in both cases, and the marginal cost of the transaction may be identical; yet the seller has managed to extract a higher price from one buyer than from

[14]A more rigorous definition says that price discrimination is the sale of a particular commodity at two or more prices that do not reflect a proportional difference in marginal costs. See George Stigler, *The Theory of Price*, rev. ed. (New York: The Macmillan Company, 1952), pp. 214–220. For this reason, the common practice of granting price discounts to customers placing larger orders is not treated as a form of price discrimination.

[15]For data on the wide variations in prices paid for the same car, see Allen F. Jung, "Price Variations among Automotive Dalers in Metropolitan Chicago," *Journal of Business* (Jan. 1960) 31–42.

the other. The occurrence of price discrimination among customers may indicate different intensities of demand or variation in consumer knowledge.

Pricing that discriminates on a *product version basis* occurs when slightly different versions of a product are priced differently but not proportionately to their respective marginal costs. An example would be the sale of an electric dishwasher with a $5 formica top for $180 and the same dishwasher with a $10 wooden top for $220. The higher premium for the latter dishwasher reflects not so much the extra production cost as the extra psychological demand. Manufacturers, however, do not always mark up the more costly version at a disproportionately higher price. In many cases the price discrimination is reversed to encourage the buyer to trade up, thereby increasing total dollar sales.

Pricing that discriminates on a *place basis* is also quite common, since place is a form of utility. The pricing of theater seats is a case in point. Although all seats cost virtually the same to install, theater managements price seats differently because of different intensities of demand for the various locations. If a relatively high price is charged for all seats, the front would be filled, but many back seats would be empty. If a relatively low price is charged, people would queue early in order to get the better seats on a first-come, first-served basis. Different prices are charged so that each customer pays close to the maximum of what he is willing to pay. The theater is filled, and theater revenue is maximized.

Pricing that discriminates on a *time basis* also takes many forms. The demand for a product is likely to vary in intensity over the business cycle, over the seasons, by the day, and sometimes by the hour. Public utilities, in their pricing to commercial users, typically vary their prices according to the day (weekend versus weekday) and even the time of day. Not long ago an economist advocated that public transportation services be priced higher at peak hours than at off-hours.[16] Generally speaking the firm whose costs are largely fixed can gain by varying prices according to temporal variations in demand.

To illustrate the profits that lie in price discrimination, we shall first develop the abstract argument and then apply it to a numerical example. Assume a market that consists of two distinct customer segments whose respective demand curves are given by

$$Q_1 = f(P_1)$$
$$Q_2 = f(P_2)$$

(12-1)

The seller who practices price discrimination will enjoy a level of profits that is

[16]This recommendation was not made in the spirit of deriving premiums from those whose demand for public transportation was more crucial—those who travel to work—but rather to try to stimulate housewives and others to shift their trips from rush-hour periods to non-rush-hour periods. In this way, the existing transportation capacity would be utilized more evenly through the day, and there would be less need for equipment to meet peak demand. See William S. Vickrey, "A Proposal for Revising New York's Subway Fare Structure," *Operations Research* (Feb. 1955) 38–68.

the difference between the sum of his revenues from the two markets less his total cost of production:

$$Z = P_1 Q_1 + P_2 Q_2 - c(Q_1 + Q_2)$$ (12-2)

To find the profit maximizing set of prices, Equation 12-2 can be differentiated with respect to Q_1 and Q_2 and each derivative is set equal to 0:[17]

$$\frac{\partial Z}{\partial Q_1} = P_1 + Q_1 \frac{\partial P_1}{\partial Q_1} - c = 0$$

$$\frac{\partial Z}{\partial Q_2} = P_2 + Q_2 \frac{\partial P_2}{\partial Q_2} - c = 0$$ (12-3)

These two conditions can be rewritten and combined:

$$P_1\left(1 + \frac{Q_1}{P_1} \frac{\partial P_1}{\partial Q_1}\right) = P_2\left(1 + \frac{Q_2}{P_2} \frac{\partial P_2}{\partial Q_2}\right) = c$$ (12-4)

The last term in Equation 12-4 represents the marginal cost of the total output. The first two terms represent marginal revenues.
Since $R = PQ$ by definition,

$$\frac{dR}{dQ} = P + Q \frac{dP}{dQ} = P\left(1 + \frac{Q}{P} \frac{dP}{dQ}\right) = \text{marginal revenue}$$ (12-5)

Thus Equation 12-4 states that a necessary condition for profit maximization is that the marginal revenue in each market must be equal to each other and to the marginal cost of the total output.[18] Otherwise the seller could increase his total revenue without affecting his total cost by shifting sales to the market showing the higher marginal revenue. To determine the prices that the seller should set in each market, we recall the following definition of price elasticity:

$$e = -\frac{P}{Q} \frac{dQ}{dP}$$ (12-6)

If we substitute Equation 12-6 into Equation 12-4, we obtain

$$P_1\left(1 - \frac{1}{e_1}\right) = P_2\left(1 - \frac{1}{e_2}\right) = c$$ (12-7)

and therefore

$$\frac{P_1}{P_2} = \frac{1 - 1/e_2}{1 - 1/e_1}$$ (12-8)

[17]Usually Equation 12-2 would be differentiated with respect to P_1 and P_2. Here it is differentiated in terms of Q_1 and Q_2 to permit discussion of the results in terms of marginal revenues, costs, and profits. It does not matter to the results whether the demand equations are of the form $Q = f(P)$ or $P = g(Q)$.

[18]A sufficient condition for price maximization requires that the marginal revenue in each market must be increasing less rapidly than the marginal cost for the output as a whole. An algebraic discussion is found in James M. Henderson and Richard E. Quandt, *Microeconomic Theory* (New York: McGraw-Hill, Inc., 1958), 171.

As long as the price elasticities differ in the two markets, the seller can maximize profits by charging different prices. His price should be higher in the market segment with the lower demand elasticity.

To illustrate this, suppose that the seller faces two distinct market segments and the demand equations along with the total cost equation are as follows:

$$Q_1 = 400 - 2P_1 \qquad Q_2 = 150 - .5P_2$$

or

$$P_1 = 200 - .5Q_1 \qquad P_2 = 300 - 2Q_2$$

and

$$R_1 = 200Q_1 - .5Q_1{}^2 \qquad R_2 = 300Q_2 - 2Q_2{}^2$$

and

$$C = 10,000 + 20\,(Q_1 + Q_2)$$

Following Equation 12-4 for a profit maximum, we find

$$200 - Q_1 = 300 - 4Q_2 = 20$$

Solving for Q_1 and Q_2 and substituting the outputs into the demand, profit, and elasticity equations, we get

$$
\begin{array}{lll}
Q_1 = 180 & P_1 = 110 & e_1 = 1.22 \\
Q_2 = 70 & P_2 = 160 & e_2 = 1.14 \\
Z = 16,000 & &
\end{array}
$$

If the seller chooses to charge a single price to the whole market instead of varying prices to the market segments, he cannot realize as much as 16,000 in profits. He would have to set the single price according to the aggregate demand curve, which is

$$Q = Q_1 + Q_2 = 400 - 2P_1 + 150 - .5P_2 = 550 - 2.5P$$

The optimal price and profits under a uniform price would be

$$
\begin{aligned}
Z &= PQ - C \\
Z &= P(550 - 2.5P) - [10,000 + 20(550 - 2.5P)] \\
Z &= -21,000 + 600P - 2.5P^2 \\
\frac{dZ}{dP} &= 600 - 5P = 0
\end{aligned}
$$

Therefore

$$
\begin{aligned}
P &= 120 \\
Z &= 15,000
\end{aligned}
$$

Consequently, price discrimination allows the seller to realize 1000 extra dollars over charging a single price.

Sellers will then face a strong temptation to set different prices in different markets to take advantage of varying demand intensities. Whether they practice price discrimination in fact depends on certain conditions holding true.[19] First, the market must be segmentable, and the segments must show different intensities of demand. Second, there should be no chance that the members of the segment paying the lower price could turn around and resell the product to the segment paying the higher price. Third, there should be little chance that competitors will undersell the firm in the segment being charged the higher price. Fourth, the cost of segmenting and policing the market should not exceed the extra revenue derived from price discrimination. Fifth, price discrimination would have to be permissible under the law, a condition that is generally not satisfied. Finally, there should be little chance that the higher paying customers will be alienated and react negatively to the company in the long run.

Competition Oriented Pricing

When a company sets its prices chiefly on the basis of what its competitors are charging, its pricing policy can be described as competition oriented. It is not necessary to charge the same price as competition, although this is a major example of this policy. The competition oriented pricing firm may seek to keep its prices lower or higher than competition by a certain percentage. The distinguishing characteristic is that it does *not* seek to maintain a rigid relation between its price and its own costs or demand. Its own costs or demand may change, but the firm maintains its price because competitors maintain their prices. Conversely, the same firm will change its prices when competitors change theirs, even if its own costs or demand have not altered.

Going-rate Pricing The most popular type of competition oriented pricing occurs when a firm tries to keep its price at the average level charged by the industry. Called *going-rate* or *imitative pricing*, it is popular for several reasons. Where costs are difficult to measure, it is felt that the going price represents the collective wisdom of the industry concerning the price that would yield a fair return. It is also felt that conforming to a going price would be least disruptive of industry harmony. The difficulty of knowing how buyers and competitors would react to price differentials is still another reason for this pricing.

Going-rate pricing primarily characterizes pricing practice in homogeneous product markets, although the market structure itself may vary from pure competition to pure oligopoly. The firm selling a homogeneous product in a *purely competitive market* has actually very little choice about the setting of its price. There is apt to be a market-determined price for the product, which is not established by any single firm or clique of firms but through the collective interaction of a multitude of knowledgeable buyers and sellers. The firm daring to charge more than the going rate would attract virtually no customers. The firm need not charge less because it can dispose of its entire output at the going rate. Thus, under highly competitive conditions in a homogeneous product market (e.g., food, raw materials, and textiles) the firm really has no pricing decision to make. In fact, it hardly has any significant marketing decisions to

[19]See Stigler, *The Theory of Price*, pp. 215ff.

make. The major challenge facing such a firm is good cost control. Since promotion and personal selling are not in the picture, the major marketing costs arise in physical distribution, and this is where cost efficiency may be critical.

In *pure oligopoly*, in which a few large firms dominate the industry, the firm also tends to charge the same price as competition, although for different reasons. Since there are only a few firms, each firm is quite aware of the others' prices, and so are the buyers. A certain grade of steel is likely to possess the same quality whether it is produced by Inland or Bethlehem, and so the slightest price difference would favor the lower-price firm unless service or contractual relationships are sufficient to overcome this. The observed lack of price competition in these industries has been explained on the basis of the individual oligopolist's demand curve's having a kink in it at the level of the present prices. The demand curve tends to be elastic above the kink because other firms are not likely to follow a raise in prices; the demand curve tends to be inelastic below the kink because other firms are likely to follow a price cut. An oligopolist can gain little by raising his price when demand is elastic or lowering his price when demand is inelastic; this is believed to explain much of the price timidity in these markets.

This does not mean that the going price in an oligopoly market will be perpetuated indefinitely. It cannot, since industry costs and demand change over time. Usually, the industry takes collective action to raise the price, or in rarer cases, to lower the price. This is not done through official channels, for that would be illegal. Typically, one firm assumes the role of price leader. The others follow any change in price by the leader. Of the twelve general price increases in the steel industry between World War II and 1960, United States Steel led in eleven cases, thus maintaining the position of price leader that began in the days of Judge Gary.[20] Occasionally, the pattern of leadership is more diffused; of thirteen price increases in the aluminum industry between 1950 and 1958, Alcoa led in nine, Kaiser in two, and Reynolds and Aluminium Limited in one apiece.[21]

In markets characterized by *product differentiation*, the individual firm has more latitude in its price decision. Product differences, whether in styling, quality, or functional features, serve to desensitize the buyer to existing price differentials.[22] Firms try to establish themselves in a pricing zone with respect to their competitors, assuming the role of either a high-price firm, a medium-price firm, or a low-price firm. Their product and marketing program are made compatible with this chosen pricing zone, or vice versa. They respond to competitive changes in price to maintain their pricing zone.

COMPETITIVE BIDDING MODELS

Many of the critical issues in setting prices are highlighted in the situation known as competitive bidding. Competitive bidding is an extremely common method of

[20]See Leonard W. Weiss, *Economics and American Industry* (New York: John Wiley & Sons, Inc., 1961), p. 294.

[21]Ibid., pp. 211–212.

[22]Other factors that desensitize buyers to price differentials are differences in personal selling, service, and buyer information. See Richard D. Sampson, "Sense and Sensitivity in Pricing," *Harvard Business Review* (Nov.–Dec. 1964) 99–105.

doing business. Many manufacturers and service organizations selling to the Defense Department, municipal governments, original equipment producers, and so forth, must bid against others for the work, the contract usually going to the lowest bidder. The seller must carefully think through two issues regarding each bidding opportunity: should he bid at all (the problem of bidding); and if so, what bid should he make (the bidding problem)?

The problem of whether to bid at all may arise for a number of reasons. Sometimes the company is working near capacity and cannot take on more work. This is not an airtight argument against bidding because the company may find it advantageous to bid very high and, if it gets the job, there would be enough profit to justify expanding capacity. Sometimes the cost of preparing a bid in relation to the expected revenue may be prohibitive. Consider the work that must go into preparing the bid for the military contract for a new plane. If the cost of this preparation is high in relation to either the value of the contract or the probability of getting it, or both, the supplier might decide to bypass this opportunity.

If the supplier decides to make a bid on a particular job, he must search for a price that is somewhere above his costs but below competitors' bids.[23] The higher the seller sets his price above his costs, the greater the conditional profit but the smaller the probability of getting the contract. These considerations have been formalized in a simple model which leads to bids that are calculated to maximize the company's expected profits.[24] The expected profit in a potential bid is the product of the probability of getting the contract and the estimated profit on the contract, that is,

$$E(Z_P) = f(P)(P - C) \qquad (12\text{-}9)$$

where $E(Z_P)$ = expected profit with a bid of P

$\qquad f(P)$ = probability of winning the contract with a bid of P

$\qquad P$ = bid price

$\qquad C$ = estimated cost of fulfilling the contract[25]

Each price the company could bid is associated with a certain probability of winning the contract; one logical criterion for pricing is for the company to choose the expected profit maximizing price.[26] Table 12-1 shows a hypothetical

[23]Under certain circumstances, the firm may be willing to set a price below its costs. In one case the company is anxious to get the contract in order to keep the plant busy, rather than discharge long term employes; in another case the company wants *a chance to work with an important buyer to get "its foot in the door."*

[24]C. W. Churchman, R. L. Ackoff, and E. L. Arnoff, *Introduction to Operations Research* (New York: John Wiley & Sons, Inc., 1957), 559–573.

[25]If the company is not good at estimating actual costs, the formula should be modified by the distribution of true cost as a fraction of estimated cost. See ibid., pp. 566–567.

[26]The use of the expected profit criterion makes sense for the large firm that makes many bids and is not dependent on winning any particular contract. In playing the odds, it should achieve maximum profit in the long run. The firm that bids only occasionally and/or may need a particular contract badly will probably not find it advantageous to use the expected profit criterion. The criterion, for example, does not distinguish between a $1000 profit with a .10 probability and a $125 profit with an .80 probability. Yet the firm that wants to keep production going is likely to prefer the second contract to the first. In other words, the dollar value of expected profits may not reflect the utility value.

situation consisting of four alternative bid levels and the associated probabilities and profits. In this example, the firm will be tempted to bid $10,000 because its associated expected profit is highest, $216.

Table 12-1 Effect of Different Bids on Expected Profit

Company's bid	Company's profit	Probability of getting award with this bid (assumed)	Expected profit
$ 9,500	$ 100	.81	$ 81
10,000	600	.36	216
10,500	1,100	.09	99
11,000	1,600	.01	16

The chief problem in using this formal bidding model is guessing the probability of getting the contract at various bidding levels. The probability of getting the contract, where price is the buyer's only concern, is the probability of submitting a lower bid than all the other competitors. The probability of submitting the lowest bid is the joint probability that the company's bid is lower than each competitor's bid (assuming competitors' bids are independently formed):

$$f(P) = f_1(P)f_2(P)\ldots f_j(P)\ldots f_n(P) \tag{12-10}$$

where $f_j(P)$ = probability that a bid of P is lower than competitor j's bid

Thus for each price the company might bid, the company estimates the probability of each competitor's bid being higher. Let us reason this out for a hypothetical competitor. The competitor forms his bid by marking up his cost. The company therefore has to estimate the competitor's cost. But generally this information is not available. As a next best thing, the company can assume that the competitor's cost in each of several past bidding situations was similar to the company's costs, the latter being known. Then one recourse for the company is to study the distribution of the ratio of the competitor's past bids to the company's past costs, that is, the ratio

$$r_j = \frac{P_j}{C} \tag{12-11}$$

where r_j = ratio of competitor j's bid to company cost
P_j = a past bid by competitor j
C = the company's cost at the time of the competitor's past bid

The ratios for several past bids of a competitor form a distribution. Distributions for three hypothetical competitors A, B, and C are shown in Figure 12-2. If these past distributions can be assumed to characterize the potential bidding behavior of the three competitors, which is the best assumption to make in the absence of additional information, then the company can proceed to estimate the probability of winning the contract for any bid it is thinking of setting in relation to its estimated cost of fulfilling the contract, that is, P/C. For the particular bid P/C shown in Figure 12-2, the probability of winning the contract is given by the *product* of the shaded areas to the right of r_j in the three distributions. These shaded areas represent the probabilities called for in Equation 12-10. In this way, the probability of winning with any company bid can be found and used in Equation 12-9 as a step in finding the profit maximizing bid.

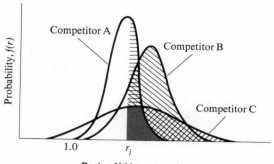

Figure 12-2   Patterns of Past Bidding Behavior

Source: Churchman, et al., *op. cit.*, p. 568.

The problem is a little more complicated if the company is not sure how many competitors will submit bids in the new situation. In this case, the company can form a bidding distribution for an "average" bidder, using all the previous ratios of competitors' bids to company costs. Then the probability that a bid P will be lower than the one submitted by an average bidder equals

$$f^1(P) = \int_{P/C}^{\infty} f^1(r)\, dr \tag{12-12}$$

where $f^1(r)$ = the probability that a bid r will be lower than one average bidder

The probability of submitting a bid lower than those of k average bidders is

$$f^k(P) = \left[\int_{P/C}^{\infty} f^1(r)\, dr \right]^k \tag{12-13}$$

The last required step is to find the probability distribution that there will be k competitors submitting bids. It is possible that the number of bidders correlate with the size of the contract or some other aspect of the bidding situation. Using available data, a gamma distribution or a Poisson distribution may be tried to see whether it gives a good fit to past data on the distribution of the number of bidders. Suppose a distribution $g(k)$ is found that describes well the past number of bidders. Then the probability that a company bid of P will be the lowest bid, when there is a probabilistic number of bidders, is given by

$$f_L(P) = \sum_{k=0}^{\infty} \left\{ g(k) \left[\int_{P/C}^{\infty} f^1(r) \, dr \right]^k \right\} \qquad (12\text{-}14)$$

This formula is used to generate the probabilities of winning a contract with any price P. These probabilities are used in the basic Equation 12-9 for determining expected profit.

Up to now, the assumption was made that the company has adequate past information on the bidding behavior of all conceivable competitors and is satisfied, using these historical data to arrive at its own bid in the current situation. Realistically, the company may be missing an adequate past history for certain competitors. In this case, management will have to develop a sub-jective probability distribution for r for each potential competitor, based on whatever information is available. Furthermore, the new situation may have factors in it which lead the company to believe that competitors may depart from their past pattern of bidding activity. In this case, management will again want to replace historical probability distributions with ones that more accur-ately reflect its subjective expectations.

The model requires further modifications to meet special circumstances that may be present in the competitive bidding situation. One circumstance is one in which the company is able to bid on several contracts at the same time, although it hopes to win only a fraction of them either because of limited resources or government restrictions on the number of contracts that any one company can obtain. In this situation the company will not simply submit the optimal bid as determined for each contract individually but modify the bids so as to maximize the total expected profit on its bids.[27] Another circumstance is that in which the company expects a sequence of opportunities to open up, one at a time and of different values, and where it cannot afford to win all the contracts because of limited resources. Here the company must decide when to bid and how much. Clearly, the availability of further opportunities will influence the company's bid in a particular case. Still another circumstance that will modify the bid occurs when the buyer is known to take other factors into consideration beside the bid such as the bidder's reputation for reliability, service, quality, proximity, past relations with buyer, and so forth. In this situation, a supplier with a good reputation may be expected to set a bid higher than his competitors by the amount of superior reputation he enjoys.[28]

Competitive bidding situations have been analyzed in a variety of mathe-matical ways, in addition to the model described here. Game theory has been used as a mode of analysis in those cases in which the company has no idea of the probability distribution of the possible bids by competitors and chooses to

[27]See footnote 24, pp. 571–573 for an illustration.
[28]See Kenneth Simmonds, "Competitive Bidding: Deciding the Best Combination of Non-Price Features," *Operational Research Quarterly* (Mar. 1968) 5–14.

bid on the basis of a maximin criterion.[29] In other situations, Bayesian decision theory has been used as a means of assessing the expected value of perfect information to a player seeking information about the value of the contract or a competitor's likely bid.[30] Payoff tables have been extensively used by Edelman of RCA to array the payoffs of each possible RCA bid against possible bids by each competitor as a prelude to determining a best bid.[31] In general, each company that does competitive bidding faces particular variables that will require adaptations of the models reviewed here.

INITIATING AND REACTING TO PRICE CHANGES

The task of pricing is not over when the company sets its prices. Circumstances are certain to change and require a reconsideration of the best price. The firm may want to give thought to a *price reduction* in order to stimulate demand, to take advantage of lower costs, or to shake out weaker competitors. Or it may want to consider a *price increase* in order to take advantage of tight demand or to pass on higher costs. Or competition may have initiated a price change calling for some reaction by the company. This section will examine various price decision models of assistance to the company in initiating or reacting to price changes.

Initiating Price Changes

The company that is planning to initiate a price change must carefully weigh the reaction of buyers, competitors, distributors, suppliers, and possibly government to its move. The decision maker must somehow integrate his expectations and uncertainties of their responses into a logical analysis for information gathering and decision making. The use of *decision tree analysis* suggests itself as a natural vehicle for model building in this area. It only requires a willingness of the executives to place subjective probabilities over various uncertain occurrences, so that the problem can be treated in expected value terms. It also has the advantage of being highly flexible for the modeling of complex event structures.

We shall describe an actual use of decision tree analysis by a company that wanted to evaluate the effect of several pricing alternatives it faced. The company, Everclear Plastics (name is fictional), had been selling a plastic substance called Kromel to industrial users for several years and enjoyed 40 percent of the

---

[29]See H. J. Griesmer and M. Shubik, "Toward a Study of Bidding Processes I, II, III," *Naval Research Logistics Quarterly*, 10, nos. 1, 2, and 3 (1963).

[30]See I. H. Lavalle, "A Bayesian Approach to an Individual Player's Choice of Bid in Competitive Sealed Auctions," *Management Science* (Mar. 1967) 584–597.

[31]Franz Edelman, "Art and Science of Competitive Bidding," *Harvard Business Review* (July–Aug.) 1965, 53–66. Edelman conducted a test in which he compared seven bids generated by his model against the bids suggested by executives without the model. In all seven cases, the bids produced by the model were better than those produced without the model; they were all under the lowest competitive bid (average rate, 2 percent).

market.[32] The management became worried about whether its current price of $1 per pound could be maintained for much longer. The main source of concern was the rapid buildup of capacity by its three competitors and the possible attraction of further competitors by the present price. Management saw the key to the problem of possible oversupply to be further market expansion. The key area for market expansion lay in the original equipment auto market that was closely held by a substitute plastic product called Verlon that was produced by six firms. This substitute product was not as good, but it was priced lower. Management saw a price reduction as a possible means to displace Verlon in the original equipment auto market. If it could penetrate this segment, there was a good chance it could also penetrate three other segments that had resisted the displacement.

The first task was to develop a decision structure for the problem in which all components would be related. This meant defining the objectives, policy alternatives, and key uncertainties. It was decided that the *objective* would be to maximize the cumulative compounded value of future profits over the next five years. Management decided to consider the four *policy alternatives* of maintaining the price at $1 or reducing the price to 93¢, 85¢, and 80¢, respectively. The *key uncertainties* were seen to be in five areas, as shown in Figure 12-3: (0) Following Everclear's choice of a price, (1) the other producers of Kromel would react in one of the four ways with respect to their prices; (2) the Verlon producers could also be expected to react in one of three ways, by standing pat, meeting the reduction halfway, or meeting the reduction fully; (3) as a result of the pricing developments, Kromel may succeed in penetrating the key segment—the original equipment auto market—in one of five future years or never; (4) the original equipment auto market will be penetrated at one of four levels, if penetrated at all; and (5) finally, Kromel may penetrate the other three recalcitrant segments at either a basic predicted rate or a slightly faster one.

The diagram in Figure 12-3 is a "collapsed" version of a full decision tree. A full tree would require repeating each successive event structure at each previous node, and obviously this would call for many pages of diagramming to describe every possible branch. *Each* of the four alternative pricing decisions has 576 ($= 4 \times 3 \times 6 \times 4 \times 2$) possible event sequences.[33] This, then, represents the logical structure of major future possibilities visualized by the decision maker.

The next task is to ascribe a payoff value and a probability to each possible event sequence. The *payoff* associated with a particular event sequence is found by calculating the revenues and costs in the sequence, using a straightforward

[32]The case is described and analyzed by Paul E. Green, "Bayesian Decision Theory in Pricing Strategy," *Journal of Marketing* (Jan. 1963) 5–14. A more detailed version is presented in "Everclear Plastics Company," in Robert D. Buzzell, *Mathematical Models and Marketing Management* (Boston, Mass.: Division of Research, Graduate School of Business Administration, Harvard University, 1964), 112-135.

[33]Actually, there are slightly fewer event sequences because the "never" branch in key uncertainty (3) nullifies the alternatives of key uncertainty (4), and because of the logical inconsistency of some other combinations.

profit formula. The *probability* associated with a particular event sequence is found by finding the joint probability of all the individual events making up the sequence. The real challenge is to secure estimates of the probabilities of the individual events. This was accomplished by asking key sales personnel to place subjective probabilities on the various possible states of the key uncertainties.

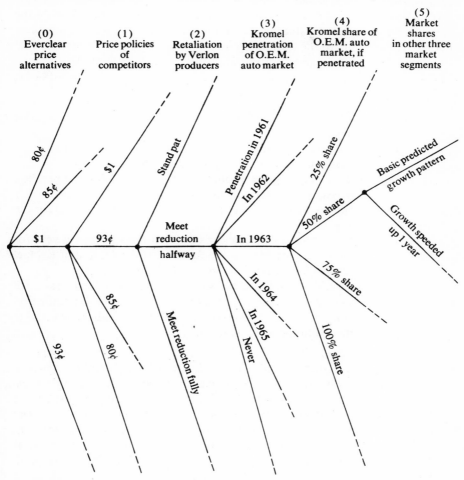

Figure 12-3 Simplified "Tree Diagram" of Possible Chains of Events for Alternative Kromel Price Policies

Source: "Everclear Plastics," *ibid.*, p. 15.

Meetings were held with the sales personnel to explain the concept of expressing judgments in the form of probabilities. For example, one question asked for the probability that the producers of the substitute product would retaliate if the company reduced its price to 93¢ per pound. On the average, the sales personnel felt that there was only a 5 percent probability of a full match, a 60 percent probability of a half match, and a 35 percent probability of no retaliation. They were also asked for probabilities for the 85¢ and 80¢ cases. The sales personnel indicated, as expected, that the probability of retaliation increased the greater the price reduction. Probabilities for the other events were also gathered and averaged for use in the model.

Armed with the payoffs and probabilities, the company could compute the cumulative compounded value of the future earnings stream for each price alternative, according to the formula.

$$E(Z_p) = \sum_{j=1}^{n} p_j \sum_{i=1}^{m} \{(1+r)^{m-1} g[(P_{ij} - C_{ij})(s_{ij} Q_{ij})]\} \qquad (12\text{-}15)$$

where $E(Z_p)$ = expected cumulative compounded net profits under a price strategy P

p_j = probability assigned to the jth outcome ($j = 1, 2, ..., n$)

r = interest rate per annum, expressed decimally

g = ratio of net to gross profits of Everclear's Kromel operation (g is assumed constant in the study)

P_{ij} = Kromel price in $/pound in the ith year ($i = 1, 2, ..., m$) for the jth outcome

C_{ij} = cost in $/pound of Everclear's Kromel resin in the ith year for the jth outcome (this cost is a function of the amount of Kromel pounds sold by Everclear, that is, $C_{ij} = f(m_{ij} Q_{ij})$.

s_{ij} = Everclear's overall market share of Kromel industry sales (in pounds) in the ith year for the jth outcome (expressed decimally)

Q_{ij} = Kromel industry poundage (summed over all four market segments) in the ith year for the jth outcome

A special computer program carried out the calculations and the results indicated that in all cases a price reduction had a higher expected payoff than *status quo* pricing; in fact, a price reduction to 80¢ had the highest expected payoff. To check the sensitivity of these results to the original assumptions, the results were recomputed for alternative assumptions about the rate of market growth (Q_{ij} in Equation 12-15) and the appropriate cost of capital (r in Equation 12-15). It was found that the ranking of the strategies was not affected by a change in these assumptions.

The analysis clearly pointed to the desirability of some price reduction in preference to the status quo. The last step belongs to management to decide on the basis of this analysis, as well as other factors that may have eluded analysis, whether to initiate the price reduction and, if so, by how much. In general, a decision tree analysis enables management to structure the problem in a flexible way and arrive at an evaluation of alternatives based on management's best estimates of the governing critical events. At the same time it uses the criterion of expected monetary value, and management may prefer to see the analysis oriented around one of the other criterion discussed in Chapter 10.

Meeting Price Changes

Here we reverse the problem and ask how can a firm that has just witnessed a price change by a competitor decide on its best course of action?

In some market situations the firm has no choice but to meet a competitor's price change. This is particularly true when the price is cut in a homogeneous product market. Unless the other firms meet the price reduction, most buyers will choose to do business with the lowest-price firm, other things being equal.

When the price is raised by a firm in a homogeneous product market, the other firms may or may not meet it. They will comply if the price increase appears designed to benefit the industry as a whole. But if one firm does not see it that way and thinks that it or the industry would gain more by standing pat on prices, its noncompliance can make the leader and the others rescind any price increases. This happened in 1962 when Inland Steel refused to match the price increases of U.S. Steel and most other steel companies; in a matter of days, prices returned to their former level.

In nonhomogeneous product markets, a firm has more latitude in reacting to a competitor's price change. The essential fact is that buyers choose the seller on the basis of a multiplicity of considerations: service, quality, realiability, and other factors. These factors desensitize many buyers to minor price differences. The reacting firm has a number of options: doing nothing and losing few or many customers, depending upon the level of customer loyalty; meeting the price change partly or fully; countering with modifications of other elements in its marketing mix.

The firm's analysis could take the form of estimating the expected payoffs of alternative possible reactions. In doing this, the answers to the following questions will take on special importance in deciding how to react:

Why did the competitor change his price? Was it to steal the market, to meet changing cost conditions, or to evoke a calculated industry-wide price change to take advantage of total demand?

Is the competitor intending to make his price change temporary or permanent?

What will happen to the company's market share (and profits) if it ignores the price change? Are the other companies going to ignore the price change?

What is the competitor's (and other firms') response likely to be to each possible reaction?

All of these questions enter directly or indirectly in the structuring of objectives, alternatives, and uncertainties, in the gathering of information and in the estimation of payoffs.

An extended analysis of company alternatives is usually not feasible at the time of a price change. The competitor who initiated the price change may have spent considerable time in preparing for this decision, but the company that must react may have only hours or days before some decisive position must be taken. The analysis and information are necessarily below the standard usually

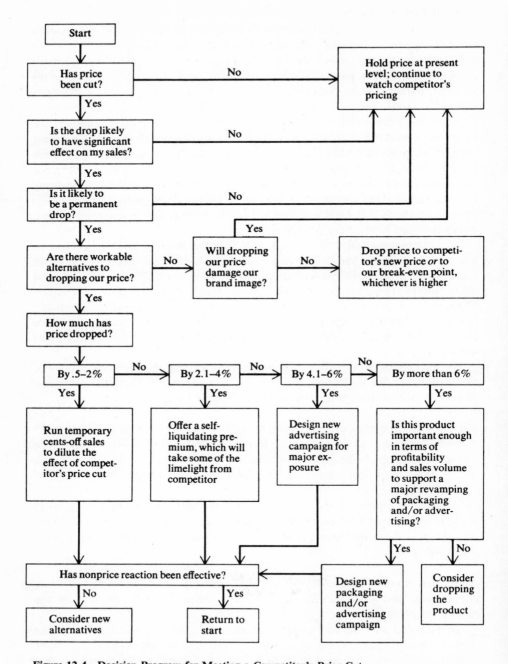

Figure 12-4 Decision Program for Meeting a Competitor's Price Cut
This is adapted and modified from an unpublished paper by Raymond J. Trapp, Northwestern University, 1964.

required for determining such an important decision as a price reaction. About the only way to place such decisions on a surer footing is to anticipate their possible occurrence in advance and to prepare a program for reaction. An example of such a program to meet a possible price cut is shown in Figure 12-4.

If a price cut has occurred, the firm asks a number of questions. First, it asks whether the competitor's price cut is likely to affect the firm's sales significantly *and* be permanent. If *both* conditions are satisfied, the firm will consider some form of reaction. The firm asks whether there are any workable alternatives to dropping price. If not, and if a price reduction would not damage the firm's brand image, it cuts its price to that of the competitor or to its own break-even point, whichever is higher. However, nonprice reactions may appear more attractive to the firm, in which case the particular nonprice reaction is geared to the magnitude of the competitor's price cut; the more substantial the price cut, the more substantial the nonprice reaction. The possibility of dropping the product is even introduced. Provision is made to evaluate the effectiveness of the nonprice reaction; if it appears effective, nothing else is done until the competitor makes a new move.

The reaction program illustrates how a firm might plan in advance to meet the price moves of a competitor. The actual program would have to be more detailed in providing for responses to price increases as well, in outlining the occasions for fractional price matches as well as full price matches, and in defining criteria for judging whether a nonprice reaction is preferable to a price reaction.

Reaction programs for meeting price changes are likely to find their greatest application in industries in which price changes occur with some frequency, where it is important to react quickly. Examples could be found in the meat-packing, lumber, and retail gasoline industries. A pilot study was conducted in one such industry by Morgenroth to determine whether the decision maker's thought processes in reacting to price changes could be spelled out in the form of a computer program.[34] Although Morgenroth did not identify the industrial situation, it is not unlike the case of price wars in the retail gasoline industry, where a major oil producer periodically confronts a price cut by another producer and must quickly decide whether to match the reduction or maintain his price.

This simulation began as a case study in 1959 and extended over three years of observation, interviewing, and analysis of executive decision behavior. Morgenroth followed a research design that involved four basic steps. First, he interviewed company executives and carefully probed for implicit models of decision making—the executives were asked to try to identify the variables relevant to pricing decisions and then to verbalize how these variables were mentally combined as the basis for a pricing decision. Flow charts were used to

[34]William M. Morgenroth, "A Method for Understanding Price Determinants," *Journal of Marketing Research* (Aug. 1964) 17–26; and John A. Howard and William M. Morgenroth, "Information Processing Model of Executive Decisions," *Management Science* (Mar. 1968) 416–428.

turn the interview data into working models of executive behavior, which in turn were shown to executives for further comment.

Second, he observed actual executive decision making. This observation provided a check for the consistency between an executive's description of his information processing and the actual availability of this information. Interest was focused at this stage on the company's communication channels.

Third, he analyzed company records of past pricing decisions and reviewed hypotheses based on these data with the executive group.

Fourth, the flow charts were used to test decision paradigms of other executives at the same level but in different regions of the country against recorded decision behavior. These four steps provided Morgenroth with a comprehensive procedure of search and feedback to represent pricing decision processes in a dynamic simulation.

The industry is made up of a few large "major firms" and several quite small "private branders." A key element in the model is the concept of a "reference marketer," the firm that has the largest share of a particular market. All firms monitor the reference marketer's pricing activity and react to it, although the reference marketer may not be the price leader if he is perceived as failing to interpret market conditions correctly. For example, a given company quickly follows a price decrease by the reference marketer but follows a price increase more slowly. These timing dynamics, together with differing pricing behavior among "majors" and "private branders," sets off the Morgenroth simulation from price decision models.

Figure 12-5 depicts a sequential binary choice process triggered by an initial price change. It can be interpreted as follows: The company first monitors the reference marketer's wholesale price in each local market at time t (box 1). If the price is not the same as the company's price, the next step is to determine whether it has increased or decreased (box 3). The direction of the price change is very important as upward price moves are much simpler than downward price moves. The rationale for this asymmetry is economic. Since the market is such that total purchases are relatively unaffected by prices changes, a mutual price rise is always profitable. Competitive reactions to price declines vary according to the company's strength in the market (as evidenced by its market share) and location of the affected market. Thus a price increase results in only three steps (boxes 4, 6, and 7) before a decision is made, while a price decrease could require up to eight steps (boxes 8–15).

The timing of price changes is also considered with a given company *delaying* more in following the reference marketer up the scale than in following him down. While several reasons are put forth for this behavior, our concern here is with the general nature of the model; so, it is sufficient to account for only the general direction and timing mechanisms.

Morgenroth tested his model on two levels. A random sample of decisions was taken from company records of the division managed by the primary executive under study. These sample data served as input to the simulation model. The output was a series of simulated pricing decisions; only the *direction* of a price change was considered. By comparing the simulated direction indicators with the actual data, Morgenroth found perfect agreement and considered the model to be confirmed by the output test.

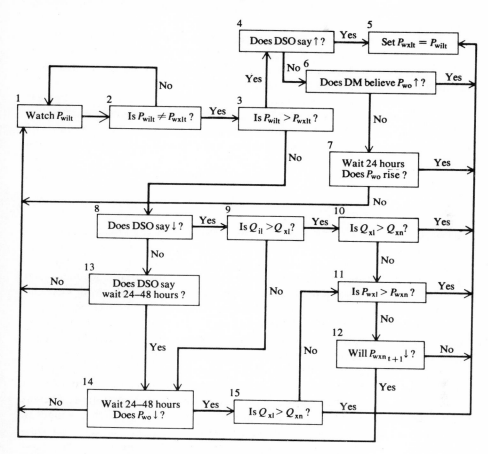

Figure 12-5   Descriptive Model of a Particular Pricing Decision Process

Symbols:
- P = price
- w = wholesale
- x = our company
- o = other major competitors in local market
- i = initiator
- t = time, at present
- Q = quantity, i.e., sales volume in physical terms
- l = local market wherein price change is being considered
- n = nearby market with funnel influences
- DSO = District Sales Office (District Sales Manager)
- ↑ = raise price
- ↓ = drop price
- DM = decision maker

Source: Howard and Morgenroth, *op. cit.*, p. 419.

Further validation was accomplished by taking extensive company data and analyzing the model shown in Figure 12-5 box by box. Here again, Morgenroth found perfect agreement and considered the model to be confirmed by the process test.

A final step in the verification procedure was to review the model with executives of other company divisions. Here both the plausibility of the decision process and the actual decisions were again tested to assure interdivisional comparability. Models such as this one make a contribution in highlighting the specific decision rules and parameters that management is following. The next logical step is to turn the model into an instrument for investigating policy changes that might improve company performance. This was not done by Morgenroth but remains an unexploited major value of constructing such models.

PRODUCT LINE PRICING

The problem of setting a price or changing a price on an individual product has been examined. Some of the preceding logic must be modified when the product is a member of a product line. In the latter case, the true quest is for a set of mutual prices that maximizes the profits of the line. This quest is made difficult because various company products are interrelated in demand and/or cost and are subject to different degrees of competition. The effects of these considerations were reviewed in Chapter 7, where the whole question of product line management was taken up. Here we shall concentrate strictly on the product line pricing issue and illustrate it with three examples of actual situations that were modeled.

The first situation was investigated by Urban and involved a company that produced three related product lines in a frequently purchased food product class.[35] Its brand in product group 1 was new and without competition; whereas its brands in product groups 2 and 3 faced direct competitors. Urban sought to determine a demand equation for the company's brand in each product class that included company and competitor *prices* and *shelf facings* as the major factors affecting sales. Urban's equation for each of the brands (illustrated here for brand 1) had the form:

$$Q_1 = a_1 P_1{}^{e_{11P}} F_1{}^{e_{11F}} P_2{}^{e_{12P}} F_2{}^{e_{12F}} P_3{}^{e_{13P}} F_3{}^{e_{13F}} S_1 \qquad (12\text{-}16)$$

where
Q_1 = company brand sales of product 1
a_1 = constant
P_i = average industry price for product i
F_i = industry total number of package facings on the store shelf for product i
e_{11P}, e_{11F} = industry price and shelf facing elasticities for product 1

[35]Glen L. Urban, "A Mathematical Modeling Approach to Product Line Decisions," *Journal of Marketing Research* (Feb. 1969) 40–47.

$$\left.\begin{array}{l} e_{12P}, e_{12F} \\ e_{13P}, e_{13F} \end{array}\right\} = \begin{array}{l} \text{cross price and cross facings elasticities, showing the effect} \\ = \text{of prices and facings of products 2 and 3 on sales of} \end{array}$$

product 1. For example, e_{12P} represents the proportional change in the quantity of product 1 that results from a percent change in the industry price of product 2, that is,

$$e_{12P} = (\partial Q_1/Q_1)/(\partial P_2/P_2)$$

s_1 = our brand share of product 1

Using data gathered from 100 test market store audits of the sales, prices, and facings for all brands in the three product classes, Urban carried out linear regression on the logs of the data and estimated an equation for the company's brand in each product group. The measured elasticities for the company brand in the first product group are

$$Q_1 = a_1 P_1^{-3.52} F_1^{-.07} P_2^{-1.33} F_2^{.94} P_3^{-.22} F_3^{-.30} s_i \qquad (12\text{-}17)$$

The price elasticities show that, if average industry prices in the other two related product groups decline, sales of the company brand in product group 1 will fall, which means products 2 and 3 are *substitutes* for product 1. However, more industry facing prominence given to product group 2 will increase the sales of the company brand in product group 1, whereas the opposite is true for industry facings of product group 3. This equation had an overall R^2 of .45 and most, though not all elasticities, were significant at the 5 percent level.

Urban analyzed the elasticities and cross elasticities for all three equations and concluded that the company's brands were *substitutes* for the competitors' brands in each product class but *complements* to each other. This means that each company brand fortified the sales of its brands, rather than take sales away from them.

Urban then turned to the task of finding optimal prices and facings for the company's three brands. This called for developing a total profit equation of the form

$$Z = \sum_{i=1}^{3} (P_i Q_i - C_i) \qquad (12\text{-}18)$$

in which the fitted demand equation would be substituted as well as the costs, including the cost of obtaining various facing levels. Optimization then requires differentiating this equation with respect to each decision variable (P_1, P_2, P_3, F_1, F_2, F_3), setting the partial derivatives equal to zero, and solving them simultaneously, followed by a check on satisfying second order conditions. Unfortunately, the resulting partial derivative equations were too difficult to solve simultaneously, so that Urban resorted to an interactive on-line search routine in the form of a conversational computer program. This routine estimated company profits for different incremental combinations of price and facing levels. This search routine led to a substantially preferred set of prices and facings for which profits would be 50 percent higher than with management's normal settings. Thus Urban arrived at a method of measuring the effect and interaction of various marketing mix elements on various products in a company's line and a way of using the computer to find improved price and shelf facing levels.

A somewhat different type of product line pricing problem is faced by the seller who introduces a new product that will partially or wholly displace a former product. An example of this in the consumer field is that of a manufacturer of a high priced brand whose sales are falling who decides to introduce a low priced brand, knowing that the new brand will consume some of its sales. An example in the industrial field is: although a manufacturer introduces an equivalent but less expensive version of his product, the buyers are held back from immediate conversion by a heavy one-time investment cost of conversion. In these and other cases, the manufacturer must decide what price to put on the new product, whether to change the price of the old product, and the optimal timing of these steps. His pricing policies will affect the rate of returned merchandise, in the consumer case, or the rate of conversion to the new product in the industrial case. His objective is to find the set of prices that will maximize his total profits over a specified time horizon.

Hess has developed simple models for these two situations to guide the manufacturer's pricing policies.[36] In the consumer case, the seller had just introduced Modern, a slightly modified version of its existing product, Ancient. Modern was priced lower to be competitive and it was expected to eventually replace Ancient in the product line. Since Ancient sold at a substantially higher price, the company expected retailers and wholesalers to return substantial quantities of Ancient for credit. The company wanted to consider possible policies to minimize the impact of returns on company profits. Three possible courses of action were identified:

1. Reduce Ancient's price to Modern's price at some time T and compensate the middlemen for their inventory losses with free quantities of Modern.
2. Recall all Ancient remaining in middlemen hands at some time T and compensate them with free quantities of Modern.
3. Do nothing and accept returns of Ancient and credit middlemen at the wholesale price.

Hess proceeded to build an equation showing total profits for the two products under each of the three alternatives. Here we shall illustrate his equation, showing the reasoning he used for evaluating the first alternative. For the first alternative, the profit is (1) the profit generated before the price cut (before T), (2) plus the profit accruing after the price cut (after T), (3) minus the costs of free quantities of Modern given to the middlemen.

[36]Sidney W. Hess, "The Use of Models in Marketing Timing Decisions," *Operations Research* (July–Aug., 1967) 720–737.

1. The profit from time 0 to time T is the profit of selling Modern less the costs of returned Ancient:

$$Z_{0T} = \int_0^T (P' - c_v' - c_f') Q_{mw}' \, dt - \int_0^T (P + c_f - c_s) Q_{wm} \, dt \tag{12-19}$$

where Z_{0T} = profit from time 0 to time T
P' = wholesale price of Modern
c_v' = variable manufacturing cost of Modern
c_f' = freight cost for Modern
Q_{mw}' = sales per month of Modern to wholesalers at time t
P = wholesale price of Ancient
c_f = freight cost for Ancient
c_s = salvage value of returned Ancient
Q_{wm} = amount of Ancient returned to manufacturer per month at time t

2. The profit after time T is the profit on net sales, that is, those achievable without free goods, less those lost because of the injection of free goods:

$$Z_{T\infty} = (P' - c_v' - c_f') \left\{ \int_T^\infty Q_{mw}' \, dt - \beta \alpha [I_w(T) + I_r(T)] \right\} \tag{12-20}$$

where $Z_{T\infty}$ = profit from time T forward
β = the fraction of free goods given to middlemen that "take away" future sales of Modern
α = units of free Modern to be given per unit of Ancient to compensate middlemen for inventory value change
$I_w(T)$ = inventories of Ancient at wholesale at time T
$I_r(T)$ = inventories of Ancient at retail at time T

3. The cost of the free Modern given to middlemen is represented by

$$C = (c_v' + c_f') \alpha [I_w(T) + I_r(T)] \tag{12-21}$$

Total profits are the sum of Equations 12-19 and 12-20 less Equation 12-21:

$$Z_{0\infty} = \int_0^\infty (P' - c_v' - c_f') Q_{mw}' \, dt - \int_0^T (P + c_f - c_s) Q_{wm} \, dt$$

$$- \alpha[\beta P' + (1 - \beta)(c_v' + c_f')][I_w(T) + I_r(T)] \tag{12-22}$$

Thus total profits are represented as a function of a single decision variable T, the time when Ancient's price should be cut to Modern's price. Since the first term in Equation 12-22 is independent of T, Hess converts the maximization problem to one of minimizing the last two cost terms. That is, total profits will be maximized when the cost of returns plus the cost of free goods are minimized.

Calculus procedures show the necessary condition for maximum profits to be

$$kQ_{wm}(T) = Q_{rc}(T) \qquad (12\text{-}23)$$

where k = a constant = $-1 + \{(P + c_f - c_s)/\alpha[\beta P' + (1 - \beta)(c_v' + c_f')]\}$

Q_{rc} = retail sales of Ancient

and the sufficient condition for maximizing profits to be

$$k\left[\frac{dQ_{wm}(T)}{dT}\right] > \frac{dQ_{rc}(T)}{dT} \qquad (12\text{-}24)$$

According to Equation 12-23, Ancient's price should be dropped to Modern's price when Ancient's sales to consumers equal k times wholesaler returns of Ancient. This equality should normally take place because Ancient's retail sales rate will fall through time, while Ancient's return rate should initially rise through time before falling as inventories are depleted. Still, there is some chance that the curves will not intersect, that is, retail sales may always stay at a higher rate than k times the return rate, in which case Ancient's price should never be cut.

Hess carried out a similar analysis for the second alternative involving recalling all Ancient, except in this case the cost of the free goods is higher. He then examined the data actually available to management; his analysis led him to recommend that the price cut was the superior alternative and it should be implemented approximately ten months after Modern's introduction. This ran counter to management's inclination to reduce Ancient's price immediately upon Modern's introduction. According to Hess' analysis, this would have been the worst time to cut Ancient's price. Management decided to delay the price reduction on the strength of Hess' analysis and use the time to observe actual retail sales and returns as clues to the next step. As it turned out, the delay was good because Modern ended by stimulating the sales of Ancient and returns never materialized.

Hess also analyzed another product line pricing problem in the same company, this time concerning an industrial chemical called Cheap that was replacing an equivalent chemical called Dear. The two chemicals performed equally well, and customers were expected to switch to product Cheap, although they would have to absorb a one-time fixed cost of conversion. In fact, the first five periods were characterized by a linear rate of conversion of product Dear customers to product Cheap. Management was not exactly happy about the rapid rate of conversion because it earned a higher profit margin on product Dear. This led management to consider the possible advantage of changing the price of product Dear to increase the total profits on the product line. Some executives in the company felt that the price of product Dear should be dropped to slow down the rate of conversion to product Cheap, thus prolonging the profits, albeit at a lower rate, of product Dear. Other company executives felt that the price of product Dear should be increased (assuming competitors would follow this price increase) in order to earn a higher premium on product Dear before it disappeared entirely. The critical issue is how the rate of conversion is affected by the price differential between the products Cheap and Dear. Hess examined the results under the assumption that the rate of conversion was proportional to either the price differential, its square, or its cube. He found that in all cases profits were higher when the price of product Dear was *increased*. He consequently recommended increasing the price of product Dear if management believed that the competitors would follow the price increase. It turned out that management had come to the same conclusion, albeit intuitively, and implemented the price increase.

Both of Hess' models show how the marketing analyst can expect to come across many real problems for which there are no ready-made marketing models, but for which he can synthesize an appropriate model from the various tools he has already acquired for expressing marketing processes and seeking optimal solutions.

SUMMARY

While nonprice factors continue to grow in importance in the modern marketing process, price remains an important element and especially challenging in certain types of situations.

In setting a price for the first time, a firm can draw guidance from the theoretical pricing model of the economists. The model indicates how the firm can find a short run profit maximizing price when estimates of demand and cost are available. However, the model leaves out several factors that must be considered in actual pricing situations such as the presence of other objectives, multiple parties, marketing mix interactions, and uncertainties surrounding the estimates of demand and cost. In practice, companies tend to orient their pricing toward either cost (as in markup pricing and target pricing), demand (as in price discrimination), or competition (as in going-rate pricing).

The problem of setting the "correct" price is highlighted in the situation known as competitive bidding. The company seeks to set a price that is above its cost but below the lowest price that competitors might bid. The higher the company's bid, the lower the probability that it will win the contract. One criterion for pricing, therefore, is to estimate the *expected profit* on each alternative bid (that is, the payoff times the probability) and use the bid that maximizes the expected profit. The key data needed by this model is the probability that the company's bid will be lower than competitors' bids. The estimation of this probability could be approached by examining the ratio of competitors' past bids to the company's past costs. If statistical information on past bids is not adequate, management may wish to use subjective estimates of these probabilities and proceed in the same manner. The model can be modified to meet special situations, such as those when a company has a chance to submit several bids and does not want to win them all, when the company has to decide whether to bid on a current job or wait for the next job, and when the buyer considers other factors in addition to price in choosing among vendors.

Pricing is also a problem when circumstances require a company to consider changing its current price. The company must weigh carefully customers' and competitors' reactions, as well as the possible reactions of suppliers, middlemen, and government. Decision trees offer a flexible format for integrating the various considerations affecting the expected profit of different alternatives. Companies also must be prepared to react swiftly to price changes initiated by competitors. Price response programs could be established to guide management's reactions to a price challenge; this was illustrated in two different cases.

Pricing is also a challenging issue when the company's various products have important demand and/or cost interrelationships. The company may wish to develop demand equations for each of the products in its line, showing demand as a function of both company and competitors' variables. Once the elasticities in the separate demand equations are estimated from data, it is possible to determine optimal prices, facings, and so forth, either by analytical solutions when the equations are simple or by numerical search procedures. Product line pricing is also a problem when a company introduces a new product to replace or supplement a previous product and must decide on the prices of the two products. Some simple but elegant models by Hess were described in this connection.

Questions and Problems

1. The Household Appliance Manufacturing Company estimates that sales of its primary product will be about 300,000 units in the coming period. Total costs at this level of sales are expected to be $3,000,000. What price should be charged for the product if the company wishes to realize:
   (a) A 15 percent profit over costs
   (b) A 20 percent profit over costs?

2. A manufacturer sells his product in two distinct markets, A and B. The demand equation associated with each market is:

$$Q_A = 400 - 2P_A$$

$$Q_B = 150 - .5P_B$$

   The firm's total cost equation is:

$$C = 10,000 + 20(Q_A + Q_B)$$

   The current selling price is $120 in both markets. Assuming that the conditions necessary for the successful practice of price discrimination hold true, could the company benefit by charging different prices in markets A and B? If so, what prices should be set in each market?

3. The ABC Plumbing Company is invited to bid for a contract to install the plumbing system in a new apartment building. The company estimates that the cost of installation as specified in the contract will be $10,000. From past experience the company has determined that the probability of winning the contract is:

$$f(P) = e^{-P/10,000}$$

Should the company make a bid? At what price? What is the company's expected profit at this price?

4. The Chemco Corporation currently sells a commercial lubricant product at $1.00 per quart and enjoys a current market share of approximately 30 percent. The company's major competitor sells a similar product of somewhat lower quality for 90c per quart and holds a market share of approximately 65 percent. Chemco management is considering reducing the price of its product to 90c in order to increase its market share. Without such a price change the company's market share is expected to remain unchanged in the coming period. If the price reduction is implemented, the competitor is expected to react in one of two ways: (a) it will maintain its price at 90¢ with probability of .4 or (b) it will lower its price to 81¢ with probability .6. If the competitor maintains its price at 90¢, Chemco's market share will either increase to 40 percent with probability of .7 or to 50 percent with probability of .3. If the competitor reduces its price to 81¢, Chemco's market share is expected to remain unchanged with probability of .8 or to decrease to 25 percent with probability of .2. Use decision tree analysis to determine if Chemco management should implement the price reduction.

CHAPTER 13
Sales Force Decision Models

Marketing planning calls not only for setting product prices and determining the best channels of distribution, but also for estimating the resources needed to promote the company products effectively to actual and potential users. A company's promotional mix consists of a judicious mixture of personal selling, advertising, sales promotion, and public relations. The first two promotional tools are the most important in terms of the resources they consume and the effects they are calculated to have on the buyers. In this chapter, we shall examine decision problems involved in the management of personal selling. The next chapter will examine advertising. The other tools, sales promotion and publicity, will not be specifically discussed in the book, although many of the principles describing personal selling and advertising apply in a straightforward way to these other promotional tools.

Personal selling could describe all efforts by employees or agents of a company to inform personally and persuade actual and potential customers to make purchases from the company. Anyone is a company salesman at the time he is trying to win business for his company; this would include officers of a company and sometimes their wives, company service men, as well as salesmen who are hired to do full-time selling. We shall restrict the term salesmen to describe those who earn their livelihood primarily through selling. Even here, the term covers a broad range of positions in our economy. It includes order takers who sit at a phone and solicit or take phone orders. It includes retail sales personnel who sell merchandise to shoppers. It includes field salesmen who travel to different customers on a regular basis to communicate product information and take orders. It includes men who sell tangible products such as vacuum cleaners, cosmetics, computers, and encyclopedias; and men who sell intangible products such as insurance, banking services, and mutual funds.

This chapter will concentrate on the type of selling known as field selling. Field selling is found in virtually every industry and involves a sales force that travels to actual and potential buyers. The salesmen may all work out of one central office or may be located in different territories, for which they have individual responsibility. The salesmen report to district sales managers who in turn report to regional sales managers who in turn report to a general sales manager.

Sales managers are faced with two basic types of problems, the first of which might be called *sales force administration* and the second, *sales force strategy*. Sales force administration includes the problems of recruiting, selecting, training, assigning, compensating, motivating, and controlling the sales force. This chapter will not deal with these questions except indirectly, because our interest lies in marketing strategy rather than in issues of internal administration. The chapter will deal with sales force strategy, which involves three problems: (1) designing and assigning sales territories, (2) developing optimal calling policies for different types of customers, and (3) setting salesmen quotas and incentives.[1]

DESIGNING AND ASSIGNING SALES TERRITORIES

Consider a company that has just been formed around an important new product discovery and is planning to hire a new sales force of n men to sell the product nationally. The field sales manager will develop policies on recruiting, selecting, training, compensating, and motivating the new men. He will also have the responsibility of dividing the United States into n sales territories to which the men will be assigned. Once these territories are developed, he will hire an appropriate number of regional and district managers based on his ideas of effective span of control.

Designing the Sales Territories

How should the field sales manager proceed to develop the n sales territories? This general problem is faced by virtually all companies, both in circumstances when a sales force is being organized for the first time and when the existing sales territories of a company must be revised because they no longer match the current distribution of demand. There are many ways to develop these

---

[1]The optimal size of the sales force is another sales force strategy decision, but the underlying theory has been treated in Part I of this text. See the example discussed in Chap. 6, pp. 157–160.

territories, and most of them are highly intuitive. We shall describe an approach used by an increasing number of companies.

1.   The first step calls for selecting some standard geographical unit (SGU) on which census information is regularly available. This unit should be smaller than the eventual sales territories that will be formed. In fact, the sales territories will be developed by aggregating a sufficient number of these small geographical unit areas that are adjacent and have certain other characteristics. Examples of candidate geographical areas are U.S. counties, U.S. census enumeration districts, and U.S. ZIP code areas.

2.   It must be possible to estimate the present and future sales potential for each of the SGUs. Sales potential will be defined as the number of units of the product that could be sold with a well-developed marketing effort in the SGU. To estimate sales potential, it is necessary to consider the number, size distribution, and purchasing power of buying units in each SGU. In the case of a consumer product, the sales potential would be related to the number of households and distribution of purchasing power in each SGU. In the case of an industrial product, the sales potential would be related to the number of firms and their buying volumes or potential in each SGU.

3.   Company management must estimate how much sales coverage each SGU requires per year. Consider an SGU with large, medium, and small customers. The company establishes a call norm for each size customer, reflecting the number of hours or calls per year that each size customer should receive. From this information it is easy to compute the yearly number of customer contact hours or calls that adequate coverage of the SGU would require. To this figure should be added an estimate of the number of hours for travel time based on the density of accounts in the SGU. When this is done, the company has a salesman "workload" figure for each SGU.

At this point the field sales manager is in a position to start aggregating SGUs to make up viable, sufficiently sized territories to be assigned to individual salesmen. We shall now make the assumption that the company *considers it highly desirable that territories of equal workloads be established.* This is a widely accepted planning objective in territory design. It means that equally able salesmen should produce comparable sales. In practice, territorial sales will differ even when territory sales potentials have been equated because of differences in the individual abilities of salesmen. Under this principle of territory design, the salesmen are less able to blame a poor sales performance on the territory, instead of their own level of performance.

Once the equal workload principle is accepted for territory design, the next step calls for a calculation of the number of hours the average salesman will have each year for customer contact, travel, and planning. Suppose the typical salesman in this industry works a forty-hour week for fifty weeks a year, or 2000 hours a year.[2] This means he can be assigned a set of several adjacent

_____

[2]The figure in practice may be less because of holidays, other responsibilities, etc. For example, Celanese Plastics uses 1500 man-hours per year as the time required by a salesman for calling and traveling. See M. A. Brice, "The Art of Dividing Sales Territories," *Dun's Review* (May 1967) 43, 93–98.

SGUs that require in total approximately 2000 hours a year to cover adequately. The problem is to put together enough adjacent SGUs to make up 2000-hour workload territories.

This step is usually carried out in an intuitive fashion in which the field manager relies on his personal knowledge of markets. He may choose certain cities whose sheer sales potential make them desirable starting points for building up territories. He then pulls in adjacent SGUs, paying attention to geographical similarity, natural geographical boundaries and barriers, and so forth. This continues until enough adjacent SGUs have been put together to constitute a viable territory.

Recently, a mathematical alternative to this intuitive approach has been proposed in the form of linear programming, particularly the form known as the transportation method. The classic use of the transportation method occurs in the determination of optimal shipment of goods from company supply points to company demand points. In such cases, the transportation method is used to find the shipment pattern that would minimize the cost of supplying the various demand points. From this original use of the method, many other uses followed. The one of direct interest here is the recent application of the transportation method to the problem of Congressional redistricting, and its analogy to the problem of creating equitable sales territories. After a series of Supreme Court decisions requiring the states to realign their voting districts to bring about closer adherence to the "one man, one vote" rule, the states sought an objective method. A few states such as Delaware and Connecticut turned to the use of computer solutions resulting from the transportation method; in a few cases the State Supreme Court accepted the computer solution with minor modifications.

If the transportation method worked to build equitable Congressional districts, it might also serve the purpose of building equitable sales and service territories for companies. This was realized by Sidney Hess who applied the method to the problem of updating and revising the service districts of IBM typewriter servicemen.[3] The same principles of his approach can be applied to any problem calling for the formation of equitable territories.

The procedure seeks to build sales and service territories that satisfy three principles as closely as possible. The first has already been mentioned, that of *equal sales workload*. The second principle is that of *contiguity*, that is, each territory must always consist of adjacent areas. The third principle is that of *compactness*, that is, the territories should be as easy to cover from a travel standpoint as possible and this means that territories should be favored which tend toward circular rather than elongated shape. (We are assuming that customers are evenly distributed throughout the territory.) Consider the two alternately shaped but equal-sized territories in Figure 13-1 as an example. Figure 13-1(a) shows a circle with a home base in the center and four equally distant outlying customers. Figure 13-1(b) shows an ellipse containing the same area with a home base in the center and four outlying customers. The first sales

[3]Sidney W. Hess, "Realigning Districts by Computer," *Wharton Quarterly* (Spring 1969) 25–30.

territory would be considered more compact, in the sense that the total travel distance to the four customers would be lower than in the case of the ellipse.

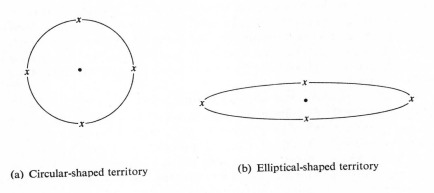

(a) Circular-shaped territory   (b) Elliptical-shaped territory

Figure 13-1 Two Equal-Sized Territories of Differing Compactness

One measure of the compactness of the shape of a teritory is the *moment of inertia*. The moment of inertia is equal to the sum of the squares of the distances from the home base to all the customers, weighted by the volume of business of the various customers, that is,

$$M_j = \sum_{i=1}^{n} v_i \, d_{hi}^{2} \qquad\qquad (13\text{-}1)$$

where M_j = moment of inertia of territory j
     v_i = sales volume of customer i
     d_{hi} = distance of customer i from home base h
     n = number of customers in territory

The lower the moment of inertia of a territory, the greater its compactness.

An example of the results of applying the transportation method to a problem in building up Congressional districts that exhibit contiguity, compactness, and equal-sized populations is shown in Figure 13-2. The results apply equally well to creating sales territories. Figure 13-2(a) is a map of the original SGUs, in this case, census enumeration districts, which are to be combined in some fashion into population territories. The first requirement is to state how many territories are to be developed and to locate a tentative initial center for each territory. Figure 13-2(b) shows a decision to build six territories and the locations of the tentative centers. The decision on the number of territories would not be arbitrary in the case of sales territories. The decision would be related to the estimated workload in the whole region divided by the workload hours per year available per salesman. Thus, if the region is estimated to require

12,000 sales man-hours for coverage, and the average salesman handles 2000 sales hours per year, then about six territories should be carved out of the region.

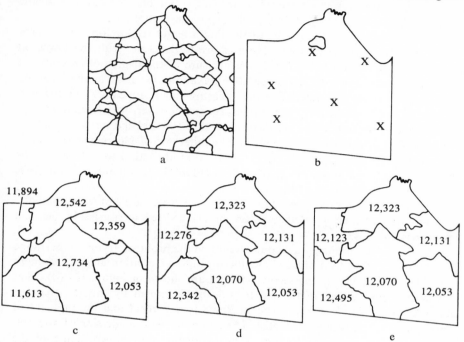

Figure 13-2   Illustration of Equal Territories Developed by a Computer Program

(a) Location of U.S. Census Enumeration Districts

(b) Set of initial guesses for the 6 legislative districts apportioned to Sussex

(c) First assignment of population to legislative districts based on guessed centers
Maximum Deviation: 5%
Moment of Inertia: 143,774

(d) Second trial—Improved assignment based on actual centers of first assignment (X's indicate towns of over 1000 population.)
Maximum Deviation: 1%
Moment of Inertia: 133,923

(e) Third trial: slightly worse results
Maximum Deviation: 2%
Moment of Inertia: 133,992
(Fourth trial—no further change)

Source: Hess, *op. cit.*, p. 17.

The initial locations of the centers of the six sales territories are also not arbitrary if certain cities stand out as having the most sales potential. Fortunately, any serious error introduced by the initial number or locations of sales centers will be corrected by a subsequent step in the computer program.

Figure 13-2(c) shows the results of the first attempt to develop the six territories. The sizes of the created territories are fairly close, with the lowest at 11,613 and the highest at 12,734. Some measure of the degree of closeness of these numbers is desirable. Hess used the maximum deviation as the measure, here 5 percent. He did not define this measure but it appears to be the percentage deviation of the size of the largest (or smallest) territory from the mean. Thus the average size of the six territories is 12,199 and the territory farthest from this size is the one with 11,613. This is a difference of 586, or approximately 5 percent of the mean. A still better measure of deviation would seem to be the coefficient of variation, $\sigma/\bar{x}$, that is, the standard deviation of the six numbers expressed as a percentage of the mean.

As shown in Figure 13-2(c), some of the territories are not very compact. The moment of inertia calculated for the six created territories in the first attempt is 143,774.

Now the computer makes a second attempt at the problem, trying to rearrange the territories so as to decrease both the maximum deviation and the moment of inertia. The results of the second attempt are shown in Figure 13-2(d). That this is an improvement in the territory design is shown by the fact that the maximum deviation has been brought down to 1 percent and the moment of inertia has been reduced to 133,923. The computer then made a third attempt, with the results shown in Figure 13-2(e), showing a slight worsening of the criteria. The fourth attempt (not shown) fared no better and at this point it appeared that the results in Figure 13-2(d) are best.

How were these various territories formed? A flow chart of the computer program that creates these territories on the basis of equal workload, contiguity, and compactness is shown in Figure 13-3. Two inputs are required. The first input is the geographical coordinates of the centers of each SGU and also each SGU's workload as derived from its sales potential. The second input is the designation of a number of centers as trial territory centers; in the example, six such centers were designated. At this point, the program has the input information it needs and begins by computing a matrix of squared distances between the center of each SGU and each of the trial territory centers. These squared distances become inputs into the linear program that assigns each SGU to a trial center for maximum compactness and equal activity. Then SGUs that are initially assigned to two different territories are reconsidered and assigned to only one territory. When this is finished, the computer program checks contiguity and estimates the compactness. The computer program also calculates desirable new trial territory centers, based on the territories formed. The new territory centers are used as improved trial territory guesses and the program reloops and produces a second solution. This continues until some solution is the same as the previous one. At this point, the program considers whether the

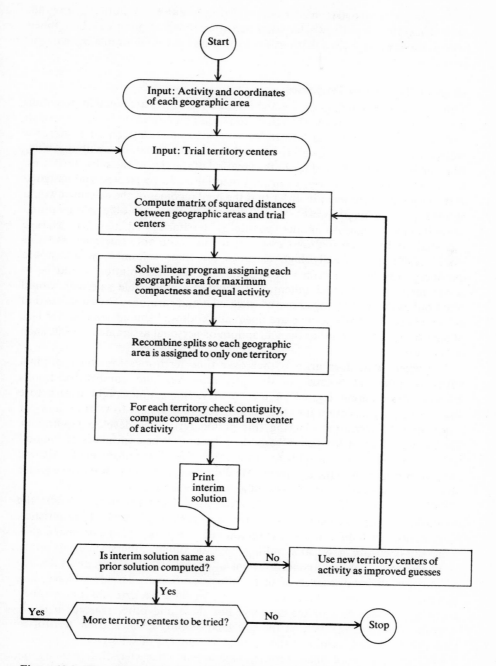

Figure 13-3 Flow Chart of Territory Design Computer Program

Source: Hess, *op. cit.*, p. 14.

field manager wants to consider more territory centers; if not, the program ends. Thus Hess has shown how mathematical programming can be applied to creating sales territories that possess properties deemed desirable by management.

Assigning Salesmen to Territories

If all salesmen are equal in ability and all sales territories are equal in potential, the salesmen could be assigned to these territories on a random basis or through a consideration of personal factors, such as the salesman's seniority and area preferences. Salesmen, however, are not generally equal in ability. Ability differences could be allowed for in the creation of the size of the sales territories. As one possibility, territories of lower potential could be created and assigned to the more able salesmen, in order that the final incomes of the salesmen would be on a parity. This, however, would discourage the more able salesmen and cause them to resign. As another possibility, territories of better than average potential could be created and assigned to the more able salesmen, but this would result in unusually high earnings for these salesmen, which would discourage the other salesmen. It appears that the best solution would be to create territories of equal potential, so that the more able salesmen would stand out as those attaining above average sales and earnings. Thus it seems that even recognizing that salesmen are unequally endowed should not alter the size of territories or lead to other than a random or personal assignment of salesmen to territories.

A problem that does arise is that over time territories lose their original parity of potential because of dynamic economic and competitive trends affecting the different regions of the country. Some time might pass before enough inequity has crept into the existing territory system to warrant a major redesigning of territories. During this period territories develop reputations among the salesmen for being "good" or "poor." When vacancies of "good" territories occur, salesmen apply for transfer and there is the problem of assigning the proper salesmen to the territories. Here the company would want to consider ability differences of salesmen, as well as seniority issues.

There is another factor that makes the assignment problem difficult: the interaction of the salesman's characteristics with the customers' characteristics. Each territory will differ in its distribution of large versus small customers, also, some salesmen are good at handling large accounts, others small accounts. Some territories will have concentrations of particular industries, and salesmen will vary in their knowledge of these industries. Some salesmen will be more effective in one part of the country because of their background and manner, others in another part of the country. For these and other reasons, it is not enough to use average data on the salesmen's ability levels and the territories' sales potential in determining the optimal assignment of salesmen.

The importance of man-territory interaction characteristics in assigning salesmen is illustrated in Table 13-1. The table shows four salesmen, A, B, C, and D, and four territories, 1, 2, 3, and 4. The four salesmen differ in their estimated ability, as shown by the marginal figures at the far right. The four territories differ in their estimated potential, as shown by the marginal figures at the bottom of the table. The figures in columns 1–4 show the sales manager's best guess as to what a particular salesman would sell in a particular territory.[4]

Table 13-1 Sales Manager's Estimates of Annual Sales of Each Salesman for Hypothetical Assignments to Different Territories

| Salesman | Territory | | | | Average expected sales |
	1	2	3	4	
A	$92,000	$95,000	$75,000	$70,000	$83,000
B	90,000	57,000	82,000	45,000	68,500
C	73,000	75,000	40,000	51,000	59,750
D	60,000	30,000	51,000	75,000	54,000
Estimated potential	$78,750	$64,250	$62,000	$60,250	

For example, salesman A (the most able salesman) whose expected sales are $83,000, is expected to sell more than this if placed in territory 1 or 2, and less than this if placed in territory 3 or 4. He would be most productive in territory 2. However, salesman C would also be most productive in territory 2. Some compromise is therefore called for when one territory is best for two or more salesmen. The problem calls for assigning one and only one salesman to each territory, in such a way as to maximize total company sales (assuming profits are proportional to sales). This is a special type of linear programming problem called the "assignment" problem for which a standard algorithm is available.[5] In the case of the simple example, it is easy to find the optimal solution by trial and error, since there are only $4! = 24$ possible assignments of four men to four territories. The reader can verify that the optimal assignment is A2, B3, C1, and D4, which would yield annual expected sales of $325,000. Where the problem involves many more than four salesmen and territories, it is clear that an algorithm would have to be used to arrive efficiently at the optimal assignment. The solution above indicates that better salesmen should be assigned the best territories in an approximate, rather than an exact, way. Assignments should reflect man-territory interactions, not just the average ability of salesmen and the average potential of territories.

[4]Different procedures have been recommended for estimating the salesman's expected sales performance in each territory. Stern recommends measuring each salesman's effectiveness with different types of customers and then using these as weights against each territory's distribution of customer types. Mark Stern, *Marketing Planning: A Systems Approach* (New York: McGraw-Hill, Inc., 1966), 69–74. King recommends measuring each salesman's probability of success in each territory, given the match between his characteristics and those of the territory, and using these probabilities along with the territories' sales potentials to estimate expected sales. William R. King, *Quantitative Analysis for Marketing Management* (New York: McGraw-Hill, Inc., 1967) 469–473.

[5]See C. W. Churchman, R. L. Ackoff, and E. L. Arnoff, *Introduction to Operations Research* (New York: John Wiley & Sons, Inc., 1957), Chap. 12, "The Assignment Problem."

DETERMINING CALL NORMS AND SCHEDULES

The development of sales territories results in assigning individual salesmen responsibility for developing the business potential of their respective territories. The business potential is found in all the present customers and prospects in the territory. The salesman's problem is to (1) decide how many calls to make per year on each customer and prospect in his territory and (2) how these calls should be scheduled during each planning period.

There are some companies in which these decisions are left entirely to the salesmen. The company establishes a sales quota for the salesman and leaves it to him to decide how to allocate his time among customers and prospects to achieve his quota. Other companies will recommend annual call frequency norms for different-size customers and prospects. These norms are usually guidelines rather than requirements. They represent economic levels of calls, that is, the salesman who makes more than the indicated number of calls on a given-size customer is drawing down the normal profit on the account, unless there is a sufficient increase in orders to offset the cost of additional calls. To offset this, the company salesman must make a certain number of calls to current customers during the year. His visits also serve the purpose of introducing new company products and of learning about new needs and developments in the customer's business.

How many calls a year should the salesman plan to make to a particular customer? The *maximum* number of calls he should make can be deduced in the following way. Suppose that a customer has been placing orders with the company amounting to $30,000 a year. Suppose, furthermore, that the company's profit margin is 10 percent before deducting the cost of the sales calls. This means that the company makes $3000 gross profit on this customer. Each sales call costs $100 when the travel time, waiting and contact time, and expenses are all accounted for. This means that the salesman should never make more than 30 calls per year on this account, for this number of calls would cost $3000 and just exhaust the gross profit.

As for determining and scheduling the specific calls to make each week or month, this is almost always left to the salesman. The company hopes through its sales training program that its salesmen will learn how to plan their weekly time effectively.

Although much of the call decision making is in the salesman's hands, we shall assume that the company has a vital interest in analyzing both the optimal number of calls and their scheduling. The optimal number of calls to customers and prospects will be analyzed first separately, and then jointly, followed by a consideration of issues in routing and scheduling.

The Number of Calls to Current Customers

A salesman must periodically contact each of his existing accounts or else they may suddenly turn up in the hands of a competitor. Competitors' salesmen will be constantly calling on them and offering inducements to switch. This conclusion rests on the assumption that the amount of business from this customer is insensitive to the number of sales calls made on the account. If the customer's purchases would rise above $30,000 with more calls than the normal level, then 30 calls would not express the maximum feasible number. The maximum feasible number of calls would require knowledge of the sales response function.

But we should not be interested in the maximum number of calls as much as the optimal number of calls. An approach that is sometimes used is for the salesman to consider the ratio of his average annual sales to the number of his annual working hours. If his average annual sales are $2 million and his annual working hours are 2000, he generally manages to get $1000 of sales per work hour. Therefore if he is dealing with an account that yields approximately $30,000 a year, he can devote about 30 work hours per year to it and maintain his annual sales rate. Suppose the customer's distance is such that a visit to this customer consumes about three hours. Therefore the salesman should plan on making about ten calls a year to this account, or a little less than one a month.

This method of reasoning however is faulty for at least two reasons. First of all, it neglects the idea that sales from an account are likely to vary with the number of calls. Second, it does not analyze the varying economic value of making calls on different accounts but only considers maintaining a parity of the present sales ratio to the number of available calling hours.

Recent discussions of the call norm problem have increasingly paid attention to the concept of the sales call response function. While it is not easy to measure the sales call response function, there have been some attempts; the concept does clarify the planning issues involved. A customer's sales call response function shows the sales per year that a particular salesman is likely to achieve from a particular customer in response to alternative call frequencies under given assumptions about the economic and competitive climate. A hypothetical example of this function is shown in Figure 13-4. It shows that the salesman receives no orders from the account if he makes zero or one call per year and he receives more business with higher call frequency. With four or more calls, sales tend to approach $12,000 a year; this can be called the sales potential of the account.

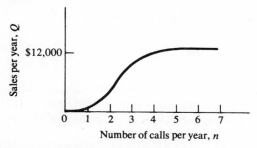

Figure 13-4   A Customer's Sales Call Response Function

If a salesman knew the sales call response function for each of his customers, he could optimally allocate his 2000 hours per year according to the principles in Chapter 6. In practice, a salesman rarely knows his customers' sales call response functions explicitly but he does proceed to select accounts intuitively in terms of their anticipated sales response.

There have been a few reported efforts to estimate the sales call response function for classes of customers, instead of individual customers and salesmen. If the functions turned up with different shapes, they would provide a basis for setting different call frequencies for different customer classes. One such study was reported by the Operations Research Group at Case Institute of Technology for the General Electric Company.[6] The operations researchers worked with data on General Electric customers in the Boston sales region. The first step consisted of sorting the customers into classes on the basis of similarity of characteristics. A number of account characteristics, including the type of business, the product involved, and the size of the customer were used to establish customer classes. The assumption was made that the accounts within each class were similar and would respond in a similar way to variations in the number of sales calls. The next step consisted of plotting all the accounts in a particular class on a grid whose vertical axis represented the account's sales that year and whose horizontal axis represented the number of calls on the account that year.[7] It was hoped that the scatter of points would be close together and show a definite positive pattern. The actual scatter of points for one of the customer classes is shown in Figure 13-5.

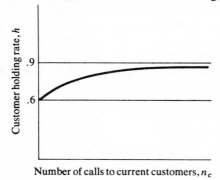

Number of calls to current customers, n_c

Figure 13-5   Scatter Diagram of Sales Volume and Number of Calls by Many Salesmen to Similar Customers

Source: Waid, Clark, and Ackoff, *op. cit.*, p. 628.

As can be seen, the scatter lies in a basically positive direction but is too diffuse to permit the fitting of a statistically significant positive curve. This lack of a strong relationship also emerged for the other customer classes. The

[6]Clark Waid, Donald F. Clark, and Russell L. Ackoff, "Allocation of Sales Effort in the Lamp Division of the General Electric Company," *Operations Research* (Dec. 1956) 629–647.

[7]The researchers said that they would have preferred to use the number of call hours per year on an account, instead of the number of calls, but they did not have information on call hours.

analysts tried other approaches, such as regressing recent changes in account sales to recent changes in account call levels, but these did not yield significantly better results. The researchers concluded that the lack of a clear positive relationship could be explained by one of three hypotheses:

1. Uniform sales response curves do not exist within groups of accounts.
2. Sales response curves exist but are difficult to measure because of imperfections in the classification of accounts and the basic data.
3. Sales response curves exist, but the data in this case reveal the upper plateaus of the curves.

The researchers rejected the first hypothesis because it went against the widely held view that a greater number of calls on a group of accounts would lead to a higher level of sales from these accounts. They rejected the second hypothesis because experienced salesmen reported that they thought the basis for classifying the accounts into different groups was sound. This left the third hypothesis, which the researchers tentatively accepted but could not prove. It implied that the salesmen on the whole were spending more time with accounts in each customer classification than was necessary. In other words, the salesmen could make fewer calls on each account and still obtain the same volume of business. This suggested a sales call function that rose sharply from zero calls to a few calls and then remained horizontal for more calls. This led the analysts to recommend to General Electric that the salesmen be advised to make fewer calls on current accounts and spend more time in prospecting.

Before accepting the third conclusion, the researchers should have tried to remove some of the scatter that might have been associated with other sources of variation than the call frequency. The major problem with the data is that they represent the historical pattern of calls, rather than the results of an experimentally predetermined pattern of calls. As a result the data reflect various uncontrolled sources of variation. One important source of variation would be in the differences among the salesmen calling on the accounts in that class. To allow for this, company management could have rated the ability of each salesman using an index number of 100 for an average salesman. While the ratings would be somewhat arbitrary, their use may be less arbitrary than ignoring individual differences altogether. How are these individual ratings utilized? Suppose a particular, above-average salesman receives a rating of 150. This means that his sales are generally 50 percent higher than those obtained by an average salesman selling to the same customers. Therefore wherever his results appear in the scatter diagram in Figure 13-5, they should be lowered vertically 50 percent to reflect the probable sales level of an average salesman selling to the same customers. All the other observations in the scatter diagram should be adjusted up or down according to each salesman's ability. Presumably, this would remove an important source of variation and the adjusted observations might show a more significant pattern.

Another source of variation occurs when the number of calls made on some of the accounts in the particular year do not represent the typical number made in the past but represent a substantial departure in order to build up sales volume. In these cases, the observations do not reflect the equilibrium relationship between the number of calls and the expected sales level. They should either be removed from the pool of observations or adjusted judgmentally to reflect the expected sales levels.

In general, it is much harder to find clear relationships in historical data than in data emerging from an experimental design in which an effort has been made to control or at least measure as many variables as possible. Unfortunately, sales management has usually resisted proposals for sales call experiments, in spite of often acknowledging their potential value. Their reasons for opposition have been many. First, no salesman is happy about halving his normal number of calls to some randomly selected accounts and doubling his number of calls to another set of randomly selected accounts. He has spent too much effort cultivating his customers to risk spoiling their loyalty in the interest of an experiment. Neither are the regional sales managers happy, because total sales might be affected and hence their bonuses. Furthermore, many sales executives are skeptical that any clear relationship will emerge, in view of the multitude of particular circumstances that surround individual accounts and salesmen. The inability of the designers of the experiment to control the number of competitive calls creates a distrust in their minds of the possible meaningfulness of the results. Cox summarized the objections of industrial firms to sales force experiments by saying:

> Experiments may involve risks of alienating customers and salesmen, possible loss of sales, and high administrative costs. The management of a firm must be convinced that the expected value of the information produced will exceed the total costs of the experiment.[8]

In spite of these problems, some companies have carried out sales call experiments and at least one case has been reported in the literature. Cox reported a study he carried out in a Cleveland company that manufactured industrial fasteners.[9] A double Latin Square experimental design, shown in Table 13-2, was selected for carrying out the study. This design calls for testing the efficacy of three different call frequency levels per quarter, specifically 0, 1, and 3 calls, respectively (called treatments A, B, and C). The experiment is carried out over three quarters to see whether the sales results are sensitive to the quarters, as well as the level of sales calls. The rows represent the quarters and the columns represent six different sequential patterns of calls. The company's customers were stratified into six different groups and eighteen customers were randomly selected to represent each of the groups, six for each quarter. For example,

---

[8]William E. Cox, Jr., "An Experimental Study of Promotional Behavior in the Industrial Distributor Market," in Raymond M. Haas, *Science, Technology, and Marketing* (Chicago: American Marketing Association, 1966 Fall Conference Proceedings), 578–586.
[9]Ibid.

salesmen were instructed to call zero times on six customers in the first quarter, one time on six other customers in the second quarter, and three times on six other customers in the third quarter. Other instructions were given to the salesmen regarding the number of calls to make each quarter on accounts in the other groups.

Table 13-2   A Double Latin Square Experimental Design for Measuring Sales Response to Call Frequency

	Account groups					
	Square 1			*Square* 2		
Quarters	Group 1	Group 2	Group 3	Group 4	Group 5	Group 6
1	A	B	C	A	B	C
2	B	C	A	C	A	B
3	C	A	B	B	C	A

Treatments: *A* = 0 calls per quarter
B = 1 call per quarter
C = 3 calls per quarter

Source: Cox, "An Experimental Study of Promotional Behavior in the Industrial Distributor Market," in Raymond M. Haas, *Science, Technology, and Marketing* (Chicago: American Marketing Association, 1966 Fall Conference Proceedings), p. 579.

When the results were in, Cox used standard *analysis of variance* techniques to determine whether the periods, groups, or call levels showed any significant differences.[10] Unfortunately, the within-cell variation was so large (that is, the variation in sales for similar accounts subjected to the same treatment in the same period) that they overshadowed any differences that might have originated because of call frequency differences, group differences, or period differences. In other words, this experiment failed to control all the significant sources of variation in sales from account to account, and some were so significant as to obscure the experimental factors. Another problem is that the alternative call levels being tested did not appear sufficiently different to create an immediate difference in sales response.

The effect of call time on current customers remains difficult to determine in practice. The effect depends on the attitude of the buyer toward increased calls, the effectiveness of the salesman, the call time put in by competitors, and so forth. Furthermore, call time has a carryover effect, as well as a current effect. The buyer may not increase his orders at the time of the sales call but may when the purchase need next arises.

[10]Analysis of variance is a set of statistical techniques for testing whether apparent differences between two or more variables found in a probability sample could have reasonably occurred by chance, and therefore are insignificant. See William S. Peters and George W. Summers, *Statistical Analysis for Business Decisions* (Englewood Cliffs, N.J.: Prentice-Hall, Inc., 1968), Chap. 13.

The Number of Calls to Prospects

Most companies require that their salesmen spend some proportion of their time in cultivating prospects in addition to serving current customers. For example, Spector Freight Systems supplies the following guidelines to its salesmen:

> You should use a call division of 75 percent active and 25 percent prospective. Therefore, each day you would have nine active accounts and three prospects. After you have made 3 calls on a prospective account with no production results, the account should be reviewed by the terminal manager or the district sales manager and yourself.[11]

There are a number of reasons why many companies try to set up a minimum requirement for the canvassing of new accounts. If left alone, many salesmen tend to spend most of their time in the offices of present customers. Present customers are better-known quantities. The salesmen can depend upon them for some business, whereas a prospect may never deliver any business or deliver it only after many months of effort. Unless the salesman receives a bonus for new accounts, he assumes the risks during the initial period. Some companies try to open new accounts by using salaried missionary salesmen exclusively.

There are two problems in missionary selling. One is which prospects should be called on and the other is how many calls should be made before giving up. As for the first problem, in many cases the challenge is to locate enough good prospects to call on. However, let us consider those situations in which the salesman has a long list of good prospects and insufficient time to call on all of them. He would like to find a way to rank them, so that he can spend his time calling on the best prospects. A useful model can be formulated by looking at this problem in terms of standard investment theory. First, the salesman should estimate the value of the prospect's business if he could be converted to a customer. The value of the prospect's business may be represented in terms of a discounted income stream lasting so many years. Specifically,

$$Z = \sum_{t=1}^{\bar{t}} \frac{m Q_t - X}{(1+r)^t} \tag{13-2}$$

where Z = present value of the future income from a new customer
m = gross margin on sales (before maintenance sales call cost)
Q_t = expected sales from new customer in year t
X = cost of maintaining customer contact per year
r = company discount rate
t = an integer respresenting year
$\bar{t}$ = number of years that this new customer is expected to remain a customer

---

[11]Ralph Westfall and Harper C. Boyd, Jr., *Cases in Marketing Management* (Homewood, Ill.: Richard D. Irwin, Inc., 1961), p. 427.

Thus the salesman estimates that this prospect if converted to a customer would make purchases from the company for i periods with a profit yield of m per unit less a certain customer contact cost.

The next step is to consider the investment necessary to convert this prospect to a customer. The investment can be described as

$$I = nc \tag{13-3}$$

where I = investment in trying to convert the prospect to a customer
$\quad\quad n$ = number of calls to convert the prospect into a customer
$\quad\quad c$ = cost per call

The number of calls to the prospect will influence the probability of his conversion, that is,

$$p = p(n) \tag{13-4}$$

The value of the prospect's business should be scaled down by this probability. Putting the previous elements together, the following investment formula emerges for the value (V) of a prospect:

$$V = p(n) \sum_{t=1}^{i} \frac{mQ_t - X}{(1+r)^t} - nc \tag{13-5}$$

According to Equation 13-5, the value of a prospect depends on the difference between the expected present value of the income stream and the investment made in prospect conversion. Both the expected present value and the investment depend in turn on the intended number of calls, n, upon the prospect. The intended number of calls should be the optimal number of calls, and this can be found by differentiating Equation 13-5 with respect to n. For the sake of illustration, suppose the probability of conversion depends upon the number of calls in the following way:

$$p(n) = \bar{p} - e^{-an} \tag{13-6}$$

where $\bar{p}$ = maximum probability of conversion, $\bar{p} \leqslant 1$
$\quad\quad e$ = 2.71 ...
$\quad\quad a$ = parameter reflecting the rate at which the maximum probability is approached with the number of calls on the prospect

By the substitution of Equation 13-6 into Equation 13-5, it can be shown that the optimal number of calls on the prospect is given by[12]

$$n^* = \frac{1}{a}\log\{[\bar{p}a/c]\sum_{t=1}^{i}[(mQ_t - X)/(1+r)^t]\} \tag{13-7}$$

Having established n^* as the optimal number of calls for this prospect, we can determine the value of this prospect, V, in Equation 13-5. Thus, each prospect

[12]See Appendix Mathematical Note 13–1.

can be ranked for his investment value, and also the number of calls that should be made on him. The formula could easily be developed into a conversational computer program, wherein the salesman sits down at a terminal, types in a set of estimates for each prospect regarding the expected volume of his business, maximum probability of conversion, and so forth, and receives back a ranking of all the prospects in order of their investment value, along with the suggested number of calls to make on each.

A possible shortcoming of Equation 13-5 is that two prospects may have the same value and yet may not seem equally worth pursuing. For example, would it be better to pursue a prospect worth $5000 with a .8 probability of conversion or a prospect worth $20,000 with a .2 probability of conversion, assuming the same call investment was involved? Individual salesmen are not likely to be indifferent toward these two prospects. If salesmen are asked to choose between them, the majority would probably prefer to pursue the surer prospect. If the surer prospects would receive too much attention, the formula would have to be modified.

The problem of how many calls to make on prospects before dropping them has also been treated by the use of Markov analysis. The Markov analysis of this problem was first suggested by Shuchman.[13] Consider a salesman who has been contacting thirty prospects each week. He never makes more than one call on any prospect in a week and he drops all prospects who have not become customers after six calls. The issue here is whether his dropping rule ($n = 6$) is optimal.

The answer will largely depend on the transitional probabilities of prospects becoming customers after different numbers of calls. Suppose the following prospect states are defined:

S_s = prospect becomes a customer (s for "sold")
S_d = prospect is dropped (d for "dropped")
S_0 = prospect has received no calls
S_1 = prospect has received one call

.

.

.

S_6 = prospect has received six calls

The first two states can be characterized as *absorbing states:* that is, once they are entered, they are never left (by assumption). The remaining states are transient states because they are occupied temporarily by prospects. Classifying prospects by the number of past calls they received assumes that members within each transient state will be fairly similar in their response to additional calls. Given these states, we can form the following matrix of transitional probabilities.

[13]Abraham Shuchman, "The Planning and Control of Personal Selling Effort Directed at New Account Acquisition: A Markovian Analysis," in *New Research in Marketing* (Berkeley, Calif.: The Institute of Business and Economic Research, 1966), pp. 45–56.

$$P = \begin{array}{c} \\ S_s \\ S_d \\ S_0 \\ S_1 \\ S_2 \\ S_3 \\ S_4 \\ S_5 \\ S_6 \end{array} \begin{array}{ccccccccc} S_s & S_d & S_0 & S_1 & S_2 & S_3 & S_4 & S_5 & S_6 \\ \hline 1 & 0 & 0 & 0 & 0 & 0 & 0 & 0 & 0 \\ 0 & 1 & 0 & 0 & 0 & 0 & 0 & 0 & 0 \\ 0 & 0 & 0 & 1 & 0 & 0 & 0 & 0 & 0 \\ .05 & .05 & 0 & 0 & .90 & 0 & 0 & 0 & 0 \\ .10 & .10 & 0 & 0 & 0 & .80 & 0 & 0 & 0 \\ .15 & .05 & 0 & 0 & 0 & 0 & .80 & 0 & 0 \\ .15 & .05 & 0 & 0 & 0 & 0 & 0 & .80 & 0 \\ .10 & .10 & 0 & 0 & 0 & 0 & 0 & 0 & .80 \\ .05 & .95 & 0 & 0 & 0 & 0 & 0 & 0 & 0 \end{array} \qquad (13\text{-}8)$$

The rows represent originating states, the columns represent destination states, and the illustrative numbers in the body of the matrix represent estimated transition probabilities. For example, the probability is assumed to be one that a sold prospect will remain a sold prospect and a dropped prospect will remain a dropped prospect, and no other transitions will take place in the first two rows. The third row shows that a prospect that is called on the first time moves to the state of being a prospect who has been called on once. In this type of selling situation, one call does not cause him to become a customer nor does it lead him to be dropped, although this is conceivable in other selling situations. The effect of a second call on a prospect (see the fourth row) may cause him to become a customer (this happens in five percent of the cases), to be dropped (this happens also in five percent of the cases), or to enter the state of being a prospect who has been called upon twice (this happens in 90 percent of the cases). The remaining rows are read in a similar way. The numbers in every row will sum to 1.

It should be noted that the matrix P is partioned into four submatrices, which can be identified as

$$P = \frac{I \mid O}{R \mid Q} \qquad (13\text{-}9)$$

where $I = 2 \times 2$ identity matrix
$O = 2 \times (n+1)$ zero matrix
$R = (n+1) \times 2$ absorbing states matrix
$Q = (n+1) \times (n+1)$ transient states matrix

The practical estimation problem facing the company that wants to develop the P matrix all lies in the R and Q submatrices, since the I and O submatrices are tautological. The nonzero entries in the Q submatrices are estimated from call records on the percentage of prospects that move into the next transient state instead of being absorbed. And the R submatrix entries are based on the respective percentages in each calling state that are converted by another call to customers or are dropped.

The matrix Equation 13-8 represents a *finite absorbing Markov process*. The system is describable as a Markov process because the probability of a prospect's entering any state depends only on his current state. It is describable as a finite absorbing Markov process because it contains at least one absorbing state (specifically two absorbing states in this case) and it is possible to enter an absorbing state in a finite number of steps from every state in the system. The matrix Equation 13-9 is said to be stated in canonical form and, as such, several interesting results can be derived from it.[14] On the basis of the transitional probabilities employed in the example, it is possible to answer the following questions:[15]

1. If the salesman see thirty prospects each period and never makes more than six calls on a prospect, how many prospects will he expect to see in each "age" group each period in the steady state?[16]

$$S_0 \quad S_1 \quad S_2 \quad S_3 \quad S_4 \quad S_5 \quad S_6$$
Answer: 5.970, 5.970, 5.373, 4.298, 3.439, 2.751, 2.201.

2. What is the expected number of prospects sold and dropped each period in the steady state?

$$S_s \quad S_d$$
Answer: 2.381, 3.589

3. What results could a salesman expect under different call cutoff policies? The answer is shown in Table 13-3.

Table 13-3

	Number of prospects entering list each period	*Expected number of conversions each period*	*Expected number of drops per period*
4 calls	7.149	2.391	4.758
5 calls	6.442	2.451	3.991
6 calls	5.970	2.381	3.589
7 calls	5.639	2.322	3.317

From the findings in Table 13-3, it appears that a cut-off policy of five calls is optimal in the long run. It produces the highest expected number of conversions per week, 2.451. Over a year's time, this policy will lead to three to four new customers than cutoff policies of four or six calls. (Naturally this criterion of five calls would have to be qualified for the value of the prospect's business, the time required for a call, etc.) Shuchman shows how variances can be calculated for these various estimates for use in setting up statistical control

[14]See J. G. Kemeny and L. J. Snell, *Finite Markov Chains* (Princeton, N.J.: Nostrand, 1959), Chap. 3; R. M. Cyert, H. J. Davidson, and G. I. Thompson, "Estimation of the Allowance for Doubtful Accounts by Markov Chains," *Management Science* (Apr. 1962) 287–303.

[15]See Appendix Mathematical Note 13–2.

[16]A steady state has been reached when the salesman adds new prospects each period equal to the number who are absorbed and he finds no advantage in changing the number of prospects in each class that he calls on.

charts that can be used by sales management to monitor salesman performance.

Subsequently, Thompson and McNeal used finite absorbing Markov processes to analyze the prospect sales call problem but they defined the prospect states somewhat differently:[17]

S_s = prospect becomes a customer
S_d = prospect is dropped
S_0 = prospect is new
S_L = prospect indicates a *low* degree of interest during most recent call
S_M = prospect indicates a *medium* degree of interest during most recent call
S_H = prospect indicates a *high* degree of interest during most recent call

Thompson and McNeal argue that their classification causes prospects to be grouped more homogeneously and the transition probabilities are more stable and meaningful for each group. Their classification also allows them to rank the relative value of additional calls on each type of prospect. The matrix they analyze is given below:

$$
P = \begin{array}{c} \\ S_s \\ S_d \\ S_0 \\ S_L \\ S_M \\ S_H \end{array}
\begin{array}{c}
\begin{array}{cccccc} S_s & S_d & S_0 & S_L & S_M & S_H \end{array} \\
\left[\begin{array}{cccccc}
1 & 0 & 0 & 0 & 0 & 0 \\
0 & 1 & 0 & 0 & 0 & 0 \\
.10 & .30 & 0 & .25 & .20 & .15 \\
.05 & .45 & 0 & .20 & .20 & .10 \\
.15 & .10 & 0 & .15 & .25 & .35 \\
.20 & .05 & 0 & .15 & .30 & .30
\end{array} \right]
\end{array}
\qquad (13\text{-}10)
$$

Thus a prospect who has evinced a *medium* interest during the last call has, if another call is made, a 15 percent chance of being sold, a 10 percent chance of being dropped, a 15 percent chance of losing some interest, a 25 percent chance of maintaining a medium interest, and a 35 percent chance of experiencing an increased interest. The other rows are interpreted similarly. With these data, the following questions can be answered:[18]

1. How many calls must be made on the average to each type of prospect to bring about absorption (a sale or a drop)?

$$
\begin{array}{cccc}
S_0 & S_L & S_M & S_H
\end{array}
$$
Answer: 2.848, 2.549, 3.461, 3.462

2. What is the probability of being sold or dropped from each transient state?

$$
\begin{array}{c} \\ S_0 \\ S_L \\ S_M \\ S_H \end{array}
\begin{array}{c}
\begin{array}{cc} S_s & S_d \end{array} \\
\left[\begin{array}{cc}
.352 & .648 \\
.261 & .739 \\
.515 & .485 \\
.562 & .438
\end{array} \right]
\end{array}
$$
Answer:

---

[17]William W. Thompson and James V. McNeal, "Sales Planning and Control Ungis Absorbing Markov Chains," *Journal of Marketing Research* (Feb. 1967) 62–66.
[18]See Appendix Mathematical Note 13–3.

3. If the cost of making a call is a constant $15, and a sale provides a constant revenue of $190, what is the gross expected value of a prospect in each state?

Answer: $24.17, $11.35, $45.93, $54.85.

The answers to these questions indicate that a salesman should use his time to call first on all of his prospects showing a high interest. Approximately three to four calls to a high interest prospect is expected to yield $54.85. If he has time left, he should budget approximately the same number of calls to each medium interest prospect. If he still has time left, he should make about three calls per period to new prospects in preference to prospects with low interest. All of this assumes he can accurately rate the level of a prospect's interest.

These conclusions from a Markov analysis of the prospect call problem are based on transitional probabilities derived from historical frequencies. Actual experimentation with different call intensities on prospects would provide an alternative methodology. One such experiment has been reported by Magee.[19] The experiment called first for sorting prospects into major classes. Each prospect class was then randomly split into three sets. The salesmen were asked, for a specified period of time, to spend less than five hours a month with prospects in the first set, 5–9 hours a month with the second set, and more than 9 hours a month with the third set. The final results of these differential efforts are summarized in Table 13-4. The results seem to demonstrate that different call intensities do have an effect on prospect conversion rates. The best call norm in this particular situation appears to be 5 to 9 hours a month for at least three months. This cannot be definitely concluded, however, until the percentage differences are tested for significance, and the expected revenues and costs of different levels of sales effort are brought into the calculation.

Table 13-4 Conversion of Prospects to Customers

	Percent converted within		
Level of effort	1 month	2 months	3 months
Under 5 hours per month	0	0	8
5–9 hours/month	10	31	53
Over 9 hours/month	25	40	40

Source: Magee, "Determining the Optimum Allocation of Expenditures for Promotional Effort with Operations Research Methods," in Frank M. Bass, ed., *The Frontiers of Marketing Thought and Science* (Chicago: American Marketing Association, 1958, p. 144.

Joint Determination of Number of Calls to Customers and Prospects

We have considered separately the questions of customer calls and prospect calls. Yet the total time at the disposal of salesman j, T_j, must somehow be

[19]John F. Magee, "Determining the Optimum Allocation of Expenditures for Promotional Effort with Operations Research Methods," in Frank M. Bass, ed., *The Frontiers of Marketing Thought and Science* (Chicago: American Marketing Association, 1958), pp. 140–156.

divided between present customers and prospects so as to produce the best overall development of profits. Companies often specify to their salesmen that they want a certain percentage of time to go to *holding effort* and the rest to go to *conversion effort*. They may even specify how much effort should be spent on established company products and new company products. An example of such a recommended division of sales call time is shown in Table 13-5.

Table 13-5 Division of Sales Effort in a Large Company (in Percent)

	Accounts		
	Active	Prospective	*Total*
Present products	70	15	85
New products	10	5	15
	80	20	100

Source: Adapted from William R. Dixon, "Redetermining the Size of the Sales Force: A Case Study," in Martin R. Warshaw, ed., *Changing Perspectives in Marketing Management*, Michigan Business Papers 37, 1962; reproduced by permission of the Bureau of Business Research, Graduate School of Business Administration, University of Michigan, Ann Arbor, p. 58.

Laying out these guidelines requires that the problem of calling customers and prospects be simultaneously analyzed. The problem has been considered in a number of ways. Three alternative modes of analysis will now be presented, the first a behavioral analysis, the second a deterministic analysis, and the third a stochastic analysis.

Behavioral analysis of salesman's call allocation problem. This will be patterned on the analysis made by a company whose name cannot be disclosed (hereafter Company X). Company X sells an industrial nondurable, fairly standardized product to a wide variety of industrial firms. It competes against six other manufacturers, the top three (which includes Company X) accounting for 80 percent of total sales. Repeat calls on customers are made because they reorder periodically and there is some chance that they would switch to competitive vendors. Calls to new prospects (including competitors' customers) are also made because the market size is fairly static or even declining and this company has to cultivate new prospects in order to keep its sales from falling.

The problem of how many calls to make to customers and prospects is compounded by the existence of two other sales tools used by the company to win business. The first of these tools is direct mail that the company can use at various levels of intensity and frequency; and the second is new catalogs that the company can send to individual customers and prospects. The management felt that there was some interaction between the call intensity, direct mail intensity, and catalogs in terms of their effect on different types of customers.

The company felt that the development of a sales call plan should be based on the estimated response of different buyer classes. The company classified all buyers into four classes: (I) those who bought exclusively from Company X, (II) those who bought from Company X and one other vendor, (III) those who bought from Company X and two or more additional vendors, and (IV) those who did not buy this product from Company X. The company then sought to learn how it was ranked in relation to competitors by the members in each of the four buying classes. An independent marketing research firm drew a sample of buyers from each class and asked them to rank the seven vendors in terms of their preference. The highest rated vendor was given a 1, and the lowest rated vendor a 7. These preference standings were then related to Company X's call margin on the various buyers. Its call margin was defined as the difference between the number of calls Company X made on a buyer per period and the number of calls on the same buyer made by the most active competitor for this buyer's account.[20] If the most active competitor made six calls per period on the buyer and Company X made eight calls, Company X's call margin was $+2$. If the most active competitor made six calls per period on the buyer and Company X made two calls, Company X's call margin was -4. The management at Company X felt that buyer ratings of vendors would be more closely related to the call margin than to the absolute number of calls. The relationship between Company X's rank and its call margin in each buying class is shown in Table 13-6.

Table 13-6   Relationship between Call Margin and Vendor Preference by Buyer Class

			Call margin			
		Deficient	Below average	Average	Above average	Excellent
Buyer class	I	1.5	1.4	1.2	1.1	1.0
	II	1.7	1.7	1.5	1.3	1.1
	III	2.7	2.3	2.1	1.3	1.2
	IV	3.7	2.7	2.3	2.0	1.7

where: I = those who bought exclusively from the company
II = those who bought from the company and one other vendor
III = those who bought from the company and two or more additional vendors
IV = those who did not buy this product from the company

The rows represent the four buying classes as described earlier. The columns represent buyers classified by the call margin they received (grouped into five levels: below -3, deficient; -2 or -3, below average; -1 to $+1$, average; $+2$ or $+3$, above average; and above $+3$, excellent.) The number in each cell represents the average preference ranking of Company X by buyers in that cell. Thus the number 1.5 in the northwest corner indicates that those buyers

[20]These were determined in a number of ways, including asking the customer or his secretary how many calls the most active competitor made per period.

who bought exclusively from Company X and received a deficient number of calls (in relation to competitors' calls) ranked Company X on the average at 1.5, that is, approximately between being the first- and the second-best vendor. The number 1.5 is an average and so some members of this cell nominated Company X as the best, others nominated it second best, and so forth. Given this interpretation, what does Table 13-6 show? First, it can be concluded that Company X's standing is better with the buying classes with which it is more involved. Second, it should be observed that Company X's standing is higher when its call margin is higher. It cannot be determined from the data whether the high positive call margins caused the preference for Company X or followed the high preference already existing for other reasons (such as product quality, delivery efficiency, etc.)

Other inferences can be drawn from the preference levels in Table 13-6 that bear on where the salesmen should be directing their sales effort. Looking at buying class I, those who buy exclusively from Company X, it appears that the call margins are excessive when they are above average or excellent. Even with an average call margin, Company X maintains a 1.2 standing with this buying class. Salesmen should therefore be advised to reduce their calls to the group of customers in class I in which their call margin is above average or excellent.

As for buyer class II and III, Company X can gain a distinct first place in preference if it makes an above average number of calls or better on these customers. Before doing this, however, it would be necessary to analyze the economic value of making more calls than the most active competitors on customers in these two buying classes. Competitive retaliation will also be a factor in that if the competitors' salesmen boost their number of calls, all of the competitors would face higher costs without having achieved increased customer preference. Company X may want to single out the larger customers in buyer classes II and III and only increase their call margin on these customers.

As for buyer class IV, the noncustomers of Company X, their preference for Company X can be improved through more calls, although the preference level of those who remain noncustomers never rises above an average of 1.7, even with an excellent call margin. Of course, the effect of calls on these noncustomers is to switch some of them into one of the other three buying classes, but those that do not switch have the preference levels as shown. Also Company X should find out from whom these noncustomers are buying and go after the noncustomers who are buying from its weaker, not stronger, competitors.

To determine how many calls to make to noncustomers, as well as optimal direct mail intensity and catalog mailings, it might be desirable to design and carry out a factorial experiment. Suppose Company X wants to concentrate on noncustomers who have been receiving an average call margin. A 2^4 factorial design experiment could be conducted as follows. Sixteen groups of accounts would be set up according to whether they would receive calls, direct mail, and catalogs, and whether they are made up of high preference or low preference prospects. The sixteen groups are listed in Table 13-7; each would be composed of an equal number of accounts. The first two groups would receive no further promotion and would serve as the control group. The results of this experiment could be analyzed to determine the best combination of promotion effort required to achieve a high preference rank for Company X and a high rate of conversion from noncustomer to customer.

Table 13-7 2^4 Factorial Experimental Design for Testing Different Marketing Mixes

1	2	3	4
No calls	No calls	No calls	No calls
No catalog	No catalog	No catalog	No catalog
No direct mail	No direct mail	Direct mail	Direct mail
High preference	Low preference	High preference	Low preference
5	**6**	**7**	**8**
No calls	No calls	No calls	No calls
Catalog	Catalog	Catalog	Catalog
No direct mail	No direct mail	Direct mail	Direct mail
High preference	Low preference	High preference	Low preference
9	**10**	**11**	**12**
Calls	Calls	Calls	Calls
No catalog	No catalog	No catalog	No catalog
No direct mail	No direct mail	Direct mail	Direct mail
High preference	Low preference	High preference	Low preference
13	**14**	**15**	**16**
Calls	Calls	Calls	Calls
Catalog	Catalog	Catalog	Catalog
No direct mail	No direct mail	Direct mail	Direct mail
High preference	Low preference	High preference	Low preference

This analysis of the sales call problem indicates in a rough way the areas in which calls may be excessive or deficient. It brings in a number of variables but does not lead to a formal solution of the optimal sales call problem. For this, we shall turn to two other models.

Deterministic model of salesman's call allocation problem. Here we consider directly the question of how many calls a salesman should make on present customers versus prospects. Assume that the salesman can make n_c calls during the year to current customers and n_p calls to prospects, so that the following identity is satisfied:

$$n = n_c + n_p \tag{13-11}$$

The number of calls that the salesman chooses to make to current customers will influence the customer holding rate, h. A hypothetical customer holding rate function is shown in Figure 13-6. This holding rate function depends upon three parameters. First, an estimate must be made of the holding rate, in the absence of any sales calls in the coming year, h_0. Here it is shown as .6, which means that the salesman can expect to hold only 60 percent of his current customers if he does not make any current calls on them but depends on their phoning or sending in their orders spontaneously. Second, an estimate must be made of the salesman's holding rate if he made a very large number of calls on his current customers, h_∞. In the example, it is shown as .9, which means that the salesman can expect to hold up to 90 percent of his current customers if he gives them all of his time. There will still be some customer attrition because of competitive activity. Third, an estimate is needed of the parameter, a, that regulates the rate of approach of the function to the upper asymptote. It will be assumed that a modified exponential function provides a reasonable theory of holding rate response to the number of sales calls. The general functional form for this three-parameter holding function is therefore:

$$h = h_0 + (h_\infty - h_0)(1 - e^{-a n_c}) \tag{13-12}$$

The term $(h_\infty - h_0)$ is a measure of the sensitivity of customer sales response to sales calls. It is a number that varies between 0 and 1. If $h_\infty - h_0 = 0$, then sales calls have no effect on customer sales response; if $h_\infty - h_0 = 1$, then calls have a substantial effect in producing sales. Note, however, that $h_\infty - h_0 = 1$ implies a customer attrition rate of 100 percent.

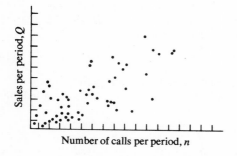

Figure 13-6 Customer Holding Rate Function

The specific equation describing the example is

$$h = .6 + .3(1 - e^{-a n_c}) \tag{13-13}$$

The parameters could vary substantially for different products. In a market in which customers feel little loyalty and switch their business quite often on the basis of specific inducements, the lower holding rate, h_0, will tend to be close to 0. That is, the salesman will lose all of his current customers if he makes no service calls during the period. The upper holding rate, h_∞, will also be lower than shown in the example because of the impossibility of matching all competitive offerings and holding every customer. On the other hand, in a market in which customers feel strong loyalties and are more sensitive to product qualities than price or sales calls, the upper and lower holding rates will be closer to 1.

Since the number of calls on current customers will affect the customer holding rate, by the same token it enables us to estimate sales from current customers. In fact, sales to current customers this period, Q_{ct}, will be the product of the customer holding rate times the total sales last period, Q_{t-1}:

$$Q_{ct} = hQ_{t-1} \tag{13-14}$$

where Q_{ct} = sales to customers this period due to the holdover effect
$\quad\quad h$ = customer holding rate
$\quad Q_{t-1}$ = total sales of company last period

This function assumes no net growth in sales per period, although this could easily be added. The customer holding rate function in Equation 13-12 can now be substituted in Equation 13-14 to estimate current sales due to the holdover effect as influenced by the number of calls made to current customers:

$$Q_{ct} = [h_0 + (h_\infty - h_0)(1 - e^{-an_c})]\, Q_{t-1} \tag{13-15}$$

The salesman will use the remainder of his time to make n_p calls on prospects. The response of prospects to sales calls will probably increase at a diminishing rate because the salesman will try to call on the prospects in the order of their expected value. Furthermore, there would be an upper limit in the sales that could be expected from prospects, even if all the call time were devoted to them. The response of prospect sales to salesman calls can be reasonably represented by a modified exponential function:

$$Q_{pt} = \bar{Q}_{pt}\,(1 - e^{-bn_p}) \tag{13-16}$$

where Q_{pt} = actual sales from prospects who are called upon this period
$\quad \bar{Q}_{pt}$ = maximum possible sales from prospects who are called on this period
$\quad\quad b$ = a response parameter

Now the salesman sees his task as one of allocating a fixed number of calls, n, between customers and prospects so as to maximize his sales (assuming his income is based on his sales). If the company's profits are the same for sales to prospects and existing customers, then the salesman's pursuit of sales maximization will coincide with the firm's pursuit of profit maximization. Thus the salesman is interested in maximizing:

$$Q_t = Q_{ct} + Q_{pt} \tag{13-17}$$

subject to the constraint

$$n_c + n_p \leqslant n \tag{13-18}$$

Combining Equations 13-17 and 13-18 into a Lagrangian expression to be maximized, and substituting Equations 13-15 and 13-16 into the equation, we get

$$L(Q_t) = [h_0 + (h_\infty - h_0)(1 - e^{-an_c})]Q_{t-1} + \bar{Q}_{pt}(1 - e^{-bn_p}) + \lambda(n - n_c - n_p) \quad (13\text{-}19)$$

Taking the three first derivatives of this function with respect to n_c, n_p, and λ, setting them equal to 0 and solving simultaneously, we find that the optimal number of calls on customers is:[21]

$$n_c^* = \frac{1}{a+b} \log [Q_{t-1} (h_\infty - h_0)a / Q_{pt} (e^{-bn})b] \quad (13\text{-}20)$$

Note that current customers should receive more calls than prospects,

the higher the sales response parameter to current calls, a (if $0 < a \leqslant 3$)
the higher the customer call sensitivity, $h_\infty - h_0$
the higher the level of sales last period, Q_{t-1}
the higher the total number of calls that can be made, n
the lower the maximum sales potential of calls on prospects, $\bar{Q}_{pt}$

The appropriate number of calls on prospects can be derived from Equation 13-20 by using the relationship in Equation 13-11. It should be noted that these conclusions are conditional on the particular forms of the chosen functions, but the general method can be applied to any reasonable functions that are assumed.

Thus the salesman will allocate his time freely between customers and prospects in a way that will maximize his sales, assuming that his income is directly proportional to his sales. His allocation is based on the respective sales response functions in a way similar to the use of such functions by the sales manager in allocating promotional effort to territories. The company can influence the salesman to make a different call allocation to his customers and prospects through particular settings of quotas and commissions, a subject that will be treated later in the chapter.

Stochastic model of salesman's call allocation problem. Instead of inquiring into how the salesman should divide a given number of calls between customers and prospects, it is possible to view the problem as determining the optimal number of calls to make to each buyer (customer or prospect) and then hiring enough salesmen, so that the time is available to make the optimal number of total calls. In practice, buyers would be stratified into groups that should receive different numbers of calls based on this analysis. This approach has been taken by Lodish, Montgomery, and Webster in a stochastic model of the sales call response process.[22] They treat the sales that might come from a

[21]See Appendix Mathematical Note 13-4.
[22]See Leonard M. Lodish, David B. Montgomery, and Frederick E. Webster, Jr., *A Dynamic Sales Call Policy Model*, Working Paper 329-68, Sloan School of Management, Massachusetts Institute of Technology, Cambridge, 1968.

specific number of calls to a buyer in period t to be a random variable drawn from a known probability distribution. If n_t calls are made on the buyer in period t and leads to Q_t sales, the profit will be

$$Z_t = mQ_t - cn_t \qquad (13\text{-}21)$$

where Z = profit from the buyer during period t
$\quad\quad m$ = gross margin on sales
$\quad\quad Q_t$ = sales to the buyer in period t
$\quad\quad c$ = cost per sales call
$\quad\quad n_t$ = number of sales calls made to the buyer in period t

Since actual sales is a random variable, so will the profits be a random variable. Suppose that the company seeks to make the number of calls on each account that will maximize the expected profit over a given time horizon. The authors show how this problem can be solved by treating it as a Markov sequential decision process.[23] Our interest, however, will be in their development of the probability distribution function for Q_t.

Instead of assuming some standard probability distribution that directly governs the random sales variable $\tilde{Q}_t$, they see it as governed by a joint probability function. The probability that a buyer will place an order of 0, 1, 2, . . . units, that is, $P(Q_t)$ is given by the product of:

1. The probability that the buyer will place an order, $P(Y)$.
2. The conditional probability of different-size orders, given that the buyer orders, $P(Q_t|Y)$.

That is,

$$P(Q_t) = P(Y_t)P(Q_t|Y_t) \qquad (13\text{-}22)$$

Now it is necessary to develop a suitable function for each of these probabilities.

The probability that a buyer will order in time period t, $P(Y_t)$, will be separately considered for customers (c) and prospects (p). If we consider a customer first, his probability of ordering in time period t is a function of three variables:

$$P(Y_{ct}) = P(Y_{ct}|H_t, N_t, n_t) \qquad (13\text{-}23)$$

where $P(Y_{ct})$ = probability that customer c will place an order in period t
$\quad\quad H_t$ = smoothed history of sales to the customer at the beginning of period t
$\quad\quad N_t$ = sales effort from past periods remembered at the beginning of period t
$\quad\quad n_t$ = sales effort expended on the customer during period t (number of sales calls)

[23]The technique is too involved to describe here. See ibid., pp. 11–17; Ronald A. Howard, *Dynamic Programming and Markov Processes* (Cambridge: The M.I.T. Press, 1960).

Let us examine these variables more closely. The more substantial the history of sales to this customer, H_t, the higher the probability that the customer will continue to place orders with this company. The customer's past sales history can be represented by the exponential smoothing equation:[24]

$$H_t = aQ_{t-1}+(1-a) H_{t-1} \tag{13-24}$$

where a = smoothing constant that determines the weight given to last period sales $(0<a\leqslant 1)$
Q_{t-1} = sales to the customer last period

Turning to N_t, the more substantial the customer's remembered sales effort, the higher the probability that the customer will continue to place orders with the company. The customer's remembered past sales effort is given by

$$N_t = bN_{t-1}+n_{t-1} \tag{13-25}$$

where b = fraction of past sales effort remembered at $t-1$
n_{t-1} = amount of sales effort in period $t-1$.

Using these variables, the authors expand on Equation 13-23 by proposing the following specific function to represent the probability that a customer will place an order in period t:

$$P(Y_{ct}) = d(1-e^{-k_1 H_t})+(1-d) [1-e^{-k_2(N_t+n_t)}] \tag{13-26}$$

where d = parameter reflecting the relative impact of sales history versus remembered and current sales effort $(0\leqslant d\leqslant 1)$
k_1, k_2 = parameters reflecting diminishing returns to sales history and remembered and current sales effort $(k_1, k_2\geqslant 0)$.

This function shows that past sales history and remembered and current sales effort are somewhat substitutable (provided that d is not too close to 0 or 1) in raising the probability that the customer will place an order. Yet each has a diminishing marginal impact on the probability as it rises.

As for prospects, Equation 13-26 has to be modified because prospects have no past sales history. The authors use the following function to represent the probability that a prospect will place his first order in period t:

$$P(Y_{pt}) = (e^{-k_3 pN_t}) [1-e^{-k_4(N_t+n_t)}] \tag{13-27}$$

where $P(Y_{pt})$ = probability that the prospect who has been called upon in p past periods will place an order in period t
p = the number of previous periods in which the prospect has been called upon and in which he has not ordered. $p = 0, 1, \ldots$
k_3, k_4 = parameters showing diminishing returns to remembered and current sales effort to prospect $(k_3, k_4\geqslant 0)$.

This probability is a product of two terms. The first term gives a probability

[24]For an earlier discussion of exponential smoothing, see Chap. 5, pp. 130–131.

of one if the prospect has never been called on before. However, the probability in the first term falls toward 0 (at a rate determined by k_3), the older the prospect (p) and the more intense the remembered sales effort (N_t). The second term gives the fraction of the first term's probability that the prospect will place an order; this is higher, the greater the past and current sales effort to this prospect.

The next step is to determine the probability that different order sizes will be placed by a buyer who orders, whether or not he is a customer or a prospect. This is given by the second term in Equation 13-22. The authors treat order size as a Poisson random variable having a mean of λ_t in period t. The probability that a customer's order size in period t is $Q_t = 0, 1, 2, \ldots$, is given by:[25]

$$P(Q_t | Y_t) = \frac{\lambda_t^{Q_t} e^{-\lambda_t}}{Q_t!} \tag{13-28}$$

The buyer's expected order size in period t is estimated to be two units ($\lambda_t = 2$). Then the probability that he will actually buy 0[26], 1, 2, 3, 4, ... units is given below:

Order size, Q_t	=	0	1	2	3	4	5	6	7...	
Probability, $P(Q_t | Y_t)$	=	.135	.271	.271	.180	.090	.036	.012	.005	= 1.00

The buyer's expected order size in period t in Equation 13-28 is considered a specific function of the following factors:

$$\lambda_t = \bar{Q}[1 - e^{-rk_5 H_t - (1-r)k_6 (N_t + n_t)}] \tag{13-29}$$

where $\bar{Q}$ = buyer's sales potential (in units per period)

r = parameter reflecting the relative importance of sales history versus remembered and current sales effort ($0 \leqslant r \leqslant 1$)

k_5, k_6 = parameters showing diminishing returns to sales history and sales effort ($k_5, k_6 > 0$).

Thus the expected order size of a buyer is higher, the greater his sales history and remembered and current sales effort. The order size approaches the customer's sales potential asymptotically. Since Equation 13-29 gives the expected order size, it is possible that the actual order size as determined by Equation 13-28 will occasionally exceed the customer's sales potential.

This completes the description of the factors underlying the probability that a specific buyer will place an order for Q_t units in period t, as originally stated in Equation 13-22. These factors are primarily the buyer's sales history, and

[25]This is the standard formula for a Poisson probability distribution. See Peters and Summers, *Statistical Analysis for Business Decisions*, p. 75.

[26]The value of 0 sounds like a contradiction. If a buyer places an order, how can his order size be 0? The authors state that this outcome reflects the buyer's intention to order but the occurrence of some factor that prevented the order from being placed in that period (such as a sudden sales decline).

remembered and current sales effort. When these probabilities are calculated for each buyer, it is possible to allocate current sales effort to current customers and prospects in such a way as to maximize expected company profits, on the assumption that there have been no competitive or other changes. The solution technique is too involved to describe here; the reader is referred to the authors' original paper for the details. Their contribution is to show how the call allocation problem can be solved simultaneously for customers and prospects in the face of stochastic sales response functions.

The Scheduling and Routing of Calls

The previous models are designed to indicate how many calls should be made to different groups of customers and prospects. This information is useful to sales managers to help them design and update sales territories and evaluate sales force effort. This information is useful to salesmen as a general guide to allocating sales effort to buyers. The salesman, however, will need additional data and judgment to solve the immediate problem facing him each week, that of planning his sales tour.

Consider a salesman whose territory contains ninety-six accounts. Suppose that his territory is shaped like a four-leaf clover with approximately twenty-four accounts in each cloverleaf. He spends each week in a different cloverleaf and in this way covers the whole territory each month. He has time to contact approximately twelve of the twenty-four customers each week. The accounts are classified into four different sales volume groups, *A*, *B*, *C*, and *D*, and are distributed irregularly through each cloverleaf. His problem is to determine which twelve accounts to call on each week and the best routing through these accounts.

A very simple solution to this problem is for the salesman to determine the optimal route through his territory and call on the first twelve accounts along the way in the first week (and return home), the second twelve accounts along this way in the second week (and return home), and so forth. Unfortunately, this solution ignores the varying values of the accounts. It is possible to improve this solution by skipping the smaller accounts every other trip.

Presumably, there are better solutions to this problem that require the development of a model that specifically considers the cost interactions of account selection and account routing. An interesting model in this connection has been proposed by Cloonan.[27] Basically, it calls for finding the optimal route through the territory and a salesman who is thinking about whether to include or skip each account along the way on the basis of the current opportunity cost. When he accumulates twelve accounts that are worth calling on, his sales tour for the week has been planned.

The first step in using the Cloonan model is to solve the optimal routing problem. This presupposes that travel cost (or distance or time) through the

---

[27]James B. Cloonan, "A Heuristic Approach to Some Sales Territory Problems," in John D. C. Little, ed., *Proceedings of the Fourth International Conference on Operations Research*, 1966, 81–84.

territory is an important factor. When travel costs are significant, they will affect the value of calling on each account and should figure in the decision of whether to include the account in the current tour. Cloonan suggests first finding the best route through the whole territory, using a "traveling salesman" solution. The traveling salesman problem is the name given to the problem of routing a salesman through n cities so that he visits each one once and the route minimizes either the travel cost, time, or distance. There are $(n=1)!$ possible solutions which are too many to evaluate by computer enumeration techniques when n gets in the range of most customer size problems. The basic data required for the solution is a matrix showing the distances (or travel cost or time) between all pairs of customers: the matrix has zero diagonal elements and is symmetric. Many solution techniques have been applied to this matrix, including linear programming,[28] integer programming,[29] dynamic programming,[30] heuristic programming,[31] and branch and bound techniques.[32] Few of these techniques yield an optimal solution for the large n case in a reasonable computation period but most offer good approximations.

After one of the above solution techniques is used to find the best route through the whole territory, the salesman starts thinking about the first account along the way and whether it would pay to call on this account on this trip or skip it. Calling on the first account will yield a certain value, V, and involve a certain cost, C. If the ratio of value to cost, V/C, is equal to or greater than a certain critical ratio R set by management, this account will be called on. Otherwise, it will be skipped.

The value of calling on this account on this trip is a function of two parameters, its maximum sales volume, M, and the elapsed time since the last call, t. Cloonan cites the following function as illustrative of the sales value of calling on an account.

$$V_{i,\,t} = \frac{M}{10}\left(-\frac{t^2}{18} + \frac{4t}{3} - 2\right) \tag{13-30}$$

where $V_{i,\,t}$ = the value of calling on account i

M = the maximum sales volume (is the basis for classifying accounts as A, B, C, or D)

t = the number of weeks since the last call on this account

The function is illustrated in Figure 13-7. It should be noted that the call

[28] G. B. Dantzig, R. Fulkerson and S. M. Johnson, "Solution of a Large-Scale Traveling Salesman Problem," *Operations Research* 2 (1954), 383–410.

[29] M. M. Flood, "The Traveling Salesman Problem," *Operations Research* 4 (1956) 61–75.

[30] M. Held and R. M. Karp, "A Dynamic Programming Approach to Sequencing Problems," *Journal of the Society of Industrial and Applied Mathematics* 10 (1962), 196–210.

[31] R. L. Karg and G. L. Thompson, "A Heuristic Approach to Solving Traveling Salesman Problems," *Management Science* (Jan. 1964) 225–248; S. M. Roberts and Benito Flores, "An Engineering Approach to the Traveling Salesman Problem," *Management Science* (Nov. 1966), 269–288.

[32] J. D. C. Little, K. G. Murty, D. W. Sweeney, and C. Karel, "An Algorithm for the Traveling Salesman Problem," *Operations Research* (Nov.–Dec. 1963), 972–989.

value is described by a parabola. The parabola, if extended back to the vertical axis, would intersect it at a negative value, indicating that a call following right upon another call would probably have a negative value. The function shows call value rising with elapsed time toward a maximum of M. If more time elapses than t_M, the customer might turn to other suppliers; the decreased value of the account is shown by the declining part of the function. Two points should be emphasized about this way of representing the value of a call. First, the value is to be taken as a relative measure, rather than a concrete number of dollars. Cloonan wishes to avoid the problem of assuming that the sales value of a call can be measured. Second, this function is the obverse of the sales call response function. For any number of calls that might be made on a customer in a given year, there is an implied elapsed time between calls. Thus a call frequency of twelve calls a year is the same as an elapsed time between calls on the same customer of one month. Treating call value in terms of elapsed time instead of the number of calls per year allows the salesman to build up his call schedule iteratively.

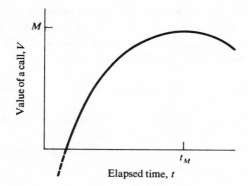

Figure 13-7   Account Call Value as a Function of Elapsed Time

The total cost of a call to the first customer, C, is made up of two specific parts: duration time of the call, C_1, and differential travel time, C_2. The duration time represents the amount of waiting and contact time the salesman expects to spend with this customer. This time can be converted into a cost figure by multiplying it by the cost of a salesman hour. The differential travel time arises because account i usually does not lie on the direct path between accounts $i-1$ and $i+1$. This means that there is some extra travel time to stop at the first account, instead of going directly from the home base to the second account. This differential travel time can be costed by the cost per mile of the particular mode of transportation used. Thus the cost of visiting the first account on this trip is $C = C_1 + C_2$.

Now the ratio, V/C, is compared to a critical ratio R established by management, and if $V/C \geqslant R$, the account will be called on. R is set at a level that will just yield approximately twelve accounts to call on out of every twenty-four, that is, it will lead to skipping one out of every two accounts on the average.

If the salesman finds that he should skip the first account because its value/cost ratio is less than R, he then considers whether he should visit the second account along the optimum route or skip it in favor of the third account. This, of course, depends on the V/C ratio for the second account, which in turn fundamentally depends upon its maximum economic value, the elapsed time since the last call, and the cost of travel and calling.

If the second account is also skipped, Cloonan's program in principle should reconsider the value of calling on the first account in relation to the third account, rather than proceed to evaluate the third account in relation to the fourth account along the way. He provides for this reevaluation though a model subroutine.

It should be emphasized that the solution procedure is heuristical rather than optimal, which is not surprising considering the complexity of the problem. To test his heuristic program, Cloonan created four different hypothetical spatial arrangements of accounts. The first two were actual configurations of the scatter of the major twenty-five cities in two different states (and were deliberately complex); the second two were artificial, one resembling a circle and another a lattice point design. Each territory has twenty-four cities plus a home base, H. Cloonan assumed six accounts of each kind (A, B, C, D) and distributed them according to the following three main patterns:

1. H $BCDA$ $BCDA$ $BCDA$ $BCDA$ No clustering of similar accounts
   $BCDA$ $BCDA$ H
2. H AAA BBB DDD CCC DDD High level of clustering and the larger
   CCC BBB AAA H accounts are close to base
3. H CCC DDD BBB AAA BBB High level of clustering and the larger
   AAA DDD CCC H accounts are far from base

The four types of spatial arrangement and the three account-size configurations provide twelve territory types. Each was used to test each of four heuristics for a total of forty-eight simulation runs. Furthermore, each simulation run consisted of a salesman making a sales call plan each week for twenty-four weeks.

Cloonan had his hypothetical salesman call on twelve customers each week, selecting them according to one of four different heuristical decision programs.

1. The simplest program called for the salesman to call on the first twelve adjacent accounts in the order of the optimal tour through the territory. The next week's tour starts with the thirteenth account and continues for twelve accounts, and so on.

2. The second program called for the salesman to make a call to 6A's, 3B's, 2C's, and 1D on each tour of twelve accounts.

3. The third program called for the salesman to evaluate the value/cost ratio for every account in the territory. The ratio is calculated by considering the value and cost of a current call on that account. The cost of making the call is the cost of call time plus the difference between going directly between accounts $i-1$ and $i+1$ and going from $i-1$ to i to $i+1$. The program determines the twelve accounts with the highest value/cost ratio; they are the ones that are called on during this tour. A subroutine is used to determine the optimum route through these twelve accounts.

4. The last program is the heuristical solution just described. It selects a starting account and then considers whether to go to the next account in the optimal territory tour or skip it. If the account's value/cost ratio exceeds a certain minimum value, it will be included. Otherwise the next account is considered for inclusion or bypassing. This reasoning is continued until twelve accounts are selected.

In a preliminary test, Cloonan found that the last three heuristical programs performed substantially better than the first one. This is not surprising, since the first program completely neglected the different size of the accounts. But the last three heuristical programs did not show much difference among themselves. Although the second program comes closest to the procedures used by salesmen in practice, and the fourth one represents a substantial sophistication of the choice procedure, the fourth one did not improve the results substantially. The last three in general were performing at over 90 percent of the optimum value as determined in an exhaustive run. This may explain why sales management has shown little interest in sophisticating account selection procedures: they may suspect that the extra cost of information and analysis may exceed the gains in better account selection.

Cloonan's invention and testing of artificial sales territories and alternative heuristics for scheduling calls on accounts is a valuable contribution to the study of the scheduling and routing problem. Further refinements can be made in the measurement of the value of an account call and in the cost of skipping a call. It is also possible that management scientists could formulate a number of alternative heuristic decision programs to test against the present four.

SETTING SALES QUOTAS AND COMMISSIONS

Salesmen are given specific territories and some broad company guidelines for allocating their selling effort among customers and prospects. They are also given specific sales quotas, commissions, and other incentives to do a good job. A small percentage of salesmen in any sales force can be expected to do their best without any special incentives from management. To them, selling is the most fascinating job in the world. These men are ambitious, and they are self-starters. However, the majority of salesmen on nearly every sales force requires personal encouragement and specific incentives to work at its best level. This is partly due to human nature because men generally will not work their hardest unless there is some special reward to be had in financial or social terms. This is also due to the nature of the field selling job, which is unavoidably subject to frequent frustration. The salesman works alone; his hours and family life are irregular; he confronts aggressive competing salesmen; he has inferior status relative to the buyer; he sometimes does not have the authority to do what is necessary to win an account or close a sale. Management, therefore, must give special thought to the development of incentives and sales targets for the salesmen.

Behavioral Model of Salesman's Response to Sales Quotas

The development of sound sales quotas and incentives requires an understanding of the determinants of the amount of sales effort a salesman will expend. Figure 13-8 is a simplified version of the quota setting problem. The company has available a control instrument, called a sales quota, which it will set for each salesman in each planning period. The quota set for each salesman, as well as personal and other factors, will affect his morale and effort. His effort, along with uncontrollable exogenous variables affecting his territory, will affect his level of sales.

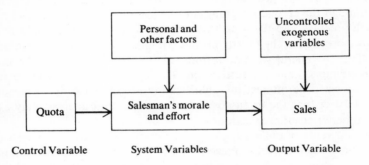

Figure 13-8 A Simplified Version of the Quota-Setting Problem

To make this version dynamic, it is necessary to elaborate the important variables and relationships in this problem. Let us start by postulating an *effort level function* that is a relationship between the quota set by the company and the resulting effort of the salesman. Realistically, the salesman's effort will not only be affected by the quota but also by his motivation level as influenced by factors independent of his quota. This effort level function is illustrated in Equation 13-31:[33]

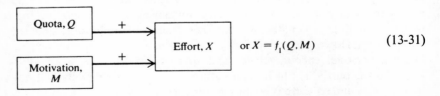

$$\text{or } X = f_1(Q, M) \tag{13-31}$$

[33]Relationships between variables are characterized in the diagrams by arrows (to show the direction of causality) and by $(+, -)$ signs (to show whether the relation is positive $(+)$, negative $(-)$, or possibly either $(+, -)$.

As a specific function, suppose that:

$$X_t = k_1 \frac{Q_t}{\bar{Q}_t} + (1 - k_1) M_t \qquad (13\text{-}32)$$

where X_t = the salesman's effort in period t ($0 \leqslant X_t \leqslant 2$, with $X_t = 1$, average effort)

k_1 = coefficient of salesman's quota-mindedness ($0 \leqslant k_1 \leqslant 1$)

Q_t = salesman's quota in period t (in dollars)

$\bar{Q}_t$ = smoothed average of salesman's past quotas, where $\bar{Q}_t = k_2 Q_{t-1} + (1 - k_2) \bar{Q}_{t-1}$. Here k_2 is the relative weight given to the most recent quota. For a new salesman, $\bar{Q}_t$ will be imputed

M_t = salesman's motivation level ($0 \leqslant M_t \leqslant 2$, with $M_t = 1$, average motivation)

This says that the salesman's effort in period t will be a weighted average of the percent increase in his quota and of his motivation level.[34] If the salesman is completely quota-oriented, then $k_1 = 1$. If the salesman is completely mood-oriented, than $k_1 = 0$. If $0 < k_1 < 1$, then both factors play a role in determining his level of effort.

The salesman's effort level decision will directly influence his expected sales. The expectation function is shown in Equation 13-33:

$$S_E = f_2(X) \qquad (13\text{-}33)$$

As a specific function,

$$S_{Et} = S_{Pt} (1 - e^{-k_3 X_t}) \qquad (13\text{-}34)$$

where S_{Et} = salesman's expected sales in period t (in dollars)

S_{Pt} = sales potential of territory during period t (in dollars)

e = base of the natural logarithms, 2.71 . . .

k_3 = coefficient of salesman's self-confidence, that is, rate of approach of expected sales to sales potential as a function of salesman effort ($1 \leqslant k_3 \leqslant 3$, with $k_3 = 2$, normal [35])

According to Equation 13-34, the salesman expects to sell an amount that approaches asymptotically his territory's potential, depending on the amount of effort he expends. The rate of his expected approach to the territory's potential depends on his coefficient of self-confidence, k_3.

---

[34]It should be assumed that this equation holds true, provided that the quota increase is not too high, say $(Q_t/\bar{Q}_t) \leqslant 1.40$. If the quota is increased in any period by more than 40 percent, the salesman reacts by reverting to an average level of effort, i.e., $X_t = 1.00$. This or some other assumption can be made about his behavior in the face of abnormal quota increases.

[35]If the salesman's coefficient of self-confidence is two, i.e., $k_3 = 2$, and he is putting out an average effort, i.e., $X_t = 1$, then he expects to achieve .86 percent of the total potential in the territory. (The 86 percent comes from solving Equation 13-34). If he puts out maximum effort, i.e., $X_t = 2$, he expects to achieve 98 percent of total potential.

The next step is to explain the salesman's actual sales. Assume that the salesman's actual sales will depend on his effort and unforeseen factors which are chance distributed, that is, the sales response function is

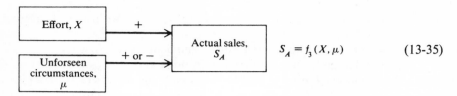

$$S_A = f_3(X, \mu) \qquad (13\text{-}35)$$

As a specific function, suppose that

$$S_{At} = S_{Pt}(1 - e^{-k_4 X_t}) + \mu_t \qquad (13\text{-}36)$$

where k_4 = coefficient of the salesman's ability

μ_t = deviation from expected sales during period t due to unforeseen circumstances, a random normal variable with mean = 0, variance, k_5

Note that the same modified exponential equation is used in the salesman's expected sales function and his actual sales function. However, the sales potential is approached differently in two cases. If $k_3 > k_4$, the salesman's self-confidence exceeds his ability, that is, he is overoptimistic and does not typically achieve the sales he expects. If $k_3 < k_4$, he is overpessimistic, and typically sells more than he expects. If $k_3 = k_4$, he is able to estimate realistically the effect of additional personal effort upon his sales. The model can be made even more flexible by assuming that the salesman is not necessarily a good estimator of true sales potential, that is, by developing S_{Pt_E} and S_{Pt_A} for sales potential as estimated, respectively, by the salesman and company. Furthermore, the sales potential term is dated to allow it to change over time in a dynamic modeling of the problem.

The company uses the relationship between its estimate of the territory's current potential and the salesman's actual sales in the past period to set the quota.[36] The quota determination function is

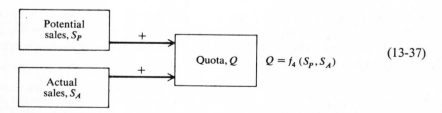

$$Q = f_4(S_P, S_A) \qquad (13\text{-}37)$$

[36]According to Crisp: "To be adequate and accurate, it (the sales quota) must be developed with a full awareness of the territorial potential and of the performance level in the territory in the preceding year." Richard D. Crisp, *Sales Planning and Control* (New York: McGraw-Hill, Inc., 1961), 241.

As a specific function,

$$Q_t = k_6 S_{Pt} + (1-k_6) S_{A, t-1} \tag{13-38}$$

where k_6 = coefficient of company orientation to sales potential $(0 \leqslant k_6 \leqslant 1)$. This says that the quota is set as a weighted average of the territory's sales potential and actual sales last period. If $k_6 = 1$, the company is strictly oriented toward realizing the territory's potential, regardless of the ability or motivation of the particular salesman in the territory. If $k_6 = 0$, the company is completely oriented toward sales, which reflect in large measure the ability and effort of the salesman. If $0 < k_6 < 1$, the company sets each salesman's quota at a level that takes both factors into account according to the relative extent they are favored.

Finally, a relationship is needed to explain how the salesman's motivation level is determined (which in turn influences his effort). His motivation level will be affected by his basic aspiration level (a personality characteristic) and the latest difference between his actual and expected sales. The motivation level function is

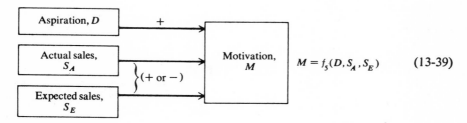

$$M = f_5(D, S_A, S_E) \tag{13-39}$$

As a specific function,

$$M_t = k_7 D + (1-k_7)(k_8)(k_9)\left(1 + \frac{S_{A, t-1} - S_{E, t-1}}{\bar{S}_{A, t}}\right) \tag{13-40}$$

where k_7 = coefficient of salesman's aspiration orientation $(0 \leqslant k \leqslant 1)$
       D = the salesman's aspiration level $(1.00 = \text{average})$
      k_8 = coefficient of salesman's direction of response to recent sales experience $(k_8 = 1 \text{ or } -1)$
      k_9 = coefficient of salesman's magnitude of response to recent sales experience $(1.00 = \text{normal})$
     $\bar{S}_{A, t}$ = smoothed average of salesman's past sales,
          where $\bar{S}_{A, t} = k_{10} S_{A, t-1} + (1-k_{10}) \bar{S}_{A, t-1}$. Here k_{10} is the relative weight given to the most recent sales. For new salesmen, $\bar{S}_{A, t}$ will be imputed.

This says that the salesman's level of motivation in period t is a weighted average of his constant aspiration level and his most recent sales experience. If $k_7 = 1$, the salesman acts entirely on his aspiration level, regardless of recent sales experience. If $k_7 = 0$, the salesman is entirely oriented toward recent sales experience and is emotionally affected by any deviation between his recent and expected sales. If $k_8 = +1$, and his recent sales exceeded his expectation, this increases his motivational level by the positive sales increase percentage (scaled by k_9); if his recent sales fell short of his expectations, this depresses him and reduces his motivational level correspondingly. If $k_8 = -1$, he responds to expectational deviations in a negative way. His motivation level falls if his sales were especially good last period or rises if his sales were especially poor last period.

The total system just described is displayed in one block diagram in Figure 13-9. Given the various functions and a set of specific parameters, it is possible to simulate the effect over time of any specific quota setting policy on any type of salesman. Alternative quota setting rules could be tested for a hypothetical sales force to see which ones lead to better sales performances. The model could also be tested for its sensitivity to different patterns of chance disturbances and to different formulations of salesman motivation and expectation levels.

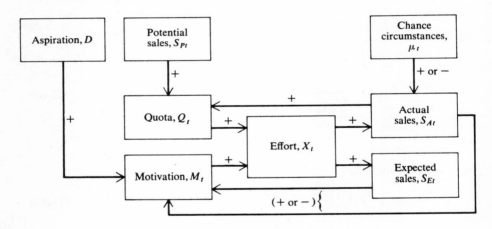

Figure 13-9   A Model of the Effect of Quota Setting on an Individual Salesman's Sales

Legend:

Exogenous variables
  D = salesman's aspiration level (index, 1.00 = normal)
  S_{Pt} = sales potential of territory in period t (in dollars)
  μ_t = deviation from expected sales in period t due to unforeseen circumstances (in dollars)

Control variable
  Q_t = sales quota in period t (in dollars)

System variables
  M_t = motivation level in period t (index, 1.00 = normal)
  X_t = effort of salesman in period t (index, 1.00 = normal)
  S_{Et} = expected sales in period t (in dollars)

Output variable
  S_{At} = actual sales in period t (in dollars)

Finally, it could be extended to take into account different systems of compensation, the effect of competition, and so forth.

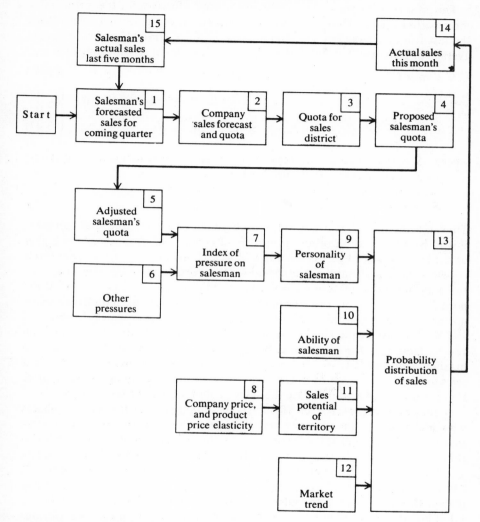

Figure 13-10 Bonini's Model of the Sales Process

Source: This flow chart is not found in Bonini, *op. cit.*, but has been developed by the author on the basis of Bonini's discussion, pp. 32-35, 47-49, 55, 64-70.

Bonini model. A somewhat different approach to the problem of modeling the effect of company incentives on salesman was developed by Bonini.[37] A flow chart of his model is shown in Figure 13-10. Much of the interest lies in

[37]Charles P. Bonini, *Simulation of Information and Decision Systems in the Firm* (Englewood Cliffs, N.J.: Prentice-Hall, 1963).

the detailed mechanisms he developed to represent the action in, and between, various boxes shown in the diagram.

The process starts with each salesman's making a forecast for the forthcoming three-period quarter (box 1). He bases his forecast on his actual sales during the last five quarters (box 15). His forecast is not a straightforward weighted average of past sales but rather the following conditional relationship:

$$\tilde{S} = \max(S_{t-1}, S_{t-2}) \quad \text{if } S_{t-1} \geqslant \bar{S} \text{ and } S_{t-2} \geqslant \bar{S} \tag{13-41}$$

$$\tilde{S} = \bar{S} \quad \text{if } S_{t-1} \geqslant \bar{S} \geqslant S_{t-2} \text{ or } S_{t-2} \geqslant \bar{S} \geqslant S_{t-1} \tag{13-42}$$

$$\tilde{S} = \frac{S_{t-1} + S_{t-2}}{2} \quad \text{if } S_{t-1} < \bar{S} \text{ and } S_{t-2} < \bar{S} \tag{13-43}$$

where $\tilde{S}$ = sales forecast (average monthly sales for the forthcoming quarter)
$\bar{S}$ = average monthly sales for the past five months
S_{t-1} = sales last month
S_{t-2} = sales month before last

Thus, if sales in the last two months are both above normal, the salesman takes this to be an indication of an upward trend and sets his forecast at the higher of the last two sales figures (Equation 13-41). If one of the last two sales levels is below the average and the other above the average, the salesman takes this to be an indication of continued normal conditions and set his forecast at the normal level (Equation 13-42.) Finally, if sales in the last two months are below normal, the salesman takes this to be an indication of a downward trend and sets his forecast at the simple average of the last two months sales (Equation 13-43.) Note that the salesman is biased toward optimism. in that he uses the maximum of recent sales for Equation 13-41 but not the minimum of recent sales for Equation 13-43. Furthermore, it is assumed that he does not manipulate his forecast in order to influence the sales quota that may be set for him.

In the next step the salesmen's forecasts are submitted to district sales managers who make some adjustments[38] and then send them on to the general sales manager. The general sales manager sums the forecasts and submits them to the executive committee which may revise them in preparing the complete quarterly plan. Box 2 covers these details of the determination of the company's sales forecast and quota. The company quota as set by the executive committee is then allocated to all of the sales districts (box 3). Each district sales manager takes his quota and then allocates it to each of the salesmen (box 4). He uses the following quota determination rule:

$$Q_{jp} = \left[.65 \left(\frac{1}{n_d} \right) + .35 \left(\frac{\bar{S}_j}{\bar{S}_d} \right) \right] 1.02 \, Q_d \tag{13-44}$$

where Q_{jp} = proposed quota for salesman j
n_d = number of salesmen in district d
$\bar{S}_j$ = sales of salesman j in last five months

[38]For the adjustment procedure, see ibid., pp. 33–34.

$\tilde{S}_d$ = sales of all salesmen in district in last five months

Q_d = district quota

This rule says that each salesman's quota will be some percentage of the district's quota. The percentage is a weighted average (here .65 and .35) of two fractions. The first fraction $1/n_d$, represents an equal sharing of the quota: thus if the district contains ten salesmen, each should be assigned one-tenth of the quota, all other things being equal. However, the second fraction, $\tilde{S}_j/\tilde{S}_d$, says that, if a salesman accounts for something other than 10 percent of the district's sales, this should also influence his quota. If a particular salesman accounts for 20 percent of district sales, then his percentage of the district quota will be

$$.65\left(\frac{1}{10}\right) + .35\left(\frac{1}{5}\right) = .135 \tag{13-45}$$

Note, finally, that the district quota is inflated by 2 percent (i.e., 1.02). This is done in order to give the district sales manager some leeway in making downward adjustments of quotas for some salesmen who complain about the proposed quota. Quotas are adjusted according to the following rules:

$$Q_{ja} = .95Q_{jp} \qquad \text{if } Q_{jp} \geqslant 1.15\tilde{S}_j \tag{13-46}$$

$$Q_{ja} = 1.10Q_{jp} \qquad \text{if } Q_{jp} \leqslant .75\tilde{S}_j \tag{13-47}$$

$$Q_{ja} = Q_{jp} \qquad \text{otherwise} \tag{13-48}$$

where Q_{ja} = adjusted quota of salesman j

Q_{jp} = proposed quota of salesman j

$\tilde{S}_j$ = salesman forecast

Thus the district manager checks the proposed quota from Equation 13-44 against the salesman's forecast and makes an adjustment in the quota if the two are widely divergent. If the proposed quota exceeds 115 percent of the salesman's forecast, the salesman is likely to complain; this is assumed to lead to a 5 percent reduction in the quota. On the other hand, if the proposed quota is 75 percent or less of the salesman's forecast, the district manager simply increases the proposed quota by 10 percent. No adjustment is made of the proposed quotas that came close to the salesmen forecasts. The end product of this process is a set of sales quotas handed to the salesman (box 5).

The first five steps describe the quota determination process used by the company. Now we shall examine the effects of these quotas (and other variables) on the actual sales level. The actual sales of each salesman this month (box 14) can be interpreted as the outcome of a random draw from a specific probability distribution of sales for each salesman's territory (box 13). A probability model of sales is used in preference to a deterministic model to reflect the many factors beyond the control of the firm that affect sales. The probability distribution itself is formulated as slightly skewed to the right to allow unusually high sales to occur occasionally. The probability distribution is essentially characterized by its mean and standard deviation. Bonini's sales model describes how various factors affect the mean and standard deviation of the probability distribution of sales in each salesman's territory.

In fact, four different factors are identified as affecting the probability distribution of sales (boxes 9, 10, 11, 12). Two factors relate to the behavior of the salesman (boxes 9 and 10) and two are set exogenously by the environment (boxes 11, 12). We shall look at the environmental factors first. The first environmental factor is the sales potential of the territory (box 11). Each territory is specified as having a certain sales potential that serves as the initial mean of its probability distribution of sales. This sales potential is a function of the price charged by the company and the price elasticity as set by the environment (box 8). The sales mean is then modified each month for the market trend, which reflects both growth and cyclicality (box 12). Specifically, mean sales are initially established as

$$\bar{S}_{At} = S_{Pj} \left[1.00167t + \frac{\sin \{(t+1)\,\pi/18\} - \sin (t\,\pi/18)}{10} \right] \qquad (13\text{-}49)$$

where $\bar{S}_{At}$ = mean of the probability distribution of actual sales in period t

S_{pj} = sales potential of territory j

Equation 13-49 says that the mean of the sales distribution is equal to the territory's sales potential modified by a trend and cyclical factor. The trend factor increases the mean by .167 percent each month, or approximately 2 percent each year. That is, the demand for the company's product is assumed to grow at the rate of 2 percent per year. Furthermore, mean demand in any period is influenced by the phase of an economic cycle which varies 10 per cent above and below the trend and whose period is three years (36 months).

The mean (and variance) of the sales distribution in period t are further modified by two behavioral characteristics of the individual salesman (boxes 9 and 10). The first is the salesman's personality (box 9) or more specifically, how he reacts to pressure (box 7) as it comes from the sales quota (box 5) and other sources (box 6). The amount of pressure felt by the salesman is summarized in an index of pressure. This index deviates from its normal level of 100 when the pressure is unusually high or low. The index is derived as a weighted average of five specific sources of pressure, each of which also centers normally on 100:

$$I_{pt} = .25I_{1t} + .40I_{2t} + .10I_{3t} + .10I_{4t} + .15I_{5t} \qquad (13\text{-}50)$$

where I_{pt} = salesman's index of pressure at time t

I_{1t} = index of pressure of salesman's superior (the district sales manager) at time t

I_{2t} = salesman's quota at time t relative to his sales in the past month, that is, Q_t/S_{t-1}

I_{3t} = sales of the "average" salesman in his district, relative to his sales at time t

$I_{4t} = .75$ plus the fraction of his products less than 75 percent of quota last period

$I_{5t} =$ salesman's total quota for the past quarter, relative to his total sales for the last quarter

Thus each period the amount of pressure on each salesman will change depending upon the five factors listed above. The effect of this pressure on the salesman, however, will vary with the salesman's "personality" (box 9). Bonini distinguishes four types of salesman. The first type reacts to increased pressure by calling more intensively on the "sure" customers and ignoring new prospects. This has the effect of increasing the mean of his sales distribution but decreasing the variance. When the pressure relaxes, he spends more time cultivating new prospects, which decreases the mean of the sales distribution but increases the variance. The specific effects of pressure on the mean of the Type I salesman are shown in Section A of Table 13-8.

The type II salesman reacts to pressure by increasing his effort in all areas, and this has the effect of increasing both the mean and standard deviation of the sales distribution. The specific changes are shown in Section B of Table 13-8. The type III salesman reacts to pressure in a negative way by slightly decreasing his sales effort. He may either resent pressure or the pressure takes the form of more sales meetings, which wastes his time without increasing his motivation. The specific effects of pressure on this salesman are shown in Section C. Finally the type IV salesman reacts to pressure by "high pressuring" his customers into buying for inventory. This increases mean sales in the current period at the cost of depressing sales in the following three periods. The complicated effects of pressure on the type IV salesman are shown in Section D.[39]

The fact that there are four types of salesmen in Bonini's model makes the analysis of company quota setting and pressure more complicated and more realistic. In thinking about quota policy, the company should be concerned with the distribution of the different types of salesmen in the sales force. A sales force with all type I salesmen should be managed differently from a sales force with, say, all type III salesmen. For the purpose of his simulation, Bonini created forty salesmen distributed as follows: Type I, 8; Type II, 20; Type III, 4; and Type IV, 8. He assigned these salesmen to the various sales districts on a random basis because sales personalities are unlikely to be related to specific districts. The results of Bonini's simulation will apply to the particular distribution of salesmen types and their assignments; the analyst has the option of testing out alternative distributions. If Type I salesmen work out better for the given company policies than Type II salesmen, this implies that the company might alter its recruitment, selection, and training policies to increase the relative number of Type I salesmen.

In addition to the effect of the salesman's personality on the probability

---

[39]It should be appreciated that the specific numbers in Table 13-8 and elsewhere in the Bonini model are illustrative. They are developed as "reasonable" magnitudes on the basis of impressionistic observation, in order to explore the impact of alternative company policies in such a system.

Table 13-8   Response of Different Salesman Types to Pressure

A. TYPE I SALESMAN

Salesman's index of pressure	Change in the mean of the sales distribution	Change in the standard deviation of the sales distribution
Less than 80	Decreased by 3.85%	Increased by 11%
Between 80 and 95	Decreased by 1.96%	Increased by 7%
Between 95 and 115	None	None
Between 115 and 130	Increased by 2%	Decreased by 11%
Above 130	Increased by 4%	Decreased by 15%

B. TYPE II SALESMAN

Less than 80	Decreased by 12%	Decreased by 12%
Between 80 and 95	Decreased by 8%	Decreased by 8%
Between 95 and 115	None	None
Between 115 and 130	Increased by 10%	Increased by 10%
Above 130	Increased by 15%	Increased by 15%

C. TYPE III SALESMAN

Less than 80	Increased by 3%	None
Between 80 and 95	Increased by 2%	None
Between 95 and 115	None	None
Between 115 and 130	Decreased by 1.96%	None
Above 130	Decreased by 2.91%	None

D. TYPE IV SALESMAN

Less than 80	Decreased by 12%	Decreased by 12%
Between 80 and 95	Decreased by 8%	Decreased by 8%
Between 95 and 115	None	None
Between 115 and 130	Moderate borrowing	
Above 130	Much borrowing	

EFFECT OF	MODERATE BORROWING		MUCH BORROWING	
	Changes in the mean	Changes in the standard deviation	Changes in the mean	Changes in the standard deviation
Current period	+20%	+10%	+30%	+15%
Following period	−35%	−15%	−40%	−20%
Third period	None	None	None	None
Fourth period				
If the index of pressure is:				
Less than 95	None	None	None	None
Between 95 and 115	+5%	None	+5%	None
Between 115 and 130	+8%	+5%	+8%	+5%
Above 130	+12%	+8%	+12%	+8%
Fifth period	Return to the normal situation			

Source: Bonini, *Simulation of Information and Decision Systems in the Firm*, pp. 65–67.

distribution of sales, his ability also affects the mean level of his sales (box 10). Bonini assigned seven different ability levels to the forty salesmen. The abilities ranged from a high of 129 per cent of "normal" to a low of 80 percent, with about one half of the salesmen standing at 100 (normal). These ability levels were assigned randomly to the various salesmen independently of their personality. The mean of the probability distribution of sales is adjusted by the salesman's ability level.

This completes the discussion of the sales model developed by Bonini as part of his larger model of the firm and its environment. In summary, each salesman's sales for the period is drawn from a probability distribution of sales whose mean and/or variance are/is immediately influenced by two behavioral characteristics (salesman's personality and ability) and two environmental factors (territory sales potential and market trend). The salesman's actual current sales, along with sales in several previous periods, influence his new forecast and the sum of salesmen forecasts influence salesmen quotas. The sales quota assigned to a salesman for the coming period acts as one of several pressures on him; he reacts to this pressure in one of four ways, depending on his personality. Bonini has presented a rich behavioral picture of the quota setting and sales process which can be refined further in many interesting ways.

An Economic Analysis of Optimal Commissions

The previous discussion displayed the various behavioral factors associated with the response of salesmen to company quotas. An analysis of salesmen's response to quotas would be incomplete if it did not bring in the commission plan under which the salesmen operate. If we are willing to make the assumption that a salesman is not interested in meeting quotas for various products so much as maximizing his commissions, it is conceivable that he will be led to allocate his selling time in ways that maximize his welfare but not the company's. This then necessitates that the company find some way to set quotas and commissions that lead the salesman's commission maximizing behavior to maximize the company's profits at the same time.

Consider a company that produces several products and pays its salesmen through commissions. If commission rates are based on total sales, the salesmen will choose to allocate their time among products in a way that will produce a mix of sales that will maximize their total commission. They will not pay attention to the varying costs of producing and selling the various products and their effort to maximize their commissions will typically not lead to profit maximization for the firm. This will be shown first and afterwards we will consider setting commission rates on gross margin instead of sales for each product, in order to lead the salesmen to sell the mix of products that will maximize the firm's profit.

The procedure will be to develop an expression of the optimization problem as it appears to the salesman and the firm, respectively, and consider under what circumstances there would be joint optimization.[40] If we consider the salesman first, his optimization problem is: maximize

$$W_j = \sum_i r_i p_i f_{ij}(t_{ij}) \tag{13-51}$$

subject to

$$\sum_i t_{ij} \leqslant T_j \tag{13-52}$$

$$t_{ij} \geqslant 0 \qquad\qquad i = 1, \ldots, m$$

where W_j = total commission earned by salesman j
   r_i = commission rate paid on total sales of the ith product
   p_i = price of the ith product
   t_{ij} = amount of time spent on the ith product by the jth salesman[41]
   $f_{ij}(t_{ij}) = q_{ij}$ = the quantity sold of the ith product by the jth salesman
   T_j = total time available to salesman j

Thus the salesman's problem is to determine how much time to spend selling each product within the limits of his total time, so as to maximize his commission (the commission rate times the sales summed for all products).

The conditions for the salesman to maximize his total commission can be found by combining Equations 13-51 and 13-52 into the Langrangian expression:[42]

$$L(W_j) = \sum_i r_i p_i f_{ij}(t_{ij}) + \beta_j (T_j - \sum_i t_{ij}) \tag{13-53}$$

where β_j = Lagrangian multipliers.

As a necessary condition for salesman maximization of $L(W_j)$, the first derivative of Equation 13-53 is set equal to 0:

$$\frac{dL(W_j)}{dt_{ij}} = r_i p_i \frac{df_{ij}}{dt_{ij}} - \beta_j = 0 \tag{13-54}$$

or

$$r_i p_i \frac{df_{ij}}{dt_{ij}} = \beta_j \qquad \text{for all } i = 1, \ldots, m \tag{13-55}$$

This condition says that the marginal increase in commissions with an extra application of effort should equal the marginal cost of increasing the time available for selling.

---

[40]The analysis in this section is adapted from Otto A. Davis and John U. Farley, "Quotas, Commissions and the Economics of the Sales Force," in Robert L. King, ed., *Marketing and the Science of Planning* (Chicago: American Marketing Association, 1968), 75–78.
   [41]Davis and Farley used time (*t*) as the scarce resource, although this could be converted into the number of calls (*n*) to make it consistent with other models discussed in this chapter.
   [42]See Chap. 6, pp. 150–153.

Turning to the firm, its optimization problem is: maximize

$$Z = \sum_i \{(1 - r_i) p_i [\sum_j f_{ij} (t_{ij})] - C_i [\sum_j f_{ij} (t_{ij})]\} \tag{13-56}$$

subject to

$$\sum_i t_{ij} \leqslant T_j \qquad\qquad j = 1, \ldots, n$$

$$\tag{13-57}$$

$$t_{ij} \geqslant 0 \qquad\qquad i = 1, \ldots, m; j = 1, \ldots, n$$

where $C_i[\sum_j f_{ij} (t_{ij})]$ = total cost to the firm of producing the ith product

Thus the firm's problem is to determine how much time each of its salesmen should spend in selling each of its products, so as to maximize its profits. The firm's profits are shown in Equation 13-56 as the difference between its total revenue after commissions and its total costs which are some function, not necessarily linear, of its respective levels of output of the various products.

The condition for an optimal solution to the firm's problem is given by combining Equations 13-56 and 13-57 into the Lagrangian expression:

$$L(Z) = \sum_i \{(1 - r_i) p_i [\sum_j f_{ij}(t_{ij})] - C_i [\sum_j f_{ij}(t_{ij})]\} + \lambda_j (T_j - \sum_j t_{ij}) \tag{13-58}$$

where λ_j = Lagrangian multipliers (not the same as multipliers β_j)

A necessary condition for maximization requires setting the first derivative of Equation 13-58 equal to 0:

$$\frac{dL(Z)}{dt_{ij}} = (1 - r_i) p_i \frac{df_{ij}}{dt_{ij}} - \frac{\partial C_i}{\partial f_{ij}} \frac{df_{ij}}{dt_{ij}} - \lambda_j = 0 \tag{13-59}$$

or

$$\left[(1 - r_i) p_i - \frac{\partial C_i}{\partial f_{ij}} \right] \frac{df_{ij}}{dt_{ij}} = \lambda_j \qquad \text{for all} \begin{array}{l} i = 1, \ldots, m \\ j = 1, \ldots, n \end{array} \tag{13-60}$$

This condition says that the company should encourage the salesmen to allocate their time among the company products in such a way that, at the margin, the company's profit on each product is the same and equal to λ_j, the marginal return on additional selling time beyond $\sum_i t_{ij}$ (λ_j = marginal cost of relieving the time constraint, i.e., increasing T_j).

Now it must be asked under what circumstances will the salesmen be allocating their time among products in such a way that their time allocation maximizes their commissions and, at the same time, the company's profits? For this to happen, there would have to be some time allocation that satisfies both Equations 13-55 and 13-60. This is very unlikely to happen. For Equations 13-55 and 13-60 to be satisfied simultaneously by the same time allocation, it would be necessary that two conditions must exist. The first is that r_i in Equation 13-55 equals $(1 - r_i)$ in Equation 13-60 (for all i), and this could only happen if $r_i = .50$.

But it is very unlikely that the commission rate of all products will be .50. The second condition is that the marginal cost of production must equal 0, that is $\partial C_i/\partial f_{ij} = 0$. This condition is unlikely. The implication of this analysis is that a system of commission rates paid on sales is unlikely to lead the salesmen to allocate their time in a way that maximizes the firm's profits. The firm might attempt to set sales quotas for the various products for individual salesmen based on its profit maximizing solution, but the salesmen are not likely to heed these quotas if they prevent the salesmen from maximizing their commissions.

A system that may reconcile the conflicting interests of salesmen and the company calls for setting the commission rates on product gross margin instead of sales.[43] The Lagrangian expression for the salesman's optimization problem becomes

$$L(W_j) = \sum_i r_i[p_i f_{ij}(t_{ij}) - C_i(\sum_j f_{ij}(t_{ij}))] + \beta_j(T_j - \sum_i t_{ij}) \tag{13-61}$$

The Langrangian expression for the company's optimization problem becomes

$$L(Z) = \sum_i \{(1-r_i)[p_i \sum_j f_{ij}(t_{ij}) - C_i(\sum_j f_{ij}(t_{ij}))]\} + \lambda_j(T_j - \sum_i t_{ij}) \tag{13-62}$$

The Lagrangian expression for the salesman's commissions is maximized when:

$$r_i\left[p_i - \frac{\partial C_i}{\partial f_{ij}}\right]\frac{df_{ij}}{dt_{ij}} = \beta_j \tag{13-63}$$

The Lagrangian expression for the company's profits is maximized when:

$$(1-r_i)\left[p_i - \frac{\partial C_i}{\partial f_{ij}}\right]\frac{df_{ij}}{dt_{ij}} = \lambda_j \tag{13-64}$$

The interests of the salesman and the company are reconciled if there is some time allocation that can satisfy Equations 13-63 and 13-64 simultaneously. Suppose that the marginal cost of producing each product is constant (though not necessarily identical) and known by each salesman. The firm's problem is to determine a set of commission rates on the various products that will maximize its total profits, taking into account how its salesmen will respond to these commission rates.

The problem of reconciling the interests of the salesmen and the company is complicated if marginal costs are increasing, instead of constant. Under increasing marginal costs the salesman no longer knows the marginal cost of selling each product in his seeking an optimal solution to his time allocation problem. The marginal cost of selling each product will be determined by the product's output level and this will be determined by the separate decisions of all the salesmen on how much time to spend in selling that product. The separate decisions of the salesmen will be influenced by the commission rates set by the company. If the company had full information about the individual salesmen's

---

[43]For an earlier article on this, see Ralph L. Day and Peter D. Bennett, "Should Salesmen's Compensation Be Geared to Profits," *Journal of Marketing Research*, (May 1964) 39–43.

time effectiveness functions, df_{ij}/dt_{ij}, it could determine the profit maximizing commission rates according to Equation 13-64. But the company usually does not have this information and, even if it did, the solution calls for solving centrally a nonlinear programming problem that may be difficult to solve for an optimum. These difficulties of inadequate information and ineffective solution technique have been the motivating force behind the search for decentralized solutions to the problem. Quotas imposed on the sales force represent centralized solutions; yet, if they do not conform to commission maximizing sales levels for the salesmen, they are not likely to be fulfilled. Davis and Farley have suggested a decentralized solution that would reconcile the salesmen's and firm's interests in principle. The firm determines alternate sets of commission rates on the various products, based on its knowledge of cost behavior (which it may not wish to reveal to the salesmen) and its price setting capabilities. These sets of commission rates are transmitted to the salesmen who transmit back "desired quotas" under each set of commissions. The company examines the discrepancies between what it would like to see sold of each product and what the salesmen indicate they would sell. The company adjusts the commission rates to bring sales force intentions into line with company intentions. Specifically, the commission rates are raised on products for which the planned sales levels are too low and lowered on products for which the planned sales levels are too high. After several iterations, a final set of commission rates on gross margins will be found that will bring planned sales into equilibrium with the company's desired sales.

SUMMARY

Most companies utilize a sales force to reach their intermediate and/or final customers. The salesmen perform a number of useful functions, including locating new prospects, communicating product information to customers, attempting to use persuasive arguments to close a sale, learning of customers' changing needs and bringing this and other market information back to the company. Many companies make a considerable investment in selecting, training, and motivating salesmen to perform these tasks effectively.

Management science has produced useful models in at least three areas of sales force management, that is, designing and assigning sales territories, developing optimal calling policies for different types of customers, and setting salesmen quotas and incentives.

Those companies in which each salesman is assigned a geographical area face the problem of setting up and periodically revising the sales territories. Desirable qualities of the territories are that they be equal in workload or sales potential, contiguous, and compact. Companies use a variety of procedures to create such sales territories, most of them intuitively based. Hess has recently developed a computer program based on the transportation method of linear programming which is capable of creating sales territories that achieve the desirable qualities. The computer program is able to design, in a rapid, explicit, and optimal way, a set of territories that are equitable, contiguous, and compact. After territories are designed, management will want to assign its salesmen to the territories in an optimal way. It is not correct that assigning the "best" salesmen to the "best" territories will produce the greatest sales. Rather it is necessary to estimate the likely sales of each salesman in each territory, taking into account interactions that may exist between the man and each territory and then to apply the standard "assignment problem" solution to maximize expected sales.

Companies vary in the extent to which they instruct their salesmen on the number of calls to make on different-size accounts and the routing to use. All companies are interested in examining this problem because a salesman's time is expensive and it is very easy for him to misplan without the proper level of training. The problem can be divided into determining how many calls to make on customers and how many calls to make on prospects and then trying to combine the two. The problem of how many calls to make on customers should ideally be guided by knowledge of the sales response function of individual customers or customer classes. Yet most of the attempts in the past to measure sales response functions of customers or customer classes have not yielded distinct sales response functions. As for the number of calls to make on prospects, this can be handled by a simple analytical model of the value of a call and/or by the use of Markov process models describing the transitional probabilities of prospects moving into new classes as a function of the number of calls they receive. The joint determination of the number of calls to customers and prospects can be carried out through either a behavioral analysis, a deterministic analysis, or a stochastic analysis. Cloonan's heuristic method can then be used to determine which accounts to call on each period and the optimal routing.

A major responsibility of the field sales manager is to motivate his salesmen to put forth their best effort. Sales quotas and commissions are two formal sales management tools that play a critical role in creating the proper motivation. The effect of salesmen quotas on salesmen's efforts is not simple but rather depends upon a complicated set of variables and feedback relationships. A behavioral model of the author's and one by Bonini illustrated how quotas and other variables affect sales performance. As for commissions, the problem is to set them in such a way that the salesman, in seeking to maximize his own income, will also automatically maximize company profits. Commissions based on product sales were shown to lead to suboptimal performance. Company and sales force interests are much better reconciled through commissions based on product gross margins. Even here, finding the optimal product commission levels calls for the solution of a complicated mathematical problem that might best be solved through decentralized procedures.

Questions and Problems

1. The sales manager of a firm selling an industrial product wishes to divide his total sales area into three territories, each containing a share of the

company's 15 customers. The following 2 arrangements are being considered:

Arrangement 1	Customer	d_{hi}	$V_i(000)$
Territory 1	1	5	5
	2	15	10
	3	20	10
	4	5	15
	5	10	5
	6	10	20
			—
			65
Territory 2	1	6	15
	2	5	30
	3	10	10
	4	25	15
			—
			70
Territory 3	1	4	15
	2	10	15
	3	8	10
	4	5	5
	5	15	12
			—
			57

Arrangement 2			
Territory 1	1	5	5
	2	15	10
	3	15	15
	4	5	15
	5	10	20
			—
			65
Territory 2	1	6	15
	2	10	10
	3	15	10
	4	5	30
			—
			65
Territory 3	1	4	15
	2	10	15
	3	8	10
	4	15	12
	5	5	5
	6	5	5
			—
			62

In the above d_{hi} represents distance from the home base, and V_i is the volume of customer i in thousands of units. Determine which arrangement is best in terms of compactness and workload.

2. An automobile parts manufacturer sells its product to three types of customers:
(a) automobile manufacturers for use as original equipment (O.E.)
(b) wholesale distributors who in turn distribute to parts retailers (W.D.)
(c) parts retailer . . . primarily jobbers and service stations (P.R.)
From past experience the company has found it most efficient to have three sales-men selling in each territory, one for each type of customer.

In a particular territory, the sales manager asks each salesman what he expects to be able to sell to each type of customer. These estimates are shown in the following table:

	Customer Type		
Salesman	O.E.	W.D.	P.R.
A	100,000	90,000	80,000
B	92,000	92,000	85,000
C	102,000	95,000	75,000

To which customer type should each salesman be assigned in order to maximize sales in the territory?

3. A salesman has 4 open calls in the next period which he would like to devote to one of 3 prospects. The probabilities that these prospects will be converted to customers after 4 calls are .6, .8, and .4 respectively (for prospects 1, 2, and 3).

If converted to customers, the respective prospects will yield the following profits to the firm in the coming 3 years:

	Year		
Prospect	1	2	3
1	2,000	2,000	3,000
2	4,000	1,000	1,000
3	2,000	2,000	6,000

If the cost of each call is $500, compute the expected rate of return for each prospect. In which prospect should the salesman invest his 4 calls? (Assume a time discount rate of 5 percent.)

4. A salesman calculates that he will be able to make approximately 720 sales calls during the coming year and wants to know how he can best allocate these calls between current customers and prospects in his territory. He has estimated his customer holding rate in the absence of sales calls at .6, and for a very large number of calls at .9. Total sales in his territory last year were $200 (in thousands). The maximum possible sales to prospects in the territory for the coming year are estimated at $100 (thousands).

Assuming that the parameters a and b take on the values .002 and .01, respectively, determine the optimal allocation of the 720 calls between current customers and prospects.

5. A salesman travels through 10 cities (A, B, C, D, E, F, G, H, I, J) on each of his trips. He must always first pass through A, B, and C, and then he is free to route

himself in any way through the remaining cities. He wants to minimize his travel cost. If he decides on the route through the remaining cities using a random device, what is the probability that his route will be optimal?

6. Using Cloonan's formulation for the value of calling on an account (Equation 13–30), determine the value of t for which V_i is greatest. How often should this account be called on? Does the value of M affect this calculation?

7. A salesman is about to select 10 out of 50 accounts to visit in the coming week. Which rule should he follow to maximize the value of his calls?
(a) Call on the 10 accounts that are most likely to place orders as a result of his calls
(b) Call on the 10 largest customers
(c) Call on the 10 accounts that he hasn't seen for the longest time
(d) Call on the 10 accounts that might conceivably place the largest orders?

8. (a) The ABC Company has five salesmen in one of its sales districts. Salesman A's sales figures (in thousands) for the last 5 months are:

Jan.	Feb.	Mar.	Apr.	May
$14	$13	$18	$15	$15

Total sales for the district over this period were $450 (thousands) and the district quota for June is $90. Using the Bonini model, determine salesman A's adjusted quota for June.
(b) Suppose the index of pressure on salesman A consisted of:

Factor	Weight
Salesman A's quota relative to actual sales last month	70
Index of pressure of district sales manager	30

Suppose the index of pressure on the district sales manager is 120 and the salesman's quota is $6000, but his sales were only $4000. What is the index of pressure on salesman A?

9. The XYZ Company is interested in finding out what makes a superior salesman. The company decides to try to identify its own superior salesmen and study their common characteristics. Are its superior salesmen those men who
(a) Rank highest in annual sales?
(b) Whose sales have shown the fastest rate of growth?
(c) Who score highest on self-confidence and energy?
(d) Who work well without supervision?

CHAPTER 14
Advertising Decision Models

One of the most important and bewildering promotional tools of modern marketing management is advertising. No one doubts that it is effective in presenting information to potential buyers; there is also widespread agreement that it can be persuasive to some extent and create or reinforce buyer preference for a company's products. These potential values of advertising are testified to by the fact that American companies are approaching the point of spending $20 billion a year in advertising, or two percent of the gross national product. Furthermore, advertising expenditures are growing rapidly in other nations, both capitalist and socialist.

Advertising is bewildering because of its typically lagged effects and also the difficulty of isolating its effects from other elements in the marketing mix. Without some sense of the functional relationship between sales and advertising expenditures, it becomes very difficult to know how much to spend on advertising. Companies in these circumstances tend to resort to simple rules for setting the advertising budget that may work satisfactorily in practice but are not likely to represent an optimal level.

In the last decade, there have been some notable attempts to formulate models of how advertising works and methodologies for measuring the effect of advertising on sales or some intermediate variable connected with sales. This chapter will examine important models with respect to major advertising decision problems facing the advertiser.

The advertiser faces five major advertising decision problems: The determining of advertising goals, creative message and copy, the best media, the best timing, and the best expenditure level. Let us consider each in turn.

1.   The advertiser must pinpoint the specific objectives that he would like to see the advertising expenditures accomplish during the period (Advertising Goals Decision). Does he see the advertising as largely passing on information to the buyers, or creating brand preference, or actually triggering purchases? These various objectives will be considered in the first section of this chapter in terms of a buyer behavior model of the effects of advertising.

2.   The advertiser must decide on a creative strategy (Creative Decision). He must determine what to say (the message) and how to say it (the copy). The number of possible messages that might be used to promote a product is typically large. The number is considerably reduced by careful product definition and target groups definition. In addition to choosing the facets of the product and company to feature, there are vital issues concerning the relative merits of one-sided versus two-sided arguments, exaggerated versus straightforward selling, the use of humor, the role of testimonials, and so on. Models for considering the creative decision are presented in the second section of this chapter.

3.   The advertiser must decide in which media he will place his messages, and when (Media Decision). This decision rests on developing solutions to several subproblems. First, there is the problem of determining the relative effectiveness of different media classes (newspapers, magazines, radio, television, and billboards). Advertisers do not generally put all their budget in one media class but rather develop a media mix that reflects their ideas of the relative effectiveness of the different media classes. Second, there is the problem of determining the specific *media vehicles* (i.e., *Life, Chicago Tribune, Ed Sullivan Show*, etc.) within each media category that are "best" in terms of their audience size and composition in relation to customer targets and media costs. Advertisers generally rate the different media vehicles in terms of the cost per thousand (weighted) exposures and seek the combination of vehicles that minimizes the cost of achieving a certain number of total exposures (or equivalently, maximizes the number of exposures for a given budget). Third, there is the problem of determining the best *media options*, that is, the size and color of ads. This is largely an issue of the trade-off value of more ads of a lower quality (smaller size or no color, in general less noticeability) to fewer ads of a higher quality.

4.   The advertiser must determine the best timing of the message over the year (Media Timing Decision). A *media insertion* will describe a specific purchase of a media option to appear at a specific time. The seller can favor a plan of steady advertising, burst advertising, or alternating advertisement.[1] The timing of advertising exposures will be highly related to the seller's ideas of the effects of advertising repetition and memory loss, as well as seasonal factors, on the

---

[1]For a schematic classification of twelve possible timing patterns, see Philip Kotler, *Marketing Management: Analysis, Planning and Control* (Englewood Cliffs, N.J.: Prentice-Hall, Inc., 1967), 485.

attitude and behavior of buyers. All of these media issues will be considered in the third section of this chapter.

5. The advertiser must determine how much money to budget for advertising (Advertising Budget Size Decision.) But the correct determination of how much to spend on any marketing resource has already been examined in Part I of this book. The decision requires, in principle, an estimate of sales for different levels of advertising expenditures. If the sales response function to advertising and other elements of the marketing mix, including competitors' outlays, are known, it is possible to determine the optimal advertising budget. Data on the response of sales to advertising expenditure can be developed experimentally or in a number of other ways, as discussed later in Chapter 19. Here we shall assume that the budget size has already been decided.

THE ADVERTISING GOALS DECISION

Advertising decisions must be made in the context of a realistic appraisal of what advertising can actually accomplish for the advertiser. In some situations, effective advertising can trigger actual purchases; in other situations it can only lay a groundwork of favorable attitudes. Furthermore, different effects may ensue, depending upon whether the stimuli are a single advertisement or a major advertising campaign. Setting objectives for advertising requires a realistic understanding of the advertising process. This process is discussed first in terms of the influence of the single advertisement on a potential buyer and then the influence of a whole advertising campaign.

The Influence of a Single Advertisement

The starting point for advertising theory and planning must be a framework for understanding what happens to a person when he confronts an advertisement. Let us represent the advertisement by

$$A_{hijkt} \tag{14-1}$$

where A = stands for an advertising insertion in a media

h = subscript for creative quality of the advertisement:[2] $h = -1$, dull advertisement; $h = 0$, neutral advertisement; $h = 1$, good advertisement; $h = 2$, highly appealing advertisement

i = subscript for media class i: $i = 1$, newspapers; $i = 2$, magazines; $i = 3$, radio; $i = 4$, television; $i = 5$, billboards; $i = 6$, other

j = subscript for media vehicle j (different for each media class)

k = subscript for media option k (different for each media class and/or vehicle: refers to size and color options)

t = subscript for time

---

[2]The quality of an advertisement is extremely difficult to measure, and the classification presented here is only suggestive. At best, the rating represents the average buyer's perception of the quality of the ad. It must not be forgotten that the initial reaction to the content of an ad wears away in time, leaving only remembrance of the company's name (called the "sleeper effect.")

Let us represent a particular person by

$$B_{mnprt} \tag{14-2}$$

where B = stands for a person

m = subscript for buyer class: $m = 0$, nonbuyer; $m = 1$, potential buyer; $m = 2$, buys from competitor; $m = 3$, buys from company

n = subscript for buyer state: $n = 0$, person is unaware of company's product; $n = 1$, person is aware but indifferent to company's product; $n = 2$, person has favorable attitude toward company's product; $n = 3$, person intends to buy company's product

p = subscript for advertising attentiveness of buyer: $p = 0$, person pays little attention to ads; $p = 1$, person pays average attention to ads; $p = 2$, person pays close attention to ads

r = subscript for the frequency of the person's exposure to media j: $r = 0$, person is never or rarely exposed to media j; $r = 1$, person is exposed to media j half of the time; $r = 2$, person is exposed to media j all or most of the time

t = subscript for time

Now let us consider a particular advertisement coming into the purview of a particular person at time t:

$$A_{hijkt} : B_{mnprt} \tag{14-3}$$

The effect of this advertisement on the person will depend on the various values of the subscripts. For example, the advertisement A_{hijkt} has no effect on the person if the person is a nonbuyer of the product ($m = 0$), pays little attention to advertising ($p = 0$), or is rarely or never exposed to media j that carries the advertisement ($r = 0$); or if the advertisement is negative or neutral in its effects ($h = -1$ or 0). Any one of these circumstances will render the advertisement a waste from the company's point of view, as far as this person is concerned. The media choice j as a whole is wasteful if it reaches a large number of nonbuyers who do not pay much attention to advertising, or if the advertisement is poor in creative quality.

At the other extreme, the advertisement insertion A_{hijkt} could have some effect on a person who is exposed all the time to the media ($r = 2$) and pays close attention to advertising ($p = 2$); and if the advertisement is perceived as good or highly appealing ($h = 1$ or 2). The effect will also depend on whether the person is a potential buyer, a competitor's buyer, or a company buyer ($m = 1$ or 2 or 3).

In between these two extremes, there will be a variable amount of wastage in the advertisement. To evaluate this, let us define the *exposure value of advertising insertion*, E_A, as the average number of persons who are exposed to the medium carrying the advertisement at that time of the year (that is, audience size). In the case of an advertisement placed in a weekly magazine such as *Life*, its exposure value is the number of persons who read or skim an issue of the magazine at that time of the year. The advertisement's exposure value is related to, but not the same as, its circulation level. Its circulation level is the number of subscriptions to the magazine plus the number of newsstand sales. The magazine may also send out an average number of complimentary copies that would raise the exposure value. Each copy will be read by one or more persons in the household and may even be passed on to other households. Copies that go to professional offices will have a large pass-on readership. Therefore, exposure value of a magazine is typically larger, and in some cases substantially larger, than the circulation level.

In the case of television, the exposure value is related to the number of TV homes but more directly to the audience sizes for the different programs. This is estimated, albeit with some error, by various TV media rating services. Advertising exposure will be of varying difficulty to estimate for the different media. We shall ignore for the present the desirability of weighing the exposures differently for the buying power of the persons exposed, a refinement that will be taken up later in the media decision section.

Only a fraction of the number of persons who are exposed to the media vehicle carrying the advertisement will actually *see* the advertisement; let this fraction be f_1. Seeing the advertisement is measured by finding out whether the person recognizes or can recall it.

Some further fraction of those who see the advertisement will *register* it; let this be f_2. Registering the advertisement is measured by finding out whether the person correctly recalls some of the content, such as the message or appeals used in the advertisement.[3] Although the advertisement has some value if it is only seen (in creating or maintaining brand identification), it has more value to the advertiser if the person can recall the appeals.

Some fraction of those who register the advertisement will be moved by the appeals (which will be related to the quality of the advertisement); let this be f_3. It is this effect that finally enters into the effective value of the insertion, $V(E_A)$. Summarizing then, the actual effective value of a single advertisement is given by

$$V(E_A) = f_1 f_2 f_3 E_A \qquad (14\text{-}4)$$

where $V(E_A)$ = effective value of a single advertising insertion

f_1 = percent of persons exposed to the medium who have seen the advertisement

f_2 = percent of persons seeing the advertisement who registered the message

f_3 = percent of persons registering the message who were favorably impressed

E_A = the average number of persons exposed to the medium carrying the advertisement

[3]There are various services that measure the degree to which advertisements have been seen or registered. These services such as Daniel Starch and staff, Gallup-Robinson, Inc. are described and evaluated in Darrell Blaine Lucas and Steuart Henderson Britt, *Measuring Advertising Effectiveness* (New York: McGraw-Hill, Inc., 1963).

Thus the effective value of a single advertising insertion is not given by its exposure value but possibly by much less, depending on the values of the various downward adjustments for audience shrinkage. Advertising readership measurement services tend to supply management with some measure of f_1 and f_2, based on controlled sampling techniques. As for f_3, it is much harder to define and measure, although it is critical in the estimation of the effective value of an advertisement.

The Influence of an Advertising Campaign

Any analysis of advertising that is confined to the effect of the single advertisement is likely to be discouraging, in that the single advertisement typically secures a low viewed score and a still lower registered score. Furthermore, the single advertisement cannot be expected to leave a lasting impression even when noted. For example, a study of print advertising concluded that recall decays sharply with time; after three months, less than 10 percent of those exposed to an advertisement can recall it.[4] Some repetition or continuity of the advertising is necessary to maintain a certain level of awareness and positive effect. One of the central questions in advertising theory and practice is how much repetition per period should the advertiser aim for. Most experts agree that, just as there may be too few repetitions of an advertisement for it to rise above the threshold level of consciousness and be noticed, there may be too much repetition from the viewpoint of either developing further awareness or strengthening affective feelings in terms of the cost. Continued exposure to an advertisement can lead the person not to notice it any more or even turn against it and the advertised brand. Therefore, a central objective of advertising decision makers is to determine the minimum exposure frequency per period that will accomplish the advertising objectives of the advertiser.

To clarify the conceptual issues posed by exposure frequency, it will help to consider the effect on one person of two or more exposures to an advertisement, with a fixed time between exposures. Two-dimensional geometric space can be used to represent the effect of advertising repetition on an individual person.[5] The space in this case is formed by two axes, one representing cognition and the other representing affect. (See Figure 14-1(a)). It will be called CA-space. The cognition axis represents the amount of knowledge that the person might have about the product. At the lowest level, he may just be aware of the advertisement, that is, he recalls seeing it. At the next level he may be able to recall the product appeals used in the advertisement. At still a higher level, he may have actual knowledge of the product and its features through past usage. Although this axis is subdivided into stages, it should be interpreted as being quite continuous.

---

[4]*The Repetition of Advertising* (New York: Batten, Barton, Durstine and Osborn, 1967), 2.
[5]The original suggestion is found and developed in Peter Langhoff, "Options in Campaign Evaluation," *Journal of Advertising Research* (Dec. 1967) 41–47. It is presented here with some modifications.

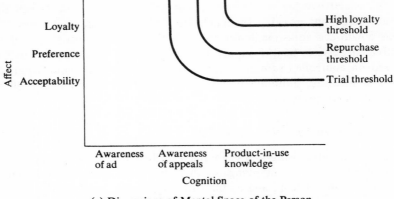

(a) Dimensions of Mental Space of the Person

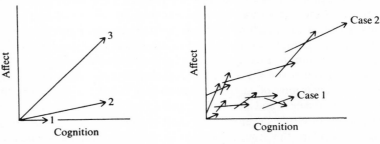

(b) Three Possible Effects of a Single Advertising Exposure

(c) Two Illustrative Paths of an Advertisement Effect through Time

Figure 14-1 Mental Space of a Potential Buyer as Affected by Ads

The affect axis represents the person's feeling about the product, which ranges from acceptability to preference to loyalty. Again this is meant to be a continuous axis and the subdivisions are simply suggestive of the growing strength of favorable feelings toward the product.

It will be assumed that the greater the product knowledge and the greater the affect, the greater the probability that this buyer will purchase this product. This could be represented by introducing a third perpendicular axis called the probability of buying this product, and the probability could be represented by a surface above the CA-space. Instead, the probability of buying has been projected down into the two-space by the device of subdividing it into areas showing a trial threshold, a repurchase threshold, and a high loyalty threshold. Thus the higher the cognition and affect, the more likely the product will be bought and repurchased by the buyer. The curves show some degree of substitution between cognition and affect in contributing to the probability of purchase.

Before a person ever sees the product or an advertisement about the product, his mental state is located at the origin. Figure 14-1(b) shows what might happen in the individual's mind as a result of an exposure to a single advertisement for the product. The effect can be represented by a vector and three illustrative possibilities are shown. For example, vector 1 shows a case in which the advertisement simply was seen but it produced no positive affect. Vector 2 shows a case in which the advertisement was noted fairly carefully by the person and it produced a small amount of interest. Vector 3 shows a case in which the advertisement was noted and produced a strong favorable affect for the product. Other possibilities also exist. For example, it is conceivable that an exposure could produce a lot of recall but a negative affect on a person, in which case the vector would fall below the cognition line and to the right. It is also conceivable that the exposure could produce a lot of preference, although most advertising men and certainly advertisers do not claim or expect a single advertising exposure to do much in the way of succeeding to create a preference for a product outside of other elements of the marketing mix.

The effect of repeated exposure to an advertisement can also be shown in the CA-space. Two hypothetical histories of the effect of repeated exposure on one individual are shown in Figure 14-1(c). Case 1 shows the person as growing in knowledge about the advertisement and the product but not growing in positive feelings. Either the advertisement is not very effective or he is too loyal to another brand to develop a positive attitude toward this brand. It should be noted that each vector seems to slip back toward the origin between exposures, because some decay takes place in both his knowledge and his feelings toward the product.

Case 2 shows the person gaining in both knowledge and affect for the product with more exposures. This, of course, is the intended effect of the advertiser but it is not guaranteed to succeed.

The effect of repetition shown in Figure 14-1(c) can be shown in another diagram with time more explicitly represented. The new diagram is shown in Figure 14-2. The horizontal axis shows time and the vertical axis shows the propensity to buy. The propensity to buy is assumed to be a positive function of the level of cognition and affect resulting from an exposure. Figure 14-2(a) shows how the repetition of an advertisement, when it is effective, raises the person's propensity to buy. In between exposures, there is some decay in the level of the propensity to buy. In this illustration, four exposures were necessary to raise the propensity to buy up to the trial threshold, and a diminishing rate of increase is noted. Figure 14-2(b) shows the difference made by a short spacing versus a long spacing between exposures. The former is known as concentrated advertising (also intensive or burst advertising); the latter is known as dispersed advertising (also uniform or paced advertising). In this case the concentrated advertising managed to bring about trial in four exposures because of the short spacing between them, whereas the dispersed advertising failed to do this in four exposures.

Figure 14-2(c) shows the interesting case in which advertising led to product trial and the product was disappointing. Figure 14-2(d) underscores how proportionately greater increases in competitive advertising can erode the propensity to buy the company's product.

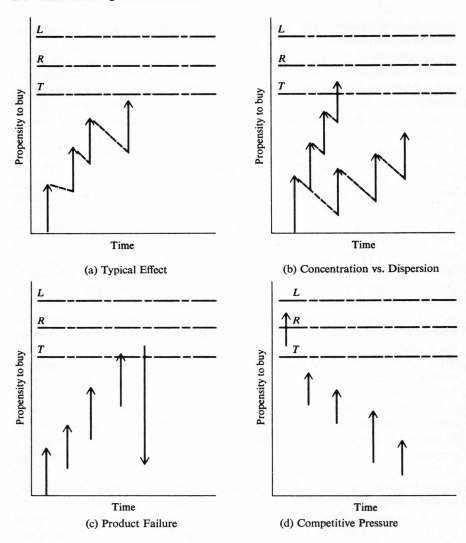

(a) Typical Effect

(b) Concentration vs. Dispersion

(c) Product Failure

(d) Competitive Pressure

Figure 14-2   The Effect of Repetition on the Propensity to Buy

Source: Langhoff, *op. cit.*, p. 47.

Setting Advertising Goals

To the extent that the advertiser has realistically appraised the manner in which advertising might influence the sales of his brand, he is able to decide on goals for the advertising program. As an example, consider a company that is preparing to set advertising objectives for two of its brands, A and B. For each brand the company has conducted marketing research to ascertain how many persons are in the market and the percentage distribution of these persons in three classes:

awareness, brand trial, and satisfaction. The results for the two brands are displayed in Figure 14-3. As for brand A, 80 per cent of the total market is aware of the brand, 60 percent have tried the brand and 20 percent of those who tried it are satisfied.[6] The distribution is quite different for Brand B. Only 40 percent of the total market is aware of Brand B, only 30 percent have tried it, and 80 percent of those who have tried it are satisfied. Clearly, these two profiles have very different implications for advertising objectives and strategy.

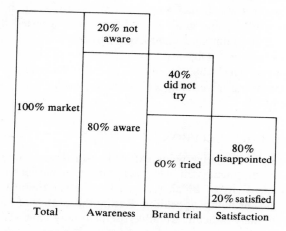

(a) Current Consumer States—Brand A

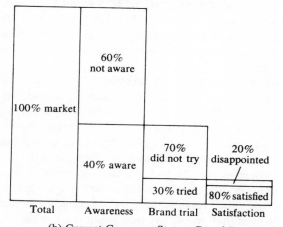

(b) Current Consumer States—Brand B

Figure 14-3 Current Consumer States for Two Brands

[6]For an interesting system for measuring these relationships, see John C. Maloney, "Attitude Measurement and Formation," a paper presented at the American Marketing Association Test Market Design and Measurement Workshop, Chicago, Apr. 21, 1966.

The market is highly aware of Brand A, but a substantial portion of those who have tried it are disappointed. This indicates that the advertising exposure schedule and creative message are effective in creating awareness but the product fails to live up to the claims. Brand B has the opposite problem. The advertising has only produced 40 percent awareness and only 12 percent of the market has tried the product. But of those who have tried Brand B, satisfaction runs in the order of 80 percent. In this case the entire advertising program, including the media, the message, and the level of expenditure may be much too weak to take advantage of the satisfaction-generating power of the brand.

The company's advertising goals for a brand are suggested by this type of analysis by which the company identifies the type of advertising job it must do and the cost of doing it. Objectives are set and the tasks that will accomplish them are determined. The "objective and task" method has been a recommended approach to developing advertising programs for many years, and is used by many major firms.[7]

MESSAGE AND COPY DECISION

Much of the effect of an advertising exposure will depend upon the creative quality of the advertisement itself. This was symbolized earlier by the h subscript to the advertisement A_{hijkt}, which referred to whether the advertisement was dull, neutral, good, or highly appealing. Rating the quality of an advertisement in practice is extremely difficult. An advertisement may have very good esthetic properties and win awards and yet not do much for sales. Another advertisement may seem crude and offensive and yet be a major force behind sales. Such properties in advertisements as humor, believability, informativeness, simplicity, and memorability still have not shown up with consistent relationships to the sales generating power of the advertisements, in spite of many research studies that have been conducted.

The reasons why an advertisement's esthetics may not be related to its actual effect are many. Sometimes advertisements that are crude and blatant catch attention better than esthetically pleasing ads. The advertisement is soon forgotten but it leaves behind greater brand awareness. Advertisements that appear to be undistinguished or even poor may have special appeal to certain kinds of people, or to unconscious processes that are difficult to assess. The effect of an advertisement also depends on many mechanical features of format and placement that are intertwined with the creative qualities of the advertisement. For these and other reasons the effect of an advertisement may not be obvious from qualities that people say they see in it when they consciously rate advertisements.

Rating the Creative Quality of Advertisements

Although the creative quality of a particular advertisement is difficult to judge, the advertiser still wants some concrete measure of the advertisement's quality

---

[7]*Printers' Ink* (Dec. 28, 1946) 26; *Industrial Marketing* (Jan. 1956) p. 65.

before agreeing to it. Any advertisement that has been prepared by an agency is a unique creation out of an infinite number of possibilities. The advertiser wants to estimate how this unique creation will actually perform in the market-place, relative to competitors' ads and relative to alternative copy that the company might have chosen. Because the problem of evaluation is so important, many measurement approaches and services have come into being to assist the advertiser in estimating the advertisement's probable effect on some cognitive, affective, or behavioral dimension of the marketplace. In principle, the advertiser is mainly interested in measuring the sales impact of the advertisement, and this is the most preferred measure. Because this is often not possible, the advertiser might try to measure the company's impact on attitudes, hoping that this measure correlates positively with sales. Less satisfactory, but still an important measure of an advertisement's quality, is its ability to be remembered, to increase the comprehension of product qualities and benefits. All other things being equal, the advertisement achieving the highest registration score is to be preferred. Finally, at the very least an advertisement is supposed to be attention-getting, that is, people should report that they have seen or are aware of the advertisement, even though they cannot recall any product qualities or benefits.

Although some progress has been made in measuring the *sales impact* of an advertisement in simpler situations through experimental design, most advertising effectiveness measurement seek to rate the advertisement's *communication effect*, that is, its effect on attitude, comprehension, or awareness.[8] Some interesting statistical work has been conducted to explain the awareness impact of an ad. Although this is the weakest proxy for sales, it remains true that an advertisement that is hardly noticed, no matter how distinguished its other qualities, is failing in a critical way.

In the case of print advertising, awareness is measured by the readership score. The readership score depends on such "mechanical" variables as size, color, the type of illustration, and the use of space. There have been several interesting multiple regression studies to isolate the influence of different content and mechanical factors on the readership score. For example, Twedt regressed the readership scores of 137 advertisements in *The American Builder* against a large number of variables and found that the parameters of size of the advertisement, size of illustration, and number of colors accounted for over 50 percent of the variance in advertising readership. Interestingly, these mechanical variables explained advertising readership variation better than many of the content variables that were also tried out in the regression.[9]

The most comprehensive regression study of the effect of advertising format

[8]See "E. I. du Pont de Nemours & Co. (Inc.), Measurement of the Effects of Advertising," in Robert D. Buzzell, *Mathematical Models and Marketing Management* (Boston: Division of Research, Graduate School of Business Administration, Harvard University, 1964), Chap. 8.

[9]Dik Warren Twedt, "A Multiple Factor Analysis of Advertising Readership," *Journal of Applied Psychology* (June 1952) 207–215.

variables on readership scores was performed by Diamond.[10] His data base was 1070 advertisements that appeared in *Life* between February 7 and July 31, 1964. For each advertisement, he had six different Starch readership scores: men-readers noted, seen-associated, and read most; and women-readers noted, seen-associated, and read most. In addition to these six Starch scores for each advertisement, he measured twelve variables related to each ad: product class, past advertising expenditure, number of ads in issue, size, number of colors, bleed-no bleed, left or right page, position in magazine, layout, number of words, brand prominence, and headline prominence. Each of the readership models was of the form

$$R_n = h + \sum_i a_i x_i + \sum_j \sum_k d_{jk} y_{jk} \tag{14-5}$$

where R_n = one of the sets of six readership measures (percent)

$\quad h$ = constant term

$\quad x_i$ = level of the ith continuous variable

$\quad a_i$ = contribution of the ith continuous variable

$\quad d_{jk}$ = level of the jth discrete variable, where k is either 0 or 1 to represent the two possible levels

$\quad y_{jk}$ = contribution of the kth state of the jth discrete variable

Diamond fitted several regression score models and used the coefficients to draw conclusions about the effect of different variables on readership score. For example, he found that the Starch score was higher the larger the advertisement, the greater the number of colors, and the fewer the number of advertisements in the issue; he found that right-hand page advertisements gained more attention than left-hand page advertisements; and that advertisements with photographs did better than advertisements with illustrations, and both did better than nonpictorial advertisements. To validate these and other conclusions, Diamond used his models to predict scores for forty-three advertisements appearing in the February 26, 1965 issue of *Life*. Although they were totally independent of the original advertisements, his equations had coefficients of determination as high as .74. With this degree of success he then placed the model on an on-line time sharing computer system to be used in planning and testing alternative advertising formats. Called ADFORS (Advertising Format Selection), the designer of an advertisement can try out different formats and in each case derive an estimate of the advertisement's likely readership score. A high readership score means that the advertisement is likely to gain attention. It is then left to the ad's inherent creativity to make a favorable impression on buyers.

How Many Advertisements Should be Created and Pretested?

When an advertising agency undertakes to create an advertisement for a client, the agency generally does not stop with the first idea it develops. The first creative

---

[10]Daniel S. Diamond, "A Quantitative Approach to Magazine Advertisement Format Selection," *Journal of Marketing Research* (November 1968) 376–387.

idea may be the best but typically it will not be. Often the client wants the agency to create and test a few alternative ideas before making a selection. The more advertisements that the agency creates and pretests the higher the probability that it will find a really first rate one. Yet the more time it spends trying to create alternative advertisements, the higher its costs. Therefore, it would seem that there is some optimal number of alternative advertisements that an agency should try to create and test for the client.[11]

If the agency were reimbursed by the client for the cost of creating and pretesting more advertisements, then the agency would go for the optimal number of advertisements to create for pretesting. Under the present commission system, in which the agency's income mainly comes as a 15 percent commission on media billings, the agency does not have an incentive to go through the expense of creating and pretesting many alternative advertisements. This question has been studied in an ingenious way by Gross who concluded that agencies generally create too few advertisements for pretesting.[12] This means that the advertiser does not typically get a very good advertisement but only the best (hopefully) of the few that have been created. Here we shall examine his reasoning.

In order to determine the optimal expenditures that an agency should make toward creating and screening advertisements, Gross developed three models dealing with: (1) the creation of alternative advertisements, (2) the screening of advertisements, and (3) the determination of the optimal expenditures. Turning to the first model, Gross visualized each of n creative men given the same data on a product and asked to create an advertisement independently. He assumes that each resulting advertisement will have a certain level of effectiveness that will have to be measured by a pretest measure. He assumes that the individual effectivenesses of the n advertisements are normally distributed. An advertisement at the center of the distribution is considered to be of average effectiveness and the other advertisements are better or worse than this. Let E stand for the relative effectiveness of an advertisement, that is, its effectiveness relative to an average advertisement. Relative effectiveness can be defined as the discounted present value of the increment in net profits which would accrue with the use of that advertisement instead of an average advertisement. Therefore, the distribution of the relative effectiveness of all possible advertisements that may be created has a mean relative effectiveness of 0, that is, $\mu_E = 0$, and a standard deviation of relative effectiveness of σ_E, as shown in Figure 14-4. Thus creating n different advertisements by an independent process is like making n independent draws from the relative effectiveness distribution. Presumably, the greater the number of advertisements generated, the better

---

[11]Although this discussion relates to advertisements (print ads, television commercials, etc.), it also applies to creating whole advertising campaigns. In either case, the agency is visualized as creating a pool of substantially different alternatives that are then pretested to discover the "best" one.

[12]Irwin Gross, *An Analytical Approach to the Creative Aspects of Advertising Operations*, unpublished Ph.D. dissertation, Case Institute of Technology, Cleveland, Ohio, Nov. 1967.

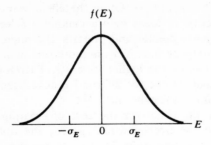

Figure 14-4 Probability Distribution of the Relative Effectiveness, E, of Advertisements Generated Independently

the best one will be. At the same time, it will be assumed that the average cost of creating an advertisement is c. Therefore the cost of creating n independent advertisements is

$$C_{cn} = cn \qquad (14\text{-}6)$$

where C_{cn} = cost of creating n advertisements at an average cost of c
$\quad\quad\quad c$ = average cost of creating an advertisement
$\quad\quad\quad n$ = number of advertisements created

The second model deals with the pretesting of the n advertisements in the interest of determining the best one. There are many different ways to pretest advertisements, and each may differ in its reliability and its validity. The observed pretest score of advertisement j on the ith replication of the pretest is given by

$$0_{ij} = \mu_0 + T_{ij} + t_{ij} \qquad \begin{array}{l} j = 1, 2, \ldots, n \\ i = 1, 2, \ldots, r \end{array} \qquad (14\text{-}7)$$

where 0_{ij} = observed score of advertisement j on the ith replication of the pretest
$\quad\quad\quad \mu_0$ = mean pretest score for all advertisements generated by the independent process
$\quad\quad\quad T_{ij}$ = the true deviation of the jth advertisement's score from the mean of all scores
$\quad\quad\quad t_{ij}$ = deviation from the true score of advertisement j introduced by random error in the ith replication of the testing procedure

Thus the observed score of advertisement j of the ith replication of the pretest is equal to the mean score of all advertisements, the true deviation of this advertisement's quality from the average quality, and the error occurring on this replication. Replication error arises because each time the advertisement is tested on a different sample of persons, some normal error will be associated with the difference between samples and the administration of the sampling procedure. It will be assumed that replication error is normally distributed with a mean of 0 and a variance of σ_t^2.

The range of variation in the quality of advertisements from each other can also be assumed to be normally distributed with a mean of 0 and a variance of σ_T^2. If a number of advertising alternatives were independently generated and tested just once each with the pretest, the observed variance, σ_0^2, would be

$$\sigma_0^2 = \sigma_T^2 + \sigma_t^2 \tag{14-8}$$

The relationship in Equation 14-8 enables us to use the following measure of reliability, R, of a particular pretest:

$$R = \left(\frac{1-\sigma_t^2}{\sigma_0^2}\right)^{1/2} \tag{14-9}$$

This measure of reliability produces a number between zero and unity. When there is no measurement variance, that is, $\sigma_t^2 = 0$, the reliability of the pretest is 1, as it should be. When there is a considerable measurement variance in relation to true quality variance, that is, $\sigma_t^2 \rightarrow \sigma_0^2$, the reliability of the pretest approaches 0. This formula for reliability is quite operational, in that the term σ_t^2 may be estimated empirically by testing the same advertisement several times and the term σ_0^2 may be estimated by observing the scores achieved by a number of alternative advertisements.

Gross defines the validity of the particular pretesting procedure to be the correlation, ρ, between the advertisement's true pretest score and its relative profit effectiveness. A correlation of $|1|$ means that the pretest measure correlates perfectly with the advertisement's relative effectiveness and a correlation of 0 means that the pretest measure is really of no use in identifying the better advertisements.

If we use these definitions of the reliability and validity of a particular pretesting procedure, what can be said about the expected relative profitability of the advertisement that achieves the higher pretest score in a sample of n advertisements. Gross is able to show that the expected relative profitability of this advertisement is

$$E_n = e_n \sigma_E \rho R \tag{14-10}$$

where E_n = expected relative profitability of the advertisement that achieves the highest score on the pretest when the sample size is n

e_n = expected value of the advertisement having the greatest relative effectiveness in a sample of size n from the standardized normal distribution of relative effectiveness[13]

---

[13]The symbol e_n is the expected number of standard deviates to the right of 0 that the best advertisement is expected to attain in n draws. In one draw, the expected value is .564. Further values are $e_2 = .846$, $e_3 = 1.029$, $e_4 = 1.163$, $e_5 = 1.267$, $e_6 = 1.352$, and so on. By $e_{20} = 1.89$, which means that the best advertisement of a set of 20 independently created advertisements is expected to be better than 97 percent of all possible advertisements. For a table of e_n values, see Donald B. Owen, ed., *Handbook of Statistical Tables* (Reading, Mass., Addison-Wesley Publishing Co., 1962).

σ_E = standard deviation of the relative effectiveness distribution

ρ = validity of the particular pretesting procedure, that is, the correlation between the true score on the pretest and the relative effectiveness of the advertisement

R = reliability of the particular pretesting procedure as defined earlier

According to Equation 14-10, the expected relative profitability of the best scoring advertisement on the pretest is higher, the higher the expected value of the advertisement (which is a function of the number of advertisements independently drawn), the higher the standard deviation in the quality of the possible advertisements, and the higher the validity and reliability of the particular pretesting procedure. If the validity and reliability of the pretest were perfect, then the relative profitability of the advertisement would depend only upon the number of advertisements drawn and the dispersion of advertising quality.

Each pretesting procedure will have its particular cost, which can be assumed to have the form:

$$C_{sn} = C_F + c_s n \qquad n \geqslant 2 \tag{14-11}$$

where C_{sn} = cost of screening n advertising alternatives over and above the cost of screening one advertisement

C_F = fixed costs of setting up for screening

c_s = marginal screening cost per alternative

n = number of alternatives to be screened

Gross is now able to bring together the two descriptive models into a decision model for determining the number of advertising alternatives to create and screen. The decision model must compare the increases in expected value and in costs from creating and testing more advertisements. At the point at which the incremental expected return is no longer sufficient to cover the incremental cost, the optimal point has been reached. Analytically, we find that:

$$P_1 = 0 \tag{14-12}$$

$$P_n = E_n - C_{c(n-1)} - C_{sn} \qquad n \geqslant 2 \tag{14-13}$$

where P_n = expected contribution to profits of generating and screening n advertising alternatives instead of just generating one

E_n = expected relative profitability of the advertising alternative achieving the highest score, exclusive of the costs of testing and the costs of creating all but the first advertisement

$C_{c(n-1)}$ = cost of generating the alternatives except the first

C_{sn} = cost of screening n alternatives

Gross is able to show, using difference relationships, that the optimal n^* is the smallest value of n for which the following relationship is satisfied:[14]

$$\Delta e_n < \frac{c + c_s}{\sigma_E \rho R} \tag{14-14}$$

[14]See Appendix Mathematical Note 14–1.

where $\Delta e_n =$ increment of the expected value of the advertisement having the greatest relative effectiveness in a sample of size n from the standardized normal distribution of relative effectiveness

$c =$ average cost of creating an advertisement

$c_s =$ average cost of screening an advertisement

$\sigma_E =$ standard deviation of the relative effectiveness distribution

$\rho =$ validity of the pretest

$R =$ reliability of the pretest

The implications of Equation 14-14 for how much of an advertising budget should be spent on creating and screening advertisements will now be illustrated with an example described by Gross. He tried to choose values for Equation 14-14 on the conservative side, in order to derive a conservative estimate. He made the following assumptions:

1. Suppose the cost of creating and screening one advertisement is about 5 percent of the media budget, D, that is,

$$c + c_s = .05D$$

2. An outstanding advertisement is one that is at the two sigma level in probability and in the long run it will return in profits an amount equal to the media expenditure (whereas an average advertisement will lead only to the recovery of the media expenditure). This means that $2\sigma_E = D$, or $\sigma_E = .5D$.

3. The correlation between the true pretest score and the true profitability, that is, the pretest's validity, is

$$\rho = .63$$

In other words, the pretest can account for 40 percent (ρ^2) of the variance in relative profitability.

4. The reliability of the pretest is

$$R = .71$$

In other words, $\sigma_t^2/\sigma_0^2 = .5$, which means that at least 50 percent of the observed variance in scores on alternative advertisements is due to measurement error.

Placing the above estimates in Equation 14-14, we find

$$\frac{c + c_s}{\sigma_E \rho R} = \frac{.05D}{(.5D)(.63)(.71)} = .224 \tag{14-15}$$

The value of .224 for Δe_n, when interpolated in a table of the values of e_n, indicates an optimal n^* of 3.[15] Under these conservative assumptions, the advertising agency should create and pretest at least three advertisements. The

[15]See note 13. The increment of .229 occurs approximately at $n = 3$. That is, $\Delta e_2 = .282$ and $\Delta e_3 = .183$.

optimal creative expenditure as a proportion of the media expenditure, d^*, is given by

$$d^* = \frac{n^*(c + c_s)}{D} \tag{14-16}$$

For the previous example, this turns out to be

$$d^* = \frac{3(.05D)}{D} = .15 \tag{14-17}$$

Under these conservative estimates of the variables, the optimal expenditure turns out to be 15 percent of the media budget, about three to five times that currently spent for this activity, according to Gross.[16]

Gross has tried to check his conclusions by testing the sensitivity of his estimate of d^* to various alternative values of the important parameters. He has also checked it against a direct mail study, in which he predicted successfully the number of advertisements that would be created and tested. If his conclusions are correct, this means that agencies should devote a larger part of their budget to creating better advertisements and a little less to direct media purchasing. The present commission system of 15 percent may have to be dropped in order to provide an incentive for agencies to test the right number of advertisements. Furthermore, it may be necessary for advertising agencies to be broken into two types, purely creative agencies and marketing agencies. The company hires a marketing agency and this marketing agency in turn hires n^* creative agencies to create advertisements from which the best one is selected.

Gross's model also yields some interesting findings for pretesting procedures. He found that the value of pretesting depended more upon the validity of the pretest than upon its reliability. Furthermore, he found that the higher the validity of the pretest, the more the justification for a large sample size to increase reliability. These and other conclusions flowed from examining different aspects of this model.

THE MEDIA DECISION

The creative decision is one of the two major areas in which advertising agencies specialize; the other is the media decision. The two, of course, interact. Sometimes, strong ideas about the proper media for advertising a product exist and

[16]Gross estimates that advertising agencies spend between 3–5 percent of their media income on creating and testing advertising. He derived this estimate from agencies statistics, showing that the creative and production departments use up about a third of agency income, which is one third of the agencies' 15 percent commission, or 5 percent. Longman maintains that Gross left out marketing research and other agency efforts that are partial cost inputs into the creative and testing process, and hence that Gross had underestimated actual agency costs. Longman also argues that an agency actually creates far more advertising ideas than ever reach the drawing boards, many of these being screened out by informal tests. Longman accepts Gross's model in principle but argues that agencies do spend the predicted optimal proportion of income on creating and testing advertisements. See Kenneth A. Longman, "Remarks on Gross' Paper," in *Proceedings of the 13th Annual Conference of the Advertising Research Foundation*, New York City, Nov. 14, 1967.

the creative decision is made around these media ideas; at other times, strong creative ideas arise first and then the agency considers the appropriate media. A major difference between the two decisions is the extent to which they are guided by economic criteria. The creative decision is typically not constrained by costs so much as imagination, whereas the media decision is essentially a cost decision. The media planner can place an advertisement in literally thousands of places. His major guide must be estimates of the respective audience exposure rates and costs of the different media opportunities.

Because of the economic nature of the media decision and the great amount of data that must be used, this problem has attracted more and varied model building efforts than any other single problem in marketing. Various approaches have been tried, including mathematical programming, stepwise analysis, and simulation.[17] Several advertising agencies in the United States, England, and France use operational versions of these models and claim important benefits with usage. Yet, to date, there has been no definitive scholarly effort to evaluate the relative performances of different models working on the same problem. The difficulty of comparing media models partly arises out of the fact that they often seek optimization of different objectives, and partly out of the fact that they employ different variables. At one extreme there are analytic models that are formulated for optimization and that are quite stark in their assumptions about the advertising influence process. At the other extreme there are models that are formulated with attention to many real world aspects of the problem but which cannot be solved optimally. Between these extremes there are analytic models with a large number of different positions on issues of the objective function, linearity, probabilistic media exposure, nonlinear cost discounts, and duplication and replication of exposure.

Basic Concepts

In this section we shall review the nature and objectives of the media selection problem as a prelude to considering some specific mathematical models that have been developed.

The media decision problem defined. The media decision problem can be stated as follows:

Given a media budget, an advertising message and copy, a set of media alternatives, and data describing the audiences and costs of the media alternatives, decide on (1) the media alternatives to use, (2) the number of insertions in each and their timing, and (3) the size and color of the media options in each case, in such a way that these decisions maximize the effect (measured in some

[17]References to specific models falling under each technique will be presented later. The following articles provide a general overview of mathematical media selection models: Dennis Gensch, "Computer Models in Advertising Media Selection," *Journal of Marketing Research* (Nov.1968) 414–424; Simon Broadbent, "Media Planning and Computers by 1970: A Review of the Use of Mathematical Models in Media Planning," *Applied Statistics* (Nov. 1966) 234–256.

way) of the media budget. The output of the media decision process is called the *media schedule*.

The choice of an objective function. The most desirable measure of the effect of alternative *media schedules* would be their impact on company profits. Since the media budget is assumed to be fixed, then the profit maximizing schedule would be the same as the sales maximizing schedule. Most media models, however, do not presume a knowledge of the current or long run sales that will be generated by advertisements placed in different media.[18] The preceding discussion has made it clear that various communication surrogates are commonly used to measure the effectiveness of advertising when sales would be difficult or impossible to measure. In media models, the surrogate that is used most often is the number of exposures to relevant members in the target audience.

An exposure does not mean that the advertisement is seen, only that the person is exposed to the media vehicle. At one time in media analysis, all exposures were counted as the same and could be obtained by simply using the circulation figures of print media or listenership figures for broadcast media. As market analysis underwent refinement and sellers recognized segments of the market of varying worth, gross audience figures for a vehicle had to be reworked into a weighted exposure value. This could be done, for example, by identifying the best segment in the market and scoring each exposure to a member of this segment as 1. Exposures to members of other segments in the market would be scored as less than 1, depending upon their relative value to the firm.[19]

Thus, for any specific advertisement placed in a particular media vehicle at a particular time, the media planner could presumably estimate a weighted exposure value:

> *Weighted exposure value.* This value is the number of persons exposed to the particular issue of the vehicle containing the advertisement, weighted by the value of the exposure to the various persons (with unity assigned to an exposure to a person in the best market segment).

The media planner also has data available on the cost of one insertion in every media alternative.[20] Consequently, he can form the ratio of the weighted exposure value of every media vehicle to its cost and select those media that deliver the highest weighted exposure value per dollar. Alternatively, he can form the inverse ratio of the cost to the weighted exposure value; multiply by 1000, forming the popular "cost per thousand" measure of media effectiveness; and find the mix of media that minimize the total cost of achieving a given number of total weighted exposures.

---

[18]For an exception, see the approach to sales maximization taken by the MEDIAC model, described on pp. 460–464.

[19]For a suggested treatment and illustration, see Philip Kotler, "Toward an Explicit Model for Media Selection," *Journal of Advertising Research* (Mar. 1964) 34–41, especially pp. 35–37.

[20]Unfortunately, these costs are not constant but fall with the number of insertions purchased per period and consequently make the problem of comparing media buys more difficult.

Most of the media models that have been proposed attempt to maximize the weighted number of exposures for a given budget B, instead of minimizing the total cost of achieving a prespecified number of exposures. The objective function typically looks like this: maximize

$$E = e_1 X_1 + e_2 X_2 + \ldots + e_j X_j + \ldots + e_n X_n \tag{14-18}$$

where E = total weighted exposure value
 e_j = weighted exposure value of an insertion in media vehicle j
 X_j = number of insertions in the media vehicle j during the period

Although this is the most popular objective function used in mathematical media selection models, it suffers from two major limitations that should be noted. *First, it does not distinguish between the reach and frequency components of the media exposures.* It will count two exposures to the same person as having the same value to the advertiser as one exposure to two persons. *Second, it does not distinguish between the replication and duplication aspects of the exposures.* It will count two exposures to different issues of the same vehicle (replication) as having the same value as two exposures to two different media vehicles (duplication).

Reach has been defined by advertisers as the net number of persons who are exposed one or more times to the company's advertising campaign. Frequency, on the other hand, is the number of exposures received by the average person who is reached at least once. Therefore the total number of exposures, E, can be expressed as

$$E = R \cdot F \tag{14-19}$$

where E = total number of exposures (also called gross impressions) during the campaign
 R = number of persons exposed one or more times during the campaign
 F = average number of exposures per person during the campaign

Alternatively, Equation 14-18 can be recast as

$$E = 1N_1 + 2N_2 + \ldots i N_i + \ldots \tag{14-20}$$

where N_i = number of persons exposed exactly i times during the campaign

This second formulation shows the distribution of the frequencies of exposure attained by the media schedule.

Why should the ideas of reach and frequency be distinguished? They are distinguished because advertisers place different emphasis on the two goals at different times and in different situations. An advertiser who is advertising a special value on a product whose message has to be heard only once or twice to be motivating would want a media schedule that would give him maximum reach. This means that almost every exposure should go to a different potential buyer in the market. On the other hand, an advertiser who is trying to build strong brand acceptance and believes that it is a function of the relative number of times his brand is mentioned in relation to all brands, will be led to seek a certain level of frequency. He is less concerned with the number of persons reached by the media schedule than with the average number of times they are reached.

The objective function in Equation 14-18 will not help the advertiser who is intent on finding the media schedule that will maximize reach or frequency, instead of the gross number of exposures. To go from Equation 14-18 to the number of persons actually reached, two things must be done. First, for each media vehicle used, the cumulative number of persons reached with X insertions must replace the gross number of exposures achieved, that is,

$$E' = r_1(X_1) + r_2(X_2) + \ldots + r_j(X_j) + \ldots + r_n(X_n) \tag{14-21}$$

where E' = total weighted exposure value with replication removed

$r_j(X_j)$ = the net cumulative audience of media vehicle j with X insertions

It should be noted that $r_j(X_j)$ is typically a concave function, showing that successive editions of the same vehicle bring in more viewers at a diminishing rate. For example, the cumulative reach of thirteen successive issues of the *Post* was 100, 109, 123, 131, 135, 137, 140, 140, 145, 147, 152, 152, and 155 (where 100 = first issue). Note that the increase is at a diminishing rate and that thirteen successive issues reached 55 percent more families than one issue.[21]

Secondly, from the set of all media alternatives that might be used, all audience duplication must be removed. If there are only two media alternatives, their reach or net coverage would be

$$E'' = r_1(X_1) + r_2(X_2) - r_{12}(X_{12}) \tag{14-22}$$

where E'' = reach of media schedule (i.e., total weighted exposure value with replication and duplication removed)

$r_{12}(X_{12})$ = number of persons in the audience of both media vehicles

With three media alternatives, their reach would be

$$E''' = r_1(X_1) + r_2(X_2) + r_3(X_3) - r_{12}(X_{12}) - r_{13}(X_{13}) - r_{23}(X_{23}) + r_{123}(X_{123}) \tag{14-23}$$

In this case, net coverage is found by summing the separate reaches of the three vehicles with the triplicated group and subtracting all the duplicated audience. Equations 14-22 and 14-23 generalize to the case of n media alternatives.

Obtaining data on the size of audience overlap between pairs, triplets, and so forth, of different sets of media vehicles requires large and expensive samples. Agostini has developed a useful estimation formula based on data from a

[21]Curtis Research Department, "Some Factors Affecting Repetition and Continuity in Advertising," Curtis Publishing Company, New York, 1953.

French study of media audience overlap, showing that total reach for magazine insertions may be estimated by:[22]

$$C = \left[\frac{1}{K(D/A)+1} \right] A \tag{14-24}$$

where C = total reach

K = a constant, estimated as 1.125

$A = \sum_{j=1}^{n} r_j(X_j)$ = total number of persons in the audiences of media $1, 2, \ldots, n$

$D = \sum_{j=1}^{n} \sum_{k=j+1}^{n} r_{jk}(X_{jk})$ = total of all pairwise duplicated audiences. If D_{ab} is the number of people simultaneously covered by a and b, then $D = D_{ab} + D_{ac} + \ldots + D_{an} + D_{bc} + \ldots + D_{bn} \ldots$ and so forth.

This relationship and parameter $K = 1.125$ has been shown to be a useful approximation for American and Canadian magazines as well.[23]

Once the reach of a proposed media schedule is estimated, the implied frequency of the schedule can be derived by the relationship shown earlier in Equation 14-19. At this point the advertiser can consider whether he would like to give up some reach for more frequency, or the reverse. Unfortunately the objective function shown in Equation 14-23 is difficult to work with in an optimization framework, in contrast to the ease of working with the exposure value objective function in Equation 14-18. The main use of Equation 14-23 is in evaluating the reach (or frequency) of a schedule after one has been selected that maximizes the number of gross exposures.[24]

Optimizing reach and frequency. We have talked about how to measure the reach and frequency of a given media schedule. Another problem is to determine the optimal reach/frequency mix that should be sought in the advertising campaign. Here some theoretical guidance is possible by the type of analysis shown in Figure 14-5. Figure 14-5(a) shows the estimated media cost of attaining different levels of reach with a given average frequency. Media costs are shown to increase at an increasing rate because it becomes progressively harder to reach the remaining potential buyers after the more accessible ones have been reached. Also note that the cost of achieving ten exposures to the average person instead

[22]M. M. Agostini, "How to Estimate Unduplicated Audiences," *Journal of Advertising Research* (Mar. 1961) 11–14. Note that, if we define $Z = C/A$ and $X = D/A$, Equation 14-24 reads: $Z = 1/(KX+1)$. Agostini found that the relationship between Z and X was best described empirically by this equation which only required estimating K.

[23]John Bower, "Net Audiences of U.S. and Canadian Magazines: Seven Tests of Agostini's Formula," *Journal of Advertising Research* (Mar. 1963) 13–21. For an analytic interpretation of the formula, see H. J. Claycamp and C. W. McClelland, "Estimating Reach and Magic of K," *Journal of Advertising Research* (June 1968) 44–51.

[24]However, see the Lee formulation of the media selection problem, which in principle can yield a media schedule that either maximizes the reach for a given level of frequency or can maximize the frequency for a given level of reach. Alec M. Lee, "Decision Rules for Media Scheduling: Static Campaigns," *Operational Research Quarterly* (Sept. 1962) 229–241.

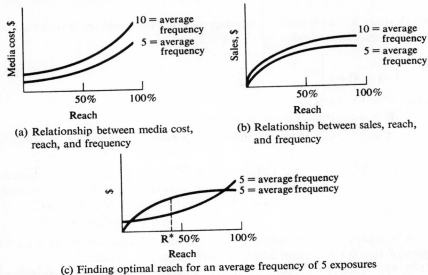

(a) Relationship between media cost, reach, and frequency

(b) Relationship between sales, reach, and frequency

(c) Finding optimal reach for an average frequency of 5 exposures

Figure 14-5 Determining Optimal Reach and Frequency

of five for any given level of reach is more expensive. Figure 14-5(b) shows the estimated sales that would be produced with different levels of reach for a given frequency. Here the sales response is shown as increasing at a diminishing rate, on the assumption that those who are harder to reach are less likely to be as interested in the product. Figure 14-5(c) puts the two curves together for an average frequency of five exposures. The optimal reach for this frequency is found where the greatest vertical distance exists between the sales curve and media cost curve. (Actually, we are assuming that profits are proportional to sales.) The next step is to repeat this analysis for pairs of curves for other average frequencies to see whether a still greater gap can be found. When the greatest gap is found, this indicates that both the reach and frequency are optimal.

This theoretical resolution of optimal reach and optimal frequency depends upon being able to estimate the appropriate curves, an admittedly difficult task. Further, it should be noted that the method considers only the average of the frequency exposure distribution and not the whole distribution. Some analysts are showing an increased interest in the whole exposure frequency distribution. Figure 14-6 shows three quite different exposure frequency distributions that have the same mean. Curve A shows a case in which most of the buyers receive a few exposures and a few receive many. Curve C, on the other hand, shows a few of the buyers receiving a few exposures and many receiving a lot. Curve B shows a more bell-shaped distribution of exposure levels. Sometimes it is useful to recast any of the curves in Figure 14-6 into cumulative form to show the number of persons who have received n or more exposures. If n exposures are considered necessary for a threshold level of response, then the percentage receiving fewer than n exposures may be considered lost as far as the campaign is concerned.

These findings on reach and frequency should ultimately be translated into their respective impact on the number of triers and the number of repeat purchasers. This possibility will be explored in Chapter 17.

Allocation of media budget over media classes and seasons. Several of the early media models were not designed to handle the allocation of the media budget to the major media classes or to different times of the year. Many were clearly intended to be used only for a particular media class, such as magazines or newspapers. Behind this was the formidable difficulty of comparing the respective exposure values of different media classes. It was felt that management should treat this as a strategic media decision and not leave it to a model. Thus, if the media budget were $500,000, management might decide that half of this, $250,000, should be spent in magazines because magazines impressed them as the most effective media class and also because competitors spent half of their budgets on magazines. Rightly or wrongly, both before media models were developed and also after the early models appeared, the allocation of the budget to the major media classes was left to the advertiser or the advertising agency's discretion.

Similarly, it was felt that the seasonal weights of advertising should be determined strategically or outside of the model. Thus, if December produced 20 percent of the company's sales, management might wish to allocate 20 percent of the magazine media budget to December, in this case, $100,000.[25] The job of the media selection model was to find the best media selections in December for $100,000, the budget having been decided outside of the model. In the case of the early linear programming models, the solution did not even specify when the insertions should be placed within December if the magazine had more than one issue in December, only how many times each magazine

[25]For the seasonal phasing of advertising expenditures, see the interesting article by Alfred A. Kuehn, "How Advertising Performance Depends on Other Marketing Factors," *Journal of Advertising Research* (Mar. 1962) 2–10. Kuehn showed that the appropriate timing pattern depends upon the *degree of advertising carryover* and the *amount of habitual behavior in customer brand choice.* Carryover refers to the rate at which the effect of an advertising impulse decays with the passage of time. A carryover of .75 per month means that the current effect of a past advertising impulse is 75 percent of its level last month, whereas a carryover of only .10 per month means that only 10 percent of last month's effect is carried over. Habitual behavior, the other variable, indicates how much brand holdover is due to habit, inertia, or brand loyalty, independently of the level of advertising. High habitual purchasing, say .90, means that 90 percent of the buyers repeat their purchase of the brand regardless of marketing stimuli.

Kuehn found that in the benchmark case of no advertising carryover and no habitual purchasing, the decision maker is justified in using a percentage of sales rule in budgeting advertising. The optimal timing pattern for advertising expenditures coincides with the expected seasonal pattern of industry sales. But, if there exists any advertising carryover and/or habitual purchasing, the percentage of sales budgeting method is not optimal. In all these cases, it would be better to "time" advertising to lead the sales curve. The peak in advertising expenditures should come before the expected peak in sales, and the trough in advertising expenditures should come before the trough in sales. Lead time should be greater the higher the carryover. Furthermore, advertising expenditures should be steadier, the greater the extent of habitual purchasing.

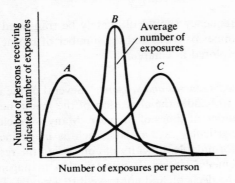

Figure 14-6 Exposure Frequency Distributions

should be bought in December. Subsequent models have aspired to comprehend both the media class allocation problem and the seasonal allocation problem within a common solution framework.

Media Selection Models

We shall now review three essentially different approaches to mathematical media selection (mathematical programming, stepwise analysis, and simulation), and then examine in some detail a model called MEDIAC, which is operational and combines many of the desirable analytical features of a useful media model.

Mathematical programming. Mathematical programming would appear to be a natural optimizing framework for analyzing the media selection problem. It is applied to problems in which there are a large number of ways to allocate scarce resources and several constraints to satisfy. The main constraints in media selection are the size of the advertising budget, the minimum and maximum usages of specific media vehicles and media categories, and the desirable minimum exposure rates to different target buyers. The choice of a "best" plan requires the specification of an *effectiveness criterion.* In media selection, the most frequently used criterion is the weighted number of exposures. Mathematical programming is a method for discovering the media mix that will maximize the weighted number of exposures.

The early applications of mathematical programming to this problem treated all the relationships as linear.[26] Table 14-1, shows a linear programming statement of the media selection problem, both in abstract form and in terms of an example. The problem is stated as one of trying to find the combination of

[26]Linear programming models are described in the following references: Ralph L. Day, "Linear Programming in Media Selection," *Journal of Advertising Research* (June 1963) 40–44; James F. Engel and Martin R. Warshaw, "Allocating Advertising Dollars by Linear Programming," *Journal of Advertising Research* (Sept. 1964) 42–48; Buzzell, "Batten, Barton, Durstine and Osborn, Inc.: Use of Linear Programming Methods in the Selection of Advertising Media," *Mathematical Models and Marketing Management,* Chap. 5; and Frank M. Bass and Ronald T. Lonsdale, "An Exploration of Linear Programming in Media Selection," *Journal of Marketing Research* (May 1966) 179–188.

Table 14-1 Linear Programming Model

		A Sample Problem
Maximize $E = e_1X_1 + e_2X_2 + \ldots + e_nX_n$	effectiveness function	$E = 3100X_1 + 2000X_2 + \ldots + 2400X_n$
subject to $c_1X_1 + c_2X_2 + \ldots + c_nX_n \leq B$	budget constraint	$15{,}000X_1 + 4000X_2 + \ldots + 5000X_n \leq 500{,}000$
$c_1X_1 + c_2X_2 + \ldots + c_nX_n \geq B_1$	media class usage constraint	$15{,}000X_1 + 4000X_2 + \ldots + 5000X_n \geq 250{,}000$

individual medium usage constraints:

$$X_1 \geq k_{1L} \qquad X_1 \geq 0$$
$$X_1 \leq k_{1U} \qquad X_1 \leq 52$$
$$X_2 \geq k_{2L} \qquad X_2 \geq 1$$
$$X_2 \leq k_{2U} \qquad X_2 \leq 8$$
$$\ldots \qquad \ldots$$
$$X_n \geq k_{nL} \qquad X_n \geq 6$$
$$X_n \leq k_{nU} \qquad X_n \leq 12$$

where E = total exposure value (weighted number of exposures)

e_i = exposure value of one ad in medium i

X_i = number of ads placed in medium i

c_i = cost of one ad in medium i

B = total advertising budget

B_1 = part of advertising budget

k_{iL} = minimum number of units to purchase of medium i

k_{iU} = maximum number of units to purchase of medium i

media that maximizes the weighted number of exposures, subject to the constraints. In the sample problem, the total advertising budget is $500,000; at least $250,000 must be spent on media class 1 (say, magazines). Media vehicle 1 gives 3100 (in thousands) effective exposures with each use and costs $15,000. It is possible to place anywhere between 0 and 52 advertisements in media vehicle 1 over a year's time. The other values are similarly interpreted. Given these concrete values, the linear programming problem can be solved for the best media mix.

The problem as stated, however, contains a number of artificialities arising out of the linear programming formulation. The four most important limitations are that linear programming:

1. Assumes that each exposure has a constant effect.
2. Assumes constant media costs (no discounts).
3. Cannot handle the problem of audience duplication and replication.
4. Fails to say anything about when the advertisements should be scheduled.

Some of these limitations can be removed by refinements of the statement of the problem. For example, if successive exposures or costs behave in a nonlinear fashion, this can sometimes be represented by piecewise linear segments and solved through the simplex method if certain concavity conditions are satisfied.[27] As for the time and place scheduling of advertisements, the unknown variables can be recast from X_i, the number of advertisements to place in medium i, to X_{ijkt}, the decision (0 = no, 1 = yes) to place in regional issue i of media vehicle j an ad of size k to appear at time t.[28] This increases greatly the number of unknown variables and the number of constraints but does get around the problem of the regionalizing, sizing, and timing of the media purchases. As for the problem of maximizing reach, this is very difficult to handle by mathematical programming.

Stepwise analysis. Stepwise analysis refers to any technique that constructs a media schedule in steps, introducing at each step the insertion that gives the greatest increase in effectiveness for the money spent (also called the gradient method, sequential method, method of steepest ascent). As an example of this method, consider the "high assay" model developed by the advertising agency of Young and Rubicam.[29] This model builds the schedule up sequentially,

[27]See Douglas B. Brown and Martin R. Warshaw, "Media Selection by Linear Programming," *Journal of Marketing Research* (Feb. 1965) 83–88. The technique of piecewise linear programming was used earlier in Chap. 7.

[28]See Willard I. Zangwill, "Media Selection by Decision Programming," *Journal of Advertising Research* (Sept. 1965) 30–36; and Stanley Stasch, "Linear Programming and Space-Time Considerations," *Journal of Advertising Research* (Dec. 1965) 40–47.

[29]This is described in William T. Moran, "Practical Media Decisions and the Computer," *Journal of Marketing* (July 1963) 26–30. Another model that uses stepwise analysis is briefly alluded to in Alfred A. Kuehn, "Models for Budgeting of Advertising," in Peter Langhoff, ed., *Models, Measurement and Marketing* (Englewood Cliffs, N.J.: Prentice-Hall, Inc., 1965), pp. 125–141, especially pp. 132–137.

rather than simultaneously. It starts with the media available in the first week and selects the single best buy. After this selection is made, all the remaining media choices are reevaluated to take into account audience duplication and potential media discounts. Then a second selection is made for the same week if the *achieved* exposure rate for the week is below the *optimal* rate. The latter is a complex function of several marketing and media variables. This continues until the optimal exposure rate for the week is reached, at which point new media choices are considered for the following week. The cycling process is shown in flow diagram form in Figure 14-7.

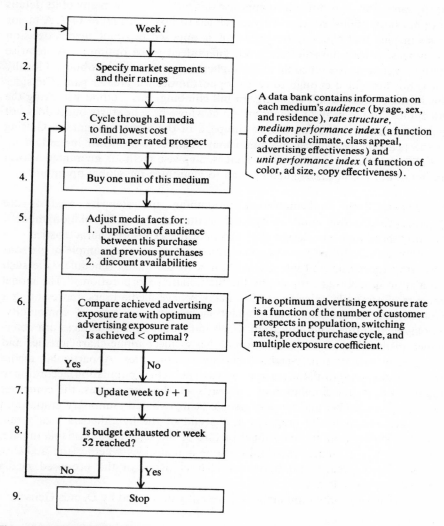

Figure 14-7 High Assay Model
Adapted from the prose description in Moran, *op. cit.*

The sequential procedure used in this model is appealing. In principle, high assay represents an improvement over linear programming because high assay:

1. Develops a schedule simultaneously with the selection of media.
2. Handles the audience duplication problem.
3. Handles the media discount problem.
4. Incorporates theoretically important variables such as brand switching rates and multiple exposure coefficients.

At the same time, it is difficult to appraise this model because many of its details have not been published, especially as related to Box 6 in Figure 14-7. A major problem, one that characterizes stepwise as opposed to simultaneous decision techniques, is that the solution is not guaranteed to be optimum. A stepwise method will bring the schedule to the highest value that can be obtained locally but is not farsighted enough to reveal opportunities for greater gain. Consider this in the context of hill climbing. In hill climbing, this method will bring the hill climber to the peak of the mountain at whose base he starts but it does not guarantee that it will bring him to the peak of the highest mountain. Getting to the peak of the highest mountain may require going down instead of up initially, descending into a valley. That is, stepwise methods guarantee a local optimum but are not farsighted enough to guarantee the global optimum.

Simulation. Both mathematical programming and stepwise analysis are designed to discover good or optimal media schedules. Simulation models, on the other hand, are designed to estimate the exposure characteristics of a given media schedule. Typically, they utilize a hypothetical sample of persons who are exposed in a Monte Carlo fashion to the media schedule. One such simulation model was designed by the Simulmatics Corporation.[30] The model consists of a sample universe of 2944 make-believe media users, representing a cross-section of the American population by sex, age, type of community, employment status, and education. Each individual's media choices are determined probabilistically as a function of his socioeconomic characteristics and location in one of ninety-eight American communities. A particular media schedule is exposed to all the persons in this hypothetical population, according to Figure 14-8. As the simulation of the year's schedule progresses, the computer tabulates the number and types of people being exposed. Summary graphs and tables are automatically prepared at the end of the hypothetical year's run, and they supply a multidimensional picture of the schedule's probable impact. The advertiser examines these tabulations and decides whether the audience profile and the reach and frequency characteristics of the proposed media schedule are satisfactory.

An alternative simulation model was recently developed by Dennis Gensch.[31]

[30]"Simulmatics Media Mix: Technical Description," Simulmatics Corporation, New York, Oct. 1962.

[31]Dennis Gensch, "A Computer Simulation Model for Selecting Advertising Schedules," *Journal of Marketing Research* (May 1969), 203–214.

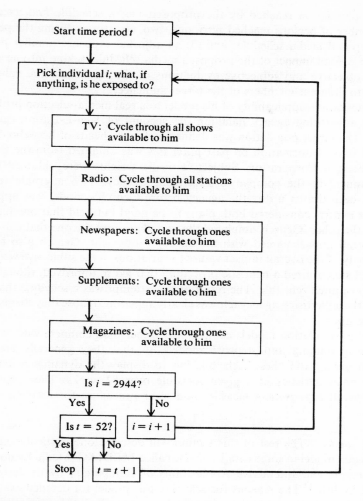

Figure 14-8 Simulation Model
Simulmatics Corp., *op. cit.*, p. 2.

The input stage of his model requires the following data: (1) the proposed media plan and schedule; (2) a set of weights for the effectiveness of different media; (3) a set of weights for the effectiveness of alternative size and color advertising forms; (4) a set of weights showing the value of different patterns of exposure frequency; (5) a list of the media cost and volume discounts; (6) a set of weights showing the value of an exposure to different types of persons in the target population; and (7) data from the Brand Rating Research Corporation showing the reading and viewing patterns over time of a real sample of individuals.

From these inputs, his computer program is able to generate weekly and cumulative output on several important variables bearing on the overall impact of the proposed media schedule: (1) the number and percentage of people in the target population reached by the proposed media schedule and its cost; (2) the number of persons reached zero, one, two, etc., times during the period by the proposed media schedule; and (3) an adjusted exposure number representing the overall impact of the proposed media schedule, taking into account all of the objective and subjective evaluations of the media and the value of exposures to different members of the target audience.

Gensch tested the applicability of his model to a real media-selection problem facing the advertising agency handling the account of Ken-L-Ration canned dog food. The target population was defined as female heads of households on a national basis. Information on past purchases was obtained from the Brand Rating Research Corporation. Subjective media weights were obtained from media planners in the company's advertising agency. Two alternate media plans had been drawn up by the agency before Gensch's model was applied. The media experts considered both plans to be good but held that one had an edge over the other. Gensch simulated the two plans, and the one that achieved higher overall impact agreed with the agency's judgment. Gensch also tested the sensitivity of the overall impact values to variations in the subjective weights.

The final step utilized a heuristic procedure that led to improved, though not necessarily optimal schedule. The result of this attempt was a schedule that the experts at the advertising agency felt was clearly superior to those they themselves had drawn up.

In general, simulation models complement rather than compete with mathematical programming and stepwise models, in that they generally are not capable of finding the "best" schedule but to display the dynamic reach and frequency characteristics of a given schedule over 52 weeks. They generally lack an overall effectiveness measure and clear procedure for arriving at an optimum.

MEDIAC model. The rest of this section will describe one particular mathematical media model in some detail, the one called MEDIAC (Media Evaluation using Dynamic and Interactive Applications of Computers) by its designers, Little and Lodish.[32] The reasons for selecting this model for detailed examination are several. First, the authors have published all the mathematical details of their model, which cannot be said for all the preceding models. Second, MEDIAC is operational on a time sharing basis in a conversational program mode and has been used by several clients to build media schedules. Third, MEDIAC handles in an analytical fashion a large number of marketing and advertising facets of the real media problem, such as market segments, sales potentials, exposure probabilities, diminishing marginal response rates, forgetting, seasonality, cost discounts, and so on.

The model assumes an advertiser who is seeking to buy media for a year

---

[32]See John D. C. Little and Leonard M. Lodish, "A Media Planning Calculus," *Operations Research* (Jan.–Feb. 1969) 1–35. Also see their earlier article, "A Media Selection Model and its Optimization by Dynamic Programming," *Industrial Management Review* (Fall 1965) 15–23.

with B dollars that will maximize his sales. The advertiser is able to identify S different segments of his market. For each segment of his market, the advertiser is able to estimate the sales potential. The sales potential of a market segment in time period t is given by

$$\bar{Q}_{it} = n_i q_{it} \tag{14-25}$$

where $\bar{Q}_{it}$ = sales potential of market segment i in time period t (potential units/time period)

n_i = number of people in market segment i

q_{it} = sales potential of a person in segment i in time period t (potential units/capita/time period)

The sales potential represents the maximally attainable sales in that segment in that time period if advertising and other company marketing resources are used maximally. Actual sales are likely to be below potential sales, depending on the per capita advertising exposure level in that segment in that time period. The more dollars spent on advertising in media reaching that segment, the higher the per capita exposure level, and the higher the percent of sales potential that will be realized. Thus the percent of sales potential realized is a function of the per capita exposure level, that is,

$$r_{it} = f(y_{it}) \tag{14-26}$$

where r_{it} = percent of sales potential of market segment i that is realized in time period t

y_{it} = exposure level of an average individual in market segment i in time period t (exposure value/capita)

As an example of one possible sales function for Equation 14-26, Little and Lodish suggest the modified exponential to show diminishing marginal returns to increased advertising exposure:

$$r = r_0 + a(1 - e^{-by}), \qquad 0 \leqslant y \leqslant \infty \tag{14-27}$$

where r_0, a, and b are nonnegative constants specific to the product. Returning to the more general function in Equation 14-26, we find that the total sales for the year is given by

$$Q = \sum_{i=1}^{S} \sum_{t=1}^{T} n_i q_{it} f(y_{it}) \tag{14-28}$$

that is, the realized sales potentials in each time period summed over all the market segments.

The next task is to indicate how y_{it}, the per capita exposure level in segment i in time period t is determined. In the absence of new advertising reaching this segment in time period t, the per capita exposure level will be some fraction, α, of last period's exposure level, that is

$$y_{it} = \alpha y_{i,t-1} \tag{14-29}$$

The fraction α represents the percentage of the advertising that is remembered from one period to the next by an average person in the segment. If there is new advertising in time period t, then the exposure level this period will be given by the more general expression:

$$y_{it} = \alpha y_{i, t-1} + \Delta E_{it} \tag{14-30}$$

where ΔE_{it} = increase in per capita exposure level in market segment i in time period t due to new advertising reaching this segment

The net effect of Equation 14-30 is to produce a pattern per capita exposure level over time that resembles that shown in Figure 14-9. Between periods of new advertising, the exposure value falls at a diminishing rate because of forgetting. New advertising, on the other hand, increases the exposure value in the segment.

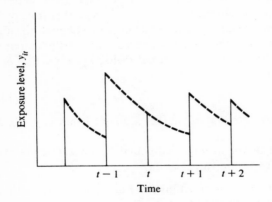

Figure 14-9 Per Capita Exposure Level Over Time in a Market Segment

Source: Little and Lodish, *op. cit.*, p. 12.

Now it is necessary to show the relationship of the increase in exposure value, ΔE_{it}, to purchases of specific media options. The advertiser must decide how many insertions he wants to buy in each available media vehicle in each time period. The increase in per capita exposure value is related to the number of these insertions in the following fashion:

$$\Delta E_{it} = \sum_{j=1}^{N} e_{ij}k_{ijt}x_{jt} \tag{14-31}$$

where e_{ij} = exposure value of one exposure in media vehicle j to a person in market segment i

k_{ijt} = the expected number of exposures produced in market segment i by one insertion in media vehicle j in time t (exposure efficiency)

x_{jt} = number of insertions in media vehicle j in time period t

Thus the advertiser's decision variable is x_{jt}. Suppose that he decides to buy

x_{jt} insertions. Each insertion in media j will yield an exposure value e_{ij}, which will be a function of:

$$e_{ij} = f(\text{media class, editoral climate of media vehicle } j, \text{ media option, market segment}) \quad (14\text{-}32)$$

The factor of media class recognizes that different media classes have different potentialities for demonstration, believability, color, and informativeness. Thus, if a food product is involved and color is important, magazines may be given a higher rated exposure value than newspapers or radio. The editorial climate recognizes that readers have images of particular vehicles that may add or subtract from the tone of believability of the advertisement. Thus *Good Housekeeping* may lend more credibility to an advertised product claim than *True Confessions*. Media option recognizes that advertising impact increases with the size and use of color in ads and should be reflected in the exposure value. Thus the exposure value of an insertion may be assumed to rise with the square root or some other function of the size of the ad. Finally, market segment recognizes that the exposure value of an exposure can vary by market segment.

The exposure value of any particular insertion in media j will be a number showing how good this insertion is in relation to a reference insertion in some media. Suppose that the highest exposure value is arbitrarily called 1 and is achieved for a particular segment by a two-page, four color ad in *Life*. Then every other possible media option that might reach this segment is assigned an exposure value in relation to this ideal value of 1.

The exposure value of a particular insertion in media j is modified further, according to Equation 14-31, by the exposure efficiency, k_{ijt}, in the particular market segment in the particular time period. The exposure efficiency will depend upon the following factors:

$$k_{ijt} = h_j g_{ij} n_i s_{ij} \quad (14\text{-}33)$$

where h_j = probability of exposure to an advertisement in vehicle j, given that a person is in the audience of the vehicle.

g_{ij} = fraction of people in market segment i who are in the audience of vehicle j (average value over a year)

n_i = number of people in market segment i

s_{jt} = seasonal index of audience size for vehicle j (average value = 1.00).

Thus exposure effectiveness will reflect the size of the media vehicle's audience at that time of the year, modified by the percent that are likely to be exposed to the advertisement if they are in the audience of the vehicle.

This concludes the descriptive part of the MEDIAC model. This descriptive part must be embodied in a mathematical programming statement designed to find the best media plan. The problem can be stated as one of trying to find the x_{jt}, for all j and t, that will maximize

$$\sum_{i=1}^{S} \sum_{t=1}^{T} n_i q_{it} f(y_{it}) \quad (14\text{-}34)$$

subject to current exposure value constraints,

$$y_{it} = \alpha y_{i,\,t-1} + \sum_{j=1}^{N} k_{ijt} e_{ij} x_{jt} \qquad (14\text{-}35)$$

lower and upper media usage rate constraints

$$l_{jt} \leqslant x_{jt} \leqslant u_{jt} \qquad (14\text{-}36)$$

budget constraint,

$$\sum_{j=1}^{N} \sum_{t=1}^{T} c_{jt} x_{jt} \leqslant B \qquad (14\text{-}37)$$

and nonnegativity constraints,

$$x_{jt},\, y_{it} \geqslant 0 \qquad (14\text{-}38)$$

In this form, the problem has a nonlinear but separable objective function that is subject to linear constraints. If the nonlinear objective function is assumed concave (as in Equation 14–27), the problem can be solved by piecewise linear approximation techniques. If the nonlinear objective function is assumed to be S-shaped, Little and Lodish show that this problem can be solved by dynamic programming if it is of modest size. If the problem is not of modest size, then the authors show that satisfactory, though not necessarily optimal solutions, can be obtained through the use of heuristical methods.

Although this model marks a major step forward in bringing in a number of phenomena left out by many previous models, some of its limitations should also be mentioned. In the first place, their statement of the problem assumes a linear cost structure for media (see Equation 14-37); whereas, in fact, the published rates are considerably more complex and even subject to negotiation in many cases. In the second place, the exposure value in Equation 14-31 should be made dependent on whether it is the first, second, third . . . , or m exposure. As it stands, the exposure value is treated as a constant for the segment and multiplied against the number of exposures. In the third place, the problem formulation in Equations 14-34 to 14-38 is not able to evaluate the effects of media duplication reaching the same market segment. However, this was corrected in a later version of the model. These and a few other problems are acknowledged by the authors who are continually introducing improvements in their model. One of their latest steps is to program their model for on-line access from a remote terminal in a conversational mode, so that the user can follow the model's logic, supply the requested data, and receive an optimal media schedule in a matter of minutes. The user can easily change the data inputs and note the effect on the media schedule. In general, the MEDIAC model remains a distinguished attempt to relate media purchases to sales and to incorporate the mechanisms of forgetting, market segment differences in response, and the effects of media class vehicle and option differences on advertising effectiveness.

SUMMARY

Advertising is one of the most potent tools available to the modern marketer for informing and possibly persuading buyers of the virtues of his product. However, its actual communication effects and sales impact are hard to establish outside of an experimental situation in which everything extraneous is held constant. To guide his budgeting, the advertiser needs whatever theoretical assistance he can get as to how advertising works and what its effect depends upon. Several interesting models have been constructed in recent years to help the advertiser do a better job in setting advertising goals, determining how much effort to put into creating and screening advertisements, and selecting the best combination of advertising media.

Advertising goals should be set in terms of a fundamental understanding of the conditions under which advertising exposure is likely to have an effect. The effect of a single advertisement depends on several qualities of the ad (its creative quality, media class, media vehicle, media option, and time of appearance) and several qualities of the potential buyer (buyer class, buyer state, advertising attentiveness of buyer, and buyer's frequency of exposure to media j). Because of these different factors, the actual effective value of a single advertisement is the total number of media exposures reduced by the number of persons who do not see the ad, or see it but do not register the message, or register the message but are not favorably impressed. As for the sales impact of an advertising campaign, this depends on the number of people in the market in such states as brand awareness, brand acceptability, and brand satisfaction and the power of the campaign to improve the ratios of triers to potential buyers and of users to triers.

Advertisers are concerned with measuring the quality of the message and copy making up the advertisement. Various measures have been developed to evaluate the impact of an advertisement or advertising campaign on sales, comprehension, and awareness. The sales impact is the most desirable effect to measure, but most of the successful work has been done at the level of measuring the market's awareness of the advertisement. Statistical regressions of readership scores on various content and mechanical features of an ad have been able to show the contribution of different variables to the size of the readership score. An advertising agency usually prepares some alternative ads before testing and selecting one as the most effective. Gross has developed a model based on the premise that the more ads an agency prepares, the better the best one will be. He came to the conclusion that advertising agencies tend to spend far too little in creating and screening ads in relation to the amount they spend on media purchases.

The media decision has perhaps received more attention from model builders than any other decision area in marketing. Most models use the weighted number of exposures as the criterion for judging the merit of a media plan. Media models have been built along the lines of mathematical programming, stepwise analysis, and simulation, with a complementary relationship possible between the last technique and the former two optimization techniques. One of the most mature media models is MEDIAC, which was reviewed in some detail because of its incorporation of many realistic facets of the media problem such as market segments, sales potentials, exposure probabilities, diminishing marginal response rates, forgetting, and seasonality.

Questions and Problems

1. A company estimates that 100,000 prospects were exposed to a medium which carried their advertisement. However, only 1000 inquiries were received by the company as a result of the ad. What factors might account for the discrepancy between the number allegedly exposed and the number positively moved? Create a hypothetical situation which will demonstrate your answer.

2. A firm has determined that the actual effective value of a single advertising insertion for its Brand A in a particular medium is 2160. It has also found that the percent of people exposed to the medium who have seen the ad (f_1) is .9, the percent seeing the ad who register the message (f_2) is .6, and the percent registering the ad who are favorably impressed is .4.
    Determine the following:

(a) The percent of the people exposed to the medium who saw the ad, registered the message, but were not favorably impressed.

(b) The percent of those exposed who saw the ad but did not register the message.

(c) The average number of persons exposed to the medium.

3. An advertising agency plans to create a number of advertisements for one of its clients and pretest them in order to select the best one. It wishes to know how many advertisements to create and test. The following information has been obtained:

(a) The average cost of creating and screening one advertisement is about $.025D$.

(b) An outstanding advertisement is one that is at the 3 sigma level in probability and in the long run it will return in profits an amount equal to the media expenditure.

(c) The pretest's validity is .7.

(d) The reliability of the pretest is .8.

Determine the optimal number of advertisements to be created and pretested, using the Gross formulation. (See footnote 13 for value of n corresponding to Δe_n.)

4. The readership of magazines A, B, and C is shown below:

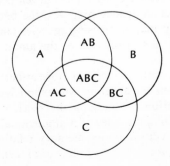

(a) Develop a formula which can be used to determine the unduplicated reach of the 3 magazines.

(b) If it is known that the readership of the 3 magazines has the following characteristics, determine the unduplicated reach of an advertisement placed simultaneously in all three media.

Read only A	10,000
Read only B	20,000
Read only C	25,000
Read both A and B	4,000
Read both B and C	8,000
Read both A and C	6,000
Read A and B and C	2,000

5. Suppose the probability equation for any person watching the *Tonight Show* is:

$$P = .04 + .20X_1 + .44X_2$$

where P = probability of watching the *Tonight Show*
X_1 = sex, with 1 for male and 0 for female
X_2 = education, with 1 for college and 0 for high school

What is the probability that a high school educated male is watching the show on a particular evening?

6. A company wishes to know how many successive advertisements it should place in each of three magazines (A, B, and C) in order to obtain the greatest total reach. Two alternative strategies are under consideration. Alternative 1 is (A, B, C) = (3, 2, 2). That is, the company would place 3 advertisements in magazine A, 2 in B, and 2 in C. Alternative 2 is (A, B, C) = (2, 3, 2). The table below shows the net cumulative audience for 1, 2, or 3 exposures in each magazine. Also shown are the pairwise duplicated audiences for each alternative.

Net Cumulative Audience (000)			
Exposures	A	B	C
1	100	150	75
2	125	180	85
3	140	200	90

Pairwise Duplication (000)			
Alternative	D_{12}	D_{13}	D_{23}
1	30	15	20
2	32	10	25

Using Agostini's estimation formula, determine which alternative offers the greatest total reach.

7. A company plans to place advertisements in two different magazines, A and B. A total budget of $250,000 has been established for these advertisements over the coming year, and the company does not wish to spend less than $100,000 of the

budgeted amount. Magazine A gives 1,500,000 effective exposures with each use, and costs $7,000. Magazine B gives 800,000 effective exposures with each use, and costs $3,000. Magazine A is a weekly publication, while magazine B is published monthly.

State the above problem as a linear programming problem, and solve it to find the optimal number of advertisements to be placed in magazines A and B in the coming year.

PART III
Models of Market
Behavior

CHAPTER 15
Sales Models for
Established Products

Part I of this book constituted a macrolevel analysis of the problem of marketing optimization. Sales and various marketing instruments were represented in aggregate form and an examination was undertaken of the theoretical relationships that might exist between them. Part II of this book undertook to reconsider the marketing instruments as subsystems of microvariables, each of which have important implications for marketing analysis and planning. Instead of considering the effect of total advertising expenditures or total sales force expenditures on total sales, the focus was on looking at the various links connecting advertising or sales force activity with sales. Now in Part III, we shall consider the dependent side of the demand equation, sales, and ways in which sales can be fruitfully disaggregated. This will allow us to investigate relationships between microlevels of sales and microlevels of marketing variables.

There are, in fact, four levels at which the sales process can be modeled. Moving from the most aggregative to the most disaggregative level, the corresponding models are:

1. Macrosales model
2. Microcomponent sales model
3. Microanalytic sales model
4. Microbehavioral sales model

A *macrosales model* is a model in which sales is represented by a single variable in total units or dollars and studied in relationship to other macrovariables. The analysis of Part I consisted almost exclusively of the construction of macrosales models. A *microcomponent sales model* is a model that shows sales as made up of additive components which can be separately analyzed in relation to marketing variables. For example, total company sales can be decomposed into company sales by product, customer, or territory. These sales components can be analyzed separately in relation to pertinent microcomponent marketing variables and lead often to interesting relationships that are hidden in the more aggregate figures. A *microanalytic sales model* is a model that looks at total sales as the product of the number of buyers in the market, the percentage who buy from the company, and the average rate of purchase. Breaking up the sales factors in this way leads to many insights into alternative strategies for improving sales. Finally, a *microbehavioral sales model* is a model that focuses on the individual customer and his probability of purchase as a function of his perception, preferences, and opportunities to buy the product. By formulating proper models of the individual buyer's knowledge, attitudes, and behavior toward products, and the factors affecting him, it becomes possible to consider micromarketing decision variables in a very direct way and to lay the groundwork for constructing sales models at higher levels of aggregation.

Since macrosales models were discussed in the earlier chapters of the book, no more will be said about them here. This chapter will take up microcomponent and microanalytic models of sales behavior and describe their uses in marketing analysis. Chapter 16 will consider microbehavioral models of sales in the context of the brand share problem. This will be followed by Chapter 17, which will examine models of the new product sales process.

MICROCOMPONENT SALES MODEL

Many analysts who have tried to find a clear relationship between total sales and the level of one or more marketing decision variables have usually been frustrated by the final results. Changes in gross marketing expenditures are not necessarily accompanied by corresponding changes in total sales. And constant levels of marketing expenditures may often be accompanied by substantial changes in total sales. The frequent failure to find a consistent relationship between aggregate sales and various categories of marketing expenditures suggests the desirability of trying out the analysis on a more disaggregative level. By sales analysis, it may be possible to turn up interesting relationships that may be buried beneath the aggregate figures.

It might seem that the executive would learn the most by examining all the individual transactions that make up total sales. He will notice that a particular call on a particular customer by a particular salesman at a particular time did or did not result in a sale of a particular company product; this may be informative. In companies with a large volume of sales transactions, however, no executive can afford to examine the individual transactions for their possible clues to marketing effectiveness or ineffectiveness. Furthermore, important sales trends could easily be missed, unless the data are summarized in some fashion. In general, executives want to work with sales data above the level of the individual transaction and below the level of the aggregate figures. Executives at different levels of responsibility in the marketing organization will typically receive sales figures at different levels of aggregation.

To appreciate the range of possibilities for breaking up sales into micro-components, it is useful to start with the basic building block of sales, namely the unit sales transaction. The sales (in dollars) of product i (in model or size m) to customer j (of industry classification k, located in region r, contacted by salesmen s) in month t will be represented by the symbol:

$$S_{i(m)j(krs)t} \qquad (15\text{-}1)$$

All of these characteristics are matters of record for those companies that issue invoices for every sale, This covers most industrial marketing transactions. Companies selling at retail and for cash typically do not know the customer's characteristics and in many cases even lose the product's identity in the course of the transaction.

When the company has a record of all of these characteristics of the transaction, and each transaction is entered on punched cards, the company can easily develop any of several useful sales figures. Its total sales of product i are S_i, its total sales to customer j are S_j, and its total sales in month t are S_t. Its total sales of all products are $\sum_i S_i$, its total sales to all customers are $\sum_j S_j$, and its total sales for the year are $\sum_t S_t$. The following identity obviously holds:

$$S = \sum_i S_i = \sum_j S_j = \sum_t S_t = \sum_i \sum_j \sum_t S_{ijt} \qquad (15\text{-}2)$$

Further desired sales figures can be derived. The company's sales of product i in month t are S_{it}. The company's sales to customer j in month t are S_{jt}. The company's sales of product i to customers in industry k are given by $S_{ij(k)}$. The company's sales of model m of product i transacted by salesman s during the year are $\sum_t S_{i(m)j(s)t}$. In a similar manner, various other sales components can be constructed.

At this point, the analyst is ready to examine the relationship between particular sales components, related marketing expenditures, and related market environment factors. For example, suppose the analyst examined three company sales regions that resembled each other closely in major marketing characteristics. Suppose that the company had formerly spent the same amount for promotion in each region. But this year it undertook an experiment and spent one half of the normal budget in one region, maintained a normal budget in the second region, and spent twice the normal budget in the third region. During the year, no other differences occurred between the regions. Suppose the analyst looks at $S_{j(r)}$ for each region and finds that market share had fallen in the first region, stayed the same in the second region, and had risen in the third region. The three observation points permit the fitting of a sales response function. This sales response function was made possible by a willingness to examine sales data on a specially chosen microcomponent sales basis.

Table 15-1   Ten Sales Reports Regularly Issued by a Manufacturer of Photographic Supplies

---

Monthly Report of Sales by Products. Total dollar sales broken down between sales of nineteen products, percentages of total shown for each product; also cumulative dollar sales and percentage of total for each product for the year to date; percentage breakdown of total sales among products shown for the previous year for purposes of comparison.

Monthly Report of Sales by Products in Physical Units. Same information presented as above, but in physical units rather than in value terms.

Monthly Sales to House Accounts. Dollar sales to wholesalers, chain stores, mail-order houses, government (direct), service accounts (Army and Navy), and other accounts handled directly from the home office; percentage of total sales made to each type of account; cumulative sales to date for the year, both in dollar figures and in percentages for each type of account.

Daily Record of Sales, Production, and Inventories in Physical Units by Products.

Monthly Reports on Sales and Commissions of Each Salesman. Net sales during past month, sales year to date; commissions earned, commissions year to date; extra commission (for introduction and sale of new products); extra commission as a percentage of the salesman's total sales.

Monthly Comparison between Actual Sales and Projected Sales by Products in Physical Units. Sales data, and percentages over or under projected sales (projections are made monthly and are used largely for production and inventory control).

Monthly Dollar Sales by Zones. Actual sales, other than to house accounts, broken down on a percentage basis between ninety-eight zones and by-products in each zone.

Quarterly Report on Sales to Key Accounts in Total and By-Products. (Like many concerns, this company makes a large proportion of its total sales to a relatively small number of key accounts; therefore, if difficulties are being encountered in any particular zone or in any particular product, an analysis of sales to key accounts may isolate the difficulty and suggest the solution.)

Occasional Study of Sales by Sizes of Account. (A frequency distribution is made of accounts by sales in dollars for a given period. Then computations are made to determine what proportions of total sales are made to various proportions of total accounts.)

Occasional Reports on the Proportion of Total Sales Made to Different Types of Buyers. (Management wishes to be informed of the increasing or decreasing importance of different types of retail stores and house accounts as outlets for the company's products.)

Source: D. Maynard Phelps and J. Howard Westing, *Marketing Management*, rev. ed. (Homewood, Ill.: Richard D. Irwin, Inc., 1960), pp. 821–22.

Even short of sales experiments, management finds value in watching key sales components throughout the year, particularly in relation to forecasts and/or quotas that had been developed for them. In this way, they can spot poor performances and hopefully interpret their causes in sufficient time to take corrective action.

Because of the large number of alternative ways to break down sales, every company has to decide which subset of sales reports would be the most useful for planning and control purposes. One manufacturer of photographic supplies regularly prepares the ten different sales reports listed in Table 15-1. A large computer manufacturer is working on a system whereby an executive could retrieve very recent sales information in detailed breakdowns much earlier than the regular report dates by requesting this information at a computer terminal. An increasing number of companies are storing their sales information on a transaction basis that permits important subanalyses to be made. All of these developments point to the growing opportunities for useful analysis through microcomponent models of sales.

MICROANALYTIC SALES MODEL

Instead of looking at total company sales as made up of additive components, company sales can be looked at as a multiplicative relationship between the number of buyers in the market, the percentage of them who buy from this company, and the average amount per period a buyer purchases from this company. In symbols, this relationship reads:

$$S = wks \qquad (15\text{-}3)$$

where S = company sales
w = number of buyers in the market
k = percentage of buyers who buy from this company
s = average amount per period a buyer purchases from this company

These three variables correspond to the three ways in which a company can hope to boost its sales:

1. Increase the total number of buyers in the market, w.
2. Increase its share of the total number of buyers, k.
3. Increase the average amount its customers buy, s.

Suppose that in period t there are four buyers in the market:

$$(S_1, S_2, S_3, S_4) = (4, 8, 9, 11) \qquad (15\text{-}4)$$

The amounts they buy from company i are

$$(S_{1i}, S_{2i}, S_{3i}, S_{4i}) = (4, 2, 3, 0) \qquad (15\text{-}5)$$

In words, buyer 1 buys all his requirements from company i, buyer 2 buys one-quarter of his needs from company i, buyer 3 buys one-third of his needs from company i, and buyer 4 buys only from competition. The following measures can be derived from Equation 15-5:

$w = 4$ (there are four buyers in the market)

$k = \frac{3}{4}$ (three-fourths of the buyers are customers of company i)

$s = 3$ (the average purchase quantity from company i is three units)

According to the analytic relation in Equation 15-3:

$$S = 4 \times \frac{3}{4} \times 3 = 9$$

which is exactly the total quantity purchased from company i.

None of these numbers is likely to stay stable over time. Each of them is subject to trends and possibly seasonal factors beyond the company's control. Each of them is subject to some random variation around the most likely levels due to a myriad of small causes. Each of them is subject to some influence by the company through its marketing program.

In the following sections, four different sales models are developed along the lines of the basic microanalytic sales equation 15-3. The first model assumes that the variables in Equation 15-3 behave in a deterministic (as opposed to stochastic) manner over time (deterministic model). The second model assumes a fixed number of company customers, n (where $n = wk$), and a random average purchase amount (fixed n, random s model). The third model assumes a random number of company customers and a fixed average purchase amount (random n, fixed s model). Finally, the fourth model assumes a random number of company customers and a random average purchase rate (random n and s model). These models constitute a sample of the many sales models that an be constructed under the basic microanalytic sales relation in Equation 15-3.

Deterministic Model

In this first case, we shall assume that each variable is subject to a deterministic behavior over time. As an example, suppose the number of buyers increases over time at a diminishing rate:

$$w_t = w_0(1 - e^{-at}) \tag{15-6}$$

where w_t = number of customers at time t

w_0 = number of customers today

e = the number $2.71\ldots$

a = coefficient regulating the rate of increase

t = time

Suppose that the percentage of all customers buying from company i at time t, k_{it}, is equal to company i's share of total industry marketing effort at time t, m_{it}:

$$k_{it} = m_{it} \tag{15-7}$$

Finally, suppose that the average amount purchased by a customer from firm i remains constant:

$$s_t = s_0 \tag{15-8}$$

Substituting Equations 15-6, 15-7, and 15-8 into Equation 15-3, we obtain the predictive equation for sales:

$$S_t = w_0 (1 - e^{-at}) m_{it} s_0 \tag{15-9}$$

Other deterministic assumptions about w, k, and s would lead to a different sales function than Equation 15-9, although the basic three-variable framework in Equation 15-3 would still underlie the equation.

Fixed n, Random s Model

In this and the following sales models, we shall leave out trends, seasonals, and specific marketing factors, in order to concentrate on building stochastic features in these models. It should be appreciated, however, that these factors can be introduced later into any of the stochastic models in the same manner as was done in the deterministic model. Our interest here is in exploring the usefulness of standard probability models (such as the binomial, Poisson, normal, and lognormal) in representing the character of sales transactions in different types of markets. Each probability model implies not only a particular manner in which sales are generated, but also provides the means of estimating the mean and standard deviation of the random variable, sales.

Binomial sales model.   Assume a company that sells its product to a fixed number of customers, n. Each customer buys one of two amounts, s_1(low) or s_2(high) each period. The probability of a customer's buying s_1 is p and the probability of buying s_2 is $(1-p)$. Given this information, we can determine the probability distribution of sales and, in particular, the mean and variance of sales.

Each customer j's purchase amount, s_j, is a binomial random variable that takes on one of two values, s_1 or s_2. The company's total sales S will therefore be a sum of n binomially distributed random variables, and therefore a random variable itself. The lowest possible sales, S_{min}, in any period would occur if every customer bought s_1. The probability of every customer's buying s_1 is very low and given by the joint probability:

$$P(S_{min}) = p_{11} p_{21} \cdots p_{n1} = p^n \tag{15-10}$$

where $P(S_{min})$ = the probability of the lowest possible level of sales taking place
p_{11} = the probability of customer 1's buying s_1, and so forth

The highest possible sales, S_{max}, in any period would occur if every customer bought s_2. The probability of every customer's buying s_2 is also very low and given by the joint probability:

$$P(S_{max}) = (1 - p_{11})(1 - p_{21}) \cdots (1 - p_{ni}) = (1 - p)^n \tag{15-11}$$

In between the lowest and highest possible sales figures, S_{min} and S_{max}, lie a great number of intermediate sales levels. In general, the probability that a sales level will correspond to r customers buying s_1 with probability p and $n-r$ buying s_2 with probability $(1-p)$ is given by the binomial probability distribution:

$$P(S|n; r; p)_B = \left[\frac{n!}{r!(n-r!)}\right] p^r(1-p)^{n-r} \tag{15-12}$$

where the first term in brackets represents the number of different ways in which r customers might buy s_1 and $n-r$ customers buy s_2, and the second term represents the joint probability of any one of these ways occurring.[1]

As a small example, assume a market consisting of three buyers, each of whom buy either one or two units of the product per week, with probabilities .7 and .3, respectively. What is the probability that the seller will sell exactly four units this week? This could happen in only three ways:

(1, 1, 2)   (1, 2, 1)   (2, 1, 1)

where each vector shows the purchase amount of each buyer, and the three amounts sum to four. The probability of the first vector's occurring, that is, that the first and second buyer will each buy one unit and the third buyer will buy two units, is $.7 \times .7 \times .3 = .147$. The probability of either of the other two vectors occurring is the same. Since the buyers can buy a total of four units in three different ways, each with a probability of $.147$, the total probability of the seller selling four units is $3 \times .147 = .441$. The same result could have been obtained directly from Equation 15-12:

$$P(4) = \frac{3!}{2! \, 1!} .7^2 .3^1 = .441 \tag{15-13}$$

The probabilities of the various possible sales levels occurring are shown below:

$$P(3) = \frac{3!}{3! \, 0!} .7^3 .3^0 = .343 \tag{15-14}$$

$$P(4) = \frac{3!}{2! \, 1!} .7^2 .3^1 = .441 \tag{15-15}$$

$$P(5) = \frac{3!}{1! \, 2!} .7^1 .3^2 = .189 \tag{15-16}$$

$$P(6) = \frac{3!}{0! \, 3!} .7^0 .3^3 = .027 \tag{15-17}$$

1.000

---

[1]See John E. Freund, *Mathematical Statistics* (Englewood Cliffs, N.J.: Prentice-Hall, Inc., 1962), pp. 66–70, for a discussion of the binomial distribution.

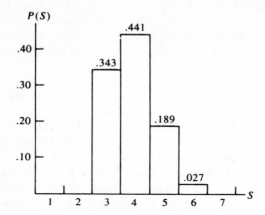

Figure 15-1 Binomial Sales Model
There are 4 buyers in the market, each buying one or two units per week, with probabilities
.7 and .3 respectively.

The corresponding binomial distribution is illustrated in Figure 15-1. Thus it is possible to calculate the probability of each possible sales level and also the probability of sales' exceeding or falling below any possible sales level. It is also possible to calculate the seller's expected sales from the following formula for the mean of a binomial distribution:[2]

$$\bar{S} = n[p \, s_1 + (1-p) \, s_2]$$
$$\bar{S} = 3[(.7)(1) + (.3)(2)] = 3.9 \tag{15-18}$$

where $\bar{S}$ = expected sales for a binomial distribution sales model.

Furthermore the variance of the seller's sales can be computed from the following formula:[3]

$$\sigma_s = np(1-p)$$
$$\sigma_s = (3)(.7)(.3) = .63 \tag{15-19}$$

where σ_s = variance of sales for a binomial distribution sales model.

The binomial sales model has been presented in its simplest possible form but is capable of additional refinement. First, it is possible to handle more than two possible sales states in an extension known as the multinomial distribution sales model.[4] Secondly, it is possible to postulate individuated probabilities for each customer's ending up in each purchase state each week. Once this is introduced, it is still possible to solve for the probabilities of various sales levels, as well as

[2]Ibid., p. 99. To check this result, multiply every possible sales level by its probability: $E(S) = (3)(.343) + (4)(.441) + (5)(.189) + (6)(.027) = 3.9$.
[3]Ibid., p. 99. To check this result, multiply every possible squared sales deviation by its probability: $V(S) = (.343)(3-3.9)^2 + (.441)(4-3.9)^2 + (.189)(5-3.9)^2 + (.027)(6-3.9)^2 = .63$.
[4]Ibid., p. 87.

the mean and variance of sales, but without the benefit of any direct formulas. The binomial sales model, although quite simple in concept, is capable of direct application to many sales situations in which there are a finite number of customers who buy at a small number of possible sales levels with a stable probability. The last assumption rules out situations in which the amount a customer buys in period t is influenced by the amount he buys in week $t-1$.

Normal sales model. Again assume a company that sells its product to a fixed number of customers, but this time each customer buys a variable amount instead of one of two amounts. The amount each customer buys is influenced by a great number of small random factors. For simplification, assume that all customers buy approximately the same amount on the average, subject to the same variance around this average. In effect, we are assuming that each customer's purchases are drawn independently from the same probability distribution. If the probability distribution describing the individual customers' purchases is normal, then total company sales will be normally distributed. This is because the sum of a set of independent and identically distributed random normal numbers is itself normally distributed. In fact, total company sales each period, S, will be a normally distributed random variable with a mean of

$$\bar{S} = n\bar{s}_i \tag{15-20}$$

where $\bar{S}$ = expected company sales
$\quad n$ = number of customers
$\quad \bar{s}_i$ = expected sales to customer i

and variance of

$$\sigma_S{}^2 = n\sigma_{si}{}^2 \tag{15-21}$$

where $\sigma_S{}^2$ = variance of company sales
$\quad \sigma_{si}{}^2$ = variance of sales of customer i

The probability of total company sales' being exactly S is given by the normal probability distribution:

$$P(S|\bar{S}, \sigma_S)_N = \frac{1}{\sigma_S\sqrt{2\pi}} \exp\left[\frac{-(S-\bar{S})^2}{2\sigma_S{}^2}\right] \tag{15-22}$$

The normal distribution is fully specified by the mean $\bar{S}$ and the variance $\sigma_S{}^2$. Figure 15–2 shows the probability distribution of sales for the case in which expected weekly sales are 100 units, the variance of sales is 400 (standard deviation = 20), and the distribution is normal. Given this information, it is possible to determine the probability of sales' falling between any two figures. For example, the probability is .68 that company sales will fall somewhere within one standard deviation of the mean, that is, between 80 and 120 units. The probability is only .023 that sales will exceed plus two standard deviations, or 140. These and other probabilities can be formed through knowledge of the sales mean and variance and the use of a standard table of areas under the normal curve.

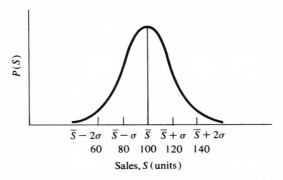

Figure 15-2   Normal Sales Model ($\bar{S} = 100$, $\sigma_s = 20$)

If the probability distribution describing individual customers' sales is not normally distributed, the results in Equations 15–20 and 15–21 still hold approximately if the number of customers, n, is large. According to the central limit theorem, the sum of a set of randomly distributed independent variables, regardless of their distribution, will tend to be normally distributed if n is large.[5]

A more serious issue with this model is that, in practice, each customer's purchases is likely to be a randomly distributed variable with its own unique mean, variance, and probability density function. If there are a small number of customers, the analyst might try to model each customer's probability density function and use the computer in a Monte Carlo fashion to simulate the distribution of total sales.

If there are many customers, each buying according to a different probability distribution function, with each distribution changing over time, then this modeling approach would be difficult to implement.

Lognormal sales model.   In some situations involving a fixed number of customers and variable purchase rates, it has been observed that monthly sales appear to be distributed in a skewed pattern, rather than a normal one. For example, Holt, Modigliani, Muth, and Simon reported the frequency histograms of monthly sales for three selected products shown in Figure 15–3[6]. The slowest moving product has a J-shaped distribution, the largest frequency being in the zero class. All three products show distributions with a pronounced skewness at the right. It is unlikely that these patterns would change with more months of observations. Clearly, there must be some characteristic of the

[5]See A. M. Mood, *Introduction to the Theory of Statistics* (New York: McGraw-Hill, Inc., 1950), p. 136.

[6]Charles C. Holt, Franco Modigliani, John F. Muth, and Herbert A. Simon, *Planning Production, Inventories, and Work Force* (Englewood Cliffs, N. J.: Prentice-Hall, Inc., 1960), p. 282.

customer sales probability distributions that produces the skewed total sales probability distributions in Figure 15-3.

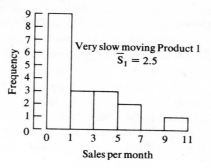

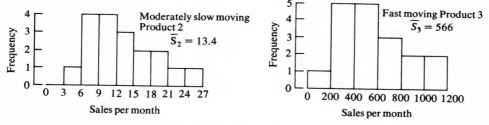

Figure 15-3   Frequency Histogram of Monthly Sales for Three Products
From Holt, *op. cit.*, p. 282.

Holt, Modigliani, Muth, and Simon and others have suggested the usefulness of the lognormal probability distribution for representing the skewness in sales distributions such as the bottom two in Figure 15-3[7]. The reasoning is as follows. Assume that each customer's purchase is a random variable determined by the product, rather than the sum, of a great many different random factors. For example, the customer may arrive at his order quantity by multiplying last period's sales rate by a weather factor, multiplied by a scrap loss factor, multiplied by several other factors, all considered as independently determined, as in Equation 15-23:

$$s_{i,t} = s_{i,t-1}(1+r_1)(1+r_2) \ldots (1+r_j) \ldots \qquad (15\text{-}23)$$

where $s_{i,t}$ = sales to customer i at time t

r_j = random adjustment factor j

Now form the log of the sales to customer i:

$$\ln s_{i,t} = \ln s_{i,t-1} + \ln(1+r_1) + \ln(1+r_2) + \ldots + \ln (1+r_j) + \ldots \qquad (15\text{-}24)$$

Thus $\ln s_{i,t}$ is the *sum* of many independent random factors. If the absolute

---

[7]See ibid., pp. 283–286; also J. Aitchison and J. A. C. Brown, *The Lognormal Distribution* (London: Cambridge University Press, 1957); Edgar A. Pessemier, *New-Product Decisions: An Analytical Approach* (New York: McGraw-Hill, Inc., 1966), 169–174.

values of the r_j's are small relative to 1, the sum will tend to be normally distributed according to the central limit theorem as the number of these random factors increases. Consequently $s_{i,t}$ the customer sales rate, would be *lognormally* distributed (showing a skewness at the right). Now if there are many customers in the market, each with a lognormally distributed sales rate, the total company sales, S, will still tend to be normally distributed according to the central limit theorem. But if there are not many customers in the market, then the lognormally distributed sales rate of each will produce a total sales probability distribution that also appears to be lognormally distributed. Holt, et al. indicate that the selected products in Figure 15–3 all represented wholesale sales data where the number of customers was not very large. The mean of company sales where they are distributed lognormally is given by

$$\bar{S} = e^{u + \sigma^2/2} \tag{15-25}$$

where $\bar{S}$ = expected company sales where sales is a lognormally distributed random variable
$\qquad e$ = the mathematical constant, 2.71 . . .
$\qquad u$ = mean of the logs of the sales observations
$\qquad \sigma^2$ = variance of the logs of the sales observations

The variance of the lognormal distribution is given by

$$\sigma_S{}^2 = \bar{S}^2(e^{\sigma^2} - 1) \tag{15-26}$$

The mean and the variance are sufficient to specify the lognormal probability distribution, which is given by

$$P(S|\bar{S}, \sigma_S)_L = \frac{1}{S\sigma_S\sqrt{2\pi}} \exp\left[\frac{-(\log S - \bar{S})^2}{2\sigma_S{}^2}\right] \tag{15-27}$$

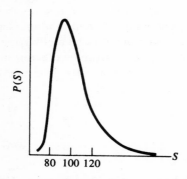

Figure 15-4 Lognormal Sales Model ($\bar{S} = 100$, $\sigma_s = 20$)

Figure 15-4 illustrates a situation in which sales are lognormally distributed with a mean of 100 and a variance of 400; this should be compared to the normal sales distribution with the same parameters shown in Figure 15-2.

Random *n*, Fixed *s* Model

Now suppose that the customers' sales rate is fixed but the number of customers varies from period to period. Then total sales will vary according to the probability distribution of the number of customers. The Poisson distribution provides one possible model for this sales situation.

Poisson sales model. Assume a market consisting of a great number of customers ($n \to \infty$), each having an extremely small probability, *p*, of buying one unit of the product each period. This might describe a situation in a mass consumer market in which weekly sales are being considered and each buyer only comes into the market once every few years: this would characterize the market for consumer durables, from small appliances to automobiles. In such markets, sales over time will resemble a series of independent drawings from a Poisson probability distribution. Expected company sales in any period will be

$$\bar{S} = p_1 + p_2 + \ldots + p_n = np = \lambda \tag{15-28}$$

where $\bar{S}$ = company sales

p_i = probability that customer *i* buys one unit this period ($p_i = p_j$ for all *i, j*)

n = number of potential customers

$\lambda = np$, assumed constant

Sales can be said to be Poisson distributed when *n* is very large, *p* is very small, and $np = \lambda$ is constant. The Poisson probability distribution is given by the formula

$$P(S|\lambda)_p = \frac{\lambda^S e^{-\lambda}}{S!} \tag{15-29}$$

where *S* is the number of units sold ($S = 0, 1, 2, \ldots$). It should be noted that the distribution depends on only one parameter, λ. It can be shown that the Poisson distribution is unique in that its mean is equal to its variance, that is[8]

$$\bar{S} = \sigma_S^2 = \lambda \tag{15-30}$$

Figure 15-5 shows the case of Poisson distributed sales with a mean and variance of 2.[9]

Random *n* and *s* Model

In the vast majority of markets, both the number of customers and the amount purchased by each customer will vary from period to period. It is as if company

---

[8]Freund, *Mathematical Statistics*, pp. 103–105.

[9]An alternative and related model considers not the number of customers per period directly but the interarrival time of customers. It is as if nature draws an interarrival time for the appearance of the next customer: by drawing interarrival times until the period is used up, the number of customers can be determined. Typically, an exponential probability distribution gives a good fitting to the interarrival time data. See Maurice Sasieni, Arthur Yaspan, and Lawrence Friedman, *Operations Research: Methods and Problems* (New York: John Wiley & Sons, Inc., 1959), pp. 125–128.

sales were generated in two steps. First, nature selects a random number n representing the number of company customers for the period; second, nature draws consecutively and independently the sales s_i for each of the n customers. These sales are summed to find company sales, S. Symbolically, S is found:

$$S = s_1 + s_2 + \ldots + s_n = \sum_{i=1}^{n} s_i \tag{15-31}$$

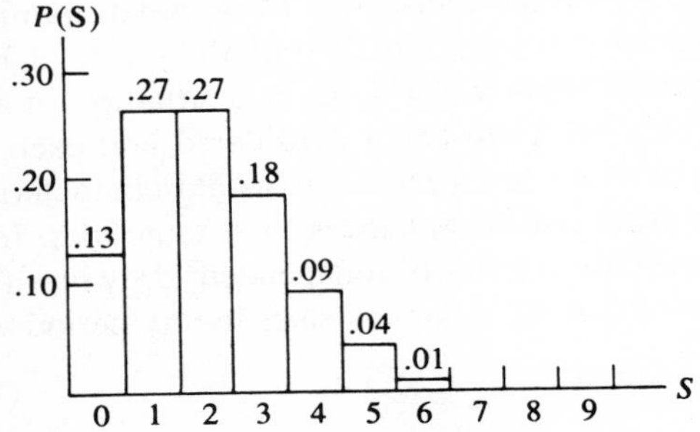

Figure 15-5 Poisson Sales Model ($\bar{S} = \sigma_s^2 = 2$)

The next step is to find the mean, variance, and probability distribution of sales where both s_i and n are random variables. Equation 15-31 can be rewritten:

$$S = \bar{s}n \tag{15-32}$$

where $\bar{s}$ is expected sales per customer.

The variance of a product of two random variables is approximately given by

$$\sigma_S^2 = n^2 \sigma_s^2 + \bar{s}^2 \sigma_n^2 + 2\bar{s}n\rho_{sn}\sigma_s\sigma_n \tag{15-33}$$

where ρ_{sn} is the coefficient of correlation between the average customer purchase rate and the average number of customers.[10]

If the number of customers and the average purchase rate are uncorrelated, then the last term in Equation 15-33 drops from the equation. In the majority of situations the two variables are likely to be correlated. For example, in periods of rising income, companies are likely to experience both a rise in the number of customers and a rise in the average purchase rate; in periods of falling income, both the number of customers and their average purchase rate are likely to fall. As a result of this positive correlation between n and s, the variance of S, according to Equation 15-33, will be greater than if n and s were uncorrelated. That is, a positive correlation between n and s will make it more difficult to forecast S accurately.

Under some circumstances, n and s may be negatively correlated. For example, the company may have a policy of easing its customer credit standards in good

[10]According to Holt, et al., *Planning Production, Inventories, and Work Force*, 297, the approximation is good when the coefficient of variation of the two random variables is "small." An exact derivation, and an application to cement sales data, are found in Haskel Benishay, "Random Sums of Random Variables as Economic Processes: Sales," *Journal of Marketing Research* (Aug. 1967) 296–302.

times and tightening its standards in bad times. Easing its credit standards generally brings more smaller customers to the company, who generally order less per period. In other words, while the number of customers rise, the average purchase rate falls. Tightening credit standards, on the other hand, generally reduces the number of customers (especially small customers) with the effect of increasing the average purchase rate. The negative correlation between n and s introduced by the policy has the effect of reducing the variance of company sales as shown in Equation 15-33, making company sales more predictable than in the case when n and s are uncorrelated.

Equations 15-32 and 15-33 gave the mean and variance of the product of two random variables. Unfortunately, it is very difficult to derive analytically the form of the probability distribution itself from a knowledge of the distribution of each variable. However, if both random variables have a lognormal distribution, company sales can be analytically derived. First take the logarithm of Equation 15-32:

$$\ln S = \ln \bar{s} + \ln n \tag{15-34}$$

Since the log of s and the log of n are assumed to be normally distributed, then the log of S is also normally distributed; S itself is therefore lognormally distributed. Were s and n to come from other distributions than the lognormal, the form of the probability distribution of the product, $S = sn$, would ordinarily have to be determined by Monte Carlo simulation.

SUMMARY

This chapter described some methods of disaggregating sales into its elements, so that particular micromarketing decision variables can be examined in relation to particular sales elements. Two types of disaggregate sales models were developed in detail. The first, microcomponent sales models, calls for breaking down company sales into additive components. Sales can be disaggregated according to product, customer, territory, or some combination of these transaction dimensions. Then micromarketing variables can be examined in relation to these components to discern relationships that might be useful in marketing planning or control.

The second, microanalytic sales models, calls for breaking down company sales into multiplicative variables, specifically the total number of buyers in the market, the percentage who buy from the company, and the average purchase rate of a company customer. The company can develop different marketing plans to influence each of these factors, and hence total sales. To simplify the exposition, the first two factors were combined into the number of company customers, n. A series of models were explored where n, the number of company customers, and s, the average customer purchase rate, were specified as either both fixed (deterministic model); or one was randomly determined from a known probability distribution (binomial, normal, lognormal, or Poisson); or both were randomly determined. By treating one or both of these as random variables drawn from specified probability distributions, it is possible to show the mean and variance of sales facing the company. A knowledge of the mean and variance of sales enables the company to improve its production scheduling, cash flow management, and balancing of risk and opportunity. At the same time, the company is even more interested in developing marketing programs that will change the mean and variance of its sales. A company would like to increase expected sales and generally reduce the variance of sales. Expected sales can be increased through marketing programs that increase the total number of buyers in the market, the number of buyers buying from the company, and the average customer purchase rate. When it comes to a choice of alternative marketing programs, this choice should rest on the likelihood of effecting each source of increased sales with each program against the required costs. The variance of sales can be reduced by reducing the variance of each of the sources of sales and by policies that bring about negative correlations between the factors in the sales process.

Questions and Problems

1. A company sells in a market consisting of 5 buyers. They buy:

    $(S_1, S_2, S_3, S_4, S_5) = (10, 13, 7, 9, 14)$

    The amounts they buy from the company are:

    $(S_{1i}, S_{2i}, S_{3i}, S_{4i}, S_{5i}) = (4, 9, 0, 7, 6)$

    Determine the values of w, k, and s and use them to calculate company sales (S).

2. A company currently sells its product in a market of 100 potential customers. Its market penetration is .6 and it sells an average of 2 units per customer each period.

    Management is considering 3 separate promotional campaigns as a means of stimulating sales. It is estimated that campaign A will increase the size of the market by 20 potential customers, while leaving penetration and average sales per customer unchanged. Campaign B will increase penetration by .1 while increasing the size of the market by 10. Campaign C will result in an increase of the average sales per customer of 1, while decreasing penetration by .1.

    Which of the 3 campaigns will most greatly stimulate sales?

3. The owner of a small restaurant wants to know how many doughnuts he should stock at the beginning of each day. By examining past sales records he determines that on 5 percent of the days examined, he sold only 10 doughnuts. The complete distribution is as follows:

Number of doughnuts sold	Relative frequency
10	.05
20	.15
30	.35
40	.30
50	.15

Each doughnut costs the owner 10c and is sold for 15c if sold on the first day. Doughnuts not sold on the first day are sold back to the supplier for 5c to be resold in his day-old shops.

In this situation, what is the expected value of stocking each of the 5 quantities of doughnuts? Which quantity should he stock?

4. A company has 5 customers in its market each of whom buys 5 or 10 units of the company's product in the next period, with probabilities of .4 and .6, respectively. What levels of sales are possible in the period? What are the probabilities of sales taking on any one of these levels?

5. A salesman's territory contains 100 thousand customers, and the probability that any one customer will purchase a unit of the company's product in this period is known to be .01. The salesman has predicted that his sales will be 2 thousand units in this period. What is the probablity that the salesman will achieve this predicted sales level?

6. Because of unexpected personal expenses the owner of a local bakery shop will be forced to take out a loan to cover operating expenses unless his sales in the next month are at least \$5000. If his monthly sales are normally distributed with expected sales of \$4000 and a standard deviation of \$500, what is the probability that he will have to take out the loan?

7. In a particular market the number of customers (n) in any month, and the average monthly amount purchased by each customer (s), are normally distributed random variables. Specifically:

$$f(n) = f_N(n|u_n = 10,000; \sigma_n = 500)$$

and

$$f(s) = f_N(s|u_s = 3; \sigma_s = 1)$$

Suppose that n and s are uncorrelated. What is the expected level of sales in any given month? What is the variance of these sales levels?

CHAPTER 16
Brand Share Sales Models

One of the critical variables that influence a company's sales is the percentage of all buyers in the market who buy from this company (see Equation 15-3). A company seeking to increase its sales must try to understand how buyers see the company's brand in relation to competitive brands and what influences their perception and preferences for the different brands. Some of the influencing factors, such as product quality, promotion, distribution, and price are under the company's control and provide the company with leverage for increasing its percentage of all customers, and hence total company sales.

This takes us into the area of buyer behavior, particularly the challenge of trying to represent buyer behavior by mathematical models that will assist in evaluating marketing plans and in predicting sales. Most of the extant models of buyer behavior are verbal. For example, theories of buyer behavior have been fashioned from grander theories of human choice behavior, leading to such prose models as the Marshallian buyer, Pavlovian buyer, Freudian buyer, Veblenian buyer, and Hobbesian buyer.[1] More recently, students of buyer behavior have begun to construct prose models out of a more inter-

---

[1]See Philip Kotler, "Behavioral Models for Analyzing Buyers," *Journal of Marketing* (Oct. 1965) 37–45.

disciplinary set of variables, drawn from psychology, social psychology, economic theory, anthropology, and information processing theory.[2]

Admittedly, the complexity of buyer behavior requires the language of prose to convey all the intricate nuances. At the same time, the divergences of these models is a direct consequence of the ambiguity of prose. This has led an increasing number of scholars to express their behavioral explanations in mathematical terms. Though this involves a high degree of simplification, it promotes increased vigor in the communication and comparison of theories. The development of mathematical behavioral models is a welcome complement to the abundant verbal formulations of individual buyer behavior dynamics.

This is not the place to present a detailed history of mathematical formulations of human behavior, but it would be desirable to cite a few major works. Some of this work stretches back into the nineteenth century when economists such as Edgeworth and Jevons first formulated their utility maximization equations of buyer behavior.[3] Early experimental psychologists described many of their findings on learning, memory, and motivation in terms of mathematical relationships between two or more variables. However, it is only recently that whole systems of equations have been developed to describe more comprehensive aspects of human behavior. A significant step in this direction occurred with the mathematical formulation by Herbert Simon in 1954 of George Homans' verbal propositions on human interaction.[4] Simon's model related the strength of positive sentiments, the amount of interaction, and the number of common activities of individuals through a series of simultaneous differential equations, each equation showing the change in one of the variables as a function of the others.

Another milestone is represented in the set of papers delivered at a conference on computer simulation and personality theory held at the Educational Testing Service, Princeton, New Jersey in June 1962.[5] These papers contain impressive speculations and suggestions as to the programming of a computer to duplicate some of the perceptual, cognitive, affective, motivational, and behavioral aspects of the homo sapiens. As for representing mathematically the more social

---

[2]Among the most interesting verbally constructed models of buyer behavior are John A. Howard and Jagdish N. Sheth, "A Theory of Buyer Behavior," in Harold H. Kassarjian and Thomas S. Robertson, eds., *Perspectives in Consumer Behavior* (Glenview, Ill.: Scott, Foresman and Company, 1968), pp. 467–487; Alan R. Andreasen, "Attitudes and Customer Behavior: A Decision Model," in Kassarjian and Robertson, *Perspectives in Consumer Behavior*, pp. 498–510; Francesco M. Nicosia, *Consumer Decision Processes* (Englewood Cliffs, N.J.: Prentice-Hall, Inc., 1966), Chaps. 6 and 7; and James Engel, David Kollat, and Roger D. Blackwell *Consumer Behavior* (New York: Holt, Rinehart and Winston, Inc., 1968), Chap. 2.

[3]F. Y. Edgeworth, *Mathematical Psychics*, 1881 (London: London School of Economics Reprints, 1932); William S. Jevons, *The Theory of Political Economy* (New York: The Macmillan Company, 1871).

[4]Herbert A. Simon, "The Construction of Social Science Models," in P. F. Lazarsfeld, ed., *Mathematical Thinking in the Social Sciences* (New York: The Free Press, 1954), pp. 430–440.

[5]Silvan S. Tomkins and Samuel Messick, eds., *Computer Simulation of Personality* (New York: John Wiley & Sons, Inc., 1963).

interactions of human beings, the recent book by James S. Coleman presents an impressive collection of mathematical tools, studies, and possibilities in this area.[6]

With regard to consumer behavior, the literature on mathematical models of individual behavior is scant. A pioneering article by Carman and Nicosia offers a formulation of buyer decision processes in terms of five simultaneous differential equations.[7] This work is an extension of the Simon approach mentioned earlier. Most of the Markov process articles on consumer brand choice deal with aggregate brand loyalty and switching tendencies, rather than with individual consumer behavior. The exceptions are found in some of the work of Amstutz, Duhamel, Frank, Lipstein, Massy, Montgomery, and Morrison.[8] Germane research of still a different character is found in Guy Orcutt's work[9] and that of the Simulmatics Corporation.[10] Orcutt has modeled individual persons who are born, age, marry, save, spend, and die. The Simulmatics Corporation has modeled the media habits of a hypothetical population of 2944 persons who choose their programs and reading material probabilistically in a way related to their varying social-economic characteristics. As for business and marketing games, hardly any of them have incorporated individual buyers as the *modus operandi* for determining market response but instead utilize total market or market segment response functions directly.

This brief review of the existing literature is intended to show that the mathematical formulation of human behavior, and particularly consumer behavior, is in its infancy. Future contributions will be achieved in different degrees, depending upon the buying situation that is being modeled and the resources and imagination of the model builder. Each buying situation makes salient a different set of consumer mechanisms and marketing factors. For example, the problem of brand choice of frequently purchased nondurables (say coffee,

[6]James S. Coleman, *Introduction to Mathematical Sociology* (New York: The Macmillan Company, 1964).

[7]James M. Carman and Francesco M. Nicosia, "Analog Experiment with a Model of Consumer Attitude Change," in L. George Smith, ed., *Reflections on Progress in Marketing* (Chicago: American Marketing Association, 1965), pp. 246–257.

[8]Arnold E. Amstutz, *Computer Simulation of Competitive Market Response* (Cambridge, Mass.: The M.I.T. Press, 1967), Chap. 8; William F. Duhamel, *The Use of Variable Markov Processes as a Partial Basis for the Determination and Analysis of Market Segments*, unpublished Ph.D. dissertation, Stanford University, 1966; Ronald E. Frank, "Brand Choice as a Probability Process," *Journal of Business* (Jan. 1962) 43–56; Benjamin Lipstein, "A Mathematical Model of Consumer Behavior," *Journal of Marketing Research* (Aug. 1965) 259–265; William F. Massy and Ronald E. Frank, "Short Term Price and Dealing Effects in Selected Market Segments," *Journal of Marketing Research* (May 1965) 171–185; David B. Montgomery, *A Probability Diffusion Model of Dynamic Market Behavior*, Working Paper 205–66, Alfred P. Sloan School of Management, Massachusetts Institute of Technology, Cambridge, May 1966; Donald G. Morrison, "New Models of Consumer Behavior: Aids in Setting and Evaluating Marketing Plans," in *Marketing and Economic Development*, Peter D. Bennett, ed. (Chicago, Ill.: American Marketing Association, 1966), 323–337.

[9]Guy H. Orcutt, Martin Greenberger, John Korbel, and Alice M. Rivlin, *Microanalysis of Socioeconomic Systems: A Simulation Study* (New York: Harper & Row Publishers, 1961).

[10]*Simulmatics Meda-Mix: Technical Description* (New York: The Simulmatics Corporation, Oct. 1962).

bread, etc.), as generally formulated in the literature, does not involve the consumer's affective or motivational mechanisms (emotions and drives) as much as his perception and learning mechanism. Thus a model of buyer behavior in this situation is likely to be most explicit on the perception and learning questions. On the other hand, most of the literature in marketing suggests that modeling the buying process for a new automobile does require the imputation of strong and conflicting drives, affective feelings, and information seeking.

It is not possible, in the brief space of this chapter, to develop models dealing with the entire range of buying situations. Instead, the chapter will focus on one particular, important, and familiar buying situation, the purchasing of grocery staple products. This has the virtue of being one of the simplest buying situations, and yet several of the concepts are transferable to other buying situations. The first part of the chapter will deal with the representation of attitudes toward competing brands, specifically brand perceptions and brand preferences. The attitude component is an important element in explaining brand choice behavior; sellers are always eager to develop product and marketing attributes that improve attitudes toward brands. The second part of the chapter considers the brand choice process itself as it takes place each week in the decision to shop for branded staple grocery items. Several models of this process are developed and contrasted to show the variety of factors that influence brand purchase behavior.

BUYERS' PERCEPTIONS AND PREFERENCES

Effective marketing planning for a brand requires a solid knowledge of what the buyers of the product class know and feel about the various brand entries. The brands may differ in price, product attributes, packaging, image, and in other ways. It is not always obvious how buyers will see the brands or rank them. Individual buyers generally lack awareness or experience with all brands, and they have a tendency to filter out a lot of product information, and distort other information. It is essential for the seller to try to see the brands from the buyers' frame of reference and seek to understand the role the product class plays in satisfying the need systems of buyers.

A most promising modeling development in this area is the use of geometric space to represent the buyers' attitudes toward the brands. To illustrate, consider an individual buyer who is asked to reflect on the brands in a particular product class, say beer. He is asked what attributes of beer stand out in his mind for judging the different brands. Suppose the consumer singles out two dimensions of the product: the beer's mildness and lightness. In his mind, a beer's mildness can range from mild to bitter and the beer's lightness can range from light to heavy. Furthermore, assume that he sees the two dimensions as independent, although this would have to be established by research. He can imagine brands possessing different combinations of mildness and lightness.

Let us assume that our beer drinker has tried eight different brands and remembers their qualities. His perceptions of these eight brands can be represented as points in geometric space, with one axis representing mildness and the other lightness, as shown in Figure 16-1.

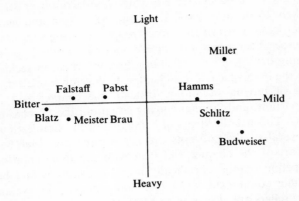

Figure 16-1 Distribution of Consumer Perceptions of Beer Brands According to Mildness and Lightness

Source: Richard M. Johnson, "Market Segmentation—A Comparison of Techniques" (a paper delivered at the 16th International Meeting of the Institute of Management Sciences, March 27, 1969).

The question can now be raised as to which brands the consumer sees as similar and which as quite distinct. A natural measure of brand dissimilarity would be the geometric distance between any pair of brands:

$$d_{ij} = \sqrt{(X_{i1} - X_{j1})^2 + (X_{i2} - X_{j2})^2} \tag{16-1}$$

where: d_{ij} = distance, or perceived dissimilarity, between brands i and j

X_{i1} = brand i's rating on attribute 1. Other X's are similarly interpreted

Applying this measure to the brands in Figure 16-1, the two brands that seem most dissimilar are Budweiser and Blatz, while the two brands that seem most similar are Budweiser and Schlitz. In general we should predict that the degree of similarity of any two brands would vary inversely with the geometric distance between them.

The question then arises whether we can predict how he would rank the brands in order of preference. The mapping of his perceptions of the brands tells us nothing in principle about how he feels about them.[11] For this, we need an additional item of information. We ask the consumer where his *ideal brand* would be in this space, whether or not it is one of the brands in existence. Suppose his ideal point is very close to Budweiser in Figure 16-1. The ideal point now provides a basis for predicting how he would rank the other brands. A natural measure of his ordinal preference for the actual brands is their distance

[11]Admittedly, there is a possible association between his perceptions and his preferences, as it might come through the selection of dimensions, and the positioning of the points in the perceptual space.

from his ideal brand. On this assumption we should predict that his preference order for the eight brands, from the most favored to the least favored, is Budweiser, Schlitz, Hamms, Miller, Pabst, Meister Brau, Falstaff, and Blatz.

All of these inferences rest on a set of at least five assumptions that should be summarized:

1. The consumer thinks consciously or unconsciously of basic dimensions when he thinks about a product class.
2. These dimensions are independent of each other and each is scalable.
3. These dimensions have equal weight in the buyer's mind.[12]
4. The buyer can indicate where each brand is located in the space.
5. The preference surface over the perceptual space symmetrically decreases in all directions from the ideal point.

Where predictions of the buyer's preferences are way off the mark, one or more of these assumptions may not be satisfied. For example, assumption 5 is illustrated in Figure 16-2. Figure 16-2 consists of Figure 16-1 represented as the floor of a three-dimensional space with the third axis representing the level of preference as it varies over the space. It may be that preference does not fall equally fast in all directions away from the ideal point, and it is even possible that the preference surface is multimodal, with the ideal point representing the highest mode.

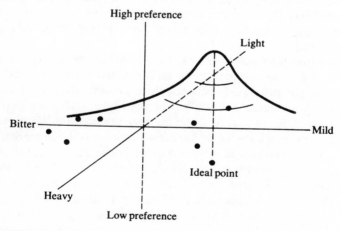

Figure 16-2 Preference Surface Mapped over the Perceptual Space

For similarity and preference mapping to be useful in marketing planning, we must go beyond the single consumer and see whether regularities show up for groups of buyers in the market. Suppose a randomly selected sample of beer

[12]If the dimensions are weighted differently by the buyer, then the simple Euclidian distance should be modified into a weighted Euclidian distance.

drinkers is interviewed with respect to individual's perceptions and preference among beer brands. The first thing we might discover is that buyers vary in the dimensions they invoke for judging beer brands. Several different attributes of beer may be mentioned in the course of the study. The situation is not hopeless if certain attribute combinations appear frequently. In fact, this finding would provide a basis for segmenting beer drinkers into distinct classes.

For simplicity, however, assume that all the beer drinkers cited the same two attributes, mildness and lightness, as important in perceiving beer brands. We now proceed to develop a separate perceptual map like Figure 16-1 for each beer drinker. When these maps are compared, two extreme results might be found, and many in between. At one extreme, we might find most of the maps differing from each other. For example, a particular brand may seem mild and heavy to some people and bitter and light to other people. Such a finding can have several meanings. One hypothesis is that people place different interpretations on the meaning of each attribute; they do not have the same conception of the meaning of a mild or a light beer. Another hypothesis is that beer brands in fact differ very little in mildness and lightness, even though people imagine they do; their low ability to discriminate leads in a random fashion to different perceptual maps. One indication of which hypothesis is more nearly correct is whether there are a few basic map types. If the maps cluster into a few distinct groups, this phenomenon might reflect the existence of market segments rather than random response behavior.

At the other extreme, beer drinkers may all report a map looking rather like the one in Figure 16-1. This extent of agreement can be taken to mean that the attributes have a shared meaning among beer drinkers and brand differences are readily discernible.

Let us suppose that high agreement has been found in the perceptual mappings. The next step is to compare the location of the various buyers' ideal points. Here we might distinguish between three possible findings. First, the ideal points may be scattered uniformly over the space, indicating that beer drinkers have quite different real or imagined beer preferences. We should be disinclined to say that there are major preference groupings in the market. The finding might suggest that the firm preparing to introduce a new beer (or change the image of its existing brand) might consider good opportunities to exist in the areas of the map where there are no brands, since some preference is found in all areas of the space. Looking back at Figure 16-1, there would be persons in this market for such new beer attribute combinations as a heavy medium-mild beer or a light medium-mild beer.

A second possible finding is that virtually all the beer drinkers place their ideal point in the same location, indicating that there is one ideal brand and that brands give less satisfaction, the further away they are from the ideal brand. In this case, we should predict that, all other things being equal (price, distribution, availability, etc.), the brand nearest the ideal point has the largest market share; the market shares of other brands fall as their distance increases from the ideal point. If all other things are not equal, such as prices, then the buyer may be willing to obtain a less preferred brand at a lower price to a more preferred brand at a higher price.

A third possible finding is that the ideal points cluster in certain distinct parts of the map. It may be that the ideal points cluster where the existing brands are found and explain the existence of these brands. On the other hand, it may be that some ideal point clusters are found where no brands exist, and this could represent an opportunity for new brand entries. Figure 16-3 shows the results of an actual study of ideal point concentrations. The larger circles represent more intense densities of preference. Note that the two largest circles (1 and 2) are near the best selling beer brands. Circle 1 may indicate that beer drinkers would like Schlitz to be even a little heavier or Budweiser to be a little less mild if the center of the circle is taken to be the most intense location of preference. Note also the existence of ideal points that are away from any existing brands (particularly 8 and 6) and therefore indicate possible opportunities for new brand entries. Finally, note that the brands at the far left do not match anyone's ideal and therefore are probably tolerated because they are less expensive.

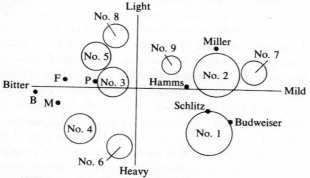

Figure 16-3   Distribution of Ideal Points in Product Space

Source: Johnson, *op, cit.*

All of these implications come out of this multidimensional model of perceptions and preferences. Previous models of brand preference typically involved only one product attribute and used the concept of a frequency distribution of preferences over the attribute.[13] Multidimensional modeling is a generalization of the more familiar one-dimensional case and represents an improvement because most products evoke two or more important attribute dimensions. Each dimension requires a decision by the seller as he designs the product. It is possible to portray up to three dimensions graphically; beyond this, the analysis can be conducted in mathematical terms. Many products probably do not involve more than 3–5 dimensions as critical in the buyer's perceptions and preferences for the brands.

[13]See Alfred A. Kuehn and Ralph L. Day, "Strategy of Product Quality," *Harvard Business Review* (Nov.–Dec. 1962) 100–110.

The discussion has implied that subjects are asked to locate their perceptions and preferences directly on scales provided to them.[14] This method, however, may bias the determination of the number of significant dimensions, their nature, and even the location of the points in the perceptual space. Some recent work in this area has proceeded on an indirect basis. For example, consumers may be asked to sort cards carrying brand names into pairs running from the most similar pairs to the least similar pairs. They may also be shown all possible pairs of brands and asked to state the brand they prefer in each pair. From this raw similarity and preference data, multidimensional scaling techniques can be used to develop dimensions and locations of points. The data need not be interval scaled; they can be in the form of ordinal or rank order measures. A statistical technique developed by Kruskal computes the configuration of points that optimize goodness of fit for a monotonic relationship between the similarity measures and the geometric distances.[15] The goodness of fit is evaluated by a quantity called "stress," which is similar to the proportion of unexplained variance. The technique seeks to find the configuration of points for a space of a given number of dimensions that minimizes the stress. It finds the best configuration for a space of one dimension, then two, and up to $n-1$ dimensions, where n is the number of brands or objects. Typically, the stress is larger with fewer dimensions because the points are more constrained. When the analyst finds an acceptable number of dimensions in terms of stress, he then uses his judgment to name each dimension. The clue to the nature of the dimension is the rank order of the brands along that dimension. The rank order might suggest some quality that the brands on one side have more of than the other. This judgmental approach to naming the dimension is similar to that used in factor analysis, which is described in Chapter 18. In the case of the beer study in Figure 16-3, the brand locations in two-dimensional space suggest that the horizontal dimension is premium quality, with high premium quality toward the right and low quality toward the left (premium quality may indicate mildness); they suggest that the vertical dimension is lightness, with light beers at the top and heavy beers at the bottom.[16]

The multidimensional model of brand perceptions and preferences has several uses in marketing planning, which are summarized below.

1. *Product and promotion strategy.* It can help the seller determine whether

---

[14]The semantic differential technique would provide one method of direct scaling. For a description of this and other methods of direct scaling, see Fred N. Kerlinger, *Foundations of Behavioral Research* (New York: Holt, Rinehart and Winston, 1965), Chaps. 27, 32.

[15]J. B. Kruskal, "Multidimensional Scaling by Optimizing Goodness of Fit to a Nonmetric Hypothesis," *Psychometrika* (Mar. 1964) 1–27; and "Nonmetric Multidimensional Scaling: A Numerical Example," *Psychometrika* (June 1964) 115–129.

[16]For good expositions of multidimensional scaling, illustrating other studies that have been conducted, see Paul E. Green, Frank J. Carmone, and Patrick J. Robinson, *Analysis of Marketing Behavior Using Nonmetric Scaling and Related Techniques* (Cambridge, Mass.: Marketing Science Institute, Mar. 1968); Volney Stefflre, "Market Structure Studies: New Products for Old Markets and New Markets (Foreign) for Old Products," in Frank M. Bass, et al., eds., *Applications of the Sciences in Marketing Management* (New York: John Wiley & Sons, Inc., 1968), pp. 251–268.

consumers have a similar or dispersed image of his brand. Even if they share a similar image of his brand, the seller may be surprised to learn where it lies. He may wish to change the image of his brand, that is, cause the point to move in a direction closer to a greater concentration of ideal points. This may lead to the revision of product attributes and/or the formulation of a new advertising campaign. After some time he can measure his brand's image again, to see whether the new marketing strategy was effective.

2. *Market segmentation.* Multidimensional models may help the seller discern the segments of the market more clearly, based on perceptions and preferences. Having determined the important segments, he may seek to determine whether any clear relationship exists between the attitudinal variables and sociodemographic variables. He may find, for example, that light mild beer is preferred by women and heavy low-mild beer is preferred by older persons with low incomes. Such findings will help him in the selection of advertising messages and media, sales promotions, and even which outlets to emphasize.

3. *New product opportunities.* Multidimensional models may help the seller locate new brand opportunities by comparing concentrations of ideal points with the locations of actual brands.

At the same time, it should be recognized that perceptual and preference mapping cannot tell the whole story about consumer behavior. Attitudes do not lead to behavior in a one-to-one fashion. We have been dealing largely with the product attribute dimension of the marketing process. Buyer choice processes are also based on other factors such as prices, deals, availability, status concerns, and so on. For this reason we shall now move directly into the question of actual behavior toward brands and attempt to develop a set of models, ranging from very simple to very complex, for explaining behavior over time in the marketplace.

THE BRAND CHOICE PROCESS

The specific problem in this section will be to formulate a mechanism that will cause a hypothetical consumer to make a weekly selection of a beer brand from three available brands called *A*, *B*, and *C*. The brands can be thought of as having some differences among them in attribute and merchandising characteristics that partly contribute to variations in buyer response. *The task is one of describing how outside stimuli and internal psychological mechanisms interact to produce individual buyer choice behavior over time.*

The problem can be made concrete by viewing consumer brand choice behavior in the larger context of the competitive marketing process. The view that shall be taken is illustrated in Figure 16-4. Assume that each week (box 1) individual consumers go to a retail outlet and buy, among other things, a week's supply of beer. Three brands are available: *A*, *B*, and *C*. They differ slightly in quality, price, sales promotion features, shelf space and position, and other marketing characteristics. In fact, each week may produce some changes in the marketing characteristics of one or more brands (box 2). The first buyer enters the store with certain brand predispositions (box 3) and makes a brand choice (box 4). Buyers continue to enter the store during the week and make brand choices. After the last buyer has made a purchase (box 5), brand shares are computed for week t (box 6); they influence through a feedback process the marketing strategies of the three competitors in the following week. This process continues week after week until the simulation is over (box 7), at which point the computer program prints out the brand selection history for each individual buyer and also the brand shares in each period (box 8). These data can be analyzed for various purposes, such as to evaluate different competitive marketing strategies, to examine the validity and reliability of current statistical techniques used to analyze demand determinants, and for other purposes.

The objective here is to review and extend current models that implement the individual buyer brand choice process in boxes 3 and 4. These models produce simulated individual brand choice histories that hopefully resemble actual consumer panel histories. To the extent that the simulated histories resemble actual histories, they lend confirmation to the underlying theory.

It is, in fact, very difficult to proceed the other way, moving from actual consumer brand histories to inferences about the underlying brand decision processes. Some analysts have sought to interpret buyer decision processes on the basis of individual buyer brand purchase histories. Consider the following ten-week purchase history: $AAABAACAAA$. The most plausible interpretation is that the buyer has a strong preference for brand A and occasionally tries other brands for sundry reasons but always returns to A. Yet this same purchase history is subject to a variety of interpretations:

1. *Brand loyalty hypothesis.* The consumer consciously prefers brand A, feels loyal to it, and buys it at every opportunity. He may occasionally buy another brand for variety but always returns to his favorite brand.
2. *Habit persistence hypothesis.* The consumer buys brand A out of habit, rather than conscious preference. He gives little thought to brand choice and simply tends to reach for the familiar. His behavior may be characterized as autonomous response behavior.
3. *Maximization of value to price hypothesis.* The consumer has no loyalty to any brand and makes his choice strictly on the basis of which current brand he perceives gives him the most for his money. He feels that brand A currently offers the most quality or quantity for the price and only buys another brand when it is on sale. If another brand is improved in quality or quantity or if its price is permanently reduced to a sufficient extent, he will buy that brand more often.
4. *Shifts in brand availability hypothesis.* The consumer patronizes a store which is well stocked only in brand A and this accounts for his choosing A most of the time.

Other hypotheses may also offer a plausible explanation of the observed purchase history. The point is that an actual purchase history can be explained by a variety of hypotheses about the buyer's brand decision processes; it is difficult to tell which holds in the absence of additional information.

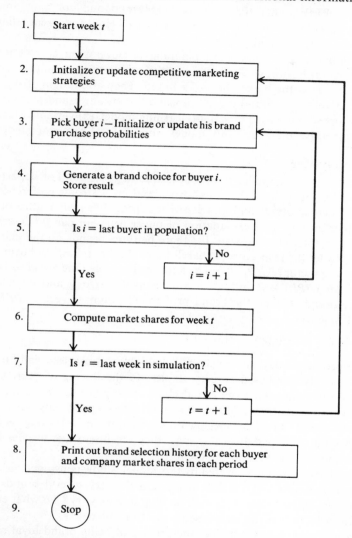

Figure 16-4   Simulation of the Competitive Marketing Process

Yet the firm must adopt some viewpoint about the determinants of buyer brand choice. The theory that a firm holds will influence its marketing strategy. For example, a view of the consumer as "stimulus-prone and high persuasible" leads to a great reliance on prior advertising, price deals, and point of purchase store displays. A view of the consumer as "a creature of habit" leads to some complacency with respect to holding present customers and some doubt in attracting new customers. A view of the consumer as "an economic calculating machine" leads to a policy of improving real values (a better ratio of quality or quantity to price), rather than emphasizing brand and company image advertising. A view of the consumer as "fantasy-prone" leads to a great reliance on imaginative advertising and packaging.

Given the importance to marketing planning of developing correct interpretations of buyer behavior, we shall now examine a succession of mathematical models describing how the buyer chooses a brand. They are, ranging from the simple to the complex: (1) brand loyalty model, (2) constant brand probability model, (3) last brand purchased model, (4) learning model, (5) variable Markov model, (6) competitive marketing mix model, and (7) total behavior model.

The Brand Loyalty Model

The first model is hardly a model at all, but it offers a good point of departure. The brand loyalty model says that the buyer develops a strong preference or habit for a particular brand and purchases it repeatedly, giving little or no thought to other brands. This explanation of buyer behavior can be described mathematically in the following way. Let there be three brands on the market, A, B, and C, and let the respective probabilities of their purchase by buyer i be represented by the vector (P_A, P_B, P_C). The latter will be called the *brand purchase probability vector* ($BPPV$). If buyer i has developed a strong and unyielding preference for brand A, then the brand probability purchase vector ($BPPV_{it}$) for buyer i at time t is

$$BPPV_{it} = (1.00, 0.00, 0.00) \quad \text{for all } t$$

That some people display this behavior is incontrovertible, especially in the buying of frequently purchased grocery staples. In the buying of beer, many consumers report buying the same brand choice in the last ten or more purchases. It may be hypothesized that these consumers spend very little time thinking about brand choice or seeking brand information. As long as their brand provides the anticipated satisfactions, they are insensitive to cues from other brands and are unlikely to try them.

An important problem not answered by this model is how consumers develop a strong brand preference in the first place. Do they try several brands and then settle on one? Or do they stick with the first one they try? To what extent are they influenced by friends, mass media, and in other ways?

In other words, this model describes the process of being brand loyal rather than becoming brand loyal. A market made up entirely of brand loyal buyers would be highly uninteresting. There would be no shifts in brand share and expenditures for price deals, advertising, and point of purchase displays would be largely wasted. Price deals would only subsidize present customers; and advertising and point of purchase store displays would mainly sustain present customer loyalties, rather than attract away competitors' customers.

In a simulation using a population of hypothetical consumers, programming some fraction of them to behave according to the brand loyalty model may well be warranted. But the behavior of many buyers is not described by this model. The model's main contribution is to describe some buyers and to provide a starting point for further model building.

The Constant Brand Probability Model

The brand purchase histories of many members of consumer panels show brand switching behavior which is inconsistent with the brand loyalty model. The task is to formulate an explanation of brand switching behavior.

Brand switching can be explained as the result of *response uncertainty*, *response change*, or some mixture of the two.[17]

Response uncertainty means that a buyer's behavior is probabilistic rather than certain, and the probabilities are fairly stable. It would be illustrated by the person who buys brand *A* approximately three out of four times, brand *B* one out of four times, and never brand *C*. His next brand choice cannot be perfectly predicted but the average frequency of each brand choice can be predicted quite well.

Response change means that a buyer's behavior is probabilistic and the probabilities undergo systematic change. It would be illustrated by the person who grows to like brand *A* more and more through time, with the result that his repurchase probability of brand *A* increases through time.

Now the problem is that observed individual brand switching histories do not immediately suggest whether response uncertainty or response change is at work. Both tend to be confounded in the observed data. Coleman has developed interesting techniques for trying to unravel the two.[18] Here, for the sake of systematic theory construction, we shall treat the case of pure response uncertainty first, under the rubric of the constant brand probability model.

This model says that it is not possible to predict exactly the next choice, but one could predict the average proportion of times each brand will be purchased by the buyer. For example,

$$BPPV_{it} = (.50, .30, .20) \quad \text{for all } t$$

says that buyer *i* will purchase brand *A* 50 percent of the time, brand *B* 30 percent of the time, and brand *C* 20 percent of the time.

Through the adoption of more extreme probabilities, one would almost be describing the brand loyalty model, subject to a small amount of response uncertainty. This is accomplished for example in

$$BPPV_{it} = (.90, .08, .02) \quad \text{for all } t$$

The buyer is highly loyal to brand *A* but for sundry reasons occasionally buys *B* and less frequently *C*.

[17]James S. Coleman, *Models of Chance and Response Uncertainty* (Englewood Cliffs, N.J.: Prentice-Hall, Inc., 1964).
[18]Ibid.

While it is easy to state this mechanism, it is not easy to provide a plausible psychological explanation of it. Clearly, the buyer does not have a random chance device in his head that he spins prior to selecting a brand. About the closest behavioral explanation is that he has some stable pattern of brand preferences such as $A > B > C$; when he goes into a store, he is subject to a large number of random influences affecting his actual choice: the presence of a point-of-purchase store display, an out-of-stock condition, a price deal on an off-brand, an advertisement in the morning newspaper, and so forth. In general, behavior may be described as having a random component when a great many small factors operate in a situation and may affect the normal predisposition of the actor.

Can observed brand switching in the beer market be explained by a model that postulates constant household brand probabilities? Frank found that this hypothesis provided a statistically satisfactory explanation of brand choice behavior in another product field, coffee.[19] It was not necessary to evoke the hypothesis of learning to explain observed brand histories.

If the constant probability model is used to describe a hypothetical population of consumers, each having a different but stable brand probability purchase vector, it is possible to derive analytically the long run implied average market shares. At the same time, the constant brand probability model has a number of shortcomings. First, it does little to promote the development of psychological theory in the area of buyer behavior. At the most, it may stimulate the development of better techniques for mapping brand preference rankings or ratings into brand probability vectors and for relating them to the individual's social-economic personality characteristics.

Second, it denies the possibility of finding systematic relationships between changing marketing stimuli and consumer response. It treats marketing stimuli on too implicit and random a level to permit a study of their effects on buyers.

Third, it denies learning, the tendency for people's predispositions to change with experience. There is much psychological evidence that favorable experiences increase the probability that people will respond in a similar way to the next occasion.

Finally, this model is unable to reproduce the serial correlation that is observed in many actual brand histories. Specifically, the data often show various length runs of the same brand purchased and such runs cannot be explained on the basis of pure random drawings.

For all these reasons we must formulate a more sophisticated model of the brand choice process, although we may have occasion to revert to this model as a benchmark for judging the more elaborate ones.

---

[19]Ronald E. Frank, "Brand Choice as a Probability Process," *Journal of Business* (Jan. 1962) 43–56. However beer brand switching seems to follow a first or even higher Markov probability process. See William F. Massy, Ronald E. Frank, and Thomas M. Lodahl, *Purchasing Behavior and Personal Attributes* (Philadelphia: University of Pennsylvania Press, 1968), Chap. 3.

The Last Brand Purchased Model

In the previous model, the buyer's brand purchase probability vector remains constant throughout the simulation, a direct denial of learning theory. Learning theory holds that a person's responses to stimuli are determined through experience. If a stimulus leads a person to try something, and if that experience is rewarding, it strengthens the habit connection between stimulus and response, so that on the next trial there is a greater probability to respond in the same way. Conversely, if a person is dissatisfied, this tends to reduce the probability that he will respond in the same way to similar cues. In either case, the brand probabilities are likely to change after the purchase.

There are a number of mathematical devices for incorporating or representing the effects of learning. The general problem is to formulate a model that makes

$$BPPV_{i,t+1} = f(BPPV_{i,t}, B_{i,t})$$ (16-3)

where $B_{i,t}$ is the last brand purchased by buyer i

As a start consider the first order Markov probability transition matrix in Table 16-1. The original marketing use of this matrix is to represent the aggre-

Table 16-1 A First Order Markov Matrix

		To	
	A_{t+1}	B_{t+1}	C_{t+1}
From $\begin{matrix} A_t \\ B_t \\ C_t \end{matrix}$	$\begin{matrix} .70 \\ .50 \\ .60 \end{matrix}$	$\begin{matrix} .20 \\ .40 \\ .20 \end{matrix}$	$\begin{matrix} .10 \\ .10 \\ .20 \end{matrix}$

gate switching and staying tendencies of the market as a whole, rather than the individual buyer. Thus it may be observed that, of those consumers who buy brand A this period, 70 percent buy A again, 20 percent switch to B, and 10 percent switch to C. The other two rows are similarly interpreted. If these percentages hold from period to period for the market as a whole, and if other assumptions are satisfied,[20] then the matrix can be used to derive a number of interesting propositions about the market, including the ultimate level of brand shares and speed of convergence to this level.[21]

The same matrix can be reinterpreted to describe the effect of the last brand choice of an individual buyer on his current brand purchase probabilities. Suppose a person purchased brand A in the last period. Then there is a .70 probability that he will buy A again and some chance that he would buy B and C. Suppose he buys B next time (the chance is .20). Then we would expect the probability of his repurchasing B to go up (assuming satisfaction with B) and the probability of his repurchasing A to decline. Both effects are captured in

[20]A. S. C. Ehrenberg, "An Appraisal of Markov Brand-switching Models," *Journal of Marketing Research* (Nov. 1965) 347–363.

[21]Richard B. Maffei, "Brand Preferences and Simple Markov Processes," *Operations Research* (Mar.–Apr., 1960) 210–218.

this matrix. The probability of his buying A (having just bought B) has fallen from .70 to .50; the probability of his buying B has risen from .20 to .40. (The probability of his buying C has been unaffected in this example. If, however, he buys C in the future, the probability of his repurchasing C will rise from .10 to .20.)

There are, however, at least two unsatisfactory features in using a first order Markov matrix to interpret the effects of the last brand purchased on the buyer's future brand probabilities. The first problem is that, while the matrix provides for probability modifications when a switch occurs, it does not provide for probability modifications when the same brand is repurchased. Thus, if A were purchased last time with a purchase probability of .70 and is purchased again, we should expect A's repurchase probability to increase from .70. It does not; therefore this model only produces learning when switching occurs, rather than when staying occurs.

A second fault is that the model is static: it builds in only one period learning. This implies that the buyer is only influenced by the last purchase and not the last n purchases. The model is static in postulating the same row vector every time the buyer returns to a particular last brand.

A frequent suggestion is to use a two or more period Markov matrix to generate period to period brand choices.[22] But it soon becomes apparent that this is a cumbersome device for expressing the impact of cumulative learning, and some better mechanism must be found.

The Learning Model

A different way to express the reinforcement effects of past brand choices uses a learning model developed by Bush and Mosteller,[23] later applied to consumer behavior by Kuehn.[24] This model postulates the existence of a pair of "learning operators" that explicitly alter current brand probabilities on the basis of the last brand choice.

The basic device is illustrated in Figure 16-5. The horizontal axis represents the probability of choosing brand j in period t and the vertical axis represents the probability of choosing brand j in period $t+1$. The figure contains a positively sloped 45° line as a norm. The figure also contains two positively sloped lines called the purchase and rejection operators. These operators show how the probability of purchasing brand j is modified from period t to period $t+1$, depending on whether brand j was just purchased or not.

For example, suppose the probability of a person's purchasing brand j this period is .60. Suppose that this is actually what he buys. What is the probability

[22]Frank Harary and Benjamin Lipstein, "The Dynamics of Brand Loyalty: A Markovian Approach," *Operations Research* (Feb. 1962) 19–40.

[23]R. R. Bush and F. Mosteller, *Stochastic Models of Learning* (New York: John Wiley & Sons, Inc., 1955).

[24]Alfred A. Kuehn, "A Model for Budgeting Advertising," in Frank M. Bass, et al., eds., *Mathematical Models and Methods in Marketing* (Homewood, Ill.: Richard D. Irwin, Inc., 1961), pp. 302–356.

that he will buy brand j again? This is found by running a dotted line up from the horizontal axis at .60 to the purchase operator line (because brand j was purchased), going across the vertical axis, and then reading the new probability. In this illustration, the new probability is .78. Thus, as a result of buying A, the person's predisposition toward A has increased from .60 to .78. If he had not purchased A, the dotted line from .60 would have extended only to the rejection operator and been read on the vertical axis. His probability of buying A next time would have fallen from .60 to .31.

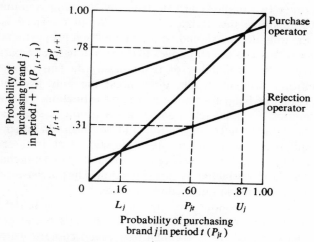

Figure 16-5 The Cumulative Learning Model

Thus the prevailing probability of buying brand j is incremented or diminished according to whether brand j is bought. And the amount of increase or decrease depends on the probability of buying brand j in period t. If brand j is purchased three times in a row, starting with a probability of .60, the probability increases each time according to the following values: .60, .78, .83, .86 (not shown).

If the consumer continues buying brand j for a long number of trials, the probability of buying brand j approaches .87 in the limit. This upper limit is given by the intersection of the purchase operator and the 45° line and represents a phenomenon known as *incomplete habit formation*. No matter how much brand j is bought, there is still some probability left that the consumer may buy another brand. On the other hand, if the consumer does not buy brand j for a long time, the probability of buying this brand falls continuously but never to 0. This is the phenomenon of *incomplete habit extinction*. There is always some positive probability that a consumer may buy a previously neglected brand.

The particular *rate* of brand habit formation or extinction, as well as the upper and lower limits, depend upon the slopes, intercepts, and curvatures of the two operators. In Figure 16-5 the operators are assumed to be parallel and linear. The parallel condition is required when there are more than two brands, in order that the probabilities sum to 1. The linearity condition greatly simplifies the estimation problem.[25] Yet it is conceivable that the actual learning process for a household is subject to more flexible operators.

Although this model represents an improvement over the last brand purchased model as a way of handling the effects of learning, it presents a number of difficulties. In the first place, the model is not stated in terms of the buyer's brand purchase probability vector but in terms of his probability of buying brand j. When his probability of buying brand j increases, the total probability of his buying the other two brands must decrease by the same amount. The problem is how to distribute the decrease between B and C. There is no a priori reason that the total decline should be distributed in a proportional way.

Another difficulty is that this model implies that the purchase of a particular brand always increases the probability of repurchasing it. This implies that there are no significant product quality differences; the only psychological process operating is that of habit formation and habit extinction. This may be a fairly safe assumption for relatively homogeneous products such as beer, coffee, bread, frozen orange juice, cigarettes, and so forth. In other cases, however, product differences are above the just-noticeable level. In these cases, it is not the choice of the brand that increases its probability of repurchase but rather the buyer's degree of satisfaction or dissatisfaction. The purchase operator is too rigid in implying inevitable satisfaction with use.

Also, this model, like the previous ones, ignores the effect on brand choice of variations in the marketing mix. It describes the buyer's brand purchase probabilities as being modified solely through past brand choices. This might be remedied by making the slopes and intercepts of the two operators a function of relative brand marketing effort. However, other methods of bringing marketing variables explicitly into the brand choice process will now be considered.

The Variable Markov Model

One of the earliest suggestions on how to incorporate marketing variables in brand switching processes was made by Alfred Kuehn and involves a novel interpretation of the probabilities in the Markov matrix.[26] Each cell probability is considered to be made up of the more basic elements shown in Table 16-2.

Table 16-2 The Variable Markov Model

$$
\begin{array}{c}
\begin{array}{ccc}
A_{t+1} & B_{t+1} & C_{t+1}
\end{array}\\
\begin{array}{c}A_t\\B_t\\C_t\end{array}
\begin{bmatrix}
r_A+(1-r_A)a_A & (1-r_A)a_B & (1-r_A)a_C\\
(1-r_B)a_A & r_B+(1-r_B)a_B & (1-r_B)a_C\\
(1-r_C)a_A & (1-r_C)a_B & r_C+(1-r_C)a_C
\end{bmatrix}
\end{array}
$$

where r_j = the unadjusted repurchase probability, $0 \leqslant r_j \leqslant 1$
a_j = the relative merchandising attractiveness of brand
j. $\Sigma a_j = 1$.

[25]James M. Carman, "Brand Switching and Linear Learning Models," *Journal of Advertising Research* (June 1966) 23–31.
[26]Kuehn, "A Model for Budgeting Advertising," in Bass et al., *Mathematical Models and Methods in Marketing*, Richard D. Irwin, Inc., 1961.

This model was formulated by Kuehn to explain aggregate switching and staying behavior but it can be reinterpreted in terms of the individual consumer. In this case, r_j represents the unadjusted probability that the buyer will choose brand j again. It reflects essentially the buyer's degree of preference for brand j after having used it. Also, a_j represents the relative merchandising attractiveness of brand j. Then the cell probability of a buyer's switching from B to A is given by

$$(1 - r_B)a_A$$

that is, the product of the degree to which he is not committed to brand B and the relative merchandising attractiveness of brand A. Similarly, the cell probability of a buyer's repeating his purchase of B is given by

$$r_B + (1 - r_B)a_B$$

that is, the degree of the buyer's loyalty to brand B, r_B, plus the extent to which his nonloyalty to B is overcome by brand B's relative merchandising attractiveness.

With this formulation, we need the parameters a_A, a_B, a_C, r_A, r_B, r_C to generate an individual buyer's behavior over time. (Actually, one of the a_j terms is redundant, since $\sum a_j = 1$.)

The a_j terms reflect the current differential attractiveness of competitive marketing appeals. For example, $a_A = .5$, $a_B = .3$, $a_C = .2$ would indicate that brand A is the most appealing brand at the time to the average customer, brand B is the next most appealing brand, and brand C is the least appealing brand. Relative brand attractiveness can change from week to week as competitors change their merchandising strategy.

Relative brand attractiveness is not measured directly but rather represents the result of averaging several dimensions of brand competition. The averaging can be accomplished in a number of ways, one of which is suggested in a later model.

The r_j terms are generally treated as constants in the original model describing aggregate behavior. However, in the application of this model to individual buyer behavior, the r_j terms can be treated as changing each period as a result of the reinforcement effect of last period brand choice. Specifically the probability of repurchasing brand j through habit should be increased if j were bought last time and reduced if it were not. This can be accomplished readily through linear learning operators.

Thus it is possible to modify the Markov model in a way that brings in two desirable effects: (1) the effect of brand learning; and (2) the effect of company merchandising variables. This approach might prove to be quite fruitful as a framework for developing specific consumer behavior hypotheses and marketing measurement techniques. At the same time, the model oversimplifies the learning phenomenon and also the dimensions of brand competition. It is with this in mind that the writer developed two further models.

The Competitive Marketing Mix Model

The variable Markov model described in the previous section used the device of a_j terms to describe the net effect of competitive merchandising strategies on brand switching behavior. From a marketing point of view it is desirable to make more explicit the specific marketing variables and their individual effects.

Assume that the current marketing characteristics of the different brands can be represented in a matrix called the *competitive marketing mix matrix*, M_t, at time t. An illustrative competitive marketing mix matrix for three brands and eight marketing variables is shown in Table 16-3.

Table 16-3   Competitive Marketing Mix Matrix

	Brand		
	A	*B*	*C*
List price	.31	.33	.36
Price deal	.33⅓	.33⅓	.33⅓
Premium	.33⅓	.33⅓	.33⅓
Packaging	.35	.33	.32
Quality	.40	.33	.27
Shelf space	.20	.50	.30
Advertising	.25	.42	.33
Store display	.33⅓	.33⅓	.33⅓

Each row represents the relative attractiveness of the three brands on a particular marketing dimension. The higher the number in a row, the more attractive the brand is on the dimension relative to the other brands. The numbers in each row add to 1.

If we consider price, brand C stands at .36, making it the most attractive brand pricewise on the market. This implies that it has the lowest list price. As for price deal, all three brands stand at .33⅓, indicating either that there are no price deals or that all the brands have the same deal. Moving to packaging, note that brand A is rated as having the most attractive package, followed by B and C; at the same time, the ratings are quite close. In the case of quality, the ratings are further apart, indicating that A is perceived to be of substantially higher quality than B and C. The brands also differ in shelf space exposure, brand B being the best exposed. Ratings are also available for advertising and store display differences among the three brands.

The competitive marketing mix matrix is used to summarize the average market perception of the three brands along the different dimensions of competition. A sample of consumers is surveyed and asked to rate the three brands on each dimension, in such a way that the ratings add up to one in each case. The ratings of all the consumers on each dimension are averaged and normalized to add to 1. It is in this sense that the matrix represents the average market perception of competitive marketing mix differences.

The competitors have the capability of influencing the average market perception through specific marketing actions. A competitor can increase his relative rating on price deals by offering one; he can improve his relative rating on advertising by finding a better message. The successful efforts of competitors to increase market favor will be reflected in the competitive marketing mix matrix.

In principle, each buyer has his own perception of the marketing mix differences among the brands. But, for our purpose, it is more useful to work with the concept of the perceptions of an average buyer. Individual variations are assumed to enter in a different manner: specifically, buyers vary the importance they attach to different marketing factors. Their individual response differences can be expressed by a second construct known as buyer i's *marketing response vector* (W_i),

$$W_i = (W_1, W_2, W_3, W_4, W_5, W_6, W_7, W_8)$$

which represents the relative weights placed by buyer i on the eight marketing variables. The weights in the vector are scaled to add to 1.00. An illustrative marketing response vector for buyer 1 is:

$$W_1 = (.08, .05, .06, .18, .20, .08, .20, .15)$$

This vector shows that buyer 1 places the most value on quality $(W_5 = .20)$, advertising $(W_7 = .20)$, packaging $(W_4 = .18)$, and store display $(W_8 = .15)$. A possible inference is that this is a middle class male interested mainly in quality and brand image, and uninterested in small price differences.

In a simulation involving a population of buyers, each buyer would face the same competitive mix matrix but would respond differently according to his individual marketing response vector. Each week the marketing mix matrix would change to reflect the latest competitive marketing actions. But the individual buyer's marketing response vectors would remain constant from week to week. In this way, brand share changes would be due entirely to marketing competition, not individual buyer changes. In a more elaborate model, individual buyer's response vectors would also change through time as a result of brand usage, learning, social influences, and other factors.

The model is set up to yield a brand probability purchase vector for each household in each week $(BPPV_{it})$. For example, the brand probability purchase vector for buyer 1 at time t is derived by multiplying buyer 1's response vector and the marketing mix matrix at time t:

$$W_1 M_t = (.08, .05, .06, .18, .20, .08, .20, .15) \begin{bmatrix} .31 & .33 & .36 \\ .33\frac{1}{3} & .33\frac{1}{3} & .33\frac{1}{3} \\ .33\frac{1}{3} & .33\frac{1}{3} & .33\frac{1}{3} \\ .35 & .33 & .32 \\ .40 & .33 & .27 \\ .20 & .50 & .30 \\ .25 & .42 & .33 \\ .33\frac{1}{3} & .33\frac{1}{3} & .33\frac{1}{3} \end{bmatrix}$$

$$= (.32, .36, .32) = BPPV_{1t}$$

The resulting brand purchase probability vector will necessarily be a unit vector because it is the product of a unit vector and a matrix composed of unit row vectors. In effect, the buyer's brand purchase probabilities depend on (1) how attractive the relative brand characteristics are, and (2) how much weight the buyer attaches to the different characteristics. In the example, the combination of the relative brand characteristics and buyer 1's weights put brand *B* ahead of the other two brands. Buyer 1's brand purchase probabilities would change from week to week as the competitive marketing mix matrix changes.

The simulation task is to derive the brand purchase probability vector for each buyer in the particular week and use Monte Carlo methods to generate the brand choices. The brand choices of all buyers are totaled each week to derive weekly brand shares.

This conceptual approach requires several refinements before it can satisfy theoretical and operational requirements for a good model. One problem is that the method does not allow for interaction effects among marketing mix variables. Because the model is linear, the effects of different changes in merchandising are treated additively. A second problem is that the brand purchase probabilities cannot fall outside the range of the lowest and highest numbers within each column of the marketing mix matrix. This is because the multiplication operation essentially amounts to taking a weighted average of the columns, which means that the results cannot fall outside the limits. Thus it would take extreme differences in relative marketing ratings to produce extremely low or high brand purchase probabilities. A third problem is that the model as it now stands does not provide for learning. As mentioned earlier, this could be remedied by updating the buyers' response vectors for the effect of recent purchases and experiences. A fourth problem is to develop a meaningful way to scale the different dimensions of competition and to talk about the average perception of the market. One of the benefits of this conceptual approach is the stimulus it gives to finding better ways to scale relative awareness and attitudes toward brand differences.

The Total Behavior Model

All the previous models dealt with one or more effects that belong in a total model for generating consumer choice behavior. At this stage, it would be worth while to restate all the effects that ideally should be designed into a model. Five effects can be distinguished:

1. The effect of current attitudes on brand choice (predisposition effect)
2. The effect of in-store stimuli on brand choice (in-store experience effect)
3. The effect of out of stock conditions on brand choice (availability effect)
4. The effect of using a brand on brand choice (usage effect)
5. The effect of interim experiences on brand choice (interim experience effect)

The relationships among these effects is illustrated in the flow diagram in Figure 16-6 and explained below.

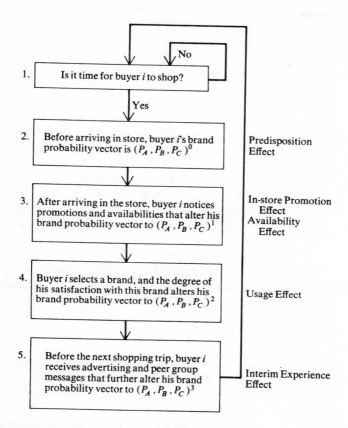

Figure 16-6   The Total Behavior Process Model

At periodic intervals, the person buys beer. The first box poses the question whether it is time for him to buy beer. In the simplest case, it will be assumed that the answer is "yes" after a week passes, although a more complex model can be developed that makes interpurchase time a stochastic function of several variables, including the consumption rate, current inventory level, social occasions, and other variables.

It is then postulated that the person goes to the retail outlet with a particular predisposition toward the available brands, represented by a brand purchase probability vector.

When he enters the store, his predisposition vector may be altered by in-store experiences, such as price deals, premiums, and point of purchase displays. This is accomplished by premultiplying his brand probability purchase vector by an in-store experience matrix.

A further adjustment is made for the chance that particular brands may be out of stock. It is assumed that each competitor spends a specific amount of money on making sure that its brand is in stock—a table is used to indicate the cost of achieving different probabilities of the brand's being in stock. The appropriate probabilities are used in the simulation. A random number is drawn to indicate whether each brand is in stock. If a brand is not in stock, the brand purchase probability vector is rescaled so that the remaining brand probabilities add to 1.

The buyer takes home the brand and his experience has some effect on his predisposition vector. If the brand is satisfying, his probability of buying it again increases and his probability of buying the other brands decreases. If the brand is dissatisfying, the opposite consequences take place. The effect of using the brand on future brand purchase probabilities is accomplished by multiplying the latest brand probability purchase vector by a usage effect matrix.

During the week, various events may happen to alter the buyer's brand probability purchase vector. The two main categories of events are impersonal communications such as advertising and personal communications from friends and neighbors.

The simplest way to handle advertising is by assuming that every advertising exposure has a positive effect on the buyer. His predispositions toward the brands will be altered in proportion to the relative number of brand messages he receives. Later, this can be modified to allow for more subtle effects such as (1) the effect of selective perception, that is, he is more likely to notice advertisements of brands he uses than of others, and (2) the effect of differences in advertising message and scheduling.

The effect of personal communications can be handled by assuming that his brand purchase probabilities are altered according to the number of brand conversations he has and whether the other person is positive or negative about the brand. In beer buying behavior, words are probably not too important a factor in brand choice. In product markets where word of mouth influence is critical, this process must be formulated carefully. Some progress has been made in incorporating word of mouth influence in some recent marketing simulations.[27]

NOMMAD model. The total behavior model takes a more comprehensive view of the factors operating in brand choice behavior than the previous models. It is represented today in at least two highly developed simulations, one by Amstutz[28] and another by Herniter, Cook, and Norek.[29] Since the former model is described in Chapter 17, we shall examine the Herniter, Cook, and Norek model, which they call NOMMAD.

Herniter et al. set out to design a model that would help explain and predict brand choice behavior toward frequently purchased low cost consumer products. They wanted a model that was applicable to pretest market forecasting and planning, test marketing, national introductions, and management of ongoing products. They wanted it to focus on the individual household's behavior and

[27]See Amstutz and Alba models discussed in Chap. 17.
[28]Amstutz, *Computer Simulation of Competitive Market Response.*
[29]Jerome Herniter, Victor Cook, and Bernard Norek, "Microsimulation of Purchase Behavior for New and Established Products," a paper presented to the University of Chicago Conference on Behavioral and Management Science in Marketing, June 1969.

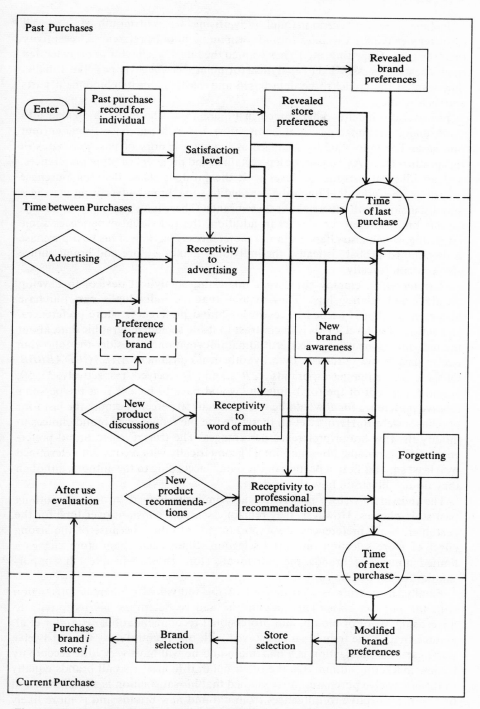

Figure 16-7   NOMMAD Simulation of Individual Purchase Behavior
Source: Herniter, Cook, and Norek *op. cit.*, p. 31.

to include several marketing stimuli (advertising, word of mouth, etc.) as well as buyer behavioral variables (brand awareness, brand preferences, receptivity to advertising, forgetting, etc.) They wanted the buyer's behavior to be generated by stochastic processes tied to analytical formulations whenever possible. Finally, they wanted the model to be data-based and verifiable in its component parts and as a whole.

The overall model is diagrammed in Figure 16-7. The figure is divided into three major sections: past purchases, time between purchases, and current purchase. The individual is visualized as having a history of past purchases in this product class. As a result, he has certain brand preferences, store preferences, and an inherent satisfaction level with the product class. Between purchase occasions, the individual might be exposed to some brand advertising messages and discussions with others about these brands. These have the effect of modifying his brand preference vector. In addition, the individual experiences some forgetting, which also alters his brand preferences. The time of his next purchase is determined probabilistically; the individual makes a store and brand choice also probabilistically.

Herniter et al. employ some very interesting analytical devices to develop the data and relationships. They assume that the individual's past purchase history is all that is needed to reveal his brand preferences, store preferences, and satisfaction level. (This is in contrast to using sociodemographic data about the individuals, or using direct attitudinal information.) Consider the following twelve past brand purchases by a hypothetical consumer: $AABACBDABBBB$. Of these twelve purchases, brands A, B, C, and D received, respectively, 33, 50, 8, and 8 per cent of the total. But one would have to believe that the person's relative preference for B would be stronger than 50 percent because the last four purchases were B. Herniter et al. therefore use the sequence of brand choices to modify the raw brand preference percentages. The true revealed brand preference vector is obtained by smoothing "geometrically with a constant determined by a least squares fit to a portion of the data," according to the authors, although they do not illustrate how this is done.

The individual's store preferences are similarly derived through smoothing past store choices. However, they remain essentially constant over time for the customer. Store preferences are important to introduce because of the strong effect of store selection on brand selection. Since each chain store carries a limited number of brands, the individual's store choice will affect his opportunities for brand choice.

Finally, a measure is also derived of the individual's inherent satisfaction with the product class. This measure is used to determine his receptivity to advertising, word of mouth, and professional recommendations. Herniter et al. assume that, if the individual has stayed with one brand during the last twelve purchases, his satisfaction is a maximum and he will have very little receptivity to new marketing stimuli. On the other hand, if he has tried all brands equally in the last twelve purchases, it is assumed that his satisfaction is a minimum and he is quite receptive to influences from old and new brands and is more likely to try any new brands. The authors apply an information measure (entropy) to the individual's past purchases to yield a numerical measure of his satisfaction.

Given the individual's initial brand preferences, store preferences, and satisfaction level, he is exposed to various influences that have the effect of modifying his brand preferences. Unfortunately, the various mechanisms are too detailed to describe here. Finally, the time of the next purchase by this individual is drawn from an Erlang probability distribution centered on his average purchase frequency. Each buyer is assigned an average purchase frequency such that the distribution of average frequencies duplicates the purchase timings in the original sample.

After the person makes a store and brand choice determined by Monte Carlo procedures, his after-use evaluation is used to modify his brand preference vector.

This model is capable of processing a population of up to 500 consumers, 10 major brands, 10 stores, and 50 time periods. It has been tested on a grocery product and a drug product. Comparisons were made in both product categories of actual and predicted brand purchase sequences, market shares, and trial and repeat purchase rates, and the fittings were reported as most satisfactory. As a result, the authors felt they could use the model to experiment with alternative advertising levels, monthly advertising patterns, and store availabilities. In one experiment they found that a particular company's advertising budget could be cut 20 percent and cause no reduction in sales if the company's seasonal pattern of advertising were revised. In another experiment, they found that withdrawing a particular brand from a particular chain did not lead to a significant reduction in its total sales because the preference for this brand was sufficiently strong to lead to changed store preferences. These and other experiments were carried out on the data-based model to predict the effect of alternative brand strategies and events such as a new brand.

Herniter et al. developed a well-conceived total buyer behavior model with several interesting features. As in all models, many questions could and should be raised. Does an individual's past purchase history reveal brand preferences as unambiguously as the authors assume? How about using sociodemographic data and attitudinal data for additional clues to brand preferences? How would multiple brand purchasing behavior be handled in their model? Should variable purchase quantities be introduced? What about the influence of various types and timings of promotions? Is the initialization and computer processing of the behavior of several hundred hypothetical buyers an efficient way to forecast total sales? While these questions can be asked, they in no way detract from the contributions of this model.

SUMMARY

Every seller is interested in the share of buyers (and their volume) that he will attract to his brand. This will depend on the brand's attributes, price, distribution, and promotion relative to competition. Consumers will tend to distribute their purchases among the brands as a function of their attitudes—brand perceptions and preferences—and other factors influencing behavior. Geometric space concepts offer a convenient way to represent the perceptions and preferences of consumers toward the brands of a product class. The major attributes of the product class are represented by right angle axes and the brands are represented as points in the resulting space. The perceived similarity of any two brands, *i* and *j*, are assumed to be inversely related to their geometric distance. In addition to consumer perceptions, consumer ideal points are located in the same space. The geometric distance of actual brands from an ideal brand can be used as a predictor of brand preference rankings. Describing consumer brand attitudes through multidimensional models can be useful in many ways, including product and marketing strategy, market segmentation, and new product opportunity identification.

Attitude is one of several factors that influence brand choice behavior over time. Several mathematical models of the brand choice process for frequently purchased staple consumer goods were described and compared. The brand loyalty model assigns a probability of one that the consumer will buy a particular brand. The constant brand probability model assigns a set of different and constant probabilities that the consumer will buy the various brands. The last brand purchased model invokes a different set of constant probabilities depending on the last brand purchased. The learning model causes the probability of the consumer's buying a particular brand to change each time, depending on whether the brand was last purchased or rejected. The variable Markov model causes the brand purchase probabilities to be affected both by the last brand purchased and the relative merchandising attractiveness of the competing brands. The competitive marketing mix model ties the consumer's brand purchase probabilities explicitly to several different marketing variables and to the relative weights placed on them by a particular consumer. Finally, the total behavior model attempts to explain brand choice in terms of a temporal process moving through the following sequence: a predisposition effect, in-store promotion effect, availability effect, usage effect, and interim experience effect. An interesting data-based model by Herniter, Cook, and Norek was recently developed along these lines.

The issue of statistically estimating the parameters of these different models from real data has not been specifically dealt with. This involves a separate and detailed discussion of underlying assumptions, data availability, and alternative estimating procedures. The estimation problems that arise even in fitting the simple models are often so tricky that many researchers have shown a bias against more elaborate model construction. Simple models have the virtue that data can be found and prediction can be tried. Complex models, on the other hand, meet the desire for a richer understanding of the phenomenon. The development of both types of models have their place, and the utility of each is to be judged by the purpose it is intended to serve.

Questions and Problems

1. A group of consumers is asked to rate 5 different brands of coffee according to 2 characteristics: strength and body. Each brand is rated on a scale from 1 to 7 for each characteristic. Each consumer is also asked to rate his "ideal" coffee. The brands are rated by the consumers in the following way:

Brand	Strength	Body
A	3	5
B	5	2
C	6	3
D	2	3
E	3	1
I (ideal)	5	5

Assume that the above perceptions are typical of the consumer group and that preference falls equally fast in all directions from the "ideal" brand.

(a) Represent these perceptions in Euclidian two-space, and order the different brands according to their probable market share if product characteristics were the only factor that counted.

(b) Suppose that the consumer is only 1/3 as concerned with body as he is with the strength of his coffee. Compute the weighted distances and reorder the brands according to their probable market shares.

2. Students and faculty at a large business school were asked to supply similarities and preference data regarding 8 professional journals. These journals included *Commentary, Harvard Business Review, Public Opinion Quarterly, Journal of Advertising Research, Journal of Business, Journal of Marketing Research, Management Science,* and *Journal of Marketing.* Which of these journals do you think were perceived as most alike? Least alike? Which journals do you think were most preferred?

3. A large marketing research firm pays a large group of households to keep a diary of their weekly grocery purchases. Suppose the record of 20 such households is examined with respect to the purchases of a particular product of which there are 3 brands: A, B, and C. The table below shows the brands chosen by these 20 households in 2 successive weeks.

House	1	2	3	4	5	6	7	8	9	10	11	12	13	14	15	16	17	18	19	20
Week 1	A	A	A	A	A	A	A	A	A	A	B	B	B	B	B	B	C	C	C	C
Week 2	A	A	A	A	A	A	A	B	B	C	A	B	B	C	C	C	B	B	C	C

Can you develop a matrix of brand switching probabilities on the basis of these 2 weeks of data?

4. Consider this brand switching matrix:

$$
\begin{array}{c}
\phantom{\text{From}} \\
\text{From}
\end{array}
\begin{array}{c}
\\
\text{A} \\
\text{B} \\
\text{C}
\end{array}
\overset{\displaystyle \text{To}}{
\begin{array}{ccc}
\text{A} & \text{B} & \text{C} \\
\end{array}}
\left(
\begin{array}{ccc}
.7 & .2 & .1 \\
.3 & .6 & .1 \\
.1 & .4 & .5
\end{array}
\right)
$$

(a) If the initial brand shares are (.10, .40, .50), what is Brand A's expected share next period?

(b) What is brand A's ultimate market share if the switching probabilities remain constant?

5. Using the first order Markov matrix shown in Table 16–1, determine the following:

(a) The probability that A will be purchased in period $t+1$, given that C was purchased in period t;

(b) The probability of A_{t+1}, given B_t;

(c) The probability of B_{t+1} and C_{t+2} given A_t;

(d) The probability of A_{t+1} and A_{t+2}, given A_t.

6. Mrs. Smith just moved into town and on her first trip to the supermarket she enters the store with a .4 probability of buying brand B. Suppose she buys brand B this time and also on her second trip. Assume that her learning operators are:

for a purchase: $P_{t+1} = .3 + .6P_t$

for a rejection: $P_{t+1} = .1 + .6P_t$

(a) What is the probability that she will buy brand B on her *third* trip to the store?

(b) If she keeps buying brand B, what is her probability of buying brand B in the limit?

7. A buyer may choose from 3 competing brands of laundry detergent, A, B, and C. The unadjusted repurchase probabilities for each brand (that is, the unadjusted probability that the buyer who has purchased the brand at time t will repurchase that brand at time $t+1$, are $r_A = .70$, $r_B = .40$, and $r_C = .20$. The relative merchandising attractiveness of each brand is $a_A = .25$, $a_B = .35$, and $a_C = .40$.

Construct a variable Markov model which describes the buyer's switching and staying behavior.

8. Given the following marketing mix matrix and the marketing response vectors of 3 customers, compute the brand purchase probability vectors for each of the 3 consumers. Are these results reasonable?

Marketing Mix Matrix

	Brand		
	A	B	C
Price	.50	.28	.22
Quality	.25	.42	.33
Packaging	.30	.35	.35
Advertising	.28	.26	.46
Store display	.34	.30	.36

Marketing Response Vectors
$W_1 = (.40, .15, .20, .10, .15)$
$W_2 = (.20, .35, .20, .15, .10)$
$W_3 = (.10, .10, .20, .45, .15)$

CHAPTER 17
Sales Models for New Products

In an economy of rising discretionary income, intense competition, and rapid technological change, no company can expect to enjoy a permanent place in the hearts and minds of American buyers on the basis of its current product line. American business history includes many examples of established companies, products, and brands that have passed into oblivion. Change is inevitable and effective management is management that plans for change. Most companies see their survival as resting on a commitment to continual product innovation.

Companies also recognize that innovation is accompanied by high costs and risks. Many product ideas that undergo research and development are never introduced into the market; many of the products that are introduced in the market are not successful; and many of the successful products tend to have a shorter life span than new products once had.[1]

The risks of innovation can be reduced through a well-conceived and professionally managed program of new product development. The four most important ingredients of such a program are effective organizational arrangements for new product research and development, professional staffing, adequate expenditures for marketing research, and explicit models for planning and forecasting new product sales.

[1]For some background statistics, see *Management of New Products*, (Chicago: Booz, Allen, and Hamilton, Inc.), 4th ed., 1965.

This chapter will focus on the last ingredient, that of new product planning and forecasting models. A number of new product decision models have been developed recently, varying in the number and type of variables considered, the level of aggregation, and the method of solution. All of these models attempt to explain and/or predict the level of sales of a new product over time as a result of behavioral and decision variables characterizing their introduction.

The chapter is divided into three sections. The first section establishes some basic distinctions for considering the new product problem, based on the product's "newness" and on its "repurchasability." The second section examines first purchase models, that is, models designed to predict the cumulative number of new product triers over time. These models serve the purpose of forecasting sales of durable goods and novelty items. The third section examines repeat purchase models, that is, models designed to predict the repeat purchase rate of those buyers who have tried the product. Predicting the sales of a repurchasable new product requires joining together an appropriate first purchase model with a repeat purchase model.

TYPES OF NEW PRODUCT SITUATIONS

A new product is introduced by a company, presumably when a favorable estimate has been made of its future sales and profits. The estimate of a new product's sales is shaped by many factors, including the size of the potential market, the nature of competition, and the company's marketing plan and resources. As the product is sold, the company receives sales data and other types of feedback, leading it to update its sales estimates, and possibly revise its marketing strategy. If sales are disappointing, management may have to consider discontinuing the product.

A periodic estimate of the new product's future sales is crucial to management planning. The appropriate sales forecasting model, however, varies greatly with the type of new product situation. New product situations can be distinguished, according to the degree of *newness* of the product and the degree of product *repurchasability*. Both of these characteristics have implications for the design of the forecasting model.

Product Newness

We shall not attempt to develop a rigorous definition of a "new" product but instead proceed to distinguish among three categories of new products that can be intuitively recognized. The first category is the new product innovation: it is a product that is fundamentally new both to the market and to the company. This is the really "new" product that establishes single-handedly a new product class to compete against other product classes. Since it is new and different, consumers have much learning to do before they respond to it. Consequently, the company may have to make a substantial investment in establishing the need for this product and overcoming resistance that might stem from the product's complexity, possible incompatibility with certain cultural or social values, and possible riskiness. Examples in their time of products in the class of innovations are television, birth control pills, household laundry detergents, transistors, and so on.

The second category of new product is the new brand, a product that is new to the company but not very new to the market. The new brand represents the effort of the company to add its own entry into an established product class. Consumers recognize the brand as part of the established product class, and less learning has to take place compared to the case of innovations. The company's task is to seek to persuade buyers of the superiority of its brand in satisfying their well-defined needs. The company must regularly collect information on brand shares and brand switching in order to evaluate its rate of brand acceptance. To some extent, versions of the competitive strategy models in Chapter 4 could serve as models for forecasting the sales of new brands.

The third type of new product is the new model, style, or package size. Here the company's product is only superficially new to the company and to the market. It is immediately recognized and understood as an extension or deepening of the company's product line. The product already has established distribution channels and an established image in the minds of buyers. The company's job is to make people aware of the availability of new features, style, or convenience. The required introductory marketing effort is small compared to the other two new product situations. Sales forecasting can proceed to a large extent on methods currently in use for the established model.

Product Repurchasibility

In addition to distinguishing degrees of product newness, it is also helpful to distinguish between products that are likely to be purchased by any buyer only once, occasionally, or frequently. Products that are likely to be purchased only once include extremely expensive goods, one-of-a-kind goods, and certain novelties. In a population of a given size, once all the potential buyers have bought the product, there will be no more sales. The sales that can be expected over time for a nonrepurchasable new product are illustrated in Figure 17-1(a). The number sold in each period rises at the beginning and later falls, until no potential buyers are left. The curve is one version of the familiar product life cycle curve and undoubtedly can be subdivided into stages (introduction, growth, maturity, decline) if clear stages seem to exist. If the curve is recast in terms of cumulative sales of the product to date, it would resemble the curve in Figure 17-1(b). In this form, the curve can be said to illustrate the rate of market penetration; it is shown approaching a limiting value representing total possible sales, that is, market potential. If the number of potential buyers is not fixed, then the curves would have to be modified. Thus the market for wedding rings (which in the majority of cases is a one time purchase) is never really exhausted because of new marriages.

Products that are purchased occasionally are exemplified by many durable goods such as automobiles, toasters, industrial equipment, and certain clothing items. These goods exhibit replacement cycles, dictated either by the physical wearing out of the product or its psychological obsolescence associated with changing styles and tastes. Most sales forecasting for this category of products consists of separately estimating new sales to first time buyers and replacement sales. We shall examine methods of forecasting new sales shortly. As for replacement sales, they are estimated from data on the age distribution of existing goods and product mortality data. When the product wears out gradually and the buyer has some discretion as to the replacement date, he will be influenced by the general state of the economy, as well as the amount of product improvement that has taken place since his last purchase. Figure 17-2 illustrates the sales life cycle of an infrequently purchased product as made up of new sales and replacement sales.

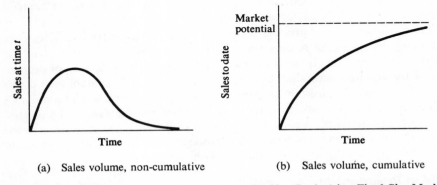

(a) Sales volume, non-cumulative   (b) Sales volume, cumulative

Figure 17-1 Sales Life Cycle for a Non-Repurchasable New Product in a Fixed Size Market

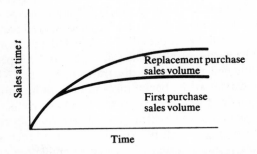

Figure 17-2 Sales Life Cycle for an Infrequently Purchased Product

New products that are likely to be repurchased frequently such as consumer and industrial nondurables have a somewhat different looking sales life cycle, as shown in Figure 17-3. The number of persons buying the product for the first time increases and then decreases as there are fewer left (assuming a fixed population). Superimposed on the first purchase sales volume is another amount representing repeat purchase sales volume, presuming that the product satisfies some fraction of people who became steady customers. The sales curve falls to a plateau level representing a level of steady repeat purchase volume; by this time, the product is no longer in the class of new products.

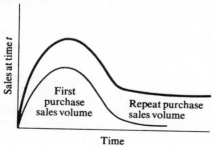

Figure 17-3   **Sales Life Cycle for a Repurchasable New Product**

Because all new products, whether they are purchased once, occasionally, or frequently, have in common a first purchase sales volume curve, our discussion will first examine models of first purchase sales volume. The second part of this chapter will examine repeat purchasing. We shall not specifically examine models of replacement sales volume.

FIRST PURCHASE MODELS

In discussing first purchase models, it would be helpful to think in terms of a new product innovation, although the general principles will approximately apply to new brands and new models as well. We shall assume a firm that is preparing to introduce for the first time a new consumer durable (such as an electric carving knife or electric toothbrush). The firm would like to make an estimate of (1) the market potential, (2) the shape of the likely approach to this potential, and (3) the rate of approach to this potential. Management can resort to one of two analytical frameworks to apply to these questions. It can think about new product sales in terms of a *diffusion process* or in terms of an *adoption process*.

Diffusion process is the name given to "the spread of a new idea from its source of invention or creation to its ultimate users or adopters."[2] To model a diffusion process, the analyst works with a few macroparameters that will locate a curve that describes the spread of the innovation through time. These parameters might represent the size of the population, the propensity to innovate and imitate, and so forth. Diffusion process models in the social sciences are often modeled after physical or biological diffusion processes such as heat transfer, the spread of epidemics, and so on.

The *adoption process*, however, focuses on "the mental process through which an individual passes from first hearing about an innovation to the final adoption."[3] Adoption itself is the act of buying the product in the case of non-

[2]Everett M. Rogers, *Diffusion of Innovations* (New York: The Free Press, 1962), p. 13.
[3]Ibid., p. 17.

repurchasable products, or the decision to use the product regularly, in the case of repurchasable products. Adoption models require a more behavioral and detailed rendering of the individual's process of moving toward the trial and use of a new product.

We shall now examine diffusion models and adoption models in more detail.

Diffusion Models

The task of a diffusion model is to produce a definite sales life cycle curve, such as illustrated earlier in Figure 17-1, usually based on a parsimonious set of parameters. The parameters may or may not have definite behavioral content. The presupposition is that they can be estimated either by analogy to the histories of similar new products introduced in the past, by consumer pretests, or by early sales returns as the new product enters the market. In this section we shall examine four different diffusion models that have been developed by those who have worked on the first purchase forecasting problem. They are the concave models, S-curve models, epidemiological models, and reliability engineering models.

Concave diffusion models. One of the earliest market penetration models is the exponential one proposed by Fourt and Woodlock in 1960 and tested against several new products.[4] Their retrospective observation of many market penetration curves showed (1) that the cumulative curve approached a limiting penetration level of less than 100 percent of all households, frequently far less, and (2) that the successive increments of gain declined. They found that an adequate approximation to these observations was provided by a curve for which "the increments in penetration for equal time periods are proportional to the remaining distance to the limiting 'ceiling' penetration." The increment in penetration for any period is given by

$$Q_t = r\bar{Q}(1-r)^{t-1} \tag{17-1}$$

where Q_t = increment in cumulative sales (i.e., sales at time t) as a fraction of potential sales
r = rate of penetration of untapped potential (a constant)
$\bar{Q}$ = potential sales as a fraction of the all buyers
t = time period

The formula is completely specified by the two parameters, r and $\bar{Q}$. To illustrate how it works, assume that a new product is about to be introduced; it is estimated that 40 per cent of all households will eventually try the new product ($\bar{Q} = .4$). Furthermore, it is believed that in each period 30 percent of the remaining new buyer potential is penetrated ($r = .3$). Therefore, the increment in new buyer penetration of this market in the first period is

$$Q_1 = r\bar{Q}(1-r)^{1-1} = r\bar{Q} = .3(4) = .12 \tag{17-2}$$

[4]Louis A. Fourt and Joseph W. Woodlock, "Early Prediction of Market Success for New Grocery Products," *Journal of Marketing* (Oct. 1960) 31–38.

The increment in new buyer penetration of this market in the second period is

$$Q_2 = r\bar{Q}(1-r)^{2-1} = r\bar{Q}(1-r) = r(\bar{Q}-r\bar{Q}) = .3[.4-.3(.4)] = .084 \quad (17\text{-}3)$$

Note that $r(\bar{Q}-r\bar{Q})$ in Equation 17-3 exactly expresses the essence of this process, that is, the increment in penetration will be the rate of penetration, r, times the untapped potential, which is $\bar{Q}-r\bar{Q}$. The increments in new buyer penetration in the third and fourth periods are

$$Q_3 = r\bar{Q}(1-r)^{3-1} = r\bar{Q}(1-r)^2 = (.3)(.4)(.7^2) = .059 \quad (17\text{-}4)$$

$$Q_4 = r\bar{Q}(1-r)^{4-1} = r\bar{Q}(1-r)^3 = (.3)(.4)(.7^3) = .041 \quad (17\text{-}5)$$

The reader should check that as $t\to\infty$, $dQ/dt\to0$. Thus Equation 17-1 produces a declining curve of new buyer sales through time. The cumulative sales curve rises monotonically in a concave fashion as illustrated in Figure 17-4(a).

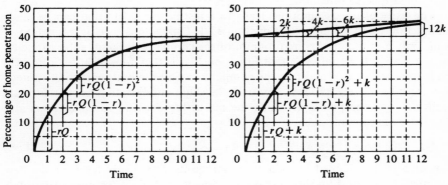

(a) Simple Model of New Buyer Penetration

(b) Advanced Model of New Buyer Penetration

Figure 17-4   Increment in New Buyer Penetration

Source: Fourt and Woodlock, *op. cit.*, pp. 33–34.

The analyst who wishes to use Equation 17-1 in forecasting market penetration for a new product first estimates $\bar{Q}$, the total potential sales volume. Here he may rely on market research studies of the percentage of persons who expressed a strong desire to buy the new product. The analyst then makes an estimate of r, the penetration rate, on the basis of how fast potential buyers are likely to learn about the product and seek to purchase it. Once the product has been introduced, and two periods have passed, the analyst can update his estimate of r by finding the ratio of the second period's new buyer increment to the difference between the ceiling level and the first period new buyer increment. In our example, this would be $.084/(.40-.12) = .3$. Another estimate of r can be made when the third period's results are received. In general, the analyst would probably want to average the past estimates of r as the data come in to determine a current r to use in Equation 17-1.

The usefulness of the latest estimated r for predicting next period's sales depends on the continuation of the marketing program and environment that characterized the former periods. Fourt and Woodlock list five assumptions underlying their forecasting model:[5]

1. Distribution will not shift greatly from the level existing at the end of the first period.
2. Promotional expenditures will not be substantially different in the second period from those during the latter part of the first period.
3. Prices will not change markedly.
4. Neither the product nor the package will be changed.
5. Competitive activity will not differ strikingly.

If any of these conditions change, the analyst should reestimate r and possibly $\bar{Q}$ in the expected direction.

The fixity of the assumptions leads to a justified criticism that can be made about Fourt and Woodlock's Equation 17-1. Diffusion is seen as a function of time only and the marketing program of the company does not enter explicitly as a variable. It would seem that Equation 17-1 is therefore of little or no help in its present form in assisting the company to find the best marketing strategy for introducing the product. Actually, a slight modification of the formula will highlight the points at which the marketing decision variable enters into the determination of sales:

$$Q_t = r(X)\bar{Q}(X)[1 - r(X)]^{t-1} \tag{17-6}$$

where X is the planned introductory marketing expenditure level for the new product. Equation 17-6 shows that the planned level of marketing expenditures can be expected to influence the level of both r, the penetration rate, and $\bar{Q}$, the potential sales level. For example, if the company adopts a marketing strategy consisting of a low price and substantial expenditures on advertising and distribution, it can be expected to achieve a higher ultimate size market at a faster rate than if it introduces the product at a high price and supports it with modest advertising and distribution expenditures. The challenge to management is to estimate the functional relationship between a specific marketing plan X and the levels of r and $\bar{Q}$. Once a functional relationship is estimated, management can use Equation 17-6 in conjunction with an appropriate cost equation to determine the marketing plan that would maximize its long run profits.

Fourt and Woodlock added one modification to their model that improved its fit to the actual data. They found a tendency of the decline in increments of buyer penetration to stretch out and approach a small positive constant, k, rather than 0. This stretch-out effect calls for revising Equation 17-1 to read

$$Q_t = r\bar{Q}(1-r)^{t-1} + k \tag{17-7}$$

and the revised model is illustrated in Figure 17-4(b). Fourt and Woodlock

[5]Ibid., p. 34.

report a rule for estimating k that works out well empirically: let k be one half of the increment of new buyers during the fourth average purchase cycle. They report that k is typically a small number, in the order of .002. More interesting is the reason they supply for the observed stretch-out effect:

> . . . consider the fact that different buyers purchase a product class and its individual brands at widely differing rates. Experience shows that, when buyers are grouped by purchase rates into equal thirds, typically the heavy buying third accounts for 65 percent of the total volume, the middle third for 25 percent, and the light third for only 10 percent. This means that, if transaction sizes are equal, heavy buyers make 6.5 purchases for every one of a light buyer, while medium buyers make 2.5, the total averaging 3.3. If the original X, r model is applied to each of these thirds separately, this difference in purchase frequency will be sufficient to induce a remarkable "stretch-out" effect in the decline of increments of penetration for all buyers combined.[6]

S curve diffusion models. The previous concave model of the diffusion process assumes that market penetration is greatest in the first period, and declines in every subsequent period. This may be true of new products that have an immediate appeal to the market, which are backed by a massive program of promotion and distribution from the very beginning. Word of mouth spreads very fast, and in a short time everyone who may be interested in the new product is aware of it. There are other new products, however, which the market may take more time to accept. A few *innovator* types will first adopt the new product because of its novelty and their desire to be different. Then *early adopters* will come along who recognize its intrinsic value or convenience value. To the extent that early adopters enjoy the respect of others as opinion leaders, they are imitated by the *early majority* whose dominant value is deliberateness; these people like to adopt new products before the average member of the social system, although they rarely are leaders. Following them are the *late majority* whose dominant value is skepticism; they adopt the new product only after the weight of majority opinion has legitimatized it. Finally, the last ones to buy the product are the *laggards* whose dominant value is tradition. They are suspicious of change, mix with other tradition-bound persons, and adopt the innovation only because it has by now taken on a measure of tradition itself.[7]

A number of innovation adoption studies have shown a normal curve to give a good fit to the data on the number of adopters through time.[8] Convenient breaks in the normal distribution are used to establish the adopter categories just mentioned. The results are illustrated in Figure 17-5(a). The innovators are defined as the first 2.5 percent of the individuals to adopt a new product, the early adopters as the next 13.5 percent, the early majority as the next 34

---

[6]Ibid., p. 33.

[7]For further discussion of these adopter categories, see Rogers, *Diffusion of Innovations*, pp. 168ff.

[8]For a summary of evidence, see ibid., pp. 156–157.

percent, and so on. There is no break between early and late laggards, because research has not produced any clear grounds for differentiating their motivations.

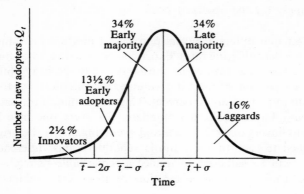

(a) Number of new adopters over time

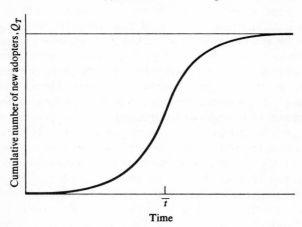

(b) Cumulative number of new adopters over time

Figure 17-5   Normal Distribution Model of the Diffusion Process

Given the anticipated history in Figure 17-5(a), we can derive the cumulative normal that will show the expected percentage of adopters to time T. The cumulative normal is illustrated in Figure 17-5(b) and given by the formula:

$$Q_T = \frac{1}{\sigma_t \sqrt{2\pi}} \int_{t=0}^{T} \exp\left[-\frac{1}{2}\left(\frac{t-\bar{t}}{\sigma_t}\right)^2\right] dt \tag{17-8}$$

This is a two-parameter distribution and is fully specified when management estimates the mean time, $\bar{t}$, when half of the potential adopters will have adopted the new product, and the standard deviation of t, σ_t. The range $\bar{t}-\sigma_t$ to $\bar{t}+\sigma_t$

represents the time span when slightly more (68.2 percent) than the middle two-thirds of the adopters will have acted. Alternatively, management can fit the early sales results of an introductory campaign to the cumulative normal and make a best estimate of $\bar{t}$ and σ_t. The results in the second case are valid, provided that the diffusion process does take the form of a normal curve.

The normal curve has, in many cases, failed to provide a good fit to new product diffusion data and researchers have had to consider other functions that produce S-shape diffusion patterns. For example, Bain found that the lognormal distribution produced a better fit to the diffusion of television sets in the United Kingdom and had a better behavioral rationale than did the normal curve.[9] In other studies, Griliches[10] and later Mansfield[11] have had good results fitting a logistic curve to their data. The logistic curve is given by the following equation:

$$Q_T = \bar{Q}[1 + e^{-(a+bt)}]^{-1} \tag{17-9}$$

where Q_T = the cumulative percentage of adoption by time T
$\quad\quad t$ = time
$\quad\quad \bar{Q}$ = the ceiling or equilibrium level
$\quad\quad a$ = a constant that positions the curve on the time scale
$\quad\quad b$ = rate of growth coefficient

The logistic describes a curve that is asymptotic to 0 and $\bar{Q}$ and symmetric around the inflection point. The rate of growth is proportional to the growth already achieved and to the distance from the ceiling. It is easy to show by algebraic manipulation of Equation 17-9 that

$$\ln \frac{Q_T}{\bar{Q} - Q_T} = a + bt \tag{17-10}$$

that is, the log of the proportion that has adopted to the proportion that has yet to adopt is a linear function of time. This enables the parameters a and b to be estimated directly by least squares.

Management's task is to estimate $\bar{Q}$, a, and b on the basis of preliminary new product tests and the inferred relationship of any contemplated marketing plan X to Q, a, and b. Presumably, more forceful marketing introductions will increase both Q and b. If the new product is tried out with distinct marketing programs in different test markets, it may be possible to derive plausible

---

[9] A. D. Bain, *The Growth of Television Ownership in the United Kingdom* (Cambridge, England: Cambridge University Press, 1964). The lognormal distribution is described in Chap. 15 of the present book. In order to use this distribution to describe the diffusion of sales over time (instead of the probability distribution of sales at a point in time), replace S with t in Equation 15-27.

[10] Z. Griliches, "Hybrid Corn—An Exploration in the Economics of Technical Change," *Econometrica* (Oct. 1967) 501–522.

[11] Edwin Mansfield, "Technical Change and the Rate of Initiation," *Econometrica* (Oct. 1961) 741–766; "Intrafirm Rates of Diffusion of an Innovation," *Review of Economics and Statistics*, 45 (1963) 348–359.

estimates of the parameters of Equation 17-9 to determine the best plan for the national introduction of the product.

Epidemiological diffusion models. A number of investigators have proposed that models of epidemics (sometimes called contagion models) provide a useful analogy to the new product diffusion process. They argue that the passage of a message or idea or product from a knower (company or adopter) to a non-knower (potential adopter) is like passage of a germ from an infected person to a susceptible person. Admittedly, catching a contagious disease lacks the human elements of cognition and volition that figure prominently in behavioral models of the adoption process. On the other hand, these human mechanisms may not be so important in the case of some new product introductions; furthermore, modifications of the model may be possible to take these higher order processes into account. Indeed, quite complicated epidemiological models have been built. Bailey has classified all of the models into three groups:[12]

1. *Continuous infection models:* epidemic has a beginning and an end and infection is occurring at all times between.
2. *Chain binomial models:* infection is limited to a short span of time and during noninfectious periods germs are either latent or incubating.
3. *Recurrent epidemic models:* the infection reaches epidemic proportions at intervals, between which it is always present in less than epidemic proportions (measles).

The last two types could conceivably describe some new product situations, although the most common situation is described by the continuous infection model.

The classic diffusion model of a continuous infection process, cast in terms of the new buyer problem, is given by[13]

$$Q_t = rQ_T(\bar{Q} - Q_T) + p(\bar{Q} - Q_T) \qquad (17\text{-}11)$$

where Q_t = the number of new adopters in the current period
$\quad Q_T$ = the cumulative number of adopters to date
$\quad r$ = the effect of each adopter on each nonadopter
$\quad \bar{Q}$ = the total number of potential adopters
$\quad p$ = the individual conversion rate in the absence of the adopters' influence

According to Equation 17-11, the time rate of change in the number of adopters is a function of two terms. The first term says that the increment of adopters is a constant proportion, r, of the product of the current number of adopters and nonadopters. The term suggests that diffusion (or infection) is due to the influence (or exposure) of adopters on the nonadopters and, implicitly, that

[12]Norman T. J. Bailey, *The Mathematical Theory of Epidemics* (New York: Hafner Publishing Company, 1957).
[13]See James S. Coleman, *Introduction to Mathematical Sociology* (New York: The Free Press, 1964), pp. 494ff.

each adopter is in contact with all nonadopters. The second term suggests that nonadopters will be converted into adopters at a constant rate, p, independent of the number of adopters. This could happen by assuming a constant source of influence (e.g., advertising) on the nonadopters.

When Equation 17-11 is integrated, it leads to an S-shaped diffusion process such as discussed earlier. Management's task is to estimate $\bar{Q}$, r, and p in order that the equation be fully specified. Management will be especially interested in the relationship between alternative marketing plans and these parameters. The number of potential adopters, $\bar{Q}$, will be influenced by the product's price and the effectiveness of the promotion in establishing multiple uses for the product. The rate of influence of adopters on nonadopters, r, will be influenced by the product's capacity to stimulate favorable word of mouth comments. The rate of influence of nonpersonal media on nonadopters will be influenced by the size and effectiveness of the advertising budget.

Some of the limitations of this epidemiological model should be pointed out. Equation 17-11 does not say anything about the dispersion of differences among people in their readiness to be adopters of this new innovation. It merely assumes there is an average rate of response of potential adopters to various forms of communication. In fact we might argue that the p (and possibly r) should decline through time, rather than stay constant, because the remaining potential adopters are less responsive to the product and associated communications.

Equation 17-11 also implies that there is full contact between all members of the social system. In reality a social system is a complicated network of groups and subgroups based on demographic, geographic, religious, and social affinities and barriers. The probability that any two persons will come into contact varies greatly with the characteristics of the two persons.

Furthermore, the equation is deterministic, whereas the diffusion process in real life is highly stochastic. The number of persons who see a particular advertisement at a point in time, or who have a chance conversation about a product, is influenced by a great number of random factors. Yet this chance-determined number will greatly influence the rate of subsequent diffusion. If the number of persons who talk about the product this week is high, this will increase the number of persons who can talk about it next week. Thus the particular cumulative adoption curve that is observed in the real history of the product is like a randomly drawn curve from a population of possible curves that might have been drawn. Yet the deterministic epidemic equation does not suggest this stochastic quality.

A modification of the classic epidemiological model has been developed by Bass and tested against real data on several new product introductions.[14] Equation 17-11 can be rewritten as

$$Q_t = (p + rQ_T)(\bar{Q} - Q_T) \tag{17-12}$$

[14]Frank M. Bass, "A New Product Growth Model for Consumer Durables," *Management Science* (Jan. 1969) 215–227.

This equation says that the time rate of change in the number of adopters is some function $(p+rQ_T)$ of the remaining number of nonadopters. (If $r = 0$, then Equation 17-12 would virtually be equivalent to the Fourt and Woodlock model.) Bass suggested that the function be modified to read:[15]

$$Q_t = \left(p + r\frac{Q_T}{\bar{Q}}\right)(\bar{Q} - Q_T) \qquad (17\text{-}13)$$

According to Bass, p is the coefficient of innovation and r is the coefficient of imitation. In each period, there will be both innovators and imitators buying the product. The innovators are not influenced in their timing of purchase by the number of persons who have already bought but they may be influenced by the steady flow of nonpersonal promotion. As the process continues, the relative number of innovators will diminish monotonically with time. Imitators, however, are influenced by the number of previous buyers and increase relative to the number of innovators as the process continues.

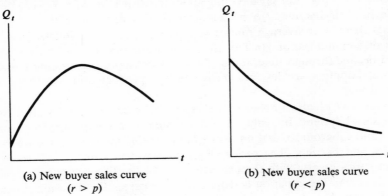

(a) New buyer sales curve
$(r > p)$

(b) New buyer sales curve
$(r < p)$

Figure 17-6   New Buyer Sales Curve: Bass Model

Source: Bass, *op. cit.*, pp. 217–218.

The combined rate of first purchasing of innovators and imitators is given by the first term, $[p+(rQ_T/\bar{Q})]$, and increases through time because Q_T increases through time. In fact the rate of first purchasing is shown as a linear function of the cumulative number of previous first purchases. But the number of remaining nonadopters, given by $(\bar{Q} - Q_T)$ decreases through time. The shape of the resulting sales curve of new adopters will depend upon the relative rates of these two opposite tendencies. In the case of a successful new product, the coefficient of imitation is likely to exceed the coefficient of innovation, that is,

[15]In Bass' notation (ibid., p. 217), the equation is

$$S(T) = \left[p + \frac{q}{m}\int_0^T S(t)\,dt\right]\left[m - \int_0^T S(t)\,dt\right]$$

This is equivalent to Equation 17-12, given the following definitional identities: $Q_t = S(T)$, $p = p$, $r = q$, $Q_T = \int_0^T S(t)\,dt$, and $\bar{Q} = m$.

$r > p$, and the sales curve will start at 0, grow to a peak, and then decay. On the other hand, if $r < p$, the sales curve will fall continuously. Figure 17-6 illustrates both cases.

Bass applied his model to the sales time series of eleven major appliance innovations, including room air conditioners, electric refrigerators, home freezers, black and white television, power lawn mowers, and so forth. In each case he used annual sales data from the year of the new product's introduction until the year when replacement sales began to be important. The equation was estimated by least squares regression after rewriting Equation 17-13 as follows:

$$Q_t = p\bar{Q} + (r-p)Q_T - \frac{r}{\bar{Q}} Q_T^2 \tag{17-14}$$

Equation 17-14 is simply a second degree equation in Q_T, the cumulative sales to time t. It has the form:

$$Q_t = a + bQ_T + cQ_T^2 \tag{17-15}$$

letting $a = p\bar{Q}$, $b = (r-p)$, and $c = -r/\bar{Q}$. The data consists of time series data on Q_t and Q_T. Equation 17-15 can be estimated as soon as data are available for the first three years of the new product's sales since three parameters, a, b, and c, have to be estimated. After these parameters are estimated, it is simple to work back to p, r, and $\bar{Q}$ in Equation 17-14. The equation can be reestimated each year as new sales data become available.

The results are illustrated for one of the new products, room air conditioners, in Figure 17-7. The predicted sales matched the pattern of actual sales quite well, with a measured coefficient of determination, $R^2 = .92$. This is quite extraordinary when one remembers that the predicted sales curve is based only on the first three years of data, not the whole time series. The observed deviations of actual sales from predicted sales are largely explainable in terms of short-term variations in national economic activity, for which there is no variable in the model. The estimated parameters of the equation,

$$p = .0104 \qquad r = .4186 \qquad \bar{Q} = 16,895,000$$

makes it possible to predict (1) the time when sales would reach its peak, and (2) the magnitude of peak sales.[16] For room air conditioners, the predicted time of peak was 8.6 years as against an actual time of peak of 7 years; the predicted magnitude of peak was 1.8 million as against an actual peak of 1.7 million. This prediction is close, and the Bass model produced reasonably good forecasts for most of the other eleven innovations studied.[17]

[16]The predicted time of peak is given by $t^* = [1/(p+r)] \ln (r/p)$ and the predicted magnitude of the peak is given by $Q_{t^*} = \bar{Q}(p+r)^2/4r$. These formulas are derived from Equation 17-13 by standard maximization procedures. See ibid., p. 218.

[17]Bass's model was recently tested against a lognormal model and a Weibull model on seven months of panel data on the introduction of a new detergent product in Lafayette, Ind. Both the Bass model and Weibull model showed up better than the lognormal model with a goodness of fit acceptable at the .95 level of significance. See Philip C. Burger, Frank M. Bass, and Edgar A. Pessemier, "Forecasting New Product Sales," Working Paper, Northwestern University, Evanston, Ill., Mar. 1968.

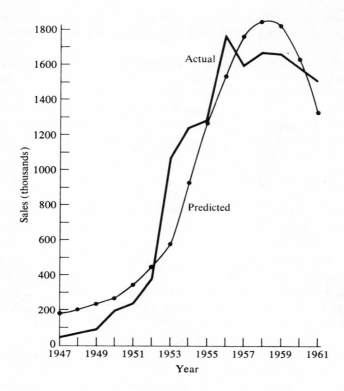

Figure 17-7   Actual Sales and Predicted Sales for Room Air Conditioners (Bass Model)

Source: Bass, *op. cit.*, p. 219.

If it is necessary to estimate p, r, and $\bar{Q}$ before a product is extensively introduced, the following possibilities exist:

1. If the new product is expected to go through the same history as some previous new product in the same product class, then the parameters for the earlier product may be used as an approximation.
2. A study of many past product introductions might reveal predictive relationships between the parameters p, r, and $\bar{Q}$, and features of the product class and/or buyer characteristics. If so, these features and characteristics for the new product under considerations are plugged into the predictive equations to find p, r, and $\bar{Q}$.
3. Data may be collected from a sample of households either in a laboratory setting, through in-home product usage tests, or limited test markets that suggest the relative magnitudes of p, r, and $\bar{Q}$.

The resulting equation can then be used for long range forecasting, particularly to predict the time of peak sales and the magnitude of peak sales for the new product. This can be of help in developing long range plans for capacity expansion and financing.[18]

It should be recognized, however, that the forecasting equation works best before replacement sales start occurring and during a period of relatively stable population.

Reliability engineering diffusion models.   Recently another model, the Weibull model, has been fitted to new product sales data with a fair amount of success and it involves a different point of view on the nature of the diffusion process.[19] Instead of originating from studies of epidemic diffusion processes, its origin is in reliability engineering theory. Applied to consumer behavior, it assumes that every potential buyer of the new product is bombarded by various stimuli which have random arrival times. The stimuli include seeing the product in a store, hearing about it from an acquaintance, seeing it on television, and so on. If any one of the several stimuli reach the buyer, it is assumed that he makes an initial purchase of the new product. Therefore, the issue is that of how much time is expected to elapse before the buyer receives a stimulus. Now suppose that the arrival time for all the stimuli have an identical gamma probability distribution.[20] Hypothetically, we now draw an arrival time for each of the stimuli and the time of arrival of the first stimulus is used to characterize when the first potential buyer adopted the product. We repeat this simulation for the second, third, . . . n buyers and end up with a distribution of waiting times for the first purchase for all the buyers. This will be a Weibull distribution because this is the form taken by the events in a parallel system of events with identical gamma distributions.[21]

The Weibull distribution supplied a good fit of the data on the diffusion of a new laundry detergent after the product triers were split into two exclusive groups: early buyers and late buyers.[22] The early buyers (those who bought

---

[18]Bass, ibid., pp. 222–226, illustrates this by making a long range sales forecast for color television, using the first three years of sales results after the product was introduced. His industry sales forecast for color television proved more accurate than many of the manufacturers' published forecasts.

[19]See Burger, et al., "Forecasting New Product Sales," Working Paper, Northwestern University, Evanston, Ill., Mar. 1968.

[20]The gamma distribution is a two parameter distribution (a, b) given by

$$P(t \mid a, b) = \frac{1}{b^a \Gamma(a)} \, t^{a-1} \exp\left(-\frac{t}{b}\right),$$

where $\Gamma(a) = (a-1)!$ See John E. Freund, *Mathematical Statistics* (Englewood Cliffs, N.J.: Prentice-Hall, Inc., 1962), pp. 127–128. The well-known exponential distribution and chi square distribution are special cases of the gamma distribution.

[21]See E. Pieruschka, *Principles of Reliability* (Englewood Cliffs, N.J.: Prentice-Hall, Inc., 1963). The functional form of the Weibull distribution is

$$P(t \mid a, b) = \left(\frac{b t^{b-1}}{a}\right) \exp\left(\frac{-t^b}{a}\right)$$

[22]See note 17.

in the first seventy days after the product's introduction in the market) were found to have a higher response rate to marketing stimuli than the late buyers; fitting separate Weibull distributions to these populations was necessary to obtain a good fit to the data.

Adoption Models

Diffusion models, as we have seen, involve postulating a few macroparameters to locate a relevant curve that might fit or predict the curve of sales for a new product. It is clear that the process of learning about a new product and making a decision to try it is more complicated than the few parameters suggest. Many analysts will sacrifice the economy and tractability of a diffusion model for the behavioral richness of an adoption model of the new product adoption process. An adoption model takes the point of view of the mental processes through which individual persons pass in learning about, and deciding to try, a new product.

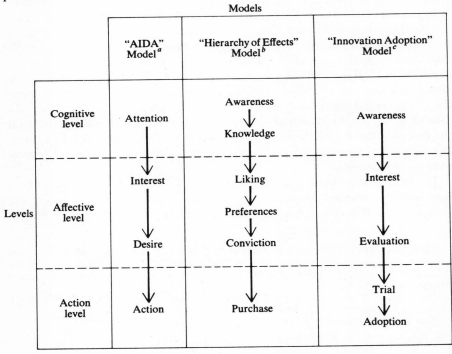

Figure 17-8   Alternate Models of Buyer Readiness Stages

Sources:
1. E. K. Strong, *The Psychology of Selling*, 1st ed. (New York: McGraw-Hill, 1925), p. 9.
2. Robert J. Lavidge and Gary A. Steiner, "A Model for Predictive Measurements of Advertising Effectiveness," *Journal of Marketing*, October 1961, p. 61.
3. Rogers, *op. cit.*, pp. 79–86. These stages were formulated by various rural sociologists and are summarized in Rogers.

Buyer readiness stages. A central characteristic of all adoption process models is the postulation of distinct stages through which the individual potential purchaser passes before he may "adopt" the new product. Figure 17-8 summarizes three of the major schemes that have been suggested in different places to describe buyer readiness stages.[23] The *AIDA* model, which arose out of studies of the effects of advertising and personal selling calls, postulates four stages. The *"hierarchy of effects"* model was proposed by Lavidge and Steiner in their studies of advertising effects and postulates six stages. The *"innovation adoption"* process model was developed by several sociologists in their pioneering studies of the diffusion of agricultural innovations; it postulates five stages.

One should observe that most of the differences among these models are semantic. They all involve three basic levels: a cognitive level, an affective level, and an action level. Each level is represented by one or two terms; if the latter, the purpose is to express a difference between a weak and a strong response in the stage. For example, knowledge is stronger than simple awareness in the cognitive stage; preference is stronger than liking in the affective stage; and adoption is stronger than trial in the action stage.[24]

All of these schemes are based on two assumptions. The first assumption is that there is a unidirectional passage through the stages toward the act of purchase. Although this may describe the experience of persons in the normal case, Palda,[25] Ramond,[26] and others have pointed out that some of the stages can be reversed. Thus it is possible for a person to become aware of something in a store, buy it without much feeling for how much satisfaction it would give, and then experience preference for it. Preference might follow, rather than precede the acts of purchase. Even awareness might follow the act of purchase if the object is presented as a gift to another person.

The second assumption is that each stage implies a higher probability than in the preceding stage that the person will purchase the product. For example, in a study of a food product involving 2800 persons, 69 percent of those reporting a preference for brand A bought it, 32 percent of those regarding it as acceptable bought it, and 9 percent of those reporting only an awareness of the brand bought it.[27] Again this is likely to be the normal case but, as we have seen, it is

[23]See Thomas S. Robertson, "Purchase Sequence Responses: Innovators vs. Non-Innovators," *Journal of Advertising Research* (Mar. 1968) 47–54, especially 48.

[24]Trial, according to Rogers, *Diffusion of Innovations*, p. 84–86, means that the individual tries the innovation on a small scale to improve his estimate of its utility; adoption means that the individual decides to make full and regular use of the innovation. For repurchasable goods, adoption is assumed to be some arbitrary number of consecutive repurchases after the initial trial. For nonrepurchasable goods, trial and adoption may be identical stages, unless the individual is allowed to rent the unit or sample it in some way before purchase.

[25]Kristian S. Palda, "The Hypothesis of a Hierarchy of Effects: A Partial Evaluation," *Journal of Marketing Research* (Feb. 1966) 13–24.

[26]Charles K. Ramond, "Must Advertising Communicate to Sell?" *Harvard Business Review* (Sept.–Oct. 1965) 148–161.

[27]John C. Maloney, "Attitude Measurement and Formation," a paper presented at the Test Market Design and Measurement Workshop, American Marketing Association, Chicago, Ill. Apr. 21, 1966.

conceivable that a person might buy the product at any stage with the same probability. Awareness could trigger the act of purchase of some goods as much as preference or desire.

If these assumptions generally hold true, they provide a basis for building models of the adoption process. Most of the buyer behavior models built out of these assumptions have been verbal but a few of a quantitative type are beginning to appear. Here we shall review four recent examples of quantitative models that deal with the adoption process.

DEMON model. DEMON, an acronym for Decision-Mapping via Optimum GO-NO Networks, was developed under the auspices of the advertising agency of Batten, Barton, Durstine, and Osborne to aid management in (1) evaluating alternative plans for the introduction of new products and (2) evaluating alternative marketing research studies that could shed light on how to improve the product's profitability.[28]

The first task is accomplished by the marketing planning model illustrated in Figure 17-9. Three different company marketing decision variables are shown to affect the number of triers: advertising, sales promotion, and distribution. The effect of advertising on sales is spelled out in the greatest detail, not surprisingly considered that the model was developed by an advertising agency. Some percentage of triers become users and their number, usage rate, and the product's price multiply out to the level of demand in dollars. Presumably, a cost model can then be brought in to yield figures that can be netted against revenue to produce a picture of expected profits.

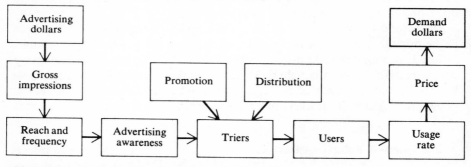

Figure 17-9 Marketing Planning Framework of DEMON

Source: Learner, "Profit Maximization Through New Product Market Planning and Control," *op. cit.*, p. 153.

[28]The authors associated with the development of DEMON are A. Charnes, W. W. Cooper, J. K. DeVoe, and D. B. Learner. Two different technical descriptions of DEMON appear in the July 1966 and May 1968 issues of *Management Science*. A useful nontechnical exposition is given by D. B. Learner, "Profit Maximization through New-Product Marketing, Planning and Control," in Frank M. Bass, Charles W. King, and Edgar A. Pessemier, eds., *Applications of the Sciences in Marketing Management* (New York: John Wiley & Sons, Inc., 1968), pp. 151–167.

We shall be interested in the relationship between the rate of trial and the rate of usage later in the chapter when we consider repeat purchase models. In the present context, DEMON is of interest in connection with the steps leading from a company decision to spend so many dollars on advertising to the effect of this on the usage rate. Figure 17-10 shows five functions that are used to trace the effect of a specific advertising expenditure level on the usage rate. The *gross impression function* shows the number of gross impressions (exposures) that the agency can attain with a certain expenditure of advertising dollars. Since media discounts are available on large volume purchases, $k > 0$. The *reach function* shows the percentage of the total audience exposed to at least one advertisement. Reach tends to increase at a diminishing rate (represented here by a logarithmic function) because successive media purchases tend to deliver fewer new persons. The *awareness function* shows the fraction of the total audience that can recall the thematic content of the brand advertising. Awareness appears to increase at first at an increasing and then a decreasing rate with reach. The *trial function* shows the fraction of aware persons who try the product at full purchase price. This function appears to be linear. Finally the *usage function* shows the fraction of triers who go on to become regular users of the product. This function also appears to be linear.

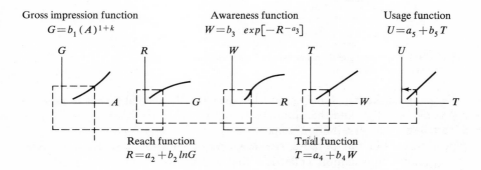

Gross impression function
$$G = b_1 (A)^{1+k}$$

Awareness function
$$W = b_3 \; exp[-R^{-a_3}]$$

Usage function
$$U = a_5 + b_5 T$$

Reach function
$$R = a_2 + b_2 \ln G$$

Trial function
$$T = a_4 + b_4 W$$

Figure 17-10   DEMON Marketing Planning Functions

These shapes were determined through least squares regression on data available on over 200 packaged goods products in sixteen product categories. Needless to say, the fits of the various functions to the available data varied in quality. The basic question is whether regression equations fitted to a cross-section of products will yield the functions sought for one product. This is known as the identification problem in econometric theory and is illustrated in Figure 17-11 for the case of reach and ad awareness. Five products are shown and they trace out the s-shaped relationship of the awareness function shown in Figure 17-10. Each product is represented only by the current observation of its reach and ad awareness. It is conceivable that if the awareness functions were known for each individual product, they might be the nearly horizontal lines shown in Figure 17-11. That is, the response of ad awareness to reach may be relatively unimpressive for each product although the curve fitted to the cross section of points observed for the products may give the appearance of a substantial S-shaped relationship.

Another criticism is that the model postulates a linked set of two way relationships whereas some of the variables depend upon additional factors. For example, trial depends not only on the amount of awareness but also on such things as advertising frequency, distribution, and price. The usage rate depends not only on the trial rate but also the amount of product satisfaction. These refinements of course can be added to the model as experience is gained with it.

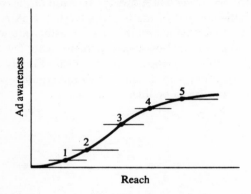

Figure 17-11   Spurious Relationship between Two Variables (Identification Problem)

Once the marketing planning model is specified, the second task is to develop a *decision model* to find the optimal settings of the controllable factors such as advertising and distribution expenditures, price, and marketing research expenditures. For this purpose, the designers of DEMON developed a model for optimum information collection that presumably leads to a marketing strategy that optimizes the company's objectives. The decision model is oriented toward the idea that a company testing a new product will have to evaluate where it stands after each test. Each evaluation can result in one of three decisions:

GO: The company should begin national marketing because the accumulated evidence indicates that the stated company objectives and requirements will all be met.

NO: The company should discontinue testing and should not market the product.

ON: The company should continue testing because the accumulated evidence is not sufficient to warrant a GO or NO decision.

An ON decision means that the company will undertake a particular market study or sequence of studies (product-use tests, TV commercial tests, economic analyses, test markets, and so on). Each alternative study has a certain cost C and is expected to yield a certain improved estimate of demand, Q. The decision problem is to find an optimal path through a total information network subject to management-specified constraints such as:

m: payback period.
n: horizon planning period.
Z_G: minimum acceptable profits for a GO decision.
Z_0: minimum acceptable profits for an ON decision.
B: total marketing research budget.
Pr_G: minimum degree of confidence (probability) needed for a GO decision, a chance constraint on Z_G.
Pr_0: minimum degree of confidence (probability) needed for an ON decision, a chance constraint on Z_0.

For example, suppose one constraint is that the expected profit by the end of the payback period should exceed the minimum level for a GO decision; that is,

$$Z_m > Z_G \quad \text{(condition for 1 GO)} \tag{17-16}$$

Suppose a second condition is that the probability of achieving this profit within the payback period should exceed the minimum degree of required confidence for a GO decision; that is,

$$Pr\{Z_m > Z_G\} > Pr_G \quad \text{(condition 2 for GO)} \tag{17-17}$$

These and other constraints delimit the feasible space of solutions on a grid similar to Figure 10-5.

The model permits an evaluation to be made of every possible path through alternative marketing studies to reach a GO decision. Each possible sequence of marketing studies involves an estimated cost and an estimated result in terms of the demand estimate. These two can be netted to yield an expected profit and risk for that sequence. The sequence with the best hypothetical profit and risk is found. It may be the sequence ON (product-use test) → ON (test market) → GO. This may appear to be better than an immediate GO decision. The company decides on ON and makes the product-use test. Now it does not make another ON decision (test market) automatically but uses the result of the product use test to reevaluate the best decision. It may be an immediate GO, NO, or some sequence of ON's.

In one reported application of the DEMON decision system, a drug company launching a new product was advised to spend less on advertising than it had planned to. (It is unusual for a model created by an advertising agency to recommend this.) The company set up two matched markets and spent the planned amount for advertising in one market and the lower amount in the other. When the sales results were in, sales were somewhat lower in the latter market but profits were higher. Thus the DEMON recommendation appeared vindicated. At the same time, the lower spending strategy may be bad in the long run because the company is not building up sales as fast as possible and competitors might move in. Unfortunately DEMON is not set up to evaluate long run profit strategies.

Urban's model. Urban developed a new product decision model in 1966 called SPRINTER (Specification of PRofits with INteractions under Trial and Error Response) which, like DEMON, was oriented toward helping management decide between a GO, ON, or NO decision respecting a new product, with the additional capability of considering any relevant interaction of the new product with other products in the company's line.[29] SPRINTER differed from DEMON in utilizing a conventional macroanalytic model of market response (similar in spirit to the models in Chapter 4 of the book) instead of a microanalytic formulation such as that found in DEMON. Subsequently, Urban reported a new model that has a definite microanalytic cast.[30] He postulates five buyer readiness stages involved in product trial: (1) awareness, (2) intent, (3) search, (4) selection, and (5) postpurchase behavior. The first stage, awareness, is divided into four levels: (a) awareness to the brand, (b) its advertisements, (c) specific product appeals, and (d) word of mouth recommendation. Each awareness level assumes that all the preceding types of awareness have taken place. And each higher level of awareness is associated with a higher probability of developing an intent to buy, according to the following behavioral rationale:[31]

The percent of people in a given awareness class who display intent to buy the product will depend upon the perceived compatability and relative advantage of the product to the people who have the specific recall of that class. It would be expected that the percent with intent would be higher in appeal recall classes since this represents more perception of relative advantage. The highest buying rates might be expected in the awareness class representing receipt of word of mouth recommendations since this group would be one in which the perceived risk is low. After the number of people intending to buy has been determined for each awareness class, they are added to get the total number of people with intent.

Those who intend to buy the product enter the stage of search. Whether they actually select the brand depends upon its availability and upon in-store stimuli such as price and point of purchase displays. The model allows for some customers who enter the store without intent to buy the particular brand. They

[29]See Glen L. Urban, "A New Product Analysis and Decision Model," *Management Science* (Apr. 1968) 490–517.

[30]Glen L. Urban, "Market Response Models for the Analysis of New Products," *Proceedings of the American Marketing Association*, Denver, Colo., Aug. 27–30, 1968 (Chicago, Ill.: American Marketing Association, 1969), 105–111.

[31]Ibid., p. 108.

are added to the number of buyers who exercised their intent to find the total number of new brand adopters.

Urban goes on to show how the first time triers may become word of mouth communicators to nontriers. He also shows how triers may move into the class of preferers, preferers may move into the class of low loyals, and low loyals may move into the class of high loyals. It might appear that his model is micro-behavioral from the description given thus far. Actually, it is microanalytic, in that it uses expected values for all the processes instead of individual persons going through the stages of the buying process. The model has been tested against a new product and is reported to have produced an unusually accurate forecast of new product acceptance.

Alba's model. We now turn to two new product adoption process models that have been formulated along microbehavioral lines. They both estimate new product demand by aggregating the actions of a population of hypothetical but representative consumers who learn about the new product and pass through the several stages of buyer readiness.

The first model was formulated by Alba to describe the adoption of the new "touch-tone" telephone.[32] He used data collected and analyzed earlier by Robertson on the diffusion of this innovation among 100 residents in the town of Deerfield, Illinois.[33] The data described the traits of each adopter (seven traits were measured: interest polymorphism, venturesomeness, cosmopolite-ness, social integration, social mobility, priviledgedness, and status concern), their sources of information about the new phone (personal influence and mass communication), and the date of their adoption. Alba's aim was to see whether he could simulate the adoption process in this community accurately enough to reproduce:

1. The actual number of new adopters each period.
2. The order in which the 100 households in the sample adopted the touch-tone telephone.

To do this, he developed the probabilities of each individual's being exposed to touch-tone telephone advertising and word of mouth communications and, in turn, exposing others. The probabilities were derived from statistical regressions on the traits of individuals. For example, the probability that an individual would be exposed to a touch-tone phone advertisement was given by

$$PE_i = .120 \frac{VE_i}{7} + .359 \frac{IP_i}{7} - .150 \frac{CO_i}{7} + .200 \frac{SI_i}{7} + .202 \frac{SM_i}{7} + .184 \frac{PR_i}{7}$$
$$+ .085 \frac{SC_i}{7} \tag{17-18}$$

[32]Manuel S. Alba, *Microanalysis of the Socio-Dynamics of Diffusion of Innovation*, unpublished Ph.D. dissertation, Northwestern University, Evanston, Ill., 1967.

[33]These data were collected by Thomas S. Robertson, *An Analysis of Innovative Behavior and Its Determinants*, Ph.D. dissertation, Northwestern University, Evanston, Ill., 1967.

where PE_i = probability that individual i will be exposed to a touch-tone advertisement

VE_i = individual i's score on "venturesomeness"

IP_i = individual i's score on "interest polymorphism"

CO_i = individual i's score on "cosmopoliteness"

SI_i = individual i's score on "social integration"

SM_i = individual i's score on "social mobility"

PR_i = individual i's score on "privilegedness"

SC_i = individual i's score on "status concern"

All scores are on a seven-point scale from 1 to 7. If an individual scores 7 (the maximum score) on all the traits that correlated with the tendency to adopt a touch-tone telephone, his probability would be 1.00. Otherwise, PE_i would range approximately between 0 and 1.

After the individual's PE is determined, a random number is drawn to determine if he saw a persuasive communication that period. If he did, then another random number is drawn to determine whether he underwent an attitude change. Alba defined an attitude change as tantamount to adopting the phone, although he notes that in most empirical studies (including his data) adoption refers to actual purchase. The probability of an individual undergoing an attitude change is affected by the level of the persuasiveness of the ad. The persuasiveness of the particular ad is rated on the basis of the message, source, transmitter, and content.

The individual who did not adopt the phone might still be exposed to a neighbor who talked about the phone. Alba formulated a model that generated a probability that any two residents of Deerfield would discuss the touch-tone phone. The probability varied directly with the degree to which the two residents shared the same traits.

Alba's steps in simulating the word of mouth process are shown in Figure 17-12. Alba distinguishes among nonknowers, knower nonadopters, and knower-adopters and he employs different probabilities of confrontation between any two categories of individuals. As confrontations take place each period, those who undergo an attitude change are considered adopters and the computer program totals the number of adopters each period.

Alba defined a simulation run as covering eight periods, each period lasting approximately two months. He replicated the process fifty times and used the mean result to compare with the actual adoption curve. The actual and simulated curves are shown in Figure 17-13. The fit is not too satisfactory: Alba's 100 simulated residents of Deerfield started out slower in their adoption rate and later adopted faster than the actual residents. By period 5, almost all of the simulated residents adopted the phone, although only 60 percent of the real residents did so in the sample. These differences were shown to be highly significant in both chi square and Kolmogorov-Smirnov tests of goodness of fit. The fault may lie in the fact that Alba did not vary the intensity of mass communications or personal influence on a seasonal basis, whereas in the real world both probably varied seasonally. If the telephone company did not advertise

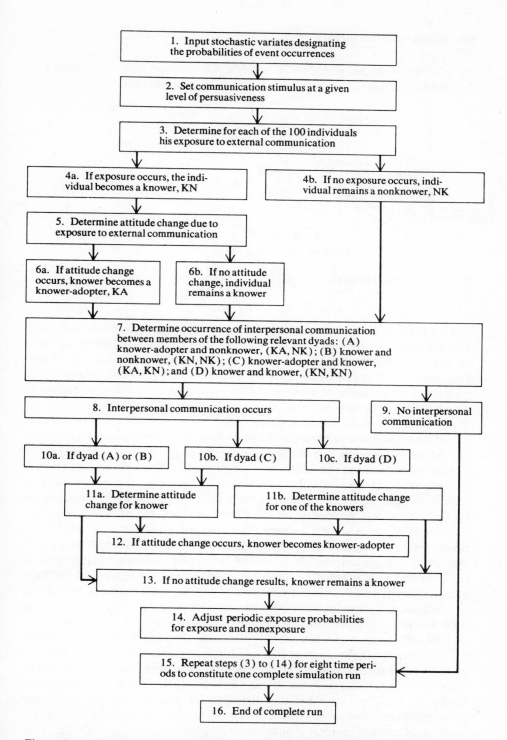

Figure 17-12   Flow Chart of Adoption Process Model (Alba's Simulation)
*Source: Alba, op. cit., p. 111.

the new phone during periods 3 to 5, while Alba continued the advertising in the simulation, this would account for some of the discrepancy.

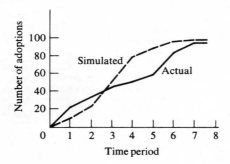

Figure 17-13   Alba's Simulation Results
Source: Alba, *op. cit.*, p. 209.

Alba fared better in his predictions concerning the early and later adopters. The rank correlation coefficient (Spearman's rho) for the times of adoption of the real and simulated residents of Deerfield was high and statistically significant. His model was also able to discriminate accurately between those residents who underwent attitude change because of mass communication influence and those whose attitude changed because of personal influence.

Alba also tested the influence that a higher versus lower level of advertising would have had in accelerating the adoption rate. He found that greater advertising did not increase the rate of adoption significantly.

Alba's simulation of the diffusion of an innovation was a pioneering attempt to determine the relative influence of *social factors*, on the one hand, and *chance*, on the other, in explaining the rate at which a sample population learned about, and decided to adopt, a new product. He worked against the limitations of an existing data bank that was not originally designed for his needs; yet he managed to develop a complex set of events and generate a plausible set of outputs that matched some of the actual occurrences fairly well. If the data had been originally collected for this project, more would have been gathered on the actual timing of advertisements, the media habits of the sample of residents, and the actual friendship or acquaintance patterns in the area. These data would have permitted the community to be modeled more concretely, and the diffusion process, still a highly stochastic one, could have been modeled more faithfully. Diffusion research has still not adequately documented the relationship between product interest levels, consumer traits, and neighbor interaction patterns and conversations about products. The main contribution of Alba's work was to show that the complex processes of individual and community adoption of new products can be studied insightfully through the medium of microbehavioral simulation.

Amstutz model.   The most ambitious microbehavioral model of sales determination is that developed by Amstutz.[34] His model is capable of providing a population of consumers, retailers, salesmen, products, advertisements, and so on, and causing these elements to interact on a stochastic basis to produce the output of ultimate interest—sales. Since it is impossible to describe the behavioral mechanisms of each of Amstutz's submodels, we shall present and evaluate perhaps his most unique model—that describing consumer behavior toward a product category.

Amstutz designed a computer program capable of performing four important tasks: (1) producing a consumer population of any desired number; (2) developing and assigning product and brand awareness and attitudes to each individual consumer; (3) putting the consumer through a set of experiences; and (4) updating the consumer's attributes as a result of these experiences.

Table 17-1 shows the computer output on the characteristics and experience of one such consumer in the week starting February 19, 1962. According to line 2, this person lives in a suburb (SU) located in the Northeast (NE). He is between twenty-five and thirty-five years of age, with an income of $8,000–$10,000, and is college educated. These characteristics could describe an actual person recorded in a sample survey. Alternatively, this person could have been created artificially through a random number generator applied to basic census data. In the latter case, the computer program randomly draws an *age bracket* from an age distribution table stored in the computer, where the chance of drawing a particular age bracket is proportional to its relative frequency in the population. Next, the computer program draws an *income* for the person from a frequency distribution of incomes within that age bracket. Finally, the computer program randomly draws an *educational level* from an education distribution. In this way, a string of characteristics is generated to create a plausible person. There is no limit to the size of the artificial population that can be bred this way. Furthermore, the population that is bred can be expected to reflect the distribution of characteristics found in the real population.

Turning to line 3, the person owns brand 3 which is now six years old. The product is assumed to be a consumer durable such as an electric floor polisher. Furthermore, the person prefers to deal with retailers 5, 11, and 3, in that order. This person also has attitudes toward twelve different product characteristics and twelve different appeals, the attitudes ranging in each case from a -5 (very negative) to a $+5$ (very positive). The person also has attitudes toward the four brands and the eighteen retailers. Finally, the person has been exposed in the past to a varying number of communications on different product characteristics and appeals for each of the four brands.

How was this information developed? Once again, the information could describe the attitudes, store preferences, brands owned, and communications recall of a real person who was interviewed in a survey. Or these characteristics could have been artificially generated from various frequency distributions compiled in earlier surveys.

[34]Arnold E. Amstutz, *Computer Simulation of Competitive Market Response* (Cambridge, Mass.: The M.I.T. Press, 1967).

Table 17-1 One Simulated Consumer in Week 117

Consumer 0109 now beginning week 117—February 19, 1962
    Characteristics–region NE SU, age 25–35, income 8–10K, education college
    Brand owned 3, 6 years old. Retailer preference 05, 11, 03
    Media available 1 0 0 1 0 0 0 0 1 1 1 1 0 0 0 0 0 0 0 0 0 0 0 0

Attitudes	1	2	3	4	5	6	7	8	9	10	11	12
Prod char's	0	+1	+1	0	−3	−1	0	+5	0	+3	0	0
Appeals	−3	0	+1	+5	0	−3	+3	0	0	0	+5	0
Brands	+2	+1	+3	+2								
Retailers	+1	−5	+3	+1	+5	−5	−5	+1	−1	−3	+5	+1
	−3	+1	−1	+3	+1	+1						
Awareness	1	0	0	0								

Memory dump follows. Brands listed in descending order 1 to 4

Product characteristic memory												Appeals memory											
1	2	3	4	5	6	7	8	9	10	11	12	1	2	3	4	5	6	7	8	9	10	11	12
2	3	15	0	5	5	4	14	8	7	1	3	8	9	7	3	1	11	7	4	4	3	9	3
8	0	6	4	9	5	4	13	0	3	6	7	6	8	0	7	0	9	2	4	3	10	3	1
0	6	15	7	0	3	11	3	5	2	5	7	0	4	8	10	9	2	14	3	9	7	9	5
7	9	3	7	3	2	7	2	6	12	14	2	0	9	7	8	13	9	11	6	0	2	5	9

Media exposure initiated
    Medium 003 appears in week 117—no exposures
    Medium 004 appears in week 117
      Exposure to ad 013, brand 3—no noting
      Exposure to ad 019, brand 4
        Ad 019, brand 4 noted. Content follows
        Prod. C 11 $P = 4$, 4 $P = 2$,
        Appeals 5 $P = 2$, 7 $P = 2$, 12 $P = 2$,

    Medium 007 appears in week 117—no exposures
    Medium 012 appears in week 117
      Exposure to ad 007, brand 2
        Ad 007, brand 2 noted. Content follows
        Prod. C 8 $P = 3$, 12 $P = 1$,
        Appeals 2 $P = 1$, 4 $P = 1$, 6 $P = 1$, 10 $P = 1$,
      Exposure to ad 013, brand 3—no noting
      Exposure to ad 004, brand 1—no noting
    Medium 016 appears in week 117—no exposures
    Medium 023 appears in week 117—no exposures
Word of mouth exposure initiated
    Exposure to consumer 0093—no noting
    Exposure to consumer 0104—no noting
    Exposure to consumer 0117—no noting
No product use in week 117
Decision to shop positive—brand 3 high perceived need
                      —retailer 05 chosen
Shopping initiated

Consumer decision explicit for brand 3—no search
Product exposure for brand 3
   Exposure to point of sale 008 for brand 3
   Pos 008, brand 3 noted. Content follows
   Prod. C 3 $P = 4$, 6 $P = 4$,
   Appeals 5 $P = 2$, 7 $P = 2$, 10 $P = 2$, 11 $P = 2$,
No selling effort exposure in retailer 05
Decision to purchase positive—brand 3, $38.50
   Delivery immediate
   Ownership = 3, awareness was 2, now 3
Word of mouth generation initiated
   Content generated, brand 3
      Prod. C 3 $P = +15$, 8 $P = +15$,
      Appeals 4 $P = +50$, 11 $P = +45$
Forgetting initiated—no forgetting
Consumer 0109 now concluding week 117—February 25, 1962
Consumer 0110 now beginning week 117—February 19, 1962

Source: Amstutz, *Computer Simulation of Competitive Market Response*, 394–395

Next, this consumer passes through a set of events and experiences resembling those which members of the real population might have passed through during the week beginning February 19, 1962. Consumer 109 is exposed to media and might or might not note advertisements pertaining to this product; he might be exposed to word-of-mouth influence, use the product during the week, make a decision to shop, deal with a salesman, and decide to purchase. Afterward he might generate favorable or unfavorable word-of-mouth influence to others. Some forgetting of his past exposures will also occur.

Each of these events in the consumer's week is regulated by mathematical functions and/or probability distributions. For example, the probability that the consumer shops in this week is related to his perceived need, which is an increasing function of his brand-attitude score, opportunity for product use, and time since last purchase; it is also dependent on the level of his income. These factors are combined in a nonlinear mathematical expression.

By generating experiences for each member of the artificial population week after week during the period under study, Amstutz is able to aggregate and summarize their purchases in the form of a simulated time series of brand shares.

Amstutz specified a multilevel validation procedure for his model. *Function-level validation* involves two steps: first, a sensitivity analysis indicating the relative sensitivity of total system performance to various functions within the system structure; and, second, a Chi-square test of the null hypothesis that observed relationships are due to random variation. *Cell-level validation* establishes that the behavior of an artificial consumer within the simulated population cannot be differentiated by an expert from that of a similar member of the real world population.[35] *Population-level* validation is undertaken to

[35]A. M. Turing, "Computing Machinery and Intelligence," *Mind* 59 (1950), 433–460.

insure that the behavior of members of the simulated population does not differ significantly from corresponding members of the real-world population. Finally, *performance validation* is the ability of the model to duplicate historical real-world population behavior. This level of validation calls for initializing parameter settings in the model to duplicate those existing in the real-world system at a particular point in time and then comparing simulated and actual results.

In a reported application of this methodology to another product area, in this case a pharmaceutical product, Amstutz and Claycamp indicate that a good fit to the data was obtained.[36] They simulated the prescribing behavior of 100 simulated doctors toward the ten brands in this product class over a year's time. There was some change in the market share ranks of the ten brands as between the beginning and end of the year. Their simulated results correctly predicted all the year-end ranks, as shown in Table 17-2. Table 17-2 also shows the same data according to market shares, and their average error in predicting year-end values was on the order of .7 percent in market share.

The overriding question raised by Amstutz's microbehavioral model is whether the extensive data gathering that this type of model requires produces enough in extra understanding or predictive ability to be worth the cost. There is no question that Amstutz's model allows considerable details of the consumer buying process to be brought in and interrelated, and this can be a real contribution to theory construction. The analyst is challenged to specify the relationships between demographic characteristics, media exposure probabilities, word-of-mouth exposure probabilities, responses to appeals and product characteristics of various kinds, and so forth. These are the kinds of variables which are worth thinking about both by the theorist searching for understanding and by the marketing practitioner searching for clues to promotional strategy. And they are worth thinking about in the operationally defined way required by simulation. But it is a different matter to justify this effort and cost as a route to developing useful forecasting and marketing planning models. In the first place, there is the question of whether the various frequency distribution data on consumer characteristics can be obtained and, if so, at what cost.[37] There is the question of how many consumers should be created for a representative sample population for trying out marketing strategies. Each consumer must be separately processed through many events and many weeks, and the computer cost of maintaining and processing all this detail is high. There is the question of the many types of errors that can creep into the data and the program and affect the results without easily being spotted because of the considerable model detail and complexity. There is the question of accurately measuring the marketing actions of competitors with respect to weekly advertising media expenditures

36Henry J. Claycamp and Arnold E. Amstutz, "Simulation Techniques in the Analysis of Marketing Strategy," in F. M. Bass, C. W. King, and E. A. Pessemier, ed., *Applications of the Sciences in Marketing Management* (New York: John Wiley & Sons, 1968).

37Amstutz does not describe how he develops or obtains the underlying conditional probability distributions for generating the demographic attributes. We can only guess that he goes back to original census data, not census summaries; that he conducts original surveys; or that he uses the marginal distribution of traits, not the conditional distributions.

Table 17-2 Actual and Predicted Brand Shares

Brand Identification	*Rank Order Brand Share Comparisons*			*Absolute Brand Share Comparison*			
	Rank as Initialized	Year End Rank		Initialization Value	Year End Value		Difference (Magnitude)
		Simulated	Actual		Simulated	Actual	
A	4	2	2	13.7%	15.0%	16.1%	−1.1%
B	5	6	6	9.7	9.1	8.7	+ .4
C	6	5	5	7.3	9.3	9.0	+ .3
D	8	8	8	5.0	3.2	2.8	+ .4
E	10	10	10	0	0	0	—
F	1	1	1	23.2	27.6	28.8	−1.2
G	2	3	3	18.1	13.0	12.7	+ .3
H	3	4	4	15.6	13.9	14.4	− .5
I	7	7	7	6.2	5.9	5.5	+ .4
J	9	9	9	1.0	2.5	2.0	+ .5
				99.8%	99.5%	100.0%	(Average) .7%

Source: Amstutz, *op. cit.*, 409–411.

and in-store promotions. Competitive intelligence is extremely difficult and costly to collect, and this model demands more detail about competitive behavior than the typical aggregative model. There is the question of validating the many functions used in the model. There are so many possible sensitivity tests that can be performed on different functions in the system that the cost of sensitivity testing can rapidly get out of hand. There is the question of performance validity, and so far only one real application has been made. Here the performance validity appeared good, but more applications are needed before it can be determined whether this was a chance result or an intrinsic accomplishment from this level of model-building.

With respect to performance validity, it must be asked whether a simpler model could have done as well. Amstutz did not test his elaborate model against possible simpler models—and such tests seem desirable. We are not doubting the value of microbehavioral simulation for stimulating theory construction and firing the imagination of practitioners; we are only raising the question of its promise in the area of practical forecasting and planning. Does Amstutz's microbehavioral model increase the degree of predictability over simpler models and, if so, to an extent justifying the substantially larger investment required? It is too early to answer this question.

REPEAT PURCHASE MODELS

A great many new products that are introduced in the marketplace are of the repurchasable kind. This includes virtually all the nondurables consumed by the household and the factory. The sellers of these products are interested in the repurchase rate even more than the trial rate. A low trial rate could be attributable to poor distribution, promotion, or packaging, all of which are correctible. Trial of a new product can be stimulated by distributing free samples, introductory pricing, etc. A low repurchase rate may suggest a product that does not meet the consumers' expectations, which is harder to correct. It is a problem that should have been solved at the product development and testing stage. Unfortunately the early aggregate sales figures do not distinguish between the two rates. A rising sales curve could mean, without further analysis, a high trying rate with a low rebuying rate (which would be a bad development) or a low trying rate with a high rebuying rate (which would be a good development). If the rebuying rate is nil, to consider an extreme case, the sales curve will turn down to zero immediately after the last trial purchases takes place. If the rebuying rate is high, the sales curve will, after the new buyer demand is finished, continue horizontally at a substantial level above zero. In between, the rebuying rate may or may not be sufficient to create a successful product.

The problem facing the marketing analyst is to define and estimate the repurchase rate in advance of the GO decision, and to keep track of it as it appears within the early sales figures. The sales taking place in any time period can be decomposed into two parts:

$$S_t = s_{Ft}N_{Ft} + s_{Rt}N_{Rt} \tag{17-19}$$

where S_t = total sales in period t

s_{Ft} = average purchase volume per period per first time buyer

N_{Ft} = number of first time buyers in period t

s_{Rt} = average purchase volume per period per repeat buyer

N_{Rt} = number of repeat buyers in period t

If there is no significant difference in the average purchase volume of trial and repeat buyers, then Equation 17-19 reduces to

$$S_t = s_t(N_{Ft} + N_{Rt})$$

(17-20)

and the analyst can focus his attention on the relative number of the two types of buyers. However, most of the evidence indicates that repeat buyers buy larger volumes per period than first time buyers, that is, $s_{Ft} \leqslant s_{Rt}$. First time buyers tend to buy a smaller quantity in order to sample it. Those who stay with the new product have found satisfaction and tend to become heavier users. Massy's data on a new food product (Table 17-3) showed the average purchase rate per period rising with the number of repeat purchases:[38]

Table 17-3

Purchase class (number of previous purchases)	Relative number of packages
1	100 (coded)
2	105
3	145
4	153
5	122
6	160
$\geqslant 7$	165

This last piece of information suggests that Equation 17-19 can be usefully expanded to read:

$$S_t = s_{Ft}N_{Ft} + s_{1t}N_{1t} + s_{2t}N_{2t} + S_{3t}N_{3t} + \ldots + s_{it}N_{it} + \ldots$$

(17-21)

where s_{it} = average purchase volume of buyers in the ith repeat purchase class at time t

N_{it} = number of repeat buyers in the ith repeat purchase class at time t

Many analysts have suggested that the seller should study not only the number of first repeat purchasers, but also second, third, ... i^{th} repeat purchasers. For example, Urban defines a really loyal purchaser as one who has purchased the

[38]William F. Massy, "A Stochastic Evolutionary Model for Evaluating New Products," Working Paper, Carnegie Institute of Technology, Pittsburgh, Pa., 1967. Also see William F. Massy, "Forecasting the Demand for New Convenience Products," *Journal of Marketing Research* (Nov. 1969) 405–413.

product at least three times and twice in succession.[39] Fourt and Woodlock have argued that the success of many products is not secured by a high ratio of first repeat purchasers to first time buyers: the seller should also watch the rate of second and third repeat purchasers.[40] Massy in his STEAM model makes a point of extending Fourt and Woodlock's basic idea of "depth of repeat" analysis. He states:

> The immediate objective in applying a depth of repeat oriented model is to predict the time paths of the cumulative proportions of one time buyers, two time buyers, and so on. These groups are handled separately because of the probable importance of purchase event feedback in the new product context. Effects of feedback are incorporated into the analysis by estimating the model's parameters separately for each depth of trial group.[41]

The following pages will describe three different models for defining and estimating repeat purchase sales.

Fourt and Woodlock Repeat Purchase Model

Basic to Fourt and Woodlock's "depth of repeat" analysis is the notion of a repeat ratio. The first repeat ratio, for example, is the fraction of initial buyers who make a second purchase. It can be thought of as the probability that a first time buyer will buy a second time. Second, third, and so forth, repeat ratios are similarly defined. In terms of the notation in Equation 17-21 these repeat ratios are

$$\frac{N_{1t}}{N_{Ft}}, \frac{N_{2t}}{N_{1t}}, \frac{N_{3t}}{N_{2t}}, \ldots \tag{17-22}$$

If these ratios are all unity, the company can look forward to a remarkably successful product. If successive ratios rapidly fall toward 0, this augurs badly for the product. Fourt and Woodlock calculated the repeat ratios shown in column 1 of Table 17-4 for a new food product that had just been introduced nationally.[42] These ratios tend to grow larger, the deeper the repeat purchase

[39]Urban, "Market Response Models for the Analysis of New Products," *Proceedings of the American Marketing Association*, Denver, Colo., Aug. 27–30, 1968 (Chicago, Ill.: American Marketing Association, 1969).

[40]Fourt and Woodlock, "Early Prediction of Market Success for New Grocery Products," *Journal of Marketing* (Oct. 1960) 31–38.

[41]Massy, "A Stochastic Evolutionary Model for Evaluating New Products," Working Paper, Carnegie Institute of Technology, Pittsburgh, Pa., p. 4.

[42]Consumer panel data are necessary to calculate repeat ratios. First, an observation period is chosen, say a year, and the numbers of new buyers, first repeat buyers, second repeat buyers, etc., are observed. Suppose that 6021 new buyers sales and 2170 first repeat sales are observed. Each figure must now be reduced by the number of buyers who just entered the class and did not have a chance, because of the length of the interpurchase time, to repurchase the product. For example, the average new buyer would not buy again for approximately four months. Therefore, those new buyers who bought in the last four months of the observation year were removed, leaving 4472 new buyers. Similarly, there were 1932 first repeat buyers, instead of 2170, after removing those who came in too late to make another purchase. The first repeat ratio was then calculated as 1932/4472 = .485, the first repeat ratio in Table 17-4. The other repeat ratios were similarly calculated.

class, indicating a growing loyalty (or habit) that occurs with use of the product.

Table 17-4 Using Repeat Ratios to Predict Sales Next Period (Fourt-Woodlock Model)

	Repeat ratios	Estimated no. at end of production period (000's)
New buyers		8141
	.485	
1st repeat		3948
	.559	
2nd repeat		2207
	.645	
3rd repeat		1422
	.593	
4th repeat		841
	.797	
5th repeat		671
	3.300	
Over 5		2214
		19,444

Fourt and Woodlock used these ratios to predict sales for the next period. First, they estimated new buyer sales in the second period to be 8141.[43] This number came from their first purchase model described earlier.[44] They multiplied 8141 by the first repeat ratio of .485 to arrive at an estimate of first repeat sales of 3948. Then they multiplied .559 × 3948 to estimate second repeat sales, in this case 2207. This was continued for the deeper repeat classes and yielded a prediction of total sales, when summed, of 19,444. The same result is given by the formula:

$$S_t = s_{Ft}N_{Ft}(1 + r_1 + r_1 r_2 + r_1 r_2 r_3 + \ldots + r_1 r_2 r_3 r_4 r_{5+}) \tag{17-23}$$

where r_1 = first repeat ratio, N_{1t}/N_{Ft};
r_2 = second repeat ratio, N_{2t}/N_{1t}; others similarly defined

The Fourt and Woodlock approach to estimating repeat sales described in Equation 17-23 requires consumer panel data for its implementation. In the absence of such detailed data, a grosser approach to estimating total sales in any period could be derived from a modification of Equation 17-19. Let us assume that a percentage r of new buyers become repeat buyers, that is,

$$N_{Rt} = rN_{Ft} \tag{17-24}$$

[43]Although Fourt and Woodlock defined repeat ratios to represent ratios of numbers of buyers in Equation 17-22, their example appears to be in terms of the ratios of sales, i.e., $s_{1t}N_{1t}/s_{Ft}N_{Ft}$, $s_{2t}N_{2t}/s_{1t}N_{1t}$, etc. This does not matter much if the average purchase volumes are approximately the same.
[44]See pp. 524–527.

Substituting this into Equation 17-19, we get

$$S_t = s_{Ft}N_{Ft} + s_{Rt}rN_{Ft} \tag{17-25}$$

or

$$S_t = (s_{Ft} + s_{Rt}r)N_{Ft} \tag{17-26}$$

In this case, the analyst has to estimate the number of first time buyers in the next period, N_{Ft} (this comes from his first purchase model), the average sales volume per period of first time buyers and repeat buyers, s_{Ft} and s_{Rt}, and the percentage of repeat buyers to first time buyers, r. This estimation model in Equation 17-26 is more appropriate for use on a period to period basis than as a long run prediction model. In the long run, the number of new buyers will go to 0, that is, $N_{Ft} \rightarrow 0$, and Equation 17-26 could imply that period sales will also go to 0, that is, $S_t \rightarrow 0$. In fact this is prevented because the ratio of repeat buyers to new buyers eventually increases, that is, $r \rightarrow \infty$. Yet, these tendencies make the formulation in Equations 17-23 or 17-26, based as it is on the ever-changing and vanishing number of first time buyers, a tenuous foundation for long run, new product sales forecasting.

Parfitt and Collins Repeat Purchase Model

As an alternative to tying the repeat purchase rate to the number of new buyers each period, as in the Fourt and Woodlock model, Parfitt and Collins relate this rate to the cumulative percent of penetration.[45] Their model is designed for long run share predictions for a new brand being introduced into an established market, rather than for a new innovation or new model. They would like to estimate, on the basis of early consumer panel data, the ultimate market share of a brand. If the forecasted ultimate brand share does not appear encouraging, management could consider withdrawing the brand, rather than dragging out expected losses.

Parfitt and Collins see ultimate brand share as the product of three factors:

$$s = p\, r\, b \tag{17-27}$$

where s = ultimate brand share
  p = ultimate penetration rate of brand (percent of new buyers of this product class who try this brand)
  r = ultimate repeat purchase rate of brand (percent of repurchases of this brand to all repurchases by persons who once purchased this brand)
  b = buying rate index of repeat purchase of this brand (average buyer = 1.00)

The definitions of these variables and the working of this formula can best be conveyed by an example. Assume that a company launches a new brand in an established product field. Its share of new buyers in this product field will rise

45J. H. Parfitt and B. J. K. Collins, "The Use of Consumer Panels for Brand-Share Prediction," *Journal of Marketing Research* (May 1968) 131–146.

from 0 to some ultimate percent as the weeks pass. Figure 17-14a shows the cumulative penetration of a new brand in the toilet soap field. The penetration rate increases at a decreasing rate from time zero. Some weeks after the brand is launched, the analyst can fit a modified exponential curve to the early results (or draw a freehand extrapolation) and predict the ultimate penetration rate, p, that is, the rate that would apply between twelve and eighteen months after the brand is launched.

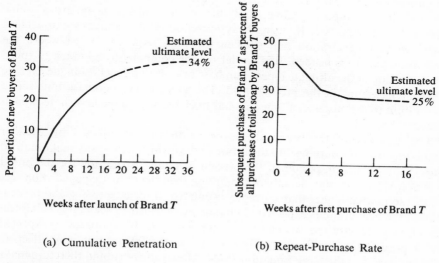

(a) Cumulative Penetration   (b) Repeat-Purchase Rate

Figure 17-14 Cumulative Penetration and Repeat-Purchasing Rate for Brand T (Parfitt and Collins Model)

Source: Parfitt and Collins, *op. cit.*, pp. 132–133.

The analyst will also examine the repeat purchase rate for this brand as the data come in. This rate shows the percent of repurchases of this brand to repurchases of all brands by those who have tried the brand. Figure 17-14(b) shows the repeat purchase rate for the new brand of toilet soap. The repurchase rate is approximately 40 percent in the first four weeks after purchase, that is, four out of ten repurchases of this product consisted of this brand. Figure 17-14(b) shows this rate as falling with the passage of time toward an asymptote of 25 percent. The earlier triers of a new product tend to like it more than the later triers.

If purchasers of the new brand buy at the average volume of purchasers of all brands in this product class, then $b = 1.00$. We are now ready to predict the ultimate brand share. According to Equation 17-27,

$$s = (.34)(.25)(1.00)$$
$$s = .085$$

That is, if 34 percent of new buyers in this market ultimately try this brand and

25 percent of their subsequent repurchases go to this brand, and those buying the brand buy an average quantity, the brand share should settle at an equilibrium level of 8.5 percent. If this brand attracts heavier than average buyers, say with an index of 1.20, then the share prediction would be 10.2 percent ($.34 \times .25 \times 1.20$); if this brand attracts lighter than average buyers, say, with an index of .80, then the share prediction would be 6.8 percent ($.34 \times .25 \times .80$).

The nice feature of this model is that ultimate share prediction can be made as soon as the penetration curve and the repeat purchase curve tend to be moving toward clear asymptotic values, and this occurs some time before a stable brand share is achieved. By using heavy promotion, the company can achieve faster market penetration and shorten the time required to see where the penetration curve is headed. It is harder for the company to do much to speed up its reading of the ultimate repeat purchase rate, as this depends on the average interpurchase time in the product field. The average interpurchase time sets a lower limit to the amount of time that has to elapse before the first share prediction can be made.

The accuracy of the brand share prediction will be affected by whether marketing factors continue into the future in the form and intensity that obtained during the prediction period. If the percent of retail distribution for the brand is expected to grow significantly in the future, then the ultimate penetration rate will be somewhat higher than currently estimated. If the advertising and promotion of the new brand is expected to change significantly in scale, this will affect the ultimate penetration rate and repeat purchase rate. If the product is expected to be priced at a significantly different level in the future, this may affect all three variables in the basic Equation 17-27. Management should therefore make allowances for expected changes in marketing factors in making ultimate brand share predictions.

When the ultimate brand share prediction is discouraging, management should consider whether it could take any action to increase either the penetration rate and/or the repeat purchase rate, before deciding to drop the brand. If the management can find a way to increase consumer satisfaction with the brand by altering its features or image, this would be worth considering if the expense of doing this were not so great as to cancel the value of a higher repeat purchase rate. It is easier to take steps to increase the penetration rate. But management often acts as if doubling the penetration rate would double the ultimate brand share. This is not necessarily true. Suppose the company ran a price special and this increased the penetration rate, especially by drawing in people who are not devoted to this brand but who want to take advantage of the value. The higher penetration rate is offset by the lower repeat purchase rate and no gain in ultimate market share need occur. Or suppose the company ran a special advertising campaign that increased the penetration rate. After the campaign was over, the penetration rate fell back to its former level. In this case, too, the ultimate brand share was not increased. Management must guard against thinking that increases in the penetration rate will be permanent, or that the repeat purchase rate will remain stable if the penetration rate rises.

The ultimate results depend on the marketing approach used to launch the new brand and the satisfaction the product gives to the buyers.

Burger Repeat Purchase Model

Still another way to look at the problem of predicting repeat sales and total sales has been proposed by Burger[46] and represents extensions of earlier work by Chatfield, Ehrenberg, and Goodhardt.[47] Burger sees total sales in period T as given by

$$S_t = S_{F,t} + S_{R,T} - S_{R,T-1} \qquad (17\text{-}28)$$

where S_t = total sales in period
$S_{F,t}$ = first purchase sales in period
$S_{R,T}$ = cumulative repurchases from period 1 to period T
$S_{R,T-1}$ = cumulative repurchases from period 1 to period $T-1$

The difference between the last two terms is the expected number of repurchases in period T. The key to estimating this value is to form a model for predicting cumulative repurchases, $S_{R,T}$. The same model will predict all other summations as well, such as $S_{R,T-1}$.

Cumulative repurchases will depend upon (1) the number of first purchasers in each period, (2) the proportion of first purchasers who repurchase the product, and (3) the expected number of repurchases per period. The relationship of these variables is exhibited in the following equation:

$$S_{R,T} = \sum_{t=1}^{T} \sum_{k=1}^{\infty} r(t) S_{F,t} k p(k = \lambda, T-t) \qquad (17\text{-}29)$$

where $r(t)$ = proportion of first purchasers who are likely to repurchase the product
$S_{F,t}$ = first purchase sales in period t
k = number of repurchases in period t (a random variable)
$p(k = \lambda, T-t)$ = Poisson distribution of the probability of arrival of k repurchases in period t, where λ is expected number of repurchases per period

This equation takes a proportion r of the first time purchases taking place in each period [the proportion is given by $r(t)$, which can change with time, since later product triers may show a lower repeat purchase rate than early product triers] and predicts and accumulates the number of repurchases they will make

[46]Philip C. Burger, "Developing Forecasting Models for New Product Introductions," in Robert L. King, ed., *Marketing and the New Science of Planning* (Chicago: American Marketing Association, 1968), pp. 112–119.

[47]C. Chatfield, A. S. C. Ehrenberg, and G. J. Goodhardt, "Progress on a Simplified Model of Stationary Purchase Behavior," *Journal of the Royal Statistical Society*, A 129, Part 3 (1966), 317–360.

to time T. The number of repurchases they will make to time T depends on the length of time between the time of first purchase, t, and the current period, T. A Poisson distribution is used because it satisfies reasonable underlying assumptions about the distribution of waiting times between repurchases.[48] Information on all of the parameters are derivable from consumer panel data; Burger reports a good fit of this repurchase model in empirical applications.

This ends our review of repeat purchase models. Each model takes a somewhat different approach to estimating repeat purchases and requires different types of data for implementation. A company has to experiment with these models and others, in order to determine the one that best fits its data and forecasting needs.

SUMMARY

Decision making takes on its most hazardous characteristics in the situation known as new product development and introduction. This is an age in which companies must introduce new products to survive, and yet do so in the knowledge that a substantial number of new products will fail. The costs involved are considerable and alert managements are taking whatever steps will help reduce the risks in the way of organization, professional staffing, marketing research, and model construction.

There has been considerable progress in the area of model building since the days of the simple break-even chart. The variety of current models for new product forecasting and planning reflects to a large extent the variety of new product situations in which companies engage. New product situations can be distinguished according to the degree of newness of the product and the degree of product repurchasability. Product newness ranges from the truly new product innovation to the new brand to the new model, style, or package size of an existing brand. Product repurchasability ranges from those which are bought only once to those which are bought occasionally to those which are bought frequently.

This last distinction enables us to separate the analysis of the first time purchase from the repeat purchases, on the idea that different factors are involved and that total period sales will be made up of the sum of these two sources of sales.

The occurrence of first time purchases can be analyzed as a diffusion process or an adoption process. A diffusion process involves working with a few macro-parameters that will locate a curve which describes the spread of the innovation through a population through time. An adoption process, on the other hand, involves modeling in more detail the behavior of the buyer as he learns and becomes interested in the product.

Treating the new product process as a diffusion process, at least four different

---

[48]See Burger, et al., "Forecasting New Product Sales," Working Paper, Northwestern University, Evanston, Ill., Mar. 1968.

diffusion-type models have been proposed. A concave model has been used by Fourt and Woodlock, which assumes that cumulative first purchases approach a limiting penetration level of less than 100 percent of all households and that successive increments of gain decline. An *S*-curve model has been used by a number of investigators to represent the cumulation of a normal curve or a lognormal curve to describe the number of adopters through time. Other investigators have analogized the new product adoption process to the spread of an epidemic through a population and have accordingly used one or another of several epidemiological diffusion models. For example, a model by Bass calls for estimating three parameters with the first three years of data on the spread of a new product. His resulting equation has been quite successful in predicting the peak time and magnitude at peak time of future sales. Finally, other investigators have used a Weibull probability distribution coming out of reliability engineering to forecast the volume of first purchases. The model assumes that the buyer is bombarded by stimuli having random arrival times and he buys the product if any of the stimuli reach him.

Adoption models, in turn, focus on the stages through which the individual passes on the way to adoption. There is a variety of such buyer readiness paradigms, all of them involving the buyer moving through a cognitive level, effective level, and action level. At least four models have been developed that take the adoption point of view. The DEMON model views marketing stimuli (advertising, promotion, and distribution) as creating a number of triers, some of whom become users and consume an average quantity that can be multiplied against price to estimate sales. Urban created a model that involves several buyer readiness stages leading up to trial, those of awareness (to the brand, the advertisements, the specific product appeals, and word of mouth recommendations), intent, search, selection, and postpurchase behavior. Alba designed an adoption model using Monte Carlo procedures to duplicate the adoptions of the new "touch-tone" telephone by 100 households in a suburban community. Amstutz developed a model which breeds a population of consumers, retailers, salesmen, products, and advertisements and causes these elements to interact on a stochastic basis to produce the output of ultimate interest, sales.

For the case of new frequently purchased products, the forecaster must develop a model to predict the repeat purchase volume. An increasing number of analysts are using the concept of depth of repeat purchase because the probability of repeat purchase varies with the number of past purchases. Fourt and Woodlock used this notion as the basis of their repeat purchase model. Parfitt and Collins chose to estimate asymptotic levels of ultimate penetration and ultimate repeat purchase rates to forecast the new brand's ultimate market share. Burger sees cumulative repurchases as depending upon the number of first purchasers in each past period, the proportion of first purchasers who repurchase the product, and the expected number of repurchases per period. Clearly, a variety of models is possible; their merits will become known only through repeated use and refinement of these models against the hard test of data.

Questions and Problems

1. Using the Fourt and Woodlock market penetration model represented by Equation (17–1), compute the increments in penetration for the first 5 periods for a company whose rate of penetration of untapped potential is .4 and whose potential sales as a percent of all buyers is .6. Verify mathematically that the sum of the individual increments approaches .6 as t goes to infinity.

2. It is stated in the chapter that from Equation 17–9

    $Q_T = \bar{Q}[1 + e^{-(a+bt)}]^{-1}$ we can derive Equation 17–10

    $$\ln \frac{Q_T}{\bar{Q} - Q_T} = a + bt.$$

    Complete this derivation.

3. For a particular product, the coefficient of innovation (p) is .05 and the coefficient of imitation (r) is .2. If the total number of potential buyers is 100,000, determine:
    (a) The time when sales will reach its peak
    (b) The magnitude of peak sales.

4. Suppose that the Bass model shown in Equation 17–14 is fitted to empirical data, resulting in the following expression:

    $$Q_t = 410 + 0.39Q_T - 10^{-6}Q_T^2$$

    From this, determine the total number of potential adopters, $\bar{Q}$.

5. In the DEMON decision model a company has to evaluate the results of each marketing research study and decide on a GO, ON or NO decision for the new product. It is likely that the company will make a sequence of ON decisions before reaching a GO or NO decision. Develop a picture of a possible sequence of marketing studies and ON decisions before a GO or NO decision is reached.

6. Suppose you are given the following Monte Carlo numbers:

Sex		Age, Male		Age, Female		Age, Unconditional	
00–49	Male	00–25	Young	00–20	Young	00–22	Young
50–99	Female	26–79	Mature	21–74	Mature	22–76	Mature
		80–99	Old	75–99	Old	77–99	Old

    What is the probability of breeding an old male on the Amstutz model?

7. A regional beverage firm has just introduced a new soft drink into its market and wishes to determine total sales of this product in the next period. It is estimated that there will be 10,000 new buyers in the period who will purchase 2 cartons, on the average, each time they buy. The repeat purchase ratios for the product are estimated as follows:

    $$(r_1, r_2, r_3, r_4, r_{5+}) = (.50, .60, .66, .70, 3.00)$$

    On the basis of these estimates, determine next period's sales.

8. The ABC company recently introduced a new product. The product has been on the market for 7 weeks, and the sales manager wishes to determine the product's long-run share of the market. The research department has provided data on the

cumulative penetration and repeat purchase rates for the product to date. These
data are presented in the following table:

Week	1	2	3	4	5	6	7
Cumulative Penetration	.13	.20	.26	.30	.33	.35	.36
Repurchase Rate		.48	.42	.37	.33	.30	.28

It is estimated that the company's customers buy somewhat less than the
average customer (index of .92 where 1.00 is average). Provide an estimate of the
product's long-run market share.

PART IV
From Theory to Practice

CHAPTER 18
The Marketing Information
System

The main purpose of this study has been to synthesize theory and examine models that can increase our understanding, prediction, and control of marketing processes. In this last section of the book, it is appropriate to turn our attention to the real problems of introducing and using marketing models in the actual practice of marketing management.

There are four major problems in attempting to move from theory to practice. The first problem is to develop the data base necessary to estimate, implement, and keep current the parameters of the model, which is the subject of the present chapter. The second problem is to develop a working understanding of how marketing decisions and plans are presently made in the company preparatory to identifying potential opportunities and difficulties for management science in marketing (Chapter 19). The third problem is to develop a strategy for "selling" marketing managers on the value of management science in marketing (Chapter 20). Finally, the fourth problem is to find a way to integrate the various specific marketing insights and model fragments into an overall corporate model for marketing planning and evaluation (Chapter 21).

Up to now, we have paid relatively little attention to whether the information required by any particular marketing model would be easy, difficult, or impossible to collect. There are a number of ways to justify the comparative neglect until now of the information and measurement problem:

1. Marketing models provide useful insights into marketing processes that may be a sufficient payoff in themselves, even in the absence of the ability to measure all the parameters.

2. Models calling for parameters that are difficult to measure are not necessarily valueless because the data may become available in the future through new measuring concepts and services.

3. In many cases, better decisions may be reached through the use of "good" models, even though they require some judgmental inputs, than through "poor" models that require only objective data. Techniques for gathering "good" judgmental data are constantly being improved. Furthermore, sensitivity analysis offers the decision maker a technique for measuring the sensitivity of the payoff measure to the uncertainties in the judgmental data.

At the same time, it must be acknowledged that poor numbers used in a good model could lead to disastrous results. Every effort should be directed at gathering the best numbers available.

The purpose of this chapter is to present a comprehensive overview of the problem of getting sound numbers for marketing models. The first section presents a design for the total marketing information system needed to support scientific marketing analysis, planning, and control. The second section describes in some detail major marketing information acquisition technologies, particularly surveys, experiments, and expert query techniques. The final section describes major statistical tools for extracting information from data, with particular emphasis on various multivariate techniques. Whole books are written on each of these topics; in this chapter we can only hope to present the highlights of the information gathering and analysis problem.

THE MARKETING INFORMATION SYSTEM

Before examining technical issues in gathering and analyzing information, we shall take a broad view of the marketing information function in a company. There was a time when firms did very little in the way of formal marketing information gathering and analysis. When firms were small and regional, their executives were in firsthand contact with buyers and dealers and they could follow market developments at close hand. Products were much simpler and so were the required marketing communication and distribution mixes. Technology, law, and culture seemed to change more slowly. For all these reasons, the seller's information needs could be satisfied simply and informally.

As company operations grew in size and complexity, company decision makers grew further removed from immediate contact with the scenes of marketing action. They had to rely increasingly on secondhand information for their picture of what was happening in the market place. The firm was involved in many more markets and products than ever before; the competitors were able to move more swiftly and deftly; and the environment of surrounding law, technology, economics, and culture was undergoing faster change.

As a result, an increasing number of firms established a formal departmental function known as *marketing research*. Sometimes this evolved out of the firm's economic research department, sometimes it was established independently. The marketing research department's tasks included gathering or buying information from published sources, arranging for special surveys, analyzing current sales and market trends, and preparing reports on special marketing problems. Much of the marketing research department's work was project oriented, that is, centered around a problem that requires some formal data collection and analysis which was to be presented in the form of a report.

At the same time, marketing executives in a firm would continue to hear, read, and gather information on their own. They would come across raw data, summary statistics, qualitative inferences, expert and lay opinions, impressions, and even rumors. The problem with this more informal information is that no provision was made for its formal evaluation, analysis, storage, or dissemination and much of its potential usefulness was lost. In fact, there is good evidence that casually gathered marketing information, even when quite important, may be lost or arrive too late to be of value.[1] This led some companies to establish a function called *marketing intelligence* to handle more formally the problem of systematically and continuously scanning the environment and disseminating intelligence items of interest to the proper executives. One large company recently appointed an ex-military intelligence officer to take over, design, and manage a marketing intelligence service for the company executives.

Marketing executives also have a third major source of information available to them in the form of *internal accounting data*. These data inform management about current and past sales broken down by product, region, and salesmen. The more advanced accounting system permits matching costs to revenue by these breakdowns and therefore allow management to determine the profit the company is earning on various products, regions, and marketing activities. The same internal accounting system also supplies information to executives on inventory levels, accounts receivables, and cash flows, all of which have bearing on the optimal marketing effort.

Thus the modern marketing executive finds himself the beneficiary of three systems designed to help him in his information needs: marketing research, marketing intelligence, and internal accounting data. That the modern marketing

---

[1]See Gerald S. Albaum, "Horizontal Information Flow: An Exploratory Study," *Journal of the Academy of Management* (March 1964) 21–33. Albaum set out to study how well information flowed from the customers of a large decentralized company through company salesmen to company executives. He arranged with a sample of company customers to pass on six fabricated pieces of market information to company salesmen. The intelligence told of the changing requirements of customers, the building of a new factory by a competitor, the price being quoted by a competitor, the availability of a new material that might be used in making the product, and the development of a competitive product made from a new material. Albaum wanted to discover how far, how fast, and how accurately this information would travel within the company. Of the six pieces of market information, only two ever traveled beyond the company salesmen! For one reason or another, the majority of the salesmen did not pass on their intelligence to anyone in their company. Of the two reports that reached company executives, one arrived in three days but was seriously distorted; the other arrived in about ten days in fairly accurate form, although its usefulness could have been impaired by its tardiness.

executive's information sources can become quite elaborate is suggested by Figure 18-1, which shows the various reports available to executives in the Mead Johnson company. These daily, weekly, monthly, bimonthly, and quarterly reports constitute quite an information system in contrast to the days when executives received little or no assistance in their information needs.

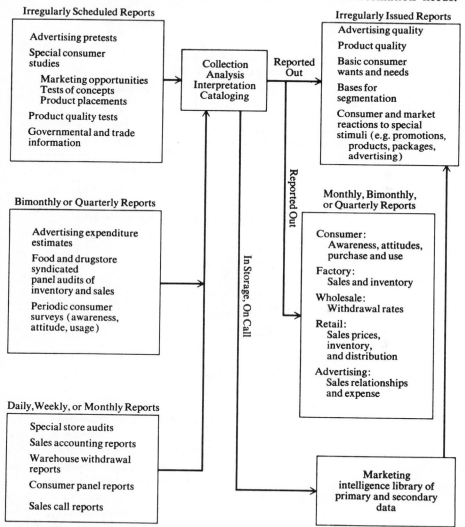

Figure 18-1   Mead Johnson's Marketing Information System

From Lee Adler, "Systems Approach to Marketing," *Harvard Business Review,* May-June, 1967, p. 111.

The real problem facing many executives today is how to stay on top of all the available information and still have time for planning and action. Many face a condition known as *information overload* in which they cannot possibly read all the material they should. This raises the issue of whether the company can take some positive steps to help its executives handle the information problem better. The answer may lie in creating a special marketing information and analysis center (MIAC) whose functions are blueprinted in Figure 18-2.

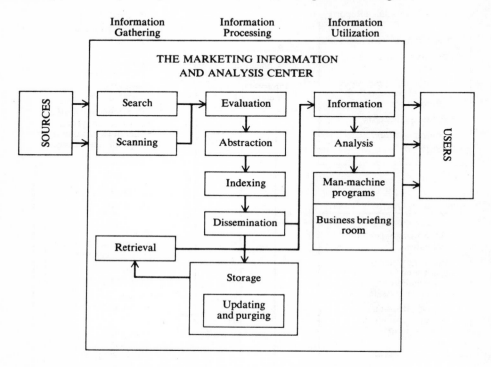

Figure 18-2   A Schematic Diagram of MIAC's Information Services

This unit is a generalization of the marketing research department into something substantially more comprehensive. MIAC would function as the marketing nerve center for the company and would not only provide instantaneous information to meet a variety of executive needs, but would also develop all kinds of analytical and decision aids for executives, ranging from computer forecasting programs to complex simulations of the company's markets.

The concept of this center can be understood best if we view its functions as being completely user oriented. It is designed to meet the total planning, implementational, and control needs of the modern marketing executive. Figure 18-2 shows the flow of marketing information from ultimate sources to and through MIAC to those who use this information. The ultimate sources consist of parties outside the firm such as customers, dealers, suppliers; and competitors and parties inside the firm such as the accounting department, the economic and forecasting department, and the field sales force. The ultimate users consist of company executives such as product managers, sales force managers, advertising managers, traffic managers, and production scheduling personnel. MIAC stands between these two groups and offers over a dozen different services to enhance and expedite the marketing information and decision making process. These services fall into three major types: information gathering, processing, and utilization.

Information Gathering

Gathering involves the effort to develop or locate information sought by company executives or deemed relevant to their needs. This function is made up of three constituent services.

The first is *search*, which is activated by requests for specific marketing information. Search projects can range from quick "information please" inquiries to large scale field marketing studies. Marketing research departments traditionally spend a substantial portion of their time in search activity.

The second information gathering service is *scanning*. This describes MIAC's responsibility for assembling general marketing intelligence. Intelligence specialists in MIAC will regularly scan newspapers, magazines, trade journals, special reports, and specific individuals to uncover any developments that might have import for one or more company executives. This partially relieves executives from the necessity to scan endless reams of written material for the sake of finding only a few items of interest. Because executives have overlapping information interests, the centralization of this function and its delegation to MIAC is likely to save considerable executive time. Its effectiveness, however, depends on how well MIAC personnel really understand the differing and specific information needs of the company's executives.

The third information gathering service is *retrieval*. When the needed information is already on file, the problem is to locate the information efficiently and speedily. This depends on the extent to which MIAC adopts advanced information storage and retrieval techniques such as computer systems, microfilm devices, display consoles, and the like. Some recent developments are:

1. *Companies are increasingly storing sales and marketing cost data on a disaggregative basis to permit executives to retrieve special configurations of information.* At Schenley an executive can retrieve current and past sales and inventory figures for any brand and package size for each of 400 distributors; or he can request the computer to list all distributors whose sales fall below a certain figure. In another company, marketing researchers are seeking to measure the effects of specific marketing inputs or specific sales by geographical area.

2. *Companies are attempting to reduce the length of time it takes for executives to learn of latest sales.* A few consumer goods companies are now able to provide executives with data on shipments that took place yesterday. Grocery goods companies are trying to figure out how they can learn of retail shelf-sales movement as it takes place. Some companies in the airline and motel industries have managed to develop *real time* information, that is, they know sales and

product availability as of the latest second. At United Air Lines the executives gather each morning in a special briefing room, where they go over the latest figures on sales, weather, and so forth, and revise their operations accordingly.

3. *Company personnel at a growing number of companies can retrieve data rapidly to service customer needs better.* Salesmen in one large paper company can dial the company computer while in a customer's office and learn in a matter of seconds whether a certain grade of paper is in stock and could be shipped to the customer to meet a target date. A large fertilizer company helps farmers decide on next year's best crops—and fertilizer—through a specially designed computer program. Several insurance companies use the computer to prepare long range insurance programs for clients.

Information Processing

The marketing information and analysis center can also offer a variety of data processing services designed to enhance the overall quality of management information. Five major services can be distinguished.

The first service is *evaluation.* One or more MIAC staffers trained in techniques of data validation would offer a technical opinion as to how much confidence can be placed in a particular piece of information. The amount of confidence depends upon how the information was gathered, the size of the sample, the reliability of the source, and other considerations that the data evaluator would immediately recognize as pertinent. This service would offset the tendency to treat all information as equally valid. The data evaluator may show that a market share figure from a particular consumer panel may vary 20 percent from the true value (at the 95 percent confidence level), and that a magazine readership estimate may vary by as much as 50 percent from the true figure. These opinions on the reliability and credibility of information will temper executive judgments in making decisions.

A second important service is *information abstraction.* Marketing information comes to MIAC in highly discursive forms. Many executives do not want to read pages and pages of reports to get a kernel of information. Trained abstracters on MIAC's staff condense and edit incoming information; they may omit important material, but this risk must be balanced against the gains accruing from a service that sharpens up information and supplies the executive with an immediate sense of what is relevant.

A third important service is that of *indexing* the information. This involves devising a set of descriptors that will permit the efficient classification of information for storage and retrieval purposes, and a ready identification of which executives might be interested in the information. For example, information about a proposed merger of two supermarket chains in California might be assigned the descriptors "supermarkets", "mergers," and "California," so that marketing executives interested in either supermarkets, mergers, or California would find this information readily. Developing a good indexing system is the key to the rapid dissemination of marketing information among the right parties and to its easy retrieval.

Dissemination is a fourth important information processing service. Dissemination involves getting information to the right people in the right form in the shortest feasible time. Among the devices used are periodic newsletters, telephone calls, teletype services, and interconnected company computers. Companies are experimenting with new and bolder dissemination procedures, as the two following examples show:

1. A large chemical company compiles during the week news of special interest to its salesmen, records the news on magnetic tapes, and sends the tapes to them. Each salesman's car is equipped with a tape recorder, and the salesmen pass many otherwise idle driving hours listening to relevant marketing and company information.
2. A large supermarket chain is considering the idea of preparing up to the minute reports of news affecting store operations, which its managers around the country can dial to obtain.

MIAC's final information processing service is that of *storage*. Every company must find an efficient way to store and compress the mountains of information that come in yearly; otherwise, it is storage without utility. Executives should be able to put their fingers on past sales figures, costs, dealer data, and other information with minimum effort. Each company must determine the economically desirable life of different types of information, so that it can be periodically updated and purged.

Information Utilization

MIAC must offer more than information gathering and processing services if it is to add substantial leverage to the executive's planning and control capabilities. The executive basically needs three types of staff assistance.

His first need is for *information* itself. Under this heading fall periodic reports, special market studies, and general marketing intelligence. We have seen how MIAC represents an improved vehicle for these services over the traditional marketing research department.

The second major need is for assistance in *analysis*. In this connection, MIAC's staff would include research specialists in statistical analysis, econometric analysis, psychometric analysis, and operations research, as well as research generalists to gauge needs and interpret results. These analysts would assist the decision maker in formulating problems and developing models for a solution. They would be able to specify the data needed and analyze the gathered data for important relationships and parameters. In this way, complex marketing decisions such as reducing a price, revising sales territories, or increasing advertising expenditures can be preevaluated and postevaluated by the scientific analysis of available data. These analysts would also help make periodic analyses of distribution costs, sales trends, expense records, and product and salesman performances.

The third major need of the executive is for *computer programs* that will enhance his power to make decisions and to control operations. Future management gains in decision making effectiveness will depend on the development of "man-computer" systems of decision making. Computer *on-line time sharing* will probably be the most potent force in making the new tools available to the marketing executives. Time sharing refers to a setup in which several remote teletype terminals are linked to a central computer and an executive can sit down at any one, dial the computer center number, type in his user number, and have access to all the power of the computer. An increasing number of computer programs will be available on a conversational basis, that is, the typewriter will type out a description of the requested program and then instruct the executive as to how he should type in his data. After the computer has received the data, it types back a solution in a matter of seconds. Conversational computer programs are already in existence for new product decision making,[2] advertising media selection,[3] sales territory design,[4] dealer site location,[5] sales prospects evaluation,[6] and marginal dealer evaluation.[7] These computer programs represent only the beginning of marketing models tailored to the problem and needs of various industries and executives. They form a part of the growing interest in improving the total information system available to executives, of which MIAC is one blueprint.

MAJOR APPROACHES TO GATHERING INFORMATION

In this section, we examine in some detail how a marketing analyst can go about gathering specific information that he needs. The information he needs may or may not presently exist. Data that already exists are called *secondary data*. Data that the firm must gather for the first time are called *primary data*.

Secondary Data

The researcher first tries to find the data he needs in existing sources. If he succeeds, he has saved time and expense. However, existing data are not always relevant, accurate, or complete enough for his purpose. Secondary data are often gathered for different purposes than the researcher may have in mind. Nevertheless, secondary data are often very useful. The two requirements for the researcher are that he be familiar with the major sources of data and that he know how to use them critically.

[2]Glen L. Urban, "SPRINTER mod 1: A Basic New Product Analysis Model," Working Paper, 397–69, Alfred P. Sloan School of Management, Massachusetts Institute of Technology, Cambridge, 1969. See Chap. 17, pp. 542–543.

[3]See J. D. C. Little and L. M. Lodish, "A Media Planning Calculus," *Operations Research* (Jan.–Feb. 1969) 1–35. See Chap. 14, pp. 461–465.

[4]See Sidney W. Hess, *Realignment of Sales and Service Districts*, Working Paper, Management Science Center, Wharton School, University of Pennsylvania, Philadelphia, July 1968. See Chap. 13, pp. 373–378.

[5]T. E. Hlavac, Jr., and J. D. C. Little, "A Geographic Model of an Automobile Market," Working Paper 186–66, Alfred P. Sloan School of Management, Massachusetts Institute of Technology, Cambridge, 1966. See Chap. 11, pp. 319–320.

[6]Private program by the author.

[7]Ibid.

Major sources of existing information. Three general sources of existing information are company files, marketing research services, and open publications.

1. *Company files.* The researcher in a large company is aware that much information is contained in various company files, such as accounting reports, detailed sales information, and special studies. The researcher should not ignore this source, nor should he overlook the possibility that useful data may exist in the files of his distributors, advertising agency, trade association, or other companies.

2. *Marketing research services.* Information is also available from marketing research firms who sell it on a fee basis. Various organizations such as A. C. Nielsen Company, Market Research Corporation of America, Audits and Surveys Company, Social Research, Gallup-Robinson, Daniel Starch, and others.

3. *Open publications.* Open publications are probably the most frequently used sources of information. An open publication is any book or magazine available to companies through libraries or purchase. The most important types are *government publications* and *commercial and trade publications.*[8]

Using existing information critically. Information in published sources is collected for a variety of purposes and under a variety of conditions that may render some of the data of limited usefulness. Often, the marketing researcher is so gratified to find some information he has been looking for in published form that he forgets to evaluate it critically. When the accuracy of the information is uncertain, its use can do more harm than if the researcher never found it. Marketing researchers and executives should check these data for four important qualities:

1. *Impartiality.* Impartiality is a quality not so much of the data as of the person or organization supplying it. The researcher generally can assume that government statistics and the data furnished by the larger commercial organizations are free from any conscious slant or bias. On the other hand, some of the data published by private organizations such as trade associations and chambers of commerce may be selected to cast the organization, industry, or area in a favorable light. The issue may not be one of conscious fabrication but of the selection of statistical measures and samples that create a one-sided picture.[9]

2. *Validity.* Validity raises the question of whether a particular number or series is a relevant measure for the researcher's purposes. An historical series of official steel prices would not be a completely valid measure of the actual prices paid for steel because the steel market has been characterized by un-

---

[8]For an annotated description of these publications, see Harper W. Boyd, Jr., and Ralph Westfall, *Marketing Research: Text and Cases*, rev. ed. (Homewood, Ill.: Richard D. Irwin, Inc., 1964), Chap. 7. Also see Steuart Henderson Britt and Irwin A. Shapiro, "Where to Find Marketing Facts," *Harvard Business Review* (Sept.–Oct. 1962) 44ff.

[9]An excellent account of these dangers is found in Darrell Huff, *How to Lie with Statistics* (New York: W. W. Norton & Company, Inc., 1954).

reported gray prices in different periods. Company data on shipments to various regional warehouses may not be a completely valid measure of sales in each region because warehouses often transship stock to other regions to meet unanticipated surges in demand.

3.   *Reliability*. Reliability raises the question of how precisely sample data reflect the universe from which they are drawn. A randomly drawn sample of 4000 housewives is likely to give a more accurate picture than a random sample of 400 housewives. Before using reported studies, management should examine the sample size and the degree of precision it implies.

4.   *Homogeneity*. Homogeneity raises the question of whether a given set of numbers is internally consistent. A time series on an industry's total advertising expenditures would not be homogeneous if the number of reporting units varied over time or if the definition of advertising costs varied.

While a researcher cannot evaluate all secondary information for impartiality, validity, reliability, and homogeneity, he should do this for the more critical information inputs. When the data's quality is in doubt, he must seriously consider whether the existing data should be used or fresh data collected.

Primary Data through Observation

When the data for a marketing problem are not found in any existing source, the company must engage in original data collection. This calls for some form of contact with company customers (actual and potential), middlemen, salesmen, competitors, or other primary information sources. The contact can take one of three forms: the information source can be observed, or involved in a controlled experiment, or interviewed. Here we shall consider observation as a method.

Partial answers to many marketing research questions can often be developed by observing the particular marketing process at work:

Two investigators recently set up a hidden television camera in the ceiling of a Pittsburgh supermarket to follow the movements of shoppers through the store. The objective was to develop generalizations on the customer flow pattern that might lead to the rearrangement of merchandise to increase customer convenience and purchases.

Another supermarket study involved stationing a hidden movie camera behind a particular canned goods display to record the eye movements of shoppers. The objective was to determine how shoppers scan the brands.

An investigator used a concealed tape recorder to record how different department store television salesmen answered his inquiry about buying a particular television set. The objective was to determine the typical sales arguments used and the degree of sales enthusiasm for the product.

Investigators observing a special display of foam rubber pillows in a department store checked the number of persons passing by, the number who stopped to look at the display, the number who handled the product, and the number who purchased it. The objective was to evaluate the effectiveness of the display.

Thus the observational method can be used to study sales techniques, customer movements, and customer responses. Its main advantage is that it generally leads to a more objective picture of overt behavior than can be expected from relying on people's accounts of how they behave. Observation avoids the problem of response bias.

The method may, however, introduce two new biases militating against an accurate picture of behavior. It assumes that the investigators are accurate and diligent observers. Instruments such as tape recorders and cameras are usually included, just to improve observational accuracy. The method also assumes that the act of observing the marketing process does not change the behavior of those being observed. This is the reason for trying to observe behavior by concealed means. Nevertheless, it yields little or no information about what is taking place under the skin of the people being observed. Their state of mind, their buying motives, their images are not revealed by this method. Even their incomes and education may not be obvious. This, coupled with the frequent costliness of the observational method resulting from the extensive time investigators must spend waiting for particular actions to take place, makes it desirable to consider other primary data collecting strategies.

Primary Data through Experiments

One of the major weaknesses of the observational method is that there is little or no control over the behavior or environment being observed. Behavior is observed in its natural setting with all the unique and uncontrollable factors that may attend it. Therefore, plain observation can rarely be counted on to yield conclusive proof of cause and effect relationships in marketing.

In order to test hypotheses about the effects of particular marketing stimuli on behavior, some controls must be introduced. The *experimental method* consists of introducing selected stimuli into a controlled environment and systematically varying them. To the extent that extraneous factors are eliminated or controlled, the observed effects can be related to the variations in the stimuli. The purpose of control is to eliminate competing hypotheses that might also explain the observed phenomena.

Many of the important decisions facing the marketing executive cannot be settled by secondary research, observation, or by surveying the opinions of customers or experts. To determine the best method for training salesmen, the best shelf arrangement for displaying a product, the best advertising media, and so forth, experimental design may be the most reliable and fruitful way to find the answers.

The experiment visualized as a system. The nature and problems of conducting marketing experiments can be understood best by thinking of an experiment as a system in which a number of inputs affect subjects and result in a number of outputs. This "systems" view of an experiment is illustrated in Figure 18-3. Each of the elements of an experiment is discussed below.

SUBJECTS. The subjects of an experiment are the units that are being acted upon and whose responses are solicited. In marketing experiments the subjects may be consumers, stores, sales territories, and the like. Because people are the ultimate subjects of marketing experiments, special techniques and precautions must be observed.[10] Some of the main problems are:

Instrumentation, or the problem of finding instruments that are sufficiently precise to measure changes in awareness, preference, or purchase behavior.

Matched groups, or the problem of developing groups of comparable subjects before the experiment begins.

Uniformity, or the problem of insuring comparable exposure of the subjects to the same environmental inputs during the experiment.

Reactive bias, or the problem of obtaining authentic behavior from people who are conscious of their participation in an experiment.

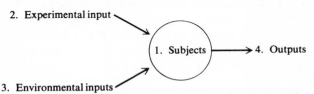

Figure 18-3   The Experiment Visualized as a System

EXPERIMENTAL INPUT. The experimental input is the variable whose effect is being tested. In marketing experiments, the experimental input may be price, packaging, display, a sales incentive plan, or some combination of marketing variables.

ENVIRONMENTAL INPUTS. Environmental inputs are all the factors affecting the experiment save the experimental input and the subjects. In marketing experiments, environmental inputs may include competitors' actions, weather changes, and uncooperative dealers.

Fortunately, many environmental inputs do not make a difference in the results. Of those that make a difference, some may be controllable, or at least measurable. The real danger comes from undetected environmental inputs or detected inputs whose effects cannot be controlled or measured.

Two precautions can be taken. One is to use a sample of sufficient size, so that the effect of exceptional environmental inputs is swamped by the normal inputs. The other is to set up a control group, namely, a group equivalent to the experimental group and differing only in not receiving the experimental input. The theory of the control group is that it catches all the effects of the uncontrolled inputs and therefore provides a measure for adjusting the contaminated experimental outputs.

EXPERIMENTAL OUTPUTS. The results of the experiment are called experimental

---

[10]An excellent discussion of the control problems posed by people in experiments is found in Donald T. Campbell and Julian C. Stanley, "Experimental and Quasi-Experimental Designs for Research on Teaching," in *Handbook of Research on Teaching*, N. L. Gage, ed. (Skokie, Ill.: Rand McNally & Company, 1963), pp. 171–246.

outputs. In marketing experiments, the results may come in the form of changes in sales, attitudes, or behavior.

Sales are the ultimate output of interest in appraising the effect of marketing stimuli. The marketing experimenter should strive to submit an experimental input to a *sales test* whenever possible. Where this is not possible, a proxy output has to be used. It should be highly correlated with sales, and, as a rule, the closer the proxy output is to the criterion output (sales), the greater the confidence.

If we assume that good control was exercised in designing the experiment, the outcomes represent information about the effects of the experimental inputs. In principle, decision rules should be established in advance of the experiment to guide the ensuing interpretation. Consider the following decision rule: "If a sales difference of a certain size or greater takes place between two types of packages, the company should produce the more popular package; if the sales difference is less than a certain size, then either package can be used; and if the sales difference falls in between the two specified sizes, a second experiment should be conducted before acting." The actual choice of the critical sales differences requires an examination of the error characteristics of the available decision rules, the economic losses implied by various possible errors, and the prior convictions of the decision maker. These are the ingredients in a Bayesian statistical analysis undertaken to find the best decision rule.[11]

The variety of experimental designs. The discussion of experimentation in marketing has pointed to a number of hazards. But many hazards also attend the interpretation of results in observational research and survey research. This discussion has a purely constructive purpose, to increase the user's sensitivity to the variables that need to be controlled in an experiment. Control itself is achieved through better experimental design.

Experimental design deals with the problem of deciding on the number of subjects, the length of the experiment, and the types of controls. These are technical problems and some of the major alternatives will be described here in terms of an example.

Suppose that a manufacturer of quality power mowers finds sales disappointing and believes they may be helped by the development of a point of purchase cutaway display. The contemplated display is expensive, however, and the manufacturer would like to try it out first on a limited basis to be sure that it stimulates more sales and profits than it costs. The following experiments can be designed, ranging from the simple to the complex.

SINGLE TIME SERIES EXPERIMENT. A simple experiment would consist of selecting some dealers, auditing their sales for a few weeks, introducing the display, and measuring their subsequent sales.

RECURRENT TIME SERIES DESIGN. Alternatively, the display can be introduced for a few weeks, removed, reintroduced, removed, and so forth, each time

[11]See Frank M. Bass, "Marketing Research Expenditures: A Decision Model," *Journal of Business* (Jan. 1963) 77–90.

noting the sales change and averaging the results. The averaging should eliminate the effects of unique events.

BEFORE-AFTER WITH CONTROL GROUP DESIGN. Alternatively, two matched groups of dealers can be selected and their sales audited for a few weeks before the display is introduced. Then the display can be introduced only into the stores of the first group of dealers, while sales are audited for both groups. The average sales for the experimental and control groups are then compared, and the difference is tested for statistical significance.

FACTORIAL DESIGN. Alternatively, the experiment can be set up to test other marketing inputs in addition to the point of purchase display. Testing only one experimental input at a time is often inefficient.[12] Suppose that the firm wants to test three displays, three prices, and three types of guarantee, or twenty-seven possible combinations of experimental inputs. By getting the cooperation of some multiple of twenty-seven dealers, it is possible to estimate the separate effect of different displays, prices, and guarantees, and also their interactions.[13]

LATIN SQUARE DESIGN. The preceding experiment involved testing twenty-seven different combinations of experimental inputs. If interaction among the experimental inputs is not thought to exist, there is a design known as a simple Latin square that can yield fairly good estimates of the separate effects of each input on the basis of testing only nine experimental combinations. This reduces considerably the scale and cost of the many factor experiment.[14]

The future of the experimental method in marketing. Experimentation in marketing will never be as easy as it is in the physical sciences or even in the agricultural sciences. Yet the experimental method remains the only research method for verifying cause and effect relationships in marketing. The existence of hurdles emphasizes that special experimental designs and precautions should be exercised, not that experiments should be dismissed.

The number of actual bona fide experiments carried out in marketing to date is quite small. Executive resistance is based on such factors as skepticism, the lack of time for carrying out experiments, difficulties in securing cooperation, and cost. In spite of these deterrents, there is evidence of increasing use of marketing experiments. Scott Paper Company and Du Pont have pioneered large scale experiments for testing the effectiveness of advertising.[15] Experiments

[12]"It was a long held scientific doctrine that good experimental procedure was to study one variable at a time holding all others constant . . . . Such a procedure is not only quite wasteful of time and resources but provides insufficient information. If there is an interaction . . . it would never be discovered by this method. The correct method is to determine the effects . . . and their interactions *simultaneously* in a single well-planned experiment." R. J. Jessen, "A Switch-Over Experimental Design to Measure Advertising Effect," *Journal of Advertising Research* (Mar. 1951) 15–22.

[13]For an example of the statistical analysis, see Kenneth P. Uhl, "Factorial Design—Aid to Management," *Journal of Marketing* (Jan. 1962) 62–66.

[14]This and the previous designs are described in more detail in Boyd and Westfall, *Marketing Research*, pp. 95–124.

[15]See, for example, James C. Becknell, Jr., and Robert W. McIsaac, "Test Marketing Cookware Coated with 'Teflon,'" *Journal of Advertising Research* (Sept. 1963) 2–8.

have also been conducted in stores, where the experimental inputs have been displays or shelf-space arrangements.[16] The experimental method has also proved useful for testing such product features as taste and color.[17] The test marketing of new products is another area in which principles of experimental design are (or should be) used.[18]

Primary Data through Surveys

The most common method of generating marketing information is through surveys. Compared with either direct observation or experimentation, surveys yield a broader range of information and are effective for a greater number of research problems. Surveys can produce information on socioeconomic characteristics, attitudes, opinions, motives, and overt behavior. Surveys are an effective way of gathering information for planning product features, advertising copy, advertising media, sales promotions, channels of distribution and other marketing variables.

Because surveys are so commonplace, there is a tendency to think that planning, executing, and interpreting them requires little training. Questions are written up, people are asked to respond, and the responses are summarized. The truth of the matter is that a good survey requires expert planning. Each step in developing survey information is subject to special problems, and the handling of these problems distinguishes the skilled researcher from the unskilled.

The research director faces many alternative ways to collect the information that will satisfy the research objectives. He must decide among *survey methods*, *research instruments*, and *sampling plans*. His decisions with respect to these three elements constitute his *research strategy*.

Suppose a company wants to draw a sample of people and interview them about their knowledge and attitudes toward the company's products. There are a large number of possible research strategies. Table 18-1 shows four of the more common ones. The first strategy is to collect a limited amount of information by making telephone calls to a small sample of households chosen in a systematic way from the telephone directory. The second strategy is to send mail questionnaires to a group of magazine subscribers. The third strategy is to take a large scale national probability sample. The fourth strategy is to carry out some depth interviewing with a small group of product users. Other permutations of these elements are possible, and this is why the researcher's skill, experience, and judgment count heavily in the ultimate usefulness and cost of the collected information. The researcher must understand the major

---

[16]See Peter L. Henderson, James F. Hind, and Sidney E. Brown, "Sales Effects of Two Campaign Themes," *Journal of Advertising Research* (Dec. 1961) 2–11; Keith Cox, "The Responsiveness of Food Sales to Supermarket Shelf Space Changes," *Journal of Marketing Research* (May 1964) 63–67.

[17]See Norman T. Gridgeman, "A Tasting Experiment," *Applied Statistics* (June 1956) 106–112.

[18]For an excellent exposition and evaluation of the experimental method in marketing, see Seymour Banks, *Experimentation in Marketing* (New York: McGraw-Hill Inc., 1965).

advantages and disadvantages of each of the major *survey methods*: telephone interviews, mail questionnaires, and personal interviews. He must be able to prepare an effective *questionnaire*, with particular attention to the types of questions asked, the form and wording of the questions, the sequencing of the questions, and the layout of the questionnaire. He must have theoretical knowledge and practical experience in designing a sampling plan, particularly with regard to who is to be surveyed (sampling unit); how many are to be surveyed (sample size); and how they are to be selected (sampling procedure).

Table 18-1   Some Alternative Research Strategies

Elements of the strategy	Strategy 1	Strategy 2	Strategy 3	Strategy 4
Survey method	Telephone interviews ↓	Mail interviews ↓	Personal interviews ↓	Personal interviews ↓
Research instrument	with a few factual questions ↓	with a 2-page questionnaire ↓	with many questions ↓	with projective tests ↓
Sampling plan	to a small sample of households chosen as every thous-andth name in telephone directory	to all sub-scribers to a magazine	to a large sample of subjects chosen on a national probability sampling basis	to a dozen people found using the product

Finally, he must know how to handle common problems in the collection of field data, such as not-at-homes, refusals to cooperate, respondent biases, and interviewer biases.

In this connection, Charles Mayer has developed a useful simulation model for estimating the probable cost of different field interviewing plans.[19] A simplified flow chart of his field interviewing model is shown in Figure 18-4. A field interviewing plan is specified. This leads to the selection of a first respondent. The computer calculates the travel time required to reach the selected respondent from the interviewer's present location, and then it determines the specific outcome of the call by generating a random number and matching it with a predetermined response probability for this respondent. Calls are continued in this manner over one or more simulated days until a predetermined response rate is achieved. When this happens, the computer prints out the total costs of the field interviewing procedure. On a particular test of the model, its forecast of costs were largely borne out in an actual field experiment.

[19]See Charles S. Mayer, "Pretesting Field Interviewing Costs through Simulation," *Journal of Marketing* (Apr. 1964) 47–50.

Primary Data through Subjective Estimation

A fourth major way to gather information for a specific marketing problem is to solicit and pool estimates from experts such as company consultants and knowledgeable company executives. A company might invite a forecast of next year's gross national product from a consulting economist, a probability estimate of hot weather in a particular market area from a local meteorologist, a market size estimate from a company salesman, or a rating of the company's advertising copy effectiveness from an advertising consultant. In all these cases, the numbers do not exist anywhere in objective form but there are experts who are expected to produce better than average estimates. The expert bases his estimate on existing objective data plus personal insights that come from experience. The distinguishing characteristic of judgmental data is that it is produced by a data transformation model that is usually not made explicit by the data producer.

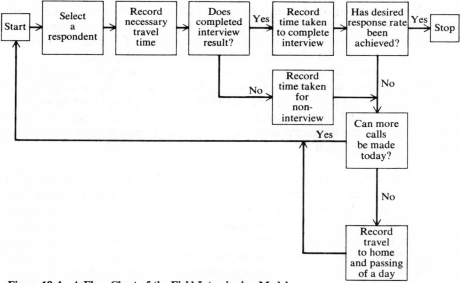

Figure 18-4   A Flow Chart of the Field Interviewing Model

Source: Mayer, *op. cit.,* p. 49.

There are those who believe that "guestimates" should be scrupulously avoided or minimized by model builders and decision makers. They would rather see models tailored to existing data than models tailored to the problem variables independent of the data availability. However, the very act of decision making in the face of uncertainty inevitably requires many personal judgments and estimates. Subjective data cannot be avoided in situations in which there is no past history or present data are poor or inadequate. The issue is not whether decision making can proceed without judgmental estimates but only whether there are strong advantages to explicating and quantifying these judgments. Our position is that the quantification of judgments yields several important benefits in the process of problem solving:

1. Executives and experts who are asked to put their judgments in the forms of numbers tend to give harder thought to the problem, especially if the numbers are a matter of record.

2. Quantification helps pinpoint the extent and importance of differences among executives with respect to the decision problem. Numbers permit the analyst to perform a sensitivity analysis to determine how dependent a decision is on particular differences in judgment.

3. Judgmental data allows the use of many interesting decision models that could not otherwise be used because of a lack of objective data. It is a mistake to think that judgmental data need be inferior and it is imaginable that they could be superior under certain circumstances to objective data. The main problem is that the analyst collecting judgmental data must exercise care in how he asks the experts for their estimates. He must form his questions with the same care he uses in interviewing customers, dealers, and others. The manner in which the questions are asked will affect the answers. Fortunately, improvements in techniques for querying experts are steadily being made.

There are two important problems in gathering and using judgmental data. The first concerns methods of obtaining useful estimates from the single expert (consultant, company executive, etc.) that can serve the purposes of the decision model. The second concerns the problem of pooling the estimates of two or more experts when there may be some divergence of opinion (this is known as the "consensus problem.")

Gathering estimates from the single expert. The marketing analyst may be faced at one time or another with the need to gather one or more of four general categories of judgmental information from experts. First, he might need a *point estimate* of the value of some independent variable or coefficient, such as a size of market estimate, a price elasticity, a unit cost figure, and so forth. Second, he might need a *sales response function*, that is, an indication of how the expert feels sales would vary with variations in the level of one or more marketing factors. Third, he might need estimates of the *uncertainty* surrounding parameter estimates, function estimates, or key events. Finally, he might need a set of *ratings and/or weights* to assign to certain variables in his model.

Obtaining a point estimate. Very often, a management decision will hinge on a certain vital estimate that is partly or wholly judgment-based. The analyst has to seek out someone who can be presumed to have better than average judgment in the area. This person may or may not be willing to be pinned down to a specific number; sometimes he may even deny any conscious knowledge or feeling about the probable size of the variable. The following dialogue is informative concerning one analyst's technique for getting an expert to admit to having a strong feeling for the probable size of a variable:

Analyst: What do you think your annual sales will be in this new territory?

Executive: I don't have the foggiest idea. I just think it will be a good territory.

Analyst: Do you think sales would go over $10 million a year?

Executive: No, that's very unlikely.

Analyst: Do you think sales will go over $8 million a year?

Executive: That's possible.

Analyst: Could sales be as low as $4 million a year?

Executive: Absolutely not. We wouldn't open the territory if we thought sales would be that low.

Analyst: Would it be more likely that sales will be around $6 million?

Executive: That's quite possible. In fact, I would say that's a little on the low side.

Analyst: Where would you place sales?

Executive: Around $7 million.

The interesting thing about this dialogue is how the executive went from a statement that he had no idea of the expected level of sales to a definite estimate as a result of a questioning procedure that confronted him with extreme possibilities. We will leave aside the question of whether the number that he finally supplied has any relation to the true, but unknown level of sales next year. The main point is that the technique managed to make the executive conscious that he did regard certain numbers as more reasonable than others.

The estimate yielded by the expert can be sensitive to the wording of the question, in which case care has to be exercised. Consider these similar-sounding questions:

"What is your estimate of the *most likely* level of sales?" (Mode)

"What level of sales would you estimate that you have *an even chance* of reaching?" (Median)

"Based on past experience, what level of sales is it reasonable to *expect?*" (Mean)

The analyst must be clear about the type of average he wants and the expert must be comfortable with the form in which the question is asked.

In the second place, the analyst should stimulate the executive to think about the estimate conditionally. A sales estimate means nothing except as it is related to assumptions about the state of the economy, the actions of competitors, the proposed marketing plan, and so forth. These assumptions should be explicated as part of the questioning procedure.

In the third place, a single point estimate should be accompanied with some indication of the confidence felt by the expert in his number. The estimate itself reveals nothing about whether the expert holds it with high confidence or low confidence. Techniques for expressing his confidence numerically will be described later.

In addition to single point estimates of values of independent variables, such as sales, costs, GNP, and so forth, the analyst often needs estimates of coefficients such as price elasticities and sales decay parameters. The problem here is that many executives do not do their thinking in terms of these concepts. The analyst in this case could explain the concept of elasticity, or a standard deviation, and then get an estimate from the executive. Or he can proceed to infer the coefficient from other data that the executives can more comfortably supply. For example, he can obtain executive estimates of sales associated with different possible price levels and derive the implied elasticity parameter himself. Many analysts favor this indirect method of deriving the needed coefficients for a model.

Obtaining an estimate of a sales response function. We have emphasized throughout the book the analytical value of thinking functionally about the relation of sales to other variables that affect sales. The causal relation between sales and other variables has been termed a sales response function and many types have been illustrated in the book. If the sales response function is to be employed in actual decision making, the analyst must determine its form, its variables and their coefficients. Ideally, the function should be measured by a statistical regression analysis of past data (described later). However, in many cases, this route is closed because past data are not extant or are insufficient or do not fully apply to the new situation. In these cases the analyst may choose to construct the function he needs out of judgmental data.

A procedure for forming such a function can now be described. As an illustration, suppose the management of a company is trying to determine whether to increase or decrease its sales force of forty men. A knowledgeable sales executive is approached and asked the following two questions:

"What do you think our sales would be with five more salesmen of average ability placed in territories A, B, C, D, and E?"
"What do you think our sales could be with five fewer salesmen of average ability taken out of territories A, B, C, D, and E?"

Note that these questions are worded in a way that encourages the estimator to think of specific levels of sales ability and specific areas of assignment. To merely talk about adding salesmen without specifying their ability level or assignment would yield less useful estimates.

Assume that the following numbers are supplied:

sales with 35 men	$5.3 million (estimated)
sales with 40 men	$6.0 million (present company sales)
sales with 45 men	$6.5 million (estimated)

These estimates suggest that the expert expects higher sales to occur at a somewhat declining rate with more salesmen. The analyst can test different functions, such as a quadratic equation, a square root equation, a modified exponential equation, and so forth, for their goodness of fit to the three observations and their theoretical plausibility. Once a function is chosen and fitted, the analyst can proceed to use it to solve the problem of the best size sales force.

In using this method it is important to query the expert about alternative sales force sizes that are sufficiently far away from the current level to allow a convincing curve to be fitted. One would not have much confidence in any shape of sales response function fitted to sales estimates for, say, thirty-nine, forty, and forty-one salesmen. In fact, a good case could be made for trying to obtain estimates of sales for several alternative sales force sizes in order to increase the confidence that the fitted curve does describe the expert's full view of the sales response function.

Obtaining probability estimates. We mentioned earlier that a point estimate does not contain any indication of how much confidence is felt by the expert in it. Yet the degree of confidence can make a great difference both in calculating the expected values of alternative strategies and quantifying the level of risk associated with each strategy. An expert will almost always acknowledge that the variable he is estimating could take on a wide range of values, even though they are not all equally likely in his mind. The information that would be most useful to the analyst would be a probability distribution estimated by the expert for the various values that he believes the variable could take on. Such a probability distribution could be obtained in two basic ways. It could be estimated directly by the expert, or it could be derived indirectly by the analyst from other numbers supplied by the expert.

It would seem that the best way to obtain an expert's subjective probability distribution is to ask him for it directly. He could be provided with graph paper and asked to draw his idea of the probability distribution for the range of possible values of the random variable. The analyst could then use this distribution directly or use a theoretical distribution to approximate it where this would facilitate the mathematical analysis. The only problem is that many executives are not acquainted with the concept of a probability distribution and would need a careful explanation before they could produce one. Analysts working in this area have found it easier to explain the concept of a cumulative probability distribution. One can be obtained from the executive by asking the following questions:

"In your opinion, what is the probability (in percent) that sales will be greater than $5 million dollars?"

"What is the probability that sales will be greater than $6 million?"

"What is the probability that sales will be greater than $7 million?" and so forth.

This sequence of questions produces a declining cumulative probability distribution. From this the analyst can derive the noncumulative probability distribution in a straightforward way. If desired, he might fit a theoretical curve to the data and use the latter in his analysis or simulation.

To obtain a well-defined distribution using the cumulative probability questioning technique, the analyst might have to elicit estimates of probability for over a dozen different values of the random variable.[20] To avoid putting the executive through this chore, which can become quite taxing, particularly if probability distributions are needed from the executive for each of several uncertain variables, the analyst might prefer to use some other procedure that only requires a few estimates from the executive and where the analyst takes the responsibility of assuming a plausible probability distribution a priori. For example, if the analyst asked for only two estimates, the mean and standard deviation of sales, he has all he needs to specify fully a two parameter probability distribution, provided that he is willing to assume one.

Even here, many executives are not familiar with the concept of a standard deviation to permit this simple estimation route to be taken. This is not fatal, however, because there is a simple three-point estimate approach that permits the analyst to derive the mean and standard deviation and proceed to construct a probability distribution. *The germ of the idea lies in asking the expert to estimate low, medium, and high values of the random variable.* These are not asked for, however, in a distribution-free sense, which was the case at one time:

"How low might sales be?"
"What is the most likely level of sales?"
"How high might sales be?"

The problem with these questions is that they afford no indication of what is meant by a low or high sales estimate. The bemused executive can retort with zero for a low estimate of sales because he is given no guidance as to how pessimistic he should be. When the lack of a probabilistic framework was grasped in the evolution of three-point estimation procedures, the questions were refined to read:

"Give me a low estimate of sales such that there is a 97.5 percent chance in your mind that we will do better." (S_L)
"Give me an estimate of the most likely level of sales." (S_M)
"Give me a high estimate of sales such that there is a 97.5 percent chance in your mind that we won't do this well." (S_H)

---

[20]However, Schussel showed how a cumulative probability distribution might be obtained with as few as five estimates. In his study of alternative sales forecasting methods for Polaroid film, he asked executives to estimate:

1.   The amount of film at which a fair bet could be made at even odds that the actual would be over or under this amount (that is, the median).
2, 3.   The amount of film at which a fair bet could be made at 3:1 odds that the actual sales would be over (upper quartile) or under (lower quartile) this amount.
4, 5.   The amount of film at which the executives would be *shocked* should actual sales be as high (upper 1 percent bound) or as low (lower 1 percent bound).

Schussel then fitted a smooth cumulative distribution function through the five estimates. See George Schussel, "Sales Forecasting with the Aid of a Human Behavior Simulator," *Management Science* (June 1967) B593–B611.

In effect, the analyst has solicited from the expert a 95 percent confidence interval; there is only a 2.5 percent chance on each side, or a 5 percent chance altogether, that sales will be outside of the $S_L - S_H$ range. If the low and high estimates are not too asymmetrical from the modal estimate, the analyst is likely to be willing to assume a *normal distribution*; the derivation of the mean and standard deviation are given by the following relationships:

$$\bar{S} = \frac{S_L + S_H}{2} \tag{18-1}$$

$$\sigma = \frac{S_H - S_L}{4} \tag{18-2}$$

Thus the mean is found by averaging the low and high estimate and the standard deviation is found by taking one fourth of the distance between the low and high estimate because approximately four standard deviations span a 95 percent confidence interval. The analyst is now able to employ the normal probability distribution in the mathematical analysis of the decision problem or as a basis for generating the Monte Carlo samples needed in risk analysis.[21]

It is convenient but not necessary to use a 95 percent confidence interval. Analysts have worked with different ranges and variants of the basic questions shown above. Some analysts find management more comfortable in using an 80 percent confidence interval. If the preceding questions based on an 80 percent confidence interval were asked and the executive's estimates were $8, $10, and $12, the standard deviation is derived from the fact that 2.56 standard deviations covers 80 percent of the middle area under the normal curve. Therefore, we can find the value of one standard deviation (σ) by

$$\sigma = \frac{S_H - S_L}{2.56} = \frac{12 - 8}{2.56} = 1.56$$

If the executive's low-high estimates are quite asymmetrical in their distance from the mode, with the high estimate being further away from the mode than the low estimate (positive skewness), the analyst may prefer to fit a *lognormal distribution* to the three estimates.[22] If sales S are assumed to be lognormally distributed, then the log of sales, that is, log S, is normally distributed. The formulas shown in Equations 18-1 and 18-2 for the mean and standard deviation of the normal distribution are now modified in a straightforward manner for the lognormal distribution:

$$\bar{S} = \frac{\log S_L + \log S_H}{2} \tag{18-3}$$

---

[21]See Chap. 10, pp. 268–276.
[22]See Chap. 15, Equations 15-25, 15-26, and 15-27.

$$\sigma = \frac{\log S_H - \log S_L}{4} \tag{18-4}$$

Another distribution for representing asymmetric low-high estimates, this time in either direction, is the *beta distribution*. (The actual beta distribution applies to a continuous variate whose admissible values lie between 0 and 1.) The distribution is widely used for estimating activity completion times in PERT projects. In our context, the analyst asks:

"What is the most pessimistic estimate of sales?" (S_L)
"What is the most likely estimate of sales?" (S_M)
"What is the most optimistic estimate of sales?" (S_H)

The mean of the beta distribution is assumed to be ⅓ of the way between the mode, S_M, and the average of the extremes, this being given by the formula:

$$\bar{S} = \frac{S_L + 4S_M + S_H}{6} \tag{18-5}$$

The standard deviation is arbitrarily established as ⅙ of the range, that is,

$$\sigma = \frac{S_H - S_L}{6} \tag{18-6}$$

The whole distribution is given by

$$f_\beta(S) = \begin{cases} 0 & \text{for } S < S_L \\ k(S - S_L)^\alpha (S_H - S)^\beta & \text{for } S_L \leqslant S \leqslant S_H \\ 0 & \text{for } S > S_H \end{cases} \tag{18-7}$$

where the parameters k, α, and β are calculated from the estimates of S_L, S_M, S_H and the required characteristics of the distribution.

The *Weibull probability distribution* has also come into favor where a flexible distribution is needed. Figure 18-5 shows some of the shapes of this two-parameter distribution. To use this distribution, the analyst asks the expert the following five questions:

"What is the most likely sales level?" (S_M)
"State a low estimate." (S_L)
"What is the probability that sales may be still lower?" (p_L)
"State a high estimate." (S_H)
"What is the probability that sales may be still higher?" (p_H)

Note that this method has the advantage of permitting the expert to select the upper and lower estimates and their corresponding probabilities, rather than limit him to specific standard deviation distances in the distribution, which may be difficult to estimate. These judgmental data are then fitted to the Weibull probability density, which is given by

$$f_W(S) = \frac{m}{\lambda^m}(S-k)^{m-1}\, e^{-[(S-k)/\lambda]^m} \tag{18-8}$$

where m = shape parameter $m \geqslant 0$
       λ = scale parameter
       k = constant $S \geqslant k$,

The terms in the equation are made operational in the three following expressions:[23]

$$\lambda = \left(\frac{m}{m-1}\right)^{1/m}(S_M-k) \tag{18-9}$$

$$1-p_L = e^{-[(m-1)/m][(S_L-k)/(S_M-k)]^m} \tag{18-10}$$

$$p_H = e^{-[(m-1)/m][(S_H-k)/(S_M-k)]^m} \tag{18-11}$$

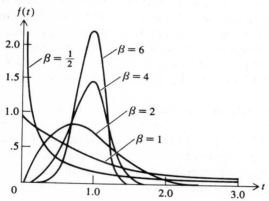

Figure 18-5   **Weibull Probability Distribution,** $\alpha = 1$

Source: Edgar A. Pessemier, *New-Product Decisions: An Analytical Approach* (New York: McGraw-Hill Book Co., 1966), p. 208.

In addition to continuous probability distributions, many decision models require discrete probabilities, describing critical events that might affect sales. Thus a decision model may require an estimate of the probability that a competitor would react fully to the company's price cut. The probability has no meaning in an objective sense because this event would not be repeated under the same conditions hundreds of times. Rather, this is a personal probability

---

[23]See W. D. Lamb, "A Technique for Probability Assignment in Decision Analysis," General Electric Major Appliance Division, No. 67MAL02; or see Edgar A. Pessemier, *New-Product Decisions: An Analytical Approach* (New York: McGraw-Hill, Inc., 1966). pp. 207–210.

reflecting the expert's degree of belief or confidence in a certain outcome. An effective procedure for eliciting this probability is to use the "standard gamble" as used in Von Neumann-Morgenstern utility theory.[24] This consists of framing a bet in terms of the utility of a consequence C and the probability of its occurrence p, that is,

$$pU(C)+(1-p)U(\sim C) \qquad (18\text{-}12)$$

The expert is asked to specify a value for p such that he would be indifferent between the utility of the above expression and the utility of some intermediate consequence C_i. Suppose C is "sales $=$ \$10 million," $\sim C$ is "sales $=$ \$5 million," and C_i is "sales $=$ \$8 million." Then, if the expert says he would be indifferent in betting when $p = 0.6$, this implies that he sees a 60 percent chance of achieving sales of \$8 million (relative to other outcomes).

Obtaining ratings and weights. Many decision models in marketing call for assignments of ratings and/or weights to certain variables. For example, the "weighted factor score model" used in evaluating new product ideas requires management to rate how well the company stands on each of several factors and also to assign weights to the factors to indicate their relative importance in new product success.[25] Many media selection models require media experts to rate media on their relative editorial suitability for a particular product. Other models require ratings of salesmen ability, channel effectiveness, and so forth, for implementation.

By their nature, rating scales do not exist in nature but must be invented for the purpose. A rating scale is any set of numbers $\{r_1, r_2, \ldots, r_i, \ldots, r_n\}$ such that $r_{i+1} > r_i$ for all i, that is, the rating numbers increase in size. Thus a rating scale must at least have ordinal properties and under certain circumstances may have interval or even ratio properties. It is clear that the analyst has a lot of latitude in formulating such a scale. The scale could be discrete, for example,

1, 2, 3, 4, 5, 6, 7, 8, 9, 10

or continuous:

0 to 100

Every scale has three orienting quantities, the two extremes r_1 and r_n, and the midpoint, $(r_1 + r_n)/2$. The analyst must decide whether he should direct the expert to rate the objects in relation to the "best" rating, r_n, or in relation to an "average" object's rating, $(r_1 + r_n)/2$. Consider the problem of eliciting ratings of a set of magazines for their editorial suitability in carrying a certain product message. According to one approach the expert is asked to suggest the "best" magazine for carrying the ad. To this magazine is assigned the number, say, 1.00. Then all other magazines will receive ratings of less than 1.00. Presumably,

---

[24]See Chap. 10.
[25]See Chap. 11, footnote 4.

0.00 will be assigned to a magazine with absolutely no value to the advertiser. It is less clear whether the rating .50 is to mean that the magazine is of average value, although the analyst could instruct the expert to think this way.

According to the other approach, the analyst could have started the inquiry by asking the expert to cite an "average" magazine for carrying the ad. This average magazine could be assigned the number 1.00 and the other magazines rated as worse than this average magazine, $r < 1.00$, or better than this average magazine, $r > 1.00$. A natural lower limit to the rating scale is $r_1 = 0$. There is no natural upper limit and here the analyst may arbitrarily set $r_n = 2$, implying that the best magazine could at the most be twice as good as an average magazine.

In addition to deciding between orienting the expert toward the best magazine or an average magazine, the analyst should seek ways to make the numbering game seem more real to the rater. For example, the previous media example may be made more meaningful if the questions are asked in the following way:

Analyst: What would you name as an average magazine for advertising a car?

Expert: Time magazine.

Analyst: Suppose that you are charged a dollar each time a potential customer for your product sees an ad in *Time*. How much would you pay for a potential customer to see your ad in *Holiday*?

Expert: I guess about $1.20.

In this way, the expert expressed the opinion that his ad in *Holiday* would carry more impact than in *Time*: he would pay 20c more. This technique could be used to produce ratings for all the other magazines in relation to the average magazine.

To make a scale clearer to the user, analysts often attach adjectives to the numbers:

Very poor	*Poor*	*Fair*	*Good*	*Very good*
-2	-1	0	$+1$	$+2$

Or they may omit numbers altogether. The semantic differential scale is often presented, so that only two adjectival extremes are listed:

Terrible service |————————————| Excellent service

The rater notches the scale at the point at which the particular entity stands in his mind between the two extremes. Not shown would be the underlying seven-point scale that permits the notch to be translated into a numerical rating.

In addition to ratings, many decision models require weight assignments to various factors to signify their relative importance. Judgmental weights are essentially rating numbers where the emphasis is on their relative level. In asking an expert to assign weights to n objects, a useful technique is to tell the expert that he is to split a certain total number of points over a set of objects in proportion to their perceived importance. Thus a sales manager may be asked to split 100 points over three sales traits, empathy, ego drive, and gregariousness to indicate his view of their relative contribution to successful selling. The intention behind constructing a set of weights is that they would have ratio scale properties, so that an object assigned twice the numerical weight as another object would be assumed to have twice the importance. But, in fact, it is very hard to construct scales with ratio properties. Even a temperature scale lacks this property, as there is no meaning in saying that this object is *twice* as hot as that object. Essentially, a ratio scale requires a nonarbitrary zero point. At the same time, some scale construction techniques are more defensible than others and will produce better scale properties. Since scale construction is a long and difficult subject, only a reference will be given here.[26]

Combining the estimates of experts. In many decision problems, the firm finds it necessary to tap the judgment of more than one expert if only because the decision maker can only imperfectly rate the experts. There are at least three different ways to extract the collective wisdom of a group of experts. They may be put together on a committee and asked to exchange views and come up with a group estimate (group discussion method). Or they may be asked to supply their estimates individually, and then some method is used by the analyst to combine them into a single estimate (pooling of individual estimates). Or they may supply individual estimates and assumptions that are reviewed by the analyst, revised, and followed by a second round of individual estimation, a third round, and so forth (Delphi method).

The group discussion method may take the form of a cooperative group in which the questions are discussed together but answered individually or a joint group in which the questions are discussed by the group until it reaches a single collective answer.[27] Although very common, this method is viewed with some misgivings because an actual confrontation of experts is likely to create certain psychological effects that might spoil the independence of the experts' estimation processes. In particular, one might be concerned with "specious persuasion, the unwillingness to abandon publicly expressed opinion, and the bandwagon effect of majority opinion."[28]

It was to circumvent this problem, while not losing the advantage of some interaction, that the Delphi technique was developed by a research group at Rand Corporation.[29] This technique calls for each expert to occupy a separate

[26]Warren S. Torgerson, *Theory and Methods of Scaling* (New York: John Wiley & Sons, Inc., 1958).

[27]Kaplan et al. performed an experiment that sought to evaluate the accuracy of prediction of individuals, cooperative groups, and joint groups. The joint group attained a success of 67 percent and the cooperative group 62 percent as compared to the 52 percent mean success of the same individuals when not participating in a group prediction. See A. Kaplan, A. L. Skogstad, and M. A. Grishick, "The Prediction of Social and Technological Events," *Public Opinion Quarterly* (Spring 1950), 93–110.

[28]See Norman Dalkey and Olaf Helmer, "An Experimental Application of the Delphi Method to the Use of Experts," *Management Science* (Apr. 1963) 458–467.

[29]Ibid.

room, where he is asked to fill out forms predicting important events in the area in question. The analyst reviews these events and develops questionnaires calling for probability estimates for these events from the experts. The experts supply these estimates which are reviewed by the analyst and then fed back to the experts. Experts whose probability estimates are extreme are asked to express their reasoning in writing. The experts, still in separate rooms, are invited to reconsider and possibly revise their earlier estimates. This process of gathering new estimates and feeding them back to the experts continues; almost invariably their estimates get closer as the information and assumptions are clarified.[30]

The third method of using experts is simply to get their individual estimates and find some way to combine them intelligently into a single estimate. If the separate estimates are substantially alike, they may be simply averaged using a mean or a median. The substantial similarity of independent estimates has the effect of heightening the decision maker's confidence in the parameter estimation. When there is substantial divergence in the estimates of two or more experts, the decision maker faces a real problem. Short of asking the experts to review or discuss their differences, he has two options. The first is to use the estimate of the "favored" expert, dismissing the others from consideration. The other is to use some set of weights for combining the estimates. The question then becomes what basis should be used for determining the proper weights. There are four logical bases:

1. Assign equal weights to the estimates if there is no further indicator of the relative expertness of each expert.
2. Assign weights that are proportional to someone's subjective ranking or rating of the experts' relative competence.
3. Assign weights that are proportional to the experts' self-ratings of their competence.
4. Assign weights that are proportional to the past predictive accuracy of the various experts.

There is no one best method of determining weights and the analyst must rely on his experience in using different procedures.[31] The analyst might also test how sensitive the decision is to different ways of pooling the estimates; often the decision is insensitive and the consensus problem becomes less serious.

---

[30]An elaborate extension and modification of this method is described in Harper Q. North and Donald L. Pyke, "Probes of the Technological Future," *Harvard Business Review* (May–June 1969), 68–76. The TRW Company sought judgmental data to assess the worth of various areas of technical work and new product development. More than 100 company experts prepared estimates of the likely technical development of 10–20 fields on the basis of a detailed set of environmental assumptions. These estimates were sifted, edited, and selectively redistributed for further estimates from more specific experts, and the process led to quite elaborate judgmental data on worthwhile technical areas for company concentration.

[31]For a further discussion, see Robert L. Winkler, "The Consensus of Subjective Probability Distributions," *Management Science* (Oct. 1968) B–61–75.

MAJOR STATISTICAL TOOLS FOR ANALYZING DATA

Anyone who has had the experience of amassing data relevant to a problem situation knows that much further work has to be done with the data to reveal underlying patterns of association or causality. It is not surprising that the marketing analyst, in seeking parameters for his decision models, will frequently resort to multivariate statistical techniques. Multivariate statistical analysis describes a broad set of techniques for analyzing relationships between three or more sets of variables. It includes such techniques as multiple regression analysis, discriminant analysis, and factor analysis. The following discussion describes the essential characteristics and purposes of each technique.

Multiple Regression Analysis

Every marketing problem involves a set of interacting variables, any one of which could be a major object of study. The marketing analyst is generally interested in one of these variables, such as sales, and seeks to understand the cause(s) of its variation over time and/or space. This variable, which the analyst seeks to explain, is called the dependent variable. The analyst next speculates on other variables whose variations over time or space might have contributed to the variations in the dependent variables. These variables are called the independent variables. Regression analysis is the technique for identifying significant independent variables and estimating an equation showing their individual contributions to variations in the dependent variable. When only one independent variable is involved, the statistical procedure is called simple regression; when there are two or more independent variables involved, the procedure is called multiple regression.

An example of multiple regression was described in Chapter 5, which showed the contribution of five variables in affecting the historical sales of Lydia Pinkham Vegetable Compound. Here we shall examine the major steps in carrying out any regression effort.

Choice of the dependent variable. The best formulation of the dependent variable is not always a straightforward matter. There may be several ways to state the dependent variable, and they may differ in the degree to which their variation can be explained. For example, the Rayco Manufacturing Company wanted to forecast sales in each of its dealerships and found that sales could be expressed in over a dozen ways, including total dollar receipts per family, total number of sets per automotive dollar expenditure, number of sets (excluding wholesale) per square mile, and so forth.[32] Sometimes there is a compelling theoretical or data reason to encode the dependent variable in a particular way; otherwise the analyst fits several different versions of the dependent variable until he finds the best fit.

---

[32]See "Rayco Manufacturing Company, Inc.," Case 3M38, Intercollegiate Case Clearing House, Soldiers Field, Boston, Mass.

Choice of independent variables. Here the analyst speculates, on the basis of theory, which variables are likely to offer the best explanation of the variations in the dependent variables. Any variable that the analyst fails to posit will be lost to the analysis. One clue to the possible association of an independent variable with the dependent variable is the simple correlation coefficient between the two series. The correlation coefficient (ρ) is a measure of the degree of association between two variables and ranges between -1 and $+1$. Its expected value is 0, when there is no true relation between the variables. A correlation coefficient of $+1$ indicates a perfectly positive relationship and a correlation coefficient of -1 indicates a perfectly inverse relationship. The closer the coefficient approaches $+1$ or -1, the greater the degree of correlation, although its statistical significance depends on the sample size. The formula for the correlation coefficient is

$$\rho = \sqrt{(\sigma_y^2 - \sigma_{y.x}^2)/\sigma_y^2} \tag{18-13}$$

where σ_y^2 = original variance in dependent variable
$\sigma_{y.x}^2$ = residual variance in dependent variable after the influence of independent variable(s) is removed. This is the square of the standard error of estimate, which measures the variation of the observations from the line of regression

From the formula, it can readily be seen that, when an independent variable has no influence on a dependent variable (i.e., is uncorrelated), the variance before and after the regression will be the same; therefore the numerator of the equation will be 0 and the correlation coefficient will be 0. On the other hand, if the dependent variable is completely determined by the independent variable, then the residual variance will be 0, that is, $\sigma_{y.x} = 0$, and ρ will equal 1.

Two things should be noted, however, about the use of the simple correlation coefficient to help point to good candidate independent variables. First, a low simple correlation does not mean that a variable is uninfluential; its effect on the dependent variable may be obscured by movements of other variables and its true relation to the dependent variable may be revealed in the regression equation after the other variables have been allowed for. Second, a high simple correlation does not prove that an independent variable is the cause of variations in the dependent variable. There can be many reasons why two variables have varied together that have nothing to do with causality. For example, a high correlation may be found between expenditures on alcoholic beverages and travel. This does not mean that alcohol influences people to take trips so much as that rising population and income is causing growth in both series.

When the variables are finally selected, the available data are gathered in the form of a *data matrix*, a table in which the columns feature the variables and the rows feature the observations. Table 18-2 illustrates a data matrix for paint sales in the United States and four posited independent variables: retail sales, population, households, and disposable income. Other variables could have been added such as average paint prices, industry marketing expenditures, number of paint manufacturers, and so forth. It is important, however, to have a sufficient excess of observations over variables. The fact that only nine years of observations are available severely limits the number of variables that can be significantly included in the final equation.

Table 18-2 Paint Industry Sales (in gallons), Retail Sales, Population, Households, and Disposable Income

Year	Y Paint sales	X_1 Retail sales	X_2 Population	X_3 House-holds	X_4 Disposable income
1958	278,700	201,549	174,914	51,217	307,568
1959	304,300	216,221	178,683	52,211	333,381
1960	319,400	219,831	181,430	53,268	358,101
1961	294,300	219,316	184,511	54,474	362,844
1962	306,100	235,283	187,291	55,280	379,991
1963	304,800	246,469	190,020	56,059	399,677
1964	330,100	259,568	192,770	56,876	428,951
1965	364,700	281,743	195,192	57,820	461,955
1966	421,100	301,526	197,208	58,784	501,527

In addition to specifying the independent variables, there is the further problem of determining the proper form of each variable. For example, it might be hypothesized that paint sales are more accurately influenced by the log of disposable income than by unlogged disposable income, to indicate diminishing marginal returns in the contribution of income to paint sales. Or the analyst may want to try out other transformations of basic variables, such as squares, square roots, and so forth.[33] Most computer programs for regression analysis allow the analyst to state the data in natural form and specify which transformations of the data should be tried in the fitting procedure.

Choice of a functional form. The goal of multiple regression is to estimate the parameters of an equation that maximizes the explanation of the variation in the dependent variable. The analyst must specify the likely form of the equation, one that makes theoretical sense. In practice, he will probably try to fit several forms. Once a functional form is specified, the statistical methodology consists of trying to find the parameters of a hyperplane that minimizes the sum of the squared vertical deviations of the actual observations from the hyperplane. This best-fit criterion is called "least squares." For example, in the case of the linear functional form,

$$Y' = b_0 + b_1 X_1 + b_2 X_2 + \ldots + b_n X_n \tag{18-14}$$

the problem is to find a set of b's that will minimize the sum

$$G = \sum_{i=1}^{n} (Y_i - Y_i')^2 \tag{18-15}$$

[33]See Ronald E. Frank, "Use of Transformations," *Journal of Marketing Research* (Aug. 1966) 247–253.

where Y_i = actual ith observation
$\quad\quad Y_i'$ = estimated ith observation

Equation 18-14 is substituted in Equation 18-15 and the partial derivatives

$$\frac{\partial G}{\partial b_0}, \frac{\partial G}{\partial b_1}, \ldots, \frac{\partial G}{\partial b_n}$$

of Equation 18-15 are taken and set equal to 0 as a necessary condition for minimization. This yields a set of *normal equations* that can be solved by standard algorithms such as the Doolittle method.[34]

Table 18-3   Multiple Regression Outputs: Paint Example

Variables:

$\quad Y\ $ = paint sales
$\quad X_1$ = retail sales
$\quad X_2$ = population
$\quad X_3$ = households
$\quad X_4$ = disposable income

Regression equation:
$\quad Y' = 903.12 + 2.39 X_1 - 16.11 X_2 + 34.24 X_3 - .05 X_4$

Multiple index of determination:
$\quad R^2 = .94$

F ratio:
$\quad F = 16.9 \quad$ where $F_{.01} = 15.98$

Since $F > F_{.01}$, accept the independent variables as having a statistically significant association with the dependent variable.

Table of residuals:

Year	Y-actual	Y-calculated	Difference	Percent
1	278.7	293.9	15.2	5.2
2	304.3	300.2	−4.1	−1.4
3	319.4	299.3	−20.1	−6.7
4	294.3	289.5	−4.8	−1.7
5	306.1	308.8	2.7	.9
6	304.8	316.7	11.9	3.7
7	330.1	329.5	−0.6	−.2
8	364.7	367.9	3.2	.9
9	421.1	417.8	−3.3	−.8
			Average percent forecasting error	2.4

Examining the statistical results. The mathematical computations in multiple regression yield a number of measures of interest, several of which are shown for the paint sales example in Table 18-3. The regression equation itself shows

[34]See Paul G. Hoel, *Introduction to Mathematical Statistics*, 2d ed. (New York: John Wiley & Sons, Inc., 1954), pp. 129ff.

paint sales as positively related to retail sales and households, and negatively related to population and disposable income. (The implausibility of the negative signs is due to multicollinearity, one of the pitfalls in multiple regression: see p. 601). The coefficients indicate the effect on the dependent variable of a unit increase in any of the independent variables. They should not be interpreted to signify the relative importance of each variable because (1) their units are related to the units in which the data on the independent variables are cast, and (2) their relative variability varies. A measure of the relative effect of each independent variable is found by transforming the regression coefficients into equivalent beta coefficients that are free of units. A beta coefficient shows the standard deviation change that would occur in the dependent variable as a result of a 1 standard deviation change in an independent variable. For example, the beta coefficient for households

$$\beta_{13} = b_{13} \frac{s_3}{s_1} = 34.24 \frac{2.56}{43.51} = 2.01 \tag{18-16}$$

where b_{13} is the regression coefficient, showing the effect of variable 3 on variable 1, and the s's are the respective standard deviations of variables 3 and 1. The result indicates that an increase of 1 standard deviation in households was accompanied with an increase of 2.01 standard deviations in paint sales. Beta coefficients can be found for the other variables in the same manner.

The second output in Table 18-3 shows the multiple index of determination, $R^2 = .94$. This says that the variation in the independent variables helped account for 94 percent of the variation in the dependent variable. It is calculated in a similar fashion to Equation 18-13 and is essentially a measure of the variance reduction produced by the functional relationship between the independent variables and the dependent variable.

The third output is the F ratio, here equal to 16.9. It is used to test the hypothesis that the estimated functional relationship might be due to chance, that is, might amount to an artifact of the random variation in the data. The theory of testing this hypothesis involves separating the variation due to regression from the residual variation and seeing whether the mean square of the latter is significantly larger than the mean square of the former. This ratio behaves under chance conditions according to the F distribution, values of which can be obtained from a standard table when the appropriate degrees of freedom for the numerator and denominator are determined. The 1 percent rejection level for the null hypothesis in our example is $F_{.01} = 15.98$; therefore the null hypothesis can be rejected. Thus it appears that the regression coefficients are significantly different from those that would exist if there were no association between the dependent and the independent variables.

The last output is a table showing the actual sales data, the calculated sales data, and the difference between the two series in absolute and percentage terms. Since R^2 is high, it is not surprising that the calculated values are close to the actual values. The maximum percentage forecasting error is in the order of 6.7 percent, with the average percentage error in the order of 2.4

percent. Thus it would appear that the four variables go a long way in accounting for variations in paint sales.

Before accepting the equation uncritically, however, several questions should be considered. With the advent of high speed computers, multiple regression is becoming an increasingly popular technique in marketing, and many marketing researchers unfortunately do not know enough about the technical aspects of the technique to interpret the results cautiously. There are five major points to check before using this equation.

1. *Too few observations.* The predictive reliability of an equation depends on an excess of observations over variables. If the analyst can use only nine years of past data, he should not attempt to fit more than two or three independent variables. If he can find twenty past observations, he should not try to fit more than four to six variables. The problem typically is that many product sales series are short; therefore the analyst cannot use more than a few independent variables.

2. *Multicollinearity.* This is a technical term to describe a condition in which some of the independent variables are not independent of each other. For example, population and households both show a strong historical upward trend and hence are highly intercorrelated. If two independent variables move more or less in the same way, it is hard to appraise their separate influence on sales as opposed to their joint influence, and their respective coefficients cannot be very meaningful. When multicollinearity is detected and strong, one of the variables should be dropped. Alternatively, it may be possible to use both variables expressed in the form of first differences (yearly changes, rather than yearly levels), if it is found that these are less correlated.

3. *Autocorrelation of residuals.* This technical term refers to a condition in which the forecasting errors (or residuals) resulting from using the equation are not randomly distributed. In the example, the residuals almost show a cyclical effect, and it would be necessary to apply a Durbin-Watson test or some other test to see whether the residuals are randomly distributed.

4. *Two-way causation.* A single demand equation implies a one-way direction of influence from the independent variables on the right to sales on the left. This is plausible in the case of paint sales but may not be true of many other equations used in marketing. For example, advertising influences sales and sales often influence the advertising budget. The presence of two-way causation unfortunately means a single demand equation is not a good model; in fact, it can be shown mathematically that the coefficients estimated for the effects of advertising or price on sales are biased and unreliable. In such cases a system of two or more equations should frame the demand analysis.[35]

5. *Forecasting relevance.* In the case of all statistical backcasting methods, the question must always be raised whether the equation is likely to apply to future conditions. Changes in environmental conditions and/or marketing

[35]A good account of simultaneous equation model building and estimation is found in Stefan Valavanis, *Econometrics* (New York: McGraw-Hill, Inc., 1959).

policies in the industry may create a new set of relationships. If management believes conditions have changed, it must resort to other means of appraising the influence of various variables on sales, including experimental methods and expert query methods.

Finally, multiple regression analysis can be a worthwhile pursuit, whether or not it results in a highly reliable forecasting equation. It should increase company knowledge of demand factors. Very often, the technique helps uncover relationships that cannot be found or measured in any other way. It stimulates the attempt to quantify demand factors and build better theories of demand in the industry. When the equation does forecast well, the analyst has an estimate of its probable error. He is also free to spend his time considering factors that in the next period may disturb the expected relationships.

On the other hand, the major danger is that the equation, if it has worked well in the past, may displace the exercise of independent judgment. New factors constantly come into play and must be assessed. The independent variables are usually stated in a gross form. For example, the disposable personal income variable reflects the level of income and not its distribution; yet the trend in income distribution may be quite important. Finally, sometimes it is as hard to forecast the independent variables as to forecast directly the dependent variable. This and other considerations mean that regression analysis like any other technique must be used intelligently and cautiously by management.[36]

Discriminant Analysis

There are many situations in marketing in which the dependent variable is classificatory rather than numerical. Consider the following situations:

An automobile company wants to explain brand preferences for Chevrolet versus Ford.

A detergent company wants to determine what consumer traits are associated with heavy, medium and light usage of its brand.

A retailing chain wants to be able to discriminate between potentially successful and unsuccessful store sites.

A credit company wants to distinguish between persons of high and low credit risk.

In all these cases, two or more groups are visualized to which an entity (person or object) might belong. The challenge is to find discriminating variables that could be combined in a predictive equation and help produce better than chance assignment of the entities to the groups. The solution to this problem is known as discriminant analysis.

Let us consider the case of finding traits that would help predict whether a

[36]For further reading on the theory and practical use of multiple regression analysis, see Norman Draper and Harry Smith, *Applied Regression Analysis* (New York: John Wiley & Sons, Inc., 1967).

person would buy a Ford or a Chevrolet.[37] Consider as an initial hypothesis that Ford buyers have lower incomes than Chevrolet buyers. This hypothesis can be tested by gathering a random sample of Ford (F) and Chevrolet (C) buyers and indicating their incomes along an income scale:

$5000	$10,000	$15,000	$20,000

F F F F F F F F F F C C C C C C C C C C

In this case, the hypothesis is born out because all of the Ford buyers are on the low side of the income scale and the Chevrolet buyers are on the high side. Of course, this was a hypothetical finding. It is also possible that the result might look like this:

$5000	$10,000	$15,000	$20,000

C F C F C F C F C F C F C F C F C F C F

Here there is no apparent relationship between income and brand choice and we would reject the hypothesis that income was a discriminating variable. Or we might have found the following result:

$5000	$10,000	$15,000	$20,000

F F F C F C C F C F F C C C C F C C C

In this case, there seems to be some relationship between income and brand choice, although income is far from a perfect discriminator. If the analyst used income to predict a car buyer's brand choice, he would be right more than 50 percent of the time but still far from completely right.

This suggests the possibility that some additional variable might improve the predictability of brand choice. Perhaps Ford owners have higher scores than Chevrolet owners on the personality trait called dominance. The analyst can plot his data on a two-dimensional diagram for a sample of car owners as in Figure 18-6. The scatter shows some tendency for Ford owners to be more dominant and also to have lower incomes. This leads us to wonder whether we can find *some linear combination of characteristics properly weighted that would be efficient in creating a score for each car owner,* where high scores would indicate, say, Ford owners and low scores Chevrolet owners, That is, an equation could be fitted of the form:

$$Y = b_1 X_1 + b_2 X_2 + \ldots + b_n X_n \tag{18-17}$$

where the X's represent the characteristics being tested for their discriminatory power, the b's represent the discriminant coefficients, and Y represents a resulting score for each person such that, if the score exceeded a certain boundary score, Y^*, the person would be classified in one group; otherwise he would be classified in the other group.

[37]For an excellent study, see Franklin B. Evans, "Psychological and Objective Factors in the Prediction of Brand Choice; Ford versus Chevrolet," *Journal of Business* (Oct. 1959) 340–369.

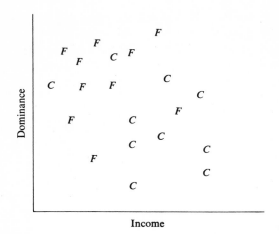

Income

Figure 18-6 Scatter of Car Owners' Incomes and Dominance Scores

The problem amounts to choosing the b's and Y^* in such a way as to maximize the probability of correct classification. Note that any choice of b's will create a number for each car owner and thus allow him to be classified. It is desirable that the b's be so estimated that the average score for Ford owners be as far away as possible from the average score for Chevrolet owners. Discriminant analysis amounts to a statistical procedure for choosing the b's in such a way that they maximize $\overline{Y}_F - \overline{Y}_C$, where these represent the respective mean scores of Ford and Chevrolet owners. But this criterion has to be modified because it turns out that, as $\overline{Y}_F - \overline{Y}_C$ increases, so does the dispersion of the respective scores increase. R. A. Fisher suggested that the statistical procedure be set up to maximize the following expression:

$$G = \frac{(\overline{Y}_F - \overline{Y}_C)^2}{\sum(y_{F_j} - \overline{Y}_F)^2 + \sum(y_{C_j} - \overline{Y}_C)^2} \qquad \text{where } j = 1, 2, \ldots, n \text{ persons} \quad (18\text{-}18)$$

That is, the technique estimates b's that maximize the ratio of the squared difference between the class means to the variances within the groups. This becomes a problem of finding the partial derivatives $\partial G / \partial b_i$, for all i, and setting them equal to 0. This results in a set of normal equations that can be solved for the b's.[38]

This technique was applied by Pessemier and Tigert to see if characteristics could be found to discriminate between owners and nonowners of gasoline credit cards. They tested twenty-four independent variables, and eight showed predictive ability. The equation is

$$Y = -4.63X_1 + .84X_2 - 6.12X_3 - 2.81X_4 - 5.02X_5 + 5.61X_6 - 2.60X_7 - 3.85X_8$$

[38]See Paul Hoel, *Introduction to Mathematical Statistics*, 1962 ed., pp. 179–184.

where X_1 = housewife's age

X_2 = housewife's education

X_3 = husband's occupation

X_4 = husband's education

X_5 = total family income

X_6 = outgoing, sociable, humorous score

X_7 = weight watcher, dieter score

X_8 = nonparticipating sports enthusiast

with a mean score for nonowners of $\overline{Y}_N = -8.10$ and owners $\overline{Y}_0 = -10.49$, and a boundary value, $Y^* = -9.29$.[39] Thus gasoline credit card owners appear to be older (if women), of a higher socioeconomic group, less outgoing, more diet- and weight-conscious, and more enthusiastic about sports. The analyst should go behind these empirical findings and find a theoretical explanation for them if they are to be a convincing basis for segmentation and market planning. The high predictive ability of the equation itself is revealed in the following "confusion matrix":

$$
\begin{array}{cc}
 & \text{Predicted} \\
\end{array}
$$

		I	II	
	I	43	7	50
Actual				
	II	8	42	50

where I = nonowners

II = owners

The number of correct classification is 85 out of 100, or 85 percent. That is, the discriminant equation led to correct classification of 85 percent of the persons in the sample, whereas the expected rate of correct classification on a chance basis is 50 percent. A significance test was performed and showed that this rate of correct classification was significant at the 1 percent level.

Pessemier and Tigert reported that three other applications they made of discriminant analysis (to heavy vs. light buyers of Crest, Duncan Hines versus Betty Crocker cake mix buyers, subscribers versus nonsubscribers of cable TV) did not yield significant results. In general the technique is worth trying but, like regression analysis, it must be carefully used and accompanied with modest expectations.

Factor Analysis

One of the problems faced in many regression studies and discriminant analysis studies is multicollinearity, that is, high intercorrelation of the independent variables. The idea in multiple regression is to use truly independent variables, independent in the sense that they influence, but are not influenced by, the dependent variable, and in the sense that each independent variable is independent of the others. The simple correlation coefficients for all pairs of variables will reveal which variables are highly intercorrelated and the analyst has the option of dropping one from each pair. Another approach is to factor-analyze

---

[39]Edgar A. Pessemier and Douglas J. Tigert, "Personality, Activity, and Attitude Predictors of Consumer Behavior," *Proceedings of the American Marketing Association* (Chicago: American Marketing Association, June 1966), pp. 332–347.

the set of intercorrelated variables, in order to derive a smaller set of factors that are truly independent of each other. More formally, factor analysis is a statistical procedure for trying to discover a few basic factors that may underlie and explain the intercorrelations among a larger number of variables. The technique assumes that the intercorrelations occur because a few basic factors are shared in common by the different variables in different degrees.

Factor analysis was originally developed in connection with efforts to identify the major factors making up human intelligence. Educational researchers did not believe that every test in an educational battery measured a different facet of intelligence. In fact, test scores for certain pairs of tests were highly inter-correlated, indicating that a more basic mental ability underlays the performance. Factor analysis was developed to explain the intercorrelations in the test results in terms of a few basic intelligence factors, subsequently identified as verbal ability, quantitative ability, and spatial ability. Since this time, factor analysis has been applied to many other problems. In the marketing area, it has been applied to determining the basic factors underlying attitudes toward air travel[40] and alcoholic beverages,[41] the constituents of corporate and product images,[42] the clustering of media program types,[43] the reduction in the number of independent variables for regression, and so forth.

The basic factor analysis model can be briefly described here. Assume that a dog owner is asked to rate fifty statements of attitudes toward dogs on a 1–4 scale of agree-disagree. Obviously, there are not fifty different attitudes one can hold toward dogs. Many of the statements must be rephrasings of the same attitudes. A few basic attitudes held by the person will determine the majority of his specific answers.

Call these basic attitudes, or factors, $\{F_k\}$, where $k = 1, \ldots, m$. Assume person i is asked to state his attitude toward j items, where $j = 1, \ldots, n$. Then person i's attitude toward item j, or Y_{ij}, can be assumed to be (in the simple case) a linear combination of the weights and factors making up that item. Thus person 1's rating of item j is given by

$$Y_{1j} = a_{1j}F_{11} + a_{2j}F_{12} + \ldots + a_{mj}F_{1m} + d_1U_{11} \tag{18-19}$$

$Y_{1j} = $ person 1's attitude toward item j

$a_{1j} = $ effect of factor 1 on item j (called a loading)

$F_{11} = $ person 1's score on basic factor 1, and so forth

$d_1U_{11} = $ residual error

The number of hypothesized factors is never more than the number of test items,

[40]William H. Reynolds and George T. Wofford, "A Factor Analysis of Air Traveler Attitudes," *Proceedings of the American Marketing Association* (Chicago: American Marketing Association, June 1966), 640–650.

[41]Jean Stoetzel, "A Factor Analysis of the Liquor Preferences of French Consumers," *Journal of Advertising Research* (Dec. 1960), 7–11.

[42]William Stephenson, "Public Images of Public Utilities," *Journal of Advertising Research* (Dec. 1963), 34–39.

[43]Arthur D. Kirsch and Seymour Banks, "Program Types Defined by Factor Analysis," *Journal of Advertising Research* (Sept. 1962), 29–32.

that is, $m \leqslant n$ and indeed is much less if there is to be validity to the view that a few basic factors underlie all the test items. Furthermore, it is assumed that the basic factors are orthogonal, that is, independent of each other. The interesting aspect of this technique is that the F's are never really measured, only the a's, or factor loadings. The statistical problem is to estimate the a's that satisfy certain desired properties. Since factor analysis is quite complicated and with many variations,[44] we shall confine our discussion to an example showing the basic inputs and outputs of factor analysis and the conclusions that can be drawn.[45]

Suppose ten persons are asked to rate how much they like each of five meat products—beef, fish, lamb, pork, and chicken—on a scale from 1 to 10, 10 indicating the highest preference. Results are shown in a data matrix in Table 18-4.

Table 18-4   Data Matrix of Preference Ratings

	Meats				
Respondents	1 *Beef*	2 *Fish*	3 *Lamb*	4 *Pork*	5 *Chicken*
1	8	3	4	7	6
2	7	3	1	5	8
3	7	2	3	5	3
4	4	2	4	5	5
5	10	1	5	6	3
6	6	5	6	5	7
7	7	4	1	4	4
8	6	3	2	8	4
9	9	4	2	4	5
10	8	1	3	6	5

Source: Heim and Gatty, *The Application of Factor Analysis to Marketing Research*, p. 9.

Let us assume that the respondents were not asked to state the factors that underlie their preferences, such as taste, cost, and so forth. It will be the analyst's task to infer these factors. The place to start is to examine the correlations in the ratings of pairs of meat products. A high positive correlation in the ratings of fish and chicken, for example, could suggest something about the nature of the underlying factor. Table 18-5 features the matrix of simple correlations between all product ratings; this reveals some medium-sized, positive and negative correlations.

One could trace through these intercorrelations and try to draw some inferences about the basic factors at work. Factor analysis is more direct, however, and is a method that will maximize the explanation of the correlations found

---

[44]An excellent book on factor analysis is Harry H. Harman, *Modern Factor Analysis*, revised ed. (Chicago: University of Chicago Press, 1967).

[45]This example is adopted with permission from Ronald Heim and Ronald Gatty, *The Application of Factor Analysis to Marketing Research* (New Brunswick, N.J.: Rutgers, Department of Agricultural Economics, Technical A.E.S., Dec. 1961).

between pairs of variables. Skipping the statistical details, the output of the factor analysis is the table of factor loadings shown in Table 18-6. The rows repeat the five meat products and the columns show factor loadings for two factors. The factor loadings resemble correlation coefficients. For example, a rough statement about the numbers in the first column is that the preference for beef is negatively related to the extent of .315 to factor I, the preference for fish is positively related to the extent of .707 to factor I, and so forth. However, the output does not tell us what factor I is—we can only make an educated guess.

Table 18-5   Correlation Matrix

		1 *Beef*	2 *Fish*	3 *Lamb*	4 *Pork*	5 *Chicken*
Beef	1	—	−0.23	−0.01	0.00	−0.24
Fish	2	—	—	−0.09	−0.33	0.46
Lamb	3	—	—	—	0.18	0.00
Pork	4	—	—	—	—	−0.11
Chicken	5	—	—	—	—	—

Source: Heim and Gatty, *The Application of Factor Analysis to Marketing Research*, p. 14.

Table 18-6   Factor Loadings Matrix

	Factors	
	I	II
1. Beef	−0.315	−0.292
2. Fish	0.707	0.100
3. Lamb	−0.198	0.316
4. Pork	−0.428	0.336
5. Poultry	0.572	0.356

Source: Heim and Gatty, *The Application of Factor Analysis to Marketing Research*, p. 24.

The major clue we have to the nature of factor I are the factor loadings. By rearranging the factor loadings from high positive to high negative, the order of the meat products is

fish, poultry, lamb, beef, pork

The analyst now speculates on what factor might explain this order and particularly the extremes. An obvious factor is that the products seem to be ordered from the one with the lowest fat content (fish) to the one with the highest fat content (pork). In the absence of other equally convincing hypotheses, the analyst might name the first factor "low fat content" and assume that this plays a strong underlying role in explaining variations in individual preferences for meats. To hypothesize the nature of the second factor, the products are again rearranged in order from high positive to high negative factor loadings:

poultry, pork, lamb, fish, beef

A hypothesis that could explain this order is cost, the products going from low to high cost. Thus without asking the respondents to explain what lay behind their preference ratings for different meat products, we inferred that two important factors might be fat content and cost.

Some other useful conclusions can be drawn from the factor loadings matrix by preparing a table showing the squares of the factor loadings. This is done in Table 18-7. At the bottom of each factor column is an average of the squares in the column; this average represents the percent of preference variation for the five meat products that is accounted for in the first factor. Considering both averages, we should say that fat content explains 23 percent of the variability in preferences for meat products, while cost accounts for another 9 percent. It should be added here that factor analysis can yield more factors than are shown, in fact up to the number of variables being analyzed. However, each additional factor that is extracted explains less of the variance and in many factor analysis procedures, the extraction process stops after a certain specified level of variance reduction is reached.

Table 18-7 Squares of Factor Loadings and Communalities

	I	II	Communalities
1. Beef	.099	.085	0.184
2. Fish	.500	.010	0.510
3. Lamb	.039	.099	0.138
4. Pork	.183	.113	0.296
5. Poultry	.327	.127	0.454
Average percentage of variation explained by factor	.230	.087	0.317

Source: Heim and Gatty, *The Application of Factor Analysis to Marketing Research,* p. 24.

Table 18-7 also contains an additional column called communalities. A communality is a measure of the amount of a variable's variance that is explained by the extracted factors. Thus the two extracted factors in the example account for 18 percent of the variability in the preference for beef. This is a low order of communality and means several additional factors are at work in the preference for beef. On the other hand, the same two factors account for 51 percent of the variance in the preference for fish. The higher a variable's communality, the more it is explained by the common factors, rather than any unique factor. The total communality shows how much of the variability in preference among all the meat products is accounted for by the two extracted factors, here .32.

The mathematics of deriving factor loadings is based on the notion that they will reproduce approximately the observed correlation coefficients, according to the formula:

$$\rho_{12} = a_{11}a_{21} + a_{12}a_{22} \tag{18-20}$$

where ρ_{12} = estimated correlation coefficient between variables 1 and 2

$\quad a_{11}$ = factor loading of variable 1 on factor 1, and so forth

To check this, we might try to reproduce the correlation coefficient between beef and fish:

$$\rho_{BF} = (-.315)(.707) + (-.292)(.100) \cong -.25$$

This checks well against the actual $\rho_{BF} = -.23$ in Table 18-5. The other correlation coefficients are similarly reproduced.

Factor analysis is essentially an exploratory technique for generating hypotheses about the nature of basic factors, rather than proving them. There are many different statistical approaches and rotation schemes[46] open to the factor analyst and it is easy to be arbitrary. Therefore, it is important that the work be performed and interpreted by persons familiar with the theory and experienced in its application.

SUMMARY

Scientific progress in marketing requires the development of better models of analysis and better data. Although models have value even in the absence of complete data, their full potential is best realized when the necessary data are available. However, since information is not a free good, every company must carefully think through the problem of rationalizing its methods of gathering and analyzing information. A large company may want to work toward the development of a marketing information and analysis center (MIAC), which performs a considerable range of functions for the executive users, including scanning, search, validation, abstraction, indexing, dissemination, storage, and analysis. These information services would help the executive manage the problem of information overload and assist him in the analysis of data. The idea of MIAC synthesizes the ideas of marketing research, marketing intelligence, and internal management information accounting.

The problem of gathering specific data for a problem can be handled in several ways. The best starting point usually is an examination of secondary sources. Further data can be gathered through observation, experimentation, surveys and expert query methods. Because the subject of expert query methods is the least developed in the literature, this chapter paid special attention to techniques of obtaining point estimates, sales response functions, probability distributions, and ratings and weights needed in marketing decision models.

Gathered data usually does not speak for itself but must be analyzed to find meaningful patterns of marketing causation. Multivariate statistical techniques provide a large answer to this need and are being used increasingly by marketing analysts. Multiple regression is a statistical technique for estimating the influence of a set of independent variables on an important dependent variable. Dis-

---

[46]The factor loadings are read as projections against orthogonal axes. These axes can be rotated according to different schemes to give a better picture of the underlying factors.

criminant analysis is a technique for determining predictive variables that are associated with an entity's likely membership in different groups. Factor analysis is a technique for reducing a set of intercorrelated variables into a smaller set of highly independent factors. These and other multivariate techniques, when carefully used, can supply the estimates and functions needed to convert general marketing decision models into immediately useful tools for solving specific marketing problems.

Questions and Problems

1. There has been a recent trend toward the centralization of information activities in large companies. What developments have led to this centralization? What are some of the advantages and disadvantages of a centralized information system.

2. One of the telephone companies in the Bell chain is considering a rate reduction. The company noticed that the percentage of homes with 1 or more extension phones was approaching a stable level of around 30 percent. There was some evidence that many families whose dwelling units were large resisted 2 phones because the 75¢ monthly charge seemed too high to them. The company was wondering how many additional extension phones would be ordered if the charge were reduced to 50¢.
   Discuss 4 ways in which the company can obtain this information.

3. An executive is asked, "What is the most likely level of sales for the new product in the coming period?" He answers 105,000 units. Next, he is asked, "What is your estimate of sales such that there is a 95 percent chance that you will do better?" He answers 80,000 units. Finally, he is asked, "What is your estimate of sales such that there is a 95 percent probability that you will not do this well?" He answers 120,000 units.
   (a) Determine the executive's implicit probability distribution, assuming normality.
   (b) Could it be argued that in this situation judgmental data might be more desirable than purely objective data?

4. A sales manager wishes to know how the probability of converting each sales prospect in a certain territory varies with the number of prospecting calls made by the salesman on the prospect. He feels that this relationship can best be approximated by the following expression:

$$P(n) = P_L + (P_U - P_L)(1 - e^{-an})$$

   where $P(n)$ is the probability of converting the prospect in n calls
      P_L is the minimum probability of conversion
      P_U is the maximum probability of conversion
   What questions would you ask the salesman in order to determine the parameters of this function for each individual prospect?

5. Prove that the formula for the mean of the beta distribution (Equation 18–5) assumes the mean to be 1/3 of the way between the mode, S_M, and the average of the extremes.

6. A model is built to explain the historical course of sales for the ABC Company. The model generates a simulated time series that does not match perfectly with

the actual time series but moves along with it in a rough way. The model builder wishes to develop a measure for the goodness of fit of the simulated to the actual data. He decides to fit a least squares linear regression line through the scatter of points (X_1, X_2) where X_1 = actual sales, X_2 = predicted sales. If the simulated and actual data showed a perfect fit, what would be the expected value of the intercept and slope of the regression equation?

7. The XYZ Company is a manufacturer of industrial solvents and relies mainly on personal selling to move its products. The vice-president of marketing has tried to determine whether any relationship exists between the number of sales calls per month and the resulting levels of sales. He chose 7 salesmen who were selling to comparable customers and recorded the following data:

Salesman	Monthly no. of calls	Monthly sales	Salesman ability rating
1	2	27.0	1.5
2	4	26.0	1.0
3	3	11.0	.5
4	3	44.0	2.0
5	4	20.8	.8
6	2	10.8	.6
7	3	13.2	.6

The last column expresses the fact that the salesmen differed in ability, with 1.0 representing an average salesman and the higher numbers representing more ability. Does it appear that there is any positive relationship between monthly sales and number of calls when salesmen's abilities are omitted? When they are included?

8. An automobile manufacturer is attempting to determine which traits are associated with successful (S), average (A), and unsuccessful (U) franchised dealers. It is hypothesized that the greater the population density, P, and the higher the disposable family income, $\overline{Y}$, in the dealer's sales area the more likely he is to be successful. A random sample of dealers is analyzed and the results plotted. In each of the following cases determine by inspection whether the results support the hypothesis.

(a)

(c)

(b)

(d)

9. A marketing researcher wanted to test how well a discriminant function would help him predict which of five FM stations (A, B, C, D, E) a person would listen to. His results are shown below:

Actual Audience	Predicted Audience Membership					Total Audience Size
	A	B	C	D	E	
A	43	13	8	21	14	99
B	16	15	15	13	13	72
C	3	5	14	5	4	31
D	2	3	5	9	4	23
E	2	1	0	4	7	14
						239

(a) Which station's audience did the discriminant function predict best?
(b) What percentage of correct predictions was made through the discriminant function?
(c) What percentage of correct predictions overall could have been expected by chance if each station had an equal size audience?

10. A large sample of people were asked to rate how much they liked each of 5 beverages—milk, coffee, tea, fruit juice, and soda pop. Through factor analysis the following table of factor loadings was obtained. What might each of the 3 factors be?

	Factors		
	I	II	III
Milk	.504	−.213	−.217
Coffee	−.209	.373	−.328
Tea	−.137	.682	.307
Fruit juice	.475	−.107	.110
Soda pop	−.368	−.645	.534

11. A marketing researcher collected information on each of the following variables for each state in the nation: number of people on relief, income per capita, population between 20–50, percentage of vacant land in urban areas.

He wanted to use these variables to explain state-to-state variations in the demand for housing. Suspecting that the set of variables was somewhat redundant, he submitted them to factor analysis and the following factor loading matrix emerged:

	Factors	
Variable	I	II
Number of people on relief	−.2	−.6
Income per capita	.2	.8
Population between 20–50	.9	−.1
Percentage of vacant land in urban areas	−.7	.0

(a) What names would you give to the two factors?

(b) How much of the variance in "income per capita" is associated with the first 2 extracted factors?

CHAPTER 19
Planning and Control Processes in the Marketing Organization

Up to now, we have dealt with the model building and information requirements for developing useful descriptions of marketing processes. We have defined the procedures that marketing executives should use in principle to set the marketing budget and allocate it over territories, products, marketing instruments, customers, and time periods in the face of carryover effects, competitive strategies, interactions with other business functions, multiple goals, and uncertainty. Combining all of these conditions in one optimizing statement of the problem is extremely hard if not impossible. Given the difficulties of modeling and measuring these processes, it is not surprising that marketing managers in practice deal with the complexity of the problem in a number of ways. They develop their own rules of thumb for allocating the marketing budget over products, territories, and so forth, and cope with their miscalculations as well as unanticipated changes in the marketplace through monitoring the results and modifying their program as circumstances warrant.

In practice, complex decision problems are rarely resolved through formal models for optimization. Management generally proceeds by breaking down complicated problems into manageable subproblems to be solved by different departments in the organization. Subproblems are simplified and handled by precedents and rules that have worked well in the past.

Even if managers were able to arrive at a sophisticated statement and resolution of their marketing problems, it is not clear that they would implement the formal solution. They may modify the formal solution in the interests of other factors and pressures. Decisions in organizations tend to be made under conditions of "bounded rationality," that is, the solution has to satisfy a number of formal and informal constraints. Managers seek to do a good job, one that satisfies the goals and expectations of others, and do not necessarily take the time and effort to search for the best possible plan.[1]

The purpose of this chapter is to consider how marketing managers carry out their planning and control responsibilities in practice and how their practice might be improved. The first section describes how annual company and marketing planning tends to be carried out in the typical firm and the roles played by the various marketing executives. The effect of interpersonal factors in the final plans is considered, along with alternative organizational models for marketing planning. The second section briefly considers the question of control processes as it relates to marketing.

THE ANNUAL MARKETING PLANNING PROCESS

Although it is convenient to describe the "firm" as making marketing decisions, these decisions actually emerge from the complex interaction of a large number of persons carrying out diverse responsibilities in the marketing organization. Marketing decision makers range from the vice-president of marketing through various functional marketing specialists (advertising manager, product managers, territory managers) down to individual salesmen. Broad marketing policies and plans are set at the top and interpreted and redefined at successively lower levels of the marketing organization. Eventually, they emerge as microactions in the marketplace such as a full-page ad in *Life* or three calls on a particular large account during the month of March. These marketing microactions were never specifically conceived at the top and yet they are the ultimate marketing actions that affect sales. As critical as this hierarchical decision process is, there is very little systematic theory and knowledge on how the marketing decisions unfold at different levels of the marketing organization.

A Hypothetical Marketing Organization

Figure 19-1 shows a hypothetical marketing organization that is charged with carrying out the firm's marketing planning, control, and information activities. At the top is the executive committee of the firm, which sets annual company goals within the broad framework of the company's long run objectives. Annual company goals include the setting of the period's target rate of return and the target sales level. The executive committee approves broad plans for the

---

[1] For a discussion of the concept of "bounded rationality," see James G. March and Herbert A. Simon, *Organizations* (New York: John Wiley & Sons, Inc., 1958), pp. 169–171. Also, the goal of "satisficing," or finding a course of action that is "good enough," has been discussed in Herbert A. Simon, *Models of Man* (New York: John Wiley & Sons, Inc., 1957), pp. 204–205.

achievement of annual goals. The goals and plans involve a balancing of production, financial, and marketing considerations and resources.

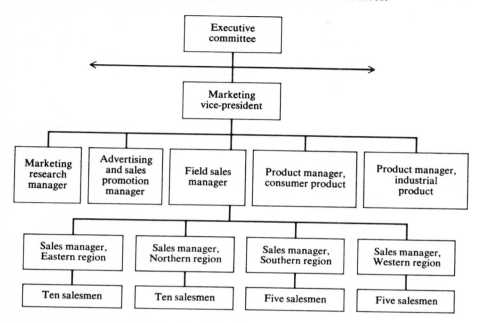

Figure 19-1 Marketing Organization of a Hypothetical Firm

The vice-president of marketing is a member of the executive committee and in this capacity influences the setting of annual company goals and plans. At the same time, he accepts the commission of the executive committee to achieve the target level of sales subject to a designated budget. He typically has the discretion of allocating the marketing budget among the various marketing activities of the firm. He is also responsible for designing marketing strategy and tactics and changing them as feedback information from the market points to the need for change.

The marketing vice-president's staff consists of a field sales manager, two product managers, an advertising manager, and a marketing research manager. The field sales manager exerts some influence on the size of the field sales budget and is responsible for deploying the budget in a way that would optimize the impact of the sales force on the number of company customers and their ordering rate. He is responsible for territorial organization, policies on sales call norms, presentation materials and messages, and many other aspects of sales force management. He works through four regional sales managers, each of whom in turn supervise several salesmen.

The four regional sales managers have the responsibility for hiring, assigning, and motivating salesmen. They must design and modernize sales territories in their region, assist in the process of developing sales forecasts, budgets and quotas, and lay plans for the effective cultivation of their region by coordinating the sales force effort with other types of marketing effort.

Salesmen in turn have the responsibility of allocating their time to existing customers and prospects to maximize the attainment of company goals. In practice, the salesmen's compensation arrangements and some aspects of the salesmen's role lead them to behave in ways that may maximize their welfare at the expense of the company.

This firm also has two product managers, one supervising an industrial product and the other a consumer product. The industrial product manager tends to concentrate on problems of pricing, production design, and customer service. The consumer product manager tends to concentrate on packaging, advertising, promotion, and merchandising. Each product line manager bids for a certain amount of resources to support his product line and is responsible for many tactical decisions.

The advertising manager's main role is to advise on promotional message, copy, media, and timing and work with the advertising agency. He may influence but he does not determine the amount of company funds spent on advertising.

The marketing research director has responsibility for developing and supervising research for the firm related to its market opportunities and marketing operations. He has a budget and some discretion over projects he will accept, as well as determining the research design he will use in obtaining information efficiently.

These men constitute a typical marketing organization of a company. They interact vertically and laterally and also with executives from other departments of the company. Out of these complex interactions emerge company marketing plans and actions.

Overview of the Annual Marketing Planning Process

We shall assume that once each year these men engage in a process of planning for the next year and making decisions on the allocation of marketing resources. Although there are many variations of the marketing planning process in practice, we shall describe a representative version that contains the major elements. An overview of the process is shown in Figure 19-2. The process starts with the top management executive committee of the company considering recent history and current outlook and setting the annual goals for profits and sales (1). The marketing vice-president as a member of the top management team has participated in setting these goals; in the next stage he takes these goals and instructs his product managers to develop tentative annual plans and budgets in the light of these goals (2). The product managers develop their plans and these move back to the marketing vice-president (3). The marketing vice-president confers with the sales manager about these various plans and the sales manager's budgetary needs for the coming year (4). The marketing vice-president then consolidates the plans and sends a master marketing plan to the executive committee (5). The executive committee considers the master marketing plan, makes modifications, and approves a final plan (6). The marketing vice-president then establishes specific budgets for the product managers and sales manager (7). The sales manager develops sales quotas for the regional sales managers (8) who develop them in turn for sales territories and salesmen (9). This, in brief, describes a fairly common planning process used by many companies.

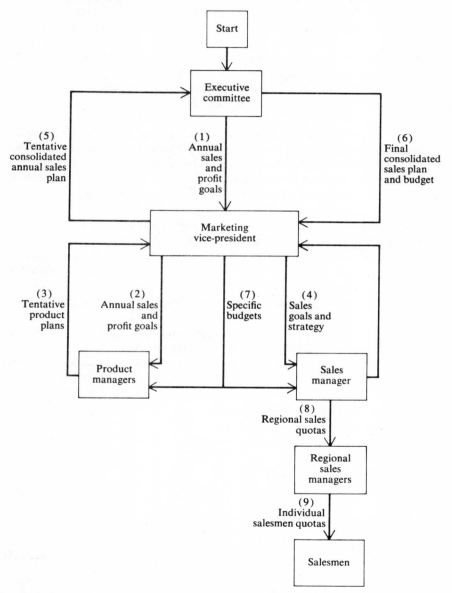

Figure 19-2   Overview of the Annual Sales and Profit-Planning Process

Decision Roles of Specific Marketing Executives in the Planning Process

Having considered the annual planning process and how it links various marketing executives, we can now look more closely at the question of how typical executives occupying specific marketing roles perform their responsibilities. Each marketing executive can be viewed as an input-output node in the system, in that certain influences impinge on him and decisions emerge from him. To understand his behavior, we must seek to answer three questions:

1. What decisions does the executive in this position typically make? (output)
2. What major factors and information does he consider? (input)
3. How are these factors and information combined and weighed by the executive to make a decision? (processor)

Executive committee. To understand the executive decision-making process, it is necessary to start with the goal setting, planning, and control practices of the top management group. Leadership of the organization is assumed to be vested in an executive committee composed of the president and the various vice-presidents of the firm. Major functions of the executive committee include:

1. Establishing the long range profit and sales objectives of the firm
2. Establishing the annual profit and sales goals
3. Reviewing and approving annual department budgets and programs
4. Reviewing each quarter the degree of attainment of annual plan goals and taking actions where needed
5. Taking interim action between quarters to meet unanticipated situations

The specific long range quantitative profit and sales objectives of the firm can be represented in vector form. (We shall ignore the long range qualitative objectives of the firm, such as to be the industry leader, etc.) Suppose that the company strives to average over the years:

An annual increase in sales of 10 percent
An annual pretax profit on sales of 20 percent
An annual pretax profit on investment of 25 percent

This can be expressed compactly as:[2]

$$G_L = (S_t/S_{t-1}, Z_t/S_t, Z_t/I_t) = (1.10, .20, .25), \qquad (19\text{-}1)$$

where G_L = long range goal vector
S_t = sales goal at time t
Z_t = profit goal at time t
I_t = investment goal at time t

---

[2]These three targets are not independent of each other. Planned sales, profit margins, and rate of return goals satisfy the relationship shown in Chap. 9, Equation 9-6.

When the executive committee comes to setting the goals in a particular year, it will deviate from G_L when opportunities in the marketplace are either significantly better or worse than usual. If an increased demand potential is visualized for the company's products, the executive committee would not be content to set this year's sales growth at only 10 percent; this would mean failing to tap the potential. Each year the executive committee will consider a host of factors in setting the goal parameters (G_A) for the year. A diagram of these influences is shown in Figure 19-3.

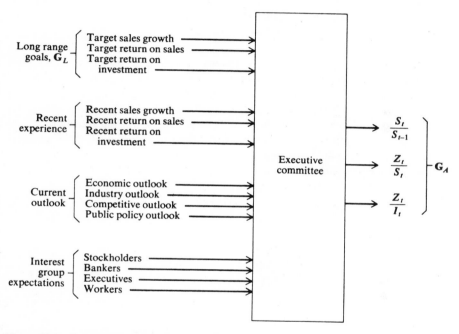

Figure 19-3   Factors Affecting the Annual Goals Set by the Executive Committee

The long range goals serve as the basic factor in orienting the annual goals. The committee is also affected by recent experience. If sales and profits have been below average for the last few years, the committee will view the challenge differently than if normal sales and profits have been achieved. Their current aspirations are also influenced by how favorable the current outlook is; in fact, this sets an upper limit to their aspirations. Finally, the need to satisfy specific interest groups that may be putting on pressure for high achievement affects the setting of the annual goals.

The job of describing how the various factors on the left are transformed into the specific outputs on the right is exceedingly complex. Each member of the executive committee weighs the factors on the left differently because of his training, personality, and position. During the committee's deliberations, subtle processes of interpersonal influence and negotiation take place. The processes of group decision making can be described to a certain extent, although there is need for considerably more theory and research. Even if a comprehensive model were available, there would remain the difficult problem of gathering all the data necessary for prediction.

After the executive committee sets G_A^-, the vice-presidents proceed to develop plans and budgets within these guidelines for their respective operations for the coming year. When these preliminary plans and budgets are ready, they are examined by the executive committee, modified in some cases, and approved. The plans include a total budget for marketing effort (B_t), a basic price (P_t), a budget for new product development (R_t), and a capital budget (I_t).

Product managers. The responsibility for developing concrete plans and budget proposals generally lies with departmental and divisional heads. In principle, the marketing vice-president prepares the plan for his operations. In practice, plans are prepared by his subordinates in consultation with him. Later he consolidates the various plans into a master marketing plan.

The actual starting point for most annual plans is at the level of the product managers. Each product manager is responsible for developing a marketing plan (V_{it}), which consists of a sales forecast, a marketing program for achieving it, and the implied budget, that is,

$$V_{it} = (S_{it}, M_{it}, B_{it}) \tag{19-2}$$

where V_{it} = marketing plan for product i in year t
S_{it} = sales forecast for product i in year t
M_{it} = marketing program for product i in year t
B_{it} = budget requested for product i in year t

The marketing program (M_{it}) can be thought of as a vector made up of levels set for price, advertising, and distribution. That is,

$$M_{it} = (P_{it}, A_{it}, D_{it}) \tag{19-3}$$

where M_{it} = marketing program for product i in year t
P_{it} = price proposed for product i in year t
A_{it} = promotion budget requested for product i in year t
D_{it} = distribution requested for product i in year t

As a result, the product manager's total requested budget can be described as

$$B_{it} = A_{it} + D_{it} + K_{it} \tag{19-4}$$

where K_{it} = administrative marketing costs for product i at time t, including marketing overhead charges, product research and development costs, and marketing research

These various decision outputs of the product managers are summarized on the right side of Figure 19-4. The left-hand side offers a classification of the multitudinous factors that affect the final planning outputs on the right-hand side. The purely rational factors are grouped first, under the term "perception of demand potential." The product manager considers the outlook for the economy and industry and then considers whether competitors are likely to undertake any special actions that may have an adverse effect on his market share. The estimate of sales he forms from these factors is then compared with the "grass roots" forecast of the sales force for his product line. The two are reconciled in some fashion. The product manager also considers possible departures from the normal marketing mix for his product and their likely impact on sales. The estimate is based on his intuitive—or researched—ideas of the response parameters of different marketing mix elements. This can be symbolized as

$$S_{it} = f(P_{it}, A_{it}, D_{it}, Y_t, C_{it}) \tag{19-5}$$

where S_{it}, P_{it}, A_{it}, and D_{it} as previously defined
Y_t = national income expectations for year t
C_{it} = expectations about competitors' marketing policies for product i in year t

In other words, the product manager's sales forecast is a function of his idea of the appropriate marketing program (P, A, D), his expectations concerning the economic outlook (Y) and competitive behavior (C), and his estimate of how sales respond to these various factors.

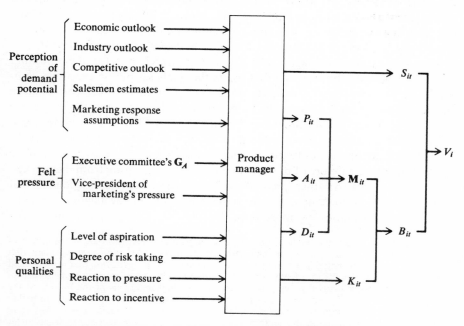

Figure 19-4 Factors Affecting the Product Manager's Annual Plan

His idea of the appropriate marketing program is a complex calculation in itself. Every possible setting of the controllable variables (P, A, D) in the sales forecasting equation has a different implication for the product's sales and costs. In the unconstrained short run case, he would choose that marketing program (P, A, D), which would maximize the product's profit return on investment (Z_t/I_t). In the constrained short run case, he searches for a marketing program that produces a level of profit, sales, and investment that will satisfy the following inequalities:

$$\frac{S_{it}}{S_{i,t-1}} \geqslant \frac{S_t}{S_{t-1}} \tag{19-6}$$

$$\frac{Z_{it}}{S_{it}} \geqslant \begin{cases} Z_{i,t-1}/S_{i,t-1} & \text{if this exceeds } Z_t/S_t \\ Z_t/S_t + k[(Z_t/S_t) - (Z_{it}/S_{it})] & \text{otherwise} \end{cases} \tag{19-7}$$

$$\frac{Z_{it}}{I_{it}} \geqslant \begin{cases} Z_{i,t-1}/I_{i,t-1} & \text{if this exceeds } Z_t/I_t \\ Z_t/I_t + k[(Z_t/S_t) - (Z_{it}/I_{it})] & \text{otherwise} \end{cases} \tag{19-8}$$

The first inequality states that the product manager will seek a marketing program that will cause his sales volume for product i to grow this year at least as much as the sales growth target rate prescribed by the executive committee. The second inequality states that the marketing program for this product must lead to a sales and cost level that leaves a profit on sales at least equal to the last period's profit on sales if this exceeds the company's goal level for all products; otherwise, the planned profit rate on sales must equal the last period's profit rate on sales, plus an improvement, where k shows the percent of the gap that must be made up. The third inequality calls for the same asymmetric attainment level as the second, this time for the profit rate on investment.

Thus the product manager is engaged in a search not for the optimum marketing program but for one that meets the goals set by the executive committee, or which at least represents some improvement over the performance of the previous year.[3] This means he has decision latitude, and this raises the question of where he will finally set his targets. This depends on nonrational factors (not necessarily irrational) that influence his judgment (Figure 19-4). One class of factors relates to the pressure to meet the goals set by the executive committee, plus a mixture of pressure and incentive emanating from the marketing vice-president. Another class of factors describes personal qualities that cause different product managers to react differently in the face of the same objective opportunities. A most important factor is the product manager's

[3]The product's long run opportunities may call for planned departures from fulfillment of current goals. The product manager may demonstrate to the marketing vice-president that he should spend substantial marketing money to develop new territories that would yield better than average profits in a few years. The marketing vice-president may agree to accept lower sales and profit goals for this year for the sake of higher returns in the future. At the same time, it should be noted that product managers who expect to advance rapidly to higher positions are likely to emphasize short run goals at the expense of long run goals. They want to produce a good showing in the short run. Usually, they are promoted and their successor inherits all the problems created by the short run emphasis.

level of aspiration, that is, how high a performance he wants to achieve. There is considerable evidence that the achievement drive varies significantly among executives. It is not clear, however, whether a high achiever will be motivated to set a modest sales forecast and then turn in an outstanding performance, or set a high sales forecast and fulfill it. This depends in part on his degree of risk taking, another personal quality that varies among executives. It is less risky to set a modest sales goal and overachieve than to set a high sales forecast and to have doubts about achieving it. The sales forecast set by the product manager is also affected by his psychological pattern of reacting to pressure or incentive. In principle, both of these should increase his sales forecast and his performance, but not all people react positively to pressure and incentive.

Any theory of sales planning by the product manager must include these factors but more studies of product managers will be needed before his responsibilities can be fully explicated.

Marketing vice-president. The preliminary plans developed by the product managers are reviewed by the marketing vice-president. He proposes modifications where they are desirable. Then he consolidates the plans and tests whether in the aggregate they satisfy the particular goals set by the executive committee. Specifically, he hopes that the following inequalities are satisfied:

$$\sum_i \frac{S_{it}}{S_{i,t-1}} \geqslant \frac{S_t}{S_{t-1}} \tag{19-9}$$

$$\sum_i \frac{Z_{it}}{S_{it}} \geqslant \frac{Z_t}{S_t} \tag{19-10}$$

$$\sum_i \frac{Z_{it}}{I_{it}} \geqslant \frac{Z_t}{I_t} \tag{19-11}$$

That is, the forecasted sales growth for the whole product line equals or exceeds the executive committee's target sales growth rate; the forecasted profit rate on sales for the whole product line equals or exceeds the executive committee's target profit rate on sales; and the forecasted profit rate on investment for the whole product line equals or exceeds the executive committee's target profit rate on investment.

If any of these inequalities are not satisfied, the marketing vice-president meets with the product managers and asks them to revise their plans. This may also require an increase in the implied marketing budget, B_t. Yet the marketing budget itself is constrained by the executive committee not to exceed some historical percentage of sales, say B/S. That is,

$$\frac{B_t}{S_t} \leqslant \frac{B}{S} \tag{19-12}$$

If the marketing vice-president wants a budget for marketing that substantially exceeds the previous year's budget, he must base his argument on this budget's generating higher sales, so that the expected marketing budget ratio to sales remains at its historical level. Sometimes, this is relaxed if marketing can make a convincing case that substantially higher spending on marketing this year will generate substantial gains in the long run.

The marketing vice-president then presents the sales forecast and accompanying budgets to the executive committee. Committee members representing production, finance, personnel, and research and development consider the sales forecast and its implications for the parts that concern them. Their data and judgments have already been presumably solicited during the sales planning process, but this allows a more formal consideration of the balance between sales budgets, production capacity, inventory levels, cash flows, capital expenditures, and other key variables. The sales plan may have to be modified in the light of these considerations. After a final plan is accepted, each vice-president knows what performance is expected and what budget he has to work with. The detailed planning now starts in the areas of capital expenditure, production scheduling, personnel hiring, and detailed marketing programming.

For the marketing department, the marketing vice-president must set sales performance targets—sales quotas—for product managers and for major sales regions, and allocate the budget in a manner to support these performances. Budgets for the product managers have already been tentatively indicated in the preliminary plan, although some adjustments may be made because of executive committee changes in the sales plan. The sales quotas and corresponding budgets for the sales regions have not yet been set, and this is a major task facing the marketing vice-president at this time. He does not arbitrarily set the regional sales quotas but works closely with the field sales manager.

The two men reach a first approximation of the desirable regional sales quotas by resorting to some simple rule, such as that a region's sales quota be proportional to the region's market potential, or share of industry sales, or share of company sales. If the new plan calls for a sales increase of 10 percent, all regions may simply be assigned the task of increasing their sales by 10 percent over last year. Usually, the results of the simple rule have to be modified because of special weaknesses in some territories and opportunities in others. Thus a good territory may be given a 15 percent targeted sales increase and an equal-volume weak territory only a 5 percent sales increase, as long as they balance out to an overall planned sales increase of 10 percent.

Field Sales Manager.   In working out the regional sales quotas and budgets with the marketing vice-president, the field sales manager injects two other considerations, bearing on the final allocations. The first is his sales manpower needs, both to replace an expected number of men who will leave the company for one reason or another, and to expand the sales force to meet the company's goals of increased sales. Hiring new salesmen will require a budget that is not likely to be matched in the first year by a commensurate increase in sales. This fact tends to constrain the number of new men hired, unless the company has been very profitable in recent years. The field sales manager's plan would also indicate the regions in which these men would be placed, and this will influence the previously mentioned setting of regional sales quotas and budgets.

The other consideration affecting regional sales quotas is regional selling expenses. There are usually marked variations among regions in the selling expense necessary to produce $1 of sales. Thus the marketing vice-president and field sales manager will want to allocate regional sales quotas so as to encourage more profitable sales. The sales quota for a region will tend to be set directly proportional to the region's market potential and inversely proportional to the region's ratio of selling expense to sales.

The field sales manager's budget will have to reflect, in addition to planned manpower needs, any expected increases in salesmen's compensation rates or expenses. These cost increases generally do not stimulate commensurate sales increases (unless they take the form of new incentives rather than offsets to cost of living increases) and to this extent increase the difficulty of meeting profit goals.

Regional sales managers.   The regional sales quotas set up by the marketing vice-president and his field sales manager must be further elaborated at a lower level by each regional sales manager into quotas for his district sales managers, who ultimately must do this for each salesman. The quotas set for the individual salesmen are based on a number of considerations, including the salesman's sales performance in the previous period, his territory's estimated potential, and a judgment of his aspiration level and reaction to pressure and incentive. Some propositions in this area are:[4]

1.   The sales quota for salesman j at time t (Q_{jt}) will generally be set above his sales in the year just ending $(S_{j,t-1})$; that is,

$$Q_{jt} > S_{j,t-1} \qquad (19\text{-}13)$$

2.   The sales quota for salesman j at time t will be higher, the greater the positive gap between the estimated sales potential of his territory S_{Pjt} and his sales in the year just ending, that is,

$$Q_{jt} \sim (S_{Pjt} - S_{j,t-1}) \qquad (19\text{-}14)$$

3.   The sales quota for salesman j at time t will be higher, the more positively he responds to pressure (E_j), that is,

$$Q_{jt} \sim E_j \qquad (19\text{-}15)$$

These three propositions can be combined in the following equation for setting a salesman's quota:

$$Q_{jt} = S_{j,t-1} + E_j(S_{Pjt} - S_{j,t-1}) \qquad (19\text{-}16)$$

Thus salesman j's quota at time t will be at least equal to his actual sales last period, plus some fraction E_j of the difference between estimated territorial sales potential and his sales last year; the more positively he reacts to pressure, the higher the fraction.

[4]See Chap. 13, pp. 407–419 for a more extended discussion.

As for control, the various sales managers watch the performance of their subordinates in relation to assigned quotas and investigate those cases of deficient performance. Depending on their diagnosis, they put more pressure on the weaker performers or budget them more funds with which to work.

Salesmen. The actual sales occurring in sales territory j at time t, (S_{Ajt}), is the result of the four factors shown at the left in Figure 19-5. The first factor is environment and includes forecastable but uncontrollable trends in the territory such as regional income growth and local competitive effort. The second factor is the corporate marketing effort in the territory to support and stimulate sales. The third factor is the ability and effort of the company's salesman. The fourth factor embraces nonforecastable and uncontrollable developments in the territory.

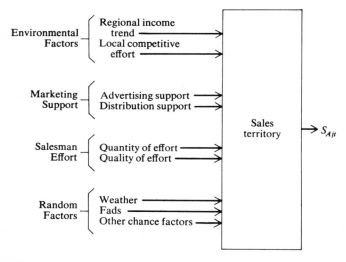

Figure 19-5 Factors Affecting the Level of Sales in a Territory

According to this interpretation, actual sales can be thought of as a random draw from a probability distribution whose mean is determined by the first three factors and whose variance is determined by the fourth factor. That is, the expected level of sales bears a determinate relationship to elements in the first three factors, while the actual level is determined by chance factors expressed by a distribution around the expected level.

Other marketing executives. The ultimate level of sales achievement is also affected by the activities of other marketing executives such as the marketing research director and the advertising manager. From one point of view, these men are not decision makers but staff advisers. They provide information and advice that is used by those responsible for the actual planning, implementing, and controlling of marketing actions. From another point of view, they are decision makers within the context of their own operations, and their decisions have an ultimate effect on sales, costs, and profits. The marketing research director decides on which research projects to carry out and influences how much is spent on each: these decisions clearly affect the quality of management forecasting and planning. The advertising manager is influential in the development of the company's advertising strategy, particularly the message, copy, and media. Not enough research has been done on the behavioral patterns of these two types of executives—what they decide, how they decide, and whom they influence.

The Effect of Interpersonal Factors on the Marketing Plan

Marketing decision makers are influenced both by normative and interpersonal factors.[5] We can imagine a marketing executive such as the field sales manager perceiving a normatively desirable solution to the problem of allocating marketing funds to each territory but modifying the solution consciously or semiconsciously in response to interpersonal factors. The left-hand side of Figure 19-6 shows a normative consideration of the problem based strictly on company goals and data on market demand and cost. The right-hand side of Figure 19-6 shows the field sales manager also subject to influence from each regional sales manager. Each regional sales manager brings a particular influence to bear on the field sales manager.

Consider regional manager i and the factors influencing him. First, he makes up his own mind as to the level of resources he would like. The budget he requests is influenced by his perception of opportunities in his region and company pressures on him. The budget request is not a straight transformation of this perception because he is also influenced by his attitude toward risk, which defines whether he will take "long shots" or only go after "sure results." The budget request is also influenced by whether he is oriented primarily toward the company's welfare or his region's welfare. The dollars he gets are effectively removed from other uses by the company, in which the marginal value might be higher. Some managers may take a more company oriented view than others.

Regional managers will vary in their effectiveness in getting the budget they want. At least three factors will influence their effectiveness: (1) there is the regional manager's persuasiveness as an individual; (2) there is his credibility, based largely on his record of fulfilling his past sales targets; and (3) there is the regional manager's status in the organization that might depend on special talents he has or support from others higher up in the organization.

The final allocation also depends upon the field sales manager's persuasibility. On the one hand, we can visualize a field sales manager who will not depart from his normative calculation of what should be spent in each territory. Regional managers will not get far with such a marketing manager, in spite of

---

[5]The following perspective on marketing executive behavior is outlined in an unpublished paper by Ronald E. Turner, *Some Organizational and Interpersonal Effects on the Allocation of Certain Resources in a Business Organization*, Northwestern University, Evanston, Ill. Mar. 1968.

their varying capacities for influencing him. On the other hand, the field sales manager might be quite persuasible. His final allocation, then, will reflect to some extent the relative persuasiveness of the individual regional managers. In general we cannot look at allocation processes in an organization as being determined by strictly rational criteria, but rather as subject to varying degrees of influence from others.

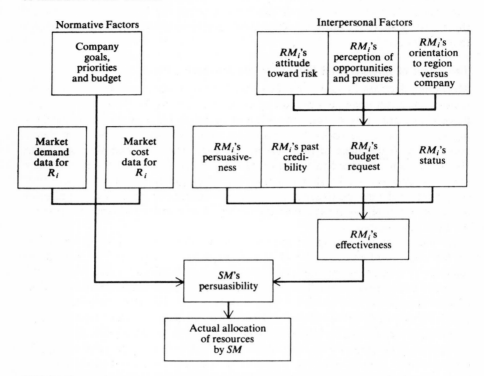

Figure 19-6   The Normative-Interpersonal Model of the Sales Allocation Process

Legend: R_i = region i
   RM_i = regional sales manager i
   SM_i = field sales manager i

Source: Adapted with modifications from Turner, *op. cit.*

Alternative Models for Annual Marketing Planning: The Centralized, Decentralized, and Semidecentralized Solutions

We have viewed the marketing planning process as involving the various echelons of management in proposing plans to top management. In this system the *local manager* (product manager, regional manager, etc.) proposes and top management disposes. The underlying implication is that top management is in the best position to know what is needed in the way of budgets by the various local managers. Let us call this a *centralized solution* to the problem of planning.

The centralized solution has certain weaknesses. Top management tends to allocate the budget to the various operations in terms of traditional percentages of various budget items to sales. It ignores differential opportunities not reflected in the current distribution of sales. It results in some operations receiving far more funds than they can use effectively and other areas receiving far less in terms of the opportunities facing them. Naturally, management at corporate headquarters does not use this solution without making judgmental modifications for exactly the reasons cited. But these modifications from normal percentage allocations tend to reflect highly subjective criteria. Furthermore, as indicated earlier, corporate decision makers are subject to influence from the more vocal, though not necessarily the more effective, local managers.

One could take the position that the centralized solution is highly inefficient in practice and the right step would be to replace it with a *decentralized solution* to the budget allocation problem. Specifically, each local manager would work out a detailed marketing plan featuring a sales forecast and a budget for its achievement. The local manager assumes responsibility for his plan and receives the budget he requests. In effect, corporate headquarters acts as a central bank, meeting the requests for "local loans" as long as the local managers' credit ratings and credibility are good. Those local managers who have demonstrated an ability to "deliver" on their promises receive the budgets they claim to need for the next period; other local managers have to make a much better case (just like poorer risks in bank credit applications) in order to secure their loans. Management at corporate headquarters sums the budget requests. If they exceed the available funds, corporate management either borrows the difference or reduces all the budget requests by some fraction.

The decentralized solution has the advantage of utilizing the knowledge-ability of the local manager about local opportunities. Furthermore, it ties up with the principle that men may work more energetically and imaginatively if they are given authority commensurate with their responsibility. The local manager is in effect treated as running a profit center and he sets the goal and is given the means to implement it. It goes without saying, however, that the decentralized solution must be accompanied by an effective system of judging and rewarding performance. The system of performance review must make provision for dealing with performance deviations, determining what proportion of the deviation was outside of the local manager's control, and relating the remainder to his performance ability.

Because both the purely centralized and purely decentralized solutions have certain disadvantages, thought should be given to the possible benefits of a mixed solution, which may be called the *semidecentralized solution*. This solution calls for corporate management to pay formal attention to the ideas of the local managers with respect to the sales response functions in their areas. Corporate management does this by asking the local managers to prepare three marketing plans for their area, one centered around the budget they received last time (adjusted upward for normal expansion), another centered around a substantially lower budget (50 percent of the normal budget), and the last one centered around a substantially higher budget (150 percent of the normal budget). Each local manager is asked to prepare independently a set of plans and forecasts for each budget level. These plans are examined at headquarters and corporate management compares the particular ideas that different local managers have of the probable sales response to additional inputs and reduced inputs of marketing expenditures. The information should be particularly helpful in identifying instances in which money could be shifted profitably from one local manager to another.

As an example, consider the case in which two local managers of sales areas each submitted three-point budget estimates that were converted into the two subjective sales response functions shown by the heavy lines in Figure 19-7.

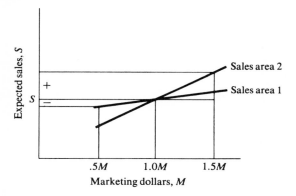

Figure 19-7   The Effect of Transfering Money between Two Sales Areas Having Different Sales Response Functions

Suppose both local managers received M dollars in the past and each achieved the same sales, S. The new information shows that local manager 2 believes he could do much more with additional marketing dollars than local manager 1. In fact, if these estimates are reliable, manager 1's budget could be reduced by 50 percent with a small resulting decline in sales and this money shifted to increase manager 2's funds by 50 percent, with a substantial increase in sales.

When the local managers begin to understand how these three-point budget estimates are used by corporate management, they will be tempted to exaggerate what they think they could achieve with higher budgets. Therefore some system of performance evaluation must be introduced. If a local manager is given a higher budget on the grounds that he could produce a more profitable level of sales, his performance at the end of the year must be compared to his forecast. His reward should be based on how close he came to predicting the actual level of sales. If his performance far exceeded his forecast, he might be considered as accountable for as much error as if his performance fell far short of his forecast. Corporate headquarters should design this system in such a way that the various local managers will have a strong incentive to think hard about their forecasts and plans and then get results.

THE MARKETING CONTROL PROCESS

Most of our discussion in this book has been on the development of optimal plans for pursuing the firm's market objectives. Planning, however, is only a part, albeit an important part, of the total process of managing a successful enterprise. A view of the total management process is presented in Figure 19-8. The total process is divided into the four subprocesses of analysis, planning, operations, and control.

The first of these, analysis, involves the management in examining the major opportunities and challenges it faces as an organization. This analysis reveals many possible futures that the firm could pursue and many possible dangers that it faces.

The second process is that of planning. Out of the examination of its opportunities, the firm adopts a set of long range and short range objectives. On the basis of these objectives, it develops a specific plan for their achievement. It also sets up specific control standards (quotas, targets) against which it will measure the subsequent performance.

The third process is that of operations; it consists of two steps: implementation and performance measurement. Implementation expresses all the concrete steps taken to carry out the plans, including advertising, sales calls, customer service, product development, and so forth. Performance measurement is then undertaken to determine the results of the implementation.

The fourth process is that of control, which is concerned with the analysis and correction of the performance. *Control is the process of taking steps to bring actual results and desired results closer together.* Control starts with the question of whether the performance is sufficiently close to the standards set in the plan. An affirmative answer means that no further analysis is necessary and operations can be carried on as usual. A negative answer, though, raises the question of whether the plan is being effectively implemented. If the implementation is not at fault, then the question is raised whether the standards set in the plan are at fault. If they appear to be sound standards for the given plan, then the next question is whether the plan itself is at fault. If the plan is sound, given the objectives, inquiry is then directed to considering the validity of the original objectives set by management. The objectives may have been appropriate, but management may now discover that the opportunity analysis was either incorrect or is now obsolete. The current situation and opportunities may require a different set of objectives and plans. If performance still continues unsatisfactory, the ultimate fault may lie in the judgment or competence of the management group responsible for the planning.

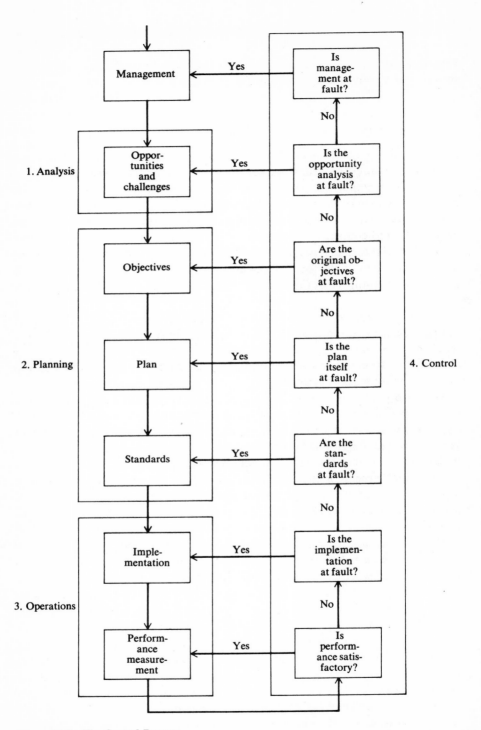

Figure 19-8 The Control Process

The Control Chart

How far this analysis should be carried and indeed whether control steps should be taken at all in the particular situation depends on how much performance deviation from the standards has occurred. When numerical standards are set it is not expected that they will be achieved perfectly. The controlling agent usually establishes a range of tolerable deviation (or tolerances) within which normal performance is expected to lie. The range should not be so broad as to excuse all degrees of performance nor so narrow as to cause investigation and/or corrective action to be applied too frequently.

The idea of normal tolerance is well conveyed in the standard quality control chart, which is increasingly being employed as a control device for marketing processes. The basic chart is illustrated in Figure 19-9. The chart is a means of observing successive levels of a particular performance indicator in relation to desired and normal levels. Suppose that a company wishes to control the advertising expense/sales ratio. Their advertising is normally set at 10 percent of sales, but may fluctuate between 8 and 12 percent because of random factors. In fact, the range 8–12 percent represents normal variation of the advertising expense/sales ratio in 99 out of 100 cases.[6] As long as the sales process is "in control," *virtually all* the future ratios are expected to be between 8 and 12 percent on the basis of chance.

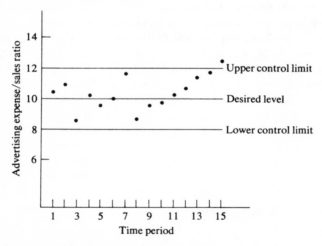

Figure 19-9   The Standard Control Chart Model

What happens when the advertising expense/sales ratio lies outside of these control limits? This happened in Figure 19-9 on the fifteenth observation of the process. One of two opposing hypotheses can explain this occurrence:

[6]The normal range used in statistical quality control is 3 standard deviations. For a lucid explanation of the theory and computations, see Chap. 6 in Edward H. Bowman and Robert B. Fetter, *Analysis for Production Management*, rev. ed. (Homewood, Ill.: Richard D. Irwin, Inc., 1961), pp. 155–194.

HYPOTHESIS A. The company still has good control over sales, and this represents one of those rare chance events. (Remember, 1 out of 100 times the ratio can exceed the control limits by chance. Furthermore, it can happen on any trial.)

HYPOTHESIS B. The company has lost control over sales as a result of some assignable cause such as a new competitor or a new distribution channel.

If hypothesis A is accepted, no investigation is made to determine whether the environment has changed. The risk in doing this is that some real change has occurred and the company will fall behind. If hypothesis B is accepted, the environment would be investigated at the risk that the investigation will uncover nothing and be a waste of time and effort.

This control model can be modified in a number of ways to make it more useful in particular circumstances. In the first place the behavior of successive observations even within the control limits should also be watched for patterns that seem difficult to explain by chance. In Figure 19-9, it should be noted that the level of the performance indicator rose steadily from period 9 onward. The probability of encountering a pattern of six successive increases in what should be a random and independent process is only one out of 64.[7] This unusual pattern should have led to an investigation sometime before the fifteenth sample.

In the second place, for some processes the controlling agent may feel that only a performance outside of one of the control limits (either the upper or the lower) will require an investigation. If the performance indicator is *market share*, for example, only a performance outside of the lower control limit may be investigated, because, it is felt, a significant slip in market share requires action, whereas a significant increase in market share is a gratuitous development. This is a difficult business, however, for a highly favorable development may point just as strongly to the occurrence of a new factor(s) in the situation, one that may repay investigation and revised programs. Some control philosophies even say that samples of performances within control should also be investigated occasionally to make sure that the results are normal for the right reasons. Generally, however, the philosophy is one of "management by exception."

Open- and Closed-Loop Control Systems

When a performance variable gets out of control, corrective action is needed. In this connection, a distinction can be made between open- and closed-loop control systems. In the *open loop system*, the executive makes the comparison between performance and standards and uses his discretion as to what type of corrective action to take. Figure 19-8 is an example of an open loop system because of the various discretionary steps that are built in. In a closed loop system, some device continuously reads the performance; when it gets out of

---

[7]There is a chance of $\frac{1}{2}$ that any succeeding observation will be higher and the same chance that it will be lower (excluding the possibility that two successive values are identical). Therefore the probability of finding six successively higher values is given by $(\frac{1}{2})^6 = 1/64$.

control, action is automatically triggered, which seeks to bring about more conformance between the performance and the standards.

When both systems are equally feasible, the closed loop model undoubtedly represents the more elegant solution. It economizes on human effort and can be depended upon to act with more swiftness and consistency. It has found many applications in physical engineering areas, such as refinery operations and missile launchings. An everyday example of a closed loop system is found in the thermostatic control of home temperature. The objective of the system is to maintain the temperature at a certain level. This means that the furnace must be switched on and off during the day. It must be switched on when the room temperature drops below a certain point, and it must be switched off again when the room temperature rises above a certain point. If the homeowner were to make these adjustments himself (an open loop system), he would be kept quite busy. Instead, this function is carried out by a thermostat, which switches the furnace on and off as the room temperature approaches the lower and upper control points, respectively.

The application of pure feedback principles in management control of marketing activities is more limited but nevertheless is found. Consider the typical company's reactions to a sharp drop in sales. Almost regardless of the cause, this event triggers off a series of predictable company actions designed to restore sales or profits. One of the first moves is to cut down discretionary costs, which unfortunately often includes advertising, marketing research, and some other expenditures whose purpose is really to build up sales in the short or long run. If this action fails, the company is next led to reduce its fixed costs by letting some personnel go. If this action fails, the company next considers selling this or some other division, some of its plant capacity, and so forth.

However explicit, decision rules and timings for these actions are rarely used. A drop in sales (as opposed to room temperature) may be caused by a company price increase, a competitor's new promotion program, a decline in business activity, or other factors. Each cause may warrant a different corrective action. Until management can develop complex interpretive and decision rules, most marketing control systems will remain of the open loop variety.

SUMMARY

The building of marketing models and the estimation of their parameters must be fitted into the larger processes of analysis, planning, operations and control making up the management system of the firm. It must be recognized that decisions in organizations are made under conditions of bounded rationality, that is, there are limits to the amount of information analysis and even motivation that affect the actors of the firm.

We have tried to draw a realistic picture of the main steps in company planning and how they involve the various marketing executives. The annual planning cycle begins with the executive committee of the company establishing particular sales and profit objectives for the year. These are influenced by various factors subsumed under long range goals, recent experience, current outlook, and interest group expectations. The way in which these influences are translated into the specific objectives set by the executive committee is a question that is too complex to consider here. The vice-president of marketing takes these objectives and asks his product managers to develop marketing and financial plans that will accomplish the sales and profit objectives set by the executive committee. These plans are reviewed by the marketing vice-president and discussed with the sales manager, who also submits a plan outlining his own resource needs and objectives. These plans are consolidated by the marketing vice-president and then sent back to the executive committee for final approval. When the plans are officially approved, they go back to the marketing vice-president, who now develops final objectives and budgets for the product managers and the sales manager. The sales manager in turn develops quotas and budgets for the regional managers, who in turn develop quotas for the individual salesmen. At each level, there are very specific decisions made by the marketing executive and very specific influences that bear on his decisions; these are indicated where possible.

In allocating funds to subordinates, decision makers are subject to both normative and interpersonal factors. A decision maker may develop an ideal allocation based on his analysis of demand and cost factors in each market area. But he is also subject to the personal influence of the various men under him who are competing for funds, and their persuasiveness depends on their personality, credibility, and status, as well as the decision maker's openness to persuasion.

Although most companies operate with a centralized model of decision making in which the "boss" decides what is best in the allocation of resources, two other organizational solutions to the allocation problem should be noted. The decentralized solution leaves the responsibility for budget determination with the local managers and they can "borrow" whatever resources they need to make the territory or product they manage profitable. They are not judged by plans so much as by results. Alternatively, a semidecentralized solution would require each local manager to submit independently plans and forecasts for three different budget levels; top management would then allocate company funds in an optimal way according to the implicit sales response functions and cost functions. The men, of course, would be held accountable for achieving their forecasts and their success would affect their credibility in the next round of budget planning.

Each of these planning models requires that careful thought be given to the problem of control. We have taken the point of view that the management process consists in analyzing opportunities, then planning (developing objectives, plans, and standards), then executing (implementation and performance measurement), and then controlling. Control is the process of taking steps to bring actual results and desired results closer together. When there is a significant performance deviation, as reflected in standard control chart procedures, management might ask in sequence whether the fault lay with the implementation, standards, plan, objectives, opportunity analysis, or the management itself. These questions would be asked in an open loop control system in the search for appropriate corrective action. In a closed loop system, which is still rare in marketing but which may come increasingly into use, a correction mechanism is automatically set in motion when a significant performance deviation is detected and continues as long as performance is out of control. Control mechanisms for the marketing operation, as well as for many other company operations, are still in need of much more theory and development.

Questions and Problems

1. Discuss the concept of "satisficing." Why do managers tend to perform in only a satisfactory manner rather than attempting to search for the optimal plan?
2. The chapter considered a decentralized decision making process in the marketing organization. Problems are successively broken down to be solved at lower operating levels. What are the main advantages and disadvantages of such decentralization?
3. What is the importance of feedback, or a two-way information flow, in the decision and planning processes of the marketing organization?

CHAPTER 20
Implementing Management
Science in Marketing

Most of this book has dealt with the problem of building useful models of marketing processes and marketing decision situations. In this chapter, we want to consider explicitly the problem of introducing management science into the marketing organization. Briefly, how might management science in marketing be marketed?

Management science and model building still have a strange sound to many marketing practitioners in spite of the number of companies that have undertaken projects in this area.[1] Those who spend their days managing a sales force, reviewing an advertising campaign, dealing with customers, and developing budgets for product lines and sales territories see a great deal in marketing that defies classification and analysis. They develop a natural suspicion about statements that mathematics and the scientific method might make a significant contribution to the understanding and solution of many marketing problems. In fact, there are many facets of the marketing process that in all likelihood will not yield to scientific treatment, facets that rely heavily on creativity, human relations, and the like. But there are other facets of marketing that have responded well to systematic observation and analysis.

[1]See Chap. 1, p. 12, for a review of companies doing management science work in marketing.

640

The attempt to get marketing executives to support the development of formal marketing models to aid their planning is unfortunately still greeted with mixed feelings that range from intense suspicion and hostility all the way to naïve and uncritical acceptance. The Preface to this book quoted a statement by Lee Adler to the effect that "a good many marketing executives . . . are artists, not analysts. For them, marketing is an art form, and . . . they do not want it to be any other way."[2] To the extent that this is true, the marketing model builder must give careful thought to the educational challenge of creating a favorable attitude toward management science. The problem of introducing the culture of management science into the marketing area shares all the difficulties found in introducing management science into other parts of the company, with the added handicaps that (1) marketing models are yet to be "proved" out, and (2) marketing processes are intrinsically less amenable to numerical analysis than production or financial processes. Nevertheless, there are some sound strategies for demonstrating the potential value of management science to marketing practitioners.

This chapter first considers the nature of the conflict between managers and management scientists and then considers five key issues in implementation: the types of persons who are likely to do effective management science work in marketing, where these persons should be placed in the organization, the educational program they should develop, the kinds of marketing problems they should try to solve first, and the desirable amount of involvement of the manager in the model building phase of the project. The chapter concludes with a brief listing and discussion of the major trends that appear to be characterizing recent management science work in marketing.

ROLE AND PERSONALITY CONFLICT BETWEEN MANAGER AND MANAGEMENT SCIENTIST

At the heart of the issue of implementation of management science in marketing is the basic issue of the relationship of line management to staff. The basic responsibility and authority for making or approving company decisions on product, price, advertising, sales force, distribution, and so forth, lies in the hands of line marketing managers. In principle, they could proceed to make their decisions without the help of staff, on the basis of intuitive feelings. There are always a handful of decision makers in every organization who proceed in this fashion, making minimal use of the information or advice of others. This is their prerogative, given the fact that they bear responsibility for the consequences. Most decision makers, however, do not operate in such an insular fashion for a variety of reasons and rely on staff resources to various degrees. In some cases they have already made up their minds but seek outside confirmation. In other cases they have not formed an opinion and sincerely want more information and analysis to cut through the issues. In still other

[2]See pp. v–viii.

cases they want staff reports primarily to have something to point to in justification of their decision, in the event that the decision turns out to be incorrect. The reports show that they took reasonable steps to research the issues before deciding. Generally, staff personnel can be used in a variety of ways by the line manager.

The staff man, however, may take quite a different view of the nature of his role and contribution to the business decision making process. Instead of seeing himself as offering services to the line manager, he may believe that his technical skills qualify him to give sound advice on the various courses of action facing the firm and, in fact, that the best decision is often implicit in the results of his research, and not something to be arbitrarily considered by the manager. In the more extreme cases, some staff would like to see the responsibility for policy making placed in the hands of a planning staff and managers asked essentially to carry out these policies.

In addition to role conflict between line and staff regarding the responsibility for decision making, there tends to be an overlay of personality conflict arising out of the fact that the two jobs tend to attract a different type of "mind," which might be superficially contrasted as the practical versus the theoretical. Leslie A. Beldo listed four conflicts in the fundamental outlook of managers versus researchers that tend to get in the way of productive relationships:[3]

Management demands	*Research offers*
Simplicity (Can't you just ask "yes" or "no"?)	Complexity (The variability of response indicates . . .)
Certainty (It is or it isn't)	Probability (Maybe)
Immediacy (Now)	Futurity (It appears that by the end of the year . . .)
Concreteness (Aren't we number one yet?)	Abstraction (Our exponential gain indeed appears favorable)

Basically, the marketing manager is seen as a person of a very practical cast of mind. He wants simple analyses and simple answers and he likes to see the research relevant and concrete. The marketing manager is preoccupied with a great many immediate issues that absorb his attention, making him more of a doer than a planner. He tends to see the unique characteristics of every problem and tends to distrust generalization and abstraction. He has insufficient training in the quantitative and behavioral sciences to appreciate their potential contributions.

[3]Leslie A. Beldo, "Introduction to Attitude Research and Management Decisions," in *Effective Marketing Coordination*, George L. Baker, ed. (Chicago: American Marketing Association, 1961), p. 584.

On the other hand, the analyst (researcher, management scientist) by training and bent is oriented to look for generalizations that will help meet future situations. While he may acknowledge the complexities in each problem, he knows that intellectual understanding is advanced by initially developing simpler models that portray the essential issues, which can be analyzed for an explicit solution. He knows that the solution arising out of a simple model may require subjective modification by the decision maker for factors left out of the picture. To help the decision maker, the analyst likes to list the assumptions underlying his research results. Often he will prepare different recommendations for the different sets of assumptions that could be adopted, leaving the choice of assumptions up to the manager. This, of course, contributes to the impression on the part of many managers that the management scientist is incapable of clear answers.

Thus we find both role conflicts and personality conflicts often plaguing the relationship between the manager and the management scientist. Opinions differ as to what is the proper and most productive relationship between the two. Churchman and Schainblatt contributed to the discussion by distinguishing between four possible types of manager-management scientist interfaces.[4] The first, or *separate function position*, holds that the researcher's function is to develop a good technical research design and solution and the manager's function is to develop a good operational solution. Neither man has an obligation to understand the details of the other man's job. The second, or *communication position*, holds that the main need is for the manager to understand the researcher and communicate his problem carefully to him; the researcher does not have the corresponding obligation. The third, or *persuasion position*, holds that the main need is for the researcher to understand the manager's needs and to gear his work toward helping the manager make and recognize better decisions; the busy manager does not have the corresponding obligation. Finally, the fourth, or *mutual understanding position*, holds that the most productive relationship is achieved when both parties set about to understand each other's work and requirements.

Dyckman followed up this classification with a survey to find out which positions were espoused by practicing managers and management scientists.[5] His results revealed that both groups took definite positions rather than neutral positions; that managers split equally over the separate-function position, while management scientists disagreed with it strongly by a margin of 5 to 1; and that both groups advocated some type of understanding as needed, although they showed more agreement with the communication or persuasion positions than with the mutual understanding position. Thus it appears that the management scientist working for a company will have to contend with a variety of views

[4]C. W. Churchman and A. H. Schainblatt, "The Researcher and the Manager: A Dialectic of Implementation," *Management Science* (Feb. 1965) B69–87. Also see the Oct. 1965 issue of *Management Science*.

[5]Thomas R. Dyckman, "Management Implementation of Scientific Research: An Attitudinal Study," *Management Science* (June 1967) B612–620.

held by managers regarding his usefulness and his most productive type of relationship to the manager.

STRATEGIES FOR INTRODUCING MANAGEMENT SCIENCE INTO THE MARKETING ORGANIZATION

Our primary interest is to consider how management science can effectively be introduced into the marketing organization. We see this problem as having five aspects:

1.   What kinds of persons make effective management scientists in marketing?
2.   Where should these persons be placed in the organization?
3.   What educational programs should they run for the management?
4.   What marketing problems should be analyzed first?
5.   What involvement should managers have in the design of the model?

Characteristics of Effective Management Scientists in Marketing

Many of the management scientists doing work in the marketing area were originally trained in the areas of production and physical distribution where operations research was first applied. These men found productive solutions to production-type problems by the application of such methodologies as linear programming, queuing theory, Markov processes, and calculus. The success of these methodologies naturally gave them confidence and they were the first techniques to be applied to marketing problems. The real problem was often distorted in order to achieve solutions with existing techniques. Thus the media selection problem was simplified so that it could be solved in straightforward linear programming terms and the brand choice problem was simplified so that it could be handled in straightforward Bernouilli or Markov process terms. These trial and error steps were necessary to the progress of theory in marketing because it soon became apparent that marketing problems deserve their own original model building to capture their particular combinations of complexities.

The newer marketing management scientists realize this and they have spent as much time observing marketing processes in their full complexity as learning the niceties of existing mathematical methodologies. The company seeking an effective person to do management science work in marketing must search for a person who knows marketing. It has two choices, each of which can be effective if carried out correctly.

1.   The company can hire the management scientist who has practiced in the more traditional areas of operations research and put him through a careful training program to learn about company marketing processes, so that he does not resort to naïve models. This means that the man will not reach his full productive potential until some time has passed, when he has learned the special characteristics of marketing problems.

2.   The company can hire the new man who has recently earned an M.B.A.

or Ph.D. with specialization in marketing and quantitative methods. This man would be ideally equipped with the tools and understanding necessary to do effective work in marketing, although he will not reach his full productive potential until he gains sufficient practical experience.

Both of these recruitment alternatives involve risks but, as mentioned earlier, each has the potential of succeeding under normal circumstances.

Organizational Placement of the Marketing Management Scientist

A frequent issue is whether the marketing management scientist should be located in the operations research department along with other management scientists or be located in the marketing department, either in a staff planning position serving the marketing vice-president or in the marketing research department. All of these locations are used in actual practice. Many large companies have a sizeable operations research department, and one or more of the men specialize in making their services available to the marketing department. The positive feature of this arrangement is that the marketing management scientist has active interaction with other management scientists and can keep abreast of new techniques that are being developed in the other areas and exchange ideas on current problems. The negative feature of this arrangement is that the marketing management scientist is removed from the scene of daily marketing decision making, which will mean that he will miss some opportunities to propose research where needed and also may be less knowledgeable about actual marketing processes. For this reason, in some companies the marketing management scientist works with the marketing group. Here the issue is one of what level of authority he should have. When he is placed close to the vice-president of marketing, he can be highly influential in infusing management science thinking into the marketing organization. At the other extreme, the management scientist might be placed within the marketing research department as a resource for model building. In this position, his skills and influence may be less visible to line management and he will be less free to choose the problems on which to work. Thus the marketing management scientist's position and location in the company will make a great difference to his ability to make headway with line managers.

Educational Programs for Line Marketing Management

The management scientist will quickly recognize that his influence in the organization will depend upon the level of management's appreciation of fundamental notions such as "models," "decision theory," "optimization," and the fundamentals of certain important solution techniques. To this end, he will want to develop in-company seminars for line management to explain the meaning and potentialities of management science for business problem solving. These seminars have taken the form of one- to three-day programs in some companies or a series of short weekly meetings in other companies. These programs are most successful when they have the endorsement of top management and their participation. One of the most successful examples of an entire company's being converted over to management science thinking is the case of the Pillsbury Company.[6] Some years ago, President Robert Keith saw the importance of his company's making more sophisticated use of the computer and he had his staff arrange a program in which outstanding management scientists described to him and his top managers the nature of modern decision theory, game theory, and linear programming. He was very impressed with the seminar and had it repeated for the next level of management. The seminar has been repeated many times, reaching down to all important levels of management. As a result of this and other steps, the conditions were established for the acceptance, and use of, management science at Pillsbury. Once top management shows an interest in management science and labels it as important, the other levels of management are ready to give it a serious hearing.

The educational effort is abetted by using good visuals, describing clear and meaningful examples of previous work, and introducing simple exercises calling for the men to apply the concepts to actual problems. One company stimulated a lot of interest by programming an analogue computer to demonstrate in a graphic manner the expected effects on sales of varying advertising and other marketing expenditures. One of the most potent demonstration tools for interesting line managers in the potentialities of models for marketing decision making is to expose them to computer on-line time sharing. A remote terminal facility has several advantages over batch processing, including greater accessibility, instantaneous results, and a large available program library. Seminars which are put on for marketing executives should feature one or more interactive programs on a remote terminal to give the executives a first-hand experience in sophisticated methods of problem solving.

Choice of Problems

The management scientist who has undertaken to work with line marketing management will undoubtedly recognize a large number of marketing problems deserving study. However, he must be judicious about selecting problems that are thought to be important and where there is a reasonable chance for early solution and payoff. For example, it would be fatal for the beginner to choose as his first assignment to build a marketing planning simulator because such a simulator will require a tremendous number of man-hours invested in model design and data collection, so that a few years would pass before any practical results would be possible. Before this time, someone is sure to question his value to the firm. Such a problem choice is also absurd because it is highly desirable to diversify the portfolio of studied problems to minimize risk: it would be better to work on several problems and achieve some successes than to rest everything on one problem, no matter how important.

6"EDP Keys New Era in Planning at Pillsbury," *Grocery Manufacturer* (Jan. 1967) 6–12; "Involvement Helps at Pillsbury," *Grocery Manufacturer* (Feb. 1967) 28–31. Also see "The Pillsbury Company: Development of Marketing Systems," case 9M-255, Harvard Business School, Boston, 1967.

There are two particular areas in marketing in which study is likely to produce improved procedures or solutions in a reasonable amount of time. The first is in the evaluation of nonrecurrent major policy proposals. Where a company is facing a marketing decision of some importance, such as shifting from one marketing channel to another, or dropping a price in an oligopoly situation, management will find its thinking considerably aided by simple decision tree analysis or simulation models, both of which are easy to understand. These techniques have an intuitive appeal and are helpful in the broadest range of situations. On the other hand, problems that involve linear programming, queuing theory, or calculus, are likely to be harder for management to understand.

The second area is in the improvement of routine management decision systems and procedures. Most companies can benefit from objective studies of their current procedures for making sales forecasts, developing budgets for territories and products, developing sales quotas for salesmen, and so on. Studies of the present systems can yield clues as to alternative decision procedures that can lead to substantial improvements in performance.

The analyst who decides to study a current company decision procedure can use one or more of five modes of research inquiry to reach the conscious and semiconscious "decision programs" of particular executives. They are, respectively, the statistical, observational, introspective, retrospective, and prospective methods.

The *statistical method* calls for the analyst to gather data on the important factors that might have influenced the marketing executive's past decisions in this area. He does not require any verbal account by the executive on how he made his decisions, only data on relevant inputs and decision outputs. The analyst draws on theory as to the possible relationships among the variables and applies correlation and regression techniques to these data, seeking to fit a statistical function that comes close to predicting the executive's past decisions. The major limitation of this method is the lack of mental process data to provide clues or confirmation of the description.

The *observational method* calls for the analyst to observe the executive in the course of his daily activities, noting the influences he is subject to and the decisions that he makes. Out of these materials the analyst seeks to evolve an explanation of the executive's decision making processes. Two limitations of this method are (1) the analyst never obtains the executive's own description of his decision making process, and (2) the presence of the analyst as observer can alter or condition the normal behavior of the executive.

The *introspective method* calls for the analyst to interview the executive for a description of the general factors and procedures he uses in making his decisions. The executive describes his general style of problem solving, and the weights he attaches to different recurring factors. Two major limitations of this method are (1) this description is apt to be too general, and (2) the executive may forget or distort certain factors that actually play a role in his decision making.

The *retrospective method* calls for the analyst to ask the executive to discuss specific past decisions, the data he had available at the time, the factors that pressed on his mind, and the weights he gave to them. This makes the discussion of his decision making style much more specific than under the introspective method. Furthermore, it gives the analyst a chance to check other information on these past decisions to verify that all the factors appear to be accounted for. The retrospective method, however, still suffers from reliance on memory and past records for its accuracy.

Finally, the *prospective method* calls for the analyst to ask the executive to think aloud through a series of new decision problems that are given to him. A verbal record (called a protocol) is made of his actual thinking process as he calls for data, ruminates over the situation, and describes how he has decided to act.[7] The analyst goes over these protocols and attempts to formalize the steps, factors, weights, and heuristics used by the executive to resolve the problem. The formal model is computerized and then is used to produce a fresh protocol for a new decision problem. The executive also produces a fresh protocol; both are then shown to a third party, such as the executive's superior, who is asked whether he can distinguish which protocol was produced by the computer model and which by the executive. If he cannot discriminate in a number of such cases better than chance, the computer model is considered good.[8]

The methods just described are not mutually exclusive, and an analyst is likely to use all or some combination of them in studying the decision processes of an actual marketing executive. Several values are served by being able to represent successfully his decision processes. First, it makes the executive more conscious of his own thought processes and gives him a chance to seek improvement of the more vulnerable facets. Second, it can serve as a means of communicating to a successor of this executive how he typically proceeds to think through decision problems that will soon face the successor. Third, it reveals to the executive's superiors how their information and policies tend to be used and interpreted down the line, and this may lead to reexamination of current procedures and policies. Finally, it may be combined with the typical decision programs of other executives in the firm into a total simulation of the firm's organizational decision processes. The simulation can show what marketing decisions are likely to be made in the firm in response to various developments in the marketplace. The consequences of these decisions on the market in turn can be explored through a model of market sales response.

At the same time, the successful development and use of executive decision process programs will not always be realizable. For problems that are unique and important, in which the executive goes through a substantial learning process, the process may lack sufficient structure to be made formal. For problems in which there is a lot of decision latitude for executives occupying

[7]See Allen Newell and Herbert A. Simon, "Computer Simulation of Human Thinking," *Science* (Dec. 22, 1961) 2011–2017.

[8]This method of testing a heuristic program is known as Turing's test. See A. M. Turing, "Computing Machinery and Intelligence," *MIND* (Oct. 1950) 433–460.

the same position, it is hard to pretend that the resulting program is typical of the job, rather than the man. Yet the values that might be obtained from successfully modeled decision programs make their development one of the most interesting and promising new tools in marketing analysis.

Degree of Management Participation in Model Building

Management scientists tend to be divided over how much involvement the manager should have in the model building and data gathering phases of the research process. In operations research work in the areas of production and physical distribution, the management scientist generally listens to the manager's definition of the problem, goes away and builds a model, and presents his solution and his evidence some months later to the manager, with a few progress reports in between. This practice reflects the straightforward nature of many of the problems in these areas and the highly technical and standardized nature of the mathematical analysis. The main weakness of this approach is that the manager rarely gets to understand the technical details of the model and often has to accept it on blind faith. In the marketing area, this would be extremely hard to expect of the manager. Management science practitioners are increasingly of the opinion that marketing managers should be involved as much as possible in the model building process. First, it is important that the manager and management scientist come to a sound conclusion as to what is the real problem; this may be more elusive in marketing than in the other areas. Second, the participation of the manager will keep the management scientist from building the wrong model or omitting important factors. Third, the manager will achieve a feeling that he understands the model, rather than the more common feeling that the model is a threat or a mystery. Fourth, he will feel that it is *his* model. Fifth, his participation is a form of education that will increase his capability of understanding and using even more sophisticated models.

Those who believe that management involvement is highly desirable hold that it is more important to develop models that managers understand and by implication will use than sophisticated models they cannot understand and will reject. By first building simple models that the manager understands and then adding refinements as the manager himself calls for them, a maximum amount of management motivation and education is achieved. Montgomery and Urban call this an *evolutionary approach* to model building.

In initial attempts to involve the "man" or the marketing manager in the MS (management science) system, it may be wise to forego the sophisticated models that could be applied to the problem. A descriptive model of how the manager makes this decision may be the best starting point for involvement of the man in the system. With this descriptive model and a retrieval system, the manager may see ways to improve his decisions. This involvement might then provide the basis for an evolution of the decision maker's model to a more normative level, which eventually results in confidence and involvement in a sophisticated management science model. The use of an *evolutionary approach* to the design of the model bank and information system may yield the greatest long-term rewards for the firm, since it will lead to utilization of management science technology to solve relevant problems and to implementation of the ensuing MS recommendations.[9]

Little has addressed himself to the same issue after noting that "the big problem with management science models is that managers practically never use them."[10] He lists the following reasons: (1) Good models are hard to create; (2) good parameterization is even harder; (3) managers do not understand the models; and (4) most models are incomplete. Then he goes on to propose the characteristics that decision models ought to have to be acceptable. They should be (1) simple, (2) robust, (3) easy to control, (4) adaptive, (5) complete on important issues, and (6) easy to communicate with.

To illustrate his philosophy of introducing management to models, Little describes his work with three product managers on an advertising model called ADBUDG:

> The development has proceeded in evolutionary steps. First a very simple advertising budgeting model was brought up and used to demonstrate concepts. Then a more complex model for advertising budgeting, one with sufficient detail to be of practical value, was brought up. Experience with it is influencing the design of a more elaborate model.

The first task is to build up a simple sales response function.[11] The managers participate in this by providing four estimates:

1. "If advertising is cut to zero, brand share will decrease, but there is a floor, *min*, on how much share will fall from its initial value by the end of one time period.
2. If advertising is increased a great deal, say, to something that could be called saturation, brand share will increase but there is a ceiling, *max*, on how much can be achieved by the end of one time period.
3. There is some advertising rate that will maintain initial share.
4. An estimate can be made by data analysis or managerial judgment of the effect on share by the end of one period of a 50 percent increase in advertising over the maintenance rate."

These estimates yield four points that allow the fitting of a hypothetical brand share response curve shown in Figure 20-1. Little suggests that the following

[9]David B. Montgomery and Glen L. Urban, *Management Science in Marketing* (Englewood Cliffs, N.J.: Prentice-Hall, Inc., 1969), p. 358.

[10]John D. C. Little, "Models and Managers: The Concept of a Decision Calculus," *Management Science* (Apr. 1970), 466–485.

[11]Ibid., p. B–471.

function is quite flexible for fitting the curve, although other response functions would also do:

$$\text{share} = \text{min} + (\text{max-min}) \frac{(\text{adv})^{\gamma}}{\delta + (\text{adv})^{\gamma}} \tag{20-1}$$

The constants δ and γ are estimated uniquely from the input data. The equation is quite general in that if $\gamma > 1$, the curve will be S-shaped and, if $0 > \gamma \leqslant 1$, the curve will be concave.

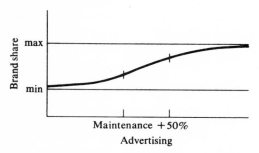

Figure 20-1   Fitting a Smooth Curve Through Two Points and Two Asymptotes
Source: Little, *op. cit.*, p. B–472.

The manager might then point out that the holdover effects of advertising are omitted in Equation 20-1. The management scientist might then suggest that this period's brand share might be viewed as related to last period's brand share reduced by a decay factor and increased by the current advertising expenditure. Equation 20-1 can be modified to read:[12]

$$\text{share } (t) = \{\text{long run min} + [\text{persistence}] [\text{share } (t-1) - \text{long run min}]\}$$

$$+ (\text{max-min}) \frac{[\text{adv}(t)]^{\gamma}}{\delta + [\text{adv}(t)]^{\gamma}} \tag{20-2}$$

where: long run min = the long run minimum value of market share in the absence of advertising (possibly zero)

persistence = (min − long run min)/(initial share − long run min)

At this point the product manager might suggest that a given dollar advertising expenditure could be more or less effective, depending upon the media efficiency and the copy effectiveness. This can be handled by establishing the following definition:

$$\text{adv}(t) = [\text{media effcy}(t)] [\text{copy effct}(t)] [\text{adv dollars}(t)] \tag{20-3}$$

and estimating indices for media and copy effectiveness in the particular situation, using 1.00 as a normal level.

[12]Ibid., p. B-471–472.

The product manager may now point out that several other factors are left out that have an effect on brand share. Here Little would ask the product manager to construct indices showing how he thinks these factors will affect

Table 20-1 Developing a Composite Index of Nonadvertising Effects

Factor	Period			
	1	2	3	4
Promotions	1.00	1.10	.98	1.00
Price	1.00	1.00	1.00	1.00
Package	1.00	1.05	1.05	1.05
Competitive action	1.00	.98	.95	1.00
Other	1.00	1.00	1.00	1.00
Composite	1.00	1.13	.98	1.05

Source: Little, "Models and Managers: The Concept of a Decision Calculus," p. B–474. See footnote 10.

brand share in each period. Table 20-1 shows a sample set of values. The composite index of nonadvertising effects may arbitrarily be estimated as the product of the numbers in each column. This composite index can be used to modify the calculated brand share level based strictly on advertising. With a few more steps, such as estimating total product class sales and a seasonal index, and adding a profit equation, ADBUDG is the simple but complete dynamic system shown in Table 20-2 readily understandable by the product managers who participated in its construction.

Table 20-2 ADBUDG: A Simple Advertising Budgeting Model

1. *Share*
   brand share (t) = [nonadv effect index (t)] [unadjusted share (t)]
   unadj share (t) = long run min + [persistence] [unadj share $(t-1)$ − long run

   $$\text{min}] + (\text{max-min}) \ \frac{[\text{adv} \ (t)]^\gamma}{\delta + [\text{adv} \ (t)]^\gamma}$$

   adv (t) = [media effcy (t)] [copy effct (t)] [adv dollars (t)]/[reference value of numerator]

2. *Brand Sales*
   brand sales (t) = [reference product class sales] [product class sales index (t)] [brand share (t)]

3. *Profits*
   contribution to profit after adv (t) = [contribution per sales unit (t)] [brand sales (t)] − adv dollars (t)

Source: Little, "Models and Managers: The Concept of a Decision Calculus," p.B–475. See footnote 10.

This simple model can be programmed for conversational input/output and the product manager can try out different advertising budget levels and sets of assumptions about other factors and get back forecasts of sales and profits. Presumably, these forecasts will be plausible because they arise essentially from a codification of the manager's insights joined with hard data when available. As he uses this model, he will get to know its forecasting reliability and, furthermore, will be in a position to introduce additional factors that call for consideration.

This philosophy of evolutionary model building has much to recommend it as a pragmatic approach to overcoming the communication and credibility gap separating many managers from management scientists. It calls for the management scientist to model the manager's ideas and move at the manager's pace, although at the price of foregoing the best model that is possible to build for the problem. For this reason, other management scientists would rather take the chance of building the best model and then educating the manager to use it. Clearly, both approaches have their merits and can be effective in different situations, the judgment of which must be left to the management scientist.

RECENT TRENDS IN MANAGEMENT SCIENCE IN MARKETING

In looking at the most recent developments in management science work in marketing, six trends stand out. Two trends can be listed under each of the three topics that interest management scientists most: problem definition, types of models, and data collection.

Two Trends in Problem Definition

The two important trends under problem definition are toward deeper problem definition and toward wider problem definition.

First, analysts reveal a growing willingness to work with microanalytic definitions of the problem. It is becoming increasingly apparent that one can fit a mathematical relationship to gross sales and still not understand the underlying processes. There is now more interest in exploring the underlying behavioral phenomena as a prelude to developing macromodels.

Second, there is increasing recognition that narrow statements of the problem may lead to optimization of one part of the system at the expense of other parts, and this has encouraged wider problem definition. For example, it is hard to settle on the best advertising level without simultaneously determining the best price and sales force size. This is because one marketing instrument is rarely varied without making correlated adjustments in other marketing instruments. In fact it is increasingly recognized that marketing optimization cannot be achieved without considering production and financial issues.

Two Trends in Model Building

Two important trends under model building are toward practice oriented models and toward adaptive models.

First, there is a growing recognition that models and systems to be useful must be designed with particular users in mind. This means starting with the problems of real product managers, sales managers, advertising managers, and so on; defining the decisions they make and their current decision rules; and working for improvements even if not optimization.

Second, there is a growing interest in decision models whose parameters are tied to a program of systematic field experimentation that allows the analyst constantly to update his estimates of likely response. These models recognize that parameters of marketing response undergo continuous change and must be tracked by systematic measurement procedures.

Two Trends in Data Collection

Two important trends under data collection are toward improved measurement techniques and toward the use of subjective data.

First, there is a growing interest in field and laboratory experimentation, more sophisticated questionnaire design and scaling instruments, better multivariate tools for analyzing data, and improved data available from commercial services. The growth of management information systems and computer facilities is making an important contribution in this area. Companies are beginning to recognize the value of building up a well-supplied data bank, statistical bank, behavioral model bank, and planning model bank, all accessible to different managers as needed. Because of the high cost of developing them, some companies are making plans to share the cost of building these banks.

Second, although analysts are enjoying increasing amounts of hard data, they are not willing to limit their variables only to ones that can be measured with hard data, for this would mean staying at the level of quite simple models. They are increasingly turning to the executives themselves for estimates of missing parameters and probability distributions, incorporating these in the models, and covering the risks of doing this through the route of sensitivity analysis.

These six trends are not free from contradiction, but contradiction as someone observed over a hundred years ago, is the reason for change.

SUMMARY

Management science is the attitude that many business problems can be considerably clarified by resort to scientific method and substantial reliance on mathematical tools. No wonder it seems alien and threatening to many managers who consider business decision making primarily a matter of art and judgment. The management scientist and manager can see themselves as having one of four relationships to each other: (1) they both work in separate spheres and need only minimal understanding of each other's work; (2) the manager should depend heavily on the management scientist and seek to understand his work (3) the management scientist should seek to maximize his usefulness to the manager by being persuasive, simple and clear; (4) both parties have an obligation to work closely together and understand each other's work. We favor the fourth position and at least insist on the third position, that the management scientist should see his role as primarily one of being helpful to the manager.

To effect these ends, it is necessary that the company employ management scientists with good mathematical training but, even more important, good understanding of the complexities of the marketing process, so that their models do not seem oversimplified or irrelevant to the manager. The management scientists working on marketing problems can be placed either in the management science department or in the marketing department (either close to the vice-president of marketing or in marketing research), each possibility offering a number of advantages and disadvantages. Wherever he is based, he should seriously consider developing some educational seminars for managers that are endorsed and supported by top management, and his programs should feature practical problems and demonstrations, particularly the use of computer programs on a time sharing basis. In addition, he should carefully select as first problems to work on those that can be finished in a reasonable amount of time with clear payoff. These usually involve the application of decision theory or simulation to a policy problem facing marketing management or the study of some important procedural area in marketing to determine how it is done and to seek improved procedures and decision rules. Finally, the management scientist should seek to involve the manager in the building of the model as a means of motivating him and educating him about the potential values of the management science approach. The whole area of management science in marketing is characterized by strong trends toward deeper and wider problem definition, practice oriented and adaptive models, and improved measurement techniques and subjective data.

Questions and Problems

1. Top management in a large manufacturing company felt that the marketing department could benefit greatly from the implementation of management science (MS) methods in the marketing operation. A group of operations research experts from the firm's centralized MS group was assigned to study marketing problems and activities. After a number of months of independent work the MS group came up with a lengthy report which included recommendations for a comprehensive restructuring of the marketing operation and the implementation of a number of sophisticated operations research models. The report was passed along to the company's marketing management with a recommendation to implement the recommended actions as soon as possible. Upon reading the report the marketing manager claimed that the recommendations were highly unrealistic and completely unworkable. He further stated that the department personnel lacked the understanding and technical ability to implement the MS proposal.

    Discuss the problems highlighted in the above situation. What should top management do to deal with these problems and to prevent their recurrence in the future?

2. The management of a company is considering the introduction of a new product.

The research department is called upon to provide information which management can use to make the necessary decision. In light of the fundamental differences in the outlooks of the two groups, what specific answers are typically sought by management in this situation, and what answers are likely to be provided by the research department?

3. A marketing manager hired an MS expert into his department, although he was doubtful of the value of MS methods in marketing operations. The management scientist immediately set to work to develop an elaborate consumer behavior simulation model. Six months later, just as the model was beginning to take shape, the marketing manager fired the MS expert, convinced that his original thoughts concerning the value of MS in marketing were justified, since the man had wasted six months on a project that promised little in the way of practical operating results. Did the management scientist go wrong?

CHAPTER 21
Developing the Corporate Marketing Model

In this chapter, we shall look at one of the newest and most far-reaching developments in marketing management science, the construction of corporate marketing models.[1] These are models that are (1) computerized, (2) industry-specific, (3) data based, (4) comprehensive, and (5) designed for developing and evaluating alternative company marketing plans. These models integrate many specific management facts and feelings about the marketplace into an orderly instrument for appraising overall product and brand marketing plans and budgets. They promise to increase the marketing manager's capacity to evaluate quickly and effectively the financial implications of alternative assumptions about the marketing environment and the market's response.

The chapter is divided into two major sections. The first section will present a general discussion of the evolution and present state of development of corporate marketing models. The second section will describe a specific approach to mapping and programming a computerized marketing planning model and illustrate it in terms of a specific company.

---

[1]This chapter is adapted from the author's "Corporate Models: Better Marketing Plans," *Harvard Business Review*, July-August 1970, 135-149. Copyright © 1970 by the President and Fellows of Harvard College.

EVOLUTION AND PRESENT STATE OF DEVELOPMENT OF CORPORATE MARKETING MODELS

The comprehensive corporate marketing planning model has its source in the general model building tradition in management science but in addition has two specific sources that give sharp focus to the idea. These sources are the corporate financial model and the marketing game.

The Corporate Financial Model

A corporate financial model is a model that represents a company's operations in financial terms. These models originated in a simple effort to computerize manual accounting procedures, so that management would have a more efficient way to prepare and alter budgets, income statements, and balance sheets. The accounting relationships would be expressed in a series of equations that could be run through the computer. Soon it became clear that the computerized accounting model could be used for a number of additional purposes. For example, it would facilitate the preparation of alternative short term budgets and profit plans. Many companies have avoided preparing alternative budgets because of the substantial man-hours required. Another use of the model is in forecasting the financial effects of different long term investment strategies. This use was adopted early by the electric utility companies, which needed a tool to help estimate the financial consequences of alternative capacity addition plans. Early models were built for the Boston Edison Company[2] and the Philadelphia Electric Company.[3] More recently, companies in the oil industry, particularly Sun Oil[4] and Standard Oil of New Jersey,[5] have pioneered large scale corporate financial models. The whole development has elicited much interest among managers. One prominent executive said:

> One of the most far-reaching new computer techniques I know of is the financial model. I have seen the kind of information that a well-planned, tailor-made corporate model can give to management. It is the kind of information responsible management has dreamed of having for years, but they have had to make do with something less because of the prohibitive manual effort involved in making projections and using a range of varying assumptions about the future. But the financial model gives management the equivalent of a 1000 man-planning department which can produce almost instant answers. This is management firepower only dreamed of before, but now available to the progressive management.[6]

[2]John M. Kohlmeier, "An Analysis of Some Aspects of Capital Budgeting Policy, A Simulation Approach," unpublished Ph.D. dissertation, Harvard Graduate School of Business Administration, Boston, 1964.

[3]Joseph K. Furst and Marvin H. Porter, "Computerized Corporate Planning Model," a paper presented at the ORSA/TIMS Joint Meeting, San Francisco, May 1–3, 1968.

[4]George W. Gershefski, "Building a Corporate Financial Model," *Harvard Business Review* (July–Aug. 1969) 61–72.

[5]D. K. Abe, "Corporate Model System for Planning," a paper presented at the TIMS International Meeting, New York, Mar. 27, 1969.

[6]Leonard Spacek, "Servicing Management in an E.D.P. Environment," *Edison Electric Institute Bulletin* (Jan. 1968).

At the same time, such models tend to be of limited interest to marketing planners because of their superficial treatment of the marketing side of the business. The Sun Oil Company's model inputs future sales volume and prices on the basis of historical projections without examining the impact on volume of different marketing strategies and costs. This limitation is recognized by the designers of the Sun Oil Company model in their statement of intended future model refinements:

> The model will also be extended and revised to determine the effect of such items as advertising, pricing, and research and development on operating departments, so that alternatives involving these expenditures can be incorporated directly into the model. . . . We will also build models for each functional area of the company. They are expected to be detailed enough to aid in operational decision making. These models will take over much of the detail that now is part of the corporate model, so that the latter's main function will be to consolidate the results of the functional model.[7]

The Industry Based Marketing Game

The other source of the corporate marketing model idea is the marketing game. Such games were originally developed as a pedagogical tool to put players through a simulated business experience. The players were expected to gain a number of insights into business decision making not available by textbook study or case discussion. More recently, investigators have realized that gaming could serve research purposes as well. Research values could arise both in attempting to design realistic marketing games, and also in studying the organizational and decision behavior of the players during the game. From this, it was a small step to recognize the potential conversion of complex games into company planning models.

The early marketing games were very simple in design, consisting usually of one product, one territory, and only a few marketing instruments such as pricing and advertising. The sales response functions were artificially developed. More recently, games have appeared that have been designed around specific industries; they have been backed up by considerable research into the industry's behavior.[8] Usually, the first version of such a game will strike actual decision makers in the industry as oversimplified and sometimes behaviorally incorrect. The game designers will revise it; after several cycles of criticism and revision,

---

[7]Gershefski, "Building a Corporate Financial Model," *Harvard Business Review* (July–Aug. 1969) 72.

[8]In addition to the two games to be described below, there is a game designed around the rubber tire market: D. C. Basil, P. R. Cone, and J. A. Fleming, *Executive Decision Making through Simulation: A Case Study and Simulation of Corporate Strategy in the Rubber Industry* (Columbus, Ohio: Charles E. Merrill Books, Inc., 1965); a retail store game: R. E. Schellenberger, *Development if a Computerized, Multipurpose Retail Management Game*, Research Paper 14, Graduate School of Business, University of North Carolina, Chapel Hill, 1965); and a wholesale supply game: W. B. Kehl, "Techniques in Constructing a Market Simulator," in M. L. Bell, ed., *Marketing: A Maturing Discipline* (Chicago: American Marketing Association, 1961) 86–102.

the final game will turn out to be quite a complicated and realistic model of the industry. It is at this point that some executives will begin to recognize the potential uses of the game for marketing planning purposes.

We shall briefly review two outstanding games to show the variety of mechanisms and approaches that can be taken. The Carnegie-Tech Marketing Game is modeled after the detergent market and the M.I.T. Marketing Game is modeled after electric floor polishers.

Carnegie Tech Marketing Game.   One of the first and most fully developed business games is the Carnegie Tech Management Game, created by faculty members at Carnegie-Mellon University Graduate School of Industrial Administration.[9] A special version called MATE (Marketing Analysis Training Exercise), developed by Kuehn and Weiss,[10] shows the marketing operation in much detail, while simplifying the production and financial aspects of the original game. MATE revolves around three firms in the packaged detergent industry, operating in four geographical regions. Each firm may market from one to three brands of detergent in each of the four regions. Each month the firm may establish or alter price, advertising expenditures, sales force size, call time allocation to the brands, and retail allowance. The firm may also purchase market survey reports containing estimates of total retail sales and market shares, retail distribution and stockouts, and competitive advertising expenditures. These estimates are subject to an amount of error varying with the funds appropriated for each survey and chance factors. Furthermore, the firm can invest in product research to find new and better products or to imitate competitors' products, with the results also dependent on how much it invests and chance factors.

On the nonmarketing side, the firm owns one factory and a factory warehouse and rents warehouse space in each marketing region. Products may be shipped directly from the factory to the regional warehouses or stored in the factory warehouse, the decision being influenced by the respective costs. Each month, the firm decides how much to produce, this amount being limited by sufficient funds to pay for this level of production and sufficient capacity. The firm may seek additional funds to augment its working capital, but this move must be approved by the game administrator. At the end of each month the decision makers receive financial and accounting information on monthly sales, cost of goods sold, operating expenses and profit, and current balance sheet figures.

The basic market model consists of an equation determining monthly total case demand for packaged detergent in each region as a function of a growth term, average income per capita, seasonality, and the company's price and sales promotion expenditures relative to competitors. Total demand in a region is then allocated among the brands competing in the region in two steps. First,

[9]Kalman J. Cohen et al., *The Carnegie Tech Management Game* (Homewood, Ill.: Richard D. Irwin, Inc., 1964).

[10]Alfred A. Kuehn and Doyle L. Weiss, "Marketing Analysis Training Exercise," *Behavioral Science* (Jan. 1965), 51–67.

the holdover or habitual demand for each brand is determined. That is, a percentage of last period's sales is repeated for each brand, this percentage varying with its customer loyalty factor. The difference between total demand and total holdover demand represents potential shifters demand; this difference is shared among the competing brands as a function of their relative product characteristics, retail price, retail distribution and availability, and advertising. Each brand consists of a particular mix of three product characteristics— washing power, gentleness, and sudsing—and the sales potency of the mix depends on their levels, relative to the market's most desired levels and also the average ability of product users to discern differences in product characteristics.

The effect of the product characteristics and the other merchandising factors on market shares are worked out in interesting detail, including attempts to incorporate realistic interaction effects. The same can be said about the modeling of the results of investments in product research and market survey studies.

M.I.T. Marketing Game.   The M.I.T. Marketing Game also models a complex and realistic marketing environment.[11] Developed around electric floor polishers for household use, this game requires the players to determine product quality, price, dealer margins, channels of distribution (including number and type of dealers), market area, advertising expenditures, advertising media and appeals, and the number and disposition of salesmen and promotion within the retail store. Like the Carnegie Tech game, the M.I.T. game is designed as a training device, specifically for advanced marketing management courses. But in contrast with most other business games, the M.I.T. simulation requires the players to make some qualitative as well as quantitative decisions. For example, players of the M.I.T. game must develop advertising plans and copy for their product that are subsequently given a quantitative rating by a "control team."

Industry sales are determined by adjusting exogenously determined "normal sales" for the effects of price, promotion, and retail margins. Market share for each company is a function of competitive prices, distribution policies, and advertising. Company sales are determined by multiplying total industry sales by market share.

The control team ratings enter the model through certain "effectiveness functions" that adjust the sales for the quality of the respective company marketing programs. While these control team's ratings are subjective, they provide an analogue of the subjective appraisal of real marketing programs by real customers. This overcomes a criticism that has been directed at most business games: they stress only the dollar allocation dimensions of competition and not the bright ideas that could make for a brilliant advertising campaign or marketing strategy.

[11]Peter S. King, et al., "The M.I.T. Marketing Game," in Martin L. Bell, ed., *Marketing: A Maturing Discipline* (Chicago: American Marketing Association, 1961), 85–102.

Examples of Some Corporate Marketing Models

The example provided by corporate financial models and industry based marketing games has led some companies to attempt to construct a corporate marketing model. One of the best-known examples is the Xerox Corporation and its work on MARS (Marketing Analysis Research System). The overall model is shown in Figure 21-1 and consists of six models.[12] MAST (Market Information Bank) acts as the data bank and contains individual establishment information arranged by market areas. TXPO (Total Xerox Potential Model) stores and calculates the company's market opportunities by market, geographic area, product line, and the size of establishment. ECO (Economic Model) generates economic indices that are used in forecasting growth rates of the various segments of the market. MAPS (Market Analysis Profile Simulator) simulates different marketing strategies and new product concepts that take into account customer buying habits, machine group interactions, technological, competitive, and economic conditions. SOMA (Share of Market Analysis) estimates the share of market Xerox and its leading competitors would enjoy for each of the next ten years under a given strategy and assumed marketing environment. Finally REAM (Resource and Effort Analysis Model) determines the allocations of corporate funds to various product lines and searches for an optimal or satisfactory profit plan. MARS as a whole is still under development, and many adjustments and changes will no doubt be made before it becomes fully operational. Nevertheless, its designers testify to many benefits that have already been yielded in decision making and information gathering by the effort to design this model.

Other companies having some involvement in the construction of corporate marketing models can be cited. Stanley Buchin helped develop for the Minute Maid Company a forecasting planning model for Minute Maid frozen orange concentrate sales as a function of such marketing variables as the case price, advertising budget, sales commission rate, and other variables.[13] The Arthur D. Little Company helped develop a market model of the fertilizer industry for forecasting long run demand for different fertilizers.[14] Claycamp and Amstutz helped develop for the LaRoche Company (pharmaceuticals) a complex model for simulating the effect of different marketing plans involving detail men, media promotion, and direct mail promotion on the rate of prescription drug sales for specific products.[15] A. M. Economos described a model for evaluating the future of the computer leasing business, given the uncertainty of such factors as the rate of market growth, the year of the introduction of fourth generation

[12]This diagram was distributed by a Xerox Company representative in a talk given at the Graduate School of Management at Northwestern University in March 1968.

[13]Stanley Buchin, "A Model of the Florida Orange Industry for Minute Maid Planning," Harvard Business School, AI270.

[14]George B. Hegeman, "Dynamic Simulation for Market Planning," *Chemical and Engineering News* (Jan. 4, 1965), 64–71.

[15]Henry J. Claycamp and Arnold E. Amstutz, "Simulation Techniques in the Analysis of Marketing Strategy," in Frank M. Bass et al., eds., *Applications of the Sciences in Marketing Management* (New York: John Wiley & Co., Inc., 1968), 113–151.

computers, and the year of decision of computer manufacturers to impede the growth of the leasing industry.[16] General Electric designed a disaggregative model of the flashbulb market, showing the response of different types of retailers to different types of trade promotions and deals.[17] The E. I. du Pont de Nemours and Company developed several simulations of specific markets and marketing plans under the general name of Venture Analysis.[18] Other companies that are active in developing complex computer models of specific markets are Pillsbury and Corning Glass. According to the managers at Corning:

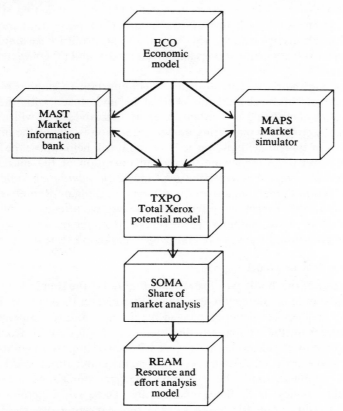

Figure 21-1 Xerox Marketing Analysis Research System (Project Mars)
Source: Company memo.

Simulation models for several new products have been developed thus far at Corning. It is intended in the next few years to have simulation models for all new products so that investments for these products might be evaluated

[16]A. M. Economos, "A Financial Simulation for Risk Analysis of a Proposed Subsidiary," *Management Science* (Aug. 1968), B–675–682.

[17]From a private memorandum.

[18]Sigurd L. Andersen, "Venture Analysis: A Flexible Planning Tool," *Chemical Engineering Progress* (March 1961), 80–83.

on a total company basis rather than on an individual basis, permitting more comprehensive investment planning, and optimum use of resources.[19]

A SYSTEMATIC PROCEDURE FOR CONSTRUCTING A CORPORATE MARKETING MODEL

Every company is a pioneer in this area because it must start fresh to create its own concepts, data base, and means of validation. The following seven concepts and tools appear to be basic to any such system: (1) core marketing system model, (2) comprehensive marketing system model, (3) input-output models, (4) functional relationship models, (5) four-quadrant profit-forecasting and -planning model, (6) mathematical sales and profit model, and (7) computerized model and output.

Before discussing these concepts in detail, it is important to emphasize that the development of the marketing model must be undertaken with the full participation of the marketing and other company executives who will be the future users of the corporate marketing model. Education is one of the important by-products of this model building activity and it will help expose the blind spots of various executives in viewing the overall operation of the marketing system. *Executives in the same company tend to see the marketing system in different terms.* It is not exceptional to find executives omitting or deemphasizing critical elements in the marketing system. The cooperative attempt to build a corporate marketing model should yield, as one of its major products, a comprehensive and consensual view of the company's marketing system.

Core Marketing System Model

In the first chapter of this book, we illustrated in Figure 1-1 the simplest marketing system, made up of a company interacting with a market through two inner flows (products and services being exchanged for money), and two outer flows (communications from the company to the market and information from the market to the company). Following this, Figure 1-2 showed important additional elements that make up a modern marketing system: competitors, marketing intermediaries, suppliers, and the encompassing environmental forces of economics, public policy, technology, and culture. These two diagrams constitute a good starting point for trying to map the marketing system of real companies.

We shall now apply all the techniques for building a corporate marketing model to a specific and real company. The specific company is a leading candy producer and we shall develop the marketing model for one of its leading products, a soft-centered, chocolate-covered candy bar.

A diagram of the company's core marketing system can be constructed showing the company, the market, and the linking channels of distribution

[19]John C. Chambers, Satinder K. Mullick, and Thomas J. Patterson, "Strategic New Product Planning Models for Dynamic Situations," a paper presented at TIMS meeting, Philadelphia, Sept. 6, 1966.

(see Figure 21-2). Some time back, the company made a major *product-market decision* to produce and sell this candy bar. Such a decision is not made lightly or frequently; it is a *strategic decision* that is followed by sizable resource committments to its pursuit. Only at long run intervals will it evaluate and decide whether to continue or drop the product.

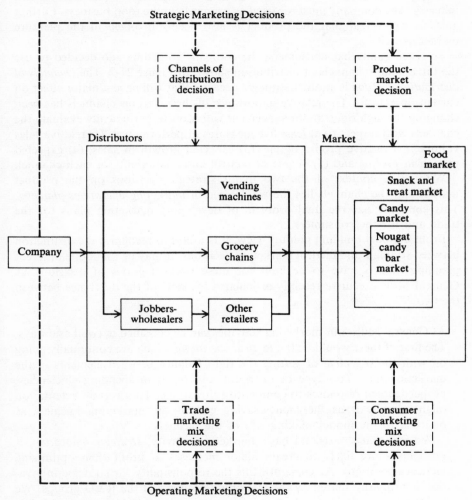

Figure 21-2   Core Marketing System Model

The right side of the diagram attempts to expand the generic market basis of this particular product. It can provide clues to spotting other opportunities and also to understanding the sources of competition. Thus a candy bar is part of a larger market, the candy market, which contains many other forms of candy that may constitute potential opportunities or competition. In turn, the candy market itself is included in a much larger market known as the snack and treat market, which represents all products that provide nourishment or taste satisfaction between major meals. Seen in this light, candy is in competition with such sundries as potato chips, soft drinks, pastry, and chewing gum. Finally, the snack and treat market represents only a small part of the food industry. The company must see itself as primarily in the food business. Further analysis will reveal that the product is also deeply involved in the pleasure market as well.

To reach candy bar consumers, the company sometime ago decided to use the three major channels of distribution shown in Figure 21-2. The *channels of distribution decision* is another strategic decision that will have a major effect on current operations. The relative importance of these various channels has been changing through time, and management will want to periodically evaluate the channels with respect to at least five measures of performance: (1) relative sales volume, (2) relative profit volume, (3) expected growth in sales, (4) expected growth in profits, and (5) degree of control and adaptability of each channel.

Within the context of the two major strategic decisions on the product market and the channels lies the whole area of *marketing operations planning*. This company has the dual problem of developing marketing plans for the trade and for the consumers.

From a model building point of view, it is useful to recognize the distinction between strategic and tactical marketing decisions. It may be that quite different planning models have to be built for these two categories of decisions. A General Mills executive recently articulated his view of the difference between the two:[20]

At General Mills, our marketing activities can be classified in two basic ways. The first of these would be the *tactical operations* which are continually going on with the objective of getting the right balance between elements in the marketing mix. This type of operation can result in spending efficiencies, proper tactical responses to competitive thrust, etc. To a certain extent, you might classify it as the money-saving end of the marketing business as opposed to the money-making end of the business.

We feel that the second basic marketing activity, *strategic innovation*, is probably more likely to create major increases in profit than optimizing tactical operations. At General Mills the responsibility for strategic innovation is primarily shared by the marketing groups and the R&D groups. We feel most strongly that only by creating major discontinuities in established marketing patterns are we going to be able to grow in profit at our targeted rate.

Clearly, if strategic innovation involves changing the system itself, the model

[20]H. B. Atwater, Jr., "Integrating Marketing and Other Information Systems," a speech presented to the 15th Annual Marketing Conference of the National Industrial Conference Board, New York City, Oct. 18, 1967, p. 7.

necessary for its evaluation may be quite different from that required for evaluating marketing operations planning which takes place within a stable system.

Comprehensive Marketing System Model

The next step calls for diagramming the company's marketing system more comprehensively to show other marketing entities and decisions and the feedback control relationships. Figure 21-3 illustrates how such a model could be constructed for the candy company. The system is logically divided into six aspects:

1. The environment, or, more precisely, those forces in the environment that affect candy demand, such as population growth, per-capita income, attitudes toward candy, and so on.
2. The company and competitors' marketing decision models.
3. The major categories of decision making in this market—product characteristics, price, sales force, physical distribution and service, and advertising and sales promotion.
4. The three major marketing channels which the company uses for this product.
5. The buyer behavior model which shows customer response to the activities of the manufacturers and the distribution channels, as well as to the environment.
6. Total industry sales, market shares and costs.

The various arrows show the flows connecting the major elements in the marketing system. The flows are numbered for ease of reference to more detailed documents. Flow "5," for example, would refer to a detailed diagram and description showing types of product characteristic decisions, the inputs used to influence each of these decisions, the source of data for each of the inputs, and so forth. Using this device, the company can develop a detailed documentary analysis of its marketing system.

Input-output Models

At this stage the marketing system is further refined by the preparation of diagrams of the inputs and outputs shown in the boxes of Figure 21-3.

As an illustration of this technique, consider the company marketing decision box which is singled out and featured in Figure 21-4. To obtain the information shown in the figures, company executives would be asked to list the major types of marketing decisions made in the company. A variety of answers can be expected, which again emphasizes the fact that managers within the same company carry in their heads only partial models of the total marketing system. Note that their answers generally seem to relate to either trade decisions or consumer decisions. The two kinds of decisions are called outputs and are listed on the right side of the figure. To influence the trade, the company uses the wholesale price, trade allowances, sales calls and service, trade advertising, co-op advertising allowances, credit policy, and delivery policy. To influence

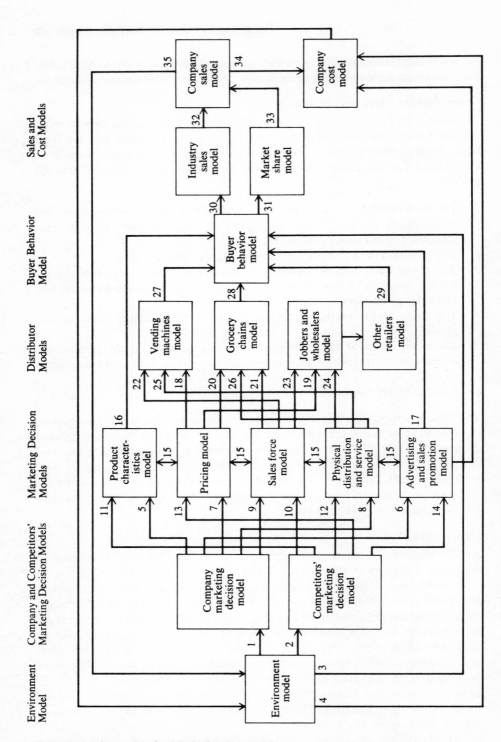

Figure 21-3   Comprehensive Marketing System Map

the consumer, the company uses product characteristics, packaging characteristics, retail price, consumer deals, and consumer advertising.

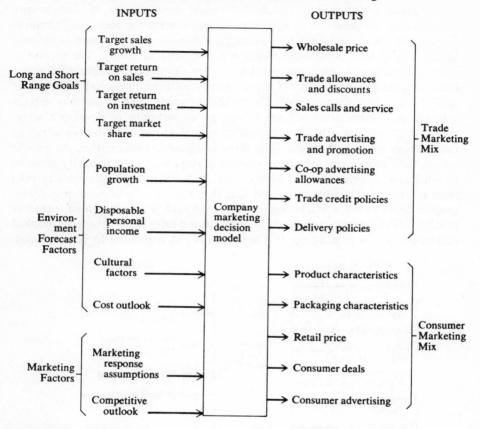

Figure 21-4 Input-Output Map of Company Marketing Decisions

Having identified the major marketing decision outputs, management then lists the various inputs and influences on these decisions which fall into one of three groups:

1. The company's long- and short-range goals for sales growth, return on sales, and return on investment.
2. Forecastable factors in the environment, such as population growth, disposable personal income, cultural factors, and the cost outlook.
3. Various assumptions about the sales effectiveness of different marketing instruments as well as expectations concerning competition.

The inputs listed on the left represent one possible way to classify the factors affecting the company marketing decisions listed on the right. Each input and output can be elaborated further. For example, in the area of cultural factors, it is possible to isolate three such factors that will have a significant effect on future candy consumption. The first is *weight consciousness*. If there is any relaxation of the pressures in American society toward the idea that "slimness is beautiful," and we return to a Peter Paul Rubens view of feminine beauty, this may lead to a substantial increase in the sales of candy. The second is *cavity-consciousness*. As better dentifrices are developed, people will worry less about the negative effects of sugar on their teeth, and this may reduce their inhibitions against eating candy. Nevertheless, worry about sugar may remain a factor, and some firms will see this as an opportunity to develop a tasty, sugarless candy that will offer the double appeal of not contributing either to tooth decay or to overweight. The third is *cigarette consumption*. As people reduce their rate of cigarette consumption in response to the publicity given to health hazards, we can expect candy, gum, and other "oral" gratifiers to take their place. All this adds up to the fact that the traditional economic-demographic factors used in marketing forecasting should be supplemented whenever possible with forecasts of cultural factors. Cultural forecasting, like technological and public policy forecasting, is a field that is just beginning to be developed.

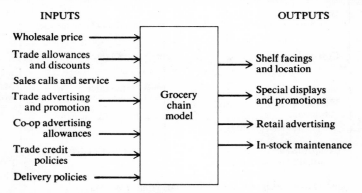

Figure 21-5   Input-Output Model of Grocery Chain Decisions

Having identified the major inputs and outputs of the company marketing decision model, we now proceed to trace how these data feed into other parts of the system. Consider the output described as the trade marketing mix. This output now becomes input into each of the distributor channels—for example, the grocery chain model (Figure 21-5). The next step is to consider the major outputs of the grocery chain model, that is, the decisions that grocery chains independently make which affect the purchase rate of this candy bar. These include: (1) the amount and location of shelf facings that will be devoted to this candy bar product; (2) the extent of store cooperation in special displays and promotions; (3) the amount of retail advertising of this candy product that each store decides to undertake; and (4) the policy of the stores toward maintaining good inventories and keeping the shelves filled with the product. These are store decisions that vitally affect the sales of this candy bar through the stores, especially considering that candy bar sales have a large impulse component. The manufacturer, however, has no direct control over the stores' decisions in this area.

This is why it is vitally important to identify the factors on the left, because they represent the "methods" that the manufacturer has in trying to influence the store decisions shown on the right. That is, the manufacturer will develop wholesale prices, trade allowances, sales calls and service, trade advertising, cooperative advertising, credit policies and delivery policies in such a way as to exert the appropriate amount of influence on the grocery chains to feature its product.

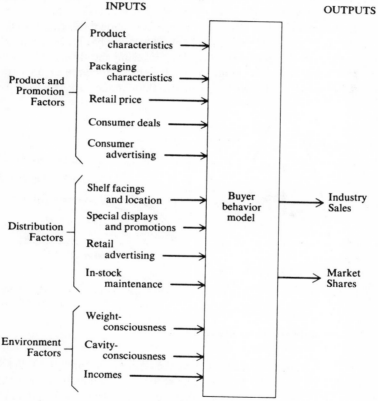

Figure 21-6   Input-Output Model of Buyer Behavior

The influence of the dealers' decisions on the final consumers is shown in Figure 21-6, along with influences coming from other parts of the marketing system. The various influences are classified into product and promotion factors (outputs coming from the company marketing decision model), distribution factors (outputs coming from the channels of distribution models), and environmental factors (outputs coming from the environment model). These factors shape consumers' buying behavior to bring about a certain level of industry sales and brand share sales of candy bars.

Functional Relationship Maps

We have illustrated how each model component can be analyzed in greater detail to define its inputs and outputs, and how the outputs of one component become the inputs to other components. The next task is to measure the functional relationships between various key elements. For instance, it is obvious that retail price and advertising affect the rate of consumer purchase; the real task is to measure by how much.

Two examples of measured functional relationships are shown in Figure 21-7. Figure 21-7(a) shows the estimated effect on candy bar sales of an important product characteristic—the relative amount of chocolate (measured as a percent of the total weight of the candy bar). The candy bar is chocolate covered and the question is how thick this chocolate covering should be. The company would like to keep this percentage down because chocolate is an expensive ingredient compared with the ingredients that make up the soft center.

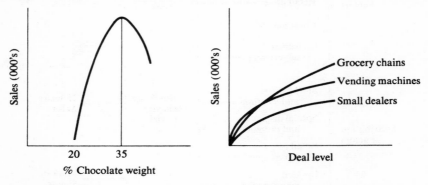

(a) Relationship between Percentage Chocolate Weight and Sales.

(b) Relationship between Deal Level and Sales Response of Different Channels

Figure 21-7   Functional Relationship Models

However, consumer tests reveal that, as the chocolate content of the bar is reduced, preference and sales decline. The soft center begins to appear through the chocolate in places and leads the average consumer to feel that the bar is poorly made. Furthermore, his palate desires more chocolate to offset the soft center. Surprisingly, when the layer of chocolate gets too thick (above 35 percent of the weight of the bar), consumer preference for the bar also falls, but for a different reason. The consumer begins to think of this, not as a soft-centered candy bar, but as a chocolate bar with "some stuff in it." He relates this bar to pure chocolate bars, and it suffers by comparison. To the best of management's knowledge, sales have the parabolic relationship to percentage chocolate weight that is shown in Figure 21-7(a).

Given this functional relationship, what is the optimum level of chocolate? If the company wishes to maximize sales, then chocolate should constitute 35 percent of the candy bar's weight. However, since the company is primarily interested in maximizing profit, management needs the ingredient cost functions, as well as the sales response function, to determine the profit-maximizing amount of chocolate.

Figure 21-7(b) shows another functional relationship, that between the amount of trade allowance (deal level) and sales. It appears that the channels of distribution differ in their response to deal offers. Small retailers are less responsive to deals than other channels. They do not handle as high a volume, nor do they calculate as closely the profit implicit in various deals. The grocery chains, on the other hand, are quick to take advantage of deals. The functional relationships can be useful in determining the optimal allocation of deal money to the different distribution channels.

Profit Forecasting Model

At some point, the various functional relationships must be put together into a model for analyzing the sales and profit consequences of a proposed marketing plan. We shall first look at a graphical method of integrating major relationships in the marketing model. Then, in the following section, we shall use this to develop a computerized version of the marketing model.

The graphical-analytical device is shown in Figure 21-8. It has been adapted for the candy company example from an idea of Robert S. Weinberg.[21] Quadrant 1 shows a relationship between population and the total sales of chocolate-covered soft-centered candy bars.[22] The functional relationship shows that sales tend to increase with population, but at a decreasing rate. The part of the curve describing candy consumption for stages in which the American population was under 200 million persons is historically derived by least-squares regression analysis. The part of the curve showing sales for future sizes of the U.S. population is extrapolated and is influenced by anticipated cultural and economic trends. The curve indicates that a population of 200 million persons consumes approximately $105 million of soft-centered candy bars.

The second quadrant shows the relationship between total sales of soft-centered candy bars and company sales. When industry sales are $105 million, this particular company enjoys sales of $70 million, that is, a market share of approximately 67 percent. The part of the curve toward the lower level of industry sales is derived from historical information; the part toward the higher levels of sales is extrapolated on the assumption that there will be no dramatic changes in company and competitors' marketing efforts. Although

[21]Robert S. Weinberg, "Multiple Factor Break-Even Analysis: The Applications of Operations-Research Techniques to a Basic Problem of Management Planning and Control," *Operations Research* (Apr. 1956), 152–186.

[22]We are assuming for the sake of illustration that the only important environmental variable is population. If two or more environmental variables are involved, a weighted combination of them may be portrayed on this axis or a mathematical analysis can be substituted for the graphical one.

the function is linear, it does not necessarily indicate that the company expects its market share to remain constant. This would be true only if the line started at the 0, 0 origin of this quadrant (not shown). Actually, the line indicates that the company expects its share of market to fall slightly as total sales increase. For example, when industry sales are $140 million, the expectation of company sales is $90 million, or an estimated market share of 64 percent as compared with 67 percent now.

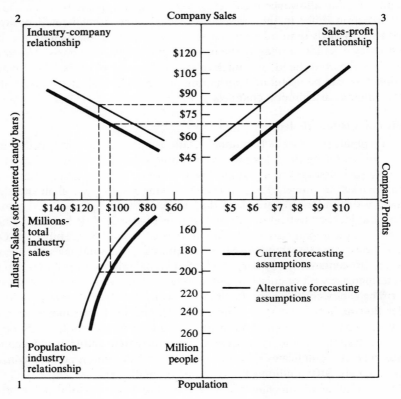

Figure 21-8   The Profit Forecasting and Planning Map

The third quadrant shows the relationship between company sales and company profits. Again, the company assumes that the relationship is basically linear. At the present time, profits are $7 million on company sales of approximately $70 million, or 10 per cent. If company sales go up to $105 million, the company expects profits of approximately $10.2 million, that is, 9.7 percent.

This kind of graphical device, which assumes that all the underlying relationships have been combined and expressed in terms of three basic relationships, allows us to visualize the effect of a particular level of an environment factor and continued marketing program on company sales and profits. To this extent, it is a forecasting device. Its use extends beyond this, however, into marketing planning as well. Suppose, for example, that the company expects the new antismoking campaign to have a big impact on candy bar sales, shifting the curve in the first quadrant to the left (Figure 21-8). Furthermore, suppose that the company is considering intensifying its marketing effort to increase its market share even further. The anticipated effect of this on company market share can be seen by shifting the function in the second quadrant to the right, as shown in Figure 21-8. At the same time the company's marketing costs increase and therefore shift the sales profit curve to the left, as shown in the third quadrant of Figure 21-8. What is the net effect of this complicated set of shifts? The result is that, although sales have increased, profits have fallen. Apparently, the cost to the company of attaining a still higher market share exceeds the profits on the extra sales. The company would be wise not to intensify its marketing effort, at least according to the specific plan it is considering and its estimated effects.

Mathematical Sales and Profit Model

The four-quadrant profit forecasting and planning model helps one to visualize the impact of a complex set of developments on final company sales and profits. It is also a very useful device for explaining a forecast or a plan to others in the company. At the same time, however, it is quite limited with respect to the number of factors that can be handled directly. For more detailed modeling we need a mathematical formulation of the candy company's marketing system.

A simplified version of this model is shown in Table 21-1. The starting point for any marketing planning model is an equation that expresses profits as a function of the variables under the company's control. Equation 21-1 shows a profit equation for company i where profit is equal to the gross profit margin $(P-c)$ times quantity (Q), minus the fixed costs (F), advertising and promotion expenditures (A), and distribution expenditures (D). It is possible to spell out the profit equation in greater detail but this form will suffice for illustration.

Typically, the most difficult variable to estimate is company sales (Q_i). The model builder's skill comes into play here as he tries to formulate an explanatory and predictive equation for company sales. Equation 21-2 is such an equation. It appears that the model builder took the easy way out by defining company sales as the product of company market share (s_i) and total sales of soft-centered candy bars (Q). However, in doing this, it is now necessary to account for the two new variables, total sales and market share.

To explain total sales, we formulate the relationship shown in Equation 21-3. Total soft-centered candy bar sales are the product of the population (N), the per-capita candy consumption rate in pounds (k), and the ratio of soft-centered candy bar sales to total candy sales (m). But now it appears that we have traded the variable Q for three new variables. Fortunately, the three variables are fairly easy to account for exogenously. The ratio of soft-centered candy bar sales to total sales is a fairly stable number. The per-capita candy consumption rate is expected to rise asymptotically in the United States from its present level $(t = 1)$ of 18 lbs per capita to 24 lbs per capita, which happens to be the per-capita

Table 21-1   Mathematical Sales and Profit Model

Company i's Profit Equation

$$Z_{it} = (P_{it} - c_{it})Q_{it} - F_{it} - A_{it} - D_{it} \qquad (21\text{-}1)$$

Company i's Sales Equation

$$Q_{it} = s_{it}Q_t \qquad (21\text{-}2)$$

Industry Sales Equation

$$Q_t = m_t k_t N_t \qquad (21\text{-}3)$$

where m_t = parameter

$k_t = 24(1 - .25^t)$

$N_t = 200(1.03)^t$

Market Share Equation

$$s_{it} = \frac{R_{it}^{e_{Ri}}P_{it}^{-e_{Pi}}(a_{it}A_{it})^{e_{Ai}}(d_{it}D_{it})^{e_{Di}}}{\sum_i [R_{it}^{e_{Ri}}P^{-e_{Pi}}(a^{it}A^{it})^{e_{Ai}}(d^{it}D^{it})^{e_{Di}}]}$$

$$(21\text{-}4)$$

Z_{it} = profits in dollars of company i in year t

P_{it} = average price per lb of company i's product in year t

c_{it} = variable cost per lb of company i's product in year t

Q_{it} = number of lbs sold of company i's product in year t

F_{it} = fixed costs of manufacturing and selling company i's product in year t

A_{it} = advertising and promotion costs for company i's product in year t

D_{it} = distribution and sales force costs for company i's products in year t

s_{it} = company i's average market share in year t

Q_t = industry sales of soft-centered candy bars in year t

m_t = soft-centered candy bar poundage as a share of total candy poundage

k_t = per capita candy consumption in pounds in year t

N_t = millions of persons in United States in year t

R_{it} = preference rating of company i's product in year t

a_{it} = advertising effectiveness index

d_{it} = distribution effectiveness index

$\left.\begin{matrix} e_R \\ e_{Pi} \\ e_{Ai} \\ e_D \end{matrix}\right\} =$ elasticities of preference, price, advertising and distribution, respectively, of company i

candy consumption level of the highest candy-consuming country in the world, Great Britain. The population (N) is rising at the rate of 3 percent a year.

The other variable in the company's sales equation, market share, is typically the hardest of the elements to formulate; yet it is crucial, in that it will reflect all of the assumptions about the company marketing decision variables. There are several ways to formulate the market share equation.[23] Equation 21-4 is one example. It shows market share as the ratio of the weighted value of the company's marketing mix to the sum of all candy companies' weighted marketing mixes. The weighted value of a marketing mix is given by the product of the company's effective preference level, price, advertising, and distribution, raised to their respective elasticities. Further refinements can be introduced to reflect the carryover effects of past promotions. The market share model, whatever its form, must synthesize the functional relationships described earlier.

Additional refinements can and should be introduced into this model. For example, cost per pound (c) may not be constant but, rather, vary with the scale of sales (via production), the preference rating for the company's product (to the extent that this involves better quality ingredients), and time itself, because of inflation. This means that some formulation of $c = f(Q, R, t)$ would be desirable. Furthermore, fixed costs may not be independent of the level of sales and production, and therefore some formulation of the form $F = g(Q)$ might be necessary. These and other refinements are introduced as part of the evolution of the model into an increasingly accurate instrument for forecasting and planning.

The model not only must be formulated, but must also be fitted and updated according to the best available information and statistical techniques. Objective data are preferred, but, when they are not available, carefully collected subjective data may be used. The effect of uncertain data inputs on the results can be estimated through sensitivity analysis.

Computer Model and Output

At some stage the model should be programmed for the computer and made available to management, preferably on an on-line basis. Marketing planners should be able to sit at a terminal, type in the latest research data, along with specific proposed settings of the marketing decision variables, and get back an estimate of the plan's expected sales and profits. The computer program should also contain, if possible, a subroutine which can search for the best plan.

As an illustration of the printout from one such computer program, consider Table 21-2.[24] The print-out shows the inputs and expected payoffs for a seven-year plan being considered for a cereal product. (This plan calls for the continuation of the past marketing strategy: two other plans were also evaluated, one calling for intensified marketing effort and the other calling for a gradual phasing out of the product.) The first item printed out is the calculated internal rate of return after taxes for the particular plan (Plan 1)—it is a substantial 45

---

[23]See Chap. 4.

[24]"The Quaker Oats Company–Life Cereal C," Harvard Business School M-311, 1968. The particular model underlying this output is much simpler than the one discussed earlier. Instead of using a sales model to derive sales estimates from planned levels of marketing decision variables, management supplies subjective estimates of sales.

Table 21-2 Sample Print-out from Computer Program

Internal rate of return (after taxes) = 45   %

Time horizon = 7   Years

Remaining undepr. P & E invest. at begin. yr. 1 = 900000   Dollars
Remaining no. of years of P & E depreciation = 3   Years
Remaining undep. bldg invest. at begin. yr. 1 = 210000   Dollars
Remaining no. of years of bldg depreciation = 21   Years

Depreciation horizon for P & E investments = 10   Years
Depreciation horizon for bldg investments = 30   Years

Opportunity cost (at beginning of period) = 2E+06   Dollars
Working capital = 13   % Sales
Salvage value (at end of period) = 10   × earnings

Year	1 Ret. price($)	2 Ret. mar. (%)	3 Whole. price($)	4 Whole. mar. (%)
1969	.577	18	.473	0
1970	.602	18	.494	0
1971	.621	18	.509	0
1972	.639	18	.524	0
1973	.659	18	.540	0
1974	.675	18	.554	0
1975	.698	18	.572	0

	5 Factory price($)	6 Variable man. cost($)	7 Variable man. cost (%)	8 Variable mktg. cost (%)
1969	.473	.191	40.4	5
1970	.494	.196	39.7	5
1971	.509	.202	39.7	5
1972	.524	.208	39.7	5
1973	.540	.214	39.6	5
1974	.554	.221	39.9	5
1975	.572	.227	39.7	5

	9 Contrib. to fixed costs and profit ($)	10 (%)	11 Fixed man. cost($)	12 Fixed mktg. cost($)
1969	.258	54.6	915000	4.25E+06
1970	.273	55.3	971000	4.90E+06
1971	.282	55.3	1.028E+06	5.50E+06
1972	.290	55.3	1.310E+06	5.75E+06
1973	.299	55.4	1.386E+06	6.25E+06
1974	.305	55.1	1.421E+06	6.85E+06
1975	.317	55.3	1.824E+06	7.60E+06

	13 *P & E invest.*	14 *Bldg. invest.*	15 *Deprec. expense*
1968	850000	0	
1969	0	0	395000
1970	0	0	395000
1971	850000	1E+06	395000
1972	0	0	213333
1973	0	0	213333
1974	850000	1E+06	213333
1975	0	0	331666

	16 *Index of* *company sales*	17 *Company* *sales (units)*	18 *Industry* *sales (units)*	19 *Market* *share*
1969	1.0	3.0E+07	1.166E+09	2.6
1970	1.1	3.3E+07	1.182E+09	2.8
1971	1.2	3.6E+07	1.198E+09	3.0
1972	1.3	3.9E+07	1.215E+09	3.2
1973	1.4	4.2E+07	1.230E+09	3.4
1974	1.5	4.5E+07	1.247E+09	3.6
1975	1.6	4.8E+07	1.265E+09	3.8

	20 *Mktg. exp.* *(% sales)*	21 *P.A.T.* *(% sales)*	22 *P.A.T. ($)*	23 *Cash flow* *(After Tax) ($)*
1968				−2.85E+06
1969	34.9	7.7	1.097245E+06	−353001
1970	35.1	8.4	1.370807E+06	1.493337E+06
1971	35.0	8.8	1.610162E+06	−110272
1972	33.1	9.9	2.014062E+06	1.953967E+06
1973	32.5	10.4	2.361914E+06	2.281351E+06
1974	32.5	10.4	2.591395E+06	667228
1975	32.7	9.9	2.723974E+06	2.722089E+06
1976				2.723975E+07

Source: "The Quaker Oats Company—Life Cereal C," Harvard Business School, M–311, 1968, p. 5.

percent.[25] The next line shows that this calculation is for a seven-year planning horizon. Some details are then printed out on the initial value of the unde-preciated plant and equipment and building investment devoted to this product line and the remaining number of years of depreciation. The depreciation horizons are also printed out, as well as the current opportunity cost of this investment and its expected salvage value at the end of the period.

The rest of the print-out shows the expected or planned year to year levels

[25]The computer program is set up to give two other payoff measures, that is, the present value of the after-tax cash flow, and the sales and market share needed to achieve 10 percent ROI after taxes.

of important variables that ultimately affect the internal rate of return. Column 1 shows that the retail price per unit is expected to rise from 58¢ to 70¢ in the course of seven years. Column 2 shows that the retail margin for this product is 18 percent and it is not expected to change. Column 3 shows the resulting wholesale prices. Since this company sells direct to the retailers, there is no wholesale margin (column 4), and the factory price (column 5) is the same as the wholesale price. Column 6 shows estimated variable manufacturing costs and they too are expected to rise over the period from a present level of 19¢ to 23¢ in 1975. The ratio of variable manufacturing costs to factory prices is shown in column 7, followed by the planned ratio of variable marketing costs to factory prices (column 8). By subtracting variable manufacturing and marketing costs per unit from the price, the result is the contribution to fixed costs and profits, which is shown in dollar and percentage form in columns 9 and 10, respectively.

The next step calls estimating fixed manufacturing costs and fixed marketing costs over the next seven years, which are shown in columns 11 and 12. The symbol, $E+06$, is computer print-out shorthand and means that the reader should move the decimal place in the associated number, six places to the right. Thus $\$1.028E+06$ means $\$1,028,000$. Columns 13 and 14 show the anticipated investments in plant, equipment, and building over the next seven years; column 15 shows the estimated total depreciation expense.

We now arrive at the estimated sales and profits. Columns 16 and 17 show management's estimates of sales (in percentage and dollar terms, respectively) over the next seven years. The figures indicate that management expects company sales (in units) to rise at the rate of about 10 percent a year, on the basis of its planned levels of marketing expenditures. Column 18 presents management's estimate of industry sales for the next seven years. The figures in column 19, market share, are derived by dividing estimated company sales (column 17) by estimated industry sales (column 18). We see that management expects market share to grow from 2.6 percent to 3.8 percent over a seven-year period. Column 20 expresses total marketing expenditures (columns 8 and 12) as a percent of sales, and this percentage is expected to fall. Examining this closer, we see that management expects sales to rise faster than marketing expenditures; hence it is assuming an increase in marketing productivity.

Columns 21 and 22 are a derivation of the implied yearly profits after taxes (P.A.T.) in percentage and dollar terms. The computer program uses the following formula to calculate dollar profits after taxes:

$$Z = (1 - t)[mQ - F - D] \qquad (21\text{-}5)$$

where Z = profits after taxes (column 22)

$\quad t$ = tax rate, here .4944

$\quad m$ = contribution to fixed costs and profit (column 9)

$\quad Q$ = sales in units (column 17)

$\quad F$ = fixed manufacturing and marketing costs (columns 11 and 12)

$\quad D$ = depreciation (column 15)

For example, the profits after taxes for 1969 are

$(1 - .4944)[(\$.258)(30,000,000) - \$5,165,000 - \$395,000]$, or $\$1,097,245$.

Column 23 shows the results of the conversion of profits after taxes to cash flow after taxes, according to the following formula:

$$Z' = Z + D - W - I \qquad (21\text{-}6)$$

where Z' = cash flow after taxes (column 23)

W = working capital in dollars, i.e., working capital as a percent of sales, times wholesale price, times sales in units

I = new investment expenditure (columns 13 and 14)

For example, the cash flow after taxes for 1969 is

$\$1,097,245 + \$395,000 - [.13(\$.473)(30,000,000)] - 0$, or $-\$353,001$.

Having calculated the cash flow after taxes, the computer now calculates the internal rate of return implicit in the cash flow in column 23. This is found by taking the opportunity cost at the beginning of the period and searching for the interest rate that would discount the future cash flows so that the sum of the discounted cash flows is equal to the initial opportunity cost; this rate turns out to be 45 percent.

Thus computer programs such as this one enables the marketing planner to determine the financial consequences implied by a particular set of costs, investments, and sales. He can easily calculate the impact on profit of any alterations in his data or assumptions. This particular computer program could be further improved by (1) including separate estimates of each marketing decision variable, instead of lumping them together as total marketing expense; (2) incorporating a sales model that estimates sales analytically from the marketing plan variables and environmental and competitive assumptions, instead of requiring direct estimation; (3) introducing a subroutine for planning territorial allocations of the marketing budget; (4) introducing risk explicitly into the program by including pessimistic, optimistic, and normal estimates; and (5) introducing a profit-maximizing algorithm that will search for the best marketing plan in the light of the assumptions and data.

SUMMARY

A corporate marketing model is a model that is (1) computerized, (2) industry-specific, (3) data based, (4) comprehensive, and (5) designed for developing and evaluating alternative company marketing plans. Its roots lie in recent work done on corporate financial models and also some of the elaborate industry-specific marketing games such as the ones developed at Carnegie Tech and M.I.T. Corporate marketing models are beginning to be developed by such companies as Xerox, Minute Maid, General Electric, Pillsbury, and Corning Glass.

Each company that undertakes to develop a corporate marketing model should involve the executives who will use it throughout the development stages, so that the model will be understandable and acceptable. Seven concepts and tools mark the stages of developing the corporate marketing model, although the particulars will have to be creatively applied to each company. Using a candy company and one of its key products, a soft-centered chocolate covered candy bar as an illustration, the first step consists of developing a core marketing system map, that is, a map showing the company, the market, and the linking channels of distribution. This map highlights the distinction between the company's strategic marketing decisions and its operating marketing decisions, suggesting the possibility that these two levels of decision making may require different marketing models. The second step is to develop the comprehensive marketing system map, showing all the key marketing entities and decisions and the feedback control relationships. The third step calls for listing, for each marketing entity separately, the major decisions made by that entity (outputs) and the major influences on these decisions (inputs). From this listing stage, it is next necessary to pass to the fourth stage of expressing functional relationships between key variables, utilizing the best objective or subjective information available to the company. The fifth step calls for integrating the key relationships into a profit forecasting and planning map, which allows the marketing planner to examine the effects of major movements along, or shifts in, three key relationships in terms of their effects on company sales and profits. The sixth step calls for reexpressing the maps into a detailed mathematical model of sales and profit determination and statistically fitting this model. Finally, the seventh stage calls for computerizing this model, so that it can be used to yield analytical results on an on-line basis. An example of the output of one such computer program was shown, consisting of a seven-year forecast of anticipated costs, investments, sales and profits, and the derived internal rate of return.

Questions and Problems

1. It has been argued that corporate marketing models are of little value, since it is impossible to operationalize such models without first understanding individual component mechanisms. What do you think?
2. List and discuss the major criteria you would use in judging a corporate marketing model.
3. Develop a core marketing system map for:
(a) A newspaper publisher in a large metropolitan area
(b) An oil company which markets a high-grade motor oil.
4. Develop an input-output map for the advertising submodel in Figure 21–3.
5. Develop a functional relationship map which shows the relationship between:
(a) Retail price and candy bar sales
(b) Advertising and candy bar sales.

Appendix:
Mathematical Notes

2-1

Show that in $Q = \bar{Q}(1 - e^{-aX})$, the marginal sales response, dQ/dX, is proportional to the level of untapped potential.

Proof: Find the marginal sales response at X:

$$\frac{dQ}{dX} = (ae^{-aX})\bar{Q} \tag{1}$$

Define the untapped potential at X to be $Q_G = \bar{Q} - Q(X)$. Then,

$$Q_G = \bar{Q} - \bar{Q}(1 - e^{-aX})$$
$$Q_G = \bar{Q}(1 - 1 + e^{-aX}) = \bar{Q}(e^{-aX})$$

or

$$\bar{Q} = \frac{Q_G}{e^{-aX}} \tag{2}$$

Then substitute Equation 2 into Equation 1:

$$\frac{dQ}{dX} = (ae^{-aX})\frac{Q_G}{(e^{-aX})}$$

Therefore,

$$\frac{dQ}{dX} = aQ_G$$

and the proposition is proved.

3-1

Given the profit function $Z = PQ - c(Q, R)Q - A - D - F$, where $Q = q(P, A, D, R)$, show that marketing mix optimization occurs when $e_P = MRP_A = MRP_D = e_R(P/c)$.

Proof: Price optimization implies

$$\frac{\partial Z}{\partial P} = Pq_P + q - cq_P - c_q q_P q = 0$$

where $q_P = \dfrac{\partial q}{\partial P}$, $c_q = \dfrac{\partial c}{\partial q}$, and $q = Q$

Therefore, $P = [q_P(c + c_q q) - q]/q_P$

$$P = c + c_q q - \frac{q}{q_P} \tag{1}$$

For optimum advertising expenditure,

$$\frac{\partial Z}{\partial A} = Pq_A - cq_A - c_q q_A q - 1 = 0$$

Therefore, $Pq_A = q_A(c + c_q q) + 1$

$$P = c + c_q q + \frac{1}{q_A} \tag{2}$$

For optimum distribution expenditure,

$$\frac{\partial Z}{\partial D} = Pq_D - cq_D - c_q q_D q - 1 = 0$$

Therefore, $Pq_D = q_D(c + c_q q) + 1$

$$P = c + c_q q + \frac{1}{q_D} \tag{3}$$

Finally, for optimum quality,

$$\frac{\partial Z}{\partial R} = Pq_R - cq_R - c_q q_R q - c_R q = 0$$

Therefore, $Pq_R = q_R(c+c_q q)+c_R q$

$$P = c+c_q q+\frac{c_R q}{q_R} \tag{4}$$

Hence, from Equations 1, 2, 3, and 4 and the condition that all partial derivatives be set to 0:

$$-\frac{q}{q_P} = \frac{1}{q_A} = \frac{1}{q_D} = \frac{c_R q}{q_R} \tag{5}$$

Taking the reciprocals, we get

$$-\frac{q_P}{q} = q_A = q_D = \frac{q_R}{c_R q}$$

Multiplying by P, we find

$$-q_P\frac{P}{q} = Pq_A = Pq_D = \frac{q_R}{c_R}\cdot\frac{P}{q}$$

or $e_P = MRP_A = MRP_D = e_R\dfrac{P}{c}$

where $e_P = -\dfrac{\partial q}{\partial P}\cdot\dfrac{P}{q}$ = price elasticity of demand

$\quad Pq_A$ = marginal revenue product of advertising expenditure (MRP_A)

$\quad Pq_D$ = marginal revenue product of distribution expenditure (MRP_D)

$\quad e_R\dfrac{P}{c} = \left[\dfrac{\partial q}{\partial R}\dfrac{\partial R}{\partial c}\dfrac{c}{q}\right]\dfrac{P}{c} = \dfrac{q_R}{c_R}\dfrac{P}{q}$ = product quality rating elasticity times ratio of price to unit cost

3-2

Given the demand equation $Q = kP^pA^aD^d$ and the cost equation $C = cQ+A+D+F$, find the decision rules for optimum price, advertising, and distribution.

Solution: Let $Z = PQ-cQ-A-D-F$

$$Z = (P-c)Q-A-D-F \tag{1}$$

For the optimum price, find the first partial derivative of Equation 1 with respect to price:

$$\frac{\partial Z}{\partial P} = (P-c)\frac{\partial Q}{\partial P}+Q \tag{2}$$

Since $\partial Q/\partial P = kA^aD^dpP^{p-1} = (p/P)Q$, then Equation 2 becomes

$$\frac{\partial Z}{\partial P} = (P-c)\frac{p}{P}Q+Q = Q(p-\frac{cp}{P}+1) \tag{3}$$

Setting the first derivative in Equation 3 equal to 0, we obtain

$$Q\left(p - \frac{cp}{P} + 1\right) = 0 \tag{4}$$

Since $Q > 0$, then

$$p - \frac{cp}{P} + 1 = 0 \tag{5}$$

Rearranging terms and solving for P,

$$P^* = \frac{pc}{1+p} \tag{6}$$

The optimum advertising expenditure is

$$\frac{\partial Z}{\partial A} = (P - c)\frac{\partial Q}{\partial A} - 1 = 0$$

Since $\partial Q/\partial A = (a/A)Q$, then

$$(P - c)\frac{a}{A}Q = 1$$

Therefore, $A^* = a(P - c)Q$

The optimum distribution expenditure is

$$\frac{\partial Z}{\partial D} = (P - c)\frac{\partial Q}{\partial D} - 1 = 0$$

Since $\partial Q/\partial D = (d/D)Q$, then

$$(P - c)(d/D)Q = 1$$

Therefore, $D^* = d(P - c)Q$
(Note: The second-order conditions are not considered here.)

3-3

Given $Q = kP^pA^a$ and $Z = PQ - F - A$, show that $\dfrac{A^*}{P^*Q} = -\dfrac{a}{p}$. $\tag{1}$

Proof: Substitute (3-29) and (3-30) for P^* and A^* and simplify

$$\frac{A^*}{P^*Q} = \frac{a\left(\dfrac{pc}{1+p} - c\right)Q}{\left(\dfrac{pc}{1+p}\right)Q} = \frac{a\left(\dfrac{pc - pc - c}{1+p}\right)}{\left(\dfrac{pc}{1+p}\right)} = \left(\dfrac{-ac}{1+p}\right)\left(\dfrac{1+p}{pc}\right) = -\dfrac{a}{p}. \tag{2}$$

4-1

Given the four equations in (4-39) to (4-42), solve them simultaneously for A_1, A_2, P_1, P_2.

Proof: Equation (4-42) gives $P_2 = 4/3$. Substituting this value into (4-39) to (4-41), we have

$$3A_1 - A_1{}^2 - 4P_1 + 6 = 0 \tag{1}$$
$$2A_1 - 2A_1 P_1 + 3P_1 - 4 = 0 \tag{2}$$
$$3A_2 - 3A_1 + P_1 - 5 = 0 \tag{3}$$

Solving equation (3) for A_2 yields

$$A_2 = A_1 - 1/3 P_1 + 5/3$$

Solving equation (2) for P_1 yields

$$P_1 = (4 - 2A_1)/(3 - 2A_1)$$

Substituting this value of P_1 into Equation (1) gives a cubic equation in A_1,

$2A_1{}^3 - 9A_1{}^2 + 5A_1 + 2 = 0$, which can be factored into
$(A_1 - 1)(2A_1{}^2 - 7A_1 - 2) = 0$

The first solution, $A_1 = 1$, yields $A_2 = 2$, $P_1 = 2$, and $P_2 = 4/3$.
The second solution, $A_1 = (7 + \sqrt{65})/4$, yields $A_2 = (7 + \sqrt{65})/4 + 4/3$, $P_1 = 1$, $P_2 = 4/3$.
The third solution, $A_1 = (7 - \sqrt{65})/4$, gives negative solutions which have no meaning.
Thus equilibrium is reached at either

$A_1 = 1.00 \quad A_2 = 2.00 \quad P_1 = 2.00 \quad P_2 = 1.33 \quad Z_1 = 2.00 \quad Z_2 = -1.67$

or

$A_1 = 3.765 \quad A_2 = 5.095 \quad P_1 = 1.00 \quad P_2 = 1.33 \quad Z_1 = -3.765 \quad Z_2 = -4.665$

In the first equilibrium situation, only firm 1 is profitable, while in the second situation, both are unprofitable. The first solution dominates the second with respect to profits.

5-1

Show that the c coefficient in the Koyck equation may reflect autocorrelation as well as the carryover effect.

Discussion: The presence of errors of estimate in the relationship between Q and X is made explicit when it is written as

$$Q_t = bX_t + bcX_{t-1} + bc^2 X_{t-2} + \ldots + u_t \tag{1}$$

where u_t is a random disturbance term.

By lagging this expression one period and multiplying it by the "decay" parameter c, the Koyck method would yield

$$cQ_{t-1} = bcX_{t-1} + bc^2 X_{t-2} + \ldots + cu_{t-1} \tag{2}$$

Subtracting Equation 2 from Equation 1, we obtain

$$Q_t = bX_t + cQ_{t-1} + (u_t - cu_{t-1}) \tag{3}$$

where $(u_t - cu_{t-1})$ may be considered to be a composite disturbance term.

Equation 3 can be estimated by least squares, and the problems of multicollinearity present in Equation 1 are largely bypassed. However, the residuals of Equation 3 will be correlated with Q_{t-1}, since they contain the related term u_{t-1}. This results in biased estimates of the b and c coefficients.

A second problem with the use of Equation 3 is that the residual terms are serially correlated, even if it can be assumed that the u_{t-1} terms are independent. This arises because any two successive residuals such as $(u_t - cu_{t-1})$ and $(u_{t-1} - cu_{t-2})$ contain the common term u_{t-1}.

Koyck developed a method for estimating b and c without bias, using the expression $u_t = ku_{t-1} + e_t$, but based his method on assumed values for k. Klein ["The Estimation of Distributed Lags," *Econometrica*, 26 (1958), 553–565] showed that the Koyck result yields a maximum likelihood estimate in the case when $k = 0$. He suggested a method for estimating b, c, and k simultaneously without having to assume values for k.

5-2

Show, given $0 \leqslant c < 1$, that

$$S = (1-c) + c(1-c) + c^2(1-c) + \ldots + c^n(1-c) + \ldots = 1.00 \tag{1}$$

Proof: From Equation 1,

$$S = (1-c)[1 + c + c^2 + \ldots + c^n + \ldots] \tag{2}$$

Since $0 \leqslant c < 1$, the expression in the brackets is the sum of an infinite convergent series whose sum is $1/(1-c)$. Therefore:

$$S = \frac{1-c}{1-c} = 1 \tag{3}$$

5-3

Given that

$$1 = \frac{zb}{(1+r)^0} + \frac{zcb}{(1+r)^1} + \frac{zc^2b}{(1+r)^2} + \ldots \tag{1}$$

show that

$$r = \frac{c}{1-zb} - 1$$

Proof:

$$1 = zb\left(\frac{1}{(1+r)^0}+\frac{c}{(1+r)^1}+\frac{c^2}{(1+r)^2}+\cdots\right)$$

$$1 = zb\left(1+\left(\frac{c}{1+r}\right)^1+\left(\frac{c}{1+r}\right)^2+\cdots\right).$$

Let $k = c/(1+r)$. Then,

$$1 = zb(1+k+k^2+\cdots)$$

But $0 < k < 1$. Hence

$$1 = zb\left(\frac{1}{1-k}\right)$$

according to Mathematical Note 5-2.

$$1-k = zb$$
$$k = 1-zb$$
$$\frac{c}{1+r} = 1-zb$$
$$1+r = \frac{c}{1-zb}$$
$$r = \frac{c}{1-zb}-1$$

Alternatively, the last expression can be rewritten as

$$r = \frac{zb+c-1}{1-zb}$$

which is the form used by Palda, *The Management of Cumulative Advertising Effects*, p. 82.

5-4

Show that $1-c^n \geqslant .95$ reduces to $n \leqslant \log .05/\log c$

Proof: From $1-c^n \geqslant .95$, we obtain $.05 \geqslant c^n$. Hence $\log .05 \geqslant n \log c$. Therefore,

$$n \leqslant \frac{\log .05}{\log c}$$

6-1

Show that Equation 6-21 in Chap. 6 reduces to

$$X_1^* = B\left[\frac{(m_1a_1)^\alpha}{(m_1a_1)^\alpha+(m_2a_2)^\alpha}\right]$$

when total costs increase linearly and marketing expenditure elasticities are identical in both territories.

Proof: When total costs increase linearly, rather than nonlinearly, with sales, the following terms in Equation 4 and 5 vanish:

$$d_1 = d_2 = e_1 = e_2 = 0 \tag{1}$$

As a result, Equation 6-20 becomes

$$(P_1 - c_1)a_1b_1X_1^{b_1-1} = (P_2 - c_2)a_2b_2(B - X_1)^{b_2-1} \tag{2}$$

Also, let the marketing expenditure elasticities be equal in both territories, that is, $b_1 = b_2$. Then designating the gross margins $(P_i - c_i)$ as m_i, where $i = 1$, 2, Equation 2 becomes

$$\frac{m_1a_1X_1^{b-1}}{m_2a_2(B - X_1)^{b-1}} = 1 \tag{3}$$

$$\left(\frac{B - X_1}{X_1}\right)^{b-1} = \frac{m_1a_1}{m_2a_2} \tag{4}$$

$$\frac{B}{X_1} - 1 = \left(\frac{m_1a_1}{m_2a_2}\right)^{1/(b-1)} = \left(\frac{m_2a_2}{m_1a_1}\right)^{1/(1-b)} \tag{5}$$

$$\frac{B}{X_1} = \left(\frac{m_2a_2}{m_1a_1}\right)^{1/(1-b)} + 1 = \frac{(m_2a_2)^{1/(1-b)} + (m_1a_1)^{1/(1-b)}}{(m_1a_1)^{1/(1-b)}} \tag{6}$$

To simplify this expression, let $1/(1-b) = \alpha$ where $\alpha > 0$ for $0 < b < 1$. Then the optimum expenditure in territory 1 is given by

$$X_1^* = B\left[\frac{(m_1a_1)^\alpha}{(m_1a_1)^\alpha + (m_2a_2)^\alpha}\right]$$

6-2

Given n sales territories, a fixed marketing budget B, and territorial sales response functions of the form $Q_i = a_iX_i^{b_i}$, show that the optimum marketing budget allocation to the ith territory is given by

$$m_1a_1b_1X_1^{b_1-1} = m_2a_2b_2X_2^{b_2-1} = \ldots = m_na_nb_nX_n^{b_n-1}$$

In the special case where $b_1 = b_2 = \ldots = b_n = b$, then

$$X_1^* = B\left[\frac{(m_ia_i)^\alpha}{\sum_{i=1}^n(m_ia_i)^\alpha}\right]$$

Proof: Let Z_i be the profit function for the ith territory:

$$Z_i = m_iQ_i - F_i - X_i; \qquad i = 1, 2, \ldots, n \tag{1}$$

The marketing budget B must be so allocated over the territories as to maximize the following Lagrangian expression:

$$L = \sum(m_i Q_i - F_i - X_i) + \lambda(B - \sum_{i=1}^{n} X_i); \qquad i = 1, 2, \ldots, n \tag{2}$$

Find the partial derivatives:

$$\frac{\partial L}{\partial X_i} = m_i \frac{\partial Q_i}{\partial X_i} - 1 - \lambda, \qquad \text{for all } i \tag{3}$$

$$\frac{\partial L}{\partial \lambda} = B - \sum_{i=1}^{n} X_i \tag{4}$$

Set the partial derivatives equal to 0 as a *necessary* condition for an optimal allocation:

$$m_i \frac{\partial Q_i}{\partial X_i} - 1 - \lambda = 0, \qquad \text{for all } i \tag{5}$$

$$B = \sum_{i=1}^{n} X_i \tag{6}$$

From Equation 5, $m_i(\partial Q_i / \partial X_i) = 1 + \lambda$. Thus a necessary condition for optimality is

$$m_1 \frac{\partial Q_1}{\partial X_1} = m_2 \frac{\partial Q_2}{\partial X_2} = \ldots = m_n \frac{\partial Q_n}{\partial X_n} = 1 + \lambda \tag{7}$$

which states that the gross margin in each territory from the next dollar of marketing expenditure is the same in each territory. Given that:

$$Q_i = a_i X_i^{b_i}, \tag{8}$$

then

$$\frac{\partial Q_i}{\partial X_i} = b_i a_i X_i^{b_i - 1} = \frac{b_i Q_i}{X_i} \tag{9}$$

and hence Equation 7 can be restated:

$$\frac{m_1 b_1 Q_1}{X_1} = \frac{m_2 b_2 Q_2}{X_2} = \ldots = \frac{m_n b_n Q_n}{X_n} \tag{10}$$

or

$$m_1 a_1 b_1 X_1^{b_1 - 1} = m_2 a_2 b_2 X_2^{b_2 - 1} = \ldots = m_n a_n b_n X_n^{b_n - 1} \tag{11}$$

According to Equation 11,

$$m_1 a_1 b_1 X_1^{b_1 - 1} = m_i a_i b_i X_i^{b_i - 1} \tag{12}$$

$$X_i = \left(\frac{m_1 a_1 b_1 X_1^{b_1 - 1}}{m_i a_i b_i} \right)^{1/(b_i - 1)} \tag{13}$$

Now if $B = \sum_{i=1}^{n} X_i$, it follows from Equation 13 that

$$B = \sum_{i=1}^{n} \left(\frac{m_1 a_1 b_1}{m_i a_i b_i} X_1^{b_1-1} \right)^{1/(b_i-1)} \tag{14}$$

For the special case where $b_1 = b_2 = \ldots = b_n = b$ (i.e., all the territorial elasticities are the same),

$$B^{b-1} = m_1 a_1 X_1^{b-1} \sum_{i=1}^{n} \frac{1}{m_i a_i} \tag{15}$$

or

$$X_1^* = \left(\frac{B^{b-1}}{m_1 a_1 \sum_{i=1}^{n} 1/m_i a_i} \right)^{1/(b-1)} \tag{16}$$

$$X_1^* = \frac{B}{(m_1 a_1 \sum_{i=1}^{n} 1/m_i a_i)^{1/(b-1)}} \tag{17}$$

$$X_1^* = B \left(m_1 a_1 \sum_{i=1}^{n} \frac{1}{m_i a_i} \right)^{1/(1-b)} \tag{18}$$

For $\alpha = 1/(1-b)$,

$$X_1^* = B \left(\frac{(m_1 a_1)^{\alpha}}{\sum_{i=1}^{n} (m_i a_i)^{\alpha}} \right) \tag{19}$$

7-1

Show that, for $Z = (P_i - c_i)(k_i - a_i P_i + b_i P_j) + (P_j - c_j)(k_j - \partial_j P_j + b_j P_i) - F$, the optimum price rule is

$$P^* = \frac{(k_i + c_i a_i - c_j b_j)(b_i + b_j) + (k_j + c_j a_j - c_i b_i)(2a_i)}{4 a_i a_j - (b_i + b_j)^2}$$

Proof: Expanding Z,

$$\begin{aligned} Z &= P_i k_i - a_i P_i^2 + b_i P_i P_j - c_i k_i + c_i a_i P_i - c_i b_i P_j \\ &\quad + P_j k_j - a_j P_j^2 + b_j P_i P_j - c_j k_j + c_j a_j P_j - c_j b_j P_i - F \end{aligned} \tag{1}$$

Gathering terms,

$$\begin{aligned} Z &= -a_i P_i^2 - a_j P_j^2 + (b_i + b_j) P_i P_j + (k_i + c_i a_i - c_j b_j) P_i \\ &\quad + (k_j + c_j a_j - c_i b_i) P_j - c_i k_i - c_j k_j - F \end{aligned} \tag{2}$$

Setting the first partial derivatives of profit with respect to each price equal to 0, we find that

$$\frac{\partial Z}{\partial P_i} = -2 a_i P_i + (b_i + b_j) P_j + (k_i + c_i a_i - c_j b_j) = 0 \tag{3}$$

$$\frac{\partial Z}{\partial P_j} = -2a_jP_j+(b_i+b_j)P_i+(k_j+c_ja_j-c_ib_i) = 0 \tag{4}$$

From Equation 3:

$$2a_iP_i = (b_i+b_j)P_j+(k_i+c_ia_i-c_jb_j) \tag{5}$$

Dividing by $2a_i$ we obtain

$$P_i = \frac{b_i+b_j}{2a_i}P_j + \frac{(k_i+c_ia_i-c_jb_j)}{2a_i} \tag{6}$$

From Equation 4:

$$(b_i+b_j)P_i = 2a_jP_j-(k_j+c_ja_j-c_ib_i) \tag{7}$$

Dividing by (b_i+b_j),

$$P_i = \frac{2a_j}{b_i+b_j}P_j- \frac{(k_j+c_ja_j-c_ib_i)}{b_i+b_j} \tag{8}$$

Setting the two partial derivatives in Equations 6 and 8 equal to each other, we find that

$$\frac{b_i+b_j}{2a_i}P_j+ \frac{k_i+c_ia_i-c_jb_j}{2a_i} = \frac{2a_j}{b_i+b_j}P_j- \frac{(k_j+c_ja_j-c_ib_i)}{b_i+b_j} \tag{9}$$

$$\left(\frac{b_i+b_j}{2a_i} - \frac{2a_j}{b_i+b_j}\right)P_j = - \frac{k_i+c_ia_i-c_jb_j}{2a_i} - \frac{k_j+c_ja_j-c_ib_i}{b_i+b_j} \tag{10}$$

$$\left[\frac{(b_i+b_j)^2-4a_ia_j}{(2a_i)(b_i+b_j)}\right]P_j = \frac{-(k_i+c_ia_i-c_jb_j)(b_i+b_j)-(k_j+c_ja_j-c_ib_i)2a_i}{(2a_i)(b_i+b_j)} \tag{11}$$

$$[(b_i+b_j)^2-4a_ia_j]P_j = -(k_i+c_ia_i-c_jb_j)(b_i+b_j)-(k_j+c_ja_j-c_ib_i)2a_i \tag{12}$$

Therefore,

$$P_j^* = \frac{(k_i+c_ia_i-c_jb_j)(b_i+b_j)+(k_j+c_ja_j-c_ib_i)(2a_i)}{4a_ia_j-(b_i+b_j)^2} \tag{13}$$

7-2

Show that given

$$L = (P_i-c_i)(k_iX_i^{a_i}X_j^{-b_i})+(P_j-c_j)(k_jX_j^{a_j}X_i^{-b_j})-F+\lambda(B-X_i-X_j)$$

the optimal level of X_j is as given in Equation 7-12, p. 170.

Proof: Find the first partial derivatives of L with respect to X_i, X_j, and λ and set them equal to 0:

$$\frac{\partial L}{\partial X_i} = (P_i-c_i)(k_ia_iX_i^{a_i-1}X_j^{-b_i})-(P_j-c_j)(k_jX_j^{a_j}b_jX_i^{-b_j-1})-\lambda = 0 \tag{1}$$

$$\frac{\partial L}{\partial X_j} = -(P_i-c_i)(k_i X_i^{a_i} b_i X_j^{-b_i-1})+(P_j-c_j)(k_j a_j X_j^{a_j-1} X_i^{-b_j})-\lambda = 0 \qquad (2)$$

$$\frac{\partial L}{\partial \lambda} = B - X_i - X_j = 0 \qquad (3)$$

Since Equations 1 and 2 are equal to 0, rearranging terms yields:

$$\frac{a_i X_i^{a_i-1} X_j^{-b_i}+b_i X_i^{a_i} X_j^{-b_i-1}}{a_j X_j^{a_j-1} X_i^{-b_j}+b_j X_j^{a_j} X^{-b_j-1}} = \frac{(P_j-c_j)k_j}{(P_i-c_i)k_i}$$

But, by Equation 3, $X_i = B - X_j$. Therefore,

$$\frac{a_i(B-X_j)^{a_i-1} X_j^{-b_i}+b_i(B-X_j)^{a_i} X_j^{-b_i-1}}{a_j(B-X_j)^{-b_j} X_j^{a_j-1}+b_j(B-X_j)^{-b_j-1} X_j^{a_j}} = \frac{(P_j-c_j)k_j}{(P_i-c_i)k_i}$$

7-3

Prove that Equation 7-34 shows the variance of a sum of weighted random variables.

Proof: Let X_1 and X_2 be two variables and let Y stand for their sum. Let y, x_i, and x_2 denote deviations of the variables from their arithmetic means. Since $Y = X_1 + X_2$, then

$$y = x_1 + x_2 \qquad (1)$$

Squaring both sides of Equation 1 and summing:

$$\Sigma(y^2) = \Sigma(x_i^2)+\Sigma(x_2^2)+2\Sigma(x_1 x_2) \qquad (2)$$

Dividing both sides by n, we get:

$$V(X_1+X_2) = V(X_1)+V(X_2)+2V(X_1 X_2).$$

Using the same method, it can be shown that

$$V(a_1 X_1+a_2 X_2) = a_1^2 V(X_1)+a_2^2 V(X_2)+2a_1 a_2 V(X_1 X_2)$$

This proof can be generalized to the sum of three or more weighted variables.

7-4

Show that the firm can find the least risk portfolio of products for any specific target return. This will be called an efficient portfolio.

Proof: The equations $E = \Sigma_{i=1}^N a_i X_i$ and $V = \Sigma_{i=1}^N \Sigma_{j=1}^N \sigma_{ij} X_i X_j$ in the case where $N = 3$, imply that the isomean (constant return) curves are a system of straight lines and that the isovariance curves are a system of concentric ellipses of which the minimum variance corresponds to the "center." See Figure A1. For the specific return E_1, the least risk portfolio corresponds to the point of tangency A with the lowest value isovariance ellipse. This defines the proportions of products 1 and 2 directly; through $\sum_{i=1}^{N} X_i = 1$, it defines the proportion of product 3 indirectly. This portfolio has minimum risk, corresponding to ellipse V_1. (The above discussion assumes that point A falls within the attainable set.)

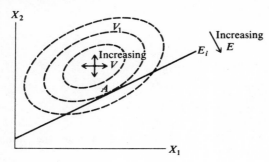

Figure A1

9-1

Maximize

$$Z = 56{,}000 + 1200P - 4P^2$$

subject to

$$1000P - 4P^2 \geqslant 50{,}000$$
$$1000 \quad -4P \geqslant 300$$
$$\qquad P \geqslant 0$$

Solution: First state the Lagrangian expression for profits:

$$L = (-56{,}000 + 1200P - 4P^2) - \lambda_a(1000P - 4P^2 - 50{,}000) - \lambda_b(1000 - 4P - 300)$$

Find the relevant partial derivatives:

$$\frac{\partial L}{\partial P} = 1200 - 8P - \lambda_a(1000 - 8P) + 4\lambda_b \leqslant 0 \qquad \text{If} <, \text{then } P = 0 \tag{1}$$

$$\frac{\partial L}{\partial \lambda_a} = 1000P - 4P^2 - 50{,}000 \geqslant 0. \qquad \text{If} >, \lambda_a = 0 \tag{2}$$

$$\frac{\partial L}{\partial \lambda_b} = 1000 - 4P - 300 \geqslant 0. \qquad \text{If} >, \lambda_b = 0 \tag{3}$$

The above conditions are based on the concavity of the objective function and the assumption of a convex set of continuously adjustable prices.

Case A. $P > 0$; $\lambda_a = 0$; $\lambda_b = 0$

From Equation 1, $1200 - 8P = 0$. Therefore $P = 150$. This is the unconstrained optimum price.

Case B. $P > 0$; $\lambda_a > 0$; $\lambda_b = 0$

From Equation 2

$$P = \frac{250 \pm \sqrt{62,500 - 50,000}}{2} = 69 \text{ or } 181$$

Substitute in Z:

$P = 69$	$Z = -56,000 + 82,800 - 19,100 = 7700$	
$P = 181$	$Z = -56,000 + 217,000 - 131,000 = 30,000$	

The revenue-constrained optimum price is 181.

Case C. $P > 0$; $\lambda_a = 0$; $\lambda_b > 0$

From Equation 3, $-4P = -700$ or $P = 175$. Therefore the quantity-constrained optimum price is $P = 175$.

Case D. $P > 0$; $\lambda_a > 0$; $\lambda_b > 0$

From Equations 2 and 3, we have the two equations:

$$1000P - 4P^2 - 50,000 = 0 \quad \text{and} \quad 1000 - 4P - 300 = 0$$

Since the second equation is a vertical line at $P = 175$, this must be the optimum price for the fully constrained problem. When $P = 175$, $Z = -56,000 + 210,000 - 122,500 = 31,500$.

Cases E–H. $P = 0$; $\lambda_a \geqslant 0$; $\lambda_b \geqslant 0$

These cases are trivial and will not be evaluated, since $P = 0$ yields the minimum $Z = -56,000$ (unconstrained), or $-50,000$ (revenue-constrained). A graphical representation of the cross-hatched feasible solution area is shown in Figure A2.

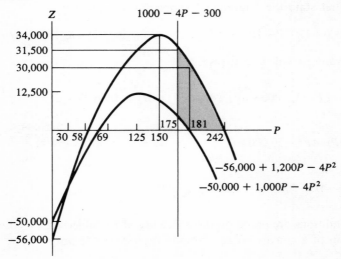

Figure A2

10-1

Given that $Q = a\sqrt{X}+bY$, where a and Y are random variables, show that the variance of Q is given by $\sigma_Q{}^2 = X\sigma_a{}^2+b^2\sigma_Y{}^2+2\rho X^{1/2}\sigma_a b\sigma_Y$.

Proof: Let $a\sqrt{X} = V$ and $bY = W$, so that $Q = V+W$ and let q, v, and w be the respective deviations from the means of the variables Q, V, and W. In general, $q = v+w$. Squaring both sides, we find that $q^2 = v^2+w^2+2vw$, and summing over all values, $\sum q^2 = \sum v^2+\sum w^2+2\sum vw$.
Dividing by N, we obtain

$$\frac{\sum q^2}{N} = \frac{\sum v^2}{N}+\frac{\sum w^2}{N}+\frac{2\sum vw}{N}$$
$$V(q) = V(v)+V(w)+2 \text{ Cov }(vw)$$
$$= \sigma_v{}^2+\sigma_w{}^2+2\rho\sigma_v\sigma_w$$

The correlation between v and w can be defined as

$$\rho = \frac{\sum vw}{N\sigma_v\sigma_w}$$

Then

$$V(q) = \frac{\sum q^2}{N} = \frac{\sum Q^2}{N} = V(Q)$$

$$V(v) = \frac{\sum v^2}{N} = \frac{\sum V^2}{N} = \frac{\sum(a\sqrt{X})^2}{N} = \frac{X\sum a^2}{N} = XV(a)$$

$$V(w) = \frac{\sum w^2}{N} = \frac{\sum W^2}{N} = \frac{\sum(bY)^2}{N} = \frac{b\sum Y^2}{N} = b^2V(Y)$$

$$V(Q) = XV(a)+bV(Y)+2\rho X^{1/2}\sigma_a b\sigma_y$$

or

$$\sigma_Q{}^2 = X\sigma_a{}^2+b\sigma_y{}^2+2\rho X^{1/2}\sigma_a b\sigma_y$$

10-2

Show how the computer can generate probabilistic values, using the Monte Carlo method.

Discussion: Suppose that sales can take on four levels (column 1) with the probabilities shown in column 2:

Sales	Probability	Cumulative Numbers
$10	.05	00–05
$12	.30	06–35
$14	.50	36–85
$16	.15	86–99

Column 3 represents the assignment of 100 cumulative two-digit numbers to the four sales levels in proportion to their probability. Now the computer draws a random number between 00–99. (This may be drawn from a table of stored random numbers or may be generated from a formula.) Suppose the random number is 39. This falls in the third block and corresponds to a sales level of $14. Thus sales of $14 are assumed to have taken place. For a good account of random number generators for different probability distributions, see T. H. Naylor, J. L. Balintfy, D. S. Burdick, and K. Chu, *Computer Simulation Techniques* (New York: John Wiley & Sons, Inc., 1966), Chaps. 3 and 4.

10-3

Given $Z = mS - X - F$ and $S = a + bX + cX^2$, show that the optimal promotion rate is given by $X^* = (mb-1)/2mc$.

Proof: Substitute the sales function in the profit function:

$$Z = m(a + bX - cX^2) - X - F$$

Find the first derivative of the profit function, set it equal to 0, and solve.

$$\frac{dZ}{dX} = mb - 2mcX - 1 = 0$$

$$2mcX = mb - 1$$

$$X^* = \frac{mb-1}{2mc}$$

10-4

For the information in note 10-3, show that the loss rate is given by $L(X) = mc(X - X^*)^2$.

Proof: The loss rate, $L(X)$, can be defined as

$$L(X) = Z(X^*) - Z(X)$$

Now substitute the profit function and carry out the necessary algebra:

$$L(X) = mS^* - X^* - F - (mS - X - F)$$
$$L(X) = m(S^* - S) + (X - X^*)$$
$$L(X) = m[b(X^* - X) - c(X^{*2} - X^2)] + (X - X^*)$$
$$L(X) = mbX^* - mbX - mcX^{*2} + mcX^2 + X - X^*$$
$$L(X) = X^*(mb - 1) - X(mb - 1) - mc(X^{*2} - X^2)$$
$$L(X) = (mb - 1)(X^* - X) - mc(X^{*2} - X^2)$$
$$L(X) = 2mcX^*(X^* - X) - mc(X^{*2} - X^2)$$
$$L(X) = mc(X^2 - 2XX^* + X^{*2})$$

Therefore

$$L(X) = mc(X - X^*)^2$$

11-1

Develop an economic analysis to show the circumstances under which producers benefit by working through middlemen. Then show *how many* middlemen will naturally arise in a given market.

Discussion: Channel theorists have found it useful to think in terms of an equilibrium number of middlemen that will grow to serve any particular channel in the presence of full information, freedom of entry and exit, and a given set of costs. The equilibrium number of middlemen is the number that minimizes the average cost of distribution to the participating producers. The equilibrium logic has been developed in a basic article by Frederick E. Balderston: "Communication Networks in Intermediate Markets," *Management Science* (Jan. 1958), 155–171, and has been refined in the recent writings of Baligh and Richartz [Helmy H. Baligh and Leon E. Richartz, *Vertical Market Structure* (Boston: Allyn and Bacon, Inc. 1967), 128–181].

First we inquire under what circumstances producers would care to work through middlemen at all; subsequently, we consider the question of the optimal number of middlemen. Assume a market in which there are m producers and n customers. Each producer separately contacts each of the n customers. Since there are m producers, there will be

mn contacts per period in the system in the absence of a middleman   (1)

If each contact cost b,

bmn is the total cost of contacts per period in the system in the absence of middlemen   (2)

For any one producer, where the costs are born equally,

bn is a producer's cost of contacts per period in the absence of a middleman (3)

A single middleman is established and all the producers sell through him. Given a middleman, the total number of contacts per period in the system is reduced to

$m+n$ contacts in the system per period with one middleman   (4)

This reduction in the number of contacts in the system effected by one middleman is shown graphically in Figure A3 for the case of three producers and three customers. A middleman effects a reduction in the number of required contacts from 9 to 6.

Now suppose that the cost of a contact between a producer and the middleman, or the middleman and a customer is $\bar{b}$. Then

$\bar{b}(m+n)$ is the total cost of contacts per period in the system in the presence of one middleman   (5)

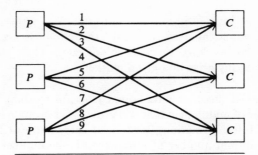

(a) Number of contacts with three producers (m) selling directly to three customers (n). Therefore, $mn = 3 \times 3 = 9$.

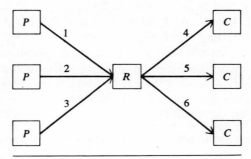

(b) Number of contacts with three producers selling through one wholesaler who sells to three customers. Therefore, $m + n = 6$.

Figure A3 How a Middleman Reduces the Number of Required Customer Contacts in a System

For any one producer, where the costs are borne equally,

$[\bar{b}(m+n)]/m$ is a producer's cost of contact per period in the presence of one middleman (6)

Therefore, a producer would prefer to work through a middleman if condition 6 is less than condition 3, i.e.,

$$\frac{\bar{b}(m+n)}{m} < bn \tag{7}$$

If $\bar{b} = b$, then

$m + n < mn$ is the condition for a producer preferring to work through a middleman (8)

This equation is always satisfied if $m > 2$ and $n \geqslant 2$ (or $m \geqslant 2$ and $n > 2$). That is, there must be more than two producers and/or two customers before a middleman is able to perform the customer contact function at less cost and therefore earn a profit.

Now we are ready to determine the equilibrium number of middlemen. Suppose that this number is w^*. The equilibrium number of middlemen will equalize the two sides of condition 8; that is,

$$w^*(m+n) = mn \tag{9}$$

or

$$w^* = \frac{mn}{m+n} \tag{10}$$

This solution makes intuitive sense. The equilibrium number of middlemen will be equal to the ratio of total customer contact cost without a middleman and with middlemen.

Admittedly, the formulation of the problem has been highly simplified. The solution in Equation 10 assumes that all producers sell to all customers; contact costs are the same for all producers and middlemen no matter who is being contacted; each middleman would contact all customers; and all contacts are equally effective, no matter who is making them. These are heroic simplifications. The analysis would have to be modified if producers or middlemen serve different customer segments; if middlemen require not only positive profits but a certain minimum rate of return on investment; if middlemen must offer rebates to existing firms to get established, etc. The basic force of this analysis is to show that the use of middlemen and their equilibrium number will be determined primarily by the extent to which they can perform the channel work more efficiently than the producers can do on their own.

11-2

Given

$$\frac{S}{P} = \frac{k_2 T}{0+(1+k_2-k_1)P} \tag{1}$$

and

$$\bar{S} = \frac{S}{P} \tag{2}$$

$$\bar{O} = \frac{T}{O+P} \tag{3}$$

$$X = \frac{S}{T} \tag{4}$$

$$N = O+P \tag{5}$$

show that

$$\frac{\bar{S}}{\bar{O}} = k_2+(k_1-k_2)X \tag{6}$$

Proof: From Equations 1 and 2, we get:

$$S = \frac{k_2 T}{O + (1 + k_2 - k_1)P} \tag{7}$$

Divide Equation 7 by $\bar{O}$

$$\frac{S}{\bar{O}} = \frac{k_2 T(O + P)}{[O + (1 + k_2 - k_1)P]T} \tag{8}$$

Simplify Equation 8

$$\frac{S}{\bar{O}} = \frac{k_2(O + P)}{(O + P) + (k_2 - k_1)P} \tag{9}$$

Substitute Equations 5 and 3 in Equation 9

$$\frac{S}{T} = \frac{k_2}{N + (k_2 - k_1)P} \tag{10}$$

Substitute Equation 2 in Equation 10

$$\frac{S}{T} = \frac{k_2}{\dfrac{N}{P} + (k_2 - k_1)} \tag{11}$$

Substitute Equation 4 in Equation 11 and rearrange

$$X \left[\frac{N}{P} + (k_2 - k_1) \right] = k_2 \tag{12}$$

Simplify

$$\frac{XN}{P} = k_2 + (k_1 - k_2)X \tag{13}$$

Substitute Equation 4 in the left-hand side of Equation 13 and rearrange. Therefore

$$\frac{S}{\bar{O}} = k_2 + (k_1 - k_2)X \tag{14}$$

12-1

Show that profits are maximized by a rigid markup policy when average costs are constant and price elasticity is constant.

Proof: The argument proceeds as follows. It can be shown that price (P) and marginal revenue (MR) are related in the following way:

$$MR = \left(1 - \frac{1}{e} \right) P \tag{1}$$

where e = price elasticity of demand, expressed as a positive number (see Equation 12-5.) Now, profits are maximized when marginal revenue is equated to marginal cost. Therefore, applying Equation 1, the optimality condition is

$$MC = \left(1 - \frac{1}{e}\right)P \tag{2}$$

Suppose that average costs are constant (special condition 1). Then $AC = MC$, and the condition for optimality is

$$AC = \left(1 - \frac{1}{e}\right)P \tag{3}$$

Equation 3 can be rearranged algebraically to yield a formula for the optimal markup:

$$\frac{P}{AC} = \frac{1}{1-(1/e)} = \frac{e}{e-1}$$

Subtracting AC/AC from both sides and simplifying, we obtain

$$\frac{P-AC}{AC} = \frac{e}{e-1} - 1 = \frac{1}{e-1}$$

or

$$\text{markup} = \frac{1}{e-1} \tag{4}$$

According to Equation 4, the optimal markup is inversely related to price elasticity. If brand price elasticity is high, say 5.0, as it might be in the case of branded sugar, then the optimal markup is relatively low (25 percent). If brand elasticity is low, say 2.0, as it might be in the case of branded frozen pastry, the optimal markup is relatively high (100 percent). Furthermore, if the price elasticity remains fairly constant over time (special condition 2), then a fairly rigid markup would be consistent with optimal pricing.

13-1

Given

$$V = \bar{p}(1-e^{-an}) \sum_{t=1}^{i} \frac{mQ-X}{(1+r)^t} - nc$$

find the number of calls, n, that will maximize V.

Discussion: Find the first derivative of V with respect to n and set it equal to 0.

$$\frac{dV}{dn} = \bar{p}a \sum_{t=1}^{i} \frac{mQ-X}{(1+r)^t} e^{-an} - c = 0$$

$$e^{-an} = \frac{c}{\bar{p}a\sum_{t=1}^{i} \dfrac{mQ-X}{(1+r)^t}}$$

$$e^{an} = \frac{\bar{p}a\sum_{t=1}^{i}(mQ-X)/(1+r)^t}{c}$$

Take the log of both sides and solve for n:

$$n^* = \frac{\log\left\{\dfrac{\bar{p}a\sum_{t=1}^{i}(mQ-X)/(1+r)^t}{c}\right\}}{a}$$

13-2

Show how the prospect matrix of transitional probabilities set up by Shuchman yields the conclusions shown on p. 389.

Discussion: To derive the results shown in the text, first find the matrix

$$N = (I-Q)^{-1} = I+Q+Q^2+Q^3+\dots+Q^n$$

This is known as the fundamental matrix of the absorbing Markov Chain. Each of the rows of this matrix N gives the proportion of prospects in each age group at the beginning of the period, which receive 0, 1, 2, ..., n calls. To obtain the average number of *new* prospects each period, sum the first row of the N matrix and divide the resulting sum into the number of prospects the salesman contacts each period. The average number of new prospects should be multiplied against every number in the first row of N to find the expected number of prospects in each group in the steady state (Question 1). To find the expected number of prospects who will be absorbed in states S_s and S_d each period, multiply the matrices NR (Question 2). The entries in the first column of NR represent the probabilities of converting the prospect in each age group to customers; the entries in the second column represent the probabilities of dropping the prospects in the respective age groups. Question 3 is answered by redoing this analysis for other customer call cutoff rules. The logic underlying these manipulations is more fully explained in Shuchman, "The Planning and Control of Personal Selling Effort Directed at New Account Acquisition: A Markovian Analysis," in *New Research in Marketing* (Berkeley, Calif.: The Institute of Business and Economic Research, 1966).

13-3

Show how the matrix set up by Thompson and McNeal yields the conclusions shown on p. 391.

Discussion: First find the N matrix, where $N = (I-Q)^{-1}$. Then find $\tau = N\xi$ where ξ is a column vector with all unity elements. The answer to Question 1 is τ. The answer to Question 2 is given by NR, where R is the absorption submatrix. The answer to Question 3 is given by

$$NR\begin{bmatrix} 190 \\ 0 \end{bmatrix} - 15\tau$$

which is a straightforward profit estimation equation (revenue minus cost). For the underlying logic, see Thompson and McNeal, "Sales Planning and Control Using Absorbing Markov Chains," *Journal of Marketing Research* (Feb. 1967), 62–66.

13-4

Show analytically that Equation 13-20 represents the optimal number of calls that a salesman should make on customers, given the Lagrangian expression:

$$L(Q_t) = h_o + (h_\infty - h_o)(1 - e^{-an_c})Q_{t-1} + \bar{Q}_{pt}(1 - e^{-bn_p}) + \lambda(n - n_c - n_p)$$

Proof: Find the first derivatives of the Lagrangian expression with respect to n_c, n_p, and λ and set them equal to 0:

$$\frac{\partial L(Q_t)}{\partial n_c} = Q_{t-1}(h_\infty - h_0)(e^{-an_c})a - \lambda = 0 \tag{1}$$

$$\frac{\partial L(Q_t)}{\partial n_p} = \bar{Q}_{pt}(e^{-bn_p})b - \lambda = 0 \tag{2}$$

$$\frac{\partial L(Q_t)}{\partial \lambda} = n - n_p - n_c = 0 \cdot \tag{3}$$

Substituting Equation 3 into Equation 2, we obtain

$$\frac{\partial L(Q_t)}{\partial n_p} = \bar{Q}_{pt}[e^{-b(n-n_c)}]b - \lambda = 0 \tag{2a}$$

But Equations 1 and 2a are equal. Hence,

$$Q_{t-1}(h_\infty - h_o)(e^{-an_c})a = \bar{Q}_{pt}[e^{-b(n-n_c)}]b \tag{4}$$

Therefore,

$$e^{-nc(a+b)} = \frac{Q_{pt}(e^{-bn})b}{Q_{t-1}(h_\infty - h_o)a}$$

$$e^{n_c(a+b)} = \frac{Q_{t-1}(h_\infty - h_o)a}{Q_{pt}(e^{-bn})b}$$

Taking the natural logarithm of both sides, we find Equation 13-20 pp. 399 in the text:

$$n_c^* = \frac{1}{a+b} \log [Q_{t-1}(h_\infty - h_o)a / Q_{pt}(e^{-bn})b]$$

The number of calls on prospects is simply $n_p = n - n_c$.

14-1

Given Equation 14-13 in the text, $P_n = E_n - C_{c(n-1)} - C_{sn}$, show that the optimal n^* is the smallest value for n for which the following relationship is satisfied:

$$\Delta e_n < \frac{c + c_s}{\sigma_E \rho R}$$

Proof: Substituting Equations 14-10 and 14-11 into Equation 14-13, we get

$$P_m = e_n \sigma_E \sigma R - C_{c(n-1)} - C_F - c_s n$$

The expected contribution to profits of generating and screening $n-1$ advertising alternatives is given by

$$P_{n-1} = e_{n-1} \sigma_E \rho R - C_{c(n-1)} - C_F - c_s(n-1)$$

The expected contribution to profits of generating n instead of $n-1$ advertising alternatives is therefore:

$$P_n - P_{n-1} = \Delta e_n \sigma_E \rho R - c - c_s$$

where $\quad c = C_c =$ average cost of creating an ad

The optimal n^* occurs when the expected contribution to profits of generating one more ad is negative:

$$0 > \Delta e_n \sigma_E \rho R - c - c_s$$

This in turn can be simplified to

$$\Delta e_n < \frac{c + c_s}{\sigma_E \rho R}$$

Name Index

Subject Index